Living with Racism

LIVING WITH RACISM

THE BLACK MIDDLE-CLASS EXPERIENCE

JOE R. FEAGIN
MELVIN P. SIKES

Beacon Press
Boston

Beacon Press
25 Beacon Street
Boston, Massachusetts 02108-2892

Beacon Press books
are published under the auspices of
the Unitarian Universalist Association of Congregations

Printed in the United States of America

99 98 97 96 95 94   8 7 6 5 4 3 2 1

Text design by Lisa Diercks

Library of Congress Cataloging-in-Publication Data

Feagin, Joe R.
Living with racism: the black middle-class experience / Feagin and Melvin P. Sikes.
p. cm.
Includes bibliographical references and index.
ISBN 0-8070-0924-5
1. Afro-Americans—Social conditions—1975– 2. Racism—United States. 3. Middle class—United States. 4. United States—Race relations. I. Sikes, Melvin P. II. Title.
E185.86.F43 1994
305.96'073—dc20   93-37530

Contents

Preface vii

Chapter One
The Continuing Significance of Racism 1

Chapter Two
Navigating Public Places 37

Chapter Three
Seeking a Good Education 78

Chapter Four
Navigating the Middle-Class Workplace 135

Chapter Five
Building a Business 187

Chapter Six
Seeking a Good Home and Neighborhood 223

Chapter Seven
Contending with Everyday Discrimination: Effects and Strategies 272

Chapter Eight
Changing the Color Line: The Future of U.S. Racism 319

Notes 365

Index 393

Preface

"WHAT is it like to be a black person in white America today? One step from suicide! What I'm saying is—the psychological warfare games that we have to play everyday just to survive. We have to be one way in our communities and one way in the workplace or in the business sector. We can never be ourselves all around. I think that may be a given for all people, but us particularly; it's really a mental health problem. It's a wonder we haven't all gone out and killed somebody or killed ourselves."

Our interviews began with this statement from a successful black entrepreneur, the first respondent of 209 African Americans we interviewed in a number of cities across the United States. She challenges us to see the personal and family losses that have resulted from decades of dealing with prejudiced whites. She summons us to understand the great tension between conforming to white standards and trying to maintain personal integrity and black identity. She dares us to look beyond the statistics of inequality conventionally provided by scholars and journalists to experience the reality and pain of recurring racial discrimination, raising the questions: How are the unique vicissitudes of my life defined? How have I survived? And at what price?

A common white credo about racial relations today holds that discrimination is no longer a serious and widespread problem and that whatever blatant antiblack hostility remains is mostly that of isolated white bigots and Klan-type groups. In particular, middle-class African Americans are not viewed as victims of discrimination, but are seen as prosperous examples of the success of equal opportunity and affirmative action programs. Indeed, middle-class black Americans are thought by many whites to be the beneficiaries of racial quotas that have gone too far, to the point of "reverse discrimination."

Middle-class black Americans appear to most whites to have secured the promises of the American dream. They and their families have sacrificed to get a good education; they have worked very hard; and they have done everything said to be required to achieve the American dream. All have achieved or will soon achieve some signs of material success—the good income, the credit cards, the nice car. They appear to be well integrated into middle-class America, and from a white perspective they have no real reason to link problems in their lives to skin color.

Yet when one engages in extended conversations with middle-class African Americans about their efforts, achievements, and obstacles, their often vivid accounts of the white hostility and discrimination they have experienced tell a different story. In this book we hope to show the image of untrammeled black middle-class prosperity and integration to be a white illusion, quite out of touch with the daily reality.

Our in-depth interviews provide windows into the black middle-class world, one not only of determination and hard work but also of frustration and rage over persisting discrimination. These African Americans show in their personal accounts that they have not been accepted as equals by many of the working-class and middle-class whites they encounter in their daily lives. In our analysis we address the character of the hostility and discrimination these middle-class respondents have experienced in public places and in traditionally white workplaces, business arenas, residential complexes and neighborhoods, and schools and colleges. They present a tragic and terrible portrait of recent and continuing experiences with white racism.

But there is more to our argument than the contention that middle-class African Americans face serious discrimination. Our data say something even more profound about the state of this nation. Clearly, no amount of hard work and achievement, no amount of money, resources, and success, can protect black people from the persisting ravages of white racism in their everyday lives. Our respondents are alternately baffled, frustrated, shocked, and outraged that the strong evidence of their hard work and personal achievements does not protect them from white discrimination. Moreover, while they may have greater resources with which to respond to discrimination than less affluent black Americans, the presence and use of these resources appear to have had little lasting effect on the magnitude of white racism in the United States today. Racial stereotyping, prejudice, and hostility still operate indiscriminately, despite the actual identities and achievements of the black individuals discriminated against. In the everyday experience of our black middle-class respondents the full attainment of the American dream is "for whites only." The implications of this continuing racism for the fundamental democratic values of this society are far-reaching. The classic American creed promises the inalienable rights of "life, liberty, and the pursuit of happiness" today for all citizens of this democratic nation. Yet after several centuries of struggle these rights are not even close to being secured for black Americans, including middle-class black

Americans. Perhaps the greatest tragedy in our findings of widespread racism is that they reveal the much-celebrated American creed to be little more than hollow words.

Over the past decade or two, mainstream white media commentators, intellectuals, and government policymakers have rarely accorded value to critical black middle-class voices. This book evolved from our own conversations as professional colleagues, one white (Feagin) and one black (Sikes). As Sikes recounted his many and dramatic experiences of racial discrimination, Feagin was moved and angered. We both found our exchanges eye-opening, and Feagin pressed Sikes to write of these experiences in an autobiography. Yet Sikes felt unable to do so, because the task would be too painful and probably fruitless, particularly after more than four decades of experience with white editors and publishers uninterested in publishing strong black accounts of everyday racism. Eventually, then, our discussions led to the decision to collect and compile accounts of the everyday experiences of a large group of middle-class African Americans.

This book has grown beyond the initial attempt to record black middle-class experience to a deep analysis of the character and impact of white racism in this society. A primary goal is to help voice rarely expressed middle-class realities, using a richness of material unavailable in surface-level analyses based on surveys and opinion polls. We hope this book is as true as it can be to the life experiences of middle-class African Americans; to the racial barriers they face; to the pain and rage they feel; and to how they react, fight, and survive.

As a current expression among African Americans puts it, "Racism in America is alive and well!" Grounded in black experience, this book is a plea for better-enforced civil rights laws and for new social policies in the public and private sectors designed to confront and extirpate persisting white racism in its many modern faces and disguises.

Acknowledgments. In conducting this research study and preparing this manuscript we incurred more intellectual debts than we can ever repay. We are especially grateful to the many African Americans who gave of their time and energy to provide us with the extensive interview materials on which this book is based. We have not been able to quote all of them in the text, but all the interviews have informed our analysis whether quoted or not. We are indebted to many other people as well. We are indebted to the many black journalists (especially Isabel Wilkerson) and other black professionals around the country who took time out to talk with us about our research materials and their own life experiences. We would like to thank Hernan Vera, Nijole Benokraitis, John Goering, Christine Williams, Raphael Allen, Charles Tilly, John S. Butler, Tony Orum, Nestor Rodriguez, Sharon Collins, Janice Allen, Nikitah Imani, Michael Hodge, and Suzanne Harper for their insightful comments on earlier drafts of this manuscript, and Nijole Benokraitis, Beth Anne Shelton, Bob Parker, Diane Smith, Robert Adams, Yanick St. Jean, Leslie Inniss, Debi Van Ausdale, Cedric Herring, Marsha Herring, Lory Jennell Dance, Barbara McDade, Bob Bullard, L. M. Bullard, Yoku Shaw-Taylor, Charles Shepherd, Brenda Shepherd, Wilmer Roberts, Megan Pulliam, Annette Adams, Kellie Barr, Joseph Delphonse, Nishon M. Holmes, Robert L. Mayers, Pansy Mcdowell, Richard Newton, Mattie Lucas, Tammy Edwards, and Virginia Reid for interviewing and research assistance. We are indebted to Clairece Feagin and Zeta Sikes for their assistance and personal support.

We would like to thank the Hogg Foundation for Mental Health and the University of Florida Division of Sponsored Research and College of Liberal Arts and Sciences for financial support for certain portions of our research. We also would like to thank the University of Oklahoma Center for Research on Minority Education for support of a working paper that developed into part of chapter 3 and the United Church of Christ's

Commission on Racial Justice for allowing us to develop an initial version of some material found in chapter 6 at their December 1991 National Symposium on Race and Housing. We would like to thank two journals for permission to use portions of two articles. An early form of portions of chapter 2 appeared as Joe R. Feagin, "The Continuing Significance of Race: Antiblack Discrimination in Public Places," *American Sociological Review* 56 (February 1991), pp. 101–116; and an early rendering of parts of chapter 3 appeared in Joe R. Feagin, "The Continuing Significance of Racism," *Journal of Black Studies* 22 (June 1992), pp. 546–578.

Chapter One

The Continuing Significance of Racism

> *Everything, everywhere I look, everywhere I turn, right, left, is white. It's lily white, it's painted with white. And it's funny, because I was reading this article about how America is synonymous with white people. I mean, I'm sure when Europeans, or Asians or Africans for that matter, think of America, they think of white people, because white people are mainstream, white people are general. "White is right," as my daddy tells me. White is right, at least they think it is. So, if you're a black person trying to assert yourself, and express your culture, there's something wrong with you, because to do that is to be diametrically opposed to everything this country stands for. And everything this country stands for is what is white.*
>
> —Student at a historically white university

THE United States and its founding documents stand for democracy, liberty, and justice around the world. Yet the founding documents, especially the U.S. Constitution, buttressed the long-term enslavement of African Americans. Centuries of slavery and decades of legal segregation finally came to an end with the civil rights revolution of the 1950s and 1960s. During the period of legal segregation white prejudice was overt and frequently crude, and the material, physical, and psychological impact of blatant discrimination on African Americans was severe. Without societal backing in the form of civil rights laws, few blacks had the resources and power to fight discrimination successfully.

Widespread societal changes came in the 1960s as African Americans moved into areas of society formerly off limits to them. Federal and state governments began the task of dismantling the legal foundations of a segregated society and granted black Americans formal equality. Some government and private employers implemented modest affirmative action programs to overcome the consequences of past discrimination. In the years of the civil rights revolution, legal segregation was gradually destroyed, and for a time the old racial order seemed to be targeted for thoroughgoing destruction. Between the mid-1970s, and the early 1990s, however, many white decisionmakers in the private and public sectors abandoned aggressive programs to redress racial discrimination and retreated to a rhetoric of formal equality. As a result, in the 1990s racial discrimination remains at the heart of U.S. society.

Yet today most white Americans do not see racial discrimination as a widespread or deeply entrenched problem in traditionally white workplaces, law courts, schools, and other institutions. White and black Americans had quite different views about the role of racism in causing the 1992 Los Angeles riot. Local and national polls after the riot found that a large majority of black Americans did not feel that they received fair treatment in the U.S. courts. In the same surveys most whites felt the courts were fair.[1] Numerous other opinion polls over the past decade have shown that the majority of white Americans do not view racial injustice in employment and other areas as a major American dilemma in need of aggressive government action. The majority of whites appear to view "racism" as certain extreme views about white superiority, as "racism in the head," to use Judith Lichtenberg's apt term.[2] Apparently, when they think about it, the majority of whites tend to look at serious racism as the prejudices and actions of extreme bigots not considered to be representative of the white majority. Even the growing number of "hate crimes" targeting black Americans tend to be blamed on a few white "extremists."[3] Whites have the luxury of looking at matters of racial discrimination with detachment. This viewpoint makes it easier for whites to deny the reality of much of the racism reported by blacks. In contrast, black Americans view racism not with detachment but in terms of their own and their relatives' *experiences* in past and present encounters with white people. Marian Wright Edelman, an African American lawyer and the founder of the Children's Defense Fund, captured this eloquently in her recent book, *The Measure of Our Success: A Letter to My Children and Yours*: "It is utterly exhausting being Black in America—physically, mentally, and emotionally. . . . There is no respite or escape from your badge of color."[4]

In this book we generally use the term *racism* in a broad sense to refer not only to the prejudices and discriminatory actions of particular white bigots but also to institutionalized discrimination and to the recurring ways in which white people dominate black people in almost every major area of this society. A National Council of Churches work group has provided a summary of this institutionalized racism: "Both consciously and unconsciously, racism is enforced and maintained by the legal, cultural, religious, educational, economic, political, environmental and military institutions of societies. Racism is more than just a personal attitude; it is the institutionalized form of that attitude."[5]

Racism is racial prejudice backed by power and resources. White domination is often rationalized by the belief that the inferiority or superiority of a group's abilities, values, and culture are linked to physical characteristics such as skin color. In the chapters that follow we provide strong evidence of the blatant, subtle, and covert discrimination that cumulates to the intricate structures and processes of institutionalized racism. Contrary to a common white view, modern racism does not consist mainly of the isolated acts of scattered white bigots, but rather has been inescapable in the everyday worlds of African Americans. Almost any encounter with whites, in workplaces, schools, neighborhoods, and public places, can mean a confrontation with racism.

The Denial of White Racism

For a short period during the late 1960s and early 1970s a new intellectual discourse characterized much scholarly and media commentary on racial relations in the United States. The earlier "culture of poverty" language was abandoned for terms such as *white racism*, *racial discrimination*, and *institutional racism*. To cite perhaps the most important example, the 1968 National Advisory Commission on Civil Disorders, a mostly white group of prominent Americans appointed by President Lyndon B. Johnson to investigate the ghetto riots of the 1960s, concluded: "Our Nation is moving toward two societies, one black, one white—separate and unequal."[6] The first pages of the commission's final report minced no words about whites' responsibility for the condition of black Americans: "Discrimination and segregation have long permeated much of American life. . . . White society is deeply implicated in the ghetto. White institutions created it, white institutions maintain it, and white society condones it. . . . White racism is essentially responsible for the explosive mixture which has been accumulating in our cities since the end of World War II."[7] For a time many white analysts in academia, government, and the mass media interpreted the oppressive conditions of black Americans in the same terms.

The perspective criticizing and blaming whites and white institutions did not last. By the mid- to late-1970s there was much discontent and resentment among whites, including many in positions of power, over race-conscious remedies and the growing power of black Americans in the economy, universities, and politics. Since that time there has been a significant shift in how many prominent white scholars, journalists, politicians, and jurists have analyzed racial issues and problems. Terms like "institutional racism" and "white racism" have become rare, apparently because they have been seen by mainstream white analysts and some black neoconservative analysts as too harsh or radical. Instead, numerous articles have been written on the theme of the declining significance of race in U.S. society. Racial discrimination has often been downplayed as a major national problem. On March 7, 1988, the authors of a *Newsweek* article argued, without conducting research on racial discrimination, that "mercifully, America today is not the bitterly sundered dual society the riot commission grimly foresaw."[8] In the Winter 1988 issue of *Policy Review*, journalist Thomas Bray argued that racism was not a central motivating factor behind the 1960s riots, that the 1968 National Advisory Commission's analysis was "deeply flawed" and its central concept of institutional racism useless for analyzing U.S. racial relations then or now.[9]

With the demise of a highly visible black civil rights movement in the 1970s and 1980s, a new language was developed by many white intellectuals, media commentators, and politicians to analyze U.S. racial relations. Terms such as *the black underclass*, *reverse discrimination*, and *the privileged black middle class* have been used by commentators as influential and diverse as Nathan Glazer, Ben Wattenberg, Thomas and Mary Edsall, Nicholas Lemann, Ken Auletta, Daniel Patrick Moynihan, Thomas Sowell, Bayard Rustin, William J. Wilson, Stephen Carter, Shelby Steele, and Jim Sleeper. These writers often stress the existence of a pathological black underclass and of a pampered and prosperous black middle class, at the same time playing down the reality of persistent discrimination against all African Americans.

Nathan Glazer, in his influential book *Affirmative Discrimination* (1975), was one of the first to articulate these themes. There he argued that the United States was winning the battle against racism, that "no one is now excluded from the broadest access" to what the U.S. economy and society make possible. Glazer celebrated the new black prosperity and attributed continuing black problems not to discrimination but mostly to a tangle of ghetto pathologies. In addition, he argued that affirmative action was wrongheaded and would not benefit impoverished blacks.[10] Writing in 1973, demographic analysts Ben Wattenberg and Richard Scammon likewise exaggerated black progress, arguing from statistical data that the number of middle-class blacks "can reasonably be said to add up to a majority of black Americans."[11] For these prominent white scholars the expansion of the black middle class seemed to signal an end to the old racist order in the United States.

Since the mid-1970s scholars in a variety of fields have developed and embellished these and related arguments. In a 1981 book *Wealth and Poverty*, once called the "Bible of the Reagan-Bush administrations," economist George Gilder declared there was no need for government action to assist black Americans because it was virtually impossible to find a serious racist in a position of power and because major discrimination had been effectively abolished in the United States.[12] Reviewing much research done on higher education in the 1980s, education professor George Keller has attributed the lack of recent black advancement in higher education to causes mostly within the black community. He downplayed racism as a major factor in blacks' problems at white colleges and universities and emphasized instead individual and family factors, including an alleged lack of black middle-class leadership.[13]

Not only white scholars but also a few black scholars discussed the decline in racial discrimination and contrasted an underprivileged underclass with a very privileged middle class. In a much cited 1978 book that triggered national discussion about race and class, *The Declining Significance of Race*, University of Chicago sociologist William J. Wilson argued that the growth of the black middle class resulted from declining racial discrimination, government remedial programs, and improving economic conditions in the 1960s and 1970s. In his view, "talented and educated blacks are experiencing unprecedented job opportunities in the growing government and corporate sectors, opportunities that are *at least* comparable to those of whites with equivalent qualifications."[14] In a later book, *The Truly Disadvantaged*, Wilson reiterated these arguments in a critique of conservative underclass theories. There he suggested that the major problem of the 1964 Civil Rights Act was its failure to improve the economic situation of the underclass, not its failure to abolish discrimination for all black Americans. Moreover, in an *Atlantic* book review, former civil rights activist Bayard Rustin went so far as to say that arguments focusing on racial discrimination and the lack of black progress only served "to alienate whites." He argued that continuing obstacles to economic and social integration for black Americans were "not primarily a result of racism" but rather had to do with family breakups and economic recessions. Since the 1970s even some black analysts like Wilson and Rustin have focused on economic and family conditions, not on antiblack discrimination, in evaluating U.S. racial relations.[15]

In *The Content of Our Character*, Shelby Steele, an English professor and a black neo-conservative analyst, deemphasized the significance of discrimination as a factor in black problems and argued that "our oppression has left us with a dangerously powerful memory of itself that pulls us into warlike defensiveness." Steele argued that this memory of past oppression is a major reason blacks do not take advantage of current opportunities. Steele further argued that a black American is "basically as free as he or she wants to be. For every white I have met who is a racist, I have met twenty more who have seen me as an equal."[16] Similarly, Yale law professor Stephen Carter has maintained that racism is "no longer the all-encompassing force it once was, and it no longer holds the entire black race in desperate thrall." The significance of racism for middle-class blacks "really *is* receding." Drawing on earlier analyses, Carter also suggested that discrimination has largely been replaced by problems of the underclass.[17]

One feature of discussions of middle-class blacks in the scholarly literature and media is a focus on the positive side of their experience, especially upward economic mobility. This approach can be found in official reports from national organizations and governmental agencies. The National Research Council (NRC) report on black Americans in the late 1980s, *A Common Destiny*, offers lengthy discussions of the problems of less well-off blacks but only a brief and generally positive assessment of the situation of the middle class.[18] Other major research reports, including *Closing the Gap*, a report from the Rand Corporation, and the *Economic Progress of Black Men in America*, a report of the U.S. Commission on Civil Rights, have emphasized the economic success of black Americans, including the middle class.[19]

Government officials joined the chorus, sometimes citing the aforementioned scholarly reports as support for government's retreat from aggressive economic opportunity and civil rights programs. In a January 1989 television interview, outgoing

President Ronald Reagan argued that civil rights leaders such as Jesse Jackson and Coretta Scott King were intentionally overstating the extent of racial discrimination and were "doing very well leading organizations based on keeping alive the feeling that they're victims of prejudice."[20] In recent years Supreme Court decisions have communicated the same official government attitude. Dissenting from a conservative decision on employment rights in 1989, liberal Justice Harry Blackmun described the attitude of the (white) majority on the nation's highest court: "One wonders whether the majority still believes that race discrimination—or, more accurately, race discrimination against nonwhites—is a problem in our society, or even remembers that it ever was."[21]

Commentators in the mass media have likewise concentrated on the prosperity and privileges of the middle class and the dilemmas of the underclass. Those in the black middle class, especially the well-educated professionals and managers, have been viewed as having achieved the American dream like the middle classes of white ethnic groups before them. The major difference between the 1960s and 1980s, suggested a *Newsweek* article celebrating black middle-class affluence, is the "emergence of an authentic black middle class, better educated, better paid, better housed than any group of blacks that has gone before it."[22] Writing in 1991 in the *Atlantic* about black middle-class prosperity and the "extraordinary integration of the races," Thomas and Mary Edsall blamed the political misfortunes of the Democratic Party in the 1970s and 1980s on white hostility toward a dangerous black underclass that whites viewed as coddled by liberal elites and government programs. In a best-selling book, *Chain Reaction*, the Edsalls, like many white media analysts, have argued that among whites there has been a "public repudiation of racism" and a "stigmatization of overly racist expression" since the 1960s.[23]

According to a 1989 article by the literary editor of *The New*

Republic, Leon Wieseltier, black leaders have exaggerated white racism as a root cause of inner city drug problems.[24] He argued that this perspective accenting racism is "madness," that "in the memory of [racial] oppression, oppression outlives itself. The scar does the work of the wound. That is the real tragedy: that injustice retains the power to distort long after it has ceased to be real." Wieseltier suggested that the scars and memories of past racial discrimination are far more serious than present racial discrimination. Moreover, in a 1991 book on New York's racial politics, journalist Jim Sleeper poked fun at black arguments about persisting institutional racism and suggested that advantaged middle-class blacks have stopped "burning the midnight oil."[25]

The argument that white racism is no longer a serious and entrenched national problem and that blacks must take individual responsibility for their problems took on juggernaut proportions in the mass media by the late 1980s and early 1990s, as books like those of Steele, Sleeper, and the Edsalls were widely celebrated. The social issues editor of *Business Week*, Elizabeth Ehrlich, praised their arguments profusely and argued that blacks' emphasis on racial victimization and redress for discrimination was both unconstructive and wrongheaded.[26] Moreover, a study of hundreds of thousands of articles and stories in several hundred mainstream magazines and newspapers published between 1978 and 1992 found only nine articles that headlined "white racism." With only two exceptions, they concerned black analysts commenting on white racism. In this fourteen-year period virtually no white journalists or editors took the central part that whites play in modern racism seriously enough to do a major article on the subject. Very few saw *white* racism as a major persisting problem for the country as a whole.[27] Even British journalists writing about the American scene have joined the white chorus, as in this 1993 comment on an African American novelist in the *Financial Times*: "[Her] subject is the central issue facing black Americans in the post civil rights era, which is no longer white racism but rather the question of identity."[28]

Influential whites are not alone in their denial of widespread white racism. A majority of the white population seems to share the view that, while discrimination still exists, it is no longer of great significance. In interviews with whites in the 1970s and early 1980s, Bob Blauner found that virtually all viewed recent decades as an era of great racial progress for U.S. racial relations.[29] In the NRC report *A Common Destiny*, editors Jaynes and Williams noted that by the late 1970s many white Americans believed that the Civil Rights Act of 1964 "had led to broad-scale elimination of discrimination against blacks in public accommodations."[30] By 1976, according to a national survey analyzed by Kluegel and Smith, 71 percent of whites agreed with the statement that "blacks and other minorities no longer face unfair employment conditions; in fact they are favored in many training and job programs." Just 12 percent agreed that "discrimination affects all black people; the only way to handle it is for blacks to organize together and demand rights for all."[31] A 1980 Gallup poll found 68 percent of whites saying that blacks now had equal standing with whites in the society.[32] And a late 1980s Louis Harris survey found that, in the case of executive-level jobs, 70 percent of the white respondents believed that blacks got fair treatment.[33] In the case of white-collar jobs in general, 69 percent of the whites did not think blacks were discriminated against. Similarly, in 1991 a National Opinion Research Center survey asked the respondents why blacks have worse jobs, lower incomes, and less desirable housing than whites. Choosing among alternative explanations, 56 percent of whites said that this was not "mainly due to discrimination."[34] From the perspective of leading white scholars, media commentators, editors, and politicians, as well as the majority of the white public, the problems of racial discrimination and injustice are not systemic or pervasive enough to require aggressive new government action.

The Continuing Significance of Racial Discrimination

In contrast to the common white view, few middle-class African Americans interviewed for this book see the significance of racism in their lives declining. Indeed, in the late 1980s and early 1990s many African Americans perceive an increase in the significance of race. We can anticipate the discussions in later chapters with this brief comment from a black professor at a northern university:

> It's just really scary, you know, to see the skinheads and the Ku Klux Klan and the white power and people like Duke, who was elected in Louisiana, with his views, being able to speak in public and get rewarded for it. . . . Right after the Sixties, there was some shame about rewarding people like that. There was a public set of rules that you just don't do that, and I think that Reagan sort of dispelled all of that. So it's open season again, so that it's okay to be a bigot, it's okay to be a racist, and "we certainly don't need all these *special* affirmative action programs and all these other things." So that sets the national tone, and I think our leadership makes a real difference.

Is this so? What do we know about the realities of racial discrimination today? In recent years a few, mostly minority, scholars have kept alive a critical perspective on the enduring white-racist social order. For example, in September 1978 the Association of Black Sociologists protested the awards given to William J. Wilson's *The Declining Significance of Race* on the grounds that he neglected "the continuing discrimination against blacks at all class levels." Since the early 1970s black scholars such as Manning Marable, Patricia Williams, Bell

Hooks, Kesho Yvonne Scott, Lois Benjamin, and Philomena Essed; Latino researchers such as John Fernandez and Rodolfo Alvarez; and white researchers such as Sidney Willhelm, Bob Blauner, and Andrew Hacker have provided important analyses of racial discrimination and inequality, drawn from demographic data, in-depth interviews, and personal experience. With one exception, Andrew Hacker's *Two Nations* (a 1992 book on racism by a white social scientist), these probing analyses have not been published by major New York trade book publishers.

During the 1960s three major surveys of African Americans were conducted by Louis Harris and Gallup and published as cover stories in *Newsweek*; three significant books were published on those surveys by Simon and Schuster. The first national survey of African Americans, conducted by Louis Harris, became a cover story for *Newsweek* in July 1963 and was soon followed by a provocative book, *The Negro Revolution in America*, which analyzed the opinion poll data in more detail in such chapters as "What It's Like to Be a Negro" and "Weapons of the Revolution." Black respondents were frequently quoted, and personal experiences with discrimination and protest were examined. Followup surveys were done in 1966 and 1969, with similar cover stories and summary books entitled *Black and White* and *Report from Black America*, respectively. All three books made use of both quantitative and qualitative data on the lives of black Americans. They, and the related *Newsweek* articles, played an important role in documenting for the white public and white policymakers the dimensions of antiblack discrimination in the 1960s.[35]

Since then no similarly systematic research on the character and breadth of the discrimination faced by black Americans in daily life has been published. A few surveys of black Americans have been conducted, but they have not dealt as much with personal encounters with discrimination as the 1960s surveys, and the data have not been so widley disseminated.[36] A 1991 review of black opinion surveys by Sigelman and Welch and the review of black surveys in *A Common Destiny* have shown that in recent years few researchers have asked black Americans specific questions about the racial discrimination they encounter in their everyday lives. When questions about discrimination have been asked, they have usually been brief and not personal, inquiring, for example, if blacks generally face discrimination in white-collar jobs, as in the 1988 Harris survey. In such surveys substantial proportions of the blacks interviewed in all regions have responded that there is significant discrimination in jobs, income, and housing.

Where a few personal questions have been asked, the answers also suggest significant and widespread discrimination. A 1978 Louis Harris survey asked: "Have you or anyone in your family been discriminated against in trying to get ahead on the job or in trying to get a job?" Thirty-nine percent reported personal or family discrimination, and another 11 percent were uncertain. Two hypothetical questions were also asked. On a job pay question just under half of the black respondents said they would probably get less pay than a white person for the same work. On a hypothetical housing question 45 percent said that if they were to get a house or an apartment "the same as a white person" they would pay more than the white person.[37] Moreover, in a 1986 ABC News/*Washington Post* poll the proportions of blacks answering "yes" to four questions about personal experience with discrimination were as follows: in getting a quality education, one quarter; in getting decent housing, one quarter; in getting a job, 39 percent; and in getting equal wages for a job, 41 percent.[38] These survey questions on black encounters with discrimination are, as Sigelman and Welch point out, "fairly crude" and ignore much racial discrimination "in the daily routines of life." They add that the extent of discrimination might be found to be even "more widespread if our measures of discrimination were more refined."[39] Opinion surveys have been brief and superficial in dealing with antiblack discrimination. They have not asked black Americans about discrimination in such important areas of everyday life as public accommodations, the street, and white-collar workplaces. The major purpose of the chapters that follow is to go beyond the bare-bones survey data to examine the character, range, and depth of the discrimination black Americans encounter, its impact, and the ways in which they cope and respond.

Racism as Everyday Experience

Much of the analysis in this book is shaped by several theoretical propositions derived substantially from close readings of our interviews with middle-class African Americans. We have found existing theories useful for interpretive purposes, but we have relied heavily on the many theoretical insights provided by our respondents. As a group, they are deeply reflective about their lives as African Americans and have constructed their own insightful theoretical frames.[40]

The first of these general propositions is that modern racism must be understood as *lived experience*. The recurring experiences of middle-class and other black Americans with whites who discriminate are the heart of the racial problem in this nation. When our respondents talk about being black in a country dominated by whites, they do not speak in abstract concepts of discrimination or racism learned only from books, but tell of mistreatment encountered as they traverse traditionally white places. Most reflect on their trials, and their interpretations of the black middle-class experience are theories grounded in their everyday lives.

Our analyses of the interviews are based on several close readings of typewritten transcripts. Rather than a collection of unrelated reflections and narratives, the interview accounts we present link together substantively at a number of different levels.

A second proposition gleaned from the interviews is that experiences with serious discrimination not only are very painful and stressful in the immediate situation and aftermath but also have a *cumulative* impact on particular individuals, their families, and their communities. A black person's life is regularly disrupted by the mistreatment suffered personally or by family members. The presence of the pronoun "we" in many black accounts of encounters with whites often suggests the collective character of the African American experience. Recurring encounters with white racism can be viewed as a series of "life crises," often similar to other serious life crises, such as the death of a loved one, that disturb an individual's life trajectory.[41] Sympathetic whites may have an intellectual understanding of the consequences of racial discrimination. Profound understanding or empathy, however, involves feeling the pain and comprehending that discrimination is a series of unforgettable life crises.

The cumulative impact on an individual of repeated personal encounters with racial hostility is greater than the sum of these encounters might appear to be to a casual observer. In addition, discrimination is seldom just a personal matter. A black victim frequently shares the account with family and friends, often to lighten the burden, and this sharing creates a domino effect of anguish and anger rippling across an extended group. An individual's discrimination becomes a family matter. Another aspect of the cumulative effect of discrimination is, of course, historical, for discriminatory incidents are freighted with centuries of racial oppression of which the black victims are consciously or unconsciously aware. Memory is a key factor. Experiences with serious discrimination are stored not only in individual memories but also in family stories and group recollections. As a result, in discussing their negative encounters with whites many respondents move easily from the "I" of their own experiences to the "we" that indicates both a broad racial consciousness and a sense of group solidarity.

The third generalization we suggest is that the repeated experience of racism significantly affects a black person's behavior and understanding of life. It shapes both one's way of living—as family members, as church members, as employees, and as citizens—and one's life perspective. By life perspective we mean one's model, one's paradigmatic assumptions about and understandings of life and of the social world. A black American's life perspective comes to embed a repertoire of responses to hostile and racist acts by whites. Like other black Americans, those we interviewed have learned to cope and contend with racial mistreatment in a variety of creative ways and somehow to maintain their equilibrium.

A fourth proposition we offer is that the daily experiences of racial hostility and discrimination encountered by middle-class and other African Americans are the constituent elements of the interlocking societal structures and processes called "institutionalized racism." Our interviews reveal much about how this discrimination works. Particular encounters with whites often hint at or reveal the influence of the larger context of institutionalized racism, for racial hostility is not inborn but learned. The reflections on black experiences and the incidents recounted in the interviews add together to show the web of intentional and unconscious discrimination across traditionally white spaces. Individual black Americans soon come to see that no amount of hard work or achieved status can protect them from racial oppression across numerous institutional arenas of this society. White discriminators typically see only the color of their skins and not their great efforts, sacrifices, and personal achievements. Moreover, through institutionalized discrimination whites not only restrict individual mobility but also social, economic, and political mobility for black Americans as a group. Indeed, to limit group mobility, to protect white privilege and power, seems to be the underlying reason for institutionalized racism.

In times of group protest by African Americans, such as the urban uprisings in cities from Los Angeles to Miami since the early 1980s, white awareness of U.S. racial problems usually increases significantly; for the most part this is temporary, however, and the majority of whites dodge the real meaning of these events. For a time whites, including scholars and media analysts, may discuss the "race relations problem" as the fault of black Americans or as an abstract problem "out there," not a problem rooted in individual whites themselves or their immediate families, social groups, and workplaces. *Time*'s front cover story soon after the 1992 Los Angeles riot was titled, "Why Race Still Divides America and Its People."[42] In reviewing mainstream media stories after the 1992 urban uprisings in Los Angeles we did not find any sustained media analysis that underscored the point our interviews dramatized: that the discriminatory *actions* of many white Americans in many institutions—and not some vague agent called "racial divisions"—are the major reason for continuing black-white problems and persisting black protest.

The Dimensions of Racial Discrimination

In the relevant social science literature racial discrimination is seldom clearly defined. In the 1944 classic, *An American Dilemma*, Gunnar Myrdal regularly used the concept but never clearly defined it.[43] Other major analysts of black-white relations from the 1940s to the 1980s, such as Blalock and Katz and Taylor, likewise give no explicit definition.[44] Among scholars who have developed definitions since the 1950s, we observe a trend toward emphasizing the macro-social level of group power and institutionalized discrimination over the micro-level of individual interaction. In *The Nature of Prejudice* (1958) Gordon Allport stressed the actions of individuals and small groups and viewed discrimination as denying "individuals or groups of people equality of treatment which they may wish."[45] By the late 1960s and early 1970s many racial relations scholars were emphasizing large groups and institutions. In a pathbreaking 1967 book, *Black Power*, Stokely Carmichael and Charles Hamilton sharply contrasted the new view of institutional racism with the older approach focusing on individual racism.[46] Similarly, Thomas Pettigrew focused on the institutional dimension: "racial discrimination is basically an institutional process of exclusion against an outgroup on largely ascribed and particularistic grounds of group membership rather than on achieved and universalistic grounds of merit."[47] While whites have the power to discriminate as individuals, much of their power to harm comes from membership in white-dominated organizations and social networks, what Randall Collins calls "enforcement coalitions."[48]

Since the 1960s we have witnessed the demise of legal segregation and the emergence of many types of informal discrimination. Blatant discrimination has been joined by much subtle and covert discrimination. Moreover, writing about present-day discrimination in Great Britain, Brittan and Maynard have noted the importance of negotiated interaction: "the terms of oppression are not only dictated by history, culture, and the sexual and social division of labor. They are also profoundly shaped at the site of the oppression, and by the way in which oppressors and oppressed continuously have to renegotiate, reconstruct, and re-establish their relative positions in respect to benefits and power."[49] What begins as one-way action by a white discriminator can become interaction, often to the surprise of the white initiator. One dramatic change in racial interaction in the last two decades is the sizeable increase in the number of middle-class black Americans with the resources to contest discrimination tacitly or explicitly.[50]

We suggest that antiblack discrimination at the interpersonal micro level can be defined as the blatant, subtle, and covert actions taken by white people, willfully or half-consciously, to exclude, restrict, or otherwise harm black people. A particular discriminatory act can become the first stage in a racial negotiation process. In addition, discriminatory actions vary on a number of important dimensions, including these often suggested in our interviews: (1) the site of the action; (2) the range of discriminatory action; (3) the impact on the victim; and (4) the character of the response. A central purpose of this book is to deepen the contemporary analysis of racial discrimination by delineating and documenting these dimensions as they recur in the accounts of our respondents.

The experience of racial hostility can vary with the character of the site where it takes place. In our interviews a black professor contrasted the protection her status gives her in certain settings with the lack of protection in other, more public, surroundings:

> If I'm in those areas that are fairly protected, within gatherings of my own group, other African Americans, or if I'm in the university where my status as a professor mediates against the way I might be perceived, mediates against the hostile perception, then it's fairly comfortable. . . . When I divide my life into encounters with the outside world, and of course that's 90 percent of my life, it's fairly consistently unpleasant at those sites where there's nothing that mediates between my race and what I have to do. For example, if I'm in a grocery store, if I'm in my car, which is a 1970 Chevrolet, a real old ugly car, all those things—being in a grocery store in casual clothes, or being in the car—sort of

> advertises something that doesn't have anything to do with my status as far as people I run into are concerned. Because I'm a large black woman, and I don't wear whatever class status I have, or whatever professional status [I have] in my appearance when I'm in the grocery store, I'm part of the mass of large black women shopping. For most whites, and even for some blacks, that translates into negative status. That means that they are free to treat me the way they treat most poor black people, because they can't tell by looking at me that I differ from that.

Protection against overt discrimination is likely to decrease as a black person moves from work settings, such as a department within a white university, into such public places as hotels, restaurants, and stores. Moreover, as black citizens move into public places such as city streets they have the most public exposure and the least protection. We will also see that in many places whites question the presence or actions of blacks. We believe that a significant dimension of modern racism is the racially motivated "blocking of space." A black person venturing into historically white spaces may learn from the attitudes, stares, or actions of whites that such sites are still "for whites only" or, at best, that it is for whites to determine who can reasonably be present.

A second important aspect of racial discrimination is its great range in character and subtlety. Allport once noted that prejudices are expressed in hostile actions ranging from antilocution to avoidance, exclusion, attack, and even genocide.[51] Today antiblack discrimination still ranges across this continuum: (1) avoidance, such as a white clerk avoiding the hand of a black customer; (2) exclusion and rejection, such as blocking a job promotion; (3) verbal attacks, such as yelling "nigger"; and (4) physical attacks, such as beatings by the police and physical assaults on college campuses. These examples are clearly overt.

More subtle forms include insults and insensitivities, which are common in everyday racism; our respondents sketch out a number of forms, including insensitivity to subcultural preferences (e.g., in music) in the workplace.

The motivations, stereotypes, and prejudices lying behind the white discrimination we examine in this book are often not clear. Still, some accounts provide some insight into white attitudes. White opinion surveys reviewed in two major books, *Racial Attitudes in America* and *A Common Destiny*, have shown that in certain subject areas white attitudes toward blacks have improved in recent decades.[52] Nonetheless, recent opinion surveys also indicate that large proportions of whites candidly express racial prejudices and stereotypes. Judging from the overtly antiblack responses to questions in 1990s opinion surveys, somewhere between 20 and 35 percent of whites are very negative and exclusionary in their attitudes toward black Americans, in regard to such matters as supporting antiintermarriage laws and keeping blacks out of white neighborhoods.[53] These percentages are very significant, especially if they do not include, as seems likely, the large proportion of whites who more or less share the same views but are unwilling to say so to a pollster. Yet if only a third or so of whites hold the most hostile antiblack views, then perhaps fifty million whites over eighteen years of age today fall into this category. This number is far greater than the total of all black men, women, and children in the United States. In addition to those whites with very hostile views, the majority of whites interviewed in recent NORC surveys have shown that they accept some racial stereotypes, such as that blacks are less hardworking and more violent than whites.[54]

In fact, in recent years social scientists have conducted few systematic, in-depth research studies of white racial attitudes or of white discriminatory actions in particular settings. Brief responses to short poll questions do not necessarily signal the true feelings of many whites. Most whites share a common historical and cultural heritage of racism centered on African Americans. While much antiblack thinking is conscious, some is so deeply embedded in white assumptions and perspectives as to be half-conscious or even unconscious. It appears that a majority of whites think in racial terms when they make important choices —choosing neighborhoods, employees, business partners, places to go in the city, and mates for themselves and their children. Indeed, the negative reactions that at least two thirds of whites in recent surveys have shown toward interracial marriages are evidence of the depths of this racial heritage.[55] Without having to think much about it, the majority of whites seem to have a racial consciousness that is more than a few prejudices, but rather a broader framework of racialized thought, a way of organizing information about black and white Americans.[56]

Another aspect of discrimination is its lasting impact. In the immediate situation or over the long haul, discrimination can generate determination, embarrassment, frustration, bitterness, anger, rage, and any combination of these feelings. Discrimination is an energy-consuming, life-consuming experience. The enduring, cumulative impact of white racism has rarely been understood by white Americans. We can illustrate it with a brief quote from a black professor who has worked in several regions of the country:

> I don't think white people, generally, understand the full meaning of racist discriminatory behaviors directed toward Americans of African descent. They seem to see each act of discrimination or any act of violence as an "isolated" event. As a result, most white Americans cannot understand the strong reaction manifested by blacks when such events occur. They feel that blacks tend to "overreact." They forget that in most cases, we live lives of quiet desperation generated by a litany of *daily* large and small events that, whether

or not by design, remind us of our "place" in American society.

Even to empathetic whites discrimination appears as discrete and isolated events. For blacks, the thick skin necessary for survival may make a given individual unaware at the conscious level, or only barely conscious, of the damage some of these instances inflict. As we noted earlier, an individual's own negative experiences are frequently shared with family and friends, relieving the victim's pain but also spreading the psychological costs. And there is the historical context to individual experience, an aspect the professor went on to explain:

> [Whites] ignore the personal context of the stimulus. That is, they deny the historical impact that a negative act may have on an individual. "Nigger" to a white may simply be an epithet that should be ignored. To most blacks, the term brings into sharp and current focus all kinds of acts of racism—murder, rape, torture, denial of constitutional rights, insults, limited opportunity structure, economic problems, unequal justice under the law and a myriad of . . . other racist and discriminatory acts that occur daily in the lives of most Americans of African descent—including professional blacks.

Surprisingly few recent analyses pay much attention to another important dimension of racial discrimination, the responses and strategies for coping of African Americans. Before desegregation in the 1960s, "old-fashioned racism," especially in the South, routinely took the form of an asymmetrical encounter in which blacks were expected to treat whites with deference. Examples included the obsequious words and gestures, the etiquette of race relations, that many black people used to survive segregation and informal mistreatment. Racially deferential behavior can still be found on the part of African

Americans, especially when there is the threat of force (for example, during police harassment) or in work situations not far removed from the old segregation. For example, Rollins found in a northeastern study that black domestic workers were commonly very deferential to white female employers.[57] Today, however, most discriminatory interactions no longer seem to involve an open show of old-fashioned deference by the black victims. Even when whites still expect it, black Americans usually do not oblige.

While many whites assert that blacks jump much too quickly to a cry of "racism," in reality the opposite reaction is more likely the case. Our interviews suggest that black middle-class people frequently respond to possible discrimination by taking a "long look," by evaluating a situation carefully before judging it discriminatory and taking action. One respondent, a clerical employee, described the "second eye" she uses: "I think that it causes you to have to look at things from two different perspectives. You have to decide whether things that are done or slights that are made are made because you are black or they are made because the person is just rude, or unconcerned and uncaring. So it's kind of a situation where you're always kind of looking to see with a second eye or a second antenna just what's going on." The term "second eye" suggests that she and others like her look carefully at white-black interaction through a distinctive lens colored by accumulating personal and group experience. We have noted in our interviews the willingness of many black respondents, using this "second eye," to give whites the benefit of the doubt in many interracial encounters.

Once a black person has spent mental energy in evaluating the situation, the active response to it may vary greatly. One strategy is to leave rather than engage in explicit conflict. Another is to ignore the discrimination and continue with the interaction, a strategy similar to the one Carol Brooks Gardner has reported in her research on women who deal with harassing remarks from men on the street.[58] In some situations resigned acceptance may be the only realistic response. More confrontational responses to hostile white actions include verbal reprimands and sarcasm, physical counterattacks, and lawsuits.

Most people want to be legitimate in the eyes of others, and this includes many white discriminators. This concern for legitimacy can give black victims some leverage in certain discriminatory situations. In subsequent chapters numerous respondents articulate an ideal of "liberty and justice for all." What is especially significant is that the equal rights ideology of these middle-class black Americans is based on this American creed, the basic American principles accepted in the abstract, if not in practice, by most whites. The American creed and the legal system are often silent partners in black battles with an often hostile white world.

What Is the Black Middle Class?

Middle class African Americans are the group within black America that, generally speaking, has had the most recent experience with whites across the broadest array of social situations. They are often the ones who are desegregating historically white arenas and institutions, including upscale restaurants and department stores, business enterprises, corporate and government workplaces, white colleges, and white neighborhoods.

Since the nineteenth century the black middle class has been held up as a model for or sign of black advancement. For many decades the importance of the middle class has been emphasized by black leaders, as in William E. B. Du Bois' advocacy of an educated black elite working for social change.[59] Since the publication of E. Franklin Frazier's *Black Bourgeoisie* in the mid-1950s, a "new black middle class" composed increasingly of white-collar workers has been the subject of some scholarly and general discussion. In this controversial book Frazier criticized the black middle class as a whole for its conspicuous consumption, its obsession with status, and its uselessness within the larger society.[60] Most subsequent assessments of middle-class black Americans have been more balanced and have recognized the important achievements and general significance of this segment of black America.

In the social science literature there is no consensus definition of this black middle class, but several social scientists have used a broad demarcation including white-collar workers, sometimes with the addition of the most skilled blue-collar workers.[61] Historically, this class has grown significantly. In 1910 about 6 percent of blacks and a quarter of whites were in what the Census Bureau defined as trade, government service, professional, and clerical occupations, categories roughly covering that demarcation.[62] A few decades later, in 1940, only 9 percent of employed blacks were in white-collar or skilled blue-collar jobs, compared with just under half of whites. Significant gains came in the next few decades, and by 1970 the proportions had risen to 32 percent of blacks and 62 percent of whites.[63]

Legal equality for blacks under the 1960s civil rights laws generated a significant expansion of a formerly small middle class. In a pathbreaking analysis Bart Landry speaks of the 1960s as creating a "new middle class" whose "emergence marked a major turning point in the life of black people in the United States."[64] Landry and William J. Wilson, among others, have demonstrated the role of Vietnam-war-related economic growth and government antidiscrimination action in opening up job opportunities and spurring the development of the black middle class since the 1960s.

The broad occupational categories used by the Census Bureau were changed in 1980, so that recent data are not strictly comparable to earlier data. However, a 1988 Bureau of Labor Statistics survey found that about half of employed blacks held white-collar or skilled blue-collar jobs, compared with seventy percent of whites.[65] Yet these data probably exaggerate black progress, for those black employees in the Census Bureau's white-collar categories are often disproportionately concentrated in lower-status jobs.

Some researchers have suggested that educational attainment and income position should be considered in estimating accurately the security and size of the black middle class.[66] In many discussions middle-class status for black Americans is associated with higher levels of education, certainly a high school education and usually some college work. In 1989 about two thirds of black Americans over the age of twenty-four had completed high school. About 28 percent had completed at least a year of college, and just 12 percent had secured a college degree.[67] Increasingly, some college work, if not a college degree, seems essential to secure placement in the middle class, and this may especially be true for black Americans. Moreover, in the existing literature there seems to be no consistent standard for what is a middle-class income for black Americans, but one might speculate that an annual income near or above the white median for individuals or families might be a very rough standard for black individuals or families, at least for those with established households. A federal report found that in 1947 only 17 percent of black families had incomes above the white median income. By 1974 the proportion of black families above the white median had grown to nearly one quarter. Since the 1970s blacks have apparently made only small gains relative to whites. From 1988 data one can estimate that a little more than a quarter of black families had incomes above the white median income for that year.[68] Since the 1970s blacks have made only small gains relative to whites. Using these educational and income data, one might estimate that from one quarter to one third of the black population is more or less securely middle class.[69] While there is as yet no consensus on which measures to use, it is clear that occupational, educational, and income criteria have been used, separately or together, by many analysts to come up with rough evaluations of the character or size of the black middle class.

African American Witnesses: Our Middle-Class Respondents

Analyses of the economic and social status of African Americans that rely on Census Bureau data and public opinion surveys are useful, but they lack experiential depth. Examination of the texture, range, and meaning of black experiences requires something more than quick responses to survey questions. Sociologist Herbert Blumer once noted that the only way to "get assurance is to go directly to the empirical world—to see through meticulous examination of it whether one's premises or root images of it, one's questions and problems for it, the data one chooses out of it, the concepts through which one sees and analyzes it, and the interpretations one applies to it are actually borne out."[70]

Listening at some length to black witnesses talking about everyday experiences is particularly important for white analysts who wish to understand the contemporary situations and experiences of black Americans. It would appear that few white Americans even begin to understand the character, pain, and meaning of the contemporary black experience with racial hostility and discrimination. In an article in the *Washington Post* written a few months before her suicide in 1984, Leanita McClain, a prize-winning black journalist, wrote how her feelings toward the whites she worked with changed as she heard them viciously attack Harold Washington, the first black mayor of Chicago: "I had put so much effort into belonging, and the whites had put so much effort into making me feel as if I belonged, that we all deceived ourselves. . . . But none of us had ever dealt with the deeper inhibitions, myths and misperceptions that this society has force-fed us."[71]

Grass-roots theorists, what Antonio Gramsci once called the "organic intellectuals,"[72] frequently develop theory out of the daily experiences of difficulties and oppression. In our research we listened, usually at some length, to the accounts of many middle-class African Americans about their experiences with racial hostility and discrimination in contemporary America. We have received valuable insights from black correspondents and informants in powerful positions in traditionally white institutions across the nation, from middle-class blacks in the audiences where we have presented lectures, and from our own black students. While we make good use of these discussions in the chapters that follow, we draw most heavily on in-depth interviews with a sample of 209 middle-class African Americans, a group that represents a range of middle-class experience. Like other qualitative studies of the contemporary American experience[73] we do not have a systematic random sample, but we have made a strong attempt to talk with a broad and diverse group of middle-class African Americans. Those interviewed were selected, in a snowball design with dozens of different starting points, from the ranks of those reputed to be middle class. All but one were interviewed by black interviewers. The sample is about half male and half female. Just over half are between thirty-six and fifty years old; another third are eighteen to thirty-six; and about a sixth are over fifty. At the time of the interview about two thirds were residents of southern or southwestern cities; about 6 percent were then in western or midwestern cities; and 29 percent were then in northern cities. In the sample, those in the South and Southwest are overrepresented relative to the U.S. black population, but in our chapter presentations we examine a large number of accounts from respondents in other regions. Wherever they reside now, many have lived in other regions, and their perspectives and comments on discrimination and related matters are often shaped by their travels and experiences in a variety of places. As we will see in the chapters that follow, racial discrimination is no respecter of region, age, gender, or socioeconomic status.[74]

Virtually all these respondents have occupied, currently occupy, or will likely soon occupy white-collar jobs and positions, or currently head their own businesses. Several are students at predominantly white colleges preparing for middle-class jobs. Most are managers, teachers, social service workers, doctors or other health care professionals, lawyers, electronics and computer professionals, government officials, college professors and administrators, journalists or others in the mass media, business owners, or clerical/sales workers. About 30 percent (including college students) reported household incomes of $35,000 or less; about a fifth, in the $36,000–$55,000 range; and about half, in the over $55,000 bracket.[75] As a whole, our sample is well educated. All have at least a high school degree, and almost all (95 percent) have done some college work. Nearly eight in ten have college degrees; and more than four in ten have done some graduate work. Practically all the respondents fall clearly into the black middle class, according to one or more of the socioeconomic criteria of "middle class" noted earlier, and many are in the upper middle class.

While we recognize that our sample is not random in the statistical sense, we have taken pains to insure that we have a broad group representing many subcategories and sectors of the black middle class. In Chapters 3 and 5 we also draw on two recent research studies by the first author that have examined the situations of other groups of African Americans, one a study of black businesspeople in a major southeastern metropolis and another of black college students and parents in an eastern state. In addition, we draw throughout the book on extensive discussions of our respondents' experiences with more than sixty black middle-class informants across the nation, including journalists, administrators, graduate students, and scholars. Drawing on their own experiences, these African Americans have often insisted on validating our respondents' accounts by telling us about recent negative encounters they or their families have had with white Americans.[76] Where possible, we also make use of other recent research studies, including survey data, that relate to topics we examine in the in-depth interview data. Drawing on these multiple sources, we feel confident that the accounts of our respondents give an accurate picture of many of the racial barriers and obstacles middle-class black Americans face in their daily lives.

The main body of the interview schedule usually consisted of open-ended questions on subjects related to life goals and recent experiences with racial discrimination. Respondents were permitted to discuss questions out of order and to digress to other subjects they considered important.[77] One of the limitations of brief surveys is that they do not let respondents assess issues in their own terms. Our open-ended questions allowed our black respondents to speak in their own terms and to present their own accounts of everyday events, as well as to indicate much about their social contexts and relationships. Many of our respondents' accounts have an important processual dimension, that is, are narratives of events that have happened to them in their daily rounds. The narratives are prisms revealing much about the racial practices and structures of the United States. Our interpretations of the black experience with discrimination and other racial matters are profoundly shaped by being in contact with the complexities of their everyday worlds.

We promised the respondents we would not reveal their names and addresses and would keep interview responses anonymous. Indeed, many talked with us only on condition of anonymity, perhaps fearing reprisals from some whites.[78] We usually opened the interview itself with a general break-the-ice question probing what it means to be black in America these days, then asked about their personal goals, their recent experiences in employment, housing, and schooling, and their coping strategies and resources, both personal and familial. Most of the respondents' retrospective accounts relate experiences from the early 1980s to about 1989, with some references to an earlier period. Our other research accounts date from the mid-1980s to the early 1990s. We concluded the interviews with some other general questions, usually about social change and the future of racial relations in the United States.[79]

In the chapters that follow we quote from these interviews, with an emphasis on those with the most detail and insights about black experiences. We use numerous quotes to indicate what the barriers to achieving the American dream are for middle-class African Americans and to show how these respondents daily contend with obstacles. Each interview can be viewed as a "case study" in itself, since we usually listened at some length to our respondents' chronicles of discrimination and coping strategies. Moreover, like other qualitative researchers we have far more in-depth interview material on black-white interactions than we can possibly present in one book. We regret not being able to quote directly from all of those African Americans who kindly gave of their valuable time to be interviewed. Yet we do make indirect use of virtually all the interviews. The wealth of material on the daily lives, experiences, and perspectives of our entire sample, as well as other middle-class informants, constantly filters into our analysis at one point or another as we attempt to present a comprehensive portrait of what it means to be black and middle class in the United States today.

Conclusion

We have shown that the commonplace discussion of the declining significance of race and racism includes a singling out of middle-class African Americans as hard evidence that all blacks who "get it together" and work hard enough can "make it" in the United States. The black middle class reveals the great progress made in U.S. racial relations and proves, it is said, that black Americans, like white immigrant groups before them, can achieve the rags-to-riches Horatio Alger dream if they try hard enough. The premier measure of personal and group success in this society is upward mobility, and middle-class mobility and achievements are the chosen measures of black progress. No group has been more committed to achieving the American dream of equal opportunity and success through hard work than the black middle class. McClain, the prize-winning journalist cited earlier, commented in an October 1980 *Newsweek* column that middle-class blacks have the same American dream as whites: "These include the proverbial dream house, two cars, an above-average school and a vacation for the kids at Disneyland."[80] The behavior and achievements of middle-class African Americans demonstrate a strong commitment to the work ethic, to the belief that each American should work hard and strive to succeed in competition with others, and to the belief that those who work hard should have equal opportunity and be rewarded with a recognition of their achievements and with middle-class symbols and resources.

Yet our analysis suggests that racial hostility and discrimination make it impossible for any African American to achieve the full promise of the American dream. We can anticipate some of the later discussion with a few brief quotes from several respondents. Take the case of a once successful black executive in the North, now out of work and suing his employer for discrimination. He recounted his dream and his struggle: "So it's affected my life in a very profound way, and for one who has attempted all his life to achieve the American dream—and I say that in terms of having gone to school, done well in school, both in college and graduate school, served honorably in the military, given many years of outstanding service in a major corporation, and lesser useful service in several other organizations—to end up in a situation where you're having to go into the courts to have your basic rights reinforced, it's a real downer." Some material goods are secured; and personal achievements can be considerable, but racial barriers are routinely thrown up by the many whites who do not want blacks to succeed. The experience of middle-class African Americans on the street and in restaurants, neighborhoods, schools, and workplaces is quite different from the ideals of justice and equality, as a professor at a western university indicated: "It's a schizoid time. You have laws on the books that say that you, that there is no discrimination, that all men are treated equal. Yet every system that you encounter discriminates against you. It's very schizoid. You have to operate in two different spheres constantly." It seems likely that most African Americans with the income and occupational standing to be considered middle class sooner or later comprehend that they can never become truly middle class, at least in the ways available to white Americans. An anchorperson for a major TV station was adamant: "[There is] no black middle class, by the way. You know that's relevant. Every time I use 'middle class,' I know that. Because a black middle-class person is still not a middle-class person." And a government administrator put it another way: "Well, I heard somebody say, or I read once, that they were a middle class person trapped in a black body. And that's really the way I feel."

To be accepted as truly American, or not to be. To be allowed to be truly middle class, or not to be. These questions are forced on African Americans by a racist social system. Writing long ago in *The Souls of Black Folk*, Du Bois described a troubled black consciousness that is created by white racism: "It is a peculiar sensation, this double consciousness, this sense of always looking at one's self through the eyes of others. . . . One feels his two-ness—an American, a Negro; two souls, two thoughts, two unreconciled strivings; two warring ideals in one dark body, whose dogged strength alone keeps it from being torn asunder. The history of the American Negro is the history of this strife—this longing to attain self-conscious manhood, to merge his double self into a better and truer self."[81]

Chapter Two

Navigating Public Places

TITLE II of the most important civil rights act of this century, the 1964 Civil Rights Act, stipulates that "all persons shall be entitled to the full and equal enjoyment of the goods, services, facilities, privileges, advantages, and accommodations of any place of public accommodation . . . without discrimination or segregation on the ground of race, color, religion, or national origin." Yet, as we approach the twenty-first century, this promise of full and equal enjoyment of the public places and accommodations of the United States is far from reality for African Americans.

Not long ago Debbie Allen, a movie star and television producer, recounted a painful experience with discrimination at a Beverly Hills jewelry store. A white clerk, possibly stereotyping Allen as poor or criminal, refused to show her some jewelry. Allen was so incensed that she used the incident as the basis for an episode on a television show. Across the country in Tamarac, Florida, a twenty-year-old black man, wearing a Syracuse University cap and hoping to invest his savings, visited a branch of Great Western Bank seeking information. After stopping at other banks, he returned to Great Western, got more information, and then went to his car to review the materials. There he was surrounded by sheriff's deputies with guns drawn, handcuffed, and read his rights. The deputies questioned him for some time before dismissing the report of white bank employees that the black man looked like a bank robber.[1]

Discrimination in Public Accommodations

In this chapter the middle-class respondents challenge us to reflect on their experiences with discrimination as they move into traditionally white public accommodations, such as upscale restaurants and department stores, and through public streets once the territory only of whites. They frequently report that their middle-class resources and status provide little protection against overt discrimination. Although there are, at least in principle, some social restraints on hostile white behavior in public accommodations, African Americans often experience hostility and mistreatment when they venture into spaces where many whites question the presence of a black person.

In the authors' experience many middle-class African Americans can relate several recent stories of being treated poorly by whites in public accommodations officially made hospitable by decades of civil rights laws. In our respondents' accounts restaurants are one site of hostile treatment, as are stores, hotels, and places of amusement. A black minister in a predominantly white denomination described his experience at a restaurant near a southern religious camp:

> We were refused service, because they said they didn't serve black folk. It was suggested that if we stayed there any longer, that there was a possibility that our tires would be slashed. We finally stayed long enough for them to say,

> "Well, I'll tell you what. We will serve you something to go, but you cannot come inside. We refuse that." And it was a situation that—I was not prepared for that. I was angry. I was humiliated, and I wanted to do something. I wanted to kick some ass.[2]

Given the threat of violence, he did not respond aggressively to this exclusion, but internalized his anger. Such encounters are not isolated events for many middle-class black Americans. The minister described yet another incident in a southern metropolis:

> I was at this place called Joe's restaurant. I had to go into Joe's because I came up in that community. Joe's is a barbecue place that is right by the auto plant, so all of the executives from the plant would come there for lunch. I went there with a guy who was successful. [I] thought I was a decent black person, came in wearing a suit and tie, sat down, and I noticed that, you know, these white boys kept coming in, and the waitress kept on looking over me. And I eventually said to her, "Ma'am, I'd like to order." She said, "Well, you're going to have to wait." And I complained to the owner and he proceeded to cuss me out. Told me that I didn't have "no goddamn business" in that restaurant telling them who they ought to serve and when they ought to serve them. Told me that. I came up in the neighborhood, been eating there for years, and it suddenly dawned on me that white folk will take your money, but to them in their minds you're still a nigger. They're able to separate economics from dealing with relationships between them and black folk. He challenged me to a fight, and this was another source of humiliation. I said to myself, "If I fought this man in his restaurant with there being a hundred white boys that'll substantiate whatever story he told, they could

> lynch me and say that I hung myself, you know." I left. I've never gone back to that place. But I've always thought about burning it down.

In spite of the 1964 Civil Rights Act black customers today encounter poor service or are refused service. Even with the growth of black economic resources, there seems to be some conflict within many white business owners between taking the dollars blacks can spend and recoiling from dealing with blacks.

In such events the person being rudely treated or ignored is usually quite conscious of the historical context of the interaction, as can be seen in the minister's allusion of lynching. In another account, a black news director at a television station described an incident in which she and her boyfriend responded very differently to an act of discrimination and the anger it provoked in them:

> He was waiting to be seated. . . . he said, "you go to the bathroom and I'll get the table. . . ." He was standing there when I came back; he continued to stand there. The restaurant was almost empty. There were waiters, waitresses, and no one seated. And when I got back to him, he was ready to leave, and said, "let's go." I said, "what happened to our table?" He wasn't seated. So I said, "no, we're not leaving, please." And he said, "no, I'm leaving." So we went outside, and we talked about it. And what I said to him was, you have to be aware of the possibilities that this is not the first time that this has happened at this restaurant or at other restaurants, but this is the first time it has happened to a black news director here or someone who could make an issue of it, or someone who is prepared to make an issue of it.
>
> So we went back inside after I talked him into it and, to make a long story short, I had the manager come. I made most of the people who were there (while conducting my-

self professionally the whole time) aware that I was incensed at being treated this way. . . . "I said, why do you think we weren't seated?" And the manager said, "well, I don't really know." And I said, "guess." He said, "well I don't know, because you're black?" I said, "bingo." "Now isn't it funny that you didn't guess that I didn't have any money (and I opened up my purse and I said, because I certainly have money). And isn't it odd that you didn't guess that it's because I couldn't pay for it because I've got two American Express cards and a Master Card right here. I think it's just funny that you would have assumed that it's because I'm black." . . . . And then I took out my [business] card and gave it to him and said, "if this happens again, or if I hear of this happening again, I will bring the full wrath of an entire news department down on this restaurant." And he just kind of looked at me. "Not [just] because I am personally offended. I am. But because you have no right to do what you did, and as a people we have lived a long time with having our rights abridged."

There were probably three or four sets of diners in the restaurant and maybe five waiters/waitresses. They watched him [her boyfriend] standing there waiting to be seated. His reaction to it was that he wanted to leave. I understood why he would have reacted that way, because he felt that he was in no condition to be civil. He was ready to take the place apart and . . . sometimes it's appropriate to behave that way. We hadn't gone the first step before going on to the next step. He didn't feel that he could comfortably and calmly take the first step, and I did. So I just asked him to please get back in the restaurant with me, and then you don't have to say a word, and let me handle it from there. It took some convincing, but I had to appeal to his sense of, this is not just you, this is not just for you. We are finally in a position as black people where there are

> some of us who can genuinely get their attention. And if they don't want to do this because it's right for them to do it, then they'd better do it because they're afraid to do otherwise. If it's fear, then fine, instill the fear.

Discrimination here was not the "No Negroes" exclusion of the recent past, but rejection in the form of poor service. Again a black person's skin color took precedence over money. The black response has changed too, since the 1950s and 1960s, from deference to indignant, vigorous confrontation. Here the assertive black response and the white backtracking are typical of "negotiation" that can occur in racial confrontations today.

In recounting this incident this black professional mentions black "rights" several times. Clearly imbedded in her response is a theory of rights that she, like many African Americans, holds as a part of her worldview. Her response signals the impact of the tradition of civil rights struggle, and civil rights laws, on the life perspective of African Americans. Also of interest here is her mention of her credit cards and other middle-class resources. A quick reading of her statement, and that of other black middle-class people who mention similar trappings of success, might lead to the conclusion that middle-class blacks expect to be treated better than poorer blacks because they have worked hard and have money. But this does not seem to be the meaning of such references. Instead, this woman is outraged that the obvious evidence of hard work and achievements does not protect her from racial discrimination. She has achieved certain elements of the American dream, but they are not sufficient.

A close look at the experience of middle-class African Americans is important to understand the racial backwardness of contemporary U.S. society, for it confirms that no amount of hard work, money, and success can protect a black person from the destructive impact of racial stereotyping and discrimination. In this book we show that middle-class black Americans, just like other black Americans, have terrible experiences with everyday racism. But we show much more than that. We also demonstrate that racial stereotyping and discrimination operate independently of the real identities and achievements of specifically targeted black individuals.

The ability of middle-class African Americans to act forcefully against discrimination by whites marks a change from a few decades ago when very few had the resources to fight back successfully. Black Americans have always fought against discrimination, but in earlier decades such fights were usually doomed to failure if not injury. In this account, the woman's ability as a professional to bring a television news team to the restaurant enabled her to take assertive action. This example also underscores the complexity of the interaction in some situations of discrimination, for not only is there a confrontation with a white manager over mistreatment but also a negotiation between the black individuals over how to respond.

It is an effective antidiscrimination strategy on the part of black Americans to make the confrontations public. An executive at a financial institution in an East Coast city recounted his experience with a pattern of poor service in a restaurant, explaining his decision to confront the discriminators:

> I took the staff here to a restaurant that had recently opened in the prestigious section of the city, and we waited while other people got waited on, and decided that after about a half hour that these people don't want to wait on us. I happened to have been in the same restaurant a couple of evenings earlier, and it took them about forty-five minutes before they came to wait on me and my guest. So, on the second incident, I said, this is not an isolated incident, this is a pattern, because I had spoken with some other people who had not been warmly received in the restau-

> rant. So, I wrote a letter to the owners . . . and sent copies to the city papers. That's my way of expressing myself and letting the world know. You have to let people, other than you and the owner know. You have to let others know you're expressing your dismay at the discrimination or the barrier that's presented to you. I met with the owners. Of course, they wanted to meet with their attorneys with me, because they wanted to sue me. I told them they're welcome to do so. I don't have a thing, but fine they can do it. It just happens that I knew their white attorney. And he more or less vouched that if I had some concern that it must have been legitimate in some form. When the principals came in, one of the people who didn't wait on me was one of the owners who happened to be waiting on everybody else. We resolved the issue by them inviting me to come again, and if I was fairly treated, or if I would come on several occasions and if I was fairly treated I would write a statement of retraction. I told them I would not write a retraction, I would write a statement with regard to how I was treated. Which I ultimately did. And I still go there today, and they speak to me, and I think the pattern is changed to a great degree.

The time- and energy-consuming aspects of publicly confronting discrimination are apparent in this account. The respondent invested much of himself in a considered response to a recurring problem. Forcing whites to renegotiate, especially by using negative publicity, can bring about changes. The arrival on the restaurant scene of middle-class black Americans with substantial resources has at least created situations that force whites into explicit negotiating.

Whites often enter into this "bargaining" situation with tacit assumptions and cultural expectations about black powerlessness. In the two previous examples we see the black professionals establishing "power credibility," as the whites decide that they are not bluffing. It is important to note that the whites here are not just the blue-collar whites often said to be the primary source of whatever bigotry remains in the United States. Those doing the discrimination include middle-class whites, a fact that signals the importance of race over class in much racial interaction.

That discrimination against black customers and employees in white-owned restaurants is widespread has become evident in several court suits filed since 1990 against national chains, including Denny's, Shoney's, and the International House of Pancakes (IHOP). In December 1991, for example, several groups of black college students were reportedly turned away from a Milwaukee IHOP restaurant and told that it was closed, while white customers were allowed in. In 1993 a federal judge ordered the restaurant to pay a settlement for the discrimination. Also in 1993, the Denny's chain, found to have a pattern of discrimination by the U.S. Justice Department, reached an agreement with the Department in which executives promised to train employees in nondiscriminatory behavior and to include more minorities in its advertising. This settlement did not affect a class-action discrimination suit by thirty-two black customers who reportedly had suffered discrimination in several Denny's restaurants in California. Moreover, in mid-1993 six black secret service agents also sued the chain, alleging discrimination at a Denny's in Annapolis, Maryland. The black agents reported that while they waited for service for nearly an hour, white agents and other white patrons were promptly served.[3] After much bad publicity, Denny's joined in an important agreement with the NAACP to work to end discrimination in its restaurants.[4]

As revealed in the court cases, restaurant discrimination has recently included long waits while whites are served, special cover fees applied only to blacks, and prepayment requirements only for black customers.[5] In the Shoney's case, the chain was sued over discrimination against black employees. According to the *St. Petersburg Times*, top officers in the white-run firm were well-known for their antiblack views, and local managers were discouraged from hiring black employees. In a 1992 landmark agreement the company agreed to pay $115 million, the most ever, to employees who could prove racial discrimination.[6]

Restaurants are only one site of discrimination. Daily life inevitably involves contact with clerks and managers in various retail and grocery stores. A utility company executive in an eastern city described how her family was treated in a small store:

> I can remember one time my husband had picked up our son . . . from camp; and he'd stopped at a little store in the neighborhood near the camp. It was hot, and he was going to buy him a snowball. . . . This was a very old, white neighborhood, and it was just a little sundry store. But the proprietor had a little window where people could come up and order things. Well, my husband and son had gone into the store. And he told them, "Well, I can't give it to you here, but if you go outside to the window, I'll give it to you." And there were other people in the store who'd been served [inside]. So, they just left and didn't buy anything.

The old white neighborhood in which this episode occurred exemplifies the racial-territorial character of many cities even today. The poor service here seems a throwback to the South of the 1950s, where deferential blacks were served only at the back of a store. This man chose not to confront the white person nor to acquiesce abjectly but rather to leave. Here the effect on the white man was probably inconsequential because there was no confrontation and interracial negotiation. The long-run importance of a service site may well affect a black person's choice of how to respond to such discrimination. The store in this example was not important to the black family just passing through the area. The possibility of returning might have generated a more confrontational response.

Another problem that black shoppers face, especially in department and grocery stores, is the common white assumption that they are likely shoplifters. This is true in spite of the fact that national crime statistics show that most shoplifters are white. For several months in late 1991 a news team at KSTP-TV in Minneapolis conducted a field study of discrimination against black shoppers in several local department stores. Members of the team took jobs as security personnel in the stores, and black and white shoppers were sent into the stores in order to observe the reactions of white security personnel. The ensuring television report, "Who's Minding the Store?" showed how many black customers became the targets of intensive surveillance from white security guards, who neglected white shoppers when black shoppers were in the stores. As a result of the documentary, local black leaders called for a boycott of one of the store chains. Soon a number of the local stores changed their surveillance and security procedures.[7] Excessive surveillance of black customers in department and other stores was reported by some we interviewed. A black professional in the North commented on how she deals with whites who harass her with excessive surveillance and other acts of rejection:

> [I have faced] harassment in stores, being followed around, being questioned about what are you going to purchase here. . . . I was in an elite department store just this past Saturday and felt that I was being observed while I was window shopping. I in fact actually ended up purchasing something, but felt the entire time I was there—I was in blue jeans and sneakers, that's how I dress on a Saturday—I felt that I was being watched in the store as I was walking through the store—what business did I have there, what

> was I going to purchase, that kind of thing. . . . There are a few of those white people that won't put change in your hand, touch your skin. That doesn't need to go on. [Do you tell them that?] Oh, I do, I do. That is just so obvious. I usually [speak to them] if they're rude in the manner in which they deal with people. [What do they say about that?] Oh, stuff like, "Oh, excuse me," and some who are really unconscious about it, say "Excuse me," and put the change in your hand. That's happened. But I've watched other people be rude, and I've been told to mind my own business. [But you still do it?] Oh, sure, because for the most part I think that people do have to learn to think for themselves, and demand respect for themselves. . . . I find my best weapon of defense is to educate them, whether it's in the store, in a line, at the bank, any situation, I teach them. And you take them by surprise because you tell them and show them what they should be doing, and what they should be saying, and how they should be thinking. And they look at you because they don't know how to process you. They can't process it because you've just shown them how they should be living, and the fact that they are cheating themselves, really, because the racism is from fear. The racism is from lack of education.

A number of racial stereotypes are evident in this account. Whites with images of black criminality engage in excessive surveillance, and whites with images of black dirtiness will not touch black hands or skin. Black shoppers at all income levels report being ignored when in need of service and the unwillingness of some whites even to touch their hands. Why such a reaction to black bodies? In a speculative Freudian analysis of white racism, Joel Kovel has argued that for centuries whites have irrationally connected blackness, and black bodies, with fecal matter and dirt. In his view, whites are somehow projecting onto the darkness of the black outgroup personal inclinations, desires, and fears that cannot be openly and honestly acknowledged.[8]

A common black response to contemporary discrimination is evident here. Rather than withdrawing when facing such discrimination, this professional sometimes protracts the interaction with verbal confrontation. She notes the surprise effect of calling whites on the carpet for discrimination, which she sees as grounded in fear and ignorance. Interrupting the normal flow of an interaction to change a one-way experience into a two-way experience forces whites into unaccustomed situations in which they are unsure how to respond.

Middle-class African Americans enter many settings where few blacks have been before. A news anchorperson for an East Coast television station reported on an incident at a luxury automobile dealer:

> I knew I wanted to buy a Porsche, but I didn't know which model. So, on my day off, I went into a Porsche dealership in the city I used to work in. . . . And I was dressed like I normally do when I'm off. I'm into working out a lot, so I'm in sweatsuits, baseball caps, sunglasses quite a bit. So I dashed into this place dressed like that, and I must have walked around the show room floor for twenty minutes. No sales person ever walked up to me and asked me, "Can I help you? Can I give you some information?" Nothing. I got the impression, the opinion, that they generally thought that this person, being black, being dressed in a sweatsuit, cannot hardly afford to be in here buying a Porsche. He's wasting my time, so I'm not even going to bother. And I knew that. So I specifically, the next day on my lunch hour, dressed in my work clothes, having just come off the air, I walked into that showroom. And I said, "Can I see the general manager?" And they got the general manager for

> me. And I said to the general manager, "I was in here yesterday." Well, I said, "First of all, I want to buy that Porsche there, the most expensive one on the floor." And I also told him, "Just yesterday I was in here, I was looking in, and I was hoping I could get some information, and oddly none of your sales people ever asked me if they could help me." . . . And there is prejudice, discrimination and racism, and things like that go on. Once they found out who I was, they bent over backwards [to wait on me].

White salespeople apparently took the cue from this man's color and clothing and stereotyped him as moneyless, an assumption that the victim challenged the next day when he engaged in an unexpected confrontation. This chronic mistreatment by white salespeople, while white shoppers are generally treated with greater respect, is infuriating for black customers. It is clear from our interviews that African Americans must prepare themselves for this sort of encounter, for they never know when they will be shown normal respect and courtesy as customers or when they must "front" (dress in a certain way, talk in a certain way) in order to receive the treatment accorded a comparable white customer.

Among several respondents who discussed discrimination at retail stores, the manager of a career development organization, who found that discrimination by clerks is common, had a repertoire of responses for dealing with it:

> If you're in a store—and let's say the person behind the counter is white—and you walk up to the counter, and a white person walks up to the counter, and you know you were there before the white customer, the person behind the counter knows you were there first, and it never fails, they always go, "Who's next." Ok. And what I've done, if they go ahead and serve the white person first, then I will imme-

> diately say, "Excuse me, I was here first, and we both know I was here first." . . . If they get away with it once, they're going to get away with it more than once, and then it's going to become something else. And you want to make sure that folks know that you're not being naive, that you really see through what's happening. Or if it's a job opportunity or something like that, too, same thing. You first try to get a clear assessment of what's really going on and sift through that information, and then . . . go from there.

In discussions with middle-class black Americans across the nation, both our respondents and a variety of informants and journalists, we heard many similar accounts of white clerks "looking through" black customers and only "seeing" whites farther back in line. Such incidents suggest that much of the hostility manifest in white actions is based on a deeplying, perhaps even subconscious or half-conscious, aversion to black color and persona. This executive also spoke of her coping process, one that begins with sifting information before deciding on action. Frequently choosing immediate action, she forces whites to face the reality of their behavior.

The dean of a black college who travels in various parts of the United States described the often complex process of evaluating and responding to the mistreatment that has plagued him in public accommodations:

> When you're in a restaurant and . . . you notice that blacks get seated near the kitchen. You notice that if it's a hotel, your room is near the elevator, or your room is always way down in a corner somewhere. You find that you are getting the undesirable rooms. And you come there early in the day and you don't see very many cars on the lot and they'll tell you that this is all we've got. Or you get the room that's got a bad television set. You know that you're being dis-

> criminated against. And of course you have to act accordingly. You have to tell them, "Okay, the room is fine, [but] this television set has got to go. Bring me another television set." So in my personal experience, I simply cannot sit and let them get away with it and not let them know that I know that that's what they are doing. . . .
>
> When I face discrimination, first I take a long look at myself and try to determine whether or not I am seeing what I think I'm seeing in 1989, and if it's something that I have an option [about]. In other words, if I'm at a store making a purchase, I'll simply walk away from it. If it's at a restaurant where I'm not getting good service, I first of all let the people know that I'm not getting good service, then I [may] walk away from it. But the thing that I have to do is to let people know that I know that I'm being singled out for separate treatment. And then I might react in any number of ways—depending on where I am and how badly I want whatever it is that I'm there for.

These recurring incidents in public accommodations illustrate the cumulative nature of discrimination. The dean first takes care to assess the incident and avoid jumping to conclusions. One must be constantly prepared on everyday excursions to assess accurately what is happening and then to decide on an appropriate response. What is less obvious here is the degree of pain and emotional drain that such a constant defensive stance involves.

Whether some of the incidents reported by the last two respondents are in fact discriminatory is a question raised by some whites to whom we have shown these commentaries. Several have said that accounts of not being served in turn or being assigned poor hotel rooms are not necessarily racial discrimination, for whites too occasionally suffer such treatment. This raises the issue of how black accounts of discrimination are credited by whites. When we have discussed these accounts with black informants and journalists, they credit them quickly because of their own similar experiences. Years of cumulative experience give these middle-class black Americans the "second eye" that one respondent described, the ability to sense prejudice or discrimination even in a tone of voice, a look, or a gesture. Having occasionally experienced poor service themselves, however, many whites accuse blacks of being paranoid in seeing racism in such incidents. Yet it is the consistent pattern of bad treatment, not only of oneself but of one's relatives and friends, by whites that is the basis for the black victims' interpretation of a particular incident as probable racial discrimination. Yet one more aspect of the burden of being black is having to defend one's understanding of events to white acquaintances without being labelled as racially paranoid.

Many incidents in public accommodations have no ambiguity whatever. In many a white mind a black person standing is certain places is assumed to be in a menial position. A physician in an eastern state described her feelings when she was staying in nice hotels: "I hate it when you go places and [white] people . . . think that we work in housekeeping. . . . A lot of white people think that blacks are just here to serve them. And we have not risen above the servant position." Middle-class blacks report this experience of being taken by whites to be in servile positions. Even Democratic party presidential candidate Jesse Jackson had such an experience. Elegantly dressed and standing by an elevator in an upscale New York hotel, right after a meeting with an African political leader, Jackson was approached by a white woman who said "I couldn't have made it downstairs without you." She put a dollar in his hand, mistaking Jackson for her black bellhop.[9]

Growing old does not eradicate the possibility of discrimination in public places. An eighty-year-old retired schoolteacher in a southwestern city recounted her experiences with whites at a drapery shop:

> The last time I had some draperies done and asked about them at the drapery shop, a young man at that shop—when they called [to him], he asked, and I heard him—he said, "the job for that nigger woman." And I said to the person who was serving me, "Oh my goodness, I feel so sorry for that young man. I didn't know people were still using that sort of language and saying those sorts of things." And that's the way I deal with it. I don't know what you call that. Is that sarcasm? Sarcasm is pretty good. . . . Well I've done that several times. . . . I'm surprised that I find it in this day and time.

Using "strategic indirection" in voicing her response not to the discriminator but to another white clerk within earshot of the insult, this teacher communicated the inappropriateness of racist remarks without giving whites the satisfaction of viewing her humiliation. With their long experience of blatant racism, older black Americans may be more likely to hurt in silence. When they do speak out, their response may often be measured and deliberate. Later this woman characterized such recurring racial incidents as the "little murders" that have daily made her long life so difficult.

Much creativity is demonstrated in the strategies for coping with whites in stores and other public accommodations. One such strategy was noted by a news anchorperson:

> And if I was seeking out a service, like renting a car, or buying something, I could get a wonderful, enthusiastic reaction to what I was doing. I would work that up to such a point that this person would probably shower me with roses once they got to see me. And then when I would show up, and they're surprised to see that I'm black, I sort of remind them in conversation how welcome my service was, to put the embarrassment on them, and I go through with my dealings. In fact, once my sister criticized me for

> putting [what] she calls my "white-on-white voice" on to get a rental car. But I needed a rental car and I knew that I could get it. I knew if I could get this guy to think that he was talking to some blonde, rather than, you know, so, but that's what he has to do deal with. I don't have to deal with that, I want to get the car.

The discrepancy between civility over the phone and discrimination in person is the acid test that proves the reality of everyday discrimination. Among the resources middle-class African Americans use to cope with bigotry is language. They often find themselves in situations where so-called "standard English" is required. They can code-switch as the situation demands it, speaking English without a distinguishable accent or grammatical variation that would make their racial identity known to whites. By erasing the so-called "black accent," which is often exaggerated in the white mind, they can sometimes avoid being victims. With creativity born of necessity this respondent uses her resources not only to secure services but also to bring some sense of her discomfort to whites caught red-handed. The idea of using artifice to get a positive outcome is an old strategy for African Americans, and here the psychological play seeks to educate rather than injure.

Some of the essential coping strategies are learned at an early age. One poignant example of discrimination took place at a suburban swimming pool, yet another type of public site. A manager at an electronics firm gave this account:

> I'm talking over two hundred kids in this pool; not *one* black. I don't think you can go anywhere in the world during the summertime and not find some black kids in the swimming pool. . . . Now what's the worst thing that can happen to a ten-year-old girl in a swimming pool with all white kids? What's the worst thing that could happen? It happened. This little white guy called her a "nigger." Then

> called her a "motherfucker" and told her "to get out of the god-damn pool." . . . And what initiated that, they had these little inner tubes, they had about fifteen of them, and the pool owns them. So you just use them if they are vacant. So there was a tube sitting up on the bank. She got it, jumped in, and started playing in it. . . . And this little white guy decided he wanted it. But, he's supposed to get it, right? And he meant to get it. And she wouldn't give it to him, so out came all these racial slurs. So my action was first with the little boy. "You know you're not supposed to do that. Apologize right now. O.K., good. Now, Mr. Lifeguard, I want him out of this pool, and you're going to have to do better. You're going to have to do better, but he has to leave . . . this pool and let his parents know, okay?"

Taking his daughter back the next day, this father watched from behind a fence to make certain the lifeguard protected her. Apparently this was the first time his daughter had been the victim of such blatant racial slurs. She was not simply the victim of a rude child; she was the target of white rudeness and racist epithets that for this black father, as for other black adults, connote segregated institutions and antiblack violence. For father and daughter this incident was not trivial but took on the proportions of a painful and serious life crisis. For many African Americans one of the public places most redolent with historical memories of racism is the swimming pool, for in earlier decades many white communities closed pools rather than allow desegregation.

Discrimination in the Street

As middle-class African Americans move from public accommodations to less protected street sites, racial hostility can become even more severe. Encounters with whites in the streets can be dangerous, as in this report by a black man, now a television commentator, who was working during the mid-1980s for a media surveying firm in a southern city:

> I was parked in front of this guy's house. . . . This guy puts his hands on the window and says, "Get out of the car, nigger." . . . So I got out, and I thought, "Oh, this is what's going to happen here." And I'm talking fast. And they're, "What are you doing here?" And I'm, "This is who I am. I work with these people. This is the man we want to put in the survey." And I pointed to the house. And the guy said, "Well you have an out-of-state license tag, right?" "Yeah." And he said, "If something happened to you, your people at home wouldn't know for a long time, would they?" . . . I said, "Look, I deal with a company that deals with television. [If] something happens to me, it's going to be a national thing. . . . So, they grab me by the lapel of my coat, and put me in front of my car. They put the blade on my zipper. And now I'm thinking about this guy that's in the truck [behind me], because now I'm thinking that I'm going to have to run somewhere. Where am I going to run? Go to the police? [laughs] So, after a while they bash up my headlight. And I drove [away].

The discrimination in this account is part of a pattern of intimidation and threats whereby whites have kept most blacks from coming into this particular suburb. A consciousness of the history of lynchings and other antiblack violence in the South makes this violence and the threat of further violence even more frightening for this man. Drawing on his middle-class resources, he had the courage to tell the attackers that his death would bring television crews to the area. For most whites threatened by assailants on the street the police are a sought-after source of protection, but this is often not the case for black men.

A college graduate recounted a threatening experience near a predominantly white university he attended:

> One night I had gone to a midnight movie on campus. I was walking back to my dorm and this big four-wheeler, you know those huge trucks that white guys drive, with the big wheels, about six feet high? It came screeching around the corner. There were about six white guys in this truck and I could tell they were drunk, so I continued walking. And he slammed his brakes and started yelling and hollering racial slurs out the window, like "nigger go home," "blackie," "spade," all types of things. And my instant reaction was to spin around, you know, and get angry, which is what I did. And they saw that I did this, so they started in even more, started hurling even more epithets. But I noticed in the back of their window they had a big old hunting rifle back there and I didn't know if they'd use it or not; I wasn't about to stick around and find out. So I looked at them again with a real stern look like I didn't appreciate it, and I spun around and kept walking. Then they turned the truck around in my direction, and if they turned around just to go a different way on the street or if they turned around just to go after me, once again, I wasn't going to stick around to find out. And I started hauling for the nearest dorm because I knew I could lose them in the dorm.

Being a black student in a college town historically accustomed only to white students increases street vulnerability—and the possibility of intimidation and violence. This graduate student maintained his composure and figured out a way to escape a potentially deadly situation.

Racially motivated "hate crimes" have increased in the streets and neighborhoods of towns and cities since the 1970s. Mandated by the recent Hate Crime Statistics Act, the FBI's first hate crime report counted 4,558 attacks for the year 1991, with only 19 percent of law enforcement agencies sending in any data. The largest proportion (36 percent) of these were antiblack crimes, including property damage and serious personal assaults like the case above.[10] And this incomplete government report doubtless records but a very small proportion of the serious attacks on black individuals or homes in that year.

Racist epithets are a major problem for African Americans as they traverse streets and other public places. Such epithets are taken seriously because they may threaten action. They may also invoke in the black mind memories of past discrimination, including antiblack violence. A professor at a predominantly white university in the Southwest described a case of unforgettable street harassment:

> I was driving. This has [happened] so many times, but one night it was especially repugnant. I think it had to be, with my son being in the car, it was about nine-thirty at night. And as I've said, my car is old and very ugly, and I have been told by people shouting at intersections that it's the kind of car that people think of as a low-rider car, so they associate it with Mexican Americans, especially poor Mexican Americans. Well, we were sitting at an intersection waiting to make a turn, and a group of middle-class-looking white boys drives up in a nice car. And they start shouting things at us in a real fake-sounding Mexican American accent, and I realized that they thought we were Mexican Americans. And I turned to look at them, and they started making obscene gestures and laughing at the car. And then one of them realized that I was black, and said, "Oh, it's just a nigger." And [they] drove away.

This incident illustrates white hostility provoked by certain signals of minority group status, including an old car and dark skin; a black person suffered from hostility aimed at other people of color by whites unable to distinguish. The darkness assured the whites' anonymity and heightened the negative impact of the incident on this woman.

In research on street remarks Carol Brooks Gardner writes of women and blacks as "open persons," particularly vulnerable targets for harassment that violates the usual rules of courtesy in public places.[11] A health care professional who lives in an East Coast city described biking with his son near a shrine of American liberty:

> My son and I were riding bicycles and we were down around Fort McHenry. . . . And we'd gotten off the bikes and we were drinking out of this water fountain. And this car pulled up; these white kids drove by. And they said, "Hey, nigger!" You know? And we turned our heads and looked up, "Hey, niggers!" They never stopped, but they were just driving by slowly. And I said, "You're damn right I'm a nigger, and I'm proud of it!"

There is a deep irony here. Freedom from racially motivated street harassment is not yet a reality for this man and his son riding near Fort McHenry, whose bombardment by the British in the early 1800s inspired "The Star-Spangled Banner," memorializing "the land of the free." This man responded by turning the epithet into a badge of honor.

For younger middle-class African Americans, especially those who have been sheltered by their parents, racial harassment can generate shock and disbelief, as in the case of this student who reported a street encounter near her university:

> I don't remember in high school being called a "nigger" before, and I can remember here being called a nigger. [When was this?] In my freshman year, at a university student parade. There was a group of us, standing there, not knowing that this was not an event that a lot of black people went

> to! [laughs] You know, our dorm was going, and this was something we were going to go to because we were students too! And we were standing out there and [there were] a group of white fraternity boys—I remember the southern flag—and a group of us, five or six of us, and they went past by us, before the parade had actually gotten underway. And one of them pointed and said, "Look at that bunch of niggers!" I remember thinking, "surely he's not talking to us!" We didn't even use the word nigger in my house. . . . [How did you feel?] I think I wanted to cry. And my friends . . . were ready to curse them, and I was just standing there with my mouth open. I think I wanted to cry. I could not believe it, because you get here and you think you're in an educated environment and you're dealing with educated people. And all of this backward country stuff. . . . You think that kind of stuff is not going on, but it is.

The desire to be accepted as an equal is strong in her comments: "We were students too!" We see a black student in pain, but who initially gave whites the benefit of the doubt. Her subsequent response was tearful acquiescence to the hostility, but her friends were ready to react aggressively, although the whites may have moved on before a considered response was possible. Note too the mention of the Confederate flag, a symbol that conjures up painful memories and associations for black Americans. This episode underscores the impact of racial coding on young people and hints at the difficulty parents face in socializing children for coping with white hostility.

Another white epithet is "welfare queen," often a thinly disguised derogatory reference to black women. Much white discussion of black women is rife with welfare stereotyping. A woman who runs a business in a southwestern city described her experience with such stereotyping in front of a grocery store:

> We had a new car . . . and we stopped at 7–11 [convenience store]. We were going to go out that night, and we were taking my son to a babysitter. . . . And we pulled up, and my husband was inside at the time. And this person, this Anglo couple, drove up, and they hit our car. It was a brand new car. So my husband came out. And the first thing they told us was that we got our car *on welfare*. Here we are able-bodied. He was a corporate executive. I had a decent job. It was a professional job, but it wasn't paying anything. But they looked at the car we were driving, and they made the assumption that we got it from welfare. I completely snapped; I physically abused that lady. I did. And I was trying to keep my husband from arguing with her husband until the police could come. . . . And when the police came they interrogated them. They didn't arrest us, because there was an off-duty cop who had seen the whole incident, and said she provoked it.

Seeing only the blackness of the black couple, the whites here react on the basis of racial stereotypes. Like several previous respondents, this woman is outraged that her and her husband's hard work and achievements did not protect her from racial abuse. Seemingly no amount of success can counter the oppressiveness of white stereotyping. The angry response undoubtedly came as a surprise to the whites. If the off-duty officer was white, which is possible here, his intervention at least suggests that times have changed; in the recent past a white officer would very likely have taken the white side in the encounter.

Patience is a signal feature of many black middle-class responses to the pervasive discrimination they encounter in public places. The aggressiveness of the response varies with the situation and the resources at hand. A parole officer in a western city recounted how he dealt with a racial epithet in an determined manner:

> I've been called "nigger" before, out in the streets when I was doing my job, and the individual went to jail. . . . [Ok, if he didn't call you a "nigger," would he have still gone to jail?] Probably not. [. . . . was the person white?] Yes, he was. And he had a partner with him, and his partner didn't say anything, and his partner jaywalked with him. However, since he uttered the racial slur, I stopped him and quizzed him about the laws, and jaywalking's against the law, so he went to jail.

In the social science literature on policing, the substantial street-level discretion available to police officers has been described in some detail.[12] Jaywalking is usually a winked-at violation, but this officer exercised his authoritative discretion to punish a racist epithet. (By "to jail" he may mean "to the police station.") Although this man was in a position of authority that might well have brought a violent retaliation to the verbal hostility if the colors of the men had been reversed, he restrained himself and used a measured but authoritative response to the negative treatment.

In addition to assault, threats of violence, and racist epithets, one commonly cited form of racial harassment in public places is the discourteous white "hate stare," an old problem for African Americans that dates back to at least the eighteenth century. This phenomenon was well described by white journalist John Howard Griffin in *Black Like Me*, his book about traveling as a black man in the South in the late 1950s. Even as a white man only temporarily dyed black, Griffin found the hate stares extremely disturbing and threatening. Hostile looks can occur anywhere blacks encounter whites; they illustrate the interstitial character of much hostile behavior.[13] One college student reported that on her way to her class she stopped at a bakery in a residential area where few blacks live. A young white couple sitting in front of the store stared intently and hatefully at her as she crossed the sidewalk in front of them and went into the bakery, and again as she returned to her car. She reported that in her experience this type of nonverbal expression of hostility was common. And a manager at a large company gave this account: "The first weekend we were here we went to have breakfast in this white neighborhood and we came out and got in our car. We got stared at until we got out of the parking lot and into the street. Noticeable stares—waitresses, patrons in the restaurant, two old guys standing outside in the parking lot. It was like, 'What are you doing here?'" Part of the story of racism is this racial coding of places, for some places are still more or less off limits to black Americans. A black person moving into these spheres learns, often immediately, that his or her presence is not wanted.

Hate stares might seem minor slights to most white observers, because again they have no history of such recurring experiences and are unaware of the historical implications. Yet for black Americans the intense stare often has a lasting impact. The last two respondents reported agonizing later over the stares. In his interview the man added that after they went home he and his wife became intensely focused on the incident and found themselves "talking about it too much." Numerous black respondents and informants have reported the difficulty of letting go of discriminatory incidents, for they can cause great pain and haunt the mind for months and years. Such unpleasant memories are potentially debilitating, interfering with performance in work and school.

Harassment by White Police Officers

Many black encounters with the police have unfavorable outcomes. Sociologist James Blackwell has reviewed research suggesting that three quarters of the white officers in certain mostly black precincts have some antipathy to black residents,[14] an antipathy that is reflected in the well-documented racist actions of some white police officers. A recent study of 130 police brutality incidents reported in regional and national newspapers across the nation found that blacks or Latinos were the victims in 97 percent of the assaults; there were only two cases in which the victim was a sole white citizen.[15] And 93 percent of the officers were white. It is clear from this and other studies that police brutality is not confined to southern cities but has been reported in most regions of the nation. Moreover, unwarranted police beatings of black men, such as the videotaped beating of Rodney King in Los Angeles in 1991, have directly or indirectly precipitated numerous riots in black communities from the 1930s to the 1990s. Given the history of police harassment and brutality, it is likely that most black men—including middle-class black men—see white police officers as a source of possible danger if not injury.

The television commentator quoted earlier described two cases of police harassment when he was working for a media surveying firm. In one incident in a southern city he was stopped by several white officers, one of whom asked, "What are you doing here?"

> I tell them what I'm doing here. . . . And so they had me spread on top of my car. [What had you done?] Because I was in the neighborhood. I left this note on these people's house: Here's who I am. You weren't here, and I will come back in thirty minutes. [Why were they searching you?] They don't know. To me, they're searching. I remember at that particular moment when this all was going down, there were a lot of reports about police crime on civilians. . . . It took four cops to shake me down, two police cars, so they had me up there spread out. I had a friend of mine with me who was making the call with me, because we were going to have dinner together, and he was black,

and they had me up, and they had him outside. . . . They said, "Well, let's check you out." . . . And I'm talking to myself, and I'm not thinking about being at attention, with my arms spread on my Ford [a company car], and I'm sitting there talking to myself, "Man, this is crazy, this is crazy." [How are you feeling inside?] Scared, I mean real scared. [What did you think was going to happen to you?] I was going to go to jail . . . just because they picked me. Why would they stop me? It's like, if they can stop me, why wouldn't I go to jail, and I could sit in there for ten days before the judge sees me. I'm thinking all this crazy stuff. . . . Again, I'm talking to myself. And the guy takes his stick. And he doesn't whack me hard, but he does it with enough authority to let me know they mean business. "I told you to stand still; now put your arms back out." And I've got this suit on, and the car's wet. And my friend's hysterical. He's outside the car. And they're checking him out. And he's like, "Man, just be cool, man." And he had tears in his eyes. And I'm like, oh, man, this is a nightmare. This is not supposed to happen to me. This is not my style! And so finally, this other cop comes up and says, "What have we got here, Charlie?" "Oh, we've got a guy here. He's running through the neighborhood, and he doesn't want to do what we tell him. We might have to run him in." [You're "running through" the neighborhood?] Yeah, exactly, in a suit in the rain?! After they got through doing their thing and harassing me, I just said, "Man, this has been a hell of a week."

And I had tears in my eyes, but it wasn't tears of upset. It was tears of anger; it was tears of wanting to lash back. . . . What I thought to myself was, man, blacks have it real hard down here. I don't care if they're a broadcaster; I don't care if they're a businessman or a banker. . . . They

> don't have it any easier than the persons on skid row who get harassed by the police on a Friday or Saturday night.

By the time they are in their twenties many black men in all income groups have been stopped by the police—often several times—simply because blackness is considered a sign of possible lawbreaking by police officers.[16] Officers in many police agencies are trained, either formally in classes or informally by other officers, to look for certain demographic cues that supposedly distinguish potential criminal offenders from other people, and high on the list are the classifications "black" and "male." This black experience with police harshness doubtless marks a dramatic contrast with the experiences of most middle-class white males. In the incident described above the respondent and his friend reacted to severe mistreatment with humiliating deference. We sense their anger that their personal achievements and symbols of success brought no protection from stigmatization and harassment.

Black women traveling the public streets may also be targets of police harassment. The professor quoted previously in regard to street harassment by white civilians spoke of her encounters with the police:

> When the cops pull me over because my car is old and ugly, they assume I've just robbed a convenience store. Or that's the excuse they give: This car looks like a car used to rob a 7–11. And I've been pulled over six or seven times since I've been in this city—and I've been here two years now. Then I do what most black folks do. I try not to make any sudden moves so I'm not accidentally shot. Then I give them my identification. And I show them my university I.D. so they won't think that I'm someone that constitutes a threat, however they define it, so that I don't get arrested.

She then added this chilling comment:

> [One problem with] being black in America is that you have to spend so much time thinking about stuff that most white people just don't even have to think about. I worry when I get pulled over by a cop. I worry because the person that I live with is a black male, and I have a teen-aged son. I worry what some white cop is going to think when he walks over to our car, because he's holding on to a gun. And I'm very aware of how many black folks accidentally get shot by cops. I worry when I walk into a store, that someone's going to think I'm in there shoplifting. And I have to worry about that because I'm not free to ignore it. And so, that thing that's supposed to be guaranteed to all Americans, the freedom to just be yourself is a fallacious idea. And I get resentful that I have to think about things that a lot of people, even my very close white friends whose politics are similar to mine, simply don't have to worry about.

This statement underscores the pyramiding character of discrimination. This professor has been subjected to excessive surveillance repeatedly by white officers. She attempts to draw on her resources for protection; she asserts her status as a professor by pulling out her university I.D. This use of credentials in dealing with white police officers marks a difference from the days of legal segregation, when a black person announcing her achievements would have been considered arrogant and increased the danger. Yet it is still degrading for a black person to have to go through a rehearsed ritual to forestall being violently harassed by white authorities. She has to use the symbols of success that are recognized as such by whites. Note again the explicit theory of rights and justice. The tension in her mind between the deferential response required in dealing with white police officers and her sense of injustice is clear in her comments about the freedom of movement theoretically guaranteed by civil rights statutes.

These situations show the vulnerability of black men and women in encounters with white officers. Even black police officers have remarked on this sense of powerlessness. Quoted recently in *Essence* magazine, Ronald Hampton, executive director of the National Black Police Association, put it this way: "It sounds crazy for me to say that you can't defend yourself, but you can't defend yourself. Police have power over citizens." He added, "if there is going to be some abuse, there will be abuse." He advised black citizens that all they can do is to try to shield themselves.[17]

Black students at predominantly white colleges have regularly reported difficulties with white police officers. These problems occur on or near the campuses where they study, attend classes, and, often, reside. In an interview one college student who lives on a nearly all-white campus discussed how campus police officers had trained spotlights on her simply because she was black. Then she continued with this statement:

> This past year there have been some incidents, some attacks on campus. And [my boyfriend] was at the gym playing basketball; and he was going to the gas station. He got out of the car at the gas station down the street. The [police] guy tells him to put his hands up, and he pulled a gun. It wasn't the campus police, but I feel they called him. Their reason was that they saw him leaving the gym, and they thought they heard a woman screaming at him. He said, "There was no woman." That doesn't make sense. I think they should be punished, it's just not right. But see, incidents happen to them, especially black men, incidents like this happen to them all the time. Have they written a letter? Have they done anything? No. They [the police] haven't bothered me but when they do, I will write a letter,

> and it will be publicized. I will make sure it is. I'm not going to take that. There's no reason that I should have to. Do you want to see my I.D.? Give me a reason. You can't just ask me for my I.D. when I'm just walking down the sidewalk. There are fifty billion other white people walking on the same sidewalk and you didn't ask them for their I.D. . . . You don't want to have your friends come here sometimes, because they'll be harassed. So, it's kind of bad. But I've heard a lot of campuses are like that, white campuses.

In recent years there have been numerous reports of local police harassing of black students at traditionally white colleges in all regions of the country. Black male students often become prime suspects for white officers investigating serious campus crimes. At the University of Nebraska (Lincoln), the campus police department photographed and interrogated five black men who were in the anthropology class of a white female student who had disappeared. Later two white men were charged with her killing.[18] Being unfairly interrogated or searched is a common occurrence for black male students. Even Harvard University's Divinity School advises its black students, during the initial fall orientation, to always carry papers of identification so that they will be prepared for the likely harassment from Harvard University and Cambridge police officers.[19]

The screening process used by a variety of police agencies to assess who is a likely criminal might be termed "stereotyped profile discrimination." When we related some of our respondents' accounts of police harassment to a black journalist at a major newspaper, she recounted a recent experience of her own. She was hustling through a major airport in a northern city on her way to an important assignment, when she was pursued by white drug enforcement officers. Rushing after her and stopping her at the door of her airport rental car bus, the agents asked who she was and where she was going. Although she showed her I.D., they persisted, getting on the bus with her. There the white agents stared at her and refused to answer her questions about what they were doing. Thinking back over the events later, she said they continued to cause her much pain: "I felt like ET, an alien in another world. I felt like I had been raped." She also remembered thinking hard about how she could prove her innocence to the agents. The only black person in a group of similarly dressed whites getting on the bus, she felt they stopped her because she fit the stereotyped police profile of a drug runner—young, black, and hurrying through an airport.[20]

It is not just police agents who operate on the basis of profiles grounded in stereotypes. A New England executive commented on the difficulty black men commonly face in getting taxi drivers to stop for them: "I traveled quite a bit during that time. You would hit the normal discriminatory actions of goings-away . . . being scrutinized very closely as to who you are and what your purposes are and so forth—the situations of trying to hail cabs in New York City, that's a classic one blacks face. No matter how businesslike they're dressed, there's a problem in that regard." The voice of this executive has a tone of resignation in it, as in his noting the "normality" of this street-level discrimination. Significantly, some middle-class informants with whom we have shared these public-place accounts have mentioned the strategies they use in street situations, such as taking pains to walk at a distance from whites or getting a white friend to hail a cab for them.

The Cumulative Impact

The cumulative impact of several of these types of street discrimination was underscored by a black student at a large, mostly white university in the Southwest. He described his experiences walking home at night from a campus job to his apartment located in a predominantly white residential area:[21]

> So, even if you wanted to, it's difficult just to live a life where you don't come into conflict with others. Because every day you walk the streets, it's not even like once a week, once a month. It's every day you walk the streets. Every day that you live as a black person you're reminded how you're perceived in society. You walk the streets at night; white people cross the streets. I've seen white couples and individuals dart in front of cars to not be on the same side of the street. Just the other day, I was walking down the street, and this white female with a child, I saw her pass a young white male about twenty yards ahead. When she saw me, she quickly dragged the child and herself across the busy street. What is so funny is that this area has had an unknown *white* rapist in the area for about four years. [When I pass] white men tighten their grip on their women. I've seen people turn around and seem like they're going to take blows from me. The police constantly make circles around me as I walk home, you know, for blocks. I'll walk, and they'll turn a block. And they'll come around me just to make sure, to find out where I'm going. So, every day you realize [you're black]. Even though you're not doing anything wrong; you're just existing. You're just a person. But you're a black person perceived in an unblack world.

In a subsequent comment this student described how white men had hurled objects and racist epithets at him as he walked home. Discrimination is every day and everywhere. This student's experience is an example of what Ralph Ellison meant when he wrote of the general white inability to "see" black Americans as individuals in *The Invisible Man*.[22] Unable to perceive this black male student's middle-class symbols of college dress and books, white individuals and couples have crossed the street, dodging cars, to avoid walking near this medium-stature black student. They are doubtless reacting to the negative image of black males. The student perceives such avoidance in a particular instance as racially motivated, because he and his male friends have often encountered whites taking similar "defensive" measures.

The common white view of black men as dangerous, held by police and civilian whites alike, is deeply rooted in the history and collective psyche of white Americans. In a pathbreaking book, *The Black Image in the White Mind*, historian George Fredrickson has demonstrated that long before the twentieth century whites had developed a view of black slaves and servants as fearful and dangerous "beasts," a stereotyped view that has often lain behind white violence such as lynchings of black men.[23] Still, this view persists. Today not just white police officers but many white media producers and commentators,[24] and a majority of whites generally, appear to view criminals who commit violent crimes against white individuals and property to be mostly black or minority males. Yet the world of crime is complex and for the most part does not fit this white image. Most (78–88 percent) of the whites who are assaulted, raped, or murdered are attacked by white assailants, according to the 1991 National Crime Victimization Survey and other government crime data. While black assailants do account for 44 percent of the assailants of white robbery victims, they account for only 17 percent of the assailants in all crimes of violence targeting white victims.[25]

In the white world black men, especially young black men, routinely suffer physical or psychological attacks from whites, yet such attacks get little publicity in the mass media, and then only when they are sensational. Attacks on whites by black men get much more media attention. For example, in a recent column about hate crimes and the First Amendment, nationally syndicated columnist James Kilpatrick focused only on one case, a racially motivated "get the white boy" attack on a white youth by some black teenagers. What is striking here is that such flagrant black-on-white cases are much less frequent than the reverse, today and even more so in the past, yet this prominent columnist did not find those white-on-black cases sufficiently newsworthy for his column.[26] The case of "Willie" Horton, a black man who raped a white woman, is a celebrated example of the same biased focus on black-on-white crime. In 1988 the George Bush campaign used Horton's image to frighten white voters. Although the overwhelming majority of the rapists who attack white women are white, the negative image of the black man as a rapist of white women is so exaggerated and commonplace among white Americans that the campaign could make use of it to attract white voters to a conservative cause.[27] Significantly, much media discussion and some scholarly dialogue have been devoted to white perceptions of black men as threatening and the justifiability of that perception. To our knowledge there has been no serious research or reporting on the very negative impact on the everyday lives of black men of white assumptions and the resulting avoidance and fear.[28]

Representing what appears to be a widely accepted view, one otherwise perceptive white analyst of discrimination has commented that whites' crossing the street to avoid black men is "a minimal slight."[29] This is far from the truth. The black student quoted above reported that repeatedly being treated as a pariah, in his own words a "criminal and a rapist," has caused him severe psychological problems. Similarly, after a phone interview with the first author on some of this research on public-place discrimination, one of the nation's leading black journalists reported that middle-class whites sometimes stop talking—and white women grab their purses—when he enters an office-building elevator in his New England city. Whereas the student said that he rarely had been able to respond to the street encounters, apart from the occasional quick curse, because they happened too quickly, the journalist noted that when possible he has reacted more assertively; he described how he turns to whites in elevators and informs them, often with a smile, that they can continue talking or that he is not interested in their purses.

Conclusion

The NRC report *A Common Destiny* found that by the late 1970s many whites believed that the Civil Rights Act of 1964 had brought a broad-scale elimination of racial discrimination in public accommodations.[30] Robert Lauer and Warren Handel have written that as black Americans get access to an outer circle "from which they had been previously excluded (such as eating at a public restaurant) they encounter inner circles from which they are still excluded (such as equal access to economic opportunities) and with an even greater hostility than that with which they were barred from the outer circles."[31] Unfortunately, our interviews and other sources indicate that deprivation of the full enjoyment of public facilities promised by the 1964 Civil Rights Act is not something of the past; attack, exclusion, rejection, and other types of antiblack discrimination persist in public accommodations today for African Americans, whatever their socioeconomic status. Streets and public accommodations are relatively unprotected sites, and African Americans are very vulnerable there to white maltreatment.

These accounts of encounters with whites in public places shaped the theoretical propositions we offered in Chapter 1. For middle-class black Americans white racism is not an abstraction generated by a militant ideology but rather a matter of ordinary experience. In these reports the emotional reaction to white hostility and discrimination in public places is explicit or just beneath the surface. Whether the incident took place in a restaurant, a store, or on the street, we usually can feel the humiliation, frustration, pain, and rage, as well as sense the stoicism and determination. The frustration and pain expressed in these accounts suggest that serious instances of hostility and discrimination can indeed be life crises. Even a single incident, such as the newscaster's encounter with knife-wielding white racists on the street, leaves painful memories that will never be forgotten. Even the hate stares, which may seem minor to whites, have a way of sticking in the mind's eye and tormenting a black person for a very long time.

Encounters with white hostility and discrimination shape the lives and perspectives of middle-class African Americans. A black person's life perspective—the personal assumptions about the world—may be shaped by discrimination to include a sense of lack of control over one's life. Research studies using the Rotter Introversion-Extroversion Scale, which measures whether an individual feels in control of his or her life, have found that black subjects tend to score differently from whites and to feel that their lives are controlled predominantly by outside forces. Reviewing this research, Mirowsky and Ross have underscored the importance of a sense of control for personal well-being and effectiveness. Without it, one feels a sense of powerlessness, creating a condition in which an individual may have difficulty in achieving desired goals.[32] For our respondents it appears that the steady dose of white racism creates a chronic dilemma of having to fight, sometimes successfully, sometimes unsuccessfully, against a realistic sense of powerlessness. One important aspect of the perspective these middle-class black Americans develop, however, is a deep commitment to securing equal rights.

The dilemma of how to deal with racism can be seen in the responses of the news director and her boyfriend to being pointedly ignored in a restaurant. The boyfriend, fearing he would lose his temper, wished to withdraw, but the news director pressed for a confrontation, asserting her professional status and her power as part of the media. Her strategy was clearly grounded in her reflection on previous experiences with racial discrimination and on her commitment to black rights. White discrimination is sometimes countered with a black comeback. In an August 31, 1981 column in the *Chicago Tribune* black columnist Leanita McClain described this situation as the "new racism": "The old racism wouldn't let blacks into some stores; the new racism assumes that any black person, no matter how well dressed, in a store is probably there to steal, not to buy. . . . The old racism didn't have to address black people; the new racism is left speechless when a black, approached condescendingly, has an eloquent comeback."[33]

Chapter Three

Seeking a Good Education

IN the spring of 1987 a white Columbia College student undertook a campaign of verbally and physically harassing black students. When asked by black students to stop the harassment, he replied, "Ah man, fuck you," and a fight between black and white students ensued. One black student was sent to a hospital, and another was chased by a white student yelling "Goddamn you fucking niggers." Black security guards trying to break up the conflict were attacked by whites. Black students said they feared for their lives. With the support of a few whites, black students organized against racist conditions on campus. Many white students reportedly viewed the black students as responsible for the problems, and Columbia's white administrators, although condemning the racial attacks, were unwilling to remedy the campus conditions cited by the black students as underlying the attacks. This episode of racial harassment and administrative insensitivity took place on a northern campus with an image of liberalism.[1]

There is not much information on the character and breadth of the discrimination faced by black youth in schools and colleges, but a few surveys are suggestive. A 1991 national survey of young people aged fifteen to twenty-four by Hart Research Associates found that 41 percent of the black youth said they themselves had been the victims of racial discrimination, but the survey did not ask where or how often that discrimination had occurred.[2] A few opinion surveys have asked general questions about discrimination in education. In a 1989 ABC News/*Washington Post* survey 37 percent of black respondents agreed that blacks generally face discrimination in getting a quality education. In an earlier 1986 survey, one quarter of the black respondents reported having personally faced discrimination in getting a quality education. Given that a significant proportion of those over the age of thirty had attended legally segregated schools, this proportion seems low. Neither in this survey nor in more recent surveys have questions been asked about the many aspects of public and private education, such as teacher-student interaction or extracurricular activities, in which racial discrimination could have occurred. And these surveys provide little information on specific patterns of educational discrimination faced by the black middle class.[3]

In this chapter middle-class African Americans discuss racially integrated or predominantly white educational institutions. At first glance, integrated schools and colleges might seem intrinsically more hospitable than the public settings we discussed previously, because many contacts with white students and teachers there occur in a context formally emphasizing collegiality and openness to learning, and because many of the whites with whom blacks interact are acquaintances, not strangers. Nonetheless, black students in substantially white schools face racial hostility in many facets of their educational experiences.

African Americans have long attached great importance to education for themselves and their children. Education has been seen as a way to be accepted, as the "great leveller" that should bring first-class citizenship.[4] This emphasis on education can be seen in responses to a 1990 National Opinion Research Center survey in which blacks were more likely than whites to favor more government spending on preschool programs (76 percent versus 57 percent), slightly more likely than whites to feel that government was spending too little on education (72 percent versus 71 percent), and significantly more likely than whites to believe that a major cause of poverty was the failure to provide a good education for all (57 percent versus 33 percent).[4] Education still looms large in black dreams of opportunity and success.

Obstacles in Elementary and Secondary Schools

Where one lives can determine where one's children go to school and the quality of their schooling. In spite of housing laws banning discrimination, our towns and cities remain bastions of racial segregation. In most towns and cities people can tell you "where blacks live" and "where whites live." Black residential areas often have poor government services. In central cities many black middle-class residential areas are adjacent to other black neighborhoods (see Chapter 6).

Black parents' decisions to live in a predominantly black or black middle-class community can give their children social support in the form of black friends and black organizations, yet the public schools available may not be as well equipped or staffed as those in white suburban areas. Black middle-class parents are aware that living in historically white areas can often provide their children public schools with better resources. Some research, such as a Hartford, Connecticut study that followed 318 black students at predominantly white suburban schools and 343 black students at predominantly black central city schools, has touted the advantages of white schools. In this Hartford study black students who attended white high schools were more likely to graduate from high school, to go to college, to complete more years of college, and later to live in integrated residential areas than those who attended the central city high schools.[5] However, this case seems to be exceptional. Other studies have reported on the subtle and blatant racism, including hate crimes, that black students at predominantly white public schools have encountered.[6] Such hostility affects school performance, and some students drop out. The short term and long term damage that discriminatory white actions in desegregated schools can often do to black children puts this Hartford study into a more critical perspective.

Black parents who put their children into historically white schools soon become aware of the racial obstacles their children face. White administrators, teachers, students, and parents can create hurdles, as a counsellor at a western university explained in discussing her daughter's school:

> [We had] to enroll my daughter in school after we moved into a different school [district]. And this particular location was pretty much white; there was some integration going on. And I knew there was something wrong when I walked into the school, because there was this hush as I walked in. I thought, OK, whatever. I mean, everyone turned to look. And this woman wanted to know if I lived in their school district. And I said, "Yes, otherwise I wouldn't be here." And she wanted me to go home and get my deed to the property, and some other documents, and not thinking, I was like, "Oh, sure, yes." And then I thought, what is this? And once again, I found myself on the phone, calling the superintendent of schools. And when I went back the next day to enroll my daughter, the woman said that I didn't have to go over her head to her superiors. And I said, "Obviously I did." And I said, "Let me tell you one other thing. If my children experience any form of retaliation because of what I did, then I'll be back."

Once again a respondent mentions subtle racial cues, the strange looks or the familiar "hush" noted by many blacks entering traditionally white spaces. Like the "hate stare" noted in Chapter 2 they are part of the fabric of everyday life. This black parent did not respond directly to these racial cues until they were confirmed when she was pressured for excessive documentation. Her aggressive response signals again the insistence on civil rights that is part of the black repertoire for fighting discrimination.

The school curriculum in both predominantly white and integrated schools often presents additional obstacles to black students. A black professional in a northern city explained what she objected to in the integrated schools her children attended:

> [The school was] expecting that my children will not be achievers, therefore not offering them challenges in their schooling. And I as a parent have to [check] with regard to reading lists, making sure that my children have the opportunity to choose books by and about black people. When they talk about classics, there are black classics, so I want my children, and other children, to be able to read those classics as well. So, I've offered additional books for the reading lists, with some struggle. [What do they say about that?] "Oh, I didn't know, I didn't know about those books," or, "Oh, that's a good idea," or "These are the books that the colleges want young people to have read, so we have to use these." And my response is "Still, you can put all of those books on the list, that shouldn't stop you from adding additional books to the list." And they recognize that the population that they are educating has other races and nationalities and languages, and so they have to put other things on the list. But it's a struggle.

Across the nation, school desegregation as it has actually been implemented mainly mixes together children and teachers of different racial backgrounds. Much else remains as before. The curriculum is often not desegregated, but continues to reflect the topical interests of the white parents. A black parent may have to fight to bring new materials on African Americans into the instruction process. Punctuating her comments with some biting laughter, the same respondent reflected on other changes she has sought:

> And then, Columbus Day holidays, we had a discussion around that—helping teachers expand the discussion, frame the questions appropriately. Not "What did Columbus discover?" But how he accidentally, when he got lost, ran aground and he was discovered! Framing history in a different way, demanding that when you talk about African Americans and their contribution to society, that we were not just slaves. And looking at the inventions and the contributions of African Americans in a much broader way.

Like many other African Americans, several respondents suggested the need for expanded multicultural courses and programs in schools, including educating all children about the contributions of Africans and African Americans to the development of the United States. In recent years prominent white critics of multicultural programs in schools and colleges have been forthright about their white Eurocentric bias. Historian and presidential adviser Arthur Schlesinger, Jr., has called the multiculturalism perspective "an astonishing repudiation" of the idea of the melting pot: "The contemporary ideal is not assimilation but ethnicity. We used to say 'e pluribus unum.' Now we glorify 'pluribus' and belittle 'unum.' The melting pot yields to the Tower of Babel."[7] Schlesinger and other white observers worry that the United States cannot survive with a vibrant pluralism of racial and ethnic groups and argue that an integrated society requires all groups to adopt "Western culture" as their rudder. These whites usually oppose most of the modest cultural diversity courses and programs proposed for or implemented in some public schools around the nation, although often without any direct experience with the schools or their programs. In contrast, much criticism of school curricula by black parents is grounded in everyday experience with cultural bias and racism in the public school system.

In assessing the current state of public schools, black parents are also critical of how their children are tracked. The negative psychological impact of tracking black and white children into separate schools was at the heart of the 1954 *Brown* school desegregation decision, yet within desegregated schools testing procedures, administered under the guidance of school counsellors and teachers, have often been used to place black children into special tracks. Conventional tracking procedures can create serious difficulties, as a social services administrator in an eastern city illustrated:

> I get a sense that often my children, as well as other black children, have been steered into vocational type subjects and given to believe that that's "best for them," quote, unquote, "best for them." And I have certainly encouraged my children that I would like [them] to take the academic courses and to do well in them. I believe that their testing and that sort of thing shows that they are able to do it. And it takes a lot to stay in there with them, and try to make sure that nobody's undermining my goals for them.

Interestingly, the stratification of schools into vocational and academic tracks, begun in the early twentieth century with the support of U.S. educational reformers, initially segregated white children by class within their racially segregated schools. Since the 1920s, children from higher-income white families have tended to be placed in college-oriented tracks; those from moderate-income and working-class backgrounds have been more likely to be assigned to a vocational track. With the great increase in racially integrated schools since the 1960s, black and other minority students have been overrepresented in the lowest tracks.[8]

The tracking decisions of white teachers and counsellors can shape the educational career of a student. A teacher in a northern city discussed her son's attempt to get into a more demanding high school:

> He went to the public schools here in the city, and he had in his mind to go to Smith Tech. But his guidance counselor had in his mind that he should go to Jones High. Of course Jones—there's this mentality that white folks seem to have about us sometime. And that mentality basically deals with the fact that, it's something that was started back in slavery days, pre-slavery days, the fact that the black man should be taught to be productive with his hands and how to behave himself in society. So, the point is that they seem to feel that black folks, instead of becoming intellectual, being able to function in jobs that require some intellectual ability, they seem to think that we're better off being mechanics and whatever else, floor sweepers or whatever type of job that seems appropriate for us as long as we behave ourselves. Anyway, this guidance counselor, she tried to push the boy—the fact that the boy had merit roll and honor roll [was neglected]—she tried to stress the fact that he should go to Jones High. And of course that's just to train mechanics. And my son wanted to go to Tech. And what I had to do, I called her up on the phone to remind her that one of the main objectives of the city public schools is for every student to attain an education and become all that he can become capable of. And therefore, since he had the frame of mind to want to enter Tech, I wanted him to take the test for Tech.

The counsellor's decision forced him to take the test late, and although he passed, he went on the waiting list for Tech. She added: "So, consequently he did go to Jones High. But at Jones, he did very well, and wound up one of the winners, out of all of the students, one of two students to win scholarships. And he's presently attending a local college in the technical engineering program."

Contending with White Prejudices and Stereotypes

The interaction of black parents and children with white teachers, parents, and children can involve contending with common antiblack stereotypes. A black teacher discussed her integrated school:

> Another example—I was STOP sponsor, these are kids who are on the verge of dropping out. So at school we can volunteer to sponsor a couple of kids, or one kid. One little girl I sponsored is very dark, very huge lips, very short hair, pleasant personality, pretty to me. Well, I went to talk to her biology teacher because she was not doing well, and she said, "Oh, I know Aunt Jemima! Was she a STOP student? Aunt Jemima! You know, she's always chewing that gum and got all that red lipstick." I called her aside. I said, "I need to talk to you." I said, "Do you call her Aunt Jemima in class?" She just smiled, "She's such a sweet child." I told her, "Now, maybe you don't know what connotation Aunt Jemima has for blacks. Maybe you don't mean any harm, but *please* don't call her that. It's very offensive to blacks." Well, I talked to the student and I asked her, "How do you feel when she calls you Aunt Jemima?" "Well, I'm trying to get out of that class because I don't like it."

The racial slur by the white teacher may not have been fully conscious; her "sweet child" comment suggests a maternalistic orientation. A best-selling pancake product made by a major

U.S. corporation still uses the Aunt Jemima image, and antique shops across the nation feature racist memorabilia of this type for sale, so it is not surprising that some white teachers can be extremely insensitive to the deeper meaning of these symbols for African Americans. Clearly, insulting remarks by teachers affect the way children think about themselves and how they perform in class.

With some resignation in her voice a professor at a northern university commented on white parents' images of her children at a mostly white private school:

> Both of our sons went to high school here in this city, and everybody, every other parent in the school, *always* assumed that our children had full scholarships. And they didn't. My husband and I struggled and paid their tuition, you know. But they assumed, because they were black, that they had full scholarships. And there were some students in the school who *did* have some scholarship help, and I think there were some black students who had had some full scholarships. So that often assumptions are made about you just because you are a minority.

Reflecting on events some years before, this woman perceives questions about scholarships not to be favorable comments on her children's performance but rather to reflect white assumptions about their income. The white public's furor over affirmative action and equal opportunity programs from the 1970s to the present has been fed by the assumption that blacks in educational institutions are there substantially because of minority scholarships.

As the minority in predominantly white schools, black children are often set apart. Apparently white children learn their prejudices at an early age. A television news manager in the North described his children's experience in a white school:

> They go to white schools and some of the kids make fun of them because my son's nose is big, or his hair is different, or skin color. They tease him about his nose. He has a big nose. He is eight and not at a stage where he can even begin to try to ignore that kind of stuff, but kids are kids I guess, and they learn that from their parents; because you take great pains in trying to teach our kids to share with other people and not call people names and to try and treat everybody as you would want to be treated, but they have a hard time. My son was concerned enough to make me concerned. He just said that the kids at school were teasing him because his nose was big, and how come we had to have a nose like that, and why was this happening. Of course, we've tried to teach our children about the differences between blacks and whites and Indians and Mexicans and Chinese, and what have you. . . . And my daughter, who really hasn't been faced with that problem, but I notice that she doesn't want to wear [braids]. We tried to put the braids on her hair at one time. "No, no, no." She gave me an indication that she didn't want to be labeled that. She wanted to fit in more than she wanted to stand out. You see, I would look at that as a way of being different and she didn't want to be different, she wanted to be the same. It just made us more aware of our jobs in trying to teach our kids who they are, what they have to do.

We feel the anguish of a father, who has given lessons about respecting racial and ethnic differences, over his children being taunted about their physical characteristics. The serious psychological impact on the children can be seen in their discomfort with their physical differences. Although most children are self-conscious about their physical appearance, at least by the time they are adolescents, African American children in desegregated settings *at a very early age* bear the extra burden of dealing with comments and taunts about their skin color, hair, and other physical characteristics. Here we can also sense the early age at which some white children have learned to abhor and racialize the distinctive physical characteristics of black children.

An administrator at an East Coast law school discussed the trials of his seven-year-old daughter in a private school where she was the only child of conspicuously African American heritage:

> So my daughter was having real [hard] times adjusting, and I couldn't understand it because she wasn't the type of child to have an adjustment problem. So I sat her down and talked to her one day, and she says, "You know, they treat me differently, and the teacher treats me differently." And she said, "All I want to do is be in a place where everybody is the same or would think of me as the same." We're talking about, this was a seven-year-old telling me. So I asked her what would she want to do? Would she want to go to an all-black school? She said, "Yes, if everybody's going to treat me like I'm just one of them." [How did they treat her?] Well, the way I got it is that she couldn't do anything right, although her grades sometimes were pretty good, and then they wouldn't include her in some of the playtime activities, and made it as though that she's the odd person out in the activities. And that tended to make her feel that she was different. She knew she looked different, but then they rubbed it in. The students did it, and then the instructor was not discouraging it and in some ways encouraging that sort of behavior. So, we have a friend of ours that's a child psychologist and she's pretty well known in her field and she'd studied this instance. And she went by the school and talked to them and also talked to my child just to see what the problem was, and she helped us get to the root of it. So it wasn't something we just thought of; we had somebody

> look into it. [Is she still there?] No! No. Absolutely not. I'm not going to pay anybody that treats me bad, or my child.

This parent tells us that the failure of the teachers to discourage the harassment gave the black child the impression of collusion. Exclusion from some playtime activities breeds a sense of quarantine and isolation. At a very young age a black child may wish for a strong solution, such as an all-black school.

Schools that are predominantly white develop their own cultures, often with a certain tolerance for conventional white prejudices and even racist symbols, as can be observed in this dentist's story about his son:

> Well, just recently in the last year, he experienced a phenomenon called PUNISH, which is a penal system that they use in the school district for children that violate certain school laws. When these infractions are made they are sent to PUNISH, which is a prison-type setting, for so many days. He became a victim of this because he got into a verbal confrontation with a young man who . . . had on a swastika pin, he had on a KKK pin, and my son and this young man got into a few words, and my son told him to go to hell. The teacher heard him and therefore sent him to the principal, and because he used profanity, my son was assigned to a PUNISH detention. I confronted the teacher in front of the principal, and it was only after a very, very heated and emotional debate was I able to get my point across.

From the early 1980s to the early 1990s the nation witnessed increasing tolerance for the symbols of the Ku Klux Klan and the neo-Nazis in many white communities across the country. Membership in these organizations grew. In this account the symbols of these groups precipitated a heated exchange, and the black youngster was the one punished. Several research studies have found that black children in desegregated schools are more likely to be punished for their infractions of the rules than are whites. One important study found that black children were more likely than whites to be suspended for subjective offenses such as personal appearance, disobedience, and disrespect for teachers.[9] This study and our vignettes suggest an ongoing clash of worlds, a conflict of values and cultures, between black children and white school authorities. Later in our interview, this father stated that the white school authorities had defended the punishment and the white child's free-speech right to wear racially offensive pins, even though the school's policy did not extend a similar right to boys wearing other expressive decorations such as earrings.

One might wonder how a white teacher or an administrator could ignore the impact on the black psyche of these flagrant symbols of racial and ethnic violence. At the heart of what Gunnar Myrdal called "the American dilemma" is the contradiction between white American ideals and the reality of discriminatory actions.[10] Black children often learn about this contradiction at an early age. In desegregated schools black children are taught "The Star-Spangled Banner" and Pledge of Allegiance along with white children, and they read many stories about freedom, liberty, and justice. But degrading experiences with whites in the same schools doubtless raise serious questions about the meaning of these ideals.

Black Students in Predominantly White Colleges

In the late 1980s a report of the National Commission on Minority Participation in Education and American Life, *One Third of a Nation*, found a significant decline in black participation in higher education.[11] The proportion of black high school graduates going to college grew during the 1960s and 1970s to a high of about 48 percent in 1977, about the same as that for whites, then decreased to 37 percent in 1986, while white rates were still rising.[12] By the late 1980s the proportion of black students attending college had increased slightly but was still a minority of high school graduates and below the comparable proportion for whites. Some analysts have attributed the problems of black participation in higher education to the rising costs of a college education and the significant decline in financial aid. Others point to the alternative of good jobs in the military. Yet others emphasize the allegedly anti-educational values of black individuals and families. As we noted in an earlier chapter, white scholars like George Keller have argued that the reasons for black educational problems lie primarily within the black family or community.[13] In recent years many white analysts have minimized the relevance of white-controlled schools and white racism within those schools to the problems of black students. Yet, as we have just seen, the obstacles placed in the way of black elementary and secondary students by white counsellors, teachers, students, and parents—and their impact on achievement, motivation, and self-concept—explain in part the troubling statistics on the scarcity of blacks in institutions of higher education. Moreover, once black students make it past elementary and secondary school, they will confront similar hurdles as they enter the halls of historically white colleges and universities.

Most assessments of the state of African American students in predominantly white colleges and universities have relied heavily on numbers, such as enrollment rates, grade point averages, and graduation rates. Yet a deeper examination of the experiences of black students in these places requires something more than numbers gathered in school records and surveys or in classroom testing. We need to listen closely to what black American students tell us about what happens to them and how they feel, act, and think. In the rest of this chapter we examine the black educational experience from the point of view of black undergraduate and graduate students on majority-white campuses. Whatever their class backgrounds, all aspire to middle-class occupations and positions. We also draw on interviews with college graduates about their experiences as students at predominantly white colleges and universities. In addition, we quote occasionally from the observations of black faculty and staff members at these colleges and universities about the barriers black students face.

On entering predominantly white colleges and universities black students soon become aware of an essentially white campus culture. An honors student at a university in the Southwest discussed her feelings about being a black person in a predominantly white institution: "Everything, everywhere I look, everywhere I turn, right, left, is white." Revealing the historical context for her evaluation, she continued:

> I'm not saying that white people are all out to get us, because I don't think they think about us that much, where they sit down and actually plot, in some dark smoke-filled room, how they're going [to] stomp on black people. They don't have to because it's ingrained in the system. So things are like that. And white people call me paranoid and stuff, because I guess they look at things in regards to like the sixties when black people were like being beaten up every damn day, and crosses [were burned] in front of yards, and it was so blatant. But now it's changed. And just because it's not blatant any more doesn't mean it's not there. In fact, I think it's worse.

Discrimination is not less burdensome because it is subtly imbedded in the values, rules, and other institutional patterns of a college or other traditionally white setting and is less violent than cross-burnings. Black students are pressured to give up their identities and to adapt to the surrounding white culture, with its distinctive white middle-class ways of talking, dressing, and acting—to become, as another black student put it, "Afro-Saxon." We see here another modern variation on the double consciousness of which Du Bois spoke in *The Souls of Black Folk*.[14]

This honors student also reported on her trip to an Ivy League university as part of the process of choosing a college:

> I applied to a lot of different schools besides here, and I got accepted to this Ivy League school. And I went up there, checked it out. And a lot of people at home were like, well, you only got in because you're black. You don't deserve to be there, or you don't deserve to go, which may be true. I may have gotten in on affirmative action, but I deserve to be there, simply because of my merit. And I felt bad; I felt out of place. One reason I didn't go there, besides the money (I couldn't afford it), one reason I didn't go was because it reeked of whiteness. And that is no joke. And I am not exaggerating. I was only there for two days, and after one day I wanted to leave. And I mean, really, it just reeked, everywhere I went, reeked of old white men, just lily whiteness, oozing from the corners! [laughs] I wanted to leave. And I knew that socially I would just be miserable. And I talked to other black students; I talked to all of them because there aren't a lot. And so I said, "do you like it here?" And they were like, "No, we're miserable." I'm like, "Well then, why are you here?" And they said, "Because I'm black; it's Ivy League. I need everything I possibly could get." So, I said, "You're willing to be miserable for this?" They were like, "Yes." And then they asked me where else I was going. And one black female told me, Mary, go to the state university, "Don't come here." Really she did; and she was dead serious!

The students reported being alienated and miserable, yet because an Ivy League degree would give them a boost in the outside white world, they were resigned to the indignities of that milieu. Surveys at several predominantly white universities suggest that the campus culture is alienating to students of color. One study of students at a California campus found black and Latino students were more isolated and alienated than the white students.[15] Another study at a midwestern campus likewise found that black students scored higher on an alienation scale and dropped out more often than white students.[16] One reason for this alienating environment is that college desegregation since the 1960s has not brought fundamental changes in the character and cultural norms of white institutions. For the most part white regents, administrators, faculty members, staff, and students have shown little willingness to incorporate black values, interests, or history into the core of campus culture.[17]

At predominantly white colleges most campus activities reflect white student and faculty interests and traditions. In a study of black students at predominantly black and predominantly white colleges Walter Allen found that 62 percent of black students on white campuses, but just one third on black campuses, felt that the campus activities there did not relate to their interests.[18] This situation encourages black students to congregate in their own groups and plan their own activities, a reaction that often brings white condemnation. An undergraduate explained how this can be problematic:

> It's a constant battle dealing with racism. It is so much a part of everything. To integrate means simply to be white. It doesn't mean fusing the two cultures; it simply means to be white, that's all. And we spend so much effort in passing into the mainstream of American society. They have no reason to know our culture. But we must, in order to survive, know everything about their culture. Racism is simply preferring straight hair to an Afro; that's certainly more acceptable in our society today. Black vernacular, it's not seen

> as a cultural expression, it's seen as a speech problem. When you look at something as simple as just a group of people talking, black people are given much more, a much higher, regard if they are seen in an all-white group than they would if they were to be seen in an all-black group. If you're seen in an all-white group laughing and talking, you're seen as respectable, and probably taking care of something important. You're not wasting time. You're all right. But if you're in an all-black group, regardless if they can even hear your conversation, white people think you're trying to, you're congregated to take over the world. It's just that basic. . . . You're just punished for expressing your black culture. . . . You're just constantly forced to take on the culture of white America.

Black students not only must learn the white culture but face whites' rejection of their personal values and preferences.

For some first-year students the encounter with a white campus brings significant culture shock. A black community leader who speaks at first-year student orientations charged that many black parents do not prepare their children adequately for what a white college setting will be like:

> Kids come to this university with blinders on, that their parents put on them. . . . They've been through the university, they've been through corporate America, because a lot of the kids who've made it to the university are coming from "middle class America," suburbia, [from] racist, white suburban high schools, which is minor league compared to what they're going to face on these campuses. If parents don't do a better job of preparing their children to come to these universities—and it will have to start before they come on campus, because once they get on campus, it's a little bit too late—they've already got this preconceived idea of what campus life is about. They think they've

> watched TV, and they're falling for some b.s. that they show on TV. And that's not real life. So when the culture shock hits them, parents need to be very up front. A lot of the parents have gone to this university. They need to relate their experiences, because the university has not changed. It has not changed.

Why do some black parents fail to prepare their children fully for racism in the outside world? Some blacks suggest that it is because black parents, like white parents, try to protect their children from pain and particularly from the pain that they have experienced themselves. Perhaps too some black parents keep hoping that the situation has improved since they were in college.

Problems with White Students

The pervasiveness of white culture on campus brings not only subtle pressures to conform to white standards of dress, language, and group behavior but also blatant discrimination. According to the National Institute against Prejudice and Violence, there were published reports of at least 250 racial incidents involving physical violence or psychological assault on college campuses between 1986 and 1990.[19] At the Citadel in South Carolina, white students dressed like Ku Klux Klan members in white sheets and hoods threatened a black student with a burnt cross. The white students were not expelled. At the University of Massachusetts a group of white students severely attacked a black student during a celebration following the World Series. Racist graffiti, fraternity and sorority parties and parades with racist themes, the distribution of racist literature on campus, and violent attacks on black students have continued into the 1990s.[20] For example, at the University of Alabama in the fall of 1991 a white sorority had a party at which pledges blackened their faces and dressed as pregnant women on welfare. And in 1993 a white fraternity at Rider College in New York reportedly had its pledges talk in "black speech" as they carried out cleaning chores.[21]

Several respondents discussed how they became fully aware of what it meant to be black in the United States when they encountered flagrant hostility and discrimination on campus. One young woman, a college graduate now working in administration for a state agency, reported on racist joking:

> I have to say that I've gotten bitter. . . . Last summer, I can remember people telling jokes, that's what I remember most, everyday there was a racial joke. And they found it necessary to tell me. It might be funny and then I'd laugh, and then I thought about it while reading that book [*Black Power*]. Even if they didn't mean any harm, how can they not mean any harm? How can they not, these people who are your classmates. And supposedly some of them are your friends. How can they not mean any harm? What do you mean they don't mean any harm? Why am I making excuses for their actions? I think that's what I was doing a lot of times was making excuses. [Why do you think you were doing that?] I think probably that's just the kind of person I am, just really very passive. [Do you think it's necessary to be that way as a black person?] No, I don't think so. Before I did: Don't make too many waves. And I still think sometimes there's a right way and a wrong way to get certain things accomplished. But if we're talking about [racism] . . . how do I deal with it, let me think, on a day-to-day basis? I don't wake up and give myself a pep talk, "You're black, you're proud!" [laughs] I don't do that, but I think that. . . . I feel it now. Maybe there was a time when I didn't feel it, but I feel it now. And yes, I never thought about it, but I don't have to say it because I feel it.

> [What makes you feel black and proud?] This university! Every time I had to go across some kind of barrier, whether it was white-America-related or not, then that made me stronger, and strengthened one area. This is it. This is the learning tree.

White students may not realize how offensive and troubling racist jokes can be; others may tell such jokes intentionally because they know the jokes cause pain. For the latter, racist humor may be an outlet for passive aggression. Half a century ago Gunnar Myrdal pointed out that white jokes, stories, and popular fiction about blacks act as a "sounding board for and as a magnifier of popular prejudices" about black inferiority.[22] A striking feature of racist joking on campus is that black students and faculty with whom we have talked about such matters have reported no comparable incidence of antiwhite jokes among black students. Racist joking on campuses appears to be one-sided.

Many white college students hold firmly to negative stereotypes about black youngsters, views they probably learned before they came to college. An administrator at a western university discussed the attitudes of some white students about "dirty" black high school students who came there for summer college preparation and athletic programs:

> Somebody will have the idea that the dorm is exclusively theirs, so therefore we can't have these "germy, diseasey, dirty, filthy" black kids live in their dormitory. So that's one obstacle that we have to deal with every year, that our kids don't belong there. The dorms rent rooms out all summer long to all different kinds of groups. But, if anything goes wrong, our group gets blamed for it. If anything . . . gets broken, it's always our group. Whether it's our group, or a black basketball team, or a baseball team, it's always the black group [that] was far worse than the other group. But

> yet, we know that other groups have destroyed the place, torn it up, but you hear, "Oh, well, they were just being kids." . . . . Black kids are seen as a gang now. They must be on drugs, or crazy or something. They perceive it as a fantastic problem rather than, they broke a door knob or something, "Oh, OK, it's no big deal." . . . When the kids eat food in the cafeteria, at first, until the college kids get used to them being there, [they say] "What are they doing here? Why don't they have a separate time and sit somewhere else? We don't want to mix and mingle with them."

A student at a university in the South also reported encountering stereotypical assumptions about black students: "That's the first question they'll ask you: 'Are you an athlete?' Professors, students, everybody here will ask you, 'Are you an athlete?' When you say, 'No,' they're like, 'Oh!' And it's like you got here because you're black." Much of the discrimination we have seen discussed so far seems blatant and motivated by malevolent intentions. However, middle-class African Americans also encounter what John Calmore has termed "subtle discrimination" resulting from a tendency to relate most easily to people like ourselves. There is an "unconscious failure to extend to a minority the same recognition of humanity, and hence the same sympathy and care, given as a matter of course to one's own group."[23] A college student gave a common example:

> Here in my dorm, there are four black girls. Me and my roommates look nothing alike. And the other two are short, and I'm tall. They [white students] called me by my roommate's name the whole semester, and I didn't understand that. [Maybe] I understood it, but I didn't want to have to deal with that whole thing. That's really upsetting. It's like they put their shutters on when they see a black person coming. And the few black people that do get along

> with the other students, they seem to sort of put on a facade. They pretend to be something they're not.

Whether the differential treatment is subtle or unconscious discrimination does not matter; it is still painful and enervating. One reaction is to confront it verbally. Another is to be resigned to it and to put on a mask that hides one's true feelings.

A young lawyer in an eastern city noted some of the other assumptions white students make about black students: "In law school, there were some whites who were offended because I was smart. The teacher would ask the question and point to me, and they didn't think I should have an answer. And I would have a correct answer. But then they started to respect me for it, and they would tell me that: 'Hey, you beat us on that; we knew you would have known that,' or 'What happened? Did you study all night?'" Like others in our study this respondent spoke about the personal testing, competency testing, that black Americans must pass to receive any degree of white acceptance. Once accepted, moreover, a new problem may kick in. Certain black students may be put in a bind if they become the measuring rods for other black students. Because black students are often in a small statistical minority on historically white campuses, some of them may come to accept white views of their accomplishments and even white views of how they should see themselves in regard to other black Americans. A graduate student at a predominantly white university in the South recently noted the pain of accomplishment in a discussion with the senior author: "One problem that you often face as a 'smart' black person is that whites have a tendency to overemphasize their admiration of your success, as if you are a strange bird among your own people."

And, as always, black students have to face the assumption that they have momentous advantages over comparable white students because of government programs like "affirmative action." A professor at a northern university commented on an incident that occurred right after she finished her Ph.D., in the 1980s:

> I was mentioning to friends in the church that finally I [had] finished my Ph.D. And most people were very congratulatory, and there were both black and white people in this group, and generally they were happy. And then one white male, whom I've known for over twenty years, who, by the way, has never finished his Ph.D., even though he started one probably twenty years ago, said, when I was speaking to, there were about three of us in a group standing there, "Yes, but now that you're, because you're a black female, now that you've finished yours, the world is open for you. You can have any job that you wish." And I quickly said to him, "Well, you know, it's very interesting that you say that, because one of the things that's true is that I've never stopped working. I've been working all along while I've been working on that Ph.D., and I'm not sure that getting it's going to change my job status or even my paycheck at all." . . . He makes this assumption that because I'm a black woman, that my getting it now means that the whole world opens up to me, and it's not going to be. And . . . I've known many blacks, specifically in academic circles, who have that thrown at them *all* the time. . . . I think it's the assumption. It's part of the racist attitude, and I think it's one of the things that blacks cope with all the time. And I think it's part of the whole business that, "What with affirmative action, you get all the breaks and we get none."

Not only do the signs of black achievement not diminish whites' racist assumptions and actions, as we saw in the last chapter, many whites question whether middle-class blacks should even be credited with their achievements. The stereotypical notion about blacks' unfair advantages is widespread. In a 1990 National Opinion Research Center nationwide opinion survey 69 percent of white Americans said it was likely that today "a white person won't get a job or promotion while an equally or less qualified black person gets one instead." Yet two thirds of the black respondents said this situation was *not* likely.[24] Conservative commentators often cite the stigma of affirmative action programs in both educational and job settings as the reason why such programs should be abolished, yet they miss the essential point that the stigma is not in the programs themselves but in the prejudices of the *whites* making the evaluations. This white stigmatization of black achievements causes black Americans much pain and frustration.

Most white students on traditionally white campuses, even those who do not engage in openly racist behavior, seem insensitive to the many negative aspects of campus culture for black and other minority students. One survey at the University of Maryland found that about one in five minority students had been the victim of at least one incident of racial harassment and that the overwhelming majority of black students felt they were potential targets. Yet two thirds of the white students were unaware that harassment ever occurred; most did not perceive antiminority prejudice to be part of the campus culture.[25] Moreover, a leading expert on racism in higher education, Jacqueline Fleming, has argued that white students are taught to ignore race as a subject, and thus "the average student does not feel responsible for the racial climate or civil rights."[26]

The stereotyping and insensitivity of many white students makes relationships with them a problem for black students. Social isolation can create a quandary, as one undergraduate student suggested in response the question, "Do you feel that you can trust white people?"

> I'm sure you could. But I just haven't been in a situation where I could find out, because most of the white people that I've met here at college all seem to be reacting on a superficial basis. . . . People that I've met living in the dorm—you know most of the time there's a majority of people who are white in the dorm, and most of the people who really develop a close friendship are just white. People I start out knowing, though, I usually get phased out with towards the end of the year. I still don't know why. I've tried to figure it out. But lately I try not to bother with it, because it will just cause me mental anguish, and I don't want to do that to myself. Now when I was in high school, it was different. We hung out with a lot of different people. We had a lot of Orientals, Mexicans—it was just a whole rainbow of friends I had in high school. I didn't think much of it, but when I came to this university, it seemed to change. I don't know if it was just me, or the environment, but somehow my view of intimacy with other people, especially white people, has soured since then.

Past experience with cultural diversity did not prepare this young man for white students reacting to him on a superficial basis. His "I don't know if it was just me" reaction signals some denial and self-blame. We sense his resigned acceptance of his fate.

Punctuating her comments with occasional laughter, a young attorney in an East Coast city reflected on her college experience a few years back:

> I lived in the dorms for a couple of years, and you sit around in the dorms and eat food with the girls, eat popcorn and watch the soaps when you didn't have classes. And I remember this particular incident, this girl, we had just socialized the night before, watching TV, having popcorn, et cetera. And I saw her on campus the next day, and

> she turned her head to make sure she didn't have to speak to me. And I had that happen more than once. And I think that was a bout with discrimination which just slapped me in the face, because it doesn't feel real good to be a friend to someone, or an associate to someone at seven o'clock, and then at eight o'clock, or eight-thirty, when they're around friends of the other race, they don't know who you are or what you are, and don't even give you the consideration of acknowledging your presence or speaking to you. I think that happens a lot. Even now, I see people that I've gone to law school with in court, and sometimes they just say, "hi." Or sometimes they just don't speak. Or, they'll look at you like, oh, you made it too, I can't believe you made it. And I'll just say, yeah, just watch me, I'll even go further!

Difficulties in making same-sex friendships are just one type of isolation black students face on campus. Several black students and informants touched on the issue of cross-sex friendships and interracial dating. One black female student talked about a liberal white male student whom she had dated. It took her a while to realize that he saw her as a "sexual object, something to try, something new or different." Here sexism mixes with racism in white stereotypes of black women, another example of "gendered racism."[27] Indeed, interracial dating has been one of the underlying issues in white-black conflict at a number of U.S. colleges and universities in the early 1990s. To take just one example, it was one of the factors leading up to verbal and other attacks by white students on black students at Olivet College in Michigan during the spring of 1992. As a result of the white hostility, most of the black students left this predominantly white college campus before the end of the spring semester.[28]

In the last few quotes we see black students uncertain whether or not they can trust white students. The reason for this uncertainty may lie in the two-faced character of some whites' behavior to black students. For example, in a 1992 study at a predominantly white eastern university, Joe R. Feagin conducted group interviews with several dozen black students. In one interview a light-skinned black student reported that he had gotten a glimpse of how some white students talk behind the scenes:

> I can hear them going, "Those black people, this." And it's like the time—it's amazing, you sit there, and they think I'm Hispanic. . . . You'd be amazed what people are saying when they don't think there are black people in the room. They're like, "Oh I can't stand that black guy." And they'll be saying "nigger this, nigger that." But when the black people are around it's like, "Hey Bob. What's up, bro?" And they play like this nice little role. . . . I'm kind of like weird in the sense that I can sit in between, and I can see all this happening.

Mainstream white analysts, including many in the media, often associate the use of racial epithets with white extremists openly committed to racial oppression. Certainly, one of the conventions of polite society is not to use racist epithets in mixed-race groups. However, accounts like this suggest that there is much overt racism being expressed backstage, when black people are not present, and even among white college students. Such racist attitudes could account for some of the ambiguous or inconsistent behavior of white students in their interactions with black students.[29]

Professors as Obstacles

White Stereotypes and White Models

Analyses of the difficulties of black students in white colleges and universities have often neglected the role of white faculty members and administrators. The research reports reviewed by Keller, for example, rarely consider how white professors create racial obstacles for black students.[30] Many observers would expect a university setting, in the North, South, Midwest, or West, to be a cosmopolitan place generally free of overt racial discrimination. The fact that professors in a particular university are drawn from many different graduate schools and regions of the country reinforces this assumption of cosmopolitanism. Yet the reality in all parts of the country seems to be that some white and other nonblack professors can create major hurdles. A student at a western university commented on her graduate school:

> And the conversation is so stiff that it just comes down to racially motivated thoughts or activities at that point. Well, I've heard different things that have happened to different students. . . . I had a professor that treated me so badly during this particular quarter in school that several white students came to the assumption—not that they said [it] to me, but they said [it] to another student that relayed it to me—that they thought that the professor was a racist. Because it had been so obvious that the treatment that I had received in the class was unfair.

Again, this student's account reveals the careful evaluation many middle-class black Americans make before coming to a conclusion of racial discrimination.

One frustrating aspect of being black on a predominantly white campus is the chronic inability of many white faculty members and administrators to "see" black students as individuals, rather than as "representatives" of their racial group, thereby failing to give them the kind of academic and professional advice they are due as students. One graduate student described a black undergraduate's experiences with the chair of her department:

> A black undergraduate in my department is doing some research on black and white achievement in college, and one of her advisers was once the head of a rather prestigious organization in my field, not to mention chair of the department. Apparently she assumed that this one undergraduate somehow spoke for all black people. And this professor would ask her things like, "Well, I don't know what you people want. First you want to be called Negro, then you want to be called black. Now you want to be called African American. What do you people want anyway? And why don't black people show up in class more? Why is it that I can't get enough blacks to sit in on my classes?" So every now and then that sort of racist mentality comes out.

In one form or another we have seen this lack of white sensitivity to black individuality in previous quotes. Again we observe an example of Ralph Ellison's point about the inability of whites to see African Americans as individuals. When looking at blacks, many whites tend to see "figments of their imagination —indeed, everything and anything except me."[31] Several students suggest in their interviews that they have had to be assertive with whites to get their uniqueness recognized.

Some white professors question the competence and potential of black students, failing to give a black student the same benefit of the doubt that they might give a white student, or assuming a student's work will be inferior. A sales manager at an East Coast company described the problems she faced as an undergraduate in a predominantly white college. She noted that discrimination often came in "borderline" grading decisions by white faculty members:

> Early in my undergraduate career . . . instructors were less inclined to give me, or other blacks, the benefits of the positive side. I mean, you were like borderline in the grading situation. And you would talk to some of your white fellow

> students who you knew had the exact same average that you had going into, you know, after completing final courses, when you get your grades, and you would find out that they had an 88 or 89. And they got an A, and you got a B plus. That happened more earlier, [but] less frequently as I continued in the program. Because I also understand that the game you have to play is making yourself known to your professors, where they feel like they know that you are a good student. And they had perceptions that blacks are not going to achieve as much or to be as good a student as the white students, particularly at a predominately white institution which I attended.

We heard this metaphor of a rigged game again and again in our interviews and in many black middle-class discussions of everyday coping with whites, not only in schools and colleges but also in employment and business settings. For middle-class African Americans the institutional game is usually controlled by whites, and in addition to the regular norms (for example, expectations of grading) there are racialized norms (for example, expectations of black incompetence), which can be changed as whites see fit. Until the student proved herself and learned to play by the rules of the white game, she had great difficulty.

Even in graduate school, a black student's work often has to be better than average to head off the assumption of incompetence, particularly in writing, as a recent Ph.D. from a northeastern university noted:

> I would say that occasionally with individual professors that I've had along the way . . . there are the kind of racist assumptions that come. They're surprised if you've done a good piece of work, especially when it comes to writing. I think there are a lot of stereotypes about blacks not being good writers, so that there's a surprise if you've done this. And *that*, I've met. And the person will compliment you,

> but they don't know that underneath that is this racist assumption.

Such stereotyping can lead to action, as a teacher in a northern school system reported:

> So, what happened one time in graduate school, I had this professor, and I didn't talk much in class, so when I did a paper, a final paper, he refused to accept the fact that I did the paper on my own ability. So, what he told me in essence, he would not accept the paper, and I wouldn't get another grade until I redid the paper, which I refused to do. I thought that was basically a discriminatory act. What he was saying was that black folks can't write this good. He didn't know my ability, what I was capable of. I didn't talk much in class, the class was boring. [So, did you do the paper over?] No, I didn't. I took the incomplete. And I talked to the head of the department and I think he put a withdrawal on it. [So you didn't get any credit for the class?] No. I refused to do it. But I didn't like that. I thought if it had been a white student who kept their mouth shut in class, and did a paper that was above what he thought, I'm quite sure that he wouldn't have challenged them.

In reaction to the commonplace white doubting of black proficiency, many black people develop a wary watchfulness.

Another common assumption among white professors and administrators is that students from black communities are not able to handle the difficult course loads and educational requirements that white, or white male, students can. A black professional in a northern city recounted her sister's reaction to this assumption:

> My sister is a surgical technician, and she's just completed getting her master's degree in nursing. And she's talked about as an older student—again the expectation, being

> from a black community in the inner city, that she would not be able to sit in the classroom with younger white students and do as well as they could. But she's proven differently. [I talked] . . . to her about her struggles with her professors, about what she is capable of doing, the course load she is capable of handling, and [her] trying to convince them that she can take on this course load, as opposed to them being supportive and saying, "Whatever you think you can do is fine, and I'll see that you get the kind of guidance and support that you need." [What exactly did they do?] Well, limit her course work. . . . They said, "You can't take this course," and she got into a fight with the dean.

White misconceptions about black competence may be magnified when the student is an older black woman, as in this case, in which her struggle to succeed against white barriers required the determination to overcome whatever obstacle she encountered.

The pervasive whiteness of the historically white college environment is conspicuous in the role models typically encountered by black students. Few, if any, of their professors will be black or provide a black perspective. A talented student at a predominantly white university in the Southwest described how an English professor evaluated her essays about the black experience:

> [He told me that] if a white person, for example, picked up one of my stories he would not understand what the hell was going on. So therefore I shouldn't write about these things. But I should write about [other] things, and he quoted William Faulkner quite liberally. I should write about things that appeal to the human heart, that everybody can appeal to and can relate to. And, see me, in my nice trusting self, I said "No, he's not saying that black people aren't people enough to be termed as universal. He's not saying that, he's meaning something else. He couldn't

> possibly be saying this to my face." I was very, very confused. I did not understand what the hell he meant by it, not just the racial implications, but the whole statement.

The professor, who was Asian American, regarded her accounts of the black experience as hard for whites to understand and not as universal as stories by a white author. By citing Faulkner he suggested to a young black woman that the relevant model for excellent writing was not only white but also male and southern.

Similarly, in Feagin's 1992 study at an eastern university, one black student observed a bias in white professors' reactions to papers on black or African issues, explaining, "It can get kind of bad when you bring up certain issues," and giving as an example a paper he wrote in an English class about how African civilization antedated other civilizations: "If it's controversial, it's not good. . . . I mean you can see it when . . . you get, you know, B's, B+'s, A's and then all the sudden you write this paper on Africa and you get a C−." In his experience and that of other students, some white professors do not respond well to papers on such topics of concern to the black students and do not grade them fairly.[32] In her work on gender issues Catharine MacKinnon has pointed out that the leading doctrine of equality in the United States has been: Be the same as the dominant group. Paraphrasing MacKinnon for racial matters we can say this: Concealed in many white evaluations of the black middle class is the substantive way in which the white standard has become the measure of things.[33] We see most of our black respondents caught in the dilemma of resisting this white middle-class standard at the same time that they must accept it to some degree in order to survive in a white world.

Some white teachers of black students have difficulty not only with the substance of their writing but also with their language and style. In an eastern city a young male banker reported an experience he had had in an English course:

> The only thing that hurt me was certain white institutions. Instead of helping you and educating you, they will browbeat [you] and downplay the educational level that you have. I turned in a paper one time at a college, and I had an instructor tell me that I was speaking black English. I was the only black in the class, and it was a freshman writing class. And she told me that I was speaking black English. And it kind of, in one sense, made me not want to be black, and, in another sense, wonder what was black English. Because I had gone to white schools from the sixth grade on, and I had been speaking—not speaking but writing—white English all my life. I couldn't understand what she was talking about. . . . If I remember right, she gave me a D in the course. She had given me D's and C's on all my papers. And I know for a fact that certain people did less research, less work than me, but she was very hard on me. That really woke me up, because that really taught me to take a lot of English writing workshops. Where now, I guess you could say, my writing skills are above average. And that's great because by her hurting me, and telling me that I was speaking black English, now I'm able to speak black English in a white format, where I can get my point across and be understood.

Another aspect of being black in a white institution can be seen in the sense of inferiority the student felt when a white teacher stereotyped his writing as "black English." The teacher's harsh evaluation of his work hurt and embarrassed him but also made him determined to become more expert in the English language and to prove himself. With his "made me not want to be black" statement this young man revealed the life-crisis character of these events. One of the most serious reactions to white insensitivity and misunderstanding is the rejection of one's own group, and thus of one's self.

Yet another aspect of using white experience as the norm is the heavy use of white-oriented screening tests, such as the Scholastic Aptitude Test (SAT) and the Graduate Record Examination (GRE), at most historically white colleges. Black parents, teachers, and students often complain about the alien character of this testing. The SAT and GRE are educational tests created by whites and are reflective in a number of ways of white culture. One study by Allan Nairn and his associates examined the SAT and the GRE and found that both the tests and their administration were biased against students from minority and blue-collar backgrounds. The language and situations used in test items generally favor those from middle-income white families.[34] Percy Bates has noted that a "test-wiseness" curriculum has not been added to most central city schools and that "predominantly white high schools are more likely to offer their students special courses on how to take tests, and white parents are more likely to invest in private coaching to improve their children's college education test scores."[35] As a result, the standardized test scores are often inadequate measures of black students' potential for future achievement.

A student at a historically white private university commented on her experiences with her SAT scores and a white professor:

> When I got here it was an ignorance, a closed-minded ignorance that I didn't know how to handle. One of my professors—I went to him as a freshman asking for help, and he asked me my SAT scores. And I told him. And [he said], "I don't know why they let you in, you're not expected to do well. There are so many people like you here

> that aren't qualified, and I can try to help you and find a tutor."

The professor assumed that because her scores were lower than the very high average for incoming students at this elite university that she was not qualified. In her interview the student continued by noting that the professor asked her about the high school she had attended. When she told him that she had graduated from a prestigious private school, "his face just went every which way, [his] eyes went big, and then he said, 'Well, I'll help you get a tutor, and we'll study, because I know you're prepared for this.'" Black students are often well aware of the views of black competence and capability that many white educators hold. Here the relatively low SAT score at first confirmed the professor's assumption of her inferiority. However, the fact that she had graduated from a tough private, and mostly white, high school made him reevaluate his estimation of her potential and offer assistance. This student reported she had similar experiences with other white professors.

Restriction and Rejection

Some white instructors seem to go out of their way to make the educational agenda of black students more difficult, as a registered nurse in an East Coast city suggested:

> It was extremely hard, when we did our clinical practice at some of the hospitals with the white instructors who always gave the black students the harder patients to do. You really, really, really got the harder patients to do. . . . I think that's been demonstrated in that, of the ten or fifteen teachers that were at that school, they had one black instructor. She was a Ph.D. psychiatric nurse. Our class grad-

> uated 115 students; ten of them were black. So, you have to make a conclusion from that. It was rough.

Black health professionals with whom we talked often reported having a difficult time in school or in the early years of practice, in that they were tested in unfair ways or were expected to fail.

In most historically white medical schools and hospitals, faculties are still composed mostly of white males, so that empathy for female students and those from different racial and cultural backgrounds is often lacking. Indeed, it was not until the late 1970s that women and minority students began to penetrate many medical schools and teaching hospitals in significant numbers. A doctor in an East Coast city reported on her internship problems in the late 1970s: "About twelve years ago, when I started my internship, I was the first black to ever train at that hospital. And at that time the discrimination was, 'So you're here to train, I hope you make it' type of thing, but they were not going to help you. You were going to have to do it all on your own. That was a rough time, but I made through it."

African Americans are often pioneers in predominantly white institutions and may be resented as interlopers. The resentment may stem from difficulty with a black person's style or perspective. A nurse commented on her recent experience at a northern university:

> Well, it was just an instructor . . . a young white male who was teaching; health care industry was a part of his curriculum. And I'd been a nurse and in the health care arena for almost thirty years; I pretty well knew a lot of things. However, it was as if he made it, instead of letting me understand his concept, he went to the extreme of making me feel somewhat uncomfortable about being in his class. It's kind of hard to explain, it really is. I knew it was happening, something very subtle was happening, but you can't pinpoint it, you can't put your finger on all of it. And as a

> matter of fact, I got the worst grade from this guy. And in all my years at this university I have *never*—now can you imagine a nurse of almost thirty years who had made A's and B's in all of her other classes and the *one* class, the one area that I have expertise in, was the area where I made a C.

An experienced white nurse might also have made this young professor uncomfortable, but, as an older black female facing a young white male, this woman concluded from subtle situational cues that the instructor treated her as he did because of her gender and her color.

Professors' discomfort with black students can be caused by the difficult questions they sometimes ask, as an accounting officer recalled:

> Looking back over the last five years of my attendance in college, I feel very strongly that I have not been given an equal opportunity in seeking my educational goals. I face constant discrimination by white students and the all-white faculty members. Once it is known that you have the knowledge they have, or your knowledge surpasses theirs, then you are watched, feared, and kept back. The students have no real control, but the professors will see to it that you fail or are given a low passing grade. Three summers ago I took a writing class. The instructor was white. From the start she did not like me because I kept questioning the things that she was teaching. She also could not give answers to some of the questions that the students would ask. To make things worse my own style of writing was very different from what she was used to. I made a D plus on my final paper and was told I would get a C for my final grade. After a long and nasty conversation between us, and no resolution, I got my grade report in the mail with a C plus for my final grade. Other instructors have tried to lower my self esteem, but after experiencing a few episodes of

> what is outright discrimination I have learned to "play the game."

Some readers might consider this respondent's sense of persecution to be exaggerated, for she is quite strong in her view of her college years as a struggle against constant discrimination. Yet if her sense of persecution is more acute or dramatically stated than some other students', it nonetheless communicates well the embattled character of the black student's experience at mostly white universities.

A problem that many college students, black or white, have with college professors is the lack of feedback on course performance. But a lack of feedback and reinforcement is doubly difficult for a black student already at sea in a white world and facing other negative reactions from white faculty members. One university student described a white professor's response to an inquiry about grading:

> I can think of several courses where I honestly feel that I was very much discriminated against. One class was an honors course in social science. And it just so happened that the criteria for getting in the course was to have made a certain grade in a previous social science course, which I did. So I took the course. . . . But when it came time for grades, the grade that I got was not the grade I earned . . . and the professor actually never even respected me enough to sit down and talk to me about my grades. The only feedback I got from the guy was when I approached him after I got the grade. And he talked to me only the amount of time that it took him to walk out of his office and go to where he had to go, and I stood there as he walked through his door. And except for that he wouldn't even give me any feedback. And essentially what he told me was that, first of all, my attendance was poor in class. And secondly he told me that some work which he

> gave as optional work—that I had done—was . . . poor work. So what I understood him to say was that he took off of my regular grade for extra credit work. And as far as attendance goes, he said that I never attended class. But in fact I only missed two classes the entire semester, and the only reason I missed those two classes was because I was required by the military to be out of town on those two days.

An important aspect of life on a white campus is the tone of the place, the sense of being welcome or unwelcome. Joseph Katz, a pioneer in research on white faculty and black students, found that black students "consistently report that white professors avoid eye contact with them and engage in other forms of behavior that limit contact and recognition of the contributions and thoughts of black students."[36] According to the account above, the white professor, incommunicative, did not fairly evaluate the student. Conceivably, he might have acted the same way with white students. However, on a student already assaulted by the many slights of racism, such insensitivity and lack of feedback, whether intentional or not, can have a very negative impact.

As we have already seen, the poor treatment of black students can result from assumptions about both racial group and class. An academic advisor at an eastern university noted the difficulty some white faculty members have in relating to black students:

> Some of the white faculty, they really don't understand the problems of students, they don't understand black students. Some of them just don't care about them. You have a group of faculty in the school of business. They're not looking at those students who are working full time with children, single mothers who have lost husbands, or maybe who never had a husband. They have kids, one woman has a kid with spina bifida, and she's trying to work hard to get

herself educated so she can make her family one where she can support them. Faculty don't look at this, they don't care about these situations sometimes that black students have.

They're paying their hard-earned money to take one course at a time. Some of them are not eligible for other kinds of financial assistance. But faculty, some of the faculty, don't even think about that. And if you're black, they think you're full of excuses. And they already have a mindset, before you get into that class, that I don't deal with you because you're black. They don't want to hear that you can't be here for class because you have an appointment with your child's doctor that you've been waiting for two months to get. . . . They tend to listen to their white students more than they would listen to black students. I had one girl come in and say a faculty member slammed a door in her face because she didn't have time for her. And all she wanted to do was ask about one problem, one question. The student is a good student, strong grade point average. The faculty member didn't even have time to talk with that girl, she wouldn't even talk to her. And then she saw some whites go into her office later and the woman let them in. . . . So, these are the kinds of things that I know that are here, because I hear them all the time. And they're not just from blacks, I've had white students come in with black students, and say, that's right, these things happen.

A few black college students with whom we have talked in informal settings have noted a counterpart to the problems of neglect mentioned here, the situation of some white professors being too solicitous and giving too much attention to a black student. While this may reflect a genuine desire on the part of a white professor to help, it can also make black students feel "different" or inferior. The racist world of the white campus brings dilemmas for all.

At the core of most predominantly white colleges is the Euro-American bias in courses, curricula, and research agendas. Several students explained that some white professors call on black students primarily to give the "black side of the story" or, conversely, avoid calling on black students who have questioned a professor's excessively Eurocentric viewpoint. One black student, noting the bias in classroom discussions on non-European cultures, described her Jamaican roommate's reaction to their American studies professor in a class on cultural and mental disorders:

> She becomes really, really irritated because he'll talk about . . . a Jamaican medium. And she tried to explain to him that some of the things that he thought were abnormal, were very normal for her culture. And he just kind of like dismissed everything, and . . . I have to like push her to go to the class because she is really, really irritated with the class. She usually doesn't say anything anymore, and she is very intelligent, I mean she has a lot to contribute to the class.[37]

The white professor's harsh normative judgments of an Afro-Caribbean culture not only irritate a Jamaican student and her black roommate but also alienate them from the class. Such incidents suggest that much in the traditionally white university environment condones stereotyped interpretations of non-European cultures.

A career counsellor, now employed in a southwestern firm, reported on a recent college experience:

> I had an incident with a professor, and he and I got into a heated argument. He was giving a lecture and he was saying that the reason that there're so many [crazy people] in

> Louisiana is because black people have polluted the white Louisiana blood. The professor said this in class and he and I got into a heated verbal exchange. And he apologized subsequently, but my rationale was, you know, "What basis do you have for saying that? You have no proof of that." But that was just his ideology; that blacks had contaminated white Louisiana blood.

The pseudo-biological thinking of "race and blood" is obviously still part of some whites' thinking about racial relations. It is significant that here the reference is to Louisiana, a state from which one of the nation's foremost white supremacy politicians, David Duke, emerged in the late 1980s. Note again that an important dimension of this encounter was the aggressive response of the black student and the backing down of the white professor.

Ironically, the subject of U.S. racial history is such a charged one for many black students that some professors avoid candid presentations of the worst abuses that occurred. One college student commented on this dilemma:

> A friend of mine was telling me that he's taking a history class. He was telling me that he was talking to some of the things that went on during slavery. His professor said that there are certain things that he simply cannot talk about in class because black people would get upset. And what makes me angry about that, I have to blame the education system on that, because that is such an example of self-denial, of shame. What I hate so much is that if this was taught on the junior high level, on the high school level, we wouldn't be running from that kind of education. We could sit through it. My friend was saying how he used to talk about the rape of black women in slavery. And he said black women would leave his class, they would be so upset they wouldn't want to hear about it.

Then she turned to whites' ignorance of this Afro-American history:

> It's because we don't share that kind of knowledge, that white people can walk around [uninformed] today. The white people who don't take any other social science classes besides history or government, if they're business students or engineering or whatever, they can walk around and still ask, "How come black people are so far behind? How come black people are so poor? How come the illegitimacy rate is so high? What's happening to them?" If [public school teachers] would talk about those things, white people could not get away with being so ignorant. The way the high school system is set up, they're not going to talk about the concrete things that happened during slavery, so when you come to college, you find yourself running out of the class, not being able to hear certain things.

This account brings to mind George Santayana's famous comment that "those who cannot remember the past are condemned to repeat it." In this student's view white students badly need to learn about U.S. racial history, especially before college. She is also critical of the schools for not teaching black students about their history earlier, for encounters with this history in college can cause great distress. She implies that one solution would be much more candid education about slavery and racism in primary and secondary school for all students.

This interview excerpt raises the issue of how African-American history has been transmitted in this country. Much African-American experience, past and present, has been carried as oral history in black families and communities because most white authors have written only from their own narrow or unenlightened perspectives, and because black scholars have rarely been able to get major white publishers to print unexpurgated accounts of that history. Often white editors see critical black writings as "too emotional" or "too pessimistic."[38] Moreover, some black writers cannot write the true history of the black experience because it is too emotionally draining. In the account above we have evidence of how that history arouses intense emotion in African Americans. When an accurate version of Afro-American history is presented, many vicariously relive the experience, including the accompanying pain and rage.

Another important aspect of the whiteness of the traditionally white campus world is the assumption about what is valid and serious research. Like members of white immigrant groups in the early 1900s, black students often see the university as a place for learning and research that can be of help to their struggling communities. A graduate student at a southwestern university noted that he has had to go outside the university to pursue his research goals; then he commented on the experiences of some friends:

> I know of people who have been in my department who have left. I can think of a black woman, who I never actually met, who left the year before I got there, who felt that the department was so constricting in terms of not only the types of research that she could do, but in terms of attitudes. Apparently, she was told at one point [that] she wasn't thought of as a black person, largely because she was doing so well. She was outperforming the white students in a class. And apparently a faculty member told her something like, "Well, we don't think of you as one of them any more." And I also know someone who was in my department, who received a very cold reception, not only in terms of the type of research he wanted to do, but also in terms of basic politeness. . . . That individual ended up switching departments. He got his doctorate but never felt at home in that department.

One reason for the black attrition at many historically white graduate schools is the attitude of some white professors to many black students' concern with research that will benefit black communities.

An assistant professor recounted her recent experience at a major West Coast graduate school. Her white adviser pressured her to specialize in a certain period of white literature, not in Afro-American literature, because she would thus be

> doing something he didn't consider most black people did. And that job offers would come in for that reason. And, further, that doing Afro-American literature was not in and of itself important intellectual work. Well, I insisted . . . and he finally gave in and gave me permission. He never stopped thinking that it was important for me not to do Afro-American literature as evidence that I was a real scholar. You couldn't do Afro-American lit and be a real scholar at the same time. And I ran into that attitude when I was on the job market.

One signal that historically white college cultures are not racially integrated is in the downplaying of humanities and social science research on African Americans, not only at the undergraduate and graduate levels, but also in college hiring practices.

One black counter to obstacles on mostly white campuses has been to organize black support groups. Although such organizing may be necessary for survival, it can result in black students being labelled as separatists or militants by white students, faculty members, and administrators. Discussing effective ways to deal with discrimination, one graduate student commented,

> When I was involved in efforts to integrate the department more fully, I did receive a rather cold reception from several faculty members. . . . [We] set up a meeting of grad students to discuss the recruitment and retention of minorities

> in the department. And a few of the faculty members there who were pretty much of the old school. . . . We had agreed that the meeting would be open and candid. Their idea of open and candid was that it would be closed to everyone else except those who had been invited to be part of the discussion. So, in that sense, the department has been quite reactionary. It seems to be acting in good faith now in terms of recruitment, but only because it has been pressured to do so. . . . But it is frustrating to realize how, not only insensitive, but ignorant, a lot of supposedly intelligent white people are. I think [of] the faculty especially in that regard. There seems to be an attitude that things are well enough now for blacks and other minorities that there's no need to rock the boat. I've certainly seen that in my own department, but I think it extends beyond that department. Indifference to a variety of issues, whether it's investment in South Africa, or faculty recruitment. . . . And when people come along who want to set things right, so to speak, they're the ones that are confronted, they're the ones that are met with . . . excuses, such as [that] divesting from South Africa would be making a political statement, where obviously remaining invested is a political statement in itself.

With the rise of successful South African political movements, race-related issues on campus have included not only localized issues such as black faculty and student recruitment but also international issues such as black empowerment in South Africa. The South African liberation movement, with its so far successful political struggle and its visible leaders, has captured the political imagination not only of black students but also of African Americans generally (see Chapter 8).

Whether as undergraduates, graduate students, or professional students, blacks have organized both for protective purposes and for larger protest and political objectives. A physician in a northern city described his medical school days:

> For me it's been a very, very hard struggle. First, to begin with, I was the first one of seven, as a group of black students entering medical school. The whites at this university were very opposed to the seven of us being admitted into medical school. There was a lot of strife around that. The white students were very rebellious. Openly rebellious to the extent that that propelled me into the forefront of fighting racism on campus. Thus, I became involved in black Students Association, Student Medical Association. . . . And we became more intensely interested in teaching . . . in the black community. For example, [we] started the black sickle cell program here and various other things like that. But it was a real struggle. I don't think at any point, during our education, we were accepted. It was always fight hard to make the grade.

The black student organization here went beyond student protection to organizing for the health interests of the black community. Over the past decade we have discussed these concerns with a number of black graduate students and faculty members who made it clear that for them the larger context of their institutions was the black community, to which, as educated Americans who have succeeded, they felt a great responsibility.

The campus climate at historically white colleges and universities is also shaped by the prejudices and discriminatory actions of white administrators, staff, and alumni. The last two accounts both allude to the role of white administrators in restricting the progress and organization of black students. And in Chapter 2 we observed the physical harassment that some black students encounter from campus police officers. In Feagin's 1992 study, one black student described the blatant difference between how white students' and black students' social events are policed by campus security personnel.

> I know when you go to a black party, and if you notice how all the police are around, you know what I'm saying. And that's the thing: you have eight police there, plus a police car outside, plus student aides right there at the party. But yet you go down to the [white] frat row, and they've got no type of security there, . . . and they end up having a big 300-people fight, and something like that. And then they are so wild. Me and my friends went to one of those white frat parties, and they are so wild it's ridiculous. And black people do not act anything like that at their parties. . . . But it's funny how you have all the security at the black functions and nothing at the white functions.[39]

He continued by describing this observed pattern as "subtle racism," for the singling out of black students for special surveillance is discriminatory. Here again the excessive policing may be motivated by the white image of black people, especially young black men, as prone to violence.

Other white staff members play a role in creating a campus bureaucracy oriented to white students. Reviewing graduate education, sociologist James Blackwell has proposed that the factors contributing to the low black attendance include the scarcity of financial aid, as well as the general character of college climates and mentoring programs.[40] The difficulty of obtaining financial aid was aggravated in the 1980s and early 1990s by the conservative Republican administrations' major cutbacks. A nurse commented on her experiences at an East Coast university:

> I worked hard at it, nobody gave me anything. I mean, I struggled as a mother of three children and then a divorced mother of three kids to put myself through an associate de-

> gree program, a baccalaureate degree and a master's. So no one really gave me anything at all in any aspect. As a matter of fact, I . . . did encounter some racism in that aspect because I found out that some monies were more available to white students than was in fact available to black students to finish the graduate program at this university. . . . I had to stand my ground and say, "I want to finish this program, I have this time frame to finish this program. I can do this program, but I need some help." And so, not that they gave me the help, but they were able to extend my payments so that I was able to still take the courses and still manage to pay the tuition. But it was not easy; they didn't just offer it to me, I had to fight to get it.

Struggles with college bureaucracies, many of which are oriented to the needs of white middle-class students, become serious when daily survival is in the balance. There is a widespread notion in this country that African American and other minority college students receive large numbers of race-exclusive financial aid packages. Indeed, during the Bush administration in the early 1990s the U.S. Department of Education targeted these race-exclusive aid programs as a major problem, thereby communicating to the nation the false impression that a large proportion, if not the majority, of minority students benefit from them. However, the Department of Education's own statistics show how inaccurate this impression is. In one recent year only 45,000 minority students benefited from race-exclusive scholarship aid. And these students constituted about 3.5 percent of all minority college students. To put it another way, less than .8 percent of all aid students are minority students receiving help from race-conscious programs. The real problem is not the one so widely discussed, but rather, as the student in the previous quote suggests, the lack of funds to assist minority students to achieve their educational goals.[41]

An Agonizing Dilemma:
Black Colleges or White Colleges?

Most black parents work hard for their children to succeed, and many see advanced education as a way up for their children. In a 1992 study in an eastern state Joe R. Feagin conducted group interviews with a number of college-oriented black parents with children of college age or children old enough for them to be considering a nearby university.[42] Significantly, when the black parents were asked about this predominantly white university, many did not see it as a strongly welcoming milieu for black students. Drawing on their own experience and that of relatives and acquaintances with this university, as well as on media accounts, many portrayed black students there as facing racial barriers set up by white students, faculty, staff, and administrators. Racial barriers are not discussed by black parents just to be argumentative, for such obstacles are at the heart of an agonizing dilemma many black parents and students face: that of choosing between a predominantly white and a predominantly black college. Black parents themselves, such as this mother in one group, talked about this choice for their children specifically as a "dilemma":

> I have a seventeen-year-old daughter who's looking at college now. . . . [She] was very set on a major black university, where many members of my family have gone. And I wanted her to go there. But I also knew that she was going to make connections in college that will last for her life. And [at a white university] the people you spend your undergrad with very often are the CEO's of tomorrow. So it was a dilemma. Do I want her to identify with who she is ethnically, or do I want her to start the groundwork for her future career?

In choosing a college, few white parents or students must consider racial discrimination, the loss of faculty and other social support, or the greater difficulty of participating in campus life that the choice of a white college frequently involves for black parents and students.

Once in a predominantly white university, many black students consider dropping out, often because of the constant questioning of their capabilities. In our national middle-class sample a business executive commented on his daughter's experience at two predominantly white universities and at a black university:

> My daughter, who graduated from a predominantly black southern university, initially began her college training at a [white] midwestern university. . . . [Later] she moved back to the southern city to be with us, with my wife, and went to a white university there. [She] then decided she needed a little more exposure and went to the black university. The thing that was so interesting to her was that at the midwestern university and the white southern university, both good schools, there was a night and day difference in how you were treated by the faculty. The faculty at the black southern university were interested in you as a person, wanted to insure that you were successful in completing courses and getting your degree. And at the midwestern university and the white southern university they could care less about you as an individual; you're more or less a number. . . . She decided in a number of instances that there were some assumptions made by her faculty at these universities that she would not be able to comprehend some of the information they were giving her. Just on an assumption! Of course, she was able to do that, had no problem. But it was just that "Well, I know the university is here, and black students are competing with the white students, and we're really not going to expect you to do too well."

Many middle-class African Americans such as this executive

and his family must constantly debate the virtues of black and white colleges. Business researcher John Butler, himself African American, has noted that for many middle-class black professionals and business people "there is a general feeling that these [black] schools prepare them well for participation in society" and that simply "because a school is attended and operated by whites, it is not automatically superior."[43]

Conclusion

Many white commentators on the crisis in black education blame the victim in their assessments of elementary and secondary education, and especially of higher education. George Keller has argued that middle-class blacks bear the greatest responsibility for the problems of black youth, arguing that

> educators and do-gooders outside academe must move beyond their naive pieties onto the treacherous, unknown ground of new realities. Petulant and accusatory black spokespersons will need to climb off their soapboxes and walk through the unpleasant brambles of their young people's new preferences and look at their young honestly. . . . They will need to encourage, lift up, and argue with those youths who do not see the urgency of education in a scientific, international, and information-choked world. . . . Critics will need to stop the fashionable practice of lambasting the colleges as if they were the central problem.[44]

In this analysis Keller provides a window into the mind of many influential whites, including policymakers, as we approach the twenty-first century. Many whites feel that the burden is on middle-class black leaders to quit being "accusatory" and to work harder to encourage black youth to view education as the main way to overcome poverty and inferiority.

These white critics are oblivious to the influence of the contemporary racial climate at traditionally white schools and colleges and fail to see white-run institutions as a source of serious problems for black students. Yet life for black students in mostly white schools often means daily struggle and recurring crises. They struggle to find out what the rules of the game are, officially and unofficially. When black students say "whiteness" is an omnipresent problem, they are not just talking about color or racial identification. They are reporting being at sea in a hostile environment. Painful difficulties with teachers, fellow students, and curricula not only accumulate year after year for black children as individuals and as a group but also regularly bring to mind the collective memory of past discrimination.

We have observed numerous ways in which encounters with white hostility shape the perspectives of students and their parents. Life perspectives and identities are challenged constantly, and some students seem to walk on the edge of denial of their own blackness. Yet most maintain their balance and meet the recurring pain and anger with a determination to excel and conquer. As we observed in Chapter 2, the array of responses to discrimination that becomes part of one's repertoire is great, ranging from resignation to open confrontation. A black professor who has worked in various parts of the country eloquently summed up the impact of white racism in creating a defensive lifestyle and life perspective:

> When a black student walks into a predominantly white environment, that student gets the same feeling that I get when I walk into a predominantly white situation. I immediately become fearful and defensive: fearful that someone will openly show hostility, that someone will openly show that I'm not wanted there; defensive, trying to set myself up so that if I face that I can deal with it. Students don't have all of the kinds of coping mechanisms held by adults and

professional adults; therefore this is more difficult for them. I still find myself uncomfortable if I walk into a strange environment where there are only whites and I'm the only black. And unfortunately, usually someone, at least one person in that environment or in that situation, will say or do something that's negative, if it's no more than just ignore you.

So, you come in defensive. . . . your fear is reinforced. That's what happens to so many of these youngsters on these campuses, they're dealing with kids who are sons and daughters of bigots. And as soon as they find a friend who accepts them, and they feel real good and start to relax, they run into this young bigot who brings back all the pain, all of the hurt, and it almost erases all of the good that's there. So, they're constantly in a state of stress. There's not a time when they feel that they can afford to let down. And when they let down, they're hurt.

Chapter Four

Navigating the Middle-Class Workplace

On May 29, 1984, one of America's most talented journalists, Leanita McClain, committed suicide. Only thirty-two years old, she had won numerous major journalism awards. She was the first African American to serve on the editorial board of the *Chicago Tribune* in its long history. Two months prior to her suicide *Glamour* magazine had acclaimed her as one of the outstanding women working in corporate America. Why did such a talented woman commit suicide? Reviewing McClain's life, Bebe Moore Campbell has assessed the culture shock blacks face having to cope with a culturally different, often discriminatory white world. In the white-normed corporate environment, "Black women consciously choose their speech, their laughter, their walk, their mode of dress and car. They trim and straighten their hair. . . . They learn to wear a mask."[1] In addition to facing particular experiences of poor treatment by whites, black employees in corporate America are under constant pressure to adapt, unidirectionally, to the values and ways of the white world.

In this chapter we examine the world faced by those African Americans who work in thousands of white-collar workplaces. Employment as white-collar workers in very large numbers in historically white workplaces is a relatively new experience for African Americans. The black middle class of professionals, managers, sales workers, clerical workers, and entrepreneurs has increased dramatically since the 1960s. In 1988 approximately 9 percent of clerical workers were black; about 6 percent of sales workers were black. The professional-technical category was 8 percent black, and the managerial category was approximately 6 percent black.[2] Black employees make up about 11 percent of the labor force, so it is evident they are still underrepresented in these white-collar categories. Furthermore, as we discussed in Chapter 1, these broad categorical data give a misleading impression of how much progress has occurred, for white-collar blacks are disproportionately concentrated in lower status sectors within each category. Moreover, these statistical data do not tell us how individuals are actually treated in the workplace. Indeed, in the three decades that have elapsed since the 1964 federal anti-discrimination law, *no* research group has to our knowledge undertaken a major national study of day-to-day discrimination faced by black men and women in the workplace.[3]

Discrimination at the Entry Stage

Black professional, managerial, and clerical employees typically work in establishments that were until recently, at least in their white-collar ranks, exclusively white. Black employees in a white-collar work milieu, unlike in public accommodations, might be expected to be somewhat sheltered from racial hostility because the workaday cast of characters is relatively constant and the workers often know one another. In addition, fair employment laws are well known, and one might conclude—

erroneously—from media discussions, well enforced. Yet the probability of experiencing discrimination and intolerance in such a workplace environment is still great.

Job discrimination questions have totalled perhaps half of the survey questions asked of national samples of black Americans on the subject of discrimination. In a 1988 *Business Week* poll 80 percent of the black respondents, but only 32 percent of the whites, felt that if an equally well-qualified black person and white person were competing for the same job, the black applicant would be less likely to be hired.[4] In a 1989 ABC News/*Washington Post* survey, a bit more than half of the black respondents were certain that black workers generally faced discrimination in getting skilled jobs; 61 percent replied in a similar way in regard to managerial jobs. On the same survey question whites generally saw far less discrimination than blacks. An earlier 1986 ABC News/*Washington Post* poll, one of very few to ask about personal discrimination, found 39 percent reporting experience with discrimination in getting a job and 41 percent reporting discrimination in getting equal wages.[5] We suspect these latter figures are low estimates of the actual proportion of black workers encountering discrimination, because the questions are very brief and do not examine the many dimensions and conditions of employment settings. In addition, the data were not reported by income level. It is possible that in the workplace middle-class black employees face an even greater range of instances of everyday discrimination than working class black employees because they are pioneers in many formerly all-white settings.[6]

Most of our respondents hold positions in the better-paying professional, managerial, technical, sales, and clerical categories. Like the business people we discuss in the next chapter, these Americans have adopted the ethic of hard work and have taken the promises of the American dream very seriously. In conventional middle-class terms they represent the most successful group of African Americans, those thought by most white Americans to "have arrived."

Hiring is the first stage in the employment process. The 1964 Civil Rights law bars differential treatment in employment, and the "equal opportunity employer" phrase used in advertising suggests that there is indeed equal job opportunity. But legal statements of rights are not necessarily statements of reality. Several respondents reported being rejected because of their race as they sought employment. One well-educated, experienced legal secretary in a southern city recounted her experience:

> Exactly five years ago I ran into an employment barrier when I first came here. The employment office sent me around to legal offices that had openings. And since I've been a legal secretary for at least fifteen years—that's my specialty in the clerical field—I've never had trouble getting a job until I came here. And when they talked to me over the telephone, they were real nice, you know, "Come on down, yes, we have an opening." But when I got there—I went to two different law offices—when I got there, I didn't get an interview. They came, they saw me, they were shocked. They went into their office and buzzed the secretary and said, "Tell her to leave her application and we'll call later; we're too busy to do it now."

Neither firm called her back. Choosing not to challenge this discriminatory behavior, she found another job. It is important to note that the whites here, as in many similar workplaces, are not the Archie Bunker hard-hat whites whom many whites think of when the term "racist" is mentioned, but rather are educated professionals or managers. Again we observe a middle-class black American who sounds "white" over the telephone to white ears initially receiving the same treatment as a white applicant.

Although the poor treatment of this respondent was relatively overt, its character makes conclusive proof of discrimination difficult. In our discussions with whites, some have raised questions about the ambiguity in certain black reports of discrimination. The question some whites might ask of this black woman, "How do you know that the rejection was on the basis of discrimination?" would likely be received as a hard blow. Whites questioning her interpretation of a situation that for her is clearly exclusionary is painful, because she, an older black woman, is experienced in the ways of white restrictions in many organizational arenas.

Stereotypes, conscious or unconscious, about the skills of black workers may cause some white personnel officers to see a middle-class black applicant either as a menial worker or a poor risk regardless of qualifications. A college graduate working for a telephone company in a western city discussed the hiring experience of a friend: "A good friend of mine was being interviewed about the jobs that are being offered at a large hotel-casino that's just opening up. A black woman was applying for a job as a manager, or a higher-skilled job. She was then told: Wouldn't you be more comfortable being a waitress? Wouldn't you rather be a maid? This happens all the time."

Race-related factors have blocked the entry of African Americans into almost every category of workplace. A director of library services gave this account of her son's attempt to achieve his dream of becoming a professional driver in auto racing:

> He has a goal; he wants to be a professional automobile racer. There are no black . . . professional automobile racers. And he's been training. He's finished three different schools for automobile racing. But he can't break into the professional ranks of that because it takes a large corporate sponsor. It takes a lot of money to do that. And he has written proposals and he has made presentations to a lot of

> large corporations. And he hasn't been successful in getting the funding, we feel mainly because he's black. He has the skills, we've been and we've seen him race, and he's been critiqued by professional racers and instructors. And they say that he has high-level skills, and he could break into professional racing, but because he's black [he cannot]—that is a white society's sport. So he can't get corporate sponsorship.

Every day, reports in the mass media support the impression that black sports figures are very successful in many different sports. Yet some major sports, such as tennis, golf, and auto racing, are off-limits to more than a token number of African Americans. The internationally famous Indianapolis 500 has so far had only one black driver, Wally T. Ribbs, who was allowed to participate beginning in 1991. Although praised by local professionals in his sport, the young black man described in the quote learned that the views of blacks by whites in corporate suites were more powerful than the views of professionals at the track.

What little recent research has been done on racial discrimination in hiring has focused on less-skilled jobs. Thus, in a 1990 study of discrimination in hiring in Washington, D.C. and Chicago, the Urban Institute sent pairs of black and white men, matched in terms of biographical characteristics, to apply for low-skilled entry-level jobs in service, retail sales, and manufacturing jobs that would typically be filled by high school graduates. Twenty percent of the black men received unfavorable and differential treatment; they did not advance as far in the hiring process as their matched white counterpart. Although it focused on less-skilled positions, this study showed that discrimination in hiring is still a serious problem for black men in major cities.[7]

Subtle forms of exclusion in the workplace can bar blacks from professional and other white-collar positions. A law professor at an East Coast university commented on the preparation necessary for being hired in law firms:

> You may move into an environment and not know the rules, and therefore not know how to play the game, and not know how to succeed. What happens, the barriers and obstacles are often that people will not allow you into the inner circle. Well, for example, let me try to be as concrete as possible. In law school, as a law professor and as a former law student myself, one of the things I recognized was that the students who get the best grades are the students who know how to talk to the law professors. They know how to take a look outside of the legal profession and see what things they'll be doing. They know how to call on their fathers and brothers and uncles to introduce them into the profession. And that's the way they approach the law, and therefore they learn legal analysis, the proper approach, the methodology, and so on. Therefore, they're ready. They also understand the social professional aspects, how to dress, how to approach people and so and so forth. . . . But the barriers [for blacks] are often that people will simply avoid talking to you. Or, they won't let you into the little social circles where you learn the tone, the tenor, the manner, the little techniques, the appearance, the dress, and so on.

The grooming game and the informal social learning that begin in law school, he continued, extend directly into the law firms in the large city where he practiced law for a time:

> What I saw was that people simply didn't share the rules. They would simply observe you, or watch you, but they wouldn't talk about the real deal, as I call it. Therefore, you don't have the opportunity to groom yourself, to be able to go into the upper echelons. You can often get an in-

> terview, and sometimes they're willing to take a few blacks. But so many times you just don't know what you need to do, how to act, how to carry yourself. Those are the obstacles. One obvious obstacle is just people simply decide not to hire you; they decide not to invite you into their social circles. But they can't make the barriers as hard and fast. There are certain [circumstances]—because the job has an opening, and because you have a right to interview, and because they want to say that they've interviewed so many blacks, and because they may want to hire a few—that may soften up the old absolute barrier of eliminating blacks. But what happens is, they might decide they really don't quite want to hire you, and often they simply don't say anything. And if you've gone through your graduate school, through your training and preparation, even though you get the degree, the certification, you often haven't learned the real social rules, the real professional rules, and that's just so key. And those in my mind are the obstacles, in addition to simply the reluctance to hire, the reluctance to accept, the reluctance to invite—somewhat similar to the old, hard fast rules of exclusion. These days, it's the more subtle rules, where they don't discuss the real rules around you. They just look at you, or they discuss superficial things, so that you never really discover what it takes. Therefore, when judgment time comes, when the decision time comes whether to hire, whether to promote, well, you just don't quite have what it takes.

The lack of proper connections and of access to social knowledge is a major employment barrier subtly or overtly linked to differential treatment later on in the professional workplace. Many white employers may not even realize that a black candidate has been excluded from the cultural socialization necessary to make it in the legal profession. Like the business networks we will examine in the next chapter, the preparatory grooming and networking that are obvious in this account provide clear examples of institutionalized discrimination.

Discrimination in Salary, Evaluations, and Promotions

A large proportion of black employees in white-collar positions are pioneers, and many have been hired as racial tokens. For the most part, their superiors are white, which means that their success or failure is being judged by whites who as a rule have little or no experience with blacks as colleagues or supervisors. In the aforementioned *Business Week* survey, 62 percent of blacks interviewed felt chances for blacks to be promoted to supervisory jobs were not as good as those for whites; and 41 percent of the whites polled agreed.[8] In the early 1980s, researcher Ed Jones, a former corporate executive himself, conducted the first survey of black managers with top business school degrees who were working in white firms. In this pioneering research Jones found that nearly all the black managers felt that blacks had not achieved equal opportunity with whites in corporate workplaces, and more than 90 percent felt that black managers had less opportunity than whites, or no chance compared with whites, to succeed in their firms on the basis of ability. In addition, two thirds felt that many whites in corporations believe blacks are intellectually inferior and that the racial climate had a negative impact on the performance evaluations, assignments, and promotions of black managers.[9] Not surprisingly, a 1989 survey by Korn Ferry International found that only .6 percent of top corporate executives were black.[10]

In a variety of workplaces wage and salary inequities have been a reality for blacks for decades. In the *Business Week* opinion survey over half the black respondents felt that most blacks are paid less than whites "doing the same job." In contrast, less than a fifth of whites agreed; most felt there was equal pay for equal work, revealing little awareness of the continuing problem for many black employees. The pattern of answers was similar in the 1989 ABC News/*Washington Post* poll.[11] Moreover, United States Census Bureau data make it clear that there is substantial and continuing inequality at all income levels. For example, in 1990 black households headed by people with four or more years of college had incomes that were still only 78 percent of those of comparable whites.[12]

One of our respondents, a social science professor, reported an unfair evaluation of her work experience when she was hired at a western university:

> I sued the university on salary equity, and I won. My salary was less than three other people who were hired at the same time that I was hired with the same degree. And the points that they gave—and none of us had taught at universities prior to that, we had only worked for agencies—and they were counting their agency experience toward giving them a higher salary and denying it [to me]. . . . And the university did not agree with my point of view in our discussions, so I sued them, and I won.

This framing of discrimination again underscores the critical impact of civil rights laws on black thinking. Going to court won her the proper salary, but she incurred significant personal losses. Later in her discussion she described relations between her colleagues and herself as one of antipathy, of "no love lost." Relations with higher administrators may also have been difficult and strained. Sometimes it appears that some top administrators, as well as chief executives in the private sector, fight a clear case of salary inequity involving a black employee just to protect the principle of white authority.

The experiences of our middle-class respondents confirm and extend the opinion survey findings about evaluations and promotions discussed above. In their white-collar workplaces they have been subjected to inappropriate negative evaluations, deliberate attempts to restrict their advancement, and exclusion from mobility ladders and mentoring networks. While employee tracking is considered necessary in many U.S. workplaces, it can become a type of racial discrimination. A young manager in an eastern city described his experiences:

> When I first started working for the bank, I went into the bank with a degree, and I had a white friend. We graduated from the same college. We both started at the bank at the same time. We both went in for management training. They put him in management training, and put me on the teller line, and told me it would be better for me to start off as a teller and work my way up from the bottom, whereas they automatically put him on the management training. Where management training automatically goes through two weeks of teller training, I had to go through a whole year of teller training.

This manager also described instances of overt hostility from fellow white employees. His cumulative experience lends credence to his sense of injustice and his perception of the discriminatory nature of tracking. Nonetheless, this man indicated elsewhere in his interview that, in spite of the racial hurdles, he has steeled himself and become even more determined to succeed in the white world.

Prior knowledge of a white supervisor's prejudices has enabled some black employees to prepare a counterstrategy. A sales account manger at a communications company discussed a performance evaluation process involving her white supervisor:

> We had a five scale rating, starting with outstanding, then very good, then good, then fair, and then less than satisfactory. I had gone into my evaluation interview anticipating

that he would give me a "VG" (very good), feeling that I deserved an "outstanding" and prepared to fight for my outstanding rating, knowing my past experience with him and more his way toward females. But even beyond female, I happened to be the only black in my position within my branch. So the racial issue would also come into play. And he and I had had some very frank discussions about race specifically. About females, but more about race when he and I talked. So I certainly knew that he had a lot of prejudices in terms of blacks. And [he] had some very strong feelings based on his upbringing about the abilities of blacks. He said to me on numerous occasions that he considered me to be an exception, that [mine] certainly [were] not what he felt the abilities of an average black person [to be]. I was of course appalled and made it perfectly clear to him. . . . But, when I went into the evaluation interview, he gave me glowing comments that cited numerous achievements and accomplishments for me during the year, and then concluded it with, "So I've given you a G," which of course just floored me. . . . [I] maintained my emotions and basically just said, as unemotionally as I possibly could, that I found that unacceptable, I thought it was inconsistent with his remarks in terms of my performance, and I would not accept it. I think I kind of shocked him, because he sort of said, "Well I don't know what that means" when I said I wouldn't accept it. I said, "I'm not signing the evaluation." And at that point, here again knowing that the best way to deal with most issues is with facts and specifics, I had already come in prepared. . . . I had my list of objectives for the year where I was able to show him that I had achieved every objective and I exceeded all of them. I also had my sales performance: the dollar amount, the products, both in total dollar sales and also a product mix. I sold every product in the line that we offered to our customers. I had ex-

> ceeded all of my sales objectives. As far as I was concerned, it was outstanding performance. . . . So he basically said, "Well, we don't have to agree to agree," and that was the end of the session. I got up and left. Fifteen minutes later he called me back in and said, "I've thought about what you said, and you're right, you do have an O." So it's interesting how in fifteen minutes I went from a G to an O. But the interesting point is, had I not fought it, had I just accepted it, I would have gotten a G rating for that year, which has many implications.

In a recent survey of black professional and managerial women, Elizabeth Higginbotham and Lynn Weber found that 42 percent had personally experienced discriminatory treatment, especially in regard to promotions and wages.[13] In the quote we see how these black women have to contend with sexism and racism. So ingrained were the male executive's negative attitudes that only after the respondent forced the issue did he award her the rating she deserved. Like similar managers in corporate and government workplaces, he was forced to negotiate with his black employee. Noteworthy too is the extra effort this black manager exerted to check her emotions, so as not to play into the stereotypes of women and blacks being too emotional and out of control.

A service manager in an electronics company explained how a white salesperson had sold an oil company the wrong computer equipment and had promised services that the service department could not deliver:

> Everything that this sales rep promised had to come from me, a black field service manager. . . . [I said] "I cannot deliver this, Mr. Customer, because of these reasons. And some of those reasons included: the sales rep sold you the wrong equipment. This will not make your computer work. So no, I cannot deliver." And so the sales guy came back to

> the office and told my boss that I was out on site airing the company's dirty laundry in front of the customer. Hence, [my] performance appraisal: "I don't think Jack has the oomph or the go-for-it to be a field service manager." . . . [This white manager] has been the most prejudiced, the most discriminating manager that I have ever worked for, and I identified every instance that I could think of. . . . So I told *his* boss: "I don't feel that I could be successful working for this guy, and I solicit your support in helping me identify new employment and new career opportunities, since this guy said that I'm not, you know." So it got to the point where it was escalated to the vice-president of field service on the East Coast.

After discussing the rejection and pain associated with his negative performance rating, this black manager proceeded in his interview to explain that in a meeting with the vice president and other high-level managers of his company, all white, he was asked to prepare an action plan that would satisfy the customer who was alienated through no fault of his own. Though hurt deeply, he did not give up but prepared, on short notice, a plan that was accepted and successful. After the incident, however, this manger was moved by higher-level white executives to a more difficult position in another city, a position he believed he was assigned to in order that he would fail. The "promotion" was not in his view to be taken at face value.

Many workers, black or white, may face some struggles related to promotions over the course of their careers. Yet for black employees the normal pressures of seeking a promotion tend to be exacerbated by restrictive racial barriers. A researcher at a major university described his frustration: "And I did an exceptional job at that; however, I never really got a decent promotion out of that. But I did all those things that they said they wanted [you] to do, and in fact, a couple of my managers wanted to promote me but they told me they were stopped, literally they just said no. . . . A white guy told me, he said, 'Listen, you're black. They're never going to promote you.'" For many middle-class black employees time spent in a white organization brings the realization that there is a "glass ceiling"—some say a "concrete ceiling"—beyond which they cannot be promoted. Indeed, this is one reason that some quit their jobs and start their own businesses, "free from 'glass ceilings' and racial tensions in white corporations."[14]

A striking feature of our interviews was that not one respondent expressed an open and generalized hostility toward all whites. Given the prevalence of white discrimination this seems somewhat surprising. Perhaps one reason is blacks' awareness—expressed in our interviews—that some whites support their quest for equal treatment. From the Underground Railroad of the nineteenth century to white support for civil rights movements and organizations since the 1950s, white support has been important to black empowerment. The situation today was described this way by a professor at a New England university: "[what] blacks have to learn to do is to find whites in the system who are supportive and helpful to them, and there are such whites. I think that you can. Even though racism is a big factor in the world . . . there are people who are white who are not racists and who are willing [to help]."

There is evidence that some whites in desegregated workplaces resent a black employee daring to do the same job as a white or to do better in performing that job. Whites often squander corporate resources by putting personal prejudices above company profits in decisions regarding black employees. An executive for a large corporation reported on what he had learned from recent company personnel decisions. He has seen evidence that white salespeople in the company have been promoted even when their sales are far less than their sales objectives ("budgets"). He gives the example of a successful black salesperson:

> [He] had a budget of six [million]; he brought in eight. The next year they gave him a budget of eleven; he brought in more than eleven million. This same black could not have aspired to a management role, and the reasons that I got when I said, "Well, why is it that this guy is not being promoted? Why does he have to fight for it? Why aren't you seeking him out? Giving him the mentorship that he needs? Because he's demonstrated his sales skills; he's brought you the money. What are you doing for him?" . . . I get these real thin, veiled excuses about, "Well, there's a perception that Jim is not sales executive or management material." I said, "What's the perception? *Whose* perception? The customer doesn't give a damn, because they're buying the product. The peers that come to him for help in order to close this business on their accounts don't seem to have a problem, because they *know* that he can help himself. So who's got the perception? *You* have the perception."

The incongruity between the outstanding performance of this salesperson and the way he was perceived by higher-up executives suggests that such white perceptions deny blacks access to positions of greater power within a corporation. This manager continued with an account of a black woman with an outstanding sales record:

> Five years, almost six, without a promotion. Company Elite Sales is a status that says you have met your sales budget every quarter in the fiscal year, and if you make this, that means you made your budget every quarter and you made your budget for the end of the year. So for five years, the lady made Company Elite Sales. That's extraordinary, okay.

> That means that you are 110 percent hitting consistently. Now if you do that over a certain number of months, you can win what's called Top Gun. Such people go on vacation overseas for two weeks with their spouses, all expenses paid. . . . Now, these same people [higher management] did not put her in for a promotion *again* because of some perception that they say exists about her, her follow-up skills and her attention to detail and a bunch of other stuff. Perception. There's a perception that she's not able to communicate effectively with senior-level management because one senior-level person at an account wanted her off. Said that he didn't want to work with her anymore, supposedly for some issue that probably was created. They wouldn't give me a lot of details. For that reason I said, "Okay, well, there may be a valid reason why she had a problem with that account. But what I'm asking you is how you make a determination about a person who is a winner by every other management standard? You say she has one problem with one account. She *still* made her Company Elite Sales. She still made her budget, and she still made Top Gun, and she is two grade levels below your turkeys that are just half making it."

An extraordinary salesperson, this black woman was not promoted because of conflict with one white executive and because of the white perception that she was not "management material." We observe here the ghostly and elusive character of some workplace discrimination. Since no one took personal responsibility for the discriminatory judgment about this black woman, there was no specific discriminator to be challenged. The presence of civil rights laws was important in this case, for the respondent relates later in the interview that he pointed out to senior management they might be facing a lawsuit because of the discrepancy between her performance and her corporate rewards. In his account the senior executives did not seem to comprehend that they were squandering corporate resources in restricting the advancement of a talented black woman. The limited opportunity for this salesperson belies the conviction of many whites that blacks now have the same or better opportunities as whites.[15]

In her research on a large industrial corporation, Rosabeth Moss Kanter found extensive discrimination against women, most of whom were white. Citing other studies that have found criteria such as the "right" class and racial background as highly important in promotions, Kanter concluded that the replacement of old white males by new white males in an organization's promotional system provides "an important form of reassurance in the face of uncertainty about performance measurement in high-reward, high-prestige positions" and that management positions "become easily closed to people who are 'different.'"[16] A human services manager in a northeastern city described the following problem in trying to get promoted to middle management:

> I did work for eight years for a private company. . . . I wanted to move up into middle management, and I had to prove myself. It was an obstacle course. There were many white males who did not have the experience that I did who were sitting in higher positions, and I fought that. Well, I got very loud about it. I threatened to go to the State Commission Against Discrimination, and they didn't want to see that happen, so they placated me by creating new positions [so] that they could eventually say, "Oh, we don't need that position anymore." That's when I knew I had to leave there. [What was the problem with you moving into one of those management positions?] Well, I wasn't necessarily the showpiece that they wanted to have in some of the front office positions. Just a year ago I started to

> press my hair, so from the time I was fifteen until a year ago, I wore my hair in its natural state. I wasn't necessarily your picture of the budding executive! . . . I think part of it, too, was that I haven't always been one who minced my words, and I've been pretty open about my thinking and thoughts and so forth, which again can be a drawback. They like us to be quiet and reserved and speak when spoken to.

A 1991 black business study, "A Blueprint for Success," found that black managers faced a concrete ceiling when it came to moving into higher management positions in corporations.[17] As a *Black Enterprise* journalist assessing this study put it, "Unwilling to bet the success of their department or pet project on a black colleague, white managers 'play it safe' putting white males into the visible positions of their companies."[18] Image is perhaps more important than performance in this corporate "cloning" of white managers in corporate and other workplaces. With her Afro hairstyle and outspoken ways, this talented woman was not the picture, for key whites, of the "the budding executive." Middle class African Americans risk punishment when they step out of the invisible "place" that they occupy in many corporate settings. When the respondent was forced to became aggressive, her superiors responded by creating what she saw as a temporary position.

In some situations one motivation for exclusion and restriction may be white employers' ignorance about or lack of experience with African Americans. Many white managers and supervisors have had little contact with blacks; they may never have seen a black executive or may have only seen blacks in menial positions or as entertainers, athletes, or criminals in the mass media. Many live in exclusively, or almost exclusively, white suburbs. A white manager with this limited experience, drawing on his or her images of blacks only from stereotypes, may select another white person over an equally or better qualified black person because of deep-lying, even unconscious, feelings that the white candidate is more compatible or competent.

Moving up the corporate ladder usually requires good mentors. All too often, however, there are few (or no) senior white managers willing to be effective mentors for black employees. And the aforementioned cloning process means there are few blacks in higher positions who can be mentors for other blacks. An assistant vice president at an East Coast bank commented on her struggle against discrimination and the absence of mentors:

> I have a constant battle. As a matter of fact, I have an ongoing discrimination suit now. It has been more or less settled, and we signed a consent decree. . . . I guess that's how, why I learned that you have to be able to know white America, and white corporate America in order to deal with them. With me, coming into an organization such as this, I didn't have any mentors, any black mentors. And the few that you have, let's face it, they didn't have to share their knowledge. I'm not going to be that way. I do it now, so that's why I feel that I can help other people, by teaching them, telling them things that I had to learn the really hard way on how to cope with some of the different problems.

This manager suggests that she would like to be more of a mentor than white executives and a few higher-level black executives she has known. However, one should not underestimate the problems blacks in higher positions face in trying to mentor. In his pioneering research, former top executive Ed Jones described a black manager (called "Charlie") who had met with other black employees seeking his advice on coping with discrimination. Feeling the problems should be brought to senior white management, Charlie arranged a meeting. However, before that scheduled meeting he encountered the company president at an informal gathering and was reprimanded with these words: "Charlie I am disappointed that you met with those black managers. I thought we could trust you."[19]

One reaction to social "cloning" in the workplace is resignation, a reaction that can lead to a cross-generational lowering of expectations. The president of a credit fund described the impact of his experience at a major corporation in an eastern city:

> As I told the senior personnel person once, blacks in the company had jobs, and whites had careers. And that is still true in most corporations today. We're employees, we're not on the fast track to the executive suite. We are needed for statistical purposes, but going to the top of the organization is not truly there. So, within that framework, I decided the job was nice, the money was delightful, and I coexisted. I did my job, but I did not do it with the intent of looking toward a goal and being frustrated, that I would be an executive of the company one day. Where some people do get involved in the American dream—thinking that they will be there—[they] become totally frustrated and disenchanted with the system. The system was wonderful to me. . . . I have a son now who just completed his first year at an Ivy League university, and one of the things I've shared with him over the years, particularly since he was in high school, is that he has to face reality in the society, no matter if he went to A&T or whether he went to Princeton, or Harvard or Stanford. This is the kind of thing he has to understand who he is. He cannot think for a moment that he's totally equal, because he's not.

Typically, whites on favored tracks can not only think in terms of careers but also secure the special in-house training that facilitates moving up.[20] This respondent lowered his expectations for corporate advancement and passed on to his son his pessimistic, yet realistic, view of real-world equality. There is no clearer example in this book of the cumulative impact of discrimination. Racism in his employment experience seems to have shaped his life perspective in basic ways. Writing about psychological costs, Mirowsky and Ross have suggested that minority status is associated "with a reduced sense of control . . . partly because for members of minority groups, any given level of achievement requires greater effort and provides fewer opportunities."[21]

Advancement in government can also be very difficult, as one southern state legislator forcefully asserted:

> It's not easy for a black woman . . . to get good committee assignments, unless you have been what is considered to be a team player. A team player is a person who normally votes and adheres very closely to the leadership. . . . I face discrimination by whites all the time, all the time. [Could you be specific?] Committee assignments is one [area]. I had been here about fourteen years before I got a committee chairmanship. It was a little do-nothing chairmanship, the chairman of rules and resolutions. Nothing but you have to watch the rules and resolutions of what people sent out, either congratulating somebody, or memorializing somebody in their district. That's what that was. [Do you think they see it as a danger by putting you in as a chairperson, or do you think it's primarily because you're black?] I think it's probably because I'm black, period. They don't want to put us in really powerful positions. I'm the chairman of the judiciary committee, and even [as] chairman of the judiciary committee, they moved out a whole lot of things that normally the judiciary committee would control. And they put it in other committees. When somebody else was the chair—of course a white had it—they had better control. They had more powers. When they made a black chairman, they reduced those powers and took them away.

A common accusation against black managers in corporate workplaces is that they are not "team players."[22] Here we see the same accusation made against a black legislator. In her detailed interview this woman gave several examples of having been excluded by the white elite in the legislature from key meetings and political advancement. With anger in her voice she explained that she protested and forced white colleagues into interracial negotiation. However, she has kept her public criticism of these influential whites within bounds lest she become even more restricted. After the tape recorder was turned off she presented an even more negative view of the white leadership than she was willing to put on the tape. For most of this nation's history, state legislative positions were off limits to African Americans, especially in the South. As recently as 1940 only 90,000 of the 3.7 million adult blacks in the South, where most then resided, voted in the general election, and in 1942 only a dozen black state legislators served the nation, not one in the South. A major enlargement of voting power came after the passage of the 1965 Voting Rights Act, and by the early 1990s the number of black elected officials in the nation as a whole had increased significantly, to about 7,400, with more than half serving in the South.[23] Yet these numbers are still far from proportionally representative. Moreover, as the account above shows, they signal only the beginning of the struggle for real organizational power. Some scholarly debate has focused on the effectiveness of black elected officials, much of it on their characteristics and performance, but to our knowledge no significant research has been done on discrimination they face within state and federal legislatures.

Marginalized in the White-Collar Workplace

In some middle-class workplaces there seem to be positions reserved just for black employees. Social psychologist Kenneth

Clark has observed that black employees in corporate America frequently find themselves tracked into "ghettos" within companies, such as departments of "affirmative action," "community affairs," or "special markets." In many firms, professional and managerial blacks "are rarely found in line positions concerned with developing or controlling production, supervising the work of large numbers of whites or competing with their white 'peers' for significant positions."[24] Among our respondents, a salesperson working for a Fortune 500 company in an eastern city gave this account:

> Even though they say you're given territories blindly, the contrary is true. It seems as though blacks are always given the least productive territory, and it's been a recurring thing too. Again, people seem to be comfortable with giving majority people the best territories because there's a fear there that white people will get mad. . . . Therefore, you find that a black is given a territory that might be identified as a "growth" area, but really [it is] one that has not really produced to the level that the other territories have.

This segregative tracking involves hiring blacks for nontraditional jobs and putting them in less desirable or powerless positions. Similarly, Kanter found that minority and female white-collar workers were often put into special or low-mobility "staff" positions, such as those in personnel or Equal Employment Opportunity (EEO) offices, where there were fewer chances for mobility and where they had to rely on white male "line" managers to implement important policies.[25]

Another example of tokenism in traditionally white institutions is the hiring of black professors for the Black Studies programs inaugurated at more than five hundred historically white colleges since the 1960s, often in response to pressure from black students and black communities. It is one thing to set up a such a program; it is another for senior white administrators and professors to support it with adequate funding and to respect it as a legitimate and major academic enterprise. The presence of black professors has helped to make white institutions seem progressive on racial matters, but the veneer of legitimacy is often not desesrved. A professor and administrator in a Black Studies program commented on his position:

> [I have] tried to speak to the administration about blacks. The way they look at it, they're not paying you to do that. They're paying you as administrators to stay in line and help them. In that sense, you're kind of a fire insurance against black people. And I've never been able to do that. I mean, whether we like it or not, we legitimatize the institution, quite frankly, just by being in it. It's an undeserved legitimatizing in some cases. It's not doing as much as our presence might connote. . . . I think that we have to raise the contradiction; we have to raise the accountability of institutions like this one for our continual push. We have to do that. I'm just not prepared to sit here and say everything's all right because they help me feed my family. I just can't do it. What's the dues? You don't get as much money, you don't get the positions, the goodies. But I've got other kinds of goodies, and other kinds of things I value. I sleep at night, because I feel I've done the best I could. But it's not easy, you swim upstream a lot.

Many colleges and universities have responded to some degree to pressure from black communities to hire more black faculty members. Still, one survey of more than 400 black faculty members at white colleges found that 41 percent thought that racism was the important barrier to black employment in their institutions, an obstacle much more important than the limited supply.[26] Moreover, black faculty members who are hired in white colleges often find themselves to be among a small number of black representatives in a mostly white world, sometimes with little chance of longterm survival there.

Tokenism as "fire insurance" can also be seen in this news anchor's account of a previous position in the Midwest:

> I was working for one of the networks in a major, major city. . . . I was the *first* primary black anchor that they had hired. Keep in mind, prior to that I was working for a [non-network] station in a midwestern city, and this network had a station in that city. I helped my station knock the network out of number one into a number three position. Plus, [at] the network's other station (that I eventually went to work for) civil rights groups were picketing in front of the station. You don't have any blacks on the air. So, my being hired by that station in that major market was a result of, number one, beating their pants off in the market I left, and helping get civil rights leaders off their front steps so to speak. But once I got there, I realized that, I think, to a large degree the only reason why I was hired was so they could say, "See, o.k., we did something about it. We did hire a minority, and black leaders you can go home now." And once the pickets stopped, and what have you, my personal services contract I felt was reneged on. I don't think I was used as I negotiated to do, and as I indicated I was going to do. Otherwise I would have never taken the job. And I can't add anything else to that happening except for the fact that I was black. And once you reach a situation like that in whatever you do, you have a choice to make. Either you can deal with it, or you can change it. And I decided to change it. I left. I quit. I decided, if you're not going to treat me fairly, I'm not interested in being a puppet for you, or someone to make you look good.

Note the multidimensional character of discrimination. There are the surface events and the hidden meanings as he saw them. This black pioneer helped one television station beat out a network's station; then that network hired him, primarily to get civil rights protestors off the third station's doorstep. He describes a racial "bait and switch" episode, rife with frustration, illustrative of the black limbo experience often overlooked by white observers. Hired under one set of rules and confident of his professional abilities, he quickly comes to realize that he is working under a new set of rules.

Tokenism and ghettoized tracking can even be seen in historically white church groups that officially profess the values of justice and brotherhood. A black minister in a predominantly white Protestant denomination explained:

> There is a great difference between being a black minister and being a white minister. One is that if you're a white minister, you have any number of career moves that you can make just based on the personal ambition. If you are a minister who is prepared, who is on the ball, more or less, has got things going for yourself, you can move within a particular conference. You can move intra-conferences and advance. If you're a black minister—and I'll use this conference as an example, we have eight black churches . . . until someone dies or someone moves to another conference, there is no mobility for me. We have not reached the sophistication where a black minister can be assigned to a white church. . . . There are people within the systems who would use the system against other folk in an oppressive manner. . . . The system is set to perpetuate racism. A black minister ran for bishop last year and withdrew his name in the first or second round, because whites just won't be supportive. There's a whole area of the conference who said, "We don't want this man, because we don't feel like a

> black man can handle our conference, so he can become bishop here, but we don't want him here."

There is support here for the old saying that "11 o'clock on Sunday is the most segregated hour of the week." Within some desegregated denominations a type of internal segregation can reappear. (In contrast to the often negative role of the white church in U.S. racial relations, the black church has been a mainstay for black survival in a racist society.)

Marginalization within a private or public institution can have other consequences as well. Commenting on the current situation of some black professionals who had been hired into corporations some time ago, a senior secretary underscored the fragile nature of their positions:

> They're tokens. Given the era that I grew up in . . . there were certain black professionals—people that I know and have been associated with—that have held certain positions and certain jobs with certain companies, large companies like IBM, Xerox. They were successful in obtaining [a job as] the manager of a certain district or a supervisor of this or that, and for whatever reasons, those jobs became surplus or were done away with. And they were not able to just walk out and walk right into another position, not paying those same salaries. And I think several of those people—just here recently—that back then in the '60s or '70s who had their heads up in the air and thinking that they owned the world and they were turning over the world, now they're not doing that. They're out there in the unemployment lines.

In her work on corporate executives, researcher Sharon Collins has argued that the black middle class is in a very vulnerable economic position. One problem is that much black advancement since the 1960s was substantially the result of federal policy pressures, which lessened in the 1980s and early 1990s. In addition, black managers and professionals hired into corporate America in the 1960s and 1970s were often new "tokens," many of whom were ghettoized in positions oriented to affirmative action, special markets, or minority communities. The withdrawal of federal supervision of private sector employment practices during the Republican administrations in the 1980s and early 1990s eroded the positions of many middle-class blacks.[27] The weakening of civil rights enforcement encouraged many firms to abandon or neglect their (typically modest) programs to diversify workforces along racial and ethnic lines, and, as the executive director of one black management group put it, the ranks of black executives were "decimated."[28] In addition, most middle-class black employees who lose their positions do not have the parental or family resources that a large proportion of middle-class whites have to fall back on.

The marginalized position of many black managers and professionals can also be seen in their daily struggles against pressures to think or become "white." White workplaces rarely accommodate basic black interests and values. Instead, black employees are expected to assimilate. Drawing on interviews with seventy-one black female managers and professionals, researcher Ella Bell has described the everyday experience of having a foot in both the black and the white worlds as a "bicultural life experience." Her respondents reported they were constantly working to prove that they were competent and that they fit into the white world, while at the same time they had to exert an equal amount of energy in maintaining their black identities and "maintaining ties to the black community."[29] The minister quoted above commented on these bicultural challenges:

> They [white coworkers] don't see you or me and say this is a talented human being. . . . No, they say "He's black, but"

> or "She's black, but." There's an exception. So to be black and be [a] successful contributor is to be an exception to what white folks see in other black folks. The temptation is that we begin to think that we are an exception to other black folks. And most of the time when we step out on that, we get burned, because we would become coopted into the white community, into the white world, and to the white value system, and to the white frame of thinking. We excise ourselves from the black community, or we stay with our Afro-Americanness and take the risk of offending our white friends.

Caught between his white denomination and his Afro-Americanness, this minister described what might be seen as a contemporary variation of the "double" black consciousness about which William E. B. Du Bois wrote so eloquently.[30]

White Supervisors, Coworkers, and Associates

Acting on their racist prejudices and assumptions, both white supervisors and white colleagues can create a hostile workplace climate. A detention officer in a southwestern police department made this clear in describing her first days on the job:

> When I was hired I was told, and I quote, "I hope *you* make it." Emphasis on *you*. And I told my new supervisor right then and there, I stopped her right in her tracks and I said, "What do you mean? I detect some sort of implication here regarding the pronoun *you*. I don't feel that you're addressing it singularly, but plural. And there's nobody here but me and you." She said, "Yeah, yeah, no black's ever made it. We never had a black person make it." So that makes you feel really good, like you've got this black cloud [laughs] coming over your head through the probation period. They don't think I'm going to make it anyway. . . .

> Now if she had said, "It's a hard position. Not many people have what it takes." If she had said something objective, I wouldn't have felt anything. But to single something about me, you know, that confused me, and I didn't know if I'd make it or not. And subsequently, I had to go the entire nine yards of my probation. People that were hired after me, which happened to be white, didn't have to go through their [full] probation.

Her white boss's admonition signalled to her that she would not be treated fairly. Whites in charge of hostile work environments create, often intentionally, conditions that contribute to poor performance and failure.

A college-educated secretary and civil rights activist working at a large corporation described discrimination in the informal rules for employee behavior:

> Across this nation millions of [non-job-related] things . . . are achieved on the job by whites. And it's done during the day on the job, with paid salaries or what not. My example would be, even just like the use of a telephone. . . . Last year I was a delegate for Jesse Jackson to the Democratic Convention in Atlanta in which there was a lot of media—television, newspaper and all of this—saying you're a national delegate. They'd come to the job, and somebody would want to take pictures of me. Many companies would have been proud to know they had somebody; and my company would have too, except that I was a delegate for a black person, Jesse Jackson. Then they call me in the office and say, "Okay, we don't want any NAACP work done on the job. We don't want any democratic [political activity]." Because part of this time I had said let's launch a voter registration drive for every employee. . . . Then they will say, "it's time for your review. Now, your outside work does not have anything to do [with your

> work here]. We don't care what you do outside, but we just don't want you to do it here. . . . The personnel manager went to a Chamber of Commerce meeting and had to come back to our plant and xerox 'x' number of copies. The Chamber of Commerce had nothing to do with them [our company]. But if I go back to the machine to run just a copy of maybe one letter, then that's personal (and I have a dime). But why do I need to give them a dime for one copy when here is a man running twenty-five or thirty-five copies. And they worry about what the little people are doing, blacks and other minorities, but it's the big company people who are ripping them off.

The company is an international firm headquartered in Europe, but this city is in the South, a part of the nation that a few years back had seen whites violently intimidating, sometimes killing, civil rights activists such as this woman. Racial discrimination can involve the intentional creation of anomie, as a black person goes beyond formal rules of fairness to discover the informal rules applied unfairly. Here a double standard is explicit in the overly close supervision of blacks by white superiors and the latter's inconsistent evaluations of civic activities by black and white employees. One gathers from the rest of her interview that in spite of her substantial qualifications, including a college education and administrative experience, she has not been considered for promotion to a higher-level white-collar position.

A registered nurse in an eastern city described her indignation at excessively close supervision by a white administrator:

> That was probably the last straw . . . I resigned and gave my resignation and left because I would not let him have the opportunity to think that he could—after I had been functioning autonomously for twelve years—all of a sudden [there] is this white male who's going to tell me when I can

go, what I have to do. And I have to ask him permission for everything—and the manner in which he stated it. I just wrote in my resignation and left before I had to deal with him, because I was *not* going to be subservient to him in any way, shape, or form. So, of course, white skin, it has played a role, and I'm convinced that if the color of my skin was different from black I would have been treated differently by that white manager. . . . who did not bother to deal with half the problems that I was saying that was occurring within that particular organization. And I've always felt that if you work for a man, speak well of him, and when you no longer can speak well of him it's time to go.

One senses here the weariness common in black accounts of coping with mistreatment. Resigning in protest can improve the situation of the victim of discrimination and, sometimes, can force whites to reconsider their actions. On occasion, the "I'm tired" feeling has motivated dramatic protest actions like that of civil rights activist Rosa Parks, whose refusal to give up her seat to a white person on a bus in Montgomery, Alabama helped to spark the civil rights movement in the 1950s.

Research on complex organizations has shown that older workers are sometimes antagonistic to new workers, in part because of their jealousy or uncertainty about the new workers' outlooks on life and work, or moral values.[31] The resentment faced by new black workers in a historically all-white milieu may be particularly intense. The director of a midwestern drug abuse program described his frustration as the lone black working with middle-class whites:

I was working in a predominantly white hospital. And I feel as though the way I was discriminated against was I always got considered or got identified as "that black counselor up

> on that unit." . . . That always qualified my experience, it always qualified my expertise, or either it discredited it, I should say. "Well, that's John, that black guy upstairs on that unit." So I had to always fight through that, and, as a result, I ended up always having to deal with people being able to accept my credibility. I mean, I was running a unit that was 99, 100 percent white, minus myself. And predominantly white middle-class females. And no offense to females in the world, but they had a hard time being able to accept leadership or orders or direction from a young black man who had some experience in some of this.

Being constantly identified as "the black whatever" is an inescapable problem for many black workers desegregating traditionally white institutions. As a result of his experience and authority being questioned, the director left the hospital to take his current position, in which his abilities have also been questioned, this time not by coworkers but by whites running a funding agency:

> The middle-management funding agency for our program was run by white males. And they sort of tried to underestimate that I, as a young black man, knew what I was able to do. . . . They try to play those little word games and try to play that little intellect game. But see, the difference is, we as black men can become as intelligent as, if not more intelligent than, them. But we've got one other thing going for us; we've learned how to survive, from a street sense.

He added that his "street" sense enabled him to sit down at the table with them and "throw things in their faces that they can't deal with." By keeping them off balance, he suggested, he not only was effective in his negotiations but also maintained his dignity. Quite evident here is the intensity of the daily struggle that black managers face.

Alliances with coworkers are critical to success for white-collar employees, especially in large firms, and black employees may have a difficult time breaking into them, making for a chilly office climate. A human services manager discussed the difficulties she encountered in her office:

> White staff may meet together to discuss a particular program and think that they may not need to discuss it with me until after they've gotten it together. [Are you the only black?] No, there's another black woman, and often times she hasn't been in that circle either, and we've been pretty vocal about bringing it to their attention. [Why did they think that you didn't need to be there?] "Oh well, we just thought we would sit down and discuss this together and get what we thought, and we'd bring it to all of us." And "we've known each other a really long time, and we're personal friends and so forth." And this is their explanation, and clearly it's like, let's get our act together before we take it to the body. . . . Oh, I confront that. I don't let it slide. I let them know I know they've met and the issues need to be put on the table, and the executive director is pretty good about nipping that kind of thing in the bud.

Informal workplace groups often form along racial lines, with whites who have been there for a time setting the informal norms. Yet in this account there are not only racist whites but also a supportive white executive.

A young lawyer in an East Coast law firm commented about the presumptions many of her coworkers make:

> They look at me as a young black, and they can't believe I'm an attorney. They still open their mouths like, "Oh,

> that's who the new attorney is!" And then it's, "I didn't know you were a [pause] woman." Well, my name is Judy, how many men named Judy do you know? So, that's not the surprise. I've had more than a number of them submit reports to my office and then call to ask me if I understand. And my response to that is, "I understand English. Did you write what you meant? Well then, yes, I understand." And I know, like with my predecessor, that did not happen. . . . By the same token, it's presumed that I can't read a clear sentence, or interpret a clear sentence, or I need some extra help. They also want to have a lot of meetings to make sure I understand. They don't like my making decisions. If I tell them that I don't think their case will win in court, or it doesn't meet the legal standard, then they tell me I don't understand law. . . . I think that a lot of white people are very intimidated by black people, especially black men who are successful, and who have degrees and goals and strength about them, and know who they are, and don't try to abuse their identity. I think it's known throughout the agency that I'm [aggressive]. One of the problems that I have is I'll say, "How ya doin'?" If I'm in the mood to say, "How ya doin'?" instead of, "Good morning, how are you?" that's part of who I am, and who I grew up to be. And I don't want to change that. By the same token, I play my music in my office, whether it insults them or not. . . . They see a problem with that.

Research has shown that high-level (usually white) women employees must carry out their jobs under greater corporate scrutiny than their male counterparts.[32] In addition to being patronized, this attorney is quite conscious of the prevailing notions of propriety in the white corporate culture, which she resists.

In the late 1980s the *National Law Journal* reported that

blacks accounted for less than 2 percent of the lawyers and less than 1 percent of the partners of the nation's 250 largest law firms. Black lawyers and judges are rare in most courtrooms. For those whose workplace is the courtroom, however, discrimination can still be a problem, as a law professor at an eastern university explained:

> I was an attorney with the justice department. And I tried cases; I met judges [who] were incredulous that a black man could try a case before them, or be a lawyer even, and certainly be one that represented the United States government in court. And often the discrimination took the form of their trying to get me to do things that would compromise my case: "Well, counselor, you don't need to interview any witnesses, do you? We can just move on; you can just chat with them; you don't have to interview them under oath do you?" [I said] "Well, your honor, you have to have them under oath because that way they may be more likely to tell the truth. Or if they don't, then we have some way of having sanctions apply." Well, that's one example. As a lawyer, I dealt with judges a lot, and some of their discrimination was relatively overt.

This lawyer displayed considerable patience while standing his ground vis-a-vis the harassment of a white judge.

Coworkers' and associates' discrimination can be blatant. A young manager of a service firm recounted numerous experiences with racial hostility:

> Probably the most racism I've ever felt has been in the workplace. One company that I worked for, I was the regional manager for five of their branches. I traveled back and forth to the different branches to make sure that everything was OK. This one particular branch that I got was in a southwestern city. The demographics for this branch were

> bad. . . . When I went to the branch, the branch manager, his face dropped as soon as he saw me, he didn't know that I was black. The other people in the office couldn't deal with the fact that they would have to take instructions from a black person. I think that I was probably one of two black people in that city, because I never saw any black people there. I remember one time, one supervisor, we became fast friends. He was white. We got along very well. And he would always tell me all the horrible things said about me, and they were primarily because I was black. I remember the second day that I was there he told me that the installation manager, of all people—he has absolutely nothing to do with my job—told him [that] he didn't understand why he was so attentive to me, so concerned about what I thought about his job. And he said, "Well, she's my supervisor. I should be concerned about what she thinks." He said, "Well, I wouldn't worry about it. Don't worry about it. She's just a black woman. It's no big deal. I'm sure they're going to get her out of here soon. It's no problem. Don't worry about it." But that was just one of so many crazy things. . . . Everybody was so conscious of the fact that I was black, and they just couldn't deal with me being somebody that they had to take instructions from. I guess if I had been the maid I would've gotten more respect. But it was just that constant struggle, constantly dealing with those people.

As the first black person to hold a supervisory position in this local firm, she was treated as a temporary aberration by whites who were unwilling to abandon their stereotypes and feelings of racial superiority. In her interview she also discussed how she learned that one of her subordinates kept racially derogatory cartoons in her desk, then added: "Our secretary at work just didn't want to do any of my reports. I mean, that's her job, and she didn't want to do any of my reports. So I had to call the divisional manager just to get her to do her job." For a long time this respondent continued with her job, but suffered much internally. She also assessed the steeling effect of the hostility she encountered: "I just really feel that going through that I could get through anything in this world. This country cannot be nearly as evil as that environment was."

One way that whites show hostility to blacks in the workplace is by making racist jokes, sometimes quite publicly, as the manager of human resources in an East Coast office of a large corporation recounted:

> I was in the auditorium doing a presentation to about a hundred and fifty people here; basically most of them were white. There were maybe five or seven blacks in the audience out of a hundred and fifty people. And I had to put a "vu-graph" up for a visual aid, and it wasn't a very clear vu-graph. In fact it was a poor vu-graph. It had been copied here at the company, and I was talking about, the subject was, minority business and the reporting we have to do as far as the government's requirements. And one of the people in the back hollered out, "It probably was done by a minority vendor." And here I am at the front of the room, microphone and everything, and it was a matter of hey, quick thinking on your feet. You know, do you blow it here and say what you really want to say, or how do you handle this? And I just smiled and said, "No, unfortunately it was done by this corporation."

The insinuation by whites that incompetence is a peculiar characteristic of minority individuals is a feature of racism that we have seen before in many workplaces. The comment was insulting both in its content and in the speaker's attempt to humiliate a black manager making an important presentation to a predominantly white audience. This incident is also an example of a point that came up repeatedly in black discussions of differential treatment: one has to be prepared constantly to assess what is happening and then to decide, often quickly, on the appropriate response.

A young project administrator for an East Coast company commented on the office climate in a firm for which he previously had worked:

> I was the only black in the company. And me, I can take a lot of ridicule and all, and there were black jokes here and there, and I can go along with it. I'm the kind of guy who's an easy target in a sense, but they just went overboard. And I was looking to stay with one of these companies for a long period of time, but they just really overlooked that, hey, I'm [an] individual. And like I said, I was eighteen or nineteen, and hey, I'm a young guy. And in a way I was reaching out for help, because I had these other guys who had experience and what have you, but they didn't really look at me, I mean, a young black man. Everything was "black this" and "black that" and "Joe black" this and that—jokes and ridicule. And at the time, like I say, I went along with it and all, and I didn't get an attitude until after hours. I wouldn't speak up. I wouldn't speak my mind because I knew how much rage it would have been. And I would just get to my car and just sit back, and talk to myself.

In a white-male-dominated workplace, masculine posturing may take a certain racial force when a black male is present. Even though the respondent was seeking help, his coworkers ignored his needs and made his work experience more miserable with racial joking. Gunnar Myrdal pointed out in *An American Dilemma* that such joking about blacks acts as a sounding board for popular white prejudices, especially notions about racial inferiority.[33] Such racist humor is made all the more painful by its coupling to other racist actions and often can, as here, create great psychological damage.

Racist insults such as barbed joking often seem to be motivated by a desire to drive out a black employee. A college-educated clerk in a parts department of a large international corporation described the persistent harassment she has faced:

> In fact for the past twelve years I've faced discrimination on my job because I work with all men. They feel that the job I do is a man's job. They've often told me, "Go home, you don't belong here. This is not the place for you." (I'm suing the company now because of that.) When I refused to leave, they started to [put up] . . . racial photographs, pictures, drawings, writings on a calendar and things of that nature to try to intimidate me into leaving. But I stayed. I'm still there. They refused to fire me and I refused to quit, but still I'm in the process of suing the company. . . . I filed with EEOC first, over a year ago. And when nothing could be settled with them, I asked for no money at that time, when nothing could be settled with them, in fact, they retaliated against me. They called me incompetent, even though I run the place alone, and had to have someone sit in while I went to listen to them call me incompetent. And I'm still running the place alone now. In fact, I replaced three men. . . . They refused to give me an increase in salary, even though my work increased. For two years, it had increased. They managed to give me \$.33 an hour in two years for a tremendous amount of work that I do. . . . There are maybe two or three who don't feel threatened by my presence. Yeah, it's sexism, racism, because I've heard the Mexican-American guys called "wetbacks," "Olympic swimmers," "taco benders." I've heard the blacks called "niggers" and "boys" and "spooks."

She continued:

> The calendar was hanging on the door in the parts room where I work—the truck parts room. It was the 19th of January. . . . Somebody wrote in that square, "Dr. Martin Luther King's Birthday." And in the square next to it they wrote, "Nigger Day Off." So I showed a couple of white guys the calendar and a couple of black guys the calendar, then I took it down and took it home. . . . So I started collecting evidence and keeping a notebook and all the little drawings and pictures, and some of the pictures were ridiculous. They had lips on these people so big it looked like turtleneck sweaters. These I found lying around in my work area. In fact, some of them were in my desk.

This woman bristled with frustration and rage as she retold her painful story. Notable are the stages of her increasingly aggressive response to overt discrimination. Beginning with verbal protests, she later filed complaints with the EEOC. When that was not successful, she sought her day in court. While the decision to fight became part of an ongoing drama of negotiation, her attempts at redress did not lead to white concessions but rather to more harassment.

After listening to many such accounts of job discrimination, the untutored observer might wonder why they are still common, especially given the fact that the 1964 Civil Rights Act and subsequent legislation make up a tough set of employment discrimination laws. Sadly, the federal agency with the mandate to enforce these laws has been inadequate to the task. In a 1990 review Herbert Hill concluded that the EEOC "operates as a claims adjustment bureau, not as a law enforcement agency. The commission seeks voluntary, negotiated settlements with emphasis upon the quick resolution of issues, usually by extended compromise. . . . As a result, there is no genuine conciliation, little threat of litigation, and minimal substantive compliance with the statute."[34] Businesses and unions know that the government civil rights enforcement agencies, especially as weakened under the Republican administrations from the 1980s to the early 1990s, are often "paper tigers." As a result, there is no real equality of opportunity for African Americans in most U.S. workplaces. Employment discrimination is one type of law violation where the *victims*, not government enforcers, are primarily responsible for dealing with the violators, even to the point of enforcing the law in their own private lawsuits.

Dealing with White Customers and Clients

Discrimination by customers can present serious difficulties for black employees who work in sales. They may be victimized by stereotyped notions of black incompetence held by white customers who may not have encountered a black person in such a role. Or they may be victimized by the concern of whites that a black salesperson knows more than they do. A black manager in an East Coast bank discussed how some of his clients viewed him:

> In the bank, I face discrimination daily. A lot of times when I'm dealing with customers—especially when you're dealing with millions and millions of dollars—nine times out of ten, you're going to be dealing with an older white person, who has just got [it] in his mind that there can't be an educated black person working in a highly respectable position in the bank. . . . In fact, there has never been a black on the board of directors at the bank that I work for. There has never been another black in my department. So, right now, I'm creating history for the bank that I'm working for. . . . And a lot of times, you know we deal with millions and millions of dollars, we have lots of accounts, we have keys out to vaults, and a lot of times I see people like even

> hiding things from me, like keys to vaults, and put them in a certain drawer, like hide them from me, like I might steal it or something.

A mid-1980s study in banking found that blacks were being brought into management at a slow rate, and that 80 percent of black managers felt their chances for promotion were not as good as those of their white peers.[35] Unaccustomed to seeing black bank tellers or managers, many white customers may assume black employees are menial or lower-paid clerical workers and treat them with discourtesy. We also see the power of the stereotype of black men as thieves. Even the man's coworkers felt they must protect the vaults against him. Such encounters with customers and coworkers are reminiscent of the degradation "rituals" forced on blacks under legal segregation.

A college senior working as a salesperson in a southern city commented on how he was viewed by white customers:

> Sometimes I don't think that I'm taken seriously. For instance, in my job situation now, since I'm in retail sales, I find myself having to prove I sell computers. So I have to prove my knowledge of computers and get past what a person's perceptions are of me. They have to listen to what I have to say, and again say, "Well, he *does* know what he's talking about. He *does* know what the equipment is. He *does* know how to set up a system, how to make it work." But I have to get past a person's original perceptions of me before I can go on. . . . Well, I deal with a lot of white customers, and they don't seem to like to deal with a black employee with knowledge of computers. I think it scares them sometimes. You have to be very patient and very discreet.

Considerable energy was expended by this man in his long-suffering approach to everyday discrimination. Many beliefs about blacks are so entrenched in white minds, that white customers may be only half-conscious, even unconscious, of their racially barbed comments and actions. Yet from the black's perspective it does not matter whether the white perpetrator causing the pain was consciously racist.

A senior psychologist at a large, historically white university commented on her experiences with white student clients:

> In the nine years that I've been here, there have been a couple of times when I've been seated with a client that I'm working with, an Anglo, white client, and I've been called a "nigger," or "nigger" has been used in the context of some discussion that the client is making in my office to my face. I've also had clients get up and leave my office. One woman told me she didn't want to work with me because I was black, that she had never worked with, or lived with, or gone to school with blacks, and she just had great difficulty with it. . . . There have been a few others. The occasional being called a "nigger" as I go across campus still happens today.

As the hostile epithets show, there is no subtlety in the white attitudes expressed here; the hostility is often conscious and flagrant. A forceful person, this professional indicates elsewhere in the interview that her reaction to such incidents is not deferential but straightforward and, when possible, vocal. The accumulating discrimination she faced at this university eventually led her to search for a position elsewhere.

Unwilling to place themselves in a role subordinate to a black person, some white students refuse to acknowledge their traditional position in the student-teacher relationship. A law professor at an eastern university gave an account of experiences with white students: "At the university, some of the discrimination you find may come from students who are reluctant to accept your authority, or your expertise. So, it may show up in the form of anything from refusal to respond to questions or [to] take them seriously to just a kind of ridicule." And a faculty member at a white university in the South spelled out the professorial authority problems in detail:

> Discrimination is an ongoing process in this environment, and you face it at all levels. All up and down the line. It makes your job more difficult, and what is worse about it, you can't always complain about it because the people who you would complain to can't imagine that you would run into the problem. Let's just take it first with the students. They're racist in the extreme. And it's not just me; I've gone to conferences and talked with other black professors, and they have the same problem. . . . You do not have the benefit of positive presumption, so you go into the classroom—white folks think you're dumb. I don't care what your degrees are. If you've got good degrees, they figure you didn't earn them. Figure someone gave it to you. So right away, you got a problem. Now these folks have never had a black person in authority over them. They take out that hostility. . . . What you have with the ethnic minority professor is you find people wanting to test you and giving you a hard time.

Both professors encountered similar challenging of their authority and questioning of their expertise. The last respondent continued with accounts of discrimination at the hands of the secretarial staff and other whites on campus, by which he illustrated the all-pervasive nature of the racism he daily faces.

Racism and Sexism in the Workplace

On occasion, some observers of U.S. racial relations have asked whether black women face more or less discrimination than black men in pursuing their employment goals and careers.

Explicitly addressing a question on this subject, our respondents were often very thoughtful in their replies. A male college graduate in the West saw some important differences:

> There are definitely systemic differences. [Black] women are perceived as being less of a threat, more passive than men. They are seen as feminine, weak. [White males] feel like they can manipulate women by virtue of their sex, manifest many different ways, through sex bias jokes, or gender type things like, that's a man's job. Or, "honey you don't want to get your dress dirty, or something." . . . Black males are perceived to be powerful, a threat.

In his view the black male image that is frightening to many whites on the street has a counterpart in the workplace. Black women are seen as less of a threat because they can be manipulated in sexist ways.

A psychologist at a major university was quite clear as to how she saw the differences:

> Well, it's hard to measure who's being discriminated against the most, and who's hurting the most. Both black men and black women are hurting. But this society shows its racism in a sexist way. Black women may be tolerated, so that then they may be more likely to be let in the door and hired. But *then* they're devalued, because we still devalue women in general, and women still make less money. And women, then, are perceived as less of a threat to male dominated systems. Black males on the other hand can compete with white males, and because they can compete, or are perceived as competing with white males, they evoke the intimidation, and they invoke lots of fear and threats from white men. So, black men get attacked in some very troublesome ways as a result of this. They are perceived as a greater threat and challenge to white male dominance.

> . . . Black men in some areas, the door is opening and slamming all at the same time. It means that society is discriminating against us, both racially and by gender. And the purpose of that is certainly to keep the community apart.

Asking whether racism or sexism has been the primary source of oppression for women of color, the Dutch psychologist Philomena Essed conducted a comparative study of small samples of black women in the United States and the Netherlands.[36] In the lives of these women Essed found both racism and sexism, often in the interactive form of the "gendered racism" noted in the last two comments.

That black women are often viewed as sex objects by white men was underscored by one of our female respondents, a successful entrepreneur:

> [White men] think they get so familiar with you that they can say certain things, or do certain things. It's just like my husband worked with this guy, Anglo guy. And he called one night, and he was drunk. And my husband was not at home. And I told [him] that he wasn't at home, and I said, "you really need to go home, because you seem like you need to get off the streets." You know, he made a pass at me. Hey, don't put your hands on me, I don't want your white hands on me! Don't touch me!

Black women encounter a variety of sexist attitudes, often mixed together with racist attitudes. An assistant vice president spoke of gender and racial hurdles:

> I've had things said to me like, "We didn't give you a certain position because we knew you had a child, and we knew that you would not want to be that far away, or, you cannot do this." It was always something that they as-

> sumed. They are trying to govern your life for you. That was one as far as being a woman. As far as being black, [with] the education that I have, I should have been in—probably in corporate headquarters now. I've seen people who were in this same management training program as myself who were white males. They have since almost tripled their salaries. And of course their titles are much more, or better, than mine. And they have, most of them, have less education than I have, have less experience than I have. Their ratings have been less, because that was one of the things that they had to produce when I brought the charges against them. They use, my lawyer said, the common defense of "what was good for the company."

There has been much debate in the stratification literature over whether race, sex, or class is the best framework for interpreting the multiple social hierarchies in the United States. Some analysts reduce one system of discrimination and oppression to another, as when orthodox Marxists insist on interpreting racial discrimination primarily in class terms, or when some feminists ignore the racial dimension in exploring the conditions women face.[37] A comparison of the workplace situations of black men and black women, as a number of respondents demonstrate throughout this chapter, provides illuminating insights. We have seen some of the ways in which patterns of racial discrimination interact with gender discrimination. Black women face a type of double jeopardy, for their hiring or advancement may be blocked by racism or by sexism. Because they are women, they may be more likely to be hired, but once they are in the door, as one respondent put it, "they're devalued, because we still devalue women in general." Black men can compete without facing gender discrimination, but for that very reason many white men may feel more threatened by the presence of black men in the workplace.

Conclusion

The few national studies, such as *A Common Destiny*, that discuss the current employment barriers that African Americans face have not analyzed in detail the situations of those in managerial, professional, and other white-collar positions.[38] Emphasizing the difficulties faced by lower-income black workers, these studies usually attribute their lack of advancement to limited education or conditions linked to poverty or a so-called "minority subculture." These national studies have not documented the discriminatory behavior that targets middle-class black employees.

The men and women whose accounts make up most of this chapter have moved into historically white workplaces in recent decades. They speak from experience about racial discrimination in the hiring process and show how success entering the workplace often does not carry over to egalitarian treatment there. In many cases, entry-level changes have not brought about the necessary internal changes in the white-collar climate. Discrimination can vary from outright exclusion, to discrimination in salary and promotions, to unpleasant and restrictive working conditions. Our interviews underscore how workplace exclusion and restriction, often carried out by white males, remain critical problems.

The psychological costs of racial discrimination are cumulative, painful, and stifling. The economic costs include lost promotions, small or no raises, and disrupted careers. Crossing the threshold of white workplaces has not meant thoroughgoing integration for black Americans, for the dominant white culture has not taken black concerns and perspectives into its core. In the employment accounts we often see normative conflict—the intentionally created anomic condition in which a black person cannot be sure what the actual governing rules are because whites may change them. Conflict between the ideal of equal opportunity and fairness and the real norms shaped by white hostility can create the humiliation, frustration, and anger audible in the accounts of mistreatment.

Each year seminars are given across the nation for black managers to help them deal with racial discrimination and related racial problems in the workplace. Judging from our data, such programs might well be expanded to cover all black employees. For African American employees it is rarely possible to go through a work week without being reminded, a least in a subtle way, of society's negative evaluation of their blackness. There is an enveloping sense of oppression. The detention officer we quoted in regard to initial job restrictions expressed the feelings of many when she spoke with biting humor of the "black cloud" hanging over her head. The adaptive reactions may be creative and successful or destructive and deadly.

In several of these accounts we again sense the influence of a strong belief in human and civil rights on middle-class black Americans. These accounts suggest how much middle-class blacks depend on civil rights legislation and court enforcement of such laws to develop white-collar careers in traditionally white workplaces. Although black employees may be skeptical about seeking court redress, many feel they must use this means to fight back.[39] Recalcitrant white employers often deliver the message: If you want to eliminate racial injustice, "you have to go the whole nine *miles*," to quote a black clerical worker who recently won an employment discrimination case against a southern university. But winning in court also means losing, for there is a fundamental contradiction between legal rights and everyday experience when a black person cannot even take the civil right of equity for granted but must fight an expensive and emotionally draining court battle.

Whites who control and run U.S. workplaces, including the corporations, are often said to be motivated mainly by concerns for business profit and growth. According to the usual business analysis, risks are held to a minimum, and social consciousness, if present, is a minor motivating factor in daily decisions. Because bringing black employees into historically white companies is often considered unnecessary or risky, middle-class blacks have often had to overcome tremendous odds in entering and excelling in them. For more than a century the preferential treatment for whites in corporate and other workplaces has not been defined as "preferential treatment," yet the relatively recent and generally modest affirmative action programs and preferential goals for African Americans are often defined by whites as unfair, if not as "reverse discrimination." A 1990 national opinion survey by the University of Michigan found that about eight in ten white adults opposed preferential hiring of black job applicants.[40] This lack of enthusiasm for affirmative action is found among younger whites as well. A 1991 national survey of young people by Hart Research Associates found that half the black youth thought that to "require companies to hire and promote adequate numbers of minorities" would "help a lot" in dealing with racial problems in U.S. society. In contrast, only 16 percent of the white youth felt such aggressive action would help a lot.[41]

In such assessments most whites focus on the operation of remedial programs and ignore the backdrop of real-world discrimination. Yet the racial discrimination documented in this chapter requires major remedies, including both private-sector and public-sector affirmative action programs.

Chapter Five

Building a Business

America's premier real estate entrepreneur in the late 1980s, Donald Trump, commented to an interviewer that "A well-educated black has a tremendous advantage over a well-educated white in terms of the job market." Then he added, "I've said on one occasion, even about myself, if I were starting off today, I would love to be a well-educated black, because I believe they have an actual advantage."[1] Trump, who wrote a best-selling book on the "art of the deal," was until his serious financial difficulties in the early 1990s a leading model of the successful entrepreneur, the type of model often held up to African Americans by advocates of black capitalism. The American dream advocated by Trump and other business leaders is predicated upon the belief that a person can work hard, put aside some money, start a business, and make good. In recent decades many white analysts and some black neoconservatives such as Thomas Sowell and Shelby Steele have argued vigorously that the solution to black economic problems is a hard-work, start-a-business philosophy.[2]

Successful black businesspeople are sometimes celebrated in

scholarly writings and the mass media as proof that there is great opportunity in the United States—that the attainment of the American dream is possible even for the oppressed. Indeed, many whites' conceptions of black opportunities go beyond this optimistic view to a broader mythology of black privilege and white disadvantage. In his comments Trump expresses the belief, apparently common among whites at various income levels, that social and economic conditions have improved so much for well-educated black Americans in recent decades that they are actually better off than affluent white Americans. This white illusion is far from the reality. A black journalist later commented on Trump's statement: "Too bad Trump can't get his wish. Then he'd see that being educated, black and over 21 isn't the key to the Trump Tower. You see there is still the little ugly problem of racism."[3]

Black capitalism is often presented as though it were a recent idea for African Americans, but in fact African Americans have worked hard and struggled against racial barriers to be entrepreneurs since the eighteenth century. Sociologist John Butler has demonstrated that as early as the 1700s there were many black businesspeople in northern and southern cities, serving black and white customers, and that over the next two centuries thriving black business communities developed in cities from New York and Philadelphia to Chicago to Durham and Tulsa.[4] Nineteenth- and twentieth-century black business activity is impressive against the backdrop of both legal and informal discrimination. The exclusion of freed slaves and their immediate descendants from much homesteading land after the Civil War made the accumulation of wealth very difficult.[5] Generally excluded from owning productive land after slavery, most black people worked as tenant farmers or low-wage agricultural and urban workers. Still, some began small businesses on a shoestring, and by the early twentieth century there were thousands of small black businesses. Yet in the 1930s the ravages of the Depression and racial discrimination decimated many of them.

In the decades since World War II there has been a resurgence of entrepreneurial activity. By the late 1980s there were 424,000 black firms, about 3 percent of all firms. Today most black businesses are small; African Americans own nearly 4 percent of the firms with receipts of less than $5,000 annually, but less than 1 percent of those with receipts of $1 million or more annually.[6] The failure rate is higher than that for whites. Only a third as many middle-class black Americans as whites have an equity in a business, and the median equity of blacks in business is only 40 percent of that of whites.[7] Interestingly, opinion surveys of black young people show that they still dream of owning their own businesses. A 1988 survey of eighth graders by the U.S. Department of Education found that 5.8 percent of the black students expected to own a business by age 30, not much less than the 6.3 percent of white students with the same expectation.[8]

Building a Business: The Difficult Rules of the Game

Many Americans put owning their own business at the center of the American dream itself. A 1992 Roper survey found that 17 percent of those in the Northeast thought "owning your own business" was a very important part of the American dream. In other regions of the country the proportion hovered around one quarter.[9] While we do not know of any similar surveys on African Americans specifically, it is clear that for many who have faced racial discrimination in the workplace being one's own boss is seen as a recourse, although a difficult one.

Some of our middle-class respondents have sought the American dream by becoming entrepreneurs and independent professionals. Contrary to the common white stereotype that blacks are "not willing to work hard,"[10] the businesspeople in our sample have worked very hard. Most have obtained a good education, saved their money, started their own businesses, and labored to succeed. Like comparable whites, they want a just distribution of rewards for their efforts. A chef at a large western hotel who tried to start his own small business on the side explained this: "I used the word 'American dream.' From childhood you're taught in order to achieve anything: Hard work. And that is the way, basically, I was raised. I was brought up believing if you're honest, hard working, then good things will happen to you."

Like desegregated schools, the business milieu might be expected to be more protected for middle-class blacks than public accommodations, yet racial discrimination remains a chronic problem in the marketplace. The entrepreneurs and independent professionals we interviewed described a wide range of discriminatory experiences, from being excluded from professional networks, to being denied credit, to having their business locations restricted. Building a new enterprise is difficult under any circumstances, but black businesspeople face an additional set of obstacles and deterrents.

Changing the informal rules of the business game to assure the exclusion of blacks is a common tactic in the white business world. The successful owner of a small consulting firm in a southwestern city described her experiences in the business world:

> They say get an education, go out and be entrepreneurs. Pull yourself up by your bootstraps. What bootstraps? Hell, we got to first get the boot in order to have the straps. We try to do all these things. We learn the rules of the game, and by the time we have mastered them to really try to get into the mainstream, the game becomes something else, be-

cause now we have learned how to play it. So, it changes constantly, constantly. It always keeps us on edge. I can give you a good example. I have a contract right now with a city government; and I practically gave my services away. I had to become very creative, you know. I wanted the contract because I know I could do the work, and I have the background and the track record to do it. However, in negotiating the contract, they wanted to give it to all these other people who never had any experience . . . simply because they're a big eight accounting firm, or they're some big-time institution. So, I had to compete against those people. But it was good because it proved that I could be competitive, I could give a competitive price, and I could finally win a contract. But it was a struggle.

She continued:

After the evaluation panel had made a decision that I had the highest points, the best management program, and the track record, they recommended me. And they took it back to their department. And the director of their department made a very racial statement, that "they were very sick and tired of these niggers and these other minorities because what they think is that they can come in here and run a business. None of them are qualified to run a business, especially the niggers." (Now, a white person, female, heard this statement, and because they had some confrontational problems—I think the only reason she really told me was because of that.) He was going to use that, not overtly, but in his mind that was going to be his reason for rejection. . . . And, I had to use that racism part to get my contract. Even though they all recommended me (I got all five consensus votes), he was going to throw it out. . . . I had to really, really do some internalizing to keep myself from be-

> ing very bitter. Because bitterness can make you lose your perspective about what you want to accomplish. Because you know there are so many roadblocks out there—it's just stressful trying to do these kinds of things—but I really had to do that just to keep from going off the deep end. So I had to handle him very professionally. . . . If I had not known [about the racist comment], I could have possibly not had this contract. I used racism to get something that I wanted. But then you have to fight continuously. You have to cross every "t" and dot every "i," you have to be much smarter, much brighter.

Small black companies start with a disadvantage in an economy where the size of a business is directly correlated with economic power. Facing exclusionary discrimination, and possessing limited economic power, these black firms may find that their only chance to secure a contract is to bid low, leaving little profit. This respondent was fortunate in having some proof of the attempt at exclusion; without such evidence many whites hearing about the rejection of a black businessperson for a contract might view the claim as paranoid. Almost apologetically she relates that she had to use this knowledge to insure fair treatment. It is important to note the fairness in the respondent's statement. She gave credit to the presumably white evaluation panel for being fair in rating her and mentioned the help of a white worker who told her about the racist decision-maker.

Racial discrimination can involve the intentional creation of normative uncertainty, similar to what sociologist Emile Durkheim long ago termed "anomie."[11] An unpredictable milieu that keeps a black person on edge produces a modern type of anomie. The rules change because blacks have learned the rules and whites in authority have decided to exclude blacks from the rewards of playing the game well. Note too that racial exclusion violates the equal opportunity canons of public law and represents a corruption of public authority.[12]

Business Networks and 'Ole Boy' Connections

Much has been made of the impersonality and formal regulation of work within corporations and government agencies, but informal networks are at least as important as formal rules and procedures in shaping the way business actually gets done. Exclusive social networks are a problem for black businesses. For example, after the 1992 riot in South-Central Los Angeles black contractors interested in some of the reconstruction business found that they were unable to break into the network of white firms recommended by insurance companies for that work.[13] Reflecting on his experiences, an auto dealer noted that

> We still operate off the 'good ole boy' syndrome, the nepotistic element of business relationships. Because black people in general, in business, have not become part of that system, they will tend to get rejected more so than the majority. We have not been around that long. We don't have those kinds of connections. We don't have that kind of fraternity with the majority. I don't think there is really too much you can do. It's just a matter of time. I think when you really become part of the total system—right now we are basically on one side and the majority is on the other side, when it comes down to the power that's involved. It's not going to happen now. It's not going to happen in the next five years. Maybe after the year 2000 we'll see a different climate.

Like many other African Americans, this man has a developed sensitivity to inequality of power and its consequences. Even partial exclusion from informal interaction with one's counterparts and from other important business contacts can be a formidable barrier to a successful enterprise. Here one senses a defensive pessimism, yet some hope, in the speculation that blacks are not an integral part of major networks because they are neophytes.

Support and exchange networks operate in complex organizational arrangements that include more than a few "good ole boys." The owner of a baking company in the Southwest described networking problems:

> I guess five years ago I was naive in the sense that I felt like if you had a better product, if you had a good product, and if you worked hard, that you could make it. And what I have found is that . . . everything is set up structurally, all the major companies and all the major forces, everything is set up structurally so that one way or another, you're going to get blocked out. . . . And the only way that you can get around it, on top of being better at everything—which you have to be first of all—on top of that, you have to use . . . political pressure if you can. You know, if they have government contracts . . . then they have an obligation to maybe local vendors, or minority vendors, or maybe both, and that writing letters about that, and maybe talking to your congressman, or people that are pretty high up who have some political power, and letting them know that you're going to do that.

To be sure, lack of access to "good ole boy" connections may hinder some new white businesses as well. Black entrepreneurs, however, face the double handicap of newness and "blackness." As this person learned, black businesses are seldom judged by the same criteria as whites; the rules of the game can shift. Blacks are excluded by subtle run-around tactics and blatant door-slamming tactics. In this case the presence of government minority participation programs did not guarantee fair treatment. This entrepreneur delineated the sabotage techniques used by several corporations that purported to support minority businesses:

> [They] made us promises that they were going to give us business and this sort of thing, and that they had a minority program, and that they wanted to help minority companies, and send us samples and send us paper work. And you know, a year and a half went by, we lived up to our obligations, but they didn't give us one bit of business. And it was just all lies and false promises, and they would usually have a black person in the company that's supposedly heading up the minority section of this company, right, but this person is just a front. He's just there, or she's just there, to make it look like they have a minority program and they really don't. And they set it up paper-wise, and they have brochures that say, "yes we have a minority program, and we want to help minorities," but that's all just show. . . . They know that they've got it set up [so that] in order to even get through the system it's going to take such a long time that as a small company you're not going to have the money to wait that long to get the business. So, you're either going to go out of business or you're going to give up in the process. . . . So, you have to go through the system that they have lined up for you, and it's very tedious and it's a very long steady process. And once you've done all those things and fulfilled all those obligations on your side of the table, then at that point, if they don't respond, and you find out that they've just been, excuse the expression, jerking you around for the last year and a half, two years, then at that point, you take other measures. As I said, using the political system, a lot of these companies have state obligations and government obligations and they're supposed to help local vendors and minority vendors. So, you can use that avenue, once you've gone

> through the process first. If that doesn't work—it's like Martin Luther King, when he did the bus boycott, and that was the only thing, the main thing that really worked, . . . when you hit them in the pocketbook.

White discriminators in the business world seem to expect their black counterparts either to ignore the discrimination or to accept it quietly as part of a natural order. But this woman, using political pressure, reacted to the mistreatment directly. An imbalance of power is recognized as the heart of the matter, and she called it by its name. One senses in her comment about "lies" more damage to the black psyche. False promises, psychologists John Mirowsky and Catherine Ross note, result in "the belief that others are unsupportive, self-seeking, and devious, which is highly distressing."[14]

In a 1990 study of black businesses in a southeastern city, Joe R. Feagin, using black interviewers, conducted interviews with seventy-six black businesspeople in the construction industry. Numerous specific barriers faced by the black construction contractors were found to be linked, directly or indirectly, to a white ole-boy network in that large metropolitan area. For example, the owner of an electrical construction company that grossed several million dollars in the last year talked about dealing with whites in the bidding process, emphasizing the "buddy-buddy" networks between white general contractors and white subcontractors that undergird long-term working relationships:[15]

> See, it's difficult to know whether or not you're the low bidder. The [white] contractor can make it whatever he wants because you are not privy to the other bids he gets. So you know, all you know is that he's not using it; he's using the same people he's been using for twenty and thirty years. So you can . . . bid low/high, and you're still not

> going to get the job, because there are still a lot, [a] buddy-buddy system.

A college-educated air-conditioning contractor also described how a white "fast shuffle" preserves the white networks:

> When you've been at this business as I have, many years, you *know* when a [white] man is giving you a fast shuffle. You know when he's not dealing fairly with you, you know. Because he can't get anybody to do the job any different. But the way in which he manages the work tells you whether he wants you to fail or whether he wants you to succeed. And these people are very sophisticated in the manner in which they discriminate. They're not going to come out and tell you, "Oh, you know, I'm not going to deal with you because you're black." They're not going to do that. You know, it's the same thing with the bidding process, right? They'll call you up for a price, but they'll ask their buddy, "Can you beat this price?" if your price is low, and the buddy will say, "Yes, put me in."

Repeated experience with discrimination has caused many black firms to be wary of white contractors. In this particular metropolitan area the local government has a special "goals" program that requires white general contractors to involve black contractors on many government projects. Yet black contractors have reported few requests for bids on private sector projects, despite having worked for white contractors on government construction projects. Whites generally prefer to work with white firms with whom they have established working relations. Some may also fear the loss of clients if they use black contractors. Like the "social cloning" of white employees noted in the last chapter, white firms are chosen to replace previous white firms in a never-ending succession.

These construction industry findings, as well as the data in this chapter, are in line with Carmenza Gallo's unpublished study of white, black, and immigrant contractors in a sector of New York's construction industry. In New York she found that successful contractors depend on social integration, "expressed by membership in industry organizations and by informal connections and the achievement of standing in the community from which the firm's clientele is likely to be drawn."[16] Ties to important industry organizations and existing informal networks in construction were found to be critical to getting good workers, to building a significant clientele, and to establishing a long-term business. The white construction firms, the best integrated in core networks, had the widest access to commercial, governmental, and residential construction projects in New York. Gallo reasoned that the disproportionate reliance of New York's black contractors on government programs for construction projects was not because they were less efficient than others or because they needed special favors, but because of the difficulties they had in finding a color-blind clientele elsewhere.[17]

Problems of Location and Capital

Building a business normally requires a place to do business, which frequently involves working through white-dominated real estate and banking networks. A parole officer in a western city, who tried to start a child care business with a friend, reported on real estate transactions:

> If you're a minority, they predominantly want you to go to black, minority areas of town and locate your business there. When in fact, all the money isn't in the black areas of town, it's in the white areas of town. Yes, . . . we wanted to open a day care center in the predominantly white area of town and it was, it was never written down,

> but we were informed later that we were two young black men, and that wouldn't look good that two young black men would open up a day care center in a predominantly white area of town. . . . When they said that the residence that we bid on was given to someone else, one could look at that and say, "Hey, that was racially motivated." Our bid was the highest. The person with the second highest bid won the bid.

Prejudice such as that described here, Herbert Blumer has argued, is not simply antipathy felt by members of the white group for blacks but rather is "rooted in a sense of group position," which may have a territorial dimension.[18] In this case the whites create and justify a condition of spatial apartheid, probably thinking that other whites would not accept black men in that type of business.

Getting the necessary loans for a business can also be a problem. It is significant that in the late nineteenth and early twentieth centuries, freed black slaves and their descendants established no fewer than 134 banks to support numerous local and regional businesses. However, over the intervening decades blatant racial discrimination, including white violence, and economic depressions took their toll, and by the late 1980s there were only three dozen black-owned banks, all with modest assets.[19] As a result, most black businesspeople today have to turn to white-owned banks for the loans and lines of credit. Substantial collateral is not available to most, for neither they nor their close relatives have had the opportunity to build the economic base many whites have developed. Even for those with collateral, bank loans are hard to acquire, a fact underscored by a number of recent research reports by government and private agencies.

A 1992 report by the U.S. Commission on Minority Business Development found that the lack of access to financing was a major barrier to the development of a black business.[20] Moreover, looking at 10,139 businesses in twenty-eight cities, economist Timothy Bates found that black entrepreneurs had a harder time getting loans than whites did, and the loans blacks did secure were about 40 percent smaller, for the same amount of business equity, as loans to whites.[21] A veteran contractor in a major city in the Midwest explained the current situation for black businesses:

> I like the challenge and independence of being in business for myself. I am in the construction business. I would like to build my business into a thirty to forty million dollar business and be very competitive with everybody and be competitive not just as a black contractor. You need to get a line of credit to be successful. If a minority contractor doesn't have this, he won't get far. This is one of the toughest things to get over. This obstacle keeps minorities down. A white contractor can get a line of credit with less collateral than a black contractor.

A dentist in a southern city, a man of considerable attainment, described the business barriers he has faced as a "glass ceiling." As he noted, discrimination in access to capital not only hinders blacks' entry into the business world but also limits blacks' success in building strong communities:

> A white with the income of mine and the assets that we have would probably have a greater access to greater dollar values, thereby allowing that person the ability to capitalize on the financial basis by which the system is done, either via credit and/or access to information. I feel as though, that at the higher income, the higher echelon you get, the less information the white man wants you to have, because he does not want you to be able to overcome his thing. But he also is conscious that the more control that he can keep

> over you through access to money, and I'm talking about millions and above, my basic kind of example of this is [a prominent white surgeon]. [This surgeon] showed in his bankruptcy proceedings that he had $93 million worth of unsecured loans, $93 million! I don't know one black man in this state today that can get $1 million worth of unsecured, or even $93 thousand worth of unsecured dollars. . . . You see, there's a parallel there between what is really the cause and effect of us developing our own direction and developing our neighborhoods. It's access.

When we asked how many of his friends had faced banking discrimination, he replied:

> All of them. All of our friends. I don't know a black man in this city that does not have a good economic discrimination suit . . . that's borrowed $20,000 compared to $50,000 to the same [white] man with the same income with the same situation. It's just rampant, it's throughout the whole system. You almost have to pawn your grandmother to get a loan.

In the previously mentioned study of black construction contractors in a southeastern city by the first author, many respondents spoke of having experienced some type of discrimination from white-controlled banking institutions. A college-educated flooring contractor with a good credit record described what happened when he tried to get a loan:

> Last year the school board had a bunch of bankers that said that they wanted to help minority people get money. We applied to a bank, which is called [Bank B]. We put [in] our paper; we did the income tax and everything, plus the fact that the job was bonded. So therefore, payments are guaranteed by my bonding company. From November 1989

> through January 1990 we couldn't even get an answer from them. The school board couldn't even get their calls answered. Finally, we sent in even more information. They said they didn't want information. We sent them information, and to this day we never heard from them. . . . [What evidence can you give that race, and not some other factor, was the reason for that poor treatment?] Well, how do you explain that you go to a bank and, first of all, when you approach anybody in a bank, okay, even the secretaries look at you like, "Is this guy come to talk to me or to stick up the bank?" That's number one. No matter how you look or how much you dress [up] you receive a lot of questions. You are investigated very thoroughly and end up getting nothing, irregardless of your record. We had rates with [a major rating firm], we have an A rating with that company. We are cleared for a million dollars in [business]. We have a record of finishing all our work. We are bonded, and yet we can't get a bank to give us a penny.[22]

This black contractor's problems at white banks start when he walks in the door and is met with suspicion. Even after intensive investigation by the bank he still does not get the loans that his accomplishments suggest he deserves. There seems to be a widespread perception among whites that blacks cannot succeed in business. Some businesspeople have devised sophisticated ways to circumvent the problem. For example, a *Money* magazine article profiled a black entrepreneur in St. Louis who sought a loan to start an independent oil change operation.[23] Although he had a good business record, he was rejected by three banks for different reasons, all lacking substance. As a result, he turned to a white friend, a developer, who obtained a loan on the land and leased it back to the black entrepreneur.

Most small businesses, black and white, secure a substantial portion of their startup funds and initial operating expenses from informal financing, such as personal or family savings, salaries foregone, or supplier credit. A study of newly created firms in Minnesota found that those started by whites secured much more formal capital than the minority firms, with real estate loans, on the average, being the most important source.[24] Commissioned by the *Wall Street Journal*, a 1992–1993 survey of 500 black entrepreneurs with an annual revenue of $100,000 or more found that more than 90 percent had been turned down by banks when seeking loans for a business. Three quarters felt that it was much more difficult for a black firm to get loans than white firms. As a result, 70 percent reported that they had used their own personal savings to finance their business. On the average, financial institutions provided only 6 percent of their total capital. And nearly two thirds felt that black-owned businesses were charged higher interest rates for capital than white-owned businesses.[25]

Perhaps the most visible impact of past discrimination can be seen in the severe racial inequality in the economic base necessary for successful entrepreneurship. In the most recent federal survey of wealth the net worth of the average white household ($39,000) was twelve times that of the average black household ($3,400); only 13 percent of black Americans had assets of $50,000 or more, compared with 44 percent of whites.[26] Punctuating his comments with some laughter, one independent professional commented on what he would like changed in the larger society:

> Distribution of wealth. It would be good if we were able to get our portion of the American dream, so that money could come, jobs, opportunities. I think that would, you know—hey, they can think what they want about black people. But hey, if we were getting the same amount of money it would help, it would help a lot. You know what I mean? The same jobs, opportunities.

Denied loans by banking institutions, black businesspeople may fall back on local organizations. The president of a community credit fund in an eastern city discussed exclusionary discrimination by lending institutions:

> I've seen some attitudes . . . within the financial community toward minority entrepreneurs . . . saying that they have no skills, they have no ability to manage, or to borrow and successfully use those borrowed funds. I've seen people who've been turned away from financial institutions, who've come to us, and we've helped them. And I cannot understand why those commercial banks, or savings and loans haven't helped them.

That this community credit fund has fostered successful black businesses argues strongly for an end to discrimination in white-controlled commercial banks. Such success may argue for the expansion of community banks as an antidote to discrimination in mainstream institutions, although the limited amount of capital they usually have does not make this approach a panacea. Federal government intervention would seem to be the way to provide adequate funds for business expansion.

Professionals in Business

In recent years some commentators have complained about the scarcity of African American health-care professionals. Lack of motivation, low educational attainment, and insufficient role models are sometimes cited as reasons, explanations similar to those given for black student attrition (discussed in Chapter 3). Too often ignored is the fact that black professionals face discrimination at every step in a medical career, from early education, to medical school, to actual practice. Until the 1950s doctors in the American Medical Association kept the organization all white and discriminated against black Americans in their organizational activities. As a result, black professionals organized separate societies, such as the National Medical Association.[27] These societies were, and often still are, the only groups that permit the kind of open professional exchange and extensive networking black professionals need for support and advancement.

Some progress has been made, but American medicine is still substantially segregated, with many black physicians having mostly black clienteles and few white doctors locating in black communities. Although many black people are patients of white doctors, others prefer black doctors because they do not have to fear unfair racial treatment.[28] The roots of the distrust of white professionals run deep in living memories, especially of older African Americans. Some remember the chilling news reports since 1972 of the Tuskegee, Alabama experiments by the U.S. Public Health Service's white doctors on black men with syphilis. About 430 black men with late-stage syphilis were regularly examined and studied for several decades from the 1930s forward to study the effects of the disease. Even after penicillin was found to be a cure in the 1940s, the study participants received no treatment from the white physicians; most were allowed to think that they were being treated for rheumatism, bad stomachs, or "bad blood." Lacking treatment, some died horrible deaths.[29] In 1973 the attorney for the surviving men sued the government, calling the study a "program of controlled genocide." The revelation of the Tuskegee experiments deepened many blacks' distrust of white doctors and undermined others' faith in white-controlled medicine. Journalist Tom Junod recently quoted the comments of a black medical outreach worker in Atlanta about the advice given by her grandparents: "Don't ever let a doctor do an experiment on you."[30]

There are also many stories of white physicians carried in the collective memories of black families. One retired black educator described an incident in his boyhood long ago in the Midwest that still infuriates him. He and his six-year-old sister were in an auto accident in which his sister sustained a broken nose and gash on her forehead: "We were taken to a white doctor, who put one stitch in a wound that later required three stitches, used nothing to deaden her pain, and did not treat the broken nose. After a three-hour drive home, our family physician, who was black, was furious at the poor treatment."

For any doctor, professional connections are crucial to developing a viable medical or dental practice. Indeed, these professions *are* networks, for without referrals and the dissemination of knowledge along networks they would not exist. Exclusion from a professional network is a major disadvantage, yet even inclusion in a network does not necessarily confer equal status on a black doctor. Some black physicians find that their white peers sometimes see them as receptacles for poor and other unwanted clients. A doctor in the Northeast commented on the selective nature of referrals he received: "I find that referrals from agencies, white agencies, to me are apt to be patients that other physicians, white physicians, would not accept. For example, patients who don't have the money to pay. Patients who may have certain forms to fill out and the white physicians won't want to bother with it. They'll send them to me."

White administrators and doctors control admission to most hospital facilities. A physician in another East Coast city described problems that her husband, who is also a doctor, has faced:

> My husband has faced discrimination. And he's a neurologist. And his problem has been because he's black, and because the hospitals that we practice in, it's very cliquish, WASP-ish. They are very threatened by him, because of course they feel that he will take their black clientele. And so they have put barriers in his way to try to hold him back—as far as monitoring his charts, holding him up for

> the operating room so that he's late for his case. I mean, he's faced obvious discrimination, much more than I have.

A physician in a southwestern city explained in some detail how this exclusion works:

> A lot of the physicians have formed contractual arrangements with different companies and different insurance companies, okay? And if you don't have a job, you don't work, and you don't have insurance, then it's difficult to be seen by one of these physicians. . . . I signed up to join a local hospital's health care organization, which provides health care to the employees of that hospital. And I was told that the reason that they weren't going to accept me into their organization was that they had too many doctors in the downtown area in the plan already. . . . I said, "Well, I'm not downtown, I practice on the south side of this city, in the black community. And all I want to do is—I just want to be able to take care of the people who live on the south side who are in the plan, okay?"

For medical professionals like this man aggressive action against discrimination can be risky, because it may endanger the often tenuous professional networks one has already established. Yet his anger at his impotence is unmistakable. This independent professional continued with a description of how black physicians are not included in joint ventures undertaken by white administrators and doctors, then discussed other impediments, such as special scrutiny:

> If you're a doctor, say, in this community . . . and they don't allow you to have hospital privileges, for instance, then that cuts you off from hospital access. And if you don't have hospital access then patients aren't going to come see you, because they say, "Well, if I get sick, he can't put me in a hospital, or come see me when I'm in a hospi-

tal." So that, in turn, can make a doctor leave a community and move to another one. . . . It used to be, like back in the '50s and before that, they just told you that because of your color you couldn't belong and then throw your application in the trash can. Now they do it a little more shrewdly, because of the civil rights law and that kind of thing. In other words, it's the same old game, it's just that the rules are different. . . . They may let you in the hospital, and then limit what you can do while you're there. Or they may let you in, but then they have you under such scrutiny that they try to find anything that they can to put you off the staff. In other words, it's a double standard. What they'll do is, like, a black physician, if he doesn't cross every "t" and dot every "i" then he's kicked off the staff. Whereas, a white physician may have had a lot of serious infractions on his record but not have been punished or reprimanded or anything like that.

A theme in our interviews is this white questioning, sometimes explicit, sometimes subtle, of black competence, whatever the setting. In a northern metropolis a doctor with a busy practice and her own nursing home explained how she was subjected to surveillance by white members of her profession:

I've had [white] people who've tried to come in and investigate my practice, who've tried to form peer reviews of my practice to see if the quality of care was up to standards, because there was no way that someone could provide a quality of care and do it as a solo practitioner and be black. Of course, nothing was found, but I did face that problem. About four or five years ago I came through it with no problems. . . . When I went through that period, it was strictly racially motivated. And I filed a countersuit against the board.

In her interview she also said that she shudders at judgments of her work based on white perspectives and values she felt to be inappropriate to her situation. Black professionals undergoing such scrutiny fear they will be held to excessively stringent standards, to higher standards than are their white counterparts.

Refusal of the mostly white dental establishment to accept a black person can lock a new professional out of a successful practice. A black dentist noted that when she started she was

> one of the only females practicing dentistry in my city, and because of that I was definitely not accepted by the white males. So I had no choice as far as my business was concerned, than to open up another, open up my own business, because I was not going to be insulted by whites in going to apply to be an associate in their office. That was just not going to happen. I also attempted to be part of various study clubs, and I was always told that they were filled, or no one ever got back with me.

In this case, she was undoubtedly excluded both as an African American and as a woman. In later comments in the interview she explained that her practice has been limited primarily to black patients, many of modest means, and for that reason she has begun a small cosmetics business on the side. Sometimes middle-class African American professionals must start a second business to supplement their below-average incomes.

Attorneys also face racial discrimination. A self-employed attorney in a southern city explained that whites sometimes have considerable control over the work that black lawyers get. Some white firms only appear willing to give black attorneys less desirable work, a situation similar to the selective referrals black medical professionals get. White firms may exclude black attorneys from important joint ventures. One lawyer observed that exclusion from the field of law in the past continues to work against black attorneys in the present, since access to some legal work in the present requires experience that past discrimination kept them from obtaining:

> We've met some resistance from some firms who think that if, let's say, the city or the county or the mass transit system here, any one of those entities, do more business with minority firms, law firms, that it will take away from what they're doing. And consequently they're resisting that. . . . So they try to minimize what work is given out, or they try to give out work that they themselves may not want to do or [that] may not generate that much revenue. . . . Or if you're talking about funding municipal bonds and things of that notion, in order to do that work you have to get in what we call "the red book." And there're so few minority attorneys, and even fewer black attorneys, in the red book that are qualified to do the work, but in order to get in the red book, you must do some of the work. So they don't want to bring in, or do joint ventures with other black law firms or black lawyers that would qualify them to be placed in the red book.

Excluding black professionals does not seem to be enough for some white firms, which also covet the small amount of business sometimes set aside for minorities by local and federal governments. In the study of the construction industry in a southeastern metropolis discussed previously, several black contractors reported that white general contractors had offered black firms money just to sign a "letter of intent" so the white firms could appear to meet minority hiring goals in bidding on local government construction projects. Yet many white contractors had no intention of actually using the black businesses.[31] The attorney quoted above described his encounter with a similar problem:

> In terms of work that's being done in this city and this county, whether it be city, county, school district, we have negotiated with certain firms, other firms, for joint venture arrangements. We have not gotten the work. Not so much because the expertise was not vast, but because in our negotiations we wanted a meaningful arrangement. Well, why should you, a predominantly white firm, engage in business with me, when you can engage in a venture with some other minority who's saying, "Give me my check and you can use my name." When you're going to probably be paying less to that person than you'd be paying to me. So why do business with me? You won't do business with me. Unless there's some moral rationale, reason. And I gave up on that a while ago, but that's what you have. And that's the reality. I don't get upset with anybody for doing that. The only thing that I'm saying is that in the long run, minorities (or people who are in business for themselves who are minorities) do themselves and all of us a disservice by engaging in—what's the word?—in joint ventures that are intended merely to circumvent the program just for a few dollars. And as long as that happens, there is not going to be any real incentive on behalf of the white companies or corporations or firms to engage in serious conversation.

When people of different backgrounds compete fairly in business, most Americans consider it fair for the more skilled person to have an advantage over the other. Yet most black businesses are not allowed to compete meritocratically on the same level with whites. Another respondent noted that when small black firms cannot get business because of discrimination, they may be "hungry enough" to cooperate with white firms illegally in such a "set-aside racket" just to survive.

White Customers and Associates

Black people in business for themselves encounter a range of problems at the hands of prejudiced whites, similar to those that black white-collar workers do, including the refusal of some whites to buy from blacks, the doubting of black capabilities, and even the hurling of racist epithets. It is difficult for black merchants to develop their businesses, serving either the public or the private sector of the economy, if whites refuse to do business with them. An auto dealer who owned a business in the Midwest from 1979 to 1985 occasionally observed customers who "would come in the showroom floor, and they would find out that a black person owned the dealership, and they'd leave."

Knowing that white prejudice exists, blacks whose business places them in direct contact with whites must be alert. Grier and Cobbs argue that black Americans must condition themselves "against cheating, slander, humiliation, physical harm and outright mistreatment by representatives of our society. If not, life will be so full of shock and pain as to be unbearable."[32] The hotel chef quoted earlier also reported his difficulty getting white customers for his new cake catering business:

> You know how employees . . . have a birthday party for another employee or a retirement party, something of that nature. And a few of the black people here were buying cakes from me. One of the supervisors here—a pretty big wheel—well anyway, the girls that work under her . . . were up in the break room talking about where are they going to get a cake. So, one of the black girls said—she was the only black one up there and there must have been about eight white girls—and she said, "Why don't we

> get Sam to do it? He works down in the kitchen." So, I stuck my head in the door and smiled. And a couple of the white girls looked up, and looked at each other. And you can tell with their eyes [they were saying] "Oh my goodness. No, no, not him." So, hey, I can take a hint. I just gave it one of these little Charlie waves and kept going. Well, they didn't order the cake from me. But you know, cool. And so that went on for about six or seven months. The only cakes that I could sell here were to other blacks. Now, one of the owners of the place here asked me to do a cake for her son. So, I said, "Sure, no problem." I did the cake for her son. I did a pretty good job. She liked it and she was telling all the other people that work here, [in] management and everywhere else. Now from that day on, it was just, I was just bombarded. It was like, "If this big, powerful, rich lady would buy a cake from him, he's what's happening. I want to buy a cake from him, too." You see? That type of prejudice I have run into quite often.

The chef's "little Charlie waves" and "cool" reaction probably masked anger and hurt at the white workers' assumption that a black person would not do as good a job as a white person. In the waves we glimpse a kind of protective device, a feigned, nonverbal expression of amiability and nonchalance. Thomas and Sillen have suggested that "a traditional feature of the racist syndrome is the interpretation of strength of feeling in the black man as primitive emotionalism,"[33] a white attitude that causes many black men and women to repress their justified anger in order not to be stereotyped by whites as out of control.

This account also illustrates the leadership role unprejudiced whites can play in discriminatory situations, setting a precedent for others. The relative ease with which whites sometimes change certain prejudiced notions and discriminatory behavior underscores Thomas Pettigrew's point that prejudice and discrimination can be changed if the benefits of change outweigh the advantages of holding firm.[34]

Dealing with prejudiced clients creates a dilemma for black businesspeople. Some brazenly prejudiced white customers are simply not worth the effort, yet not putting forth that effort leaves the black person vulnerable to the accusation of being lazy. The owner of a chemical distributing company in the Southwest reported that

> You're going to find some racist buyers out there. You have to recognize when that situation occurs and move on to something else. . . . There've been times when I've told our salespeople to move on to some other account. For various reasons, this person's not being fair with you. I don't know if it's because it's just that he's not a fair person or because of skin color. One or two, [maybe a] combination. Then you just move on to something else.

Black businesspeople can realistically expect to be insulted, and most prepare themselves to cope with the insults and, if possible, to negotiate with the white antagonist. In a business context, restraint may stem from fear of losing a client or of being the target of white retaliation for being aggressive. Here, as in other black dealings with whites, a restrained response can bring distress from the feeling of impotence, which in turn may contribute to stress-related physical disorders such as the hypertension that plagues African Americans.[35]

No matter how experienced and able they may be, black businesspeople may be subject to the automatic assumption from whites that their products or services are inferior. A successful contractor in the Midwest explained: "It's not as easy for a black contractor to negotiate design changes as it is for a white contractor. The stereotype is that your qualifications are not up to par." A lawyer in a southern metropolis explained that he was treated as competent by officials who knew him but not by strangers:

> When I pick a jury of strangers who don't know me, I have to constantly be on guard of the potential racial ideas that those jurors might have. When I interact with court personnel who may not know who I am, I run into an assumption sometimes that because he's a black lawyer, he must not be as sharp as his white counterparts, or his pleadings might not be as good, or basically he's just not as good a lawyer. And when I interact with my black clients, who have been victims of racism, some of them have apprehensions sometimes with having a black lawyer represent them, because they feel for whatever reasons that maybe he's not going to be as good as a white lawyer. Or, conversely sometimes, I have white clients who come and I represent, and I feel that I have to prove to them that even though I am black, I'm a hell of a lawyer. Those are all examples of the way racism is still alive and well in the American judicial system.

Doubtless most black clients know there are competent black lawyers, but many choose white representation because they fear the prejudices of a white jury or judge or because they too feel white is better.[36]

Another distressing attitude black businesspeople encounter is a lack of respect from white customers. A respondent in an eastern city related her husband's experiences: "I know that the [white] attitudes may not change, but I'd like to see the behaviors change. An example of that: My husband had his own business in the south part of the city. There are white people there who are on welfare who consider themselves better than he. They still consider all black people, even though they're destitute, to be lower than they are." Poor whites' condescension and emphasis on blacks' racial status over the class status they have achieved have a long history in this society.[37]

Reflecting on years of consulting experience, a retired professor commented on how he had been treated by white clients and on the marked discrepancy between the respect and compensation he received compared with his white peers.

> In my consulting, I have great difficulty getting half of what a white man would get for doing the same job. There was an instance where I did some consulting at the state Department of Corrections. I worked teaching their counselors for months. I became ill, had a heart attack, and sent another [white] young man to complete the two or three days of work. He went in and did an excellent job, completed the job. Months later when I came back on the job, I looked on his wall and saw a certificate of appreciation for all he had done for the Department of Corrections counselors and what he had meant to them. And not one even sent me a card while I was ill. . . . And right now, blacks are limited in consulting because whites really don't want to pay them the same fee they pay a white person for doing less.

The devaluation of professional activity reported here reminds us of the defective white vision about which Ellison wrote in *The Invisible Man.* What might seem to some white readers as hypersensitivity in the professor's interpretation of these events as discriminatory is the result of decades of experience with racial insensitivity and animosity consulting in this and similar government agencies.

Doing business with whites who devalue one's abilities is bad enough, but there is always the additional possibility of the racist epithet, the crude racial remark in the business setting. Racist comments sometimes come from white workers who supposedly have lower social status in the workplace than black businesspeople, or racial slurs come from business associates at the same status level. In the 1990 study of the construction industry the first author found a number of black contractors who had been taunted by comments on the job. A well-educated steel contractor from the Caribbean described his experience with whites while working for a white-run firm:

> Oh, with [XYZ company], ho. They come along, and they'll yell on the job. And they'll be asking you,"Why you all leave where you are from and come here to work?" "Which boat you land on?" It's a common thing, alright? They come around, and you're doing the work. And they say, "You know, the place where your forefathers come from, they don't do this kind of work, they use only sticks and leaves to make buildings!" And you know, it's kind of degrading, like, "Hey, you see that we can do the work, you see we are doing the work." And I always say I'm from the islands . . . and as far as I'm concerned you don't have any building here that we don't put up there. Alright? And it's always, it's aggravating. . . . So we're tired of it. . . . As soon as it became a black crew on the job, you go into the restroom: "Niggers, we don't want you here." "Niggers, go use the bush."

In settings like these the black businessperson senses viscerally the whites' view that blacks are less than human, a perspective with an ideological lineage running back through legal segregation to slavery.

Another example from a quite different work setting was given by a black attorney who recounted an incident with a white associate at the end of a work day:

> I was sitting in the offices one day after 5:00 P.M. You know, people come together in the office, and everybody's talking and shooting the b.s. . . . they were talking about the attorneys or the people or the clients and everybody's laughing, and everybody's getting loose. And then one [white] attorney said, "Yeah, that nigger." And you're sit-

> ting there. . . . Well, they say what you do in private comes out in the light of day, so he must have been saying it other places. And it just came out. When he said it, everybody else heard it. He recognized it when he said it. I'm sitting there and I said nothing. I wasn't going to say anything. I did not laugh at it, but I wasn't going to say anything. And my point was, he knew he said it, they knew he said it and they heard it, and they knew that I heard it. Now let their own consciences deal with it. Now, maybe in another setting, I may have commented or I may have said something, but there was no need to say anything, you know? So my attitude was: I won't say anything, you know I heard it, now I'll let you think what I'm thinking.

Laughing periodically, he discussed subsequent events:

> So for the next two or three days, he'd come to my office, see how I'm doing, you know. [I'd say] "I'm doing fine. Because I knew you were racist way before you said it; all you did was confirm what I had already thought." . . . Like I told him, I said, "Y'all are sick. My attitude is that you white Americans are in general sick. Y'all need help. And my training and where I was brought up, you help the sick, feed the hungry, clothe the naked. I can't get mad at you for your racism; you're sick." And I think that's the attitude that black America must have towards white America, especially those who pronounce racist views or hold racist views or practice discrimination, and that is that those individuals are sick. And instead of us getting so bent out of shape and angry and frustrating ourselves, we treat them as patients. And for some, you can nurse back to health; for others, you must diagnose as being terminally ill.

Again we observe what being black in a white world means on a daily basis, for one must be prepared to assess a situation rapidly and then exert energy to decide on the appropriate response. We see here a reluctance to confront his colleague aggressively at the time of the remark; he decided instead not to display any response and in a measured reaction forced the white man to reflect on his ill-considered action.

Conclusion

Some white scholars view African Americans as just another immigrant group that can work its way up if it adheres to the American work ethic. Sociologist Nathan Glazer has argued that although differences exist between the experiences of black Americans and of white-ethnic immigrants, there are more similarities than differences: "The gap between the experience of the worst off of the ethnic groups and the Negroes is one of degree rather than kind. Indeed, in some respects the Negro is better off than some other groups."[38] Thus relatively recent nonblack immigrants to the United States, such as the mostly white Cubans who migrated to Florida beginning in the late 1950s, have been viewed by many white analysts as more or less comparable to black Americans in the difficulties they have faced getting into business. They are celebrated among those advocating "free enterprise" solutions for black Americans.[39] If these Cuban immigrants "have made it," this reasoning goes, so can African Americans if they will only come to terms with their weaknesses and work much harder. Yet this common white view ignores the major dissimilarities in the situations of African Americans and immigrants such as the Cubans. There are, for example, differing times of entry into major cities and significantly different amounts of wealth and other resources to consider. And there is the virulence of antiblack discrimination among whites. Discussing the Cuban American community in Florida, Alejandro Portes and Robert Bach have argued that a chief reason that the mostly white Cubans have done well economically is that they migrated not as poor individuals but rather as an officially recognized group with substantial economic, educational, and political resources. Many came with the education and credentials that enabled them to become professionals or businesspeople. The Cuban immigrants were also covered by federal legislation providing a substantial social welfare program that helped many get a new start, including a start in business. They did not "make it" only on their own.[40]

Unlike Cuban Americans, African Americans have faced major racial barriers in getting into business for several centuries and have not benefitted from a concerted, large-scale governmental effort to break down business barriers. Our respondents speak eloquently of obstacles to building a business, either as a merchant, contractor, or independent professional, and of the deliberate and unconscious discriminatory actions of whites, which can be impediments to success in business. More than one respondent told of being the victim of behind-the-scenes maneuvering by white officials working against their bids for contracts. Examining racial barriers in her study of discrimination in the New York construction industry, Gallo concluded that a businessperson's reputation depends more on subjective factors such as social acceptability than on objective criteria such as cost and efficiency.[41]

One of our respondents commented simply that many whites do not want blacks to have a "piece of the pie." Because of barriers to black opportunity, whites can command larger segments of business markets than they would under free competition. A self-employed lawyer put his desire for changes in the business world and other areas of daily life this way:

> If I had the magic wand and could wave and get an instant result, I would create in white folk an attitude that would allow them to disregard considerations of race when it came to making judgments about us. I think Martin Luther

> King's dream is very, very apropos. I'd like to see this society in which the worth of an individual is measured in terms of the content of the mind and the character, as opposed to the color of the skin.

Our respondents show how discrimination in business and experiences with white racism shape their approach not only to business but also to life itself. For example, we see a certain resignation to the inevitability of discrimination in such comments as, "It's not going to happen now" and "Maybe after the year 2000 we'll see a different climate." One glimpses in the interviews humiliation, frustration, and anger. A black businessperson pays a heavy psychological price in order to gain access to the white world. One entrepreneur spoke of the emotional strain:

> You always have to watch and really think and really concentrate about what you're saying, so that you're not emotional, because you know black people are "so emotional" and "so defensive," and so you have to always be cognizant of that. And that's a mental strain and a mental drain on you.

Asked what she does to keep a balance, she replied with some laughter:

> I come in here and scream! I talk to my friends. I come in here and talk to my assistant. She's even seen me cry because I'm so angry 'til I am to the point of violence. But I know that I have to really, really be cognizant of what I'm doing, because why go to jail for nothing? . . . So I just call my friends and get it off my chest with them, because they understand.

Particular incidents of discrimination not only have a devastating impact on African Americans but also perpetuate institutionalized racism. The recounted incidents and others alluded to give us a picture of the web of discrimination faced by black businesspeople in traditionally white business sites. The market does not work fairly or freely with ole-boy or buddy-buddy networks at its heart. Frequently the white discriminators in these accounts are not the stereotyped blue-collar bigots but rather middle-class whites. Significantly, Walter Rodney considers the notion that "free enterprise," individualism, and great effort will pay off handsomely for African Americans to be destructive: "It is a common myth within capitalist thought that the individual through drive and hard work can become a capitalist. The acquisition of wealth is not through hard work alone, or the Africans working as slaves in America and the West Indies would have been the wealthiest group in the world."[42]

Over a lifetime of facing racial discrimination in America, an African American comes to see that the promise of truly equal opportunity is a "white lie," a betrayal that the professor with his own consulting business feels keenly:

> I feel angry. I feel betrayed. Sometimes I feel very cynical. Most of the time I feel that I live in a country where I'm still not respected as a person. I lived at a time when I was told that if I got a good education, did all the right things, that I could be anything I wanted to be. I got a good education. I did all the right things, but even today I run into situations where my opportunity structure is limited because I am black. So, I found that all along that no matter what I did, no matter how hard I tried, limitations were placed on me strictly because of the color of my skin.

Chapter Six

Seeking a Good Home and Neighborhood

At the top of the list of material goods promised by the American dream to those who get a good education and work hard is a decent apartment or house in a pleasant neighborhood. Like middle-class whites, middle-class African Americans greatly value this promise. Speaking of conversations with her husband, a teacher articulated this dream: "I would like to have my dream home in the next year, and I'm serious. Because no matter what you do, no matter how much money you make, you're always going to owe somebody. So I said, why not go ahead and get our dream home now?" A house is a visible manifestation of accomplishments, one's standing in society, even one's character. For homeowners the house is also a sign of equity, of wealth that can be passed to subsequent generations. Yet racial discrimination has historically played a major role in keeping most African Americans from building up much housing wealth. Today they are still less likely to be homeowners than whites; according to the U.S. Census Bureau just 43 percent of black Americans own their homes, compared with 67 percent of whites.[1]

Home as a Place of Refuge

To black families, home represents one of the few anchors available to them in an often hostile white-dominated world. Home is for African Americans the one place that is theirs to control and that can give them refuge from racial maltreatment in the outside world. Putting the point succinctly, a corporate executive said: "The only place it probably doesn't affect me, I guess, is in my home; specifically, actually, in the interior portions of my home. But outside one's home, it always affects me." A manager at a major electronics firm commented, "Well, I think you really kind of lead dual lives," one at home among black people and one at work among white people. And a substance abuse counsellor explained that home means support: "Because I can come home and talk about the situations. That's one thing that I have in my favor, because my family, they are understanding, and if anything like this should happen, I can come home and talk about it and get it resolved." Numerous respondents criticized the air of unreality in the portrayal of the lives of black middle-class families on television. The nearly perfect family on the Bill Cosby Show, for example, does not face racism from its white neighbors or coworkers. In this regard the Cosby show is mythological, because it shows neither the racism that middle-class blacks ordinarily experience nor the role of the family in helping individual family members cope.

Even white friends are rarely able to relate to blacks in the intimate way that family and black friends can, as an airline manager suggested:

> So I can't discuss it with white friends, and I do have white friends, but they're just, I mean, like I said, in the industry,

> the neighborhood, the situations that I'm in, there just aren't that many black people. So my husband and my family become the stabilizing force for bouncing off situations.

A student at a mostly white university described retreating to home regularly during his freshman year because of his difficulty dealing with the culture of his university:

> Everything in the environment here [causes stress]. Everything. Every single thing—the parties, the music, the teachers, the classroom discussions, the meals, the new prejudices, the new stereotypes. . . . I think part of the reason I went home every weekend in [my] freshman year is so I wouldn't have to listen to [white students'] music that I didn't necessarily want to listen to, blasting all Saturday night, all Sunday night.

Home is the place where one can get support in an intimate way to deal with problems beyond the home. While we will return to this matter in detail in the next chapter, two brief comments will underscore the valuable functions performed by the black home. A professor in an eastern city pointed out how home serves him as a place to laugh at insults:

> For my own self, I think one copes, I cope with the experience of the work world by having a very secure, good family life and things that, you know, when you can come home and laugh at many of the things that are very outrageous and insulting [laughs], but you can come home and laugh about it, in a sense, because you know very well that it's not true.

The black home can be the one place where one does not have to be on guard, as a business manager at a mostly white university described: "The [white] smiles and so forth, understanding what those mean, and so therefore my intent is I've got to be suspicious and that's just survival. So I live in a world of survival in that sense, in terms of what it is to be black. The place where I don't have to justify, in a sense, and can let down that guard is, yes, it's at home and with my family."

Segregated Housing: U.S. Laws and White Attitudes

Without the foundation of home and family there would be no black middle class. In the search for a decent house and a safe, well-equipped middle-class neighborhood in which to build home-castles, the black middle class faces the major dilemma of whether or not to venture into white residential areas. From the late-nineteenth century to the last third of the twentieth century, municipal ordinances, state laws, private deed restrictions, and brute force were used to keep African Americans out of most white communities, North and South. From the 1930s to the 1960s Federal Housing Administration (FHA) policies reinforced or increased racial segregation by effectively restricting FHA housing loans to segregated areas and by locating public housing for African Americans in historically black communities. Only in the late 1960s was federal protection from blatant housing discrimination officially extended to most black Americans. Although government-backed housing segregation has not been the rule for more than two decades, the United States still remains a very segregated society. One 1989 report on the twenty-five largest cities noted very high levels of residential segregation in 1980, with only a modest 7 percent decline in the continuing high levels of segregation over the civil rights era between 1950 and 1980.[2] And a recent study by Douglas S. Massey and Nancy A. Denton of housing segregation in the thirty northern and southern metropolitan areas with the largest black communities found little change in the massive patterns of residential segregation since 1980. The very small declines in their indices of housing segregation for 1980 to 1990 were even less than for 1970 to 1980. As of 1990 the indices indicated that, on the average, 67 percent of the black residents of southern cities and 78 percent of the black residents of northern cities would have to move from their present neighborhoods (census tracts) in order for there to be a completely desegregated housing pattern.[3]

This continuing segregation is by no means voluntary on the part of African Americans, for their housing choices are constrained immediately or indirectly by white attitudes and actions. Opinion surveys show that today many white Americans believe housing discrimination by white homeowners should be government-sanctioned. In a 1990 NORC opinion survey nearly four whites in ten said they favored a law giving a white homeowner the right *not* to sell a house to a black person over a law prohibiting such discrimination.[4] And a substantial majority of whites have a negative reaction to the presence of blacks as neighbors when the numbers increase beyond token levels to a significant proportion. In a 1976 Detroit study only one in six whites said they had a favorable reaction to the idea of moving to a neighborhood that was half white and half black. Most black Americans, in contrast, prefer this type of blended neighborhood. The Detroit study found blacks' ideal choice was an area 55 percent white and 45 percent black.[5] This desire for a mixed neighborhood still seems to be the ideal for many black Americans. With this desire for integrated housing, and with the proportion of whites with negative views of black neighbors so high, there is a likelihood that many black families will encounter discrimination when seeking to buy or rent a home.

Several housing audit studies show that racial discrimination by white landlords, homeowners, and real estate agents is a primary cause of residential segregation. Over the last two decades studies in dozens of metropolitan areas have sent a black and a white auditor of similar socioeconomic backgrounds to white real estate agents selling homes and to white agents renting apartments. Whites were more likely to be shown or told about more housing units than blacks. In a recent federal survey involving 3,800 test audits in twenty-five metropolitan areas, black renters faced some type of discriminatory treatment about half the time, while black homeseekers faced discriminatory treatment 59 percent of the time. Discrimination was found in discrepancies in information about housing availability and during the transaction with the seller or agent.[6]

A 1989 ABC/*Washington Post* opinion poll found that half the black respondents felt there was serious discrimination against blacks in getting decent housing; the proportion had increased a little since a similar 1986 survey. Also, in that earlier survey 26 percent of the black respondents reported personally having experienced racial discrimination in getting decent housing.[7] This latter percentage seems low; the proportion reporting discrimination might have been higher if more specific questions about the finding and financing of housing had been asked. In addition, survey data for middle-class black homeseekers have not been reported separately. Because middle-class black families often seek housing outside of traditionally black communities, they may be the most likely to face housing discrimination. In a 1990 NORC national opinion survey 46 percent of all black respondents felt there was housing discrimination, while among the most educated respondents the proportion climbed to nearly three quarters.[8]

Renters: Seeking and Securing Housing

In cities or suburbs blacks are less likely to own their homes than whites are, because of historical and contemporary patterns of discrimination in employment, income, wealth, and housing.[9] Many black Americans in their search for houses or apartments to rent report having been mistaken for whites over the phone, then rejected in person, such as this minister in an eastern city: "Now, at the present location that we're living at, we've had to deal with whites, and we've faced discrimination. At first, they didn't realize that we were black in applying for the housing. And when my wife was persistent, she found out on the phone that they had vacancies. And then when we got there, we found out there were no vacancies. But in our persistence, we found out that there was an opening for us that wasn't there before." Good housing opportunities may appear in the search and be promised over the phone but then evaporate suddenly. Aware of the problem of accepting black renters over the phone, some savvy whites may listen carefully to the accent of the potential renter, as in this example given by a high school teacher in a northern city:

> I had a friend who was an LPN. And she wanted an apartment, and she saw one in the paper. She called, and they told her that the apartment was rented. And she called me on the phone and said, "I'd like for you to call them." I said, "Why?" And she said, "Because you sound like a white person." And I called, and the apartment was still unrented. So . . . this hasn't been a hundred years ago. This is like in the last two or three years that this happened.

The intentional use of a "white-sounding" voice, either one's own or a friend's, is one painful strategy middle-class black homeseekers have developed to get around some discrimination.

A HUD researcher commented recently on the great variety of strategies white landlords use to exclude blacks: "HUD gets plenty of instances in which the person shows up after a phone call and the agent suddenly has to leave; doesn't open the door; says the apartment was just taken; slams the door in their face; tells them they'd be unhappy there; unleashes the dog."[10] White homeowners who are landlords play a role in this exclusionary behavior, as in this case reported by university administrator in a northern city: "But I think one incident that made an impression on me was a woman [who] answered the door when I came to look at a house. This was to rent. And she just laughed, just started laughing when she saw my black face, and closed the door in my face. And didn't even respond."

Since the 1950s, housing discrimination laws have had an effect on many white landlords; the laws have made the old forms of outright exclusion on racial grounds less likely. Yet there are many ways to reject a black renter other than by slamming the door. One runaround strategy was described by a public administrator in an eastern city: "I remember specifically, I would go by this apartment building a lot of times. There was one apartment in particular that I really wanted to live in [in] this apartment building, and I applied. They said there were no vacancies. And I asked them, please, put me on the waiting list." Continuing with the account, she laughed and said, "And it's been over five years, and they've not called me yet, and I know people have moved out of that building!"

A drug abuse counselor discussed a creative excuse for exclusion:

> Recently we went to rent a house, and probably they weren't expecting us [to be black] after they spoke to us on the phone. . . . when we got there and we saw the place, they had no recourse or anything like that to say that they couldn't rent us a place. She made a promise that she was going to rent us a place and everything. And then when she did the financial check, she came back with an excuse, like "Well, you know, people [like you] normally move, and we want someone who is going to be staying there for a period of time."

When racial characteristics cannot be used overtly as grounds for exclusion, contemporary discriminators may attempt to use income and other class characteristics thought to be associated with racial group, a point illustrated by the experience of an engineer in a southwestern metropolis:

> When I talked to the lady, she said, "Oh yes, come on in and we can approve your application while you're here," and all that. And then when I got there, it was going to take two days to approve. And they checked everything out thoroughly and the guy who referenced me to the apartment was a white guy. And he got his approved in one day. And he's saying, "Oh, why don't you go there, and it doesn't take any time to get it approved." They went so far as to call my job. And one of the people who works for me answered the phone, and the lady from the apartment complex said, "Is it conceivable that he makes X amount of dollars a month?" I mean, that's not something—first of all, if you want to know, call personnel or ask me, but you don't ask somebody who works for me. Well I know they have to have verification of the stuff that you put on your application, but . . . I think that if they want to know bad enough they'd say, by the way, bring in a copy of one of your pay statements.

Intensive background checks can be used to discourage or stall black applicants. Not only was the respondent forced to endure a runaround once color became salient, but he had to go through the degradation of a check with one of his workplace subordinates. Such instances of housing discrimination provide clear indications not only of the energy cost to the victims but also of the processual character of some present-day discrimination.

Another barrier for black renters is quotas that allow only a certain number of minority renters to move into a complex. An accountant described what it was like when she lived in New York City:

> There're certain apartment buildings that you are denied

> living there strictly because of your color. . . . There was one particular incident, and it ended up being in the paper. And it wasn't because of me, but I had applied during that same time. There was a huge apartment complex; it's like a city within a complex. They had their own stores, their own schools, everything is right there within walking distance. And they had a quota. The quota was 25 percent minorities, period, which included blacks, Hispanics, whatever. There was a big issue because there were qualified black people that applied and they were denied housing strictly because the management said that they had their quota. . . . And a lot of people got a little angry because they did apply and they couldn't get in and they met all the requirements. And it came out that the housing, the people, management said that they were not going to put any more blacks in there or other minorities because they had met their quota as far as—I assume there was a minority requirement—that they had to have in order to continue to get whatever [government] money they were getting.

This privately owned complex had received federal housing subsidies and had set up a quota (actually closer to 40 percent) in order to limit the proportion of minorities. Such "integration maintenance" programs use race-conscious quotas to maintain "balance," because the white demand for integrated housing is usually weak, and small changes in the proportion of minority residents can trigger white flight or keep whites from moving in. Yet much of the human cost of this type of managed housing integration is paid for by potential minority renters, who must again adapt to the racial prejudices of whites. In most cases the effect is to keep black residents as the statistical minority in the complex and to create very long waiting lists for black families seeking such housing. Meanwhile, white waiting lists tend to be short. Some white developers and landlords have learned to use federal housing loan and development programs to their advantage, knowing such programs can provide essential capital, and perhaps expecting little surveillance by federal authorities to enforce housing justice.[11] In this case they miscalculated, for the Department of Justice did sue the management for racial discrimination.

Having overcome barriers in the search for rental housing, a black person who moves into a substantially white complex may find that the facilities provided are inferior, as a flight attendant in a western metropolis discovered:

> I guess one funny thing happened when I took an apartment in a well known area of California, and I did the application for the apartment over the telephone. And when I went in to sign the lease, the owner in fact emphasized the fact that I did the application over the telephone. And I distinctly felt as though they didn't know I was black. And then when I showed up and I was black, he just came right out and said, "Oh, you did the interview over the phone." I think he said it without really thinking about what he was even implying when he said it. . . . At that point, there was really nothing he could do, because it had been approved. [So, was it your feeling that if he had known you were black there might have been a problem?] Oh, for sure, because of the way he said it. . . . After I got moved into this particular apartment, I wanted to get a parking space there. And they told me that my apartment didn't come with a parking space. But next door to me, a white guy lived there, and we had the same exact apartment. In fact, he was paying a few dollars more than I was only because he moved into the building after I did, and his apartment came with a parking space. And when I asked the owners about it, they tried to tell me that his did and mine didn't. But my question was, but we have the same exact apartment, why

> does his, and why doesn't mine? And after some discussion, after about twenty minutes, I actually had to accuse the owners of discriminating, because I couldn't find any other reason why I couldn't have a parking space. The owner relented and did give me a parking space. So, I had to assume that there was no real reason why I didn't have one.

Not only did the respondent encounter a landlord who had apparently taken her to be white over the phone, but she had to struggle to get the same facilities as a white renter. Middle-class black renters can demand fair treatment, but the personal energy costs can be high. Some we interviewed suggested that they found discriminatory treatment to be so unbearable that they had moved out, or considered moving out, perhaps permitting a white landlord to say "Well, I rented it to them. I can't be responsible for whether they stayed or not."

Homeowners: Seeking and Securing Housing

The 1980s were the first decade since the Great Depression in which there was a decline in the proportion of U.S. homeowners. The reason: the increasing cost of houses relative to incomes. While home ownership is still central to the American dream, buying a house has often become more difficult. This situation has become especially serious for African Americans. Nonetheless, since the 1970s significant numbers of middle-class black families have sought the American dream of owning their own homes, often in predominantly or entirely white areas.

Denial of access is the most basic constraint facing black families seeking housing in formerly all-white areas. We cited earlier the federal study of U.S. metropolitan areas that found black homeseekers faced a better than 50–50 chance of encountering racial discrimination. Attempts to secure suburban housing can involve great expenditures of energy. In particular cases the attempts to exclude blacks can be complex and involve extended racial bargaining, as in this one described by a dentist in a southern city:

> My first encounter with discrimination in my present location ironically had to do with a very basic thing that most people look forward to, and that's their home. . . . That evening she [the white real estate agent] called me at home and said she thought she'd accidentally stumbled onto something that might interest me and would I be interested in looking? I said yes. She arranged to show me the home, which turned out to be the first one that I bought here. It was a home owned by a major insurance company executive who had been transferred to another city 100 miles away. . . . We contacted the owner by phone. She conveyed an offer; he countered. I countered; he accepted it. I signed the papers; we sent them to him. We never got them back. The real estate owner that she [our salesperson] worked for was totally uncooperative with assisting her. Days went by; weeks went by; over a month went by. At this particular time, every brokerage house in town was anxious to show this house. The young lady, who happened to be white, who showed me that home went out of town; she took the keys to the home. She told her children not to give word that she was home. She did everything humanly possible to keep from letting that house be shown again. She confronted the owner of the real estate company; he refused to help her. He refused to look to find out why we had not gotten the papers back. He simply stated [that] without two signatures, the home was up for grabs. Well, she knew at that interest rate, and having known what the owner [now

> in another city] accepted, that house would be sold to someone else out from under me in a matter of seconds. And she wanted to keep her word.
>
> It was only after about five, six weeks I said to her: "Don't bother to hide the key any more. Put it back in the office. I'll handle it." And it was at that time that I formulated a letter, and I sent a copy of it to the president of that insurance company, explaining what had happened and stating that we could not understand why there was a delay. I also made note that I sent a copy of that letter to the general secretary of the NAACP. My point in sending a copy of the letter and making note on the president's letter of this fact was not anything that was very casual or accidental. I did it deliberately. Within 24 hours I got a call from the general counsel of that insurance company. He made one statement and he was very emphatic. He said, "Doctor, if any of our executives gave you their word that they accepted the offer on your house, whether it was written or whether it was his word, he has no job if he goes back on it. So don't worry; the house is yours."

Several white actors, including a homeowner and the owner of a real estate firm, play a major role in this mini-drama. We see a white real estate agent denying herself a quick commission for the sake of principle, a sign of some change from the recent past. Yet she was blocked by other whites, including her own boss. The dentist reacted forthrightly to the runaround and attempted exclusion by writing a measured letter to the president of the insurance company, with a copy to a civil rights organization known for litigation victories. Significantly, this man did not make direct use of fair housing laws or government enforcement agencies. Judging from our interviews, black homebuyers rarely consider the possibility of using government enforcement agencies to fight housing discrimination, perhaps because of a distrust of the generally weak fair housing agencies at all government levels and a sense of futility because racial discrimination in housing is so widespread.

Sometimes a group of whites may work together to exclude black residents, as the president of a community credit fund in an eastern city recounted: "When we first came to the neighborhood, the people were very upset, because the neighborhood association wanted to sell all of the homes and therefore control who came in. We happened to make friends with a black family who was already there, and that's when we came in. The gentleman who ran for governor, his wife led the neighborhood association that really did not want blacks in." Here it was members of the local elite rather than working-class whites who led the effort to exclude blacks. The black family's assertive action, facilitated by a family already there, was successful, which signals some changes from the recent past of rigid housing segregation.

In the United States the real estate industry is about as segregated as residential housing.[12] White real estate brokers are often linked together in informal networks through which they circulate information about houses for sale and make homebuyer referrals. Homes-for-sale information is usually printed in multiple listing services' books, listings that may only encompass mostly white suburban areas and certain city areas. Distribution of these lists tends to be limited to the white real estate brokers who have listed houses in such areas. This type of marketing of housing restricts the information that is available to black homeseekers currently living in segregated areas, since real estate brokers serving black areas are often not well integrated into the white real estate networks.[13] As a result, the searches of black homebuyers for housing are usually less efficient than for comparable whites.

A university administrator in a northern city reported that her experiences trying to rent a place were so unpleasant that she turned to buying. Here she discussed the reaction of a white woman who was apparently a real estate agent:

> So I worked two jobs so that I'd be able to buy a house, and saved the money from the second job to be able to buy the house with, because it took all the money from the first job just to live, because I have a large family. And I had a woman tell me on the phone that I would like the neighborhood because there were no blacks in it. And I said, "Well, my dear, you're in for a big surprise, because if I buy it, there will be a black there then, because I am now, I am a black." And she gasped, you know, and just hung the phone up.

White realtors and their agents use several mechanisms to perpetuate racial mapping. The procedure whereby black and other minority homebuyers are systematically shown neighborhoods different from those of their white counterparts is often called *steering*. A 1991 federal study of housing discrimination found the steering of minority homebuyers in a fifth of the cases where white and minority auditors were shown housing or where addresses were recommended.[14] With an angry tone to his reply, the director of a drug abuse program in a midwestern city commented on several recent instances of poor treatment:

> Have I ever been discriminated [against] in housing? Oh, yes! . . . We saw [a house] in the newspaper, called the girl up and told her we wanted to look at this house. We got out of the car and we could see the lady sitting at the table, the owner of the home, as we got out of the driveway. And I actually saw the expression on her face change as she saw this young black couple walking up the driveway. I guess she figured we couldn't afford a house, or else she didn't want to give us one in this neighborhood.
>
> The area I live in is called Stonebridge, which is predom-

> inantly white. Right across the street is Stonebridge Heights, which is 85 percent black, and across the street from there is Stonewoods, which is 99 percent black. So after [the agent] got through showing us this one house, she drove all the way to the other side into Stonebridge Heights to show us another house. The house that I bought eventually was right around the corner from the original house we saw, which is a 99 percent white neighborhood. We're the only blacks in the neighborhood, on the corner. And the other thing that made me realize that it was discrimination—how many of you have ever seen a real estate agent who has never called back a prospective buyer? This woman *never* called us back, never wanted to know if we were still looking or interested. And so, yeah, I have experienced it. It pissed me off.

The housing of this particular city is substantially segregated along racial lines, much like the rigidly segregated housing of an earlier era. Unlike earlier black homebuyers, however, this man had the ability to thwart the attempted steering by a white salesperson. Reviewing his experience, he added this comment:

> As far as being discriminated [against], I mean, they're going to discriminate against us till we leave here! And I don't let other folks' problems become mine, as far as discrimination is concerned. That's their problem, you know; they got more of a problem with me being black than I got with being black!

Our respondents use their middle-class resources to fight mistreatment by homeowners and real estate agents. A financial analyst at a Fortune 500 company reported:

> I hired a realtor to show me around. And I gave her the requirements I was looking for—the price range, the type of house, and so forth. And at one point in time she steered

> me toward a certain section of town which made me feel a little uneasy. And henceforth I had a new realtor within a day or two.

This professional's ability to find a cooperative white agent again marks a significant change from the 1950s and 1960s when few such agents could be found in any city in the nation.[15] Our respondents mentioned a variety of innovative coping tactics. Replying to a question about discrimination in real estate, a teacher replied in an exasperated tone:

> Oh! Geez! Yes! I think that's been our problem here in this city. And we've been tempted to get a white friend to—the house that we love—to be the face for us. You know, bargains we've heard of . . . that work for other people, they don't work for us. And I think it's simply because of the neighborhoods that we're looking in. . . . And I think a lot of discrimination goes on as far as housing here in this city.

Even when a sale is well underway, racial barriers may be erected. A manager at a large corporation explained how he foiled an attempt to discriminate against him during the closing process:

> We found a house that we wanted. The [white] people, for whatever reason, assumed that upon the closing of the house, they were going to make us aware of some things that they hadn't before, [that] we would not be able to financially follow suit with the house that we wanted. But I think that it was probably because some of the neighbors had indicated that they had not had any blacks in the neighborhood, and they figured out some way of not allowing this particular family into the neighborhood. So when the person presented this [money] figure to us, they kind of indicated, "Well, we know you put down your earnest money and you put down too much earnest money. This

> will probably be a lesson to you that, don't put down a bunch of earnest money. . . . So we listened, and [I said] "Well, you haven't asked us if we could meet that financial obligation." And I wrote a check for the amount, and the person was just kind of flabbergasted. I found out later from some neighbors that a certain influential neighbor had put up this particular company to figure out some way of not allowing us to buy the house.

The employment of black agents in formerly all-white real estate firms marks a significant change from the era of legal segregation. While black agents in white firms may feel great pressure to cooperate in steering and otherwise discriminate against black homeseekers—indeed, their jobs may be on the line—they may still be a welcome source of additional information. A newspaper publisher recounted her experience with a white realtor and a black realtor in the same firm:

> From a white realtor, one time when I was looking for a house I had asked about certain properties that I was interested in seeing, and he told me that all of them were sold. And he showed me another section in a black area where he thought I should be, I assume. And I proceeded to call back to his same agency and ask if there was a black salesperson. And a black salesperson came on, and I asked about the other houses. And the other houses were not gone.

Clearly, black real estate agents selling in a white housing world face difficult problems, as an administrator at an eastern law school who had previously sold real estate described:

> There have been times when I used to sell real estate that I know that the other realtor will not want to give me a key to show the house because he thinks that the client that I'm showing the house to is black. And that happened about

> four years ago, where the house was in an exclusive white area. The other broker thought that my clients were black, but as it turned out, both of my clients were white, and more than that, my client's father knew the broker. And when they discovered what was happening, that I wasn't getting the key so they could see the house, they wanted to buy this house, she just stopped. She said, "Stop right here at this phone booth in the middle of the street." And called her father. Her father called him. And immediately when I went back to the office, the key was available. That's the way it works. . . . Yeah, it was all based on their belief that I had a black client.

From the tone of the respondent's comments one can conclude that it was galling for him to see white clients use their own social networks to secure easy access to a house—a result underscoring the blatancy and the cumulative character of some housing discrimination.

Interestingly, a few respondents suggested that housing discrimination often took the form of "green discrimination" and that income, not skin color, was what mattered. A university administrator when asked whether he had recently faced housing discrimination answered, "Not really. And you know why? It's that thing I talked about before. If I were making 30 or 40 or 50,000 dollars a year less, then my answer would inevitably be 'yes.' But this is a capitalist society. And I make lot of money and so, therefore, my color does not mean near as much as the color of my money!" Whites with prejudices may be swayed by money. An administrator at a western university made a similar comment.

> I know my way around. I don't rent, I don't have a landlord. I pay a mortgage company. The dollar bill counts for a lot. They don't care. If you've got the bucks, you can live almost anywhere. And so, I live in a predominantly white neighborhood, I don't live in the ghetto by choice. So, find-

> ing my house was easy. The realtor that helped us get it—I lucked upon somebody that was real nice.

The final comment does suggest that luck as well as money enabled him to avoid discrimination in this particular case.

It was a corporate manager in an eastern city who suggested the term "green discrimination" for the limitations imposed by income:

> I purchased a home some ten years ago. And it was in a redeveloping area. In fact, I moved from a predominantly white area to the inner city where the home had been renovated. It's like a carriage home. So, basically, it's a mixed neighborhood, more blacks, but we do have whites in the neighborhood. I haven't faced any discrimination. If any kind of discrimination, it's economically. If you don't have the money, you can't go or move certain places. You can't do certain things. That's what I find the biggest discriminatory factor nowadays. Not so much race, or color, but green discrimination.

Although he did not explain why, it is interesting that he moved from a white area to a racially mixed, gentrified area where he is now more comfortable. Here too we note an illustration of the effects of government subsidized redevelopment and gentrification on the housing opportunities of middle-class African Americans. Some areas like this have become scattered exceptions to the usual segregated urban housing patterns. Still, gentrifying areas with reasonable income and racial mixes account for only small portions of the housing market in U.S. cities.[16]

Racial Transition and Resegregation

Often linked to the practice of steering is the illegal practice of "blockbusting," the practice of actively working to shift an area from white to black. This is often done so that white real estate agencies can reap profits from panicky whites willing to sell for less to get out of an area. As a result, many middle-class black families find themselves living in residential areas, including suburbs, once substantially or entirely white, that have become mostly black. Responding to a question about his neighbors, a school principal explained: "Most of them are black. When I moved out here in '67, you couldn't see a black here until you saw my family or the next door people. . . . My son was the only black in the second grade. Now this place is predominantly black. That church was white; once the Methodist church was white. Now it is one of the biggest Methodist churches in the South and it's predominantly black." With a tone of resignation in his voice an engineer at a computer firm in the Southwest described how areas become reserved by realtors for blacks:

> [In] the suburb I moved into, I have seen a tendency of them gearing, seems like, only blacks to where we live. There are few whites. When I first moved in that neighborhood, there were only about twenty families living there; now it's about over a hundred families live in that neighborhood. It was about fifteen white families and five black families. As the neighborhood grew and the homes began to close out throughout that building [area], I saw a tendency of—it seemed that the realtors were only selling to black people. Seemed like they were trying to set us in one location. I mean, you saw it go from 80 percent white and 20 percent black, to now almost 80 percent black and 20 percent white now. And I often wondered, what happened? I began to see homes go up for sale of the few white families, and the neighborhood is excellent. Beautiful homes, lawns, things are kept up nice. And the neighborhood's only been there two and half years. But every white I

> would see, 95 percent of them, that "For Sale" sign put up from their home. Because it seemed like the realtors were only gearing black people toward that neighborhood, so the whites started moving out when the blacks started moving in.

The short time that it took this suburban area to go from predominantly white to mainly black probably signals cooperation among real estate agents to blockbust the area. The engineer observed that agents were selling there only to black households. This deliberate concentration of middle-class blacks in certain suburban areas, resulting in a hopscotch pattern of black-white segregation, contradicts the arguments of some scholars, such as William J. Wilson, about the black middle class moving out of black inner city communities and successfully integrating themselves into formerly all-white areas.[17] Middle class families sometimes bypass older central city areas, yet find themselves facing resegregation in a variety of suburban areas.

A manager at a computer firm in a large southern city noted the role of whites in shaping the population map in his city:

> I came here as a result of a move with a major computer firm. And this neighborhood—I was open to move into any neighborhood, and what ended up happening is that we were somewhat directed, or steered, out to this neighborhood. And when we moved out into this neighborhood, it was one third black and 60 percent white, with the remaining percentage being Hispanics. So at this point the neighborhood has become now probably 80 percent black and probably 15 percent white, and the remaining percentage Hispanics and Orientals. So the neighborhood has changed, and from what I understand—after we've moved here and several years later—this whole southwest quadrant was in fact designated to become black. But that was after the fact, and realtors being very sophisticated in how they han-

> dle these things. . . . I was totally at the mercy of the realtors when I came here. We came here in '71; I did not know anybody. And so we just went to realtors, and the realtors in turn just showed us homes and, ironically, most of the homes we were ever allowed to see were in the minority quadrant.

Typical of many blacks looking for a better home, this man is not fussy about the racial population mix. Yet he has little control over it. Housing patterns involve more than the preferences of individual homeowners, black or white. The reported shift in mapping from majority white to mostly minority in the respondent's immediate area, as well as in that quadrant of this major city, again shows that much discrimination is not spontaneous but rather represents the policy of many in the real estate establishment to concentrate black families in certain residential sectors.

A law professor at a southern university commented on local segregation:

> Right around this campus, there's one community that's predominantly white, has been for years. And the major realtors in the area take great pride in discriminating against black folks. It's breaking down just a little bit just now. Again, I've been here ten years. I remember one of my colleagues was looking for a house, and he came to relay this story because this realtor was showing him houses. And this realtor proudly told him how he had kept blacks out of there for a number of years. Proudly. Told him because he was white, and he didn't think he'd be offended. . . . I live in a nice neighborhood. It's near here, predominantly black. And I've had colleagues come who wouldn't even look in my area. I've had other people look for places. And then I would say, "Well, look, we've got some houses for sale over there near me." And I had one say to me, "Any white peo-

> ple live over there?" Now look, that's a quote. He didn't say, "Any other professors?" He didn't say, "Any middle class folk?" He didn't say anything like that. He said, "Any white people?" And not, not, not "educated people?" No! Just "any white people" is what he said. It's not a joke. It was a serious question. But it spoke volumes, you know. . . . I didn't make a big deal out of it at the time; I haven't since.

Here one of the respondent's white colleagues informed him of intentional steering, while another asked crudely about the racial composition of a neighborhood. Revealing here is the way in which some whites, in this case the real estate agent, are willing to talk about discrimination with other whites in what they believe to be complicity and mutual understanding. It is significant too that this black lawyer has not taken legal action against the realtors' discrimination.

Over the course of U.S. history new groups moving into cities or suburban areas in significant numbers have seen the racial or ethnic groups already there move out, either gradually or suddenly. However, some city neighborhoods undergoing residential succession can remain significantly diverse for some period of time. Some of our interviews suggest that the whites likely to remain in such areas often may not be a representative sample of the white population. A vice president at an East Coast bank commented on the mix in her neighborhood:

> Well, now it's about half and half. When I first lived there ten years ago, it was predominantly white. It's older Jewish type of families that live there, but now it's about half and half. [And during that time, how were you treated by your white neighbors?] Really very friendly. I didn't really have a lot of problems. They really stay to themselves. They would speak, "Hi, how you doing?" And that was it. They didn't make me feel they didn't want me in the neighborhood.

A few respondents mentioned that their mixed neighborhoods included Jewish neighbors. A self-employed attorney in a southern city described his neighborhood as "a little U.N.": "We've got Asians and Indians and whites and blacks. But how is my relationship with my neighbors? It's been good." Some racially integrated communities develop a certain stability, at least for a time, as a black professor observed of the neighborhood in a western city: "This neighborhood that I'm in is somewhat mixed. And it's not, I guess, totally typical, because in many, many cases neighborhoods tend to, once they start to being mixed, they tend to resegregate. And once one group moves in, other groups start to moving out; and then so different sections tend to . . . resegregate it sometimes. But in this particular case, I think there's not much of a problem because the balance is reasonable." It is clear in the interview that the respondent's preference is for a racially mixed neighborhood. Not much research has been done in recent years on what keeps neighborhoods like this from resegregating; the commitment of black and white residents to maintaining a balance seems crucial. A few historically white residential areas have tried a type of "managed integration" similar to that we noted for a rental housing complex earlier in the chapter. Suburban areas like Shaker Heights, Ohio and Oak Park, Illinois have made aggressive attempts to keep white homeowners from fleeing; white community leaders help white buyers get special loans, provide insurance to protect the value of white property, prohibit "For Sale" signs in front yards, and encourage realtors to steer potential white buyers into the area. While such solutions can maintain desegregation, they are in effect bribing whites to live in integrated neighborhoods and, as Massey and Denton have argued, "ultimately they operate by restricting black residential choice and violating the letter of the Fair Housing Act."[18] Again we see that much of the burden of desegregating U.S. residential communities has been placed on the backs of African American families.

Discrimination by Lenders

White-controlled banks have a long history of discriminating against African Americans. For decades the federal government intentionally fostered racial discrimination in lending. The Federal Housing Administration's manual discouraged desegregation of housing in its stipulation that loans would not be approved if made in racially mixed areas. Title VIII of the 1968 Civil Rights Act and the Equal Credit Opportunity Act prohibited discrimination in lending. By the 1970s federal housing regulations had eliminated the most blatant exclusionary discrimination in lending.[19] In Senate hearings in the early 1990s lending regulators reported that there was little evidence of widespread overt discrimination in lending and that there were few discrimination complaints filed against lenders.[20] Yet serious questions about differential treatment in lending remain. A 1989 report of the federal Office of Thrift Supervision found that, nationwide, black mortgage loan applicants were rejected by savings and loan associations at twice the rate of white applicants.[21] A Federal Reserve Board study of more than six million mortgages made by 9,300 financial institutions in 1990 found that 34 percent of black applications were rejected, compared to only 14 of white applications.[22] And a report sponsored by the Federal Home Loan Mortgage Corporation found that lenders rely heavily on white realtors for referrals and are biased in favor of white areas in their loan-related assessments of residential stability.[23]

Today African Americans face not only exclusion from loans for homes and businesses, but also more subtle and covert discrimination in the form of poor information, getting the runaround, and added restrictions for loans. Providing a sense of the struggle, a professor of nursing in a southwestern city discussed her experience:

> One of the major sources of discrimination is in the housing market and in the mortgage financing aspect in trying to buy houses. Now, we're skilled home buyers, we're skilled lookers. And we recognize as African American people that any time we approach a mortgage company to buy anything that exceeds $60,000 in cost we're going to have a problem. And we're going to have a problem in the arena of a black moving into a white neighborhood, so to speak. Redlining is not uncommon in this city, just like it is in Atlanta and a lot of other cities that have upwardly mobile African American families. And that's one of the things that we have to deal with, and on a number of occasions in the process of purchasing six homes we've had to challenge that issue. . . . We were denied information about housing, the threat of denial of the mortgage, of [not] being able to purchase a particular home for various and sundry reasons, none of which had to do with our ability to pay the mortgage or our credit rating.

Commenting on her persistence with one bank, a manager in a social services agency in an eastern city highlighted some mortgage problems:

> My husband and I have owned our present home for the last thirteen years. . . . we live in a nontraditional area for blacks within the city. And we were discriminated against in getting a mortgage for our house. We were very much aware of that. That whole—well—the lending institution to which we went, where we have always dealt with our banking needs, was reluctant to give us a mortgage. And it was only through applying pressure, that it was given to us.

In practice, white bankers can decide on the basis of their subjective judgments where it is appropriate for a middle-class black family to live. A probation officer in a southern city described one of his encounters with a bank:

> I owned some property, an acre of land. It's in a predominantly, as a matter of fact, an all-black subdivision area of the city. And I wanted to build a $100,000–$150,000 house. In my opinion, it'd probably [be] valued at more. I went to three different banks—had to post $2500 in their loan processing—and each time they found some reason to deny me the loan. Basically what they were saying in essence is the type of house that I wanted to build couldn't be built in that area for that particular price. And I know—because I've done contracting before and I have been a contractor—so I know what the costs were going to be. I had figured out all the costs, plus added their 20 percent into it. And I know that for $120,000 I could have built that house. I only wanted $90,000 to borrow. Also I'm going to put $30,000 invested money into it. Plus I've got land there, so it was very well secured. So that pissed me off, and it upset me so much that I just went out and bought a house where the "establishment" says that you can apply. And they made the loan real easily. Of course, the house wasn't valued at quite as much. For the money I got a comparable house. But it's not what I want, because my lifetime ambition is to build this dream home. [Do you feel that if you'd been white it would've been different?] Certainly!

Because the house was to be built in an all-black subdivision, the white bankers denied the respondent a loan that probably would have been only 60 to 70 percent of the value of house and lot and thereby killed his housing dream. In making loans white-controlled banks and thrifts have considerable power to shape how, and whether, urban communities grow. Thus when they have decided to finance office towers in central cities, they have contributed to the growth of new administrative centers. When the white real estate elites decide to deny loans to black homeowners in certain areas, they reduce black housing options and help to configure city residential patterns according to their conceptions and interests.

After the Move: White Neighbors

Whether a black family owns or rents, the move into a traditionally white neighborhood typically begins a new phase in the struggle to create a safe and supportive family milieu. In such neighborhoods the white repertoire of negative responses can range from violence, to surveillance, to grudging accommodation. Whatever the white response, including acceptance, the dimension of race usually hovers in the background. One report by the Southern Poverty Law Center covering just two years (1985–1986) counted forty-five cases of move-in violence targeting minority Americans, the majority of these being African Americans.[24] In the 1990s cross burnings aimed at black families moving into white areas continue to occur in all regions of the country.[25] These areas have included DuPage County, Illinois; Pasco County, Florida; Marshall County, Ohio; Suffolk County, New York; Orange County, California; Vidor, Texas; Winter Garden and Orlando, Florida; St. Paul, Minnesota; Phoenix, Arizona; and Bellevelle, Illinois, to name just a few. In the early 1990s a dozen black families had crosses burned outside their homes in Dubuque, Iowa; the cross burnings were part of a broader protest by local whites against a small-scale minority-recruitment plan proposed by a local task force to increase the racial diversity of the city.[26] That such action could take place in a midwestern city with a black population of less than 1 percent suggests that racism is not necessarily generated by whites' contact with black Americans and that such white racism is probably omnipresent in the United States. Black families moving into white areas have been shot at, have had their windows broken, and have fled when their houses were firebombed. In our interviews a former secretary, now a hair stylist, recounted the experiences of a friend in a large midwestern city in the 1970s: "I had a girlfriend. When [she and her husband] bought in the same area that we were buying in, their house got fired on three times, you know, before they even got a chance to move in. Her husband had to sit there and sleep with a shotgun. And we are still talking about the 1970s in that city. So you knew, you knew your place." Since the 1970s this city has experienced a series of similar incidents. In such situations some black homeowners have fled, while others have responded by arming themselves and standing their ground.[27]

Several in our sample reported vandalism with overtones of personal violence. A newspaper publisher discussed her sister's experience in an industrial city in the South: "She had a new car, one of those little sports cars. I can't think of what it's called. They kept 'keying' her car, taking a key and running down, scraping the side of it. And she was the only—there are only about four or five blacks who live in this little exclusive complex in the city. Her car got keyed three times, and the insurance company canceled her. And she moved. Nobody else's car was getting keyed." Similarly, one of the black interviewers for our project, a graduate student who was living in a large city in New England in the early 1990s, reported that her car was vandalized in a residential area where there were no other black renters. Nearby cars belonging to whites were not damaged, but hers was dented and defaced several times by unknown vandals. In both cases the destruction of property and implied personal threat pressured the women to move out of the white areas.

Sometimes the opposition of whites, while not violent, is

openly hostile. After describing the hate stares he had encountered at a local restaurant, a manager at an electronics firm in the Southwest discussed his reaction to finding racist graffiti in his nearly all white neighborhood:

> [In] the same neighborhood, a half-block down the street, is a junior high school. And my wife and I, you know, we're middle-aged, forties, and we're getting a gut so we wanted to start walking. So they built a brand-new asphalt track at this high school. So we went over there one afternoon to walk. And as we walked around the track, we came on the far end of the track and there was this big brick wall and all across this wall were negative slurs: "Go home, nigger," "Jews die," the German swastika all over the place, "White power," "White supremacy." Now again, in a totally white neighborhood—and when I say totally I'm talking about the year I was there I saw *two* black families—totally white neighborhood and a few Asian, Indian, Arabic-descent families around, but again, white. Now why would we see that type of graffiti on a wall at a white school? Unless the parents had instilled that in those kids. Because those kids don't know negative [things about] blacks, because they don't even live with them, they don't go to school with them, they don't go to church with them. So that had to come from the parents, and that made me want to move. Not because I was running from it, it was that I didn't *have* to be in it, and I was putting myself in it for nothing.

In this case, the hate stares in restaurants and the threat suggested in the graffiti were so disturbing that the respondent and his family moved from the subdivision. Such racially motivated hate crimes, which include racist graffiti and similar vandalism targeting African Americans, have increased in the United States since the early 1980s. This incident did not occur in an innercity neighborhood, where such graffiti might be more likely, but rather in an exclusive white suburb with manicured lawns and high family incomes.

Most black middle-class families are not the objects of serious acts of violence, but do encounter racist reactions from some of their neighbors, ranging from excessive surveillance, to spreading misconceptions and rumors, to harassment, to white flight. A physician in an eastern city noted two different reactions of her current neighbors in a white suburb: "A lot of people became very threatened and moved. Then it was this, 'How can they afford this, or how can they do this.' Not realizing that I work sixteen hours a day, and so does my husband."

Many white homeowners, fearful about the crime and "status contamination" that they expect to come with their black neighbors, engage in some extra surveillance of the newcomers. A student counselor at a western university related her experience with unneighborly scrutiny:

> When we moved in there was a lot of glaring, and I guess when they see you do normal things, things that other people do, then it's almost like you see them breathe a sigh of relief. . . . I, one afternoon, had come in from work early. And this house [we were renting] had trees in front of it, and it was just annoying me that these leaves were always—the lawn was always covered with leaves. So, this particular day, I come in early from work, so I decide to take off my street shoes. And I put on some garden shoes and just grabbed a broom and decided I'm getting rid of these leaves right now. Only to have my neighbor come along, who is white, and say, "Gee you push that broom real swell!" [And you felt that he was making a comment?] He was making a racist comment, he was always making racist comments. He would say things like, "By god, where do you think all those colored folks get all those fine cars that they drive?"

Here the surveillance was reduced when the white neighbors were satisfied that the black renters did not fit the feared stereotypes. This woman noted that she had also felt under surveillance in an elite white suburb where she had rented previously: "But typically I find that the more affluent the neighborhood, the more suspiciously they look at you if you're a black person —trying to, in my mind, trying to figure out how you got there, where you get your money from, how can you afford to live there? In that elite suburb I was a student at the time, and not really working a full-time job, and I really felt that there was a lot of animosity towards me." An experience with white scrutiny contributes to the accumulating fund of knowledge blacks use to judge new encounters with whites.

As we have noted previously, the image of blacks, especially black men, as criminals is deeply imbedded in many white minds. One professor in a southwestern city was informative about her white neighbors' reactions:

> I think when we first moved in it was pretty clear that they were a little bit nervous. And once they saw that people weren't driving up to our house at midnight, you know, purchasing small packages of white powders, then they relaxed. And you could see them relax after a couple of months, and then they would wave, and occasionally they would come over and ask if they could take the persimmons off our tree, because I wasn't interested in doing anything with persimmons. And they loosened up quite a bit, but the first couple of months, you could sort of watch the way they behaved, the way they peered out of their curtains, the way they were careful to cut their grass and not look at our house, but looking at our house very closely when a car pulled up. They were very reassured when friends from the department came over, we knew white people, so we were probably OK. And they were reassured

> by the middle class appearance of our black friends. So, they saw that clearly these were not people who were going to be having shoot-ups in the front yard!

Such accounts suggest the price black families pay for white stereotyping and paranoia. But there are also costs to this behavior for the fearful whites. Working with a graduate student, the first author has done some research on an upper-middle-class, predominantly white suburb in a southeastern city into which two formerly poor black families moved after winning millions in a state lottery. The suburban subdivision of expensive houses experienced some turmoil and rumor mongering, and several white homeowners on the street with the lottery winners put their houses up for sale. Rumors circulated inside and outside the subdivision about alleged drug dealing in the houses of the black families. Many white real estate agents steered white clients away from the subdivision, and in an interview with the first author the white developer estimated that because of this steering he had lost a million dollars in home sales. In this case, as in the respondent's account above, there was no substance to the rumors of criminality on the part of the black families, but again the negative association of "blacks and drugs" had seized the minds of many of the white homeowners.

White suspicions of black men as dangerous result in more drastic defensive actions than glaring. A television anchorperson in an eastern city recounted an incident that occurred on the day of his interview:

> I've been in my townhome in this particular city; I bought it as probably one of the first owners in the complex I'm in . . . and I just recently returned to this city, moved back into my home here . . . And these people know who I am. Little [white] girl riding her bicycle in front of my house on the sidewalk. Well, her home is just a little ways off, can't be anymore than like thirty yards away. And I was coming

> out of my house to get into my car to come back to the station, and as the little girl was riding past me, I noticed that her mother ran out of the house in what appeared to be a fluster to keep an eye on her little girl who was in close proximity to me. Now here I am a black professional man. I'm a homeowner who's been in this complex longer than these people have, probably make ten times the amount of money that their household does. But at the same time the stereotyping of a little white girl in proximity of a black man, regardless of whether he's professional or not, whether he's wearing a suit or not, that's ignorance. Now if I had let something like that get me angry, I'd be miserable. I like to turn it around and think, if they want to be miserable worrying about the imaginary, then let them be miserable. I mean, the little girl knows who I am. I said, "Hi Sally, how you doing'?" And she says, "Hi Sam, see you on T.V. tonight!"

It appears that the conception of the menacing black man haunts the mind, not of a stranger, but of a neighbor. White imaginings about blacks not only prevent real neighborhood integration but also have a significant psychological impact on victim and perpetrator. While this newscaster tries not to let such episodes anger him, the intensity of his comments here and elsewhere in his interview signals the impossibility of that.

Many whites, including one's neighbors and local police officers, often assume that blacks in traditionally white neighborhoods are not residents. An optician in a southwestern city noted how a wealthy friend was treated by neighbors: "She was at the door. And she was approached—because of the type of house that she was in, it was about a $350,000 house—they said, 'Well, are Mr. and Mrs. so-and-so, are they here?' And she said, 'I'm that person.' And they said, 'Oh, well, we were just coming to meet our neighbor.' They had no idea that their [black] neighbor could afford, in this day and time, that price range." Similarly, a college counselor in a western city described her experience with occasional salespeople in an exclusive white suburb: "I live in a middle- to upper-class neighborhood. It's my home. Oftentimes, though, when I go to the door, for those salesmen who come around, they are shocked. They ask if 'the lady of the house' is at home."

Not all slights suffered by middle-class pioneers in white neighborhoods are so obvious. Many white slights seem to be linked to prejudices that are half-conscious or even unconscious. Recounting the mixed signals given off by his white neighbors, an engineer provided this account:

> Well, when I first moved in and to buy a house, our white neighbors came down and made us feel welcome. Brought cakes and cookies and brought sandwiches down when we were moving in. It was great! . . . [My wife's] white neighbor friend came down after everything was moved in and said . . . she was speaking to her husband—and I'll never forget this. . . . "Honey, do you see that? They have a brand new house, brand new furniture, and his wife doesn't even work!" And she was amazed. [How did you feel about that response?] I laughed. I said to myself, "Hmm, we're not supposed to have nice things. Or I'm not supposed to be able to put on a tie or a shirt and go to work, too? I'm not supposed to be able to manage and save like the other people." I just laughed at it because I knew that most of them think like that; we're not supposed to be able to live like them.

Perhaps the white neighbor did not recognize the implications of her comment; this type of ostensibly sociable reaction indicates the subliminal character of some white images of black men and women. Usually one thinks of home and neighborhood as places where one can relax and enjoy the fruits of his or her labors. For blacks coming to a home and neighborhood can mean not peace and enjoyment, but frustration, anger, and emotionally generated illnesses. Even within the confines of family space, frequently purchased at great cost, middle-class blacks may find themselves threatened with psychological, if not physical, harm.

In these historically white residential areas black children can bear a heavy burden. In our interviews we observed a range of white reactions to black children, from harassment to friendly acceptance. A college administrator recalled the behavior of one of his white neighbors: "Well, when they were smaller and they were out on the sidewalk riding their bicycles and throwing the ball and things like that, if they happened to kick the ball into his yard or something, he would get into a heated [rage]. He had an encounter with one of the fathers out there in the neighborhood about one of the kids, and this was a Hispanic family. And it only happens with the Hispanic and black kids."

Commonplace neighborhood tensions can be aggravated by an overlay of racial tensions. An attorney in an eastern city who had just moved in described her and her child's experience with their new white neighbors:

> They were like, "Maybe you should lock [the door] when the [black] neighbors are outside the door," like, "Oh god, what is she doing here?" I think for kids it's hard. I have a five-year-old. And my neighborhood is, I guess, sixty-forty white. And I noticed, like the second week we moved there, there are like five or six kids on the block. And he went over and spoke with them and played with them for awhile. [A] mother invited the five white kids into the house for Kool-aid. . . . He was not invited, which to me was just outright discrimination. There was no other basis for it. It's just unexplainable what black people go through, be they middle class or low class.

Exclusion can begin at an early age, as this five-year-old learned. The exclusion was initiated by a white adult, but in other cases the discrimination comes both from adults and children, as in the case of a high school principal and his son in a southern city:

> I found out he's a KKK'er, but as I told him, I was here before you came. . . . My son was on his bike out there. And [my neighbor] had three boys and a girl. And he [my son] was riding up and down the sidewalk. And the wife would be standing inside the screen porch watching them push him off the bike. I said: "I don't want to talk to you; I'll wait until your husband comes." They had a KKK meeting over there one day. They were barbecuing out there because the air conditioner broke down, so they had to go outside so they could have some kind of air and everything. So they didn't have on the sheets or anything; they just had their arm bands and things like that. So, I told them, I said: "The next time your kids put their hands on my child, I'm going to sue you."

He later added that the neighbor eventually "moved to the city where the Grand Wizard lives." This black man took strong action against adults who were organized racists, but again the price in terms of personal energy was high, for this principal knew that he was risking serious reprisals. Implicit too is the perspective on black rights we have seen in numerous accounts of black responses to maltreatment.

White children can also cause pain for black adults, as a flight attendant in a western city illustrated:

> Well, the neighborhood that my sister and my mother live in is, I guess you would say, 95 percent white. When my nephew and my sister first moved onto the block, the little children, the little white kids wouldn't play with him. . . . In fact, though, I was walking up the street one day, not

> long after they had moved there. And a little boy, he couldn't have been more than four years old, he was walking with his mother, and he turned around and looked at me, and he said, "What are you doing in this neighborhood?" And his mother turned around and she was appalled and she apologized to me. And I thought, well, where could a little boy of four years old even think of something like that if he hadn't heard it in his house.

There is more than white prejudice evident here. The mother did apologize for her son's behavior. The mixed, often unpredictable messages given off by whites in neighborhood interactions can confuse black residents and may signal the difficulties many white families have in casting off the legacy of racism. A dentist in the South described his son's experience at a local country club in an established white area: "Well, my son, as I told you, when he was a youngster about eight, he experienced probably his first direct confrontation with racism. I say that because *he* realized it was a racist situation. He was denied the opportunity to eat lunch during a tournament break in the country club that had invited him to play tennis, and that was something that he had never, ever experienced before. . . . He had never faced the overt name-calling." Discrimination is doubly damaging when there is no warning and when a youngster has never encountered flagrant discrimination before. The boy's experience was probably especially painful because he was expecting a pleasurable experience.

White neighbors' acceptance of black families varies from one neighborhood to the next. In many cases some type of *modus vivendi* is worked out. A minister in a southwestern suburb characterized his white neighbors as "kind, in their own way," going on to explain,

> I think they're as kind as their perceptions of blacks will allow them to be. I think many of them have an institu-

> tionalized racism; whether they want it or not, it's there, it seems. And when they see us coming, the stereotypes come with us. They try, they try, but they keep their distance. We've not been invited over for dinner. There was not a welcome committee or anything like that. But the same can be said of us. We didn't invite any white folk over, either. But my wife goes walking with this one woman who happens to be white sometimes in the evening, and they claim to have a pretty good relationship. But it's always in the back—and maybe I'm projecting, but it's always in the back of our minds. My wife is going walking, not just with a *woman*, but with a *white woman*. And I think that my wife knows she's just been walking with a white woman. It's there, at all times.

The consciousness of race hovers as a constant presence between blacks and whites, even in a friendly relationship.

Another black minister, this time in an eastern city, described the effects of residential integration more hopefully:

> I have white neighbors on each side of me where I live now, and I guess the initial reaction when we first moved in, was hostility, and "Uh, oh, more minorities in the neighborhood." But the one thing that I think is important, is when any neighbors, no matter what color they are, that we learn to live together, and work together. And there's a kind of bonding now with the neighbors, if they see anybody at our door, they want to find out if that's a strange person or whatever. Once you live together with people, they sort of learn to live together.

This man's view, perhaps because he is a minister, may be unduly optimistic, but time and familiarity can engender the possibility of bonding. The willingness to "learn to live together" marks a dramatic change from the recent American past. Some black and white residents in certain historically white neighborhoods like this one and the community of Shaker Heights mentioned earlier are beginning to renegotiate traditional black-white relations. However, it is possible the racial atmosphere described in this comment marks the positive limit of relations among black and white neighbors for the foreseeable future.

Black Residential Areas

Numerous popular and social science commentators on the state of black America have argued that middle-class families have been moving out of traditionally black residential areas and that huge numbers are now living in isolation from other black families.[28] This view of urban reality is exaggerated, for while housing segregation decreases for most American ethnic groups as education and income increases, it does not do so for black Americans. The national report on U.S. racial relations, *A Common Destiny*, cites data showing that blacks at every income level are to a substantial degree segregated from whites of similar income. In metropolitan areas affluent black families are about as residentially segregated from whites as those with lower incomes.[29]

The majority of middle-class black Americans live in substantially black or resegregating residential areas. Some choose black communities because of fear of whites; others, out of pride; and yet others, out of a concern for preserving black institutions. Expressing this sense of pride, a supervisor of vocational education programs described her neighborhood: "I've lived in a black neighborhood that's at least a hundred years old. And there's no discrimination in my neighborhood." A school board member in a northeastern city echoed this comment in her reply to a question asking if she had faced discrimination in housing: "No, only because the area where we live is predominantly African American." Living in a predominantly black neighborhood provides protection from the hostility and harassment faced by the middle-class families who venture into historically white residential areas. With a strong sense of territoriality, a dentist in an eastern city commented on his neighborhood: "Well, I don't have white neighbors. Well, this is funny. I got whites a block away. I live in the inner city, the Sugar Hill area, but I haven't been discriminated against. I'm there, and they know I'm there, I'm not going anywhere. We outnumber them, so I don't have to worry about any crosses being burned or anything like that!"

Those middle-class families who live in mostly black communities provide living contradictions to the argument that middle-class black Americans are abandoning traditional communities for white neighborhoods. Yet, the lives of middle-class black families, wherever they live, remain constrained by patterns of institutionalized discrimination. The anguish stemming from the choice between a traditional black community and a white residential area was poignantly described by a judge in the Southwest:

> I guess that one of the problems of being black [is that] I stay in a black neighborhood. And you know, staying in a black neighborhood, that's discrimination. Well, what I'm saying is, I think it's important being a black judge, being a black person, that I identify with the black community and that I reside in the black community. But with regard to services, not so much city and government services, but [with] regard to private services, in terms of grocery stores, department stores and that type of thing, that is not available in the black neighborhoods. So I feel shortchanged, and my family feels shortchanged because we're not able to do some things here, we have to ride across town to get these services. If I stayed in a white, middle-class neighborhood, all the services would be right there.

While this respondent affirms his support for the black community and its value to him as a psychological and political anchor, he acknowledges that his choice means some inferior services. There are other tradeoffs to living in black areas as well, as a university administrator stressed in describing her choice to live in a central area of a northern city:

> My friends that have done that and have moved into some areas of the suburbs are very uncomfortable, particularly if they have young black sons, you know, and the dating situation. And they're driving back and forth all the time. But I opted to live near the center of the city because I want to be near the things that I enjoy doing. The concerts, the films, I love to go to plays; the things that I like to do are in the city. Plus, I try to do business with blacks as much as possible and to be near. I like living among my own people, so I live in a mixed neighborhood. And I like that, and I'm respected because I'm a Ph.D.

Comparing her situation to that of friends, this administrator highlights a troubling feature of the landscape for black families moving into traditionally white districts. Even in relatively liberal white residential areas, interracial dating and marriage are probably anathema to most white parents.

Relatively poor services may be part of the price a middle-class family pays for staying in black communities. The dean of students at a black college in the South described the mistreatment and neglect of his neighborhood by white officials:

> You get discriminated not necessarily in that you are denied use of this house, but if you live in a black neighborhood, you'll also see that they will allow a salvage yard, as an example, right down the street to be organized in your neighborhood. Even though the neighbors protested, they didn't want this. And they [city officials] said, "Well we'll require

> them to put up a fence, a side-barring fence." And of course someone ran into the fence and knocked a hole in it, and it's been like that for five or six years now, where you can see through it. Plus the junk got piled up so high it came up over the top of the fence. So these are discriminatory acts that happen in your neighborhood. Also there is a code that requires vacant lots to be cleaned up and grass cut and underbrush cut, but somehow in the black neighborhoods these things don't get done. So you get discrimination in public services, public utilities and so forth, which also affects your housing. It affects the value of your property and things of that sort.

This respondent's difficulties with weak zoning enforcement are not unusual. Zoning processes often discriminate against African Americans. Research by sociologist Robert Bullard on what he calls "environmental racism" has shown that in many U.S. cities the location of dump sites, including toxic waste facilities, tends to be in or near minority residential areas.[30] We can see in this dean's comments how poor public services not only bring immediate costs but also reduce the value of property, making it difficult for black Americans to accumulate family wealth in real estate, a result with serious consequences for the mobility of future generations.

Conclusion

From a distance the racial ecology of U.S. cities is not unlike the geography of legal segregation, with most African Americans living in mostly black areas and most white Americans living in almost all-white areas. But up close, the patterns have changed in substantial ways. The racism of the late twentieth century is somewhat different from the racism of earlier decades, for at least a few black families live in some historically white areas in most cities in the United States. Equal housing opportunity has been a major goal of the civil rights movement, and state and federal laws now make housing discrimination illegal.

Contrasting the real experiences of African Americans with the ideal embodied in civil rights laws, one of our respondents, a professor at a western university, noted that "There is legislation. And there are policies that say it's one way, but in actuality it's totally different. Take any of the services—housing. They say there's no discrimination in housing. Yet, many blacks will show up to buy housing, or to rent an apartment, and they will be told it's filled." As we previously noted, middle-class black Americans rarely turn to government enforcement agencies to deal with discrimination. Although the 1968 Civil Rights Act banned most housing discrimination, it included weak enforcement provisions. The Department of Housing and Urban Development could negotiate settlements only in response to complaints; the Department of Justice could go to court only if the case showed a pattern of discrimination or was of "general importance." The 1988 amendments to the 1968 act added stiffer penalties and new enforcement mechanisms, and between 1989 and the early 1990s there was an increase in the number of housing discrimination complaints filed. In 1990 there were 7,664 discrimination complaints filed with the federal housing agency; about half have involved racial discrimination.[31] There have also been a few successful lawsuits brought under the 1988 act, especially in regard to rental housing.

Nonetheless, most whites who discriminate need have no fear of being punished. The enforcement of fair housing laws remains weak, and state and federal enforcement agencies are often handicapped by a lack of political will on the part of officials and legislators to provide adequate funding and to pursue substantial remedies for discrimination. As housing expert John Goering has commented, "So while the federal government now has a unique and powerful set of tools to attack housing discrimination it is less and less clear that there is any comparable responsibility or willingness to affirmatively expand this mandate."[32] The magnitude of the problem can be seen in the testimony of the HUD general counsel before a federal hearing, in which he estimated there are *more than two million cases* of housing discrimination each year in the United States. Federal agencies bring only a handful of "pattern and practice" suits each year, and the number of enforcement officers is very modest compared with the magnitude of the housing discrimination problem in the United States.[33]

Weak government enforcement puts the burden on black individuals. If African Americans wish to expend the energy and resources required, they can consider going to court as individuals. Since the 1968 housing act only a few hundred fair housing cases have been decided. Massey and Denton have assessed the current situation succinctly: "Whereas the processes that perpetuate segregation are pervasive and institutionalized, fair housing enforcement has been individual, sporadic, and confined to a small number of isolated cases."[34]

As a result, racial polarization is still fundamental to the residential layout of U.S. towns and cities. The consequences of this polarization are many, and we have observed in the comments of black men and women what happens when they try to break out of the traditional confines of housing segregation and seek homes in historically white areas. Some whites vehemently object to their presence, even fleeing as they move in, while white realtors and lenders have too much power over middle-class blacks' housing alternatives. Many black Americans seeking housing in traditionally white areas must struggle assertively to get better housing. They must often repeatedly call back, change realtors and banks, confront racist whites, or secure legal assistance. John Goering has noted that blacks' residential "choices reflect a complex overlay of fears of white rejection and hostility, desires for better residential services for themselves and their children, preferences for those like themselves, and dislike of deteriorating conditions in older, segregated neighborhoods."[35]

Washington Post journalist Joel Garreau has written of the suburban black middle class as "remarkable only for the very ordinariness with which its members go about their classically American suburban affairs."[36] Yet our respondents report that their lives as pioneers in white suburbia are often anything but ordinary and easy. For many the housing struggle brings anger mixed with resignation. The costs of this struggle were described by a counselor at a western university:

> First of all, just the attitude of taking you out to look at property. They take you to what they think you can afford based on the color of your skin. We did this three times; we had to *ask* to be taken, or to be shown, what they were calling middle-class homes. . . . Once you realize what's happening, you become so resentful. But then you figure, well, I can't spend my life [being upset]—I was born this way. I'm going to be black for the rest of my life, and I'm going to encounter discrimination. So for it not to have a negative [effect] on my life in terms of health, I think that you have to adjust. I wonder who else in this world has two, you might say even two lives, or two ways that they have to live, in order to function.

Housing problems will likely provoke much frustration, anger, and conflict for African Americans at all class levels for many years to come. The major 1992 riot in Los Angeles, the four major black riots in Miami since 1980, and the serious riots in other cities in the years between 1980 and 1993 were precipitated in part by anger over housing problems in racially polarized cities. Some time ago, the 1968 National Advisory Commission reporting on riots in the 1960s warned that the

United States was resegregating itself into two "separate and unequal" societies.

Racial segregation poses serious problems not only for black Americans but also for white Americans. Take the city of Chicago, a city with one of the most aggressive fair housing groups, the Leadership Council for Metropolitan Open Communities. In spite of much fair housing activity and a number of major court victories for fair housing, Chicago remains one of the most segregated of the nation's metropolitan areas.[37] In a 1992 *New York Times* series profiling two adjacent, highly segregated working-class suburbs of Chicago, one white and one black, journalist Isabel Wilkerson reported that the whites live in an insulated world where they "live out entire lives without ever getting to know a black person." Wilkerson found that there was racial fear and suspicion of the other racial group in both suburban communities. Yet the blacks were "fearful because much of their contact with white people was negative," while "whites were fearful because they had little or no contact."[38]

Housing segregation has costs for whites. A leading white scholar of school desegregation, Gary Orfield, has argued that future white leaders who grow up in suburban enclaves will have "no skills in relating to or communicating with minorities."[39] This social isolation will become even more of a serious handicap for whites as the United States moves into the twenty-first century, during which whites will eventually become a minority in the U.S. population. Even today, living in all-white enclaves does not prepare white Americans for dealing with a world that is composed mostly of people of color.

Chapter Seven

Contending with Everyday Discrimination: Effects and Strategies

A FEW months before he died of AIDS in 1993, the black tennis star Arthur Ashe was asked if that deadly disease had been the most difficult challenge he had faced in his life. Reflecting on his battle with AIDS, which he had contracted through a blood transfusion, Ashe replied that another challenge was greater: "Being black is. No question about it. Even now it continues to feel like an extra weight tied around me."[1] In previous chapters we have seen the extra weight that discrimination imposes on black lives. We have discussed the character and impact of specific instances of discrimination in public places, businesses, schools, and neighborhoods, and touched briefly on countering strategies middle-class African Americans have used in particular cases. In this chapter we focus in detail on the important lifesaving skills and coping strategies that African Americans rely on to survive the ordeals of modern racism.

To our knowledge the recent social science literature contains no systematic analysis of the survival skills African Americans have developed in confronting bigotry. A few psychological studies have recognized the stress caused by discrimination and identified some of the psychological strategies devised in response. Humphrey noted that "an ethnic group's perception of another ethnic group's effect on the distortion of the rules of distributive justice will predict a sense of anomie among its members and consequently disturb their emotional homeostasis."[2] He suggested that facilitating a sense of powerfulness in a group reduces psychological anomie. Similarly, Thomas and Sillen have noted that racial stress can stimulate important coping mechanisms. Individual reactions to this stress may range from constructive adaptation to a breakdown of normal functioning. Significantly, many victims of discrimination have marshalled resources that were not previously obvious or strengths of which they were not aware.[3] Much more social science research, in our view, needs to be done on black approaches to bias and discrimination.

Among middle-class African Americans there is much discussion of survival strategies. The oral tradition is a major source of the wisdom that has helped our respondents in struggling against everyday racism. Some programs within black organizations teach defensive survival tactics. A sophisticated repertoire of methods and tactics that have helped overcome racism becomes critical in a black person's life approach and life perspective.

With great persistence and patience, middle-class blacks pursue personal dreams of achievement and prosperity in the face of discriminatory encounters. Dreams must not, a hospital administrator argues, be given up in the face of discrimination. He explained forcefully what is it like to persevere despite meeting racism:

> Being aware that the opportunities are there for black Americans to achieve, and also realizing that though the

> opportunities are there for achievement, the types of blockage or the types of pitfalls that are there—and also recognizing that the opportunities may be there to excel, but you may not have all the working tools and all the necessary mentors to open the doors for you. . . . There's going to be discrimination and racism out there, and as long as you can accomplish what you have set forth to accomplish, recognize it for what it is, understand it for what it is, and don't let it deter you from your dreams, don't let it deter you from your goals. When that *does* happen, though, then you have to formulate a plan of action to still accomplish your goal and let that be your number one priority. Don't let attacking racism and attacking discrimination cause you to lose sight of your goal. You keep that aside, and understanding that this is something that you had to deal with as you continue to pursue your goal. Because what happens when you start putting all your energy in trying to deal with a racist act that is preventing you from trying to accomplish something, you won't accomplish it. You have to understand that this is an obstacle that you're going to have to deal with, but while I'm dealing with this, I'm going to keep moving straight ahead.

He continued emphatically: "And I'm saying that we can't afford to get caught up in just attacking racism without pursuing on a continued basis our goal to accomplish our goals and to accomplish our dreams. My thoughts and my feelings are, yes, recognize racism, recognize discrimination, try to deal with it as you are continuing to pursue your dreams and your goals."

The Array of Situational Strategies

Prior to the 1960s the legalized mistreatment of black Americans, especially in the South, often demanded that they subordinate themselves to whites and routinely respond to them with obsequiousness. Today, even when whites expect obsequiousness, most middle-class blacks do not oblige. Indeed, as many of our respondents have described, there has been a significant increase in the number of African Americans with the professional and financial resources to fight discrimination, often directly. In examining specific examples of discrimination, we have seen that responses to everyday prejudice or mistreatment range from careful assessment to withdrawal, resigned acceptance, verbal confrontation, physical confrontation, or legal action. We will now turn to the more general discussions in our interviews of the impact, character, and meaning of these antidiscrimination strategies.

One way to deal with discrimination is to try to avoid situations where it might occur, even at some personal cost. A physician in a southwestern city responded to a question about dealing with discrimination this way: "It just depends on what the situation is, whether or not it's personal, business; it just kind of depends on what, you know, exactly what it is. I usually don't go places where I'm not wanted, so I'm not the kind of person that trailblazes—where people tell you that they don't want you in a certain situation and you persist. It's kind of a hard question to answer." Seen here is the tragic legacy for black Americans of having to "know one's place." One senses fear of physical harm and psychological pain in his words.

Yet avoidance helps only in certain situations, since being middle class almost by definition means venturing daily into a white-dominated world. As we have seen in accounts of discrimination in previous chapters, in that white world a common initial response to discrimination is to carefully evaluate or read the situation. A teacher commented on this evaluation procedure:

> First of all, within myself I try to analyze it. I try to look at all the pros and cons, all the ways in which the situation

> could've happened. Did I do my part, not necessarily as a black person but just as a person? Did I do everything that I was supposed to do in the particular situation, whether or not it was a conversation, whether or not it was being hired for a job, or whatever. . . . Then what I do is, again, I just say what I think, in a very professional way. I try not to get into stereotyping myself by becoming very loud, and loud and aggressive, because I think that's the way white people feel as though we are going to handle ourselves. But if I'm faced with it, I try to be professional and assertive. Because I believe with whites you have to deal with them the way that they are accustomed to being dealt with. And that is, putting something on paper, and being professional, assertive but not aggressive. And that's the way I deal with it. I identify the problem. I say, "This is what I feel has happened here." And I give the steps or the reasons that I feel like it has happened, what has drawn me to this conclusion.

This woman captures well the preference of many black Americans to see, if possible, negative action against them as rooted in some factor besides color. Discrimination creates a psychological dilemma. A standard psychological recommendation for dealing with life problems is to face them head on.[4] From this perspective it may be healthier for blacks to say internally about mistreatment, "Yes, this is racism," for once a problem is named, it is often easier to solve. As we have suggested previously, many whites feel that black people are paranoid about discrimination and rush quickly to charges of racism. But the reality is often the opposite, as most middle-class blacks seem to evaluate a situation carefully before judging it discriminatory. We judge from our interviews that much discrimination is overlooked if possible. There is white hostility that blacks must ignore just to reduce the pain and to survive. If one can name racial discrimination something else, it may not hurt as much. For example, if blacks can attribute discriminatory acts to economic causes, then they can envisage how conditions might be changed to eliminate the negative behavior. They cannot change the color of their skins, and it is most disheartening to be damned for something over which one has no control.

Accuracy in assessing whites is usually necessary, as an administrative clerk in a publishing firm stressed:

> I'd say don't open your mouth and say anything that you're not 100 percent sure of. Don't have doubt. If you know this is where you want to go, and you know that these things are accurate, you shouldn't have doubt about it, no matter who comes through. . . . I don't care what the next person tells you. I've had people on my job to tell me, "well, it's your imagination." [Even] black people now, that say, "Maybe it's just your imagination that this is going on." No, it's not my imagination. . . . Take Susan, one of the supervisors. [They say] "This is just her nature to treat people this way." No. That didn't make me doubt for a moment. It didn't make me have a second thought and say, "Well, is this really the way she is and that she's really not discriminating?" No. She's discriminating.

Beneath the surface we sense the psychological toll taken on a person who must fight to have her view of what is going on in her workplace acknowledged. Having to assess potentially discriminatory situations carefully before responding can create a strain on the energy and psyche of African Americans. What is at stake is often more than whether one is right in a particular assessment. A less obvious aspect of modern racism is the great difficulty black victims often have in establishing their perceptions as legitimate. Full racial integration of historically white institutions requires a change in white views and practices, as well as an increase in power for blacks. Such a major change will result in the power of African Americans to establish their own situational readings and constructions as legitimate in interactions with the whites. In addition, some black Americans say, "The right I want most as an American of African descent is the right to be wrong." Blacks in white institutions feel constantly scrutinized and that they can never "let down" or make a mistake. True racial integration would include the right to make a mistake without abnormal or racial repercussions.

Several respondents discussed how they reassess maltreatment after it has occurred. A manager in an electronics firm described how he applies a self-evaluation technique he learned in a management program:

> When something happens, I'll take it and toss around in my head, replay it like a recorder, and see if there's maybe something that I did that could have caused it, or something I could have done differently that would have made the outcome different. Then once I feel comfortable with what I've analyzed, the one thing I'll do is I'll present, if need be, my argument to whoever it is that I'm dealing with, be it my manager or someone else.

Not every situation requires the same reaction. Punctuating his comments with some laughter, the owner of a chemical company described how he sometimes chooses to ignore minor incidents:

> It depends on the importance of the situation that I'm dealing with. If it's in the grocery store, hey, I don't get upset about somebody [who] gets in front of me, tries to pretend I'm not there. It depends on how I'm feeling that day, but, you know, life is too short to get upset about something like that. If it meant that they wanted to short-change me in the line, you know just because I'm black, then we've

> got some problems. And we will deal with it head on. So we have to put it in the proper perspective because, like I said, there's always going to be discrimination and you just have to learn to deal with it; you just don't jump up and down in every instance.

A theme throughout many discussions of coping in our interviews is the struggle to keep some kind of balance and to contain one's frustrations in searching for the best response. In one situation, resigned acceptance is preferred; in another, active confrontation.

After the initial assessment of a situation one possible response is to retreat. Some street incidents, such as those discussed in Chapter 2, allow only for a quick exit. Some type of acquiescence is another response forced on black Americans. A computer specialist for an East Coast bank described one such response, a "blocking out" method:

> My first way of dealing with discrimination is usually . . . acting like it doesn't exist. Back in the sixties, in my parents' days, Martin Luther King's days, it was outward, it was blatant. Now, you can't holler discrimination, because they're going to think that you're trying to get a lawsuit, or trying to [get] a free meal or something, so you really can't come out and say, "I'm being discriminated against." You've got to handle it in a more mature, more adult way, a more, I guess you could say, a more timid way. You've got to just know it's there, do all you can to avoid it.

Such acquiescence may sometimes be necessary, yet, as we suggested earlier, it may not be a psychologically healthy technique. It is possible too that by "a more timid way" he refers to an indirect or subtle means of deflecting discrimination.

The heavy price paid psychologically for this adaptation strategy can be seen in the comments of a banking executive in an eastern city:

> You become a chameleon. You take on the characteristics of what's going on there. It goes everything from patterns of speech, your philosophies, your thinking. Because I don't think all the time you're openly, I mean, you're not totally honest. You know what [white] people want to hear more than anything else and you give them back your feedback; you regurgitate back to them what you think they need to hear. There are times when you go against it, bucking the system, and then you just tell them your gut feelings or how you really feel about something, but most people that I know will hold that back until it's at the point when it needs to be said. But they don't normally, as a routine basis, do it.[5]

Some agree that the struggle with whites requires acquiescence, but only up to a point; that is, they take the "run to fight another day" approach. In an earlier chapter we discussed a black lawyer's measured response to a white attorney who used the word "nigger" in his presence. Although he appeared at first to ignore the remark, when the white attorney later came by to ask how he was, he with some humor pressured him by suggesting that many white people need "help" in dealing with their sickness called racism. In his interview the black lawyer added these words:

> I think many blacks have lost out because we have become frustrated. We see what we're dealing with. And then it appears so hopeless, and we just say, "Oh, I can't help it." And we just throw in the towel. . . . It's a world in which they may have the advantage, but there's nothing that says it has to continue to be that way. And so our job then be-

comes: How do we turn whatever disadvantages may be ours into advantages. And I think there're certain ways to do it. But the strategy must sometimes vary, and we must control our tempers and our emotions. And then there are some times when we must just hide to live another day, which means, "I see what you're doing, I don't particularly care for what you're doing, but nothing will be gained by me pointing it out to you today." So I'll take it, and there'll be another day.

Confronting White Racists

Withdrawal and acquiescence are by no means the only strategies our respondents described. Confrontation is a common strategy for dealing with the racist attitudes and actions of white Americans. Indeed, there has been a long history of active resistance to racism on the part of African Americans, from the time the first Africans were enslaved on ships bound for the new American colonies. Historian Herbert Aptheker found evidence of 250 American slave revolts or conspiracies to revolt, a count that did not include the numerous mutinies aboard slave ships.[6] Later, during legal segregation, some blacks took great risks by confronting whites openly. In Blauner's interviews with blacks and whites in California, several black respondents reported acquaintances reacting aggressively to racial discrimination prior to the 1970s.[7] After saying that "you have to choose your battles," a professor at a New England university commented on how she deals with racist remarks: "I would say, 'I don't think that's very funny,' you know. 'Look at what it is that you're [saying].' And they would say, 'Oh, it's *only* a joke.' But it isn't *only* a joke, you know. And I think it's really not uncommon even if it's not jokes given about blacks, but given about Arabs, for example. And I think that black people need to say, 'I don't think that's funny.'" Some whites have told the authors that the "black jokes are harmless" and that blacks should "lighten up" and laugh at them, the suggestion being that said jokes are a sign of integration into the core culture. While some middle-class blacks find themselves in situations where they feel pressured to laugh at antiblack and other ethnic jokes told by whites, this professor does not agree with such assent to joking.

By regularly confronting whites verbally, black Americans run the risk of being ostracized or labeled. Emphasizing an aggressive approach, a professional who directs a social welfare program in the Midwest spoke of confronting discrimination:

> There was a job that I just went through and filed a grievance like a big dog. And I called up all of the people that I know that would help raise hell—hell raisers—and that's what, really, what I did. I have never taken the back seat intentionally if I knew that I was taking the back seat. And I tell them. You know, when I came out of high school we had—in the seventies—we had a lot of pride, and one of the things we were taught is that you fought for what you believed in, regardless of how people felt about you, you did that. So as far as discrimination, you know, in my city people know me as a hell-raiser.

Called a "troublemaker," a social worker in an eastern city described her approach to white denial:

> Generally, I get myself into difficulties because I deal with it head on. And generally, I'm considered a troublemaker, or someone who's constantly looking at race, and someone who's looking to argue. . . . And what disturbed me and continues to disturb me is that whites will try to tell you that they're not being racist, when they can't tell you what you perceive, or how you've experienced something. And what they try to do is to deny your experience, and then invalidate it. And then in other words, you walk around like,

well, I know this is happening to me, but you're telling me this is not happening to me, so it's not? No, it means you don't want to acknowledge that it's happening, so what I tend to do is say, "you are doing this to me," and whether you acknowledge it or not, that's the way I experience it. So, I try to deal with it head on.

Again and again in the interviews we see that living with modern racism is a matter of accumulating experience. And it is the extensive experience that most African Americans have that makes them outraged at the common white denials of the reality of everyday racism.

A bank manager characterized her direct, but careful approach: "Being very direct, I tend to put them on the defensive. I don't, I'm not argumentative, but I always try to ask questions. I'm very direct with my accusations. I just don't fly off the handle. I usually have facts. I go right to the people involved, and I let them explain to me why things are happening. And it seems to shake them up a little bit, that someone can be as direct about the black-white issue."

A lawyer quoted previously sometimes deliberately uses a matter-of-fact but casual retort to racist comments: "Instead of just throwing temper tantrums, say, 'Oh, that's just because you're a racist.' They don't like to be called racist. . . . That's the exciting part. It's not always bad being the underdog. It's not. It's good to see people go through the mental gymnastics, you know." This lawyer characterizes his white antagonists as racists with a smile, using humor as an equalizer, but from the white point of view such a direct yet unheated accusation is disarming and it can provoke vigorous denials.

It is remarkable how many middle-class African Americans see it as their task to educate white Americans about racism and to remind them of the implications of the "liberty and justice" creed whites supposedly honor. One theme in some interviews is calling whites on the carpet, as a southern newspaper publisher explained:

> I think most people don't know what racism is. They consider it just part of the way of doing things. I think the most horrifying thing to me has been that when people have been racist and I have turned around and said, "That was very racist," it's almost been shocking to them. "Racist! I'm not a racist!" And then you explain to them how that's racist, and it's like, "Oh, I never thought of it like that." That's always been mind-boggling. Their perception is that it's not racist—that's the way they think, that's the way they function. So, if I had a choice, more black people would educate white people about what is racist.

The experience of being a victim often seems to generate considerably more thought and reflection about the character of U.S. racial relations than the experience of being white victimizers.

In Chapter 2 we discussed a television anchorperson's account of being discriminated against while attempting to buy a luxury car. In his interview he also described the educational approach he sometimes uses:

> I have found that probably the most effective way—at least it makes me feel better—you realize that basically discrimination is based on ignorance, so you try to educate people. And the best way to educate people I have found is to point out in a very subtle way, and a very intellectual way, the stupidness—I don't know how better to put it—the ignorance basically of why they are prejudiced. For example, the incident that I cited to you about my buying the car, and the people, based on the [casual] way I was dressed, based on the fact that I was black, assuming that I was

> not in a position, or was not interested in purchasing that car. That's based on ignorance, and that's based on stereotyping.

As we have seen in every previous chapter, racially insensitive or hostile remarks are the scourge of middle-class African Americans moving into formerly all-white situations. With an air of disapprobation, a management assistant in an eastern county government office recounted her reaction to a colleague's remark:

> Another incident in that same department—somebody had said that an ambulance company had picked up a person that was so dirty and had lice, and they were appalled. And the next comment was, "And the person wasn't even black." Well, again . . . and they looked at me, because they knew that that would be offensive to me and they also knew that I would have a retort for this person. And I said to him, "Do you think black people have a monopoly on dirt?" And the comment was made by the others in the group, which was said in jest, but probably very true, that the person who made the comment had no idea what the word monopoly meant. But they knew that he had offended me, and it was interesting. The refreshing thing about that was that the other people in the group were white and had very little exposure to blacks but because of my presence had become more sensitive.

Her presence and her quick response to racially barbed remarks apparently sensitized other whites in her work circle who had no experience with blacks.

For some middle-class black Americans, this desire to educate whites about a range of issues informs their everyday professional activities, as in the case of this professor who has taught at universities in the North and the Southwest:

> Most of my class isn't black, two-thirds of any class I teach is white. And so when I'm politicizing black students, I'm also politicizing white students. And I do that because I think that as folks who are going to be participants in the big middle class, they probably won't be as well-off as their parents were, they might be at some point people who are interested in breaking the stranglehold that ideology has on the way we see the world. I think for example that a white male, who is just going to be the equivalent of a middle manager in an insurance company, can see the fact that what is happening to him is not tied to black people, but tied to the way the economy works, that individual will then be someone who in his own life interrupts the process of scapegoating another group. It's the only way I can think of to intervene, short of becoming part of a revolutionary group. Do you know what I mean? I mean, if I wasn't teaching, I'd be standing on a street corner with a machine gun, because I can't imagine what else I would be doing.

Mixing her commentary with occasional laughter, a black professional in a northern state discussed how her approach to educating whites depends on the situation and who the white person is:

> I have very little tolerance for white people who expect me to change my behavior to make them comfortable. They don't change their behavior to make me comfortable. I am who I am. Either they sit with me and work with me respecting that, or you can't sit and work together. But I don't—and I see them uncomfortable, and I think to myself, "Well, that's unfortunate." But, no, I don't go to any great lengths to make them any more comfortable in dealing with me. I sometimes see them choking on words, trying to find ways to say things. And I let them choke! But

> I'm serious! Why should I help them phrase it. Sometimes I think they're trying to say something about, "Well, do you think the other black members . . ." "Excuse me?" And I wait for them to come forward with it, and often times they end up not saying it because they're afraid of what my response will be. So they work around it, and I say, "Well, I think that's inappropriate." Then there are other people, who are personal friends, who may make a racist statement, and it's really based on their ignorance and their lack of understanding, and I'll take the time to deal with it. There's a young white woman that I work with now, and she's really not worked with a lot of different people of color, and she uses the term, "you people," and I bring it to her attention, and she's like, "oh, oh," and so it's an education, we're working together.

Differentiating between whites whose statements reflect ignorance and those whose comments show hostility, this professional takes the time to educate the former. Such a response seems to us to be psychologically healthy, for it offers a real solution to a chronic problem and gives the individual black person a sense of accomplishment.

In their everyday rounds some middle-class African Americans have the moxie and opportunity to create situations in which whites must come face to face with their racist views and assumptions. A manager for a southwestern computer firm described a "victory march":

> One thing that used to always happen to me—[white] customers don't see me a lot, and their assumption is that I'm white when I talk to them over the phone. . . . I would go to a customer site, with one of my engineers. And they would come, and they would always talk to the engineer as though I was working for him. And what I would always do is have a game: I would make sure that I would walk to

> the other side of the room. And then the conversation would soon come to a point where the engineer would say, "I'm not the one that's going to get your problems resolved, that's my boss over there." I would make them come to me, sort of like a victory march!

Although calculated, the manager's response is more one of teaching a lesson than of seeking revenge—and again is wrapped in the commonplace black humor rather than in overt hostility.

Judging from our interviews it is very rare for black Americans to set out to annoy whites just out of vindictiveness. However, we did find a somewhat humorous example of a "payback time" reaction. A student at a predominantly white university recounted, with some laughter, how she and her black friends set up situations and took chances in taunting whites:

> It's, I don't know, it's a sense of control in a way, I guess. And it's an acceptable way for me to lash out at white people, you know "acceptable." Because my friends and I, we'll do that a lot. We'll go to a restaurant and we'll talk so loud about racial issues, and we will just trip people out! We did that last Sunday at a restaurant as a matter of fact, no joke. And they would just turn around, and look and drop food and stuff! We would make sure that we sat around the most white people that we possibly could; and we would just talk about them, and just talk about them. And have the best time! I mean, I know it's mean, I know it's evil, but hell. Ok, I have no justification for it, I don't. I admit it, but I can't help it. I can't help myself. It's payback!

Specific incidents of racial discrimination often provoke a personal and collective sense of powerlessness. This pay-back action gives this young woman and her friends some sense of power and the confidence that they often do not feel in the white university environment. The retaliation strategy works, it should be noted, only because some whites overreact to loud black comments on racial issues. Significantly, the young respondent shows concern over the meanness of her actions. Judging from our interviews—surprisingly, perhaps, given the scale of the racial hostility they face—even more aggressive revenge against whites is not an openly expressed goal of middle-class African Americans.

Many if not most whites grow up with few significant or intimate contacts with African Americans. Some may have had contact with a black domestic or yard worker; and some may have had fleeting contacts with black clerks in stores or one or two black employees in the workplace. Some have no contact at all. For that reason white preconceptions about black Americans stem mostly from parents, friends, teachers, and the mass media. Still, white prejudices can change with greater contact with black Americans, but the character of that contact is very important. Contact between those of unequal status, such as between servants and employers, will seldom have major positive effects. The racial "contact hypothesis" discussed in social science research proposes that contacts between blacks and whites must be between those of roughly equal social status for the contact to lessen white prejudices and stereotypes.[8] A research administrator at a southern university talked about how he helped a white associate deal with his prejudices:

> I'll tell you something that happened to me when I was in banking, I worked in the commercial finance division and I was supposed to go out and interview with somebody. I was the trainee, and this guy who was going out was an old-timer and stuff like that. But he told me, he said, "Listen, I never worked for black people." And in fact, he

> didn't like black people because he told me that his grandfather told him black people were no good and to watch out for them, that they were cheats and liars. I said, "You know, my mother told me the same thing. Watch out for white people. They're cheats, liars and thieves, and I've got to be very careful around them!" And he realized over the course of our relationship that all the things that he had been taught was just rhetoric, but he says, "I can't change. I've been taught this all my life." And by the time my little tour of duty in that area was over, we became very good friends. And that happens over and over and over again. I've worked with people, I was almost the only friend of this particular white guy that worked in this company. But all he had seen, because he grew up in areas—people may not believe this—but there are areas where white people haven't actually seen a real black person.

Some of the whites described in this section belong to that segment of white America for whom equal status contact with middle-class blacks seems to have changed certain antiblack attitudes. Yet a striking characteristic of the black middle-class experience is that so many middle-class whites seem to be little affected, especially in deep and lasting ways, by an increase in contacts with these middle-class black Americans. The attainment by the black middle class of a status more equal to that of the white middle class has not brought the fully integrated society that equal-status theory, and equality of opportunity laws, would seem to have foretold.

Using Official Channels and Court Suits

A more formal or official response to discrimination can range from writing a letter of protest to complaining to the relevant government agencies or filing a lawsuit. An administrator at a western university told the story of his wife driving past a white police officer who had given her an unclear signal. The officer hit her car hard with his fist, held her up in the middle of traffic, and then told her to get "that junk out of here." Reviewing the story, the administrator commented on how he prefers to handle mistreatment by working through channels:

> When I was younger, I dealt with it confrontation-style. But when I got older and smarter I dealt with it nonconfrontational-style. I deal with it through calling the proper people, writing the proper authorities, going through the proper channels and so forth. . . . Oh, for example, that same situation with that police officer who beat on the car and told her it was a piece of junk and told her to pull over. What she should have done was written down his badge number and then phoned it in. And enough people do things like that, a pattern clearly develops against policemen who do things like that.

This emphasis on using proper channels of institutional authority is remarkable given the problems that Africans Americans, including some in our sample (see Chapter 2), have with white police officers. In the recent past this type of protest would probably have been futile, if not dangerous. Yet this man's style signals how many middle-class African Americans have come to feel that the police system should be there to serve them. His resources have given him the grounds to demand respect as a citizen and taxpayer.

As we have documented in previous chapters, a number of our respondents have had to resort to threatening lawsuits or actually going to court to rectify maltreatment. A strong sense of justice and legal rights is evident in many of their specific accounts of discrimination. One account was given by an unemployed corporate executive in a northern state, who explored the implications and consequences of the litigation approach:

I got to a certain level, which is to say a middle-management level of the corporation. I was in line for a *major* increase in position, and that position was given to a white male who was brought from outside the area, outside the area of expertise of the project. . . . He had lesser education, he had lesser experience, so it would seem fit to use the old boy network to bring him into it and to see evidence that that probably happens to many people. And I believe the reaction on the part of a lot of the other blacks is to either resign themselves to putting up with it, and a large number of others end up simply quitting and going elsewhere, and all the effort that they've put into getting where they've gotten at that point in time goes down the drain. . . . Now in my particular case, I am currently unemployed; you know, I'm pursuing a lawsuit. And I'm unable to gain other employment since it's well known in the area where I live at that I am suing my previous employer. And since there is a protective order in place whereby I cannot discuss the specifics of the case, specifically what information we got from the various interrogatories and discovery material laying out what was done to me. But I cannot properly defend myself in front of potential employers, and, as a consequence, I'm affected so far as not being able to get employment. . . . It just kind of pulls you in and further essentially isolates you. . . . It's affected the way former associates, in the town I live in, particularly white associates, perceive and deal with me. It's a very overt avoidance at this point in time. It's even made black friends somewhat hesitant—black friends prior to the time I had to sue my previous employer, black friends who were very friendly toward me—after I had to sue and go into the situation I'm in right now, has made them hesitant so far as their relationships with me.

Seeking redress from discriminators in court, even if one wins, can be devastating professionally and personally. Given the isolation and possibility of retaliation, it is surprising that some middle-class black employees muster the courage to seek legal redress and jeopardize their current situations. Yet the black tradition of civil rights drives many to seek fair play. Despite the few legal recourses available to them, middle-class African Americans have in recent decades provided great and reinforcing support for the old U.S. tradition of protesting injustice.

Personal Coping Styles and Defenses

In addition to strategies for countering specific instances of white discrimination, middle-class black Americans have developed broader personal philosophies, coping styles, and protective defenses for dealing with the accumulating impact of racism on their psyches and lives. Broader life philosophies and perspectives are required because of the harshness, intensity, and prevalence of modern racism. Some costs of white racism are material; others are psychological. Psychiatrists William Grier and Price Cobbs have written that "people bear all they can and, if required, bear even more. But if they are black in present-day America they have been asked to shoulder too much. They have had all they can stand. They will be harried no more. Turning from their tormentors, they are filled with rage."[9]

Most white Americans do not have any inkling of the rage over racism that is repressed by African Americans. Asked how often she got angry about actions by white people, a professor at a western university replied:

> Any time there's any injustice either done to me, or I see it or read about it, it makes me angry. I don't think any human being has the right to feel superior, or act superior, or

> do things that say they're better than someone else, just because of the color of their skin. And every time I hear [about] incidents I get angry, it upsets me greatly. [So, would you say that's once a day, once a week, once a month?] In my profession you can hear it fifteen times on some days, it just depends on who you're seeing on that day, and what's going on in their lives.

The level of intensity this anger can reach is revealed in this vigorous comment of a retired professor in reply to the question, "On a scale of one to ten, where do you think your level of anger is?"

> Ten! I think that there are many blacks whose anger is at that level. Mine has had time to grow over the years more and more and more until now I feel that my grasp on handling myself is tenuous. I think that now I would strike out to the point of killing, and not think anything about it. I really wouldn't care. Like many blacks you get tired, and you don't know which straw would break the camel's back. . . . And I'm angry at what's happening to our young people. I call it impotent rage, because it's more than anger, it's a rage reaction, but something that you can't do something about and that makes it even more dangerous when you do strike out.

Repressed rage over maltreatment is common, this professor argues later in the interview, to *all* African Americans. The psychological costs to African Americans of widespread prejudice and discrimination include this rage, as well as humiliation, frustration, resignation, and depression. Such high costs require major defensive strategies.

One strategy African Americans in all income classes use to cope is to put on their defensive "shields," the term used in a conversation the first author had with a retired music teacher. Now in her seventies, this black informant contrasted her life with that of a white woman, who, like her, bathes, dresses, and puts on her cosmetics before leaving the house each morning. Unlike the white woman, this black woman suggested, she must put on her "shield" just before she leaves the house. When quizzed about this term, she said that for decades, before leaving home she has had to be prepared psychologically and to steel herself in advance for racist insults and acts, to be prepared even if nothing adverse happens on a particular day. One of our respondents, a physical education teacher, spoke to us of her "guarded position" in life: "I feel as though most of the time I find myself being in a guarded position or somewhat on the defense. I somewhat stay prepared to be discriminated against because I never know when it's going to happen to me." A teacher in the Midwest put it this way: Middle-class blacks "can't sit back and relax at all; you have to be vigilant at all times; if you don't you'll be back in chains." Psychologists Thomas and Sillen have argued that such a defensive approach is realistic; in order to survive, they suggest, a black person should assume that "every white man is a potential enemy unless he personally finds out differently."[10]

The high energy costs of this vigilance and of actually dealing with white racism over a lifetime were described by the retired professor quoted earlier:

> If you can think of the mind as having 100 ergs of energy, and the average man uses 50 percent of his energy dealing with the everyday problems of the world—just general kinds of things—then he has 50 percent more to do creative kinds of things that he wants to do. Now that's a white person. Now a black person also has 100 ergs; he uses 50 percent the same way a white man does, dealing

> with what the white man has [to deal with], so he has 50 percent left. But he uses 25 percent fighting being black, [with] all the problems being black and what it means.

One way that African Americans consume personal energy is in determined efforts to succeed in the face of racism, including overachieving to prove their worth in the face of whites' questioning black ability and competence. A college graduate in a western city described how he felt about having to prove himself:

> It's being constantly reminded that you're different, that you're not good enough, that you have to prove yourself, that you have to be better than average, just to be considered normal. . . . I am to the point now where when someone has a problem with my race, or my color, or my ability to be a human, and they only see me as an object, a black guy, a "blackie," I deal with it. When they have a problem, I leave it as their problem. I make sure that they understand that this problem that they're having is only theirs. If they have a problem with how I look, who I am, then maybe they should stop looking at me, stop associating with me.

The distress that comes from having to prove oneself in most situations has led this young black man to develop a defensive repertoire that includes making whites aware of who is at fault.

The professor quoted above explained a general approach many employ in dealing with whites:

> I think sometimes I use the same strategy I've seen others use. I'll say that doesn't bother me, knowing it does. It's a matter of not letting it destroy you. So it's a matter of psychological strength. And I think most blacks have a tremendous amount of psychological strength. We're able to say this is unfair, but I won't let it destroy me. And that bull-

> dog determination that you will not be destroyed, you will not be torn up, helps you to get over what I call many of the humps.

He tells blacks to recognize that discrimination is unfair, but to work to prevent it from destroying them.

Several respondents felt that it was common for black employees trying to prove themselves in white settings to overachieve, doing more than white employees with similar resources and credentials would have to do. Sprinkling his comments with some laughter, a professor at an eastern law school expounded on this strategy:

> There's a lot of pressure, but one thing that there is, there is a byproduct of that that's good, because once you succeed, you *know* that you have the ability. There's no question about it, because you've had to do a little bit more than the next guy to even get through. Whereas we used to say when we were growing up, "If you're white you don't have any excuse for not succeeding in America." And if you're black and get into a position to pursue a certain goal, yes, you might have to work much harder, but that makes it a little bit better in the end, and a little bit more assured of your own ability. The way that things are done now is that everything that a black person does—not everything, but most of the things that some black people do—they try to discount it, say it's not as good, which is not true. And if you fall for that you really have a problem, but it's all a little game.

There is clearly a psychic cost to such an approach, yet there is also the benefit of knowing one has substantial ability when forced to demonstrate it.

Our interviews repeatedly demonstrated the importance of the inner strength required when African Americans enter indifferent or hostile white worlds. A professor at a historically white university underscored the need for a healthy self-concept:

> You must develop some skills, but you also must develop a love of yourself, a liking of yourself. It's very important for you to do that. Now, the skills, that's difficult, because that's a very broad subject. You've got to put yourself in a position where you can learn, and sometimes you may be in a painful position, but once you have that confidence and the skills, you can make it. The liking of yourself is broader than just skills. . . . When you go to a predominantly white situation where people don't care about you, or a lot of them, and it's maybe even hostile at times, you need to love yourself. You truly need it. You need to get up in the morning and feel very self-contained.

This respondent links avoiding self-blame to liking oneself. Several of those with whom we talked discussed working to overcome excessive self-blaming inclinations, including this executive officer at a predominantly white chamber of commerce:

> Well, I think the thing that works for me is I know it's not me. And you're right, a lot of times when these crazy things happen, I'll sit down and call a friend. And then not even discuss that issue, but talk about something else. But the first part of my coping is to realize that I'm not the problem. I don't internalize it. And realize that I'm the victim, and so I don't blame the victim. I'm gentle on myself.

Psychologists Thomas and Sillen have suggested that, among blacks, anger at whites may be replacing self-derogation as a response to oppression. They suggest that this shift is a healthy sign, for it is saying, "I am condemning you for doing wrong to me."[11] From this perspective a positive means of coping results from a realistically targeted anger.

Young or old, the need to buttress one's self-image is a constant problem for our respondents. One college student, who has had epithets hurled at her by white students, explained that Stokely Carmichael's book *Black Power* had helped her strengthen her sense of self worth:

> This is crazy because I'm twenty-four, and all along I was thinking, "OK, he called me 'nigger,' he was just one, there's not a whole lot of them here." . . . But reading *Black Power*, I mean, we've always heard about the civil rights movement, and we've always heard about this, that, and the other, but *Black Power* to me was a little bit more in-depth than that. This man had a plan of what we needed to do in order to, I guess, consolidate or to establish some kind of solidarity. And he explained in a very, just rational, manner why it was needed. Because before, yes, we need to get together, you'd hear that all the time, "Unity, unity." But it seems like we've been doing OK without it—that was a lot of the older attitude. I can see that attitude. But reading that book I understand a little bit more about just how hard it [unity] is.

Exposure to the black power literature provided the student with a stronger sense of linkage to other black Americans and thus more confidence in dealing with the white campus culture.

Our respondents reported an array of creative approaches they find effective in keeping their sanity in the face of white racism. For some a candid dialogue with God is one approach, as in this statement of a state legislator:

> It's quite frustrating. I chew God out sometimes. I don't mean it in a blasphemous way, or cursing, but I mean like some of the minor prophets did, you know, "God what's your problem? You're not moving; you're not acting. What's the deal here? Why aren't you doing something

> about this?" You see what I'm saying? You know, that kind of thing, and it's very frustrating. It's very hurting, because you go through the [black] community and when people say, "Oh, there's legislator Jones," and you tell people about being a good American, and doing this, and doing that, and you know really, you can't promise them much, not very much at all really.

Taking a Jeremiah-like stance, this legislator has addressed God to express her anger over how little she can do to help her constituents. Reflecting the deeply-felt religious heritage of African Americans, a probation officer in the South emphasized the importance of prayer and positive thinking:

> Oh, I get angry. Frustrated. And then again, I pray. I remember back, I don't know, someone said, "What the mind can conceive and believe it can achieve." I've been a student of positive thinking, and I know if anybody can, I can. And that's the type of attitude I have to reach deep within myself to deal with that. . . . If not, it will eat you away and you'll wind up doing what we're seeing more and more of. I can remember when I grew up and I was growing up as a little kid, we didn't hear of suicides among blacks. But the older I get, the more prevalent suicides among blacks has taken place. A little godchild of mine, three months ago, took his life. Prime of his life. All because of these outside pressures, and he wasn't able to deal with them, a twenty-one-year-old kid. That's what I'm saying. You have to have an innermost strength to reach down and draw [on].

Using religious insights and resources to face racism has been at the core of black survival since slavery. The slave spirituals and much other prized religious music often refer to such conditions as a "home in Heaven" or to "rest, peace, and no more pain." Religion remains very important for many because the present life is so difficult that African Americans hope that somewhere there is a better life. African American religion, including spirituals and other religious music, has long spoken of comfort and hope, as well as of resistance to oppression. From the beginning African American religion has been a foundation from which to critique white oppression and to work to try to transform a racist society.[12]

One other resource is often critical for black survival—the ability to laugh at one's fate and one's tormentors. In *An American Dilemma* Myrdal discussed the ways in which black southerners in the 1930s and 1940s used humor to deal with the gaping discrepancy between the American creed and discriminatory white behavior.[13] Throughout this book we have seen middle-class black respondents using humor and laughter to deal with poor treatment by whites. With great amusement a political consultant described how she and her husband were a fighting team: "Matter of fact, our hobby is to fight discrimination and challenge discrimination; that's a hobby for us. We've been doing it all our lives. We like it!" In conversations reviewing their encounters with whites, blacks sometimes say things like "I cut him, and he didn't even know he had been cut", or "I cut him so sharp, he didn't even bleed." In a particular situation such humor can be a means of covert retaliation, sometimes not even recognized by the white party but totally understood by other blacks. Such humor can help defang the white enemy, thereby protecting against retaliation. In difficult conditions humor can function to take some of the sting out of a situation or to side-step an action so that it goes by relatively harmlessly.

Numerous respondents chuckled or laughed as they gave accounts of encounters with whites. A college counselor at a western university explained this coping strategy:

> Well, you know, one of the things that we've been able to use as a survival method is laughter. And there have been

> times and situations where friends, feeling like I do now, we've been able to talk about something that was quite serious, but we've been able to make light of it. Well, not to make light of it, but to laugh at it, at how bad something really is, just turn it over. That's a survival method. . . . It's very important, in order not to be a statistic in terms of stroke or heart attack.

Chuckling at painful events helps lessen the stress and perhaps decreases the probability of greater anguish. Here laughing at tragedy is part of social interaction; this circle of friends is trying to manage psychologically the effects of mistreatment.

The ability to laugh at pain rather than being overwhelmed is at the heart of heroic advice a lawyer in a southern city had for younger blacks:

> Having said all that, enjoy life. That'll get worked out over all these problems. There's a time to be serious, and there's a time to build, and there's a time to enjoy your life. And when all is said and done, don't be overcome by what you see, and by all means, don't let anybody else steal your joy. . . . And my attitude is real basic and simple, and that is, I may not live to see the struggle, the battle won, but my joy is just being right at this day in the struggle. We know how to get to the Promised Land. I just want to live to be in the fight.

Sources of Social Support

As we discussed briefly in Chapter 6, social and psychological support from family and friends is crucial in surviving daily struggles with whites. This may appear surprising to some white readers who have seen much discussion of black families as pathological, dysfunctional, and unable to provide their members sufficient sustenance.[14] However, the everyday reality is usually different, for most black families in all income classes have been strong enough to provide havens of refuge for generations. A law professor described this heroic heritage:

> Well, the love and the support and the understanding, they're important. It just happens that this past weekend, I went to a family reunion. And we traced our families' roots and we had a chance to all sit around and talk about the kinds of values that are important. My family comes from the South, and they were slaves. And we talk about the people who were slaves, but [with] a great sense of family, and a real understanding of the meaning of the concept of fear. Again, as I said, my people were slaves, they lived through Jim Crow, through the Depression, and found their way to the sustaining concepts, the sustaining philosophies, the sustaining wisdom, love, family, and support. Understanding the concept of emotional and psychological healing, then you are always making a move to make the wound heal. You also understand how to avoid wounds. You know there are situations where you may not go head on against racism, you may step aside, you may deflect it. And I think that my family has put a lot in me that has helped me to be able to at least lessen some of the effects.

Family support as a means of coping with oppression has a long history among African Americans. Harriette McAdoo has researched the family in many areas of Africa and compared it with the African American family. Among the salient dimensions of African family life are (1) an emphasis on kinship groups and tribal survival and (2) a guiding principle of humanitarianism and interdependence of members. Historically, there was a xenophilic rather than a xenophobic dimension to many African societies. Strangers were not automatically considered enemies.[15] Long before the intrusion of European slave traders and the enslavement in the Americas, the family system in west

Africa generally encompassed every person. This system proved its importance during slavery in North America. Despite the many and varied tribes, customs, and languages, and the inhuman destruction of many family bonds by white slaveholders, enslaved African Americans forged strong bonds in order to survive and escape. The importance of strong family bonds under slavery and segregation has been demonstrated by Herbert Gutman and other historians over the last two decades.[16]

A woman who worked as a clerical employee in the Midwest, then moved to the South where she holds a personal service job, discussed the role of family and friends:

> Oh, we discuss, you know, naturally blacks always get together and talk about it and what we're going to do. It's discussed, but most of my friends and even my family, my mother has always been afraid for me. Especially when, me moving here, because she knows that I'm not going to take anything, you know. So, she would always say, "Now, Jane, you know they're not like they are up here. You have to watch your mouth. You have to watch the way you say things to people because you know, you can be real cutting verbally." And I know I can. And she's just afraid that I might be one that they hang on a tree. Like my sons. I've always taught them to be proud and strong and they've had a couple incidents down here we had to discuss it, you know.

The half-joking reference to lynching is striking as a reminder of the psychological currentness of brutal practices that persisted into the 1980s.

Emotional support in the face of everyday racism is critical, as a corporate executive quoted earlier made clear: "[My family has given] me the, I guess, warm emotional support one needs that says, 'Keep pushing. Don't give up. Hang in there, and don't let things make you do things you'll regret later. Just do the positive thing and recognize that it's going to take a long time.'" In managing encounters with racism middle-class black Americans are beginning to go to psychologists and psychiatrists. Until recently the great majority of mental health professionals have been white. These professionals, tending to make judgments in the form of white-normed diagnoses, have sometimes been considered the "enemy" in black communities. For example, for many years the anger and suspicion seen in black patients was too often diagnosed as paranoid schizophrenia. In recent years, however, mental health workers have examined these diagnoses more carefully and have found that for many black patients the feelings of anger and suspicion are reality-based and do not signal a psychosis. Very often the emotions have been generated by experiences with whites.[17]

The social support of black friends is grounded in shared experiences, a point accentuated by a social worker:

> Well, I think I have some friends who validate my experience which keeps me sane. I think it's real important that you have blacks that you can go to, that you can say, this has happened to me, it is disturbing me. The [white] person will not acknowledge what they have done. Can you help me validate whether this is off or not? Having somebody that you trust, that's objective, that will tell you, "Hey, you were off there, you shouldn't have said that. They probably were being racist, but you should have dealt with it a different kind of way." But I think that my friends help me balance, because when you're in the midst of it, you get so hurt and so angry. It's like these two emotions running at the same time. It's like how dare they do this to me, that's the anger. Don't they realize that I'm a human being too? So, you have all these emotions happening at the same time inside of you, and you just need somebody to say, yea, this probably is happening to you, and this is how you can deal

> with it. And my family, I was raised in a Christian home, and raised that you treat people the way you want to be treated.

Discussions with friends help by validating a black person's experience, as well as confirming one's sense of what is right and just.

Black organizations can also be places of refuge and sources of support. For example, one important survival tactic for black students encountering poor treatment at predominantly white colleges is to link up with local black organizations. A hospital supervisor and civil rights activist who lectures to black college students offered the following advice to those newly arrived at white campuses: "They should look up the black student organization on campus. . . . It is very important that they do this. A lot of what happens to black students that come to this university—I'm sure it happens in all of the big universities—is that their parents have mislead them. That's the reason the majority of them can't survive on that campus." She felt strongly that black students must join together on a white campus:

> It is important that they hook up and become a very strong black organization member, to be there for each other. You can't walk that alone. You cannot be a lone black in a group of whites, because eventually that's going to wear so thin. . . . you need to first and foremost develop a real close relationship with the black organization. Go into the community, that's important, whether it's to the church, church activity, or a black organization in the community, but be a part of the community as well as part of the school community. Those are things that parents should tell their children.

From this point of view survival as an individual alone is impossible; only collective efforts ensure success. Thinking in a similar vein, one engineering student we interviewed on a white campus said: "I would have sought out more support groups."

The Role of Helpful Whites

In discussions with middle-class black Americans one senses a recognition that the problems of color discrimination in the United States will not be solved by either white or black Americans acting separately. Cooperation is deemed essential by most. On occasion, white reporters and colleagues of the authors have asked how helpful whites have been to middle-class African Americans as they have sought their personal goals in this society. Our respondents' answers to this question vary but most seemed to fall into two general categories: either they said they had not been helped by whites, or they cited one or two whites who had been important to them, often at a specific point in their lives. Into the first category fall respondents like this salesperson for an electronics firm, who was asked if any whites had been helpful in achieving his goals: "I wish I could think of someone, but realistically I really can't. And God forgive [me] if there was, and I don't remember. Maybe the system's had that much effect on me that . . . I can't bring it up to a conscious level."

Other respondents had a mixed reaction to the question. A human services manager in a northern city initially replied, "I can't think of any," but then qualified her answer with this comment:

> I've had white colleagues who have been very helpful in skills development. I tend not to be a numbers person, and hate dealing with the financial part of my job. I'm getting better at it, but there's a white woman at work who's been very good at helping me to do that. And at my old job, there was a white woman who—it's very funny, from a

> very, very, wealthy family in the United States, worth millions, but acted very much in the manner in which it was comfortable for me, did not flaunt that station or position in life, and we got to be very close personal friends. In fact, she worked with me, and no longer lives in this city, but at that particular job, she was very helpful in helping me, in fact, to gain the skills, computer skills, and connection skills, that I needed to do that job well, and for that I'll always be grateful.

The whites mentioned here were helpful in particular areas of skill development, yet this woman made it clear in her interview that no white person had been broadly and fundamentally helpful to her achievements.

The response of a clerk in a vehicle parts department to a question about whether whites had been especially "helpful to you in achieving your goals?" was positive:

> Yes. I would think so. They encouraged me. In fact, when I was deciding that I would bring this lawsuit against the company that I work for, I talked to this young guy—he's about thirty—and I asked him, I said, "I've decided I'm going to sue the company, so who should I go to for support, since the company's so large and I can't possibly do this on my own. Should I go to the National Organization for Women or the NAACP?" He said, "Why not go to the National Organization for Women because they are very visible and vocal. The NAACP is an old organization and they haven't done anything in a long time." This is a young white guy, He's now supervisor down where I work, but he wasn't then. He's still my friend, though. . . . I have, oh, the French class that I have, I study, all of those ladies support me and what I do. . . . There's a lady who works with me, she's part-time on this job, and the regular women in there won't associate with her for some reason or another. She's a

> Mediterranean lady, a white lady, and we've become very good friends.

This woman found a white male supporter in a workplace where a number of whites had racially and sexually harassed her. Similarly, a banking executive in an eastern city mentioned some white friends as helpful, but not as central to her goal pursuits: "I've had some white friends who were there if I needed help, but no one who's pushed me and said, you can do it if you do this and do that, and you can achieve what you want. I think it's my own inner self who really wanted to do it, and went for it."

White friends are usually not knowledgeable enough about, or sensitive enough to, the U.S. racial situation to relate in a truly intimate way to the problems that their black friends face. Thus black students have noted that it is difficult to make close white friends, since few whites are willing to listen to their detailed accounts of or frustrations about racism on campus. We suggested in Chapter 5 that many white males, including some who see themselves as liberals, are defensive in the presence of black men, a point emphasized in an interview with a security supervisor in a western city: "I don't feel that I have too many close white male friends. . . . Just associates at work, but I really can't consider them close friends, because there's nothing that we share together. Most white males have a tendency to be defensive and not honest as to their relationship with a black male." He added that he had an easier time relating to white women at work. An airline customer service representative in the South spoke of the limitations of white friendships:

> As sympathetic as white friends are, they don't understand. They just don't. They think: well, because we're friends, then surely they're not racist, so what's the whole problem, why are you even bothered about it? So I can't discuss it with white friends, and I do have white friends. . . . in the

> industry, the neighborhood, the situations that I'm in, there just aren't that many black people. So my husband and my family become the stabilizing force for bouncing off situations. And I guess just knowing that I'm not the only one who's experiencing it, you know, that safety in numbers.

This woman spoke of the insensitivity of even sympathetic white coworkers and neighbors to racist speech and action. For black Americans the most trustworthy white people may be those who candidly see themselves as "recovering racists."

The effort on the part of middle-class black students and employees to find nonracist or antiracist whites who are helpful and supportive can be vital to survival because most historically white organizations, including colleges, corporations, and governmental agencies, do not have enough black Americans for there to be a critical mass and supportive social networks. A professor at a northeastern university recommended seeking out sympathetic whites, in spite of the difficulties.

> And then I think the other thing that blacks have to learn to do is to find whites in the system who are supportive and helpful to them, and there are such whites. I think that you can. . . . Some, even if they may have some attitudes that aren't totally liberated, they can sometimes still be helpful to people. And I think blacks have to learn how to utilize those kinds of resources, because if we don't, we won't make it, because there just aren't enough blacks in the system to serve that purpose.

Some respondents suggested that their relationships with whites in the outside world were strategic, somewhat like a chess game. A professor at a southwestern university explained how in some cases she was able to outthink whites with whom she was dealing, then added:

> I'm also very good at figuring out who has the power to make decisions—of someone I might be talking to. I'm pretty good at getting the occasional white person to be interested enough in what I do to intervene on my behalf. And I think that's a skill, [finding out] who makes the decision, who because of a particular idiosyncrasy might be sympathetic to your case. And then you learn how to go to those white people, and make your case before them, and get them to intervene.

Preparing Children to Face Discrimination

Black middle-class parents face the daunting task of preparing their children for racial slights and obstacles. Many know well what playwright August Wilson has written: "Blacks know more about whites in white culture and white life than whites know about blacks. We have to know because our survival depends on it. White people's survival does not depend on knowing blacks."[18] In an important research study James Jackson and his associates found that black parents took several different approaches to teaching children about racial issues. Some avoided the issue and gave no information; some imparted messages stressing the equality of blacks and whites; and some taught their children to distrust whites and stand up for their own rights.[19]

In our interviews we found a greater variety of messages. Thus a law school administrator discussed his parents' view of whites:

> I think they have subtly prepared me for different things. My father was always very conscious and said, "There're just a lot of things that you have to do to make sure that things are going to be okay for you. You've got to be care-

> ful of what people think and how people see you." And I think those are the basic things that they've passed on to me, not suggestions of how to deal with discrimination, but how to avoid it. It's just like preventive medicine. We waste a lot of money trying to cure people instead of spending more money trying to prevent illness.

The father's cautionary socialization was based upon the preventive medicine of avoiding difficult situations. His warning to be careful of what white people think suggests another dimension of the black double-consciousness. In their book on counselling black clients, Peter Bell and Jimmy Evans have argued that in normal social interaction whites need to think mainly of how they see themselves and how other whites see them.[20] For middle-class blacks, however, social interaction is usually much more complicated. Seeing themselves in relation to how other blacks see them is compounded by the requirement to orient themselves to whites' (mis)understandings. African Americans must work through a psychological maze as they develop the necessary relationships with white Americans. Not only must they determine how they see the variety of whites (from blatant racists, to covert racists, to the culturally ignorant, to the truly color blind), they must ascertain how they see themselves *in relation to* whites (as inferior, equal, superior, powerless, or powerful). Such determinations start at an early age, and parents are a major source of advice on how to handle white hostility and discrimination. This means devoting considerable time and energy to a task with which white parents are not burdened.

Lessons are taught by example as well as by mouth. And avoidance is not the only lesson taught by parents. A television anchorperson in a southwestern city described his mother's strong personal example:

> The [white] lady in front did not have to have her I.D. checked, and my mother had hers checked. Now the wom-

> an in front was not even from the town, but then they asked my mom. And my mom was like, "Wait a minute, I've been shopping here for X amount of years, been living here all my life." She didn't tell them who she was. And she said, "and you're going to ask for my I.D.? I don't even want the groceries." And she left. But then she thought about it and said, "No, I'm going back and get the manager." And [once there she] said, "hey, I supply some money to this store, and I've been shopping here for years. And my son's in town, and my people are from here." And the guy was like, "Mrs. James, I know that name." Because he knew me. She said, "don't give me the green light because of what my son does. He's younger than me. I was here before he was, so [don't] think because he's an athlete that that's going to be the green light for me to write a check in this store and not get my I.D. checked. So, I saw her do that kind of stuff. So, it's rubbed off on me.

Notable here is the discretionary character of white power in moments of interaction with black customers. Assertive adults can create outspoken children; this man reported responding aggressively to the discrimination he encountered in his own daily rounds as an adult.

The theme of a legacy of collective wisdom about racism was touched on or discussed by numerous respondents. Alluding to this inherited wisdom, a hospital administrator in a northern city discussed the conflict she felt:

> My goals, in terms of for myself and for my family, are in trying to teach them those inherited ways that others have learned and the wisdom that was passed on as to how to overcome racism, how to overcome discrimination, how to make yourself as good as anyone else to achieve and to accomplish. And I guess I can get hung up on the racism and discrimination, which is going to be there, but I think that

> I'd rather get hung up on *my* attributes, on *my* success, on *my* qualifications, on *my* skills, on *my* intellect, and being able to overcome with strengths within myself the racisms that might be, you know, some of the stumbling blocks.

In the socialization of children there is some tension between teaching an unclouded knowledge of racism's realities and communicating a sense of personal strength and capability. In this woman's view black children should be taught there are major barriers, but they also need to be taught that they can be overcome—a difficult balancing act for parents.

However, a newspaper publisher suggested a cautionary note about teaching children too much optimism about American promises of equal opportunity: "I think we owe an obligation to our children to teach them about racism and how to deal with it, instead of giving them the false impression that if you get a good education, if you go to the better schools, if you appease the white man, then you will not have to really deal with racism." In the United States there is much exhortation to work hard and strive to succeed as individuals. In this philosophy of life personal failure is to be accepted as one's own fault. But this philosophy only makes sense if the social game is fair. An executive officer at a white chamber of commerce spoke of teaching young blacks the hard lesson that the game is rigged against them:

> I think that, again, our children have got to realize that things really aren't fair, that there are barriers out there, that there are additional barriers, there are barriers in this world, and that everything that we face isn't because we're black. But we're going to face a certain amount of things that are because we're black. And I think if we teach our children on the front end of that tunnel, that that doesn't have to stop anything. We may have to figure out a different strategy, we may have to decide that instead of running

IBM, we're going to run our own multinational corporation.

In her view, teaching black children about racial hostility is important, but so is teaching them how to circumvent the barriers they will face.

Not surprisingly, a number of respondents urged young black people to fall back on friends and family to bolster their sense of self. A university professor had the following recommendations for black youth:

> [I recommend] that they talk to other people about it constantly, because I think you need every sense of reinforcement that you can get—that you can get from your friends, people that are going through the same things, from your family, from your teachers, from any well-intentioned human being, who seems to have some inkling that when you say that things are happening to you, you are telling nothing but the truth, that you are not imagining that things are going wrong, that you are not imagining that you're being oppressed. What you need is to have constantly reinforced your sense that the world is not fine, and you are . . . fine, and doing the best that you can under circumstances that are fairly horrendous. That's what I tell my students all the time, because what they tend to do is blame themselves for what happens to them.

White denial that the discrimination individual black Americans face is serious adds the burden of reality testing and fighting self-doubt to the burden of the discrimination itself.

Emotional support is critical to the black struggle. One mother, a therapist at a hospital, was blunt about getting black children, and black males generally, to share their pain: "I encourage my boys to share feelings. Not none of that macho shit where you fall down, and your knee's hanging off and you say,

'Don't cry, be a man.' And that's where a lot of our black men have gotten totally messed up at. It hurts, you cry."

Sharing one's pain and frustrations about life's troubles, including white oppression, was also recommended for blacks of all ages. A drug program director in the Midwest made this point:

> There is a population of older blacks, though, that are—like, my grandmother died when she was ninety-one—that don't like to talk a lot about that emotional pain that's there. . . . But there's an older population of blacks, when you start asking some of those [discrimination] questions, and they will choose not to talk about it because it hurts too bad. So, I agree we need to talk. But we need to also be encouraged by, and encourage, those [black Americans] because a lot of times they don't want to talk about it.

A social welfare program director, also in the Midwest, commented on the cost to all African Americans of repressing anger and rage over racism:

> [We need] to teach them, our people, how to talk about it and how to identify what it is. Because quite a lot of what we keep inside of us prevents us from being comfortable about who we are and where we want to go. I really believe that. I feel that a lot of us hold back our frustration and emotional pain because either we have not been able to have that permission or learn how to talk about those things. . . . We can get out of that negative environment of feelings in the mind.

Conclusion

We cited in Chapter 1 the view of Brittan and Maynard that the terms of racial and gender oppression are "profoundly shaped at the site of the oppression, and by the way in which oppressors and oppressed continuously have to renegotiate, reconstruct, and re-establish their relative positions in respect to benefits and power."[21] Today the interaction of blacks and whites in discriminatory situations has some similarities with that of the era of rigid segregation, but there are significant differences. The arrival on the scene of significant numbers of middle-class African Americans with substantial resources and power has created many situations where white Americans are forced into more explicit racial negotiation and where whites' assumptions of low black power are challenged. In the examples we have examined we frequently observe middle-class blacks establishing "power credibility," as whites realize that the blacks are not bluffing. Whether this perception will last beyond the particular incident is not clear, but it is a major change from the old racism.

Consequential too in this period of modern racism are the changing legal structure, the institutionalization of civil rights laws, and black Americans' belief in legal rights and civil justice. These statutes are momentous not only in themselves but also in the effect they have had of reinforcing the robust sense of justice that is a part of the black middle-class approach to everyday racism. In numerous accounts we have noted this black sense of justice due, of the right to fair play. The irony is that these African Americans are simply demanding to be treated like the average white person in this ostensibly democratic society.

Changes in interpersonal negotiation have not meant that the costs of discrimination have been eliminated. Throughout this book we have reported the individual and collective price paid in dealing with life crises created by the omnipresent white discriminators. The anger of many middle-class black Americans is intense, if often repressed, or channelled into overachieving and hypertension. We have also observed the remarkable and pervasive ability of African Americans to laugh at adversity. And we have seen the vital support of family and friends. The tremendous energy drain caused by discrimination has taken a toll on black achievement and performance. The exceptional achievements of these Americans have come in spite of, and in the face of, energy sapping racism. A central dilemma in fighting the internal stress of racism is how to cultivate a strong self-image, not only in oneself but also in one's children. At the heart of this positive self-image must be an enduring appreciation of black achievement and group worth, an avoidance of self-blame, and a recognition of the persisting flaws in the U.S. social system.

Chapter Eight

Changing the Color Line: The Future of U.S. Racism

TODAY blatant, subtle, and covert discrimination against African Americans persists in virtually all aspects of their public lives. Racism is central to the lives of white Americans too, even though many whites deny its presence or effects. Racial discrimination is pervasive, and cumulative and costly in its impact. Is there any hope for significant change? Near the end of most interviews with our middle-class respondents we asked several questions about future U.S. racial relations: whether they saw things getting better or worse for black Americans in the next few years; what major changes they would most like to see in white society; and what they feel black Americans should be doing to fight discrimination. Their responses open up interesting windows into how they view this society's racial order now and in the future.

But their responses offer more than just another view of the racial order. Understanding their perspective is crucial to taking major steps to combat white racism. Why should white Americans listen to these black voices? When one considers the loss of prestige and honor for the United States when governments and the mass media overseas critique outbursts of U.S. racism; when one calculates the human costs and multibillion dollar property losses of racial riots in the last decade in cities from Miami to Los Angeles; when one reads numerous reports of escalating hate crimes against black and other minority Americans; when one becomes aware of the terrible loss of human energy, talent, and achievements that results from black struggles with everyday racism; and when one examines the disintegration of the social fabric of cities where many black youth have lost hope of attaining the American dream, a white person has excellent reasons to listen to the voices of those most affected by racism.

But these voices must not only be listened to, they must be *heard.* Sadly, black and white Americans mostly live in separate worlds and often do not speak the same language. Our respondents regularly show how they and other African Americans are often not "seen" or "heard" by white Americans in everyday settings. Too often whites see no reason why they should "know" blacks, except perhaps in a special situation where a token black person will be called on to speak for all black Americans. Unless we find better ways to communicate, for whites to listen to black Americans, the "two societies, one black, one white—separate and unequal" that the prophetic Kerner Commission envisioned will never change, and racial violence will become all but inevitable. The recent call of some Ku Klux Klan leaders and other white supremacists for a racial war against people of color comes doubtless because they feel the time is ripe to attack.

A first step toward change is for white Americans to admit the reality of current white racism, a point underscored by a university researcher:

> I get sick and tired of seeing things on television, white people saying that "people aren't racist any more." That's a lie. They are racist. They don't want to recognize it, they refuse to recognize it. They say, "Let's not think about the past." Well, how do you go forward in the future if you don't think about the past? . . . You still have people in 1989 saying that same stuff. They do studies on the size of people's brains; they do studies on whether or not a black athlete is better than a white athlete, and this kind of stuff, which in itself says that this place is still racist. So, I would like for them to go ahead and, you know, it's almost like being an alcoholic. Admit that you're an alcoholic and go on to solve the problem.

Until whites recognize that they have been raised in a racist society and harbor its hidden influence even when they deny it, until whites recognize that they too must take action to deal with personal and societal racism, no matter how subtle, and to eradicate it, the racial situation in the United States will only worsen. Once most whites recognize that they and the system their ancestors created are deeply racist, then most black Americans will doubtless be willing to cooperate and be patient as real programs to eradicate racism are created. This task of educating white Americans will not be easy, but it is possible. Once the problem is admitted, the solutions can at least be envisioned and implemented.

The Present and Future

Few respondents were strongly optimistic about the future of racial relations in this nation. The majority realistically and candidly characterized the present and the immediate future as bad or getting worse. Among those who expected the situation to get worse, some pointed to internal community problems such as drugs and changing family structure, and some focused on racism in the external society. In a pessimistic comment a high school teacher in the North took the position that the larger society will continue to stagnate: "I don't see that there's going to be a horrendous amount of change. I think that if we had a president who was a little bit more dynamic, or a little bit more helpful to blacks, there might be some. But as it is, . . . I see no change in the way things have gone." Some made an even stronger argument that the progress in rolling back racial discrimination from the 1950s to the 1970s had been reversed between the early 1980s and the early 1990s. An academic counsellor commented: "It seems that things are getting worse. It seems like one minute things are going well, and we're progressing. But then within a short period of time, it looks like it's reverting and going back into a backwards kind of situation. One time we felt that prejudice and discrimination was in the past. But now, it seems like it's worse than ever." She continued with a mixture of hope and pessimism: "You would think that by now everybody would be loving each other and caring, but it's just not working out that way. There's always something bad to keep it from being what it should be. I think it's going to get worse before it gets better again. It's kind of bleak when you look at it."

Government action to eradicate prejudice and discrimination has oscillated in recent decades. From the early 1980s into the 1990s African Americans experienced a conservative backlash against an aggressive expansion of civil rights and economic opportunities for minority Americans. A survey of young Americans by Hart Research Associates found that the younger generation has a pessimistic view of the present and future. Among black youth a majority thought U.S. racial relations were "generally bad," and just under half of the white respondents agreed. On a related question, the black youth were more likely than the white youth (46 percent versus 30 percent) to feel that racial relations were getting worse.[1]

Our respondents mentioned specific reasons for being pessimistic about the future of racial relations. There was great concern about the conservatism on racial issues in the U.S. political and judicial systems, especially the decisions of the conservative U.S. Supreme Court since 1980. Several major decisions in the mid- to late-1980s made it much harder for blacks to sue for redress for racial discrimination. One of these cases was *Wards Cove Packing Co. v. Atonio* (1989), an employment decision decided in favor of the employer that made it more difficult for minority plaintiffs to establish a prima facie case of discrimination and reduced employers' responsibility to justify business practices that have discriminatory effects.[2]

Noting that things are "definitely getting worse," a bank manager in an eastern city explained the backward movement: "Supreme Court decisions are already reversing all the civil rights legislation. It's going to be harder for you to prove discrimination. Everything is being turned around." She observed that African Americans had become complacent rather than vigilant:

> And I think that's becoming so because we have gotten so relaxed and laid back and thinking that everything is on the up and up, when it's not. I think that they have given us a false sense of security by letting some of us achieve our goals. We're being carefully manipulated by them, because I probably am a token. I know I'm a token. But you're going to have that in this society, because we don't have the economic strength to put ourselves in these positions. But I think we have a false sense of security, and they're just going to put a double whammy on us, because sooner or later they're going to start reducing whatever we had before.

A strong sense of the history of U.S. racial relations underlies most of our interviews, together with a sharp awareness of the possibility of retrogression in public policy. Numerous respondents explicitly or implicitly indicated that current gains, including their own, represented a tenuous advancement that was being, or could be, rescinded by whites in power. A law school administrator was explicit about the signal the Supreme Court was sending:

> I think I see it getting worse. I mean, the recent Supreme Court decisions will tell you that. Those decisions are eroding away or taking away all the gains that—when I was coming along, we used to march and protest to get the laws passed, Title VII and the laws against discrimination. Okay, that [court action] sends a signal to the rest of the, to the white community, that, "Hey, you don't have to treat them as well as you used to."

With some laughter he noted the gallows humor at his law school:

> And in fact that's one of the jokes around here at the law school, between whites and blacks, is that every time they come out with a new decision, they say, "You better start learning how to shuffle again." "Tap dance, or something, because it looks like they're trying to put you back into slavery, right?" And that's the attitude. And employers—once they see this, I mean, that's just a green light for them to not use affirmative hiring procedures and promotions.

Several respondents touched on the damage to the black cause done by the Republican administrations in the 1980s and early 1990s. The director of a midwestern drug treatment program denounced governmental cutbacks in safety net programs:

> Worse, primarily because we just went through eight years, the last eight years presidentially have taken away everything that was done in the sixties and the seventies. I mean, like we were talking about how Bush's new drug plan, the money that he's allocating is not even putting us back up to where we were before Reagan came back. Educationally, they've taken away programs that we fought for in the sixties and the seventies. Head Start programs, programs like that, are consistently being cut out.

Since the 1960s the Republican party's stance on civil rights issues has been perceived by a majority of African Americans as retrogressive and inimical to black interests. The historical evidence, though not yet compiled in a systematic way, seems supportive of their view. In his research Chandler Davidson has shown that, during the lifetimes of our respondents, the Republican party has intentionally abandoned black voters for a strategy targeting the concerns of white voters. From Barry Goldwater in the 1960s to Ronald Reagan and George Bush in the 1980s and 1990s, the Republicans' political campaigns adopted a strategy of aggressively seeking the votes of white suburbanites and Southerners to reinvigorate the party. Racial codewords such as "quotas," "busing," and "crime in the streets" have often been used, and white-oriented media campaigns have been developed, even though they are often offensive to the nation's black citizens.[3] As a professor at a western university put it, one sees "in the Reagan and Bush administration a dismantling of the whole Civil Rights acts . . . [and] that says racism is alive and well and kicking, and we will allow it to flourish."

Questioning the Republican administrations' cuts in social programs, our middle-class respondents expressed their concern for poorer blacks. In recent years, authors on the right and on the left have been critical of middle-class blacks' alleged insensitivity in forgetting the black poor or the larger black community.[4] In a 1980 *Newsweek* column Chicago journalist Leanita McClain, who saw herself as "uncomfortably middle class," replied to such critics of the black middle class: "The truth is we have not forgotten; we would not dare. We are simply fighting on different fronts."[5] Similarly, there is little evidence in our in-depth interviews of a lack of middle-class concern or sense of responsibility for blacks who are less affluent. Expressing a sense that things are getting worse, a psychologist in the Southwest was articulate on who suffers most:

> I worry. It really feels like a struggle. Yes, you know, the "good little colored folks," and those handful of folks that are bright enough, talented enough, and at the right place at the right time where they let the one in the door, they're going to do o.k. So, you and I will do fine. It's this other class of folks who are not quite as advantaged as we are, who didn't have quite the academic skill, who don't have quite the family money resources, or who come from a little more unhealthy families, that I really worry about.

In some of the later interviews we asked specifically whether the respondents felt that middle-class black people have a special responsibility for their poorer brothers and sisters. There was substantial agreement that the black middle class had such a responsibility, as role models, educators, supporters, and advocates. The range of "dues" owed was suggested by a college graduate working for a western telephone company:

> We owe them our respect. We owe them our identity. See, we owe them much more than what we can give them. We not only have to be role models for them, but we have to help them, we have to encourage them by any means possible. Not by financing their entire existence, not giving them

> a hand out, but teaching them to beat the system, by studying hard, getting good grades, and using this thing called scholarships and grants and work study programs to get an education. We need to educate them on how to build their self-esteem and their self-respect, so that they can stand firm and lift their chin and be proud of who they are and what they are. . . . We have to break the arm of the oppressor on our necks. We have to lift each other up by supporting each other, being a guide, a road map, a light in the darkness.

In our observations many, if not most, African Americans in the middle class have reflected regularly on their obligations and duties to the larger black community. Many of our respondents would agree with a central proposal in *Rethinking the American Race Problem*, a recent book by Roy Brooks, a black law professor. Brooks proposes that middle-class black Americans should take an even more active role in helping working-class and poor black Americans, acting as role models, giving financial support, and teaching consumer savvy and racial survival techniques.[6]

Evaluating the present and future, some of those we interviewed were concerned about the need for broad economic changes. The drug program director commented on worsening economic conditions: "I find it very difficult to be black in white America. And I think that it didn't used to be that way, it's changed. And the changes aren't positive. Anymore, you see change and it's not as positive. There are fewer people working in the workplace, there've been many replacements and removals of blacks. It's just, you know, we need to make strides for us, and we've seen some backwards movement." Reflecting on similar issues, the owner of a small business in the Southwest noted the decline of U.S. industry and the excessive reliance on products from overseas:

> I see things, unfortunately, I see things getting worse for blacks in the next few years. Not only for blacks. Things will get worse for America, for all Americans, over the next few years, as I stated earlier. . . . American industries are shutting down everyday. We're getting all our products from some other country, which means that those jobs that people had are no longer there. So, if America is going downhill in terms of job market and everything else, then certainly that includes blacks even more so, because unfortunately blacks are already behind in the job market and what their earnings are.

Economic restructuring, sometimes called deindustrialization, has been offered as one major explanation for the development of a black "underclass" in central cities by scholars as diverse as Sidney Willhelm and William J. Wilson.[7] The capitalist market has become increasingly global over the last two decades, and many U.S. corporations now operate and employ around the world. This global employment market has made cheaper labor available to U.S.-based firms, and as a result millions of industrial workers have lost jobs because of plant closings or employment cutbacks. Following restructuring layoffs, black and other minority workers have often had the most difficulty finding new employment.[8]

A staff assistant to a state legislator noted how deindustrialization has affected middle-class black Americans:

> You know, manufacturing is no longer the thing, we're an information economy, whatever that means, and increasingly the economic opportunities that come open are going to be fewer and fewer for us on a lot of different levels for a lot of different reasons, so I think things are getting worse, so I think that's going to force us to get up off our butts and do something. I've often said that, I said back in 1980, I think Ronald Reagan getting elected is going to be

> the best thing in the world that could happen to black folks because it was going to jar us into believing that everything wasn't o.k. Well, eight years did a lot for us, I think. I think the Reagan presidency was the absolute most anti-African American presidency in recent decades. And I think that was good for us, because we had too many of our black middle class people saying that everything's o.k. now, I have mine, now you get yours, but they saw that they were only one paycheck away from those 'bobo niggers' that they always talked about on the east side. So, when they started to lose those paychecks they started to understand.

Mixing economic analysis with commentary on some middle-class blacks who, if only temporarily, turned their backs on the poor, this young activist emphasized a point most respondents seem to sense, that those who have moved into the middle class find themselves no more protected from racism than the less fortunate. As we have suggested earlier, there is a chilling political dimension to current U.S. economic restructuring, for since 1980 there has been a resurgence of white supremacy groups and perspectives, the latter only thinly disguised in the electoral campaigns of men like Louisiana's Republican senatorial candidate and presidential hopeful, David Duke, an ex-Nazi and an ex-Ku Klux Klan leader.

With some frustration a university professor commented on the broader implications of restructuring in the U.S. economy:

> I see things getting worse, and that has to do with the way the dominant society is using and allowing blacks to be scapegoated. It's a market economy that's failing at certain sites, and that's at the life of most human beings, and succeeding wonderfully at the site of upper-class economic participation. Given that it's failing, and that one way to make sure that an economy that's failing that many people, is that you find a group or groups that you can blame for the

> failure. And black folks exist as a group that everybody can blame for what's going wrong. We can blame the economy on them, because we can say they're not a productive group and a lot of the economy is being spent taking care of them. Because, of course, Americans don't read that a lot of the economy is being spent taking care of wealthy people in the defense industry. But since most Americans don't see it that way, black folks are causing us to spend money because they're poor, and they don't contribute anything, because they're criminals and it costs a lot to maintain them, because they're drug addicts and drug pushers, and we have to spend a lot in order to stop the drug trade. With all that being played out, I don't see how things can get better, because Americans as a group are not taught to think about what's happening to them.

Thomas and Mary Edsall have explained the 1980s' white backlash against social welfare and civil rights programs in terms of what they view as the pro-black actions of liberals in the Democratic party since World War II. As these authors see it, the white middle class as a group has accepted equality of opportunity for black Americans and has accepted the civil rights laws of the 1960s, but has never approved of affirmative action and other aid programs for black Americans, programs that in the Edsalls' view were forced on white voters by liberal white elites. Adopting a white-voter strategy, the Republican party attacked these liberal-elite policies in order to establish a new conservative ideology radically opposed to "special preferences and quotas" for black Americans.[9] Widely accepted by other white commentators on racial matters in the United States, this argument views white liberals as abandoning the needs of other whites and cozying up to blacks, whose needs are somehow exaggerated. Few of our respondents show any inclination to buy into such an argument. They do not feel coddled by elite white actions and programs. They do not see the white majority as strongly committed to truly equal opportunity or the enforcement of civil rights laws. In the view of the professor above the central problem of U.S. society lies not in the modest social programs supported for a time by white elites, but in the fact that the capitalist market economy (capitalists' actions) has failed large numbers of workers and their families, in all racial and ethnic groups, while from 1980 to 1993 the rich often got richer under conservative economic and political policies. African Americans like this professor are aware that blaming the problems of a declining or stagnating capitalist economy on black Americans has a long history."

Changes Sought: The Dominant White Society

The solutions to racial conflict proposed by some prominent white scholars contrast sharply with the views of most of our respondents. For example, George Keller, a prominent white educator, has played down the centrality of racial discrimination and blamed black leaders for black problems in education: "Petulant and accusatory black spokespersons will need to climb off their soapboxes and walk through the unpleasant brambles of their young people's new preferences and look at their young honestly."[10] In recent years this blame-the-victim perspective has resurfaced with vigor, taking hold on much white thought about racial issues, yet it is fundamentally out of touch with the black experience of persisting racism.

The contrast with the social changes sought by middle-class black Americans is indeed striking. When we asked the respondents what they would most like to see changed in the larger white-dominated society, most of the changes fell into two broad categories: either political, economic, and educational reforms, or changes in attitude among whites. At the societal level they call, among other things, for new economic support programs, for new educational programs that deal realistically with black Americans and white racism in U.S. history, for enforcement of civil rights laws, and for greater equality and the redistribution of power. At the personal level they call for major changes in whites' stereotypes about African Americans, in whites' understanding of the black struggle and the courage it requires, and in whites' commitment to fair play and equal opportunity. African Americans are clearly one of the important carriers of the radical American tradition of championing full social, economic, and political rights.

Only in times of national prosperity and expansion does it appear that the majority of white Americans are willing to consider serious government programs to address the needs of less privileged citizens, especially those who are not white. Even then, most whites do not view the stratified character of this society as especially problematical.[11] In contrast, the middle-class black Americans with whom we talked often think in terms of power and inequality and underscore the justice of redistributing resources from the privileged to those in need. A director of planning at a university called for restructuring the support system for those without adequate food and shelter:

> It's a easy answer, and an impossible one to achieve, probably. I'd like to see change [in] the process and structure of providing the wherewithal for people to live in the country. This society is . . . sufficiently wealthy to enable those who are less fortunate to live in decent housing, to be able to give birth to children who have a chance to survive, to be able to provide the kind of nourishment that will facilitate the growth and development of offspring and to be educated in a way that does not demean their children. This may sound revolutionary, and if that's what it is, then so be it. . . . You have children who . . . lack a lot of the basic

> things that they need in order to survive. And you have a system that says that they lack these things because they are not as able as other children. What nonsense, what nonsense!

These words describe basic economic support programs as "revolutionary," only a quarter century after President Lyndon Johnson's War on Poverty and a half century after President Franklin Roosevelt's statement calling for implementation of a broad economic bill of rights, which included the "right to earn enough to provide adequate food and clothing" regardless of "race or creed."[12] In a similar vein, a college professor commented on the economic education of affluent whites. In her view these middle-class whites must experience the economic misery of people of color in order to see who the real economic oppressor is: "What I think, unfortunately, has to happen for things to get better, is for large groups of white people to be even more oppressed than, say, poor white people are oppressed now, and for them to be oppressed to the extent that they can no longer escape the fact that it's not the fault of blacks, or Chicanos, or Vietnamese boat people."

Real change requires many whites to make major sacrifices, to give up power and privilege. A student at a historically white university proposed that whites must sacrifice because of the history of racial exploitation:

> Oh, yes, they sit around and talk about, "Yes, we want equality for everybody." They want it on their own damn terms. They want it when they are ready. They want it when they don't have to sacrifice shit. And that's why they're mad about affirmative action because they have to sacrifice. I mean to get any long-run gain, logically, you do have to sacrifice. I'm sorry, black people have been doing the sacrificing for the last couple of hundred years, I think it is the white man's turn, thank you.

For many whites the image of Dr. Martin Luther King, Jr., is one of a moderate leader, yet in an interview not long before his death, King argued that whites must sacrifice for real change: "White America must recognize that justice for black people cannot be changed without radical changes in the structure of our society."[13]

In the last decade numerous media discussions have focused on the changing demographics of the United States; white Americans are projected to lose their voting majority in the twenty-first century, a diminishment of power that alarms many whites. Among those we interviewed, several saw the erosion of white power as underway; a manager in an East Coast firm was eloquent:

> I would like to see the [white] fear to be gone. Because it really is a matter of fear, in my view. And fear is really a false expectation about reality. But, you see, one needs to understand how this whole thing operates. The whole discrimination issue is really one of power. And it's one of money. And it's one of knowledge. And that white power base has been eroded over the years, because of some of those struggles of our parents, and their parents, and so forth. And now we are, we certainly have access to the knowledge, and to the education, in ways we never did before. And some of us are getting access to the money. But still, when you look at the statistics, we're not nearly where, we're not nearly comparable in terms of our earnings compared to our white counterparts.

In the United States the changing demographics, the growing number of Americans with non-European roots, do not necessarily entail a speedy shift of power to the underdog. This manager commented on the chilling prospect of a shift in the direction of a society such as South Africa: "When I look forward—you may be familiar with some of the information on Workplace

2000, when people of color in the population will exceed white people in this country. And unless that's really managed very carefully, at the worst end you could have a South Africa, where you have the whites still in power and the minorities just kind of out here trying to get it."

One institution targeted for change by our respondents is the U.S. educational system. A student at a mostly white university wanted education changed for the sake of black children:

> I think the educational system is very important because there are a lot of young blacks who go around in life not knowing a thing about themselves and their past, because all their days in school they've been taught about Christopher Columbus, the Greeks, Charles Darwin, and all the rest of these so-called great Europeans in history. And they're not taught anything about their own past dealing with ancient African history, the accomplishments of blacks in history in America, etcetera. And as a result, black people still have a deep inferiority complex when they go out in the world, which in effect in many ways affects their self-esteem, their self-worth, their self-pride.

Black children are not the only ones shortchanged by white-dominated school curricula. A southern newspaper publisher argued for more fundamental changes in how black and white children are taught:

> I think that if our children, and I say, our children, I'm not talking about just black children, I'm talking about white children, if they were educated with black history, not as black history, but as a part of American history, if black teachers were encouraged in the classroom, if parenting were taught in school as a class, then I think those factors would contribute more to changing America than anything. Because I have seen where you cannot legislate mental atti-

> tudes, you cannot politicize mental attitudes, you cannot purchase mental attitudes, you have to educate. And education starts at a very, very early age, kindergarten. The point is that if we could ever get to that extent to where when you open the history book, you not only see the George Washington Carvers and the Booker T. Washingtons and the Martin Luther Kings, but you see the Charles Drews, and you see all the other people that we don't read about, and the fact that black people created mathematics—those things aren't taught.

Adding another angle to this perspective, a student at a private university felt strongly that whites must learn to respect black opinions and priorities:

> The white world and the European world and the majority culture have to start taking the Third World and black people and minority cultures seriously and treat them as adults and respect them and respect their opinions. That's it. They're just going to have to stop telling us what's best for us and giving us what's best for us, and we're going to have to start making what's best for us and taking what's best for us.

Since the late 1970s some educators, black and white, have called for the integration of the school curriculum at all levels, and many discussions and debates have centered on the need for multicultural materials and teaching. Protesting the many multicultural courses and programs that have been implemented, white, especially conservative white, commentators in a series of influential books and articles have attacked multiculturalism as a bastardization of the curriculum.

In our view black demands for educational change are sensible and realistic—if this nation wishes to survive to the end of the next century. The so far modest changes in the direction of a multicultural curriculum in U.S. schools and colleges do not yet go nearly far enough. Much more multiculturalism in every aspect of U.S. schooling is necessary. Multicultural teaching must be tough and deep; it must examine the racist history and present of the United States. This type of broadened education is one way to begin to eradicate white racism. The attacks on multicultural education led by such white luminaries as Arthur Schlesinger, Jr., in recent years are shortsighted, even in terms of the self-interest of white Americans. We agree with some of our respondents that a better and broader education for whites is essential.

Changing White Attitudes

A better curriculum in the schools and colleges should ameliorate whites' misunderstanding of U.S. racial history, but white attitudes toward blacks derive from more than cultural and historical ignorance. Some opinion survey data on whites' racial views indicate a significant improvement in recent decades.[14] Yet there are problems with these data, as the lives of the African Americans we have examined document. The surface-level character of white responses often may not tap the deeper feelings of many whites in regard to black Americans. In addition, if one examines the blatantly racist responses to some recent survey questions, some 20 to 40 percent of whites show themselves to be very racist, if not segregationist. And other recent surveys show that a majority of whites hold some racist stereotypes of blacks as lazier than whites and as more violent than whites.

Middle-class African Americans, like other African Americans, express great concern about these racist attitudes; our respondents had several suggestions for bringing about changes in them. Whites must learn to understand the black experience with racism and to feel black pain and anger. A school administrator asserted the need for whites to walk in a black person's shoes:

> Whites need to become educated. White folks need to make an all out effort to learn what it is to be black. They need to see America from Africa to these shores; they need to live and process me. When I say me, I'm talking about what it is to be black. Learn me, try to process what I've been through. Try to understand what I've been through in order to think the way I think. Try to see things the way I see them, or I've seen them.

Answering a question about required changes in white society, a southern television broadcaster asked that, rather than "lumping us all together and still seeing us the way their mothers and their fathers saw us," whites abandon "ingrained attitudes about black people." She pled for a better understanding of the heroism blacks exhibit:

> I don't think they really understand how brave and courageous and strong and all those wonderful, positive things we are, but if they would just think for a minute how we were able to survive slavery, they would understand then. You know? If you asked them, if you sit down and let them look at "Uncle Tom's Cabin," which was on cable the other night, and say, "Do you think you could've survived that? Do you think you could've survived the beatings and the hangings and your daughter being taken away from you and taken to the massa's house to sleep in his bed?" And you know, I mean, we survived that, and we still came out reasonably sane.

A receptionist at a major corporation in the South expressed her wish that whites would understand the reality of racial inequality and oppression:

> In the dominant white society I would like to just for one time in life, to see them be real, if they know what being real is. . . . Being real is to stop asking black people, "What do you want or what else do you want? We've given you this, What else?" Being real is that you have the jobs. Most jobs that you go on, the companies are white owned or foreign owned, or Japanese, etc., but even though you have the jobs, even though you are supervisors and all, to treat people not like underclassmen, noncitizens, but to treat them like they are real people, and to not feel like—and not only feel like—you know, like I'm in a class of my own. Because I think really white people do not really know that we all will live together or die together. . . . So I would say that same thing to white America. Whatever is good for him is good for me and in the same manner that he gets it. . . . I want to be wanted not by having to force the issue for affirmative action and all this sort of thing, but because the white man knows within his conscience that's just the right thing to do.

After commenting that she is tired of hearing that the United States is color blind, she concluded forcefully: "I don't think it's going to ever be color blind. You can always look at a person, and I look at a person, and I know that person's white and I know that person's black, but behind the blackness and the whiteness there is a mental mind that no one can put a color on. That's why I'd like to see white people come to grips with life." Our respondents also called for a renewed commitment to affirmative action and the enforcement of existing civil rights laws and lambasted the recent conservative notions of "reverse discrimination."

During the 1980s such conservative notions resulted in a restructuring of the U.S. Commission on Civil Rights and of the U.S.

Department of Justice, so that both formerly pro-affirmative-action agencies in effect became opponents of aggressive affirmative action. An aide to a state legislator commented:

> I got into a long discussion with a white guy here at the Capitol . . . he was bellyaching about affirmative action, which is the biggest farce. There's never really been any affirmative action in this country. It's never really been enforced, and it's only been on the books little more than fifteen years. And stack that up against four hundred years of slavery and another hundred years of Jim Crow, and you see how ludicrous the whole reverse discrimination argument is. There can't be reverse discrimination unless, miraculously, tomorrow for four hundred years white people were enslaved and then they had another hundred years of Jim Crow and then we were in charge of things, *then* you could talk to me about reverse discrimination. . . . And he was saying, "You know, well I didn't have any thing to do with what happened in the past, and I don't feel like I should suffer, and I should be penalized, and blah, blah, blah." And I told him, "What did your grandfather do?" [He said,] "My grandfather was a mechanic. He worked a good union scale job back in the 1900s." [I asked] "Then, what did your dad do?" [He said,] "Well, my dad went to college, and got out of college, and he's an engineer now." And I said, "Well, how do know—we won't even go back four hundred years like we should, but let's just go back three generations—how do you know that because of Jim Crow and because of segregation and because of overt racial oppression, the mechanic that your grandfather was and the job he had wouldn't have been held by my grandfather, had he been allowed to. How do you know that my dad would not have been able to attend Georgia Tech and become an engineer, had he been allowed to and had his

> grandfather had a good union scale job and could afford to send him? How do you know?" So, yes, white people today, even young white people today, are still benefitting from past segregation.

It is discrimination, past and present, that requires the present remedy of affirmative action programs. We agree with our respondents that the U.S. government must enact and enforce them aggressively if traditionally white institutions are to respond adequately to the reality of racial discrimination in the lives of all black Americans.

In recent years there has been much discussion among white commentators and scholars about the alleged "immorality" and "destructive values" of black Americans, especially poor blacks in the so-called black underclass.[15] In contrast, some blacks with whom we spoke were critical of the values of whites, including those at the top of the social and economic pyramid. Reviewing events in the lives of Wall Street investors, a professor at a northeastern university commented on white values:

> I think that the dominant white society is driven by all the, what I consider the, wrong human values: competition, money is the top-valued thing. See, what we have in the dominant white society, you have the Ivan Boeskys, the white-collar crime, you have all of that being done. And it has a kinder, gentler face than people shooting people over crack in the neighborhoods, or a teenager saying, "Hey, if I can be a lookout for the drug guys, and just by standing on this corner and alerting them to the fact that the cops are coming I can earn a couple hundred bucks a day, you think I'm going to work at Burger King? No way." Well, that's the same set of values that drives an Ivan Boesky to say, "I can cut corners or I can do insider trading and all the rest.". . . We don't see how that relates to the behavior of

> young people in this country, and particularly young blacks who may be involved in easy money from drugs and that sort of thing. And it just happens that the penalties are much higher for the young people who get involved in drugs and that kind of quick and easy money.

Important to a deeper moral analysis of the situation of young or poor black Americans is the character of the prevailing role models, and not just the black middle-class role models that analysts like Keller and Wilson examine. At least as important is the standard set by powerful whites in the society's dominant institutions.

Running through many interviews is a strong call for *all* whites to move in the direction of fair play and truly equal opportunity, as this bank manager emphasized: "I would like to see both black men and women just given a fair shot. I don't necessarily need anyone to give me anything. However, if I qualify and work for it, just let me move along. I feel that if possibly myself, I wasn't black, a black woman, I would be much further along than what I am now." Discussing white stereotypes, an East Coast public administrator said that one thing she would like to see is the "realization that blacks as a people are as capable as the majority, and that we deserve a fair share in this country, a fair share." She continued:

> And that's all we've ever wanted, and somehow, that's gotten lost I think in all of this. An opportunity to have access to some kind of job, educational opportunity, some kind of housing. And there might be a lot of lip service to that, but then they change the rules of the game. What will happen is, "Yeah, you can move into my community." And then what will happen next is people will start selling their homes at twice the price, and move to another subdivision, up the price, and make it out of the reach of the average

> black American. I mean, there are all kinds of games that are played under the guise of equal opportunity, when in fact it is not.

The issue of opportunity and the theme of the rules of the game we have encountered in previous commentaries. Recall the sentiments of the black entrepreneur who was the first one interviewed for our project: "We learn the rules of the games, and by the time we have mastered them, to really try to get into the mainstream . . . then they change the rules of the game." From this perspective, whites in positions of authority must stop excluding blacks from the rewards that should accrue from having played the opportunity game according to the official rules.

How does one bring about significant changes in white attitudes? Only a few racial relations training programs have a record of success in the United States. And for the most part they are small or localized in one corporation or one community. Often they take the form of sensitivity training or group discussions between whites and people of color about prejudices and stereotyping. There are some inherent problems in much of this awareness training. Some training focuses on cultural differences and not on racist behavior. And one reason for the failure of racial relations education and training to reach large groups of white Americans is the lack of backing by most top corporate and U.S. government officials. One exception is the backing given to racial change in the U.S. military, especially the U.S. army. A computer engineer cited as a model for new programs to sensitize whites the relatively successful program of racial relations training conducted in the U.S. armed forces:

> We need to let them [whites] know that racism and discrimination is still alive, even though we're not carrying the picket signs, walking up and down the street. We need to let them know that we want to be done equally. How do

> we do that? Example, like in the military. In the military you have a course called "Race Relations." This is what you go through all the time in all branches of the military, and I really believe that helps. They need to have more race relations courses.

Many thousands of U.S. citizens who have served in the U.S. military in the last two decades have received some training in understanding racial and ethnic groups other than their own. Although some African Americans have criticized this military program as too brief or too modest, in this respondent's view it does at least provide one model for broader application. It seems ironic that the one large organization that currently is the most racially integrated and has the most developed program to improve racial understanding is the U.S. army. Clearly, however, military organizations have the hierarchical structure to implement change that most civilian organizations do not have.

Noting that understanding should be a reciprocal process for blacks as well as whites, a probation officer made this plea:

> I see a sensitivity, I think, to all ethnic minorities, even by ethnic minorities themselves. I'd like to see a much more moral development take place in this entire country. . . . I think by and large most often white America and black America, too, I think is entirely focused on what we like and what we need and not necessarily sensitive to what other people's concerns are. I don't know that white males are really in tune to the impact that unfairness can have and how far-reaching it can be with black people generally.

Some respondents put their hopes for improvement in the development of closer relationships between blacks and whites, especially younger whites. Optimistic about current change, a corporate sales manager in the Southwest commented that what he would like to see changed in white society are some of the stereotypes about blacks:

> I think it's improved a lot and I think it's going to continue to improve because you have more and more exposure to each other. My kids have white friends that they are dear to, and it's pure friendship. And I was probably twenty-two years old before I had a real relationship, a one-on-one relationship with a white person that I considered my friend. And that person and I have had a friendship for twenty years; probably one of my best friends. My kids are experiencing that at four and five and six and seven years old. I think that's going to make a difference in white society, people having that exposure.

The "equal status" contact we have previously discussed may be increasing in some sectors of U.S. society. Studies have shown that white prejudices are most affected by such contacts if they are not highly competitive but informal and friendly.[16]

An airline representative, with some laughter, argued that the whites in control have to be replaced by younger whites before there can be real change:

> I think about Eddie Murphy's [spiel] on Saturday Night Live—"Kill the white people!" [laughs] I'm sorry. Let's see, what changes? I guess for the people in control to just fade away. Because I see some hope with younger people, I really do. And I think that the grandmothers still have the influence, and no matter how you feel in your heart and what you know is right and how you feel is right, the grandmothers still have the influence, and I think until the grandmothers die we're still going to have the problem. . . . And so I see some hope with young people, and I think that's the salvation, if they can stay on the right track.

Black Action to Bring Change

In our view the burden of changing this racist society should lie primarily on the shoulders of white Americans. White Americans and their ancestors created a racist society, and white Americans are most responsible for taking action to eradicate this racism. And changing the system of racial inequality will require much concerted white action. This fact is recognized by many African Americans, including our respondents. But it is also clear that our respondents ask of themselves what they can do to accelerate positive changes in the state of U.S. racial relations. In the preceding chapters we have discussed the tactics and strategies used by individual black Americans as they cope with everyday racism. From the beginning of slavery African Americans have gone beyond individual strategies to consider what they as a group should be doing to deal with external racism and its internal effects on black communities. Among middle-class black men and women today one still finds a recurring concern with community and collective action. According to a dentist in a southern city the battle against racism must be carried out at several levels: "I think it has to be something that must be approached at different levels with different people. Some people are able to handle it better in the board room, on the floor of the House of Representatives and what-have-you, but I think we as a race of people must begin to support and encourage people to deal with it on every level in black society."

The white and black neoconservatives who have dominated much recent writing about U.S. racial relations prefer to target black individuals and communities as the source of contemporary black problems. A few of our respondents articulated a similar theme, although they usually acknowledged the role of racism in the problems. An administrator at a western university accented the need for community action:

> Stop this black on black crime. Start caring about being educated and start caring about their lives. Because a lot of the problem stems from blacks themselves. See, black folks are so busy killing each other and ripping each other, it's the crab syndrome. It's like a barrel full of crabs, as soon as one starts to crawl out, the rest of them pull him down, and they all try to struggle to get to the top on each other's back. We've got to learn cooperation, learn how to learn to work together and help each other.

Recognizing the need to struggle against racism in the outside world, the dentist quoted above emphasized the necessity of blacks' dealing with such community problems as "hopelessness and the despair that manifests itself in the black community with all the illegitimate children.":

> To many black young ladies, a baby is something to love and to love back, and they have so little of it. And there's no future in their eyes out there for them. I think we as blacks have many, many, many roles and many, many, many places to put our efforts and our time and our love and our patience to help black people that "have not been able to keep on keeping on."

This man's concern for the poor became clearer as he recounted a story of counselling in his office a young black woman with sexual and marital problems. In contrast to the neoconservative perspective, the respondents' assessments of community problems generally show a greater awareness of the direct and indirect role of racism in black crime and illegitimacy. And they envisage working on these internal problems while at the same time confronting racial discrimination.

Building up community pride and increasing black assertiveness, especially among young people, are goals for many middle-class black Americans. Community pride is an old concern in the writings of black leaders from William E. B. Du Bois to Malcolm X, Martin Luther King, Jr., and Jesse Jackson. Assessing the need for black action, a bank manager emphasized the necessity of teaching young people: "I think our future lies in our young people. We're going to have to train them, teach them how to live in this world, how to deal economically, how to be proud of ourselves. And when I say proud, not necessarily meaning because you want to straighten your hair or what have you that you're 'being white,' but mentally being proud. Being aware of who you are."

In racial and ethnic struggles across the globe one sees the central role of collective memory in the maintenance and development of group pride and community solidarity. This collective memory includes a central recognition of the history of African Americans and of the scale of the continuing struggle against white racism. Discussing this historical perspective, a high school teacher cited the collective memory of Jewish Americans as a model:

> I think that we cannot let that [memory of racial oppression] hinder us, and I like to use the example of the Jewish people. You never, ever will be alive and be allowed to forget the Holocaust. But that group of people does not let the Holocaust keep them back. They just keep it in front of you because they don't want it to happen again and they want you to always be apprised of what that was and how terrible it was. And periodically it's on T.V., and they're this and they're that, and they're always doing something about the Holocaust to keep it on everybody's mind. But they keep moving along. They keep moving along. And that is the one thing that I think we don't do as well. I think that we should never forget slavery. We should never forget from whence we have come.

In one way or another all of our middle-class respondents reveal that they participate in the collective memory of African Americans. This man is aware of the way the collective memory of slavery and other oppression can be debilitating, but he advocates the Jewish model of using the memory of oppression as a spur to achievements and to fuel the fight in human rights struggles.

An emphasis on black pride, black solidarity, and the memory of historical oppression are major pillars of an Afrocentricity movement in the United States.[17] Since the beating of Rodney King by Los Angeles police officers in 1991 and the subsequent Los Angeles riots in 1992, we have seen a reinforcement of black middle-class interest in concrete solidarity-building actions and a renewed commitment to "buying black" among some middle-class blacks. For example, in a *New York Times* story based on seventy interviews with middle-class black people in Los Angeles after a 1993 trial led to the conviction of only two of the four officers who had brutalized Rodney King, reporter Isabel Wilkerson found that many of these middle-class Angelenos were bitter and spoke with resignation about the need for black community solidarity and separation.[18] Many were moving their patronage from white to black businesses. This buy-black, build-black response seems to have been triggered by the view that one major way to deal with white racism today may be for African Americans to create economically stronger communities less dependent on whites. A newspaper publisher in our sample put it this way:

> I feel very comfortable about putting black people on the spot about not asking for a black sales rep. Often times these people are paid on commission, often times they will be more supportive. But then you have a group of people, like my mother, who believes that a white doctor is better than a black doctor. But yet, her daughter is in business, and she pushes her in business. Now, to me, that's a double

> standard. She's very critical of the black [emphasis], because I use all black doctors. And, anything I can get service-wise, I ask for a black person, because my thing is to keep that dollar within the black community. Now, for some people that may be interpreted as racist. I think often times our community says, "Oh, black people don't do a good job, or oh, black people are higher [in price]." And then after they try one black, they'll go to a white. The point is if they used a white, then if that white messed up they'd go to another white. So, my point is, why not go to another black? It's not a racist thing, it's a conscious effort to try to rebuild the economic structure of the black community.

The negative impact of western culture on African Americans reveals itself in the view among some black buyers that "white is better." The liberating strategy envisioned here is greater black solidarity.

One of our informants, a graduate student interviewed in 1992 after we finished the primary sample, called himself a "social revolutionary":

> I am a social revolutionary. It is my belief that black people will never receive from this society the rights and privileges that others possess. Therefore, it becomes incumbent upon blacks, along the lines of Frantz Fanon's alternative-systems thesis, to develop mechanisms within their own communities which will redress the discrepancies between the realities of a racist society and communal needs and objectives. I am a future teacher in the sense that I am teaching my people the knowledge of Afrocentric values.

Interestingly, this young man sees a type of social revolution in pressing for community action and the inculcating of an Afrocentric perspective to enhance and expand black pride.

Throughout our research many respondents advocated explicitly or implicitly a personal strategy of confronting white discriminators: African Americans must act, must confront, must argue in dialogue with whites. A corporate secretary commented this way:

> Speaking out, for one thing. Speaking out, but doing it at a minimum. Not doing it to get everybody angry. Do it with some sense. Stop covering it up. Stop talking about it only among your black friends. The black friends already know racism exists. The black friends are not the ones who created racism. Why talk to them about it? If you're going to talk to them about it, talk to them about which white friend you're going to go talk to about it.

An administrator at a northern university emphasized the need to continue a long-term dialogue with whites:

> I think they have to continue the dialogue, because as people get older, like me, I'm no longer patient enough to stop and explain to ignorant older white folks the practical realities. I think I would rather spend the time that I have left working with younger people, who're going to bring along the next generation, who're going to be the next generation out there operating, keeping things pretty good, for my grandchildren. . . . Is it up to blacks? I don't think you have too much choice; you have to do *something*, but certainly it takes more energy than I really have at this stage of the game, more energy or more patience. But the dialogue has to continue; you have to have it. If you can't sit down and talk in a rational manner about some of the conflicts, and at least if people don't buy your ideas, they have been exposed to them. And they may go back and think about them and be more fair in their dealings with us.

Throughout our interviews there is a recurring concern for the education of children, black and white. An attorney for a hotel chain, emphasizing that aggressive action against white barriers should be taught by example to children, argued forcefully that blacks should "be learning more about how to deal with the white racist world. Pushing ahead enough. Not making what these people think we are, or should be, come true:"

> A lot of people say, "Oh, I'm not going to get the job. Nobody's going to give it to me." So they don't even try. Or, "I don't care, I don't want to send my kid to that school." "To go to a school because it's all a white school," and "they'll take advantage of that kid and the kid's not going to learn." They should stop seeing that and look at it where I have as much right to be there as that white person. And teach the kid to overcome the obstacles that may stand in their way as they go about it.

His message, for black adults and young people, is not to be defeated by a sense of futility and to attack the barriers vigorously and assertively.

In addition to working for change within the African American community and for more aggressive individual protests, numerous respondents stand proudly within the distinguished black tradition of collective identification, organization, and protest in attempts to change white society. Over the last century organized black protest has ranged from legal strategies, to voter registration, to nonviolent civil disobedience, to violent attacks on the system. Some respondents called for more organization and more protest action. While they supported individual action, they assumed the importance of collective action in bringing social change. A human services manager in the Northeast commented about the benefits of activism among young people:

> All is not lost! There's hope! I'm encouraged by a newfound revolutionary spirit. I was very encouraged by the

> Howard University students demanding the resignation of Lee Atwater [campaign manager for George Bush in 1988]. That was wonderful! That kind of revolutionary fervor was just exciting to me. I'm excited by seeing black students do the black college tour that some of the agencies in this city operate each year. And I'm encouraged when I see black young people looking to black colleges for higher education. I'm encouraged when I see local activists in our community fighting for eminent domain and control of the land in this city, and getting it. I'm encouraged by that. And people are organizing and people are fighting, so I'm encouraged by that. While I said that I think in the short-run things will get worse, it will only, I think, ignite our fire to struggle more, and struggle in the collective fashion.

Other respondents also noted revolutionary stirrings in black America. A self-employed political consultant felt major changes were coming in the 1990s:

> The reality is, brothers and sisters have started moving toward Afros, towards the braids. We started moving toward the African attire. Okay, whenever you see that, revolution's on its way. But it's subtle, it's subtle. You see, I see it because I'm everywhere, you know; I'm not just locked up in this city, and I see it everywhere. . . . I'm telling you, girl; it's coming. And what's going to happen is, they're going to force us, America is forcing us . . . you're going to see a whole different America, because, honey, we're going to take names and kick ass. . . . So they're trying to hold on and control, but we saying, "Uh-uh, we not taking that anymore." And *we are*; I'm telling you, we're going to prove that in the '90s. And it's not going to be a whole lot of ranting and raving going on. Some cities, you might have to go through the '60s behavior.

Some respondents pressed for blacks to take political action within the existing political framework, both as individuals and in groups. They were aware of the heritage of the 1960s' civil rights movement that forced Congress to pass the Voting Rights Act of 1965, which encouraged voting in the South. An administrative clerk at a publishing corporation spoke of determined political action:

> Stop letting white folks push them around. One thing, we need to get out and *vote*. That's our number one priority. We do not go to the polls. We can't get any changes if we don't take the numbers out there to change them. "Oh, I'm not going to vote because . . ." You know, I've heard people say that, and I had never thought about it until I really, in the last five years, started working with the voter registration. "Why should I vote? It's not going to help anyway." And I can't believe that they actually believe that their vote won't count.

Similarly, a telephone company employee spoke of the need for community activism and political organization at the city level:

> Well, I think that we need to get more involved with what's going on around us. We need to be involved with our school systems. We need to be involved with our city councils. We need to be registered to vote. We need to have some kind of power base. And when you're dealing with a society that is built on power, and the wielding of power, sometimes you have to respond with power. Responding hate for hate does not work. But the only thing that power understands is more power. We must become educated, we must feed ourselves, for if we are not fed we cannot look up, we have to look down. We have to help our fellow brothers and sisters.

When asked in a follow-up question if the need for civil disobedience is past, he answered: "No, I think that it is a very real thing today, for our world is in for many changes, very recently. And we will be forced to either make a statement or be crushed by our oppressor. The only way we can fight the system is to stand up and fight. We cannot sit down and wait for the other guy to step in. . . . No, power has to be taken by force." The low visibility of the civil rights movements in the early 1990s seems to have lulled many into the view that African Americans will take most any indignities that are handed out. Yet the level of anger in many of our interviews is high, and this man's response suggests that more of the aggressive black activism and civil rights organization of the past could return.

The search for effective leadership has been an issue for African Americans from the beginning of racial oppression. In the last decade numerous white commentaries on the state of black Americans have been very disparaging of, if not hostile to, current black leadership. None of the blacks with whom we talked was so disparaging of black leaders as a group, although the owner of a landscaping business did comment on the need for better leaders today: "Well, unless somebody comes along, unless the good Lord drops us another Martin Luther King down here in the next few weeks, I'll tell you what, it's still going downhill. . . . Ever since that happened, we haven't had a leader, you know. We've got some out there that's defending themselves as leaders, but it's for their own personal goals."

The memory of Martin Luther King, Jr., is strong among these middle-class black Americans, and the desire for new leaders of his caliber may be nearly universal among black Americans. Numerous respondents mentioned the importance of black leaders like King, Malcolm X, or William E. B. DuBois to their own perspectives on the continuing black struggle. A southern newspaper publisher noted how the leadership styles of Martin Luther King, Jr., and Malcolm X were complementary models for the black rights struggle: "Martin Luther King, his whole thing was, wage the racism battle. But the way he did it; the finesse he did it with. Also the counterpart of the Malcolm X thing: take the racist monster and kill it. . . . I think the two balance each other off . . . if you had to choose between these two, which one would you choose?"

A professor at an eastern university called for inventive leaders, black or white, who could encourage intelligent thinking and action about racism in the United States:

> Well, it's hard to isolate one particular thing that I would like to see the most. And this is asking the impossible, but it's to ask for, to try to see someone take the lead, like the president of the United States, take the lead in encouraging some sincere thinking about race relations. Martin Luther King did it. Timing was important, but he did it. I don't think that would ever occur, but that's what I would like to happen.

The International Oneness of the Black Struggle

Reviewing issues of color coding in ancient civilizations, the late St. Clair Drake argued that "Crucial in the Afro-Americans' coping process has been their identification, over a time span of more than two centuries, with ancient Egypt and Ethiopia as symbols of black initiative and success long before their enslavement on the plantations of the New World."[19] African Americans have long drawn on the history, spirituality, and symbolism of Africa as part of their individual and group strategies for coping with the white-dominated society. Since the early 1980s black writers and scholars have probed more deeply and extensively than ever before into the significance of African history and cultures for African Americans.[20]

Several of those we interviewed wanted all blacks to develop a stronger knowledge of and solidarity with Africa as a way of fostering group solidarity and strong self- concepts. After noting the powerful ties of American Jews to Israel, a sales representative at a major corporation was persuasive on the urgency of developing similarly robust black ties to Africa:

> The way I see it is there is either conflict, or there is an understanding from black people that we are related to African brothers. We have to interact, the brothers have to see that also. For instance, my heart pains for what happens in South Africa. But I very easily have been able to accept the media's presentation of the issue now. And so, what I'm saying is, that should affect me, and I'm conscious of it, and most, a lot of other black brothers are conscious of it, it affects me. I know that shit is wrong, I know we ought to be doing more than we're doing. So, I guess what I'm saying is that the only way that gets better is we have to finally decide that we're one. We have to finally decide that black people around the world are one. I heard Stokely Carmichael say one time, that if you grow corn in Africa, it's corn. If you grow it in the U.S. it's corn. And what I believe he meant by that, is that the African Americans are dispersed all over the world, we're still Africans. You have some roots, you have some ties, . . . that are very important to you, in terms of you understanding the betterment of your life.

Speaking to the same theme, a nursing professor at a southwestern university said that things were worse now than a few years ago, but she found hopeful signs in the freedom movements in South Africa:

> Now, in order for it to get to be better in five years, something is going to happen. We see the crumbling of walls everywhere. The release of Nelson Mandela was a very big step forward, but not enough of a step forward. With the barriers falling in Africa, I *know* that something's going to

> happen in this country, and it's just a matter of what and who will be the impetus for leading it. . . . African Americans have always viewed themselves as being the freed people and our brothers in Africa as being oppressed. Now, when you get to a situation where the oppressed have made the decision and are willing to fight and die to say, "I will no longer be oppressed, I will have more say." Okay. With the walls crumbling in South Africa, the oppressed are standing up and saying, "I don't want to be oppressed any more." Then we, as African Americans who have supposedly had all these freedoms, we have to start to open our eyes and take a look and see that we really, in actuality, don't have all these freedoms.

Significantly, the freedom struggle in South Africa has put many white Americans in a conceptual bind. One woman, an active community volunteer, noted that white criticism of South African apartheid is hypocritical: "And too often, I have found that white Americans are more comfortable dealing with the point of apartheid; and they cannot see the tip of their nose. That here they are living an all-white life themselves. And I think it's going to take saying that and having them realize that, you know, are you kidding?"

Conclusion

> *We hold these Truths to be self-evident, that all Men are created equal, that they are endowed by their Creator with certain unalienable Rights, that among these are Life, Liberty, and the Pursuit of Happiness.*
>
> U.S. Declaration of Independence

> *We the people of the United States, in order to form a more perfect union, establish justice, insure domestic tranquility, provide for the common defense, promote the general welfare,*

and secure the blessings of liberty to ourselves and our posterity, do ordain and establish this constitution for the United States of America.

Preamble, U.S. Constitution

All too will bear in mind the sacred principle, that though the will of the majority is in all cases to prevail, that will to be rightful must be reasonable; that the minority possess their equal rights, which equal law must protect, and to violate would be oppression.

Thomas Jefferson, Inaugural Address

All persons born or naturalized in the United States, and subject to the jurisdiction thereof, are citizens of the United States and of the State wherein they reside. No State shall make or enforce any law which shall abridge the privileges or immunities of citizens of the United States; nor shall any State deprive any person of life, liberty, or property, without due process of the law; nor deny to any person within its jurisdiction the equal protection of the laws.

Fourteenth Amendment, U.S. Constitution

These pronouncements and constitutional guarantees form the foundation of our democratic government. They were initially written by whites, including some white slaveholders, but the intervening centuries have seen their meaning broadened to include justice and equality for Americans of all creeds and backgrounds. Writing in the 1940s in *An American Dilemma*, Gunnar Myrdal noted that most blacks, like most whites, were under the spell of the American creed, the "ideals of the essential dignity of the individual human being, of the fundamental equality of all men, and of certain inalienable rights to freedom, justice, and a fair opportunity."[21] The basics of the American dream include not only liberty and justice but also the pursuit of happiness, which can be seen as including a decent-paying job, a good home, and a sense of personal dignity.

Can all Americans achieve this dream? The logic of equal rights and equal opportunity would dictate that a black person who has reached middle-income status should have no difficulty in realizing the promises of the American dream. Middle-class African Americans have paid their dues and are asking to be accepted for their contributions and their ability to contribute, rather than to be viewed in terms of skin color. Yet the experiences of these African Americans with discrimination in traditionally white institutions are often destructive of their hopes and ambitions, of their ability to achieve true equality of opportunity and the multifaceted dream of being middle class. Recall the television broadcaster who argued forcefully that there is "no black middle class, by the way. You know that's relevant. Every time I use 'middle class,' I know that. Because a black middle-class person is still not a middle-class person."

In this book we have reported on concrete black *experience* with everyday racism. As we suggest in Chapter 1, racial discrimination is not an abstraction for these Americans, nor is it mainly a problem of the recent past. For most of these Americans racial discrimination is not a matter of isolated incidents, but instead a succession of negative experiences with whites from the early years of childhood to the last years of adulthood. Our interviews also put whites into the spotlight. We observe in the accounts that a large proportion of the discriminators are indeed middle class whites with power and resources.

Mainstream discussions emphasizing the benefits to black Americans of expanded employment in white-collar jobs often neglect the fact that as a group middle-class blacks are subordinate to middle-class whites in wages, salaries, and workplace power.[22] Typically the white-collar workplace offers no shelter from white racism, for it is a site where white peers and supervisors may isolate black employees, sabotage their work, or restrict their access to better jobs and good promotions. Nor does the university or college provide reliable security and support. Black students in mostly white colleges face many hurdles and pitfalls, from epithets to social isolation, professorial indifference, and, often, a Eurocentric curriculum. Even one's home and neighborhood may not be a place of refuge from white hostility; white realtors and homeowners may try to keep blacks out of white neighborhoods, and white neighbors may be insensitive or hostile. In public accommodations African Americans still experience a range of discrimination, from poor treatment in restaurants and department stores to hostility in pools and parks. In street sites white hostility can be especially dangerous and threatening, for a black person never knows when a racist epithet signals violence to come.

As of this writing, what is missing in the mass media and the mainstream intellectual literature is a single in-depth article or book on the role of white racism in creating the foundation for current racial conflict. What is missing not only in the mass media but in the nation is white Americans, especially middle-class whites and powerful white leaders, taking responsibility for the widespread prejudice and discrimination that generate rage and protest among black Americans. It was white Americans who created slavery and the segregation of African Americans, and it is white Americans who today are responsible for most continuing discrimination against African Americans.

Even some white liberals see the racial relations dilemma as a problem of everyone's prejudices. In 1992 the liberal organization People for the American Way published the results of a survey they commissioned on young Americans. They concluded from their research that "benign neglect" was no longer the answer for U.S. racial problems and that it was time to get young people in all racial and ethnic groups to reconsider their racial attitudes. They recommended that an "assignment of blame" should be avoided and that it was time to "find common ground." They continued by underscoring a vicious cycle of mutual resentment: "Minority citizens believe with more certainty that whites are responsible for the hostility between the races; whites believe the same thing about minorities with equal certitude. This is an exercise in bitterness that is bound to have no affirmative or beneficial end."[23] This important survey of young Americans provided valuable information and some useful suggestions for change, but its conclusions were much too weak. The U.S. racial problem, now and in its origin, is fundamentally a white problem, for whites have the greatest power to perpetuate or alter it. The conditions of antiblack discrimination have specific creators, and the creators are mostly white Americans.

As a nation we have been misled by an influential group of mainstream liberal and neoconservative analysts, most of whom are white, who have told us that the primary cause of persisting racial tensions and problems in this country is not white racism, but rather the black underclass, or black families, or black dependency on welfare. These apologists have blamed the underclass for its immorality and the black middle class for not taking responsibility for the underclass. To deny white racism and blame the black victims of racism have become intellectually fashionable in recent years. Our respondents call for a new racial education for most white Americans. White Americans must be exposed to the real history of the United States, including a starkly realistic revelation of the ravages of slavery, of the delay and failure of civil rights laws, and of the lack of courage of white presidents and legislators to demand equity in education, employment, housing, and other sectors of this society. What being white in the United States means can only be understood by delving deeply into the white-on-black history too often left out of the public discussions of American racial relations. Our respondents do not ignore the responsibility of black Americans to attend to problems of discrimination, but they also stress that white Americans have to confront and fight against white racism.

In *Faces at the Bottom of the Well*, legal scholar Derrick Bell has argued very forcefully that "Black people will never gain full equality in this country. Even those herculean efforts we hail as successful will produce no more than temporary 'peaks of progress,' short-lived victories that slide into irrelevance as racial patterns adapt in ways that maintain white dominance."[24] For Bell, an African American and former professor at Harvard Law School, the goals of racial equality and justice have been laudable, but in the final analysis they are usually sacrificed by whites to their own interests in day-to-day political struggles. This veteran of legal battles for civil rights is very pessimistic, and as a result he provides little in the way of concrete proposals and plans, beyond writing a better history of black struggles and a contemporary "defiance" of whites, for continuing the black struggle. Our black middle-class respondents are also veteran grass-roots theorists of white oppression, and they too take a broad view of the past, present, and future of this society—its strengths and hopes, as well as its weaknesses and destructiveness. Although many seem to share, to some degree, Bell's despair over the permanence of white racism, for the most part they continue to believe in or work for practical solutions to some of the nation's major race-related problems: good jobs for all black Americans, decent housing for all black Americans, vigorously enforced antidiscrimination laws, the re-education of whites away from racist attitudes, and the strengthening of solidarity in black communities. Against all odds, and in spite of the terrible obstacles, most somehow retain some hope for change in the future.

In our interviews, as well as in other accounts, African Americans have often hinted at or expressed openly the hope for future empowerment, not a wish for black domination of whites, but rather a humanist vision of shared development, one that stresses self-respect, self-determination, and self-actualization for all Americans. Indeed, expanding such an encompassing humanist and egalitarian vision *among whites* may be the only hope for a peaceful and prosperous future for the United States. Considering the discriminatory conditions black Americans face today, a majority of white Americans show little or no empathy; they seem to have lost the ability to "walk in another person's shoes."

Securing full human rights for African Americans will necessarily bring benefits for all Americans. Nearly a century ago Du Bois showed how the African slave trade not only dehumanized African Americans but also white Americans.[25] White racism has long been inseparable from white identity, white history, and white culture and has greatly demeaned and sabotaged the ideals of liberty and justice prized by all Americans. If a humanist and egalitarian vision is to be realized, whites must no longer deny the power inequality and the attitudinal imperialism at the heart of white racism. Giving up racism means not only giving up racist attitudes but also giving up substantial power and privilege. In a famous speech at an 1881 civil rights mass meeting in Washington, D.C., Frederick Douglass declared that "No man can put a chain about the ankle of his fellow man without at last finding the other end fastened about his own neck."[26]

Notes

1. The Continuing Significance of Racism

1. Lawrence D. Bobo, James H. Johnson, Melvin L. Oliver, James Sidanius, Camille Zubrinsky, *Public Opinion before and after a Spring of Discontent* (Los Angeles: UCLA Center for the Study of Urban Poverty, 1992), p. 6; Lynne Duke, "Blacks and Whites Define 'Racism' Differently," *Washington Post*, June 8, 1992, section A, p. 1.

2. Judith Lichtenberg, "Racism in the Head, Racism in the World," *Philosophy and Public Policy* 12 (Spring/Summer 1992), p. 3.

3. Nearly 4,600 hate crimes were recorded by the FBI for 1991. See "FBI Issues First Data on Hate Crimes," *The Race Relations Reporter*, March 15, 1993, p. 8.

4. Marian Wright Edelman, *The Measure of Our Success: A Letter to My Children and Yours* (Boston: Beacon Press, 1992), p. 23.

5. Quoted in Itabari Njeri, "Words to Live or Die by," *Los Angeles Times Magazine*, May 31, 1992, p. 23.

6. National Advisory Commission on Civil Disorders, *Report of the National Advisory Commission on Civil Disorders* (Washington, D.C.: U.S. Government Printing Office, 1968), p. 1.

7. Ibid., pp. 1, 5.

8. "Black and White in America," *Newsweek*, March 7, 1988, p. 19.

9. Thomas J. Bray, "Reading America the Riot Act," *Policy Review* 43 (Winter 1988), pp. 32–35.

10. Nathan Glazer, *Affirmative Discrimination* (New York: Basic Books, 1975), pp. 6–7, 71–72.

11. Ben Wattenberg and Richard Scammon, "Black Progress and Liberal Rhetoric," *Commentary* (April 1973), p. 35.

12. George Gilder, *Wealth and Poverty* (New York: Basic Books, 1981).

13. George Keller, "Black Students in Higher Education: Why So Few?" *Planning for Higher Education* 17 (1988–1989), pp. 50–56.

14. William J. Wilson, *The Declining Significance of Race* (Chicago: University of Chicago, 1978), p. 151.

15. William J. Wilson, *The Truly Disadvantaged: The Inner City, the Underclass, and Public Policy* (Chicago: University of Chicago Press, 1987), p. 146. Bayard Rustin, review of *The Myth of Black Progress*, in *The Atlantic*, vol. 254, October 1984, p. 121.

16. Shelby Steele, *The Content of Our Character* (New York: St. Martin's Press, 1990), pp. 151, 175.

17. Stephen L. Carter, *Reflections of An Affirmative Action Baby* (New York: Basic Books, 1991), pp. 249, 221.

18. Gerald D. Jaynes and Robin Williams, Jr., eds., *A Common Destiny: Blacks and American Society* (Washington, D.C.: National Academy Press, 1989), pp. 169–171.

19. J. P. Smith and F. R. Welch, *Closing the Gap: Forty Years of Economic Progress for Blacks* (Santa Monica: Rand Corporation, 1986); U.S. Commission on Civil Rights, *The Economic Progress of Black Men in America* (Washington, D.C.: U.S. Government Printing Office, 1986).

20. Andrew Rosenthal, "Reagan Hints Rights Leaders Exaggerate Racism," *New York Times*, January 14, 1989, section 1, p. 8.

21. *Wards Cove Packing Co. v. Atonio*, 109 S. Ct. 2115 (1989).

22. "Black and White in America," *Newsweek*, March 7, 1988, p. 19.

23. Thomas B. Edsall and Mary D. Edsall, "When the official subject is presidential politics, taxes, welfare, crime, rights, or values—the real subject is race," *The Atlantic*, vol. 267, May 1991, pp. 53–55; Thomas B. Edsall, with Mary D. Edsall, *Chain Reaction* (New York: Norton, 1992), p. 15.

24. Leon Wieseltier, "Scar Tissue," *New Republic*, June 5, 1989, pp. 19–20.

25. Jim Sleeper, *The Closest of Strangers* (New York: Norton, 1991), pp. 172–176.

26. Elizabeth Ehrlich, "Racism, 'Victim Power,' and White Guilt," *Business Week*, October 1, 1990, p. 12.

27. Joe R. Feagin, "A Preliminary Analysis of Media Treatment of White Racism," Unpublished research paper, University of Florida, January 1992. The analysis used Mead Data Central's Nexis database.

28. Max Rodenbeck, "Dashed Good Yarns," *Financial Times*, May 8, 1993, p. xix.

29. Bob Blauner, *Black Lives, White Lives* (Berkeley: University of California Press, 1989).

30. Jaynes and Williams, *A Common Destiny*, p. 84.

31. James R. Kluegel and Eliot R. Smith, *Beliefs about Inequality* (New York: Aldine de Gruyter, 1986), pp. 186–187.

32. Cited in Joel Kovel, *White Racism*, rev. ed. (New York: Columbia University Press, 1984), p. xviii.

33. Louis Harris Associates and NAACP Legal Defense and Educational Fund, *The Unfinished Agenda on Race in America* (NAACP Legal Defense and Educational Fund, 1989), pp. 6–10.

34. National Opinion Research Center, "General Social Survey" (Chicago: National Opinion Research Center, 1991). Tabulated by authors.

35. William Brink and Louis Harris, *The Negro Revolution in America* (New York: Simon and Schuster, 1963); William Brink and Louis Harris, *Black and White* (New York: Simon and Schuster, 1966).

36. Louis Harris did a survey for the NAACP Legal Defense Fund in 1988, but no personal questions were asked about discrimination respondents had faced; see Louis Harris Associates, *The Unfinished Agenda on Race in America.*

37. Cited in Lee Sigelman and Susan Welch, *Black Americans' Views of Racial Inequality* (Cambridge: Cambridge University Press, 1991), pp. 53–55.

38. Ibid., pp. 55–57. When the respondents in the 1986 survey were asked two similar questions rephrased in regard to "blacks generally," the proportions citing discrimination increased substantially.

39. Ibid., p. 59. Philomena Essed found in her Netherlands study that some blacks do not categorize certain negative experiences with whites as discriminatory, even though they are. Philomena Essed, *Understanding Everyday Racism* (Newbury Park: Sage, 1991), p. 78.

40. We are indebted to Hernan Vera for his insightful comments here.

41. On life crisis, see Lydia Rapoport, "The State of Crisis: Some Theoretical Considerations," in Howard J. Parad, ed., *Crisis Intervention: Selected Readings* (New York: Family Service Association, 1965), pp. 22–31.

42. "Why Race still Divides America and its People," *Time*, May 11, 1992, front cover.

43. Gunnar Myrdal, *An American Dilemma* (1944; New York: McGraw-Hill, 1964).

44. Hubert M. Blalock, *Toward A Theory of Minority-Group Relations* (New York: Wiley, 1967); Phyllis A. Katz and Dalmas A. Taylor, eds., *Eliminating Racism* (New York: Plenum, 1988), pp. 1–18.

45. Gordon Allport, *The Nature of Prejudice*, abridged ed. (Garden City, N.Y.: Anchor Books, 1958), p. 50.

46. Stokely Carmichael and Charles V. Hamilton, *Black Power* (New York: Vintage, 1967).

47. Thomas Pettigrew, ed., *Racial Discrimination in the United States*, (New York: Harper and Row, 1975), p. x.

48. Randall Collins, *Theoretical Sociology* (New York: Harcourt, Brace, Jovanovich, 1988), p. 406.

49. Arthur Brittan and Mary Maynard, *Sexism, Racism and Oppression* (Oxford: Basil Blackwell, 1984), p. 7.

50. See Samuel B. Bacharach and Edward J. Lawler, *Bargaining: Power, Tactics, and Outcomes* (San Francisco: Jossey-Bass, 1981), p. 74.

51. Allport, *The Nature of Prejudice*, pp. 14–15.

52. Jaynes and Williams, *A Common Destiny*, pp. 119–129; Howard Schuman, Charlotte Steeh, and Lawrence Bobo, *Racial Attitudes in America* (Cambridge: Harvard University Press, 1985), pp. 139–162.

53. Among whites, 39 percent favored a law permitting whites to *refuse* to sell a home to a black person; a fifth favored laws banning racial intermarriage between blacks and whites and favored the view that whites have a right to keep blacks out of their neighborhoods. National Opinion Research Center, "General Social Survey" (Chicago: National Opinion Research Center, 1991). Tabulated by authors.

54. National Opinion Research Center, "General Social Survey" (Chicago: National Opinion Research Center, 1990).

55. See, for example, the 1990 survey cited above.

56. Charles R. Lawrence, "The Id, the Ego, and Equal Protection," *Stanford Law Review* 39 (January 1987), pp. 317–323; T. Alexander Aleinikoff, "The Case for Race-Consciousness," *Columbia Law Review* 91 (June 1991), pp. 1060–1080.

57. Judith Rollins, *Between Women* (Philadelphia: Temple University Press, 1985).

58. Carol Brooks Gardner, "Passing By: Street Remarks, Address Rights, and the Urban Female," *Sociological Inquiry* 50 (1980), p. 345.

59. William E. B. Du Bois, "The Talented Tenth," in *The Negro Problem*, ed. Booker T. Washington et al. (1904; New York: Arno Press, 1969), pp. 31–75.

60. E. Franklin Frazier, *Black Bourgeoisie*, rev. ed. (New York: Collier Books, 1962), p. 195.

61. See Bart Landry, *The New Black Middle Class* (Berkeley: University of California Press, 1987), pp. 2–10; and John Macionis, *Sociology* (Englewood Cliffs, N.J.: Prentice-Hall, 1989), p. 263.

62. Bureau of the Census, *The Social and Economic Status of the Black Population, 1790–1978* (Washington, D.C.: U.S. Government Printing Office, 1979), p. 72. These figures include all employed persons ten years old and older.

63. Ibid., p. 74.

64. Landry, *The New Black Middle Class*, p. 3.

65. Bureau of Labor Statistics data, as cited in Bureau of the Census, *Statistical Abstract of the United States, 1991* (Washington, D.C.: U.S. Government Printing Office, 1991), p. 400.

66. See, for example, Roy L. Brooks, *Rethinking the American Race Problem* (Berkeley: University of California Press, 1990).

67. Bureau of the Census, *Statistical Abstract of the United States, 1991* (Washington, D.C.: U.S. Government Printing Office, 1991), p. 38.

68. Bureau of the Census, *The Social and Economic Status of the Black Population, 1790-1978*, p. 32; Bureau of the Census, *Statistical Abstract of the United States: 1990* (Washington, D.C.: U.S. Government Printing Office, 1990), p. 450.

69. On journalistic views, see Edsall and Edsall, *Chain Reaction*, p. 16. The socioeconomic indices indicate a group about the same size as is suggested by answers to self-placement questions in surveys. In a 1989 survey two thirds of black respondents identified themselves as "working class," while 30 percent identified themselves as "middle class" and 3 percent as "upper class." Among whites, however, 51 percent saw themselves as middle class and 4 percent as upper class. National Opinion Research Center, "General Social Survey" (Chicago: National Opinion Research Center, 1989). Tabulated by authors.

70. Herbert Blumer, *Symbolic Interactionism* (Berkeley: University of California Press, 1969), p. 32.

71. Leanita McClain, "How Chicago Taught Me to Hate Whites," *Washington Post*, July 24, 1983, reprinted in *A Foot in Each World*, ed. Clarence Page (Evanston, Ill.: Northwestern University Press, 1986), p. 36.

72. Antonio Gramsci, *Letters from Prison*, trans. by Lynne Lawner (New York: Harper and Row, 1973), pp. 43–44, 183–185.

73. See, for example, Robert N. Bellah, Richard Madsen, William M. Sullivan, Ann Swidler, and Steven M. Tipton, *Habits of the Heart* (New York: Harper and Row, 1986), pp. viii–ix. This major analysis has been faulted for not involving any interviews with black Americans. See Vincent Harding, "Toward a Darkly Radiant Vision of America's Truth: A Letter of Concern, An Invitation to Re-creation," in *Community in America*, ed. Charles H. Reynolds and Ralph V. Norman (Berkeley: University of California Press, 1988), pp. 67–83.

74. There are no lists of the members of the black middle class, especially those in the upper middle class, and they live in areas scattered across major cities, sometimes mixed in small numbers among whites and sometimes segregated in middle-class black residential areas. In most cases the initial respondents were suggested by knowledgeable black observers of the middle class in the cities chosen; other respondents were suggested by our black interviewers and by those first interviewed. Few of those we contacted refused to be interviewed, although some were not interviewed because of scheduling problems. The number of respondents for the demographic distributions here and in the next paragraph varies a little (from 189 to 209) because of missing data. A substantial majority in the South/Southwest category resided in Texas cities at the time of the interview, although, like respondents elsewhere, their accounts often cover experiences in other cities and regions.

75. In most cases the income reported is household income, but apparently several did report only their personal incomes.

76. We are greatly indebted to these black professionals for their support and encouragement in this difficult project.

77. In most interviews we asked questions about racial barriers

encountered in housing, education, and the workplace (or business), as well as about the personal impact of discrimination and coping strategies and support networks.

78. To protect the anonymity of these respondents, some of whom are the only blacks in their fields in particular cities, we will not list the cities. We have also disguised place and company names, and occasionally occupation, in chapter quotes.

79. After testing questions for communicability, we secured black interviewers to conduct all but one of the interviews, using a set of mostly open-ended questions. We added a few additional questions as we proceeded with the interviewing; latitude was allowed for digressions, so not all questions were covered in each interview. The interviews, conducted in 1988–1990, averaged about one to two hours each. In a few cases several respondents, such as a husband and wife, were interviewed together. Five interviews were done by black respondents who answered protocol questions on tape without an interviewer. A few short quotes in the text are presented verbatim from a taped interview of the second author by a black interviewer doing an early pilot interview for the first author before the second author became involved with this book.

80. Leanita McClain, "The Middle-class Black's Burden," *Newsweek*, October 13, 1980, reprinted in Page, *A Foot in Each World*, pp. 12–13.

81. William E. B. Du Bois, *The Souls of Black Folk* (1903; New York: Bantam Books, 1989), p. 3.

2. *Navigating Public Places*

1. Lena Williams, "When Blacks Shop, Bias often Accompanies a Sale," *New York Times*, April 30, 1991, pp. A1, A9.

2. Names and places in interview quotes have been disguised or eliminated to protect anonymity. Some quotes have been lightly edited

for grammar and to delete excessive pause phrases like "you know" and "uh."

3. National Public Radio, "Weekend Edition," May 29, 1993.

4. Associated Press, "Denny's to Monitor Treatment of Blacks," *Gainesville Sun*, May 30, 1993, p. 7A.

5. Judy Pasternak, "Service Still Skin Deep for Blacks," *Los Angeles Times*, April 1, 1993, p. A1.

6. Martin Dyckman, "Lawyers can be Heroes too," *St. Petersburg Times*, April 11, 1993, p. 3D.

7. Bill McAuliffe, "Black Leaders Call for Boycott of Local Carsons Stores," *Star Tribune*, December 10, 1991, p. 1B.

8. Joel Kovel, *White Racism*, rev. ed. (New York: Columbia University Press, 1984).

9. Walt Harrington, "On the Road with the President of Black America," *The Washington Post Magazine*, January 25, 1987, p. W14.

10. "FBI Issues First Data on Hate Crimes," *The Race Relations Reporter*, March 15, 1993, p. 8.

11. Carol Brooks Gardner, "Passing By: Street Remarks, Address Rights, and the Urban Female," *Sociological Inquiry* 50 (1980), p. 345.

12. David C. Perry and Paula A. Sornoff, *Politics at the Street Level* (Beverly Hills: Sage, 1973).

13. John Howard Griffin, *Black Like Me* (Boston: Houghton Mifflin, 1961).

14. James E. Blackwell, *The Black Community* (New York: Harper-Collins, 1991), pp. 456–457.

15. See Kim Lersch, "Current Trends in Police Brutality: An Analysis of Recent Newspaper Accounts," Gainesville, University of Florida, unpublished master's thesis, 1993.

16. See E. Yvonne Moss, "African Americans and the Administration of Justice," in *Assessment of the Status of African-Americans*, ed. Wornie L. Reed (Boston: William Monroe Trotter Institute, University of Massachusetts, 1990), vol. I, pp. 79–86; and Dennis B. Roddy,

"Perceptions Still Segregate Police, Black Community," *The Pittsburgh Press*, August 26, 1990, p. B1.

17. Les Payne, "Up Against the Wall: Black Men and the Cops," *Essence*, November 1992, p. 74.

18. Michelle N-K [sic] Collison, "Black Students Complain of Abuse by Campus Police," *Chronicle of Higher Education*, April 14, 1993, pp. A35-A36.

19. Bonnie J. Morris, "The Pervasiveness of Campus Racism," letter to editors, *The Chronicle of Higher Education*, May 12, 1993, p. B5.

20. Isabel Wilkerson, personal interview with the author, 1992.

21. This quote includes a clarification from a brief follow-up interview.

22. Ralph Ellison, *Invisible Man* (New York: Vintage Books, 1989), p. 3.

23. George M. Fredrickson, *The Black Image in the White Mind* (Middletown, Conn.: Wesleyan University Press, 1971), pp. 251- 275.

24. See Doris A. Graber, *Crime News and the Public* (New York: Praeger, 1980).

25. Bureau of Criminal Justice Statistics, *Criminal Victimization in the United States, 1991* (Washington, D.C.: U.S. Government Printing Office, 1992), p. 61, and *Sourcebook of Criminal Justice Statistics, 1991* (Washington, D.C.: U.S. Government Printing Office, 1992), p. 403.

26. James Kilpatrick, "Hate Crimes not Protected by the First Amendment," *Austin American Statesman*, May 19, 1993, p. A19.

27. For a discussion of major distortions in the Horton ad campaign, see Kathleen Hall Jamieson, *Dirty Politics: Deception, Distraction, and Democracy* (New York: Oxford University Press, 1992).

28. On the black image as threat, see Mark Warr, "Dangerous Situations: Social Context and Fear of Victimization," *Social Forces*, 68 (1990), pp. 905–906.

29. Judith Lichtenberg, "Racism in the Head, Racism in the World," *Philosophy and Public Policy*, 12 (Spring/Summer 1992), p. 4.

30. Gerald D. Jaynes and Robin Williams, Jr., eds., *A Common Destiny: Blacks and American Society* (Washington, D.C.: National Academy Press, 1989), p. 84.

31. Robert H. Lauer and Warren H. Handel, *Social Psychology: The Theory and Application of Symbolic Interactionism* (Boston: Houghton Mifflin, 1977), p. 330.

32. John Mirowsky and Catherine E. Ross, *Social Causes of Psychological Distress* (New York: Aldine de Gruyter, 1989), pp. 10–21.

33. Leanita McClain, "The Insidious New Racism," in *A Foot in Each World*, ed. Clarence Page (Evanston, Ill.: Northwestern University Press, 1986), pp. 20–21.

3. Seeking a Good Education

1. Eric L. Hirsch, "Columbia University: Individual and Institutional Racism," in *The Racial Crisis in American Higher Education*, ed. Philip G. Altbach and Kofi Lomotey (Albany: SUNY Press, 1991), pp. 199–211.

2. People for the American Way, *Democracy's Next Generation II* (Washington, D.C.: People for the American Way, 1992), p. 65.

3. Lee Sigelman and Susan Welch, *Black Americans' Views of Racial Inequality* (Cambridge: Cambridge University Press, 1991), pp. 55–58.

4. National Opinion Research Center, "General Social Survey" (Chicago: National Opinion Research Center, 1990). Tabulated by authors.

5. "Study Shows Social Mix Good for Blacks," *Newsweek*, September 18, 1985, p. 3.

6. Ansley A. Abraham, *Racial Issues on Campus: How Students View Them* (Atlanta: Southern Regional Education Board, 1990); and Leslie Inniss, "Historical Footprints: The Legacy of the School Desegregation Pioneers," in *The Bubbling Cauldron*, ed. Michael P. Smith

and Joe R. Feagin (Minneapolis: University of Minnesota Press, forthcoming).

7. Quoted in Itabari Njeri, "Beyond the Melting Pot; In America, Blending in was once the Ideal," *Los Angeles Times*, January 13, 1991, p. E1; see Arthur Schlesinger, Jr., *The Disuniting of America: Reflections on a Multicultural Society* (New York: Norton, 1991).

8 "Separate and Unequal," *Minority Trendsetter* 1 (Summer 1988), p. 4.

9. J. Eyler, V. Cook, and L. Ward, "Resegregation: Desegregation Within Desegregated Schools," Paper presented at Annual Meeting of American Education Research Association, as summarized in Russell W. Irvine and Jacqueline Jordan Irvine, "The Impact of the Desegregation Process on the Education of Black Students: Key Variables," *Journal of Negro Education* 53 (1983), p. 415.

10. Gunnar Myrdal, *An American Dilemma* (1944; New York: McGraw-Hill, 1964).

11. American Council on Education and the Education Commission of the States, *One-Third of a Nation* (Washington: The American Council on Education, 1988).

12. Gerald D. Jaynes and Robin Williams, Jr., eds., *A Common Destiny: Blacks and American Society* (Washington, D.C.: National Academy Press, 1989), pp. 338–339; for earlier studies see A. W. Astin, *Minorities in Higher Education* (San Francisco: Jossey-Bass, 1982); see also Reynolds Farley and Walter R. Allen, *The Color Line and the Quality of Life in America* (New York: Oxford University Press, 1989), p. 208.

13. George Keller, "Black Students in Higher Education: Why So Few?" *Planning for Higher Education* 17 (1988–1989), pp. 50–54.

14. William E. B. Du Bois, *The Souls of Black Folk* (1903; New York: Bantam Books, 1989), p. 3.

15. Chalsa M. Loo and Garry Rolison, " Alienation of Ethnic Minority Students at a Predominantly White University," *Journal of Higher Education* 57 (January/February 1986), pp. 64–67.

16. Hoi K. Suen, "Alienation and Attrition of Black College Students on a Predominantly White Campus," *Journal of College Student Personnel* 24 (March 1983), pp. 117–121.

17. See Philip G. Altbach and Kofi Lomotey, eds., *The Racial Crisis in American Higher Education* (Albany: SUNY Press, 1991).

18. Walter Allen, *Gender and Campus Race Differences in Black Student Academic Performance, Racial Attitudes and College Satisfaction* (Atlanta: Southern Education Foundation, 1986).

19. Howard J. Ehrlich, *Campus Ethnoviolence and the Policy Options* (Baltimore: National Institute against Prejudice and Violence, 1990), p. iii.

20. Denise K. Magner, "Blacks and Whites on the Campuses: Behind Ugly Racist Incidents, Student Isolation and Insensitivity," *Chronicle of Higher Education* (April 26, 1989), pp. A27-A29.

21. William Celis, "Hazing's Forbidden Rites are Moving Underground," *New York Times*, January 27, 1993, p. A19; William C. Rhoden, "College Football," *New York Times*, November 30, 1991, section 1, p. 29.

22. Myrdal, *An American Dilemma*, p. 101.

23. John O. Calmore, "To Make Wrong Right: The Necessary and Proper Aspirations of Fair Housing," in *The State of Black America 1989* (New York: Urban League, 1989), p. 89.

24. National Opinion Research Center, "General Social Survey" (Chicago: National Opinion Research Center, 1990). Tabulated by authors.

25. Reported in Ehrlich, *Campus Ethnoviolence and the Policy Options*, pp. 12–13.

26. Quoted in Magner, "Blacks and Whites on the Campuses," pp. A27-A29.

27. Philomena Essed, *Understanding Everyday Racism* (Newbury Park, Calif.: Sage, 1991), pp. 30–32.

28. In 1992 this liberal college of 700 students had about 55 black students. See Isabel Wilkerson, "Racial Tension Erupts, Tearing a College Apart," *New York Times*, April 13, 1992, p. A14.

29. Joe R. Fengin and Nikitah Imani, "Black in a White World," unpublished research report, 1993. University authorities requested that the university not be identified.

30. See Keller, "Black Students in Higher Education."

31. Ralph Ellison, *Invisible Man* (New York: Vintage Books, 1989), p. 3.

32. Feagin and Imani, "Black in a White World."

33. Catharine MacKinnon, *Feminism Unmodified* (Cambridge: Harvard University Press, 1987), p. 34.

34. Allan Nairn, *The Reign of ETS: The Corporation that Makes Up Minds* (Washington, D.C.: Allan Nairn and Associates, 1980).

35. Percy Bates, "Teaching Children to be Test Wise," *Breakthrough* 15 (Summer 1988), p. 23.

36. Joseph Katz, "White Faculty Struggling with the Effects of Racism," in Altbach and Lomotey, *The Racial Crisis in American Higher Education*, p. 193.

37. Feagin and Imani, "Black in a White World."

38. The second author and his black colleagues have had this happen to them.

39. Feagin and Imani, "Black in a White World."

40. James E. Blackwell, "Graduate and Professional Education for Blacks," in *The Education of Black Americans*, ed. Charles V. Willie, Antoine M. Garibaldi, and Wornie L. Reed (Boston: William Monroe Trotter Institute, University of Massachusetts, 1990), pp. 103–110.

41. Stephen L. Carter, "Color-Blind and Color-Active," *The Recorder*, January 3, 1992, p. 6.

42. Joe R. Feagin, Nikitah Imani, and Hernan Vera, "The Views of Black Parents," unpublished research report, 1993.

43. John S. Butler, *Entrepreneurship and Self-help among Black Americans* (New York: SUNY Press, 1991), p. 259.

44. Keller, "Black Students in Higher Education: Why So Few?" p. 55.

4. *Navigating the Middle-Class Workplace*

1. Bebe Moore Campbell, "To Be Black, Gifted, and Alone," *Savvy* 5 (December 1984), p. 69.

2. David H. Swinton, "The Economic Status of African Americans during the 1980s: 'Permanent' Poverty and Inequality," in *The State of Black America*, ed. Janet Dewart (New York: National Urban League, 1991), p. 63; see also Gerald D. Jaynes and Robin Williams, Jr., eds., *A Common Destiny: Blacks and American Society* (Washington, D.C.: National Academy Press, 1989), pp. 310–317.

3. See William B. Gould, "The Supreme Court and Employment Discrimination Law in 1989: Judicial Retreat and Congressional Response," *Tulane Law Review* 64 (June 1990), pp. 1485–1514.

4. James E. Ellis, "The Black Middle Class," *Business Week*, March 14, 1988, p. 65.

5. Lee Sigelman and Susan Welch, *Black Americans' Views of Racial Inequality* (Cambridge: Cambridge University Press, 1991), pp. 55–57.

6. The 1990 General Social Survey asked why blacks have worse jobs, income, and housing than whites. Choosing among alternative explanations, two thirds of blacks said it was "mainly due to discrimination," compared to 35 percent of whites. And 78 percent of college-educated blacks said it was mainly due to discrimination. National Opinion Research Center, "General Social Survey" (Chicago: National Opinion Research Center, 1990). Tabulated by authors.

7. Margery Austin Turner, Michael Fix, and Raymond J. Struyk, "Opportunities Denied: Discrimination in Hiring," Urban Institute Report 91–9, August 1991, Washington, D.C.

8. "The Black Middle Class," *Business Week*, March 14, 1988, p. 65.

9. Ed Jones, "Beneficiaries or Victims? Progress or Process," unpublished research report, South Orange, New Jersey, January 1985.

10. Ellis Cose, "To the Victors, Few Spoils," *Newsweek*, March 29, 1993, p. 54.

11. "The Black Middle Class," *Business Week*, March 14, 1988, p. 65; Sigelman and Welch, *Black Americans' Views of Racial Inequality*, p. 57.

12. Swinton, "The Economic Status of African Americans," in Dewart, *The State of Black America: 1991*, p. 67.

13. Elizabeth Higginbotham and Lynn Weber, "Workplace Discrimination for Black and White Professional and Managerial Women," in *Women and Work: Ethnicity and Class*, ed. Elizabeth Higginbotham and Lynn Weber (Newbury Park, Calif.: Sage, forthcoming).

14. Marcus Mabry, "An Endangered Dream," *Newsweek*, December 3, 1990, p. 40.

15. Kluegel and Smith report on a 1976 survey in which 71 percent of whites agreed that "blacks and other minorities no longer face unfair employment conditions. In fact they are favored in many training and job programs." Only 12 percent of whites agreed with the statement that "Discrimination affects all black people. The only way to handle it is for blacks to organize together and demand rights for all." James R. Kluegel and Eliot R. Smith, *Beliefs about Inequality* (New York: Aldine de Gruyter, 1986), pp. 186–187.

16. Rosabeth Moss Kanter, *Men and Women of the Corporation* (New York: Basic Books, 1977), pp. 50–61, 63.

17. Cited in Dawn M. Baskerville, "Are Career Seminars for Black Managers Worth It?" *Black Enterprise*, December 1992, p. 122.

18. Ibid.

19. Ed Jones, "What It's Like to Be a Black Manager," *Harvard Business Review* (May–June 1986), pp. 84–93.

20. See Kanter, *Men and Women of the Corporation*, p. 158.

21. John Mirowsky and Catherine E. Ross, *Social Causes of Psychological Distress* (New York: Aldine de Gruyter, 1989), p. 16.

22. See Baskerville, "Are Career Seminars for Black Managers Worth It?" *Black Enterprise*, December 1992, p. 122.

23. Joe R. Feagin and Clairece Booher Feagin, *Racial and Ethnic*

Relations, 4th ed. (Englewood Cliffs, N.J.: Prentice-Hall, 1993), pp. 237–239.

24. Kenneth B. Clark, "The Role of Race," *New York Times Magazine*, October 5, 1980, p. 30.

25. Kanter, *Men and Women of the Corporation*, p. 158.

26. Kenneth W. Jackson, "Black Faculty in Academia," in *The Racial Crisis in American Higher Education*, ed. Philip G. Altbach and Kofi Lomotey (Albany: SUNY Press, 1991), p. 143.

27. Sharon M. Collins, "The Making of the Black Middle Class," *Social Problems* 30 (April 1983), pp. 369–381.

28. John N. Odom, as quoted in Thomas B. Edsall and Mary D. Edsall, *Chain Reaction* (New York: Norton, 1992), p. 163.

29. Ella L. Bell, "The Bicultural Life Experience of Career-oriented Black Women," *Journal of Organizational Behavior* 11 (1990), p. 475.

30. William E. B. Du Bois, *The Souls of Black Folk* (1903; New York: Bantam Books, 1989), p. 3.

31. Everett Hughes, *Men and Their Work* (Glencoe, Ill.: Free Press, 1958), pp. 109–110.

32. Kanter, *Men and Women of the Corporation*, pp. 210–212.

33. Gunnar Myrdal, *An American Dilemma* (1944; New York: McGraw-Hill, 1964), vol. 1, p. 101.

34. Herbert Hill, "Critique of Chapter 6, 'Blacks in the Economy,'" in *Critique of the NRC Study, A Common Destiny: Blacks and American Society*, ed. Wornie L. Reed (Boston: William Monroe Trotter Institute, University of Massachusetts, 1990), p. 15.

35. Edward Irons, *Black Managers: The Case of the Banking Industry* (New York: Praeger, 1985).

36. Philomena Essed, *Understanding Everyday Racism* (Newbury Park, Calif.: Sage, 1991), pp. 30–32.

37. See Catharine A. MacKinnon, *Toward a Feminist Theory of the State* (Harvard University Press, 1989), pp. 2–10; and Joe R. Feagin and Clairece B. Feagin, *Social Problems*, 3d ed. (Englewood Cliffs, N.J.: Prentice-Hall, 1990), pp. 18–21.

38. Jaynes and Williams, *A Common Destiny*, pp. 169–171.

39. On skepticism about courts, see Julius L. Chambers, "Black Americans and the Courts: Has the Clock been turned back Permanently?" in *The State of Black America, 1990*, ed. Janet Dewart (New York: National Urban League, 1990), pp. 9–24.

40. Cited in John Hill, "Senate Race Showed State's Racial Woes," Gannett News Service, October 14, 1990, n.p., Lexis/Nexis database.

41. People for the American Way, *Democracy's Next Generation II* (Washington, D.C.: People for the American Way, 1992), p. 70.

5. *Building a Business*

1. Quoted in David. D. Porter, "What must blacks go through? An experiment will let you see," *Orlando Sentinel*, September 13, 1989, p. G1.

2. See Thomas Sowell, *Markets and Minorities* (New York: Basic Books, 1981).

3. Porter, "What must blacks go through?" *Orlando Sentinel*, September 13, 1989, p. G1.

4. John Sibley Butler, *Entrepreneurship and Self-help among Black Americans* (New York: SUNY Press, 1991), pp. 165–226, 282–330.

5. Lerone Bennett, *Black Power U.S.A* (New York: Pelican, 1969), p. 37.

6. *1987 Survey of Minority-Owned Business Enterprises -Black* (Washington, D.C.: U.S. Government Printing Office, 1990).

7. Walter L. Updegrave, "Race and Money," *Money*, December 1989, p. 162.

8. National Center for Education Statistics, "Expected Occupations of 8th Graders at Age 30 by Selected Student and School Characteristics: 1988," *Digest of Education Statistics* (Washington, D.C.: U.S. Dept. of Health, Education and Welfare, 1989), p. 130.

9. Shearson Lehman Brothers, "Life in America," telephone survey, as reported in Julia Belcher, *USAir Magazine*, October 1992, p. 13.

10. See James R. Kluegel and Eliot Smith, *Beliefs about Inequality* (New York: Aldine de Gruyter, 1986), pp. 186–196.

11. Emile Durkheim, *Suicide* (Glencoe, Ill.: Free Press, 1951), pp. 241–296.

12. We draw here on Hernan Vera and Joe R. Feagin, "Racism as Anomic Action: The American Case," unpublished research paper, University of Florida, 1992.

13. Richard W. Stevenson, "Blacks Push for Jobs Rebuilding after Riot," *New York Times*, June 10, 1992, p. A16.

14. John Mirowsky and Catherine E. Ross, *Social Causes of Psychological Distress* (New York: Aldine de Gruyter, 1989), p. 14.

15. The quotes are from Joe R. Feagin and Nikitah Imani, "Black Contractors and Subcontractors in the [Southeastern] County Construction Industry: A Portrait of Discrimination," unpublished research report prepared for the Board of County Commissioners, [Southeastern] County, July 1991.

16. Carmenza Gallo, "The Construction Industry in New York City: Immigrant and Black Entrepreneurs," Working Paper, Conservation of Human Resources Project, Columbia University, New York City, 1983, p. 25.

17. Ibid., pp. 22–33.

18. Herbert Blumer, "Race Prejudice as a Sense of Group Position," *The Pacific Sociological Review*, 1 (Spring 1959), pp. 3–7.

19. Butler, *Entrepreneurship and Self-Help among Black Americans*, pp. 125–142.

20. Cited in Udayan Gupta, "Cash Crunch," *Wall Street Journal*, February 19, 1993, p. R4.

21. The study is summarized in Updegrave, "Race and Money," *Money*, December 1989, p. 162.

22. Feagin and Imani, "Black Contractors and Subcontractors in the [Southeastern] County Construction Industry."

23. Updegrave, "Race and Money," *Money*, December 1989, p. 160.

24. Paul D. Reynolds and Brenda Miller, "Race, Gender, and Entrepreneurship," paper presented to American Sociological Association, Annual Meeting, 1990.

25. Gupta, "Cash Crunch," *Wall Street Journal*, February 19, 1993, p. R4.

26. Bureau of the Census, *Household Wealth and Asset Ownership: 1984* (Washington, D.C.: U.S. Government Printing Office, 1986), Table 4, n.p.; Billy J. Tidwell, "Black Wealth: Facts *and* Fiction," in *The State of Black America 1988*, ed. Jane Dewart (New York: National Urban League, 1988), pp. 193–210.

27. Gunnar Myrdal, *An American Dilemma* (1944; New York: McGraw-Hill, 1964), vol. 2, p. 816; Herbert M. Morais, *The History of the Negro in Medicine* (New York: Publishers Co., 1967), pp. 86–100.

28. Lois C. Gray, The Geographic and Functional Distribution of Black Physicians: Some Research and Policy Considerations," *American Journal of Public Health* 67 (1977), pp. 519–526.

29. James H. Jones, *Bad Blood* (New York: Free Press, 1981), pp. 1–23.

30. Tom Junod, "Deadly Medicine," *Gentleman's Quarterly*, June 1993, pp. 164–169.

31. Feagin and Imani, "Black Contractors and Subcontractors in the [Southeastern] County Construction Industry."

32. William H. Grier and Price M. Cobbs, *Black Rage* (New York: Basic Books, 1968), p. 178.

33. Alexander Thomas and Samuel Sillen, *Racism and Psychiatry* (New Jersey: The Citadel Press, 1972), p. 54.

34. Thomas Pettigrew, *Racially Separate or Together?* (New York: McGraw-Hill, 1971).

35. See Gerald D. Jaynes and Robin Williams, Jr., eds., *A Common Destiny: Blacks and American Society* (Washington, D.C.: National Academy Press, 1989), p. 422, note 3.

36. See E. Yvonne Moss, "African Americans and the Administration of Justice," in *Assessment of the Status of African-Americans*, ed. Wornie L. Reed (Boston: William Monroe Trotter Institute, University of Massachusetts, 1990), vol. I, pp. 79–86; and Melvin P. Sikes, *The Administration of Injustice* (New York: Harper & Row, 1975).

37. See John Hope Franklin and Alfred A. Moss, *From Slavery to Freedom*, 6th ed. (New York: Knopf, 1988), pp. 233–238.

38. Nathan Glazer, "Blacks and Ethnic Groups: The Difference, and the Political Difference It Makes," *Social Problems* 18 (Spring 1971), p. 459.

39. See George Gilder, *The Spirit of Enterprise* (New York: Simon and Schuster, 1984), pp. 110–112.

40. Alejandro Portes and Robert L. Bach, *Latin American Journey* (Berkeley: University of California Press, 1985), pp. 200–220.

41. Gallo, "The Construction Industry in New York City," p. 26.

42. Walter Rodney, *How Europe Underdeveloped Africa* (Washington: Howard University Press, 1984), p. 280.

6. Seeking a Good Home and Neighborhood

1. Census Bureau, *Statistical Abstract of the United States, 1991* (Washington, D.C.: U.S. Government Printing Office, 1991), p. 726. The black figure is "black and other."

2. Robert G. Schwemm, "Fair Housing Enforcement," *One Nation, Indivisible* (Washington, D.C.: Citizens' Commission on Civil Rights, 1989), p. 272.

3. Douglas S. Massey and Nancy A. Denton, *American Apartheid: Segregation and the Making of the Underclass* (Cambridge: Harvard University Press, 1993), pp. 221–223.

4. National Opinion Research Center, "General Social Survey" (Chicago: National Opinion Research Center, 1990). Tabulated by authors.

5. Cited in Gerald D. Jaynes and Robin Williams, Jr., eds., *A Common Destiny: Blacks and American Society* (Washington, D.C.: National Academy Press, 1989), pp. 142–146.

6. Margery Austin Turner, Raymond J. Struyk, and John Yinger, *Housing Discrimination Study: Synthesis* (Washington, D.C.: U.S. Government Printing Office, 1991), pp. ii-viii.

7. The polls are cited in Lee Sigelman and Susan Welch, *Black Americans' Views of Racial Inequality* (Cambridge: Cambridge University Press, 1991), pp. 57–59.

8. Another NORC question asked why blacks have worse jobs, income, and housing than whites. Choosing among alternative explanations, two thirds of blacks said "mainly due to discrimination," compared to 35 percent of whites. Seventy-seven percent of college educated blacks but only 41 percent of college-educated whites, said it was mainly due to discrimination. National Opinion Research Center, "General Social Survey" (Chicago: National Opinion Research Center, 1990). Tabulated by authors.

9. Gary Orfield, "Minorities and Suburbanization," in *Critical Perspectives on Housing*, ed. R. Bratt, C. Hartman, and A. Meyerson (Philadelphia: Temple University Press, 1986), pp. 223–225.

10. John Goering, Department of Housing and Urban Development, letter to senior author, May 1991.

11. See Joe R. Feagin and Robert Parker, *Building American Cities* (Englewood Cliffs, N.J.: Prentice-Hall, Inc., 1990), pp. 132–138.

12. Massey and Denton, *American Apartheid*, pp. 232–233.

13. Ibid., p. 232.

14. Margery Austin Turner, *Housing Discrimination Study: Analyzing Racial and Ethnic Steering* (Washington, D.C.: U.S. Government Printing Office, 1991), pp. ii–v.

15. See Joe R. Feagin and Clairece Booher Feagin, *Discrimination American Style* (Englewood Cliffs, N.J.: Prentice-Hall, 1978), pp. 87–105.

16. See Feagin and Parker, *Building American Cities*, pp. 129–147.

17. William J. Wilson, *The Declining Significance of Race* (Chicago: University of Chicago Press, 1978).

18. Massey and Denton, *American Apartheid*, p. 226.

19. See John M. Goering, *Housing Desegregation and Federal Policy* (Chapel Hill: University of North Carolina Press, 1986).

20. Goering, letter to senior author, May 1991.

21. Office of Thrift Supervision, *Report on Loan Discrimination* (Washington, D.C.: Office of the Treasury, 1989), p. 2; Statement of Jerauld C. Kluckman, Director, Compliance Programs, Office of Thrift Supervision, U.S. Department of the Treasury, Before the Subcommittee on Consumer and Regulatory Affairs of the Senate Committee on Banking, Housing and Urban Affairs, May 16, 1990.

22. Paulette Thomas, "Federal Data Detail Pervasive Racial Gap in Mortgage Lending," *Wall Street Journal*, March 31, 1992, p. 1.

23. ICF Incorporated, "The Secondary Market and Community Lending through Lenders' Eyes," prepared for the Federal Home Loan Mortgage Corporation, February 28, 1991.

24. Klanwatch Project, "'Move-in' Violence: White Resistance to Neighborhood Integration in the 1980s," Montgomery, Alabama, Southern Poverty Law Center, undated (circa 1987).

25. See "2 Klan Leaders Indicted on Cross-burning Charges," *Atlanta Constitution*, June 27, 1992, section D, p. 7.

26. Major Garrett, "Democratic Hopefuls Unload on Bush," *Washington Times*, November 24, 1991, p. A4.

27. For a discussion see Theodore Cross, *The Black Power Imperative* (New York: Faulkner, 1984), pp. 114–116.

28. See Wilson, *The Declining Significance of Race*.

29. Jaynes and Williams, *A Common Destiny: Blacks and American Society*, pp. 144–146; see also Douglas S. Massey and Nancy A. Denton, "Trends in Segregation of Blacks, Hispanics and Asians, 1970–1980," *American Sociological Review*, 52 (1987), pp. 802–825. Housing discrimination has been neglected in national reports on the state of black America. In *A Common Destiny*, for example, fewer

than six pages out of 600 are devoted to housing issues, and half of that is on white public opinion.

30. See Robert D. Bullard, "Solid Waste Sites and the Black Houston Community," Unpublished paper presented at the Annual Meeting, Southwestern Sociological Association, March 17–20, 1982, pp. 6–20.

31. John Goering, letter to first author, May 1991; see also U.S. Department of Housing and Urban Development, *The State of Fair Housing* (Washington, D.C.: U.S. Government Printing Office, 1989).

32. John Goering, "Are Size of Place Differences Worth Talking About?" Commentary paper, Conference on New Perspectives on Racial Issues, 1991.

33. Testimony of John J. Knapp, General Counsel, U.S. Department of Housing and Urban Development, in *Issues of Housing Discrimination*, vol. 2 (Washington, D.C.: U.S. Commission on Civil Rights, November 13, 1987).

34. Massey and Denton, *American Apartheid*, p. 224. They cite a figure of four hundred resolved fair housing cases.

35. John Goering, "The Racial Housing Question in England and the United States," revised version of a paper presented at the Annual Meeting of the International Sociological Association, Madrid, Spain, July 11, 1990, p. 21.

36. Joel Garreau, *Edge City* (New York: Doubleday, 1991), p. 146.

37. Massey and Denton, *American Apartheid*, p. 225.

38. Isabel Wilkerson, "The Tallest Fence: Feelings on Race in a White Neighborhood," *New York Times*, June 21, 1992, section 1, p. 18.

39. Quoted in George J. Church, "The Boom Towns," *Time*, June 15, 1987, p. 17.

7. *Contending with Everyday Discrimination*

1. Rachel Shuster, "Arthur Ashe; 1943–1993; Ashe Legacy Goes beyond Sports, Race," *USA Today*, February 8, 1993, p. 1C.

2. James H. Humphrey, *Human Stress* (New York: AMS Press, 1986), p. 63.

3. Alexander Thomas and Samuel Sillen, *The Theory and Application of Symbolic Interactionism* (Boston: Houghton Mifflin Company, 1977); see also John Mirowsky and Catherine E. Ross, *Social Causes of Psychological Distress* (New York: Aldine and de Gruyter, 1989).

4. See, for example, Mirowsky and Ross, *Social Causes of Psychological Stress.*

5. This commentary on the requirements for survival reminds one of the black folk song: "Got one mind for white folks to see. Another for what I know is me. He don't know, he don't know my mind. When he sees me laughing, laughing just to keep from crying."

6. Herbert Aptheker, *American Negro Slave Revolts* (New York: International Publishers, 1943), pp. 12–18, 162.

7. Bob Blauner, *Black Lives, White Lives* (Berkeley: University of California Press, 1989).

8. Gordon Allport, *The Nature of Prejudice*, abridged ed. (Garden City, N.Y.: Anchor Books, 1958), pp. 251–253.

9. William H. Grier and Price M. Cobbs, *Black Rage* (New York: Basic Books, Inc., 1968), p. 4.

10. Thomas and Sillen, *The Theory and Application of Symbolic Interactionism*, p. 54.

11. Ibid., p. 54.

12. In his analysis of black slave revolts in the United States, historian Sterling Stuckey has shown that African culture and religion were one source of the revolutionaries' philosophy and inclination to rebel. Sterling Stuckey, *Slave Culture* (New York: Oxford University Press, 1987), pp. 27, 42–46.

13. Gunnar Myrdal, *An American Dilemma* (1944; New York: McGraw-Hill, 1964), vol. 1, p. 38.

14. See, for example, Daniel P. Moynihan, *The Negro Family: The Case for National Action* (Washington, D.C.: U.S. Government Printing Office, 1965); Ken Auletta, *The Underclass* (New York: Random House, 1982).

15. Harriette P. McAdoo, *Black Families*, 2d ed. (Beverly Hills, Calif.: Sage, 1988).

16. See Herbert Gutman, *The Black Family in Slavery and Freedom, 1750–1925* (New York: Random House, 1976).

17. See Peter Bell and Jimmy Evans, *Counseling with the Black Client: Alcohol Use and Abuse in Black America* (Center City, Minn.: Hazelden, 1981).

18. Quoted in Betty Sue Flowers, ed., *Bill Moyers: A World of Ideas* (New York: Doubleday, 1989), p. 173.

19. James S. Jackson, Wayne R. McCullough, Gerald Gurin, "Race Identity," in *Life in Black America*, ed. James S. Jackson (Newbury Park: Sage, 1991), pp. 246–253.

20. Bell and Evans, *Counseling with the Black Client.*

21. Arthur Brittan and Mary Maynard, *Sexism, Racism and Oppression* (Oxford: Basil Blackwell, 1984), p. 7.

8. Changing the Color Line

1. People for the American Way, *Democracy's Next Generation II* (Washington, D.C.: People for the American Way, 1992), p. 63.

2. *Wards Cove Packing Co. v. Atonio*, 109 S. Ct. 2115 (1989).

3. Chandler Davidson, *Race and Class in Texas Politics* (Princeton: Princeton University Press, 1990). Other research has demonstrated that at all three Republican conventions in the 1980s there were very few black delegates. Joe R. Feagin, "White Elephant: Race and Electoral Politics in Texas, *Texas Observer*, August 23, 1991, pp. 15–16.

4. See Shelby Steele, *The Content of Our Character* (New York: St. Martin's Press, 1990).

5. Leanita McClain, "The Middle-class Black's Burden," *Newsweek*, October 13, 1980, reprinted in *A Foot in Each World*, ed. Clarence Page (Evanston, Ill.: Northwestern University Press, 1986), p. 13.

6. Roy Brooks, *Rethinking the American Race Problem* (Berkeley: University of California Press, 1990), pp. 17–21.

7. Sidney Willhelm, *Black in a White America* (Cambridge: Schenkman, 1983); William Julius Wilson, *The Truly Disadvantaged: The Inner City, the Underclass, and Public Policy* (Chicago: University of Chicago Press, 1987).

8. See Joe R. Feagin and Clairece B. Feagin, *Social Problems*, 3d ed. (Englewood Cliffs, N.J.: Prentice-Hall, Inc., 1990), pp. 358–360.

9. Thomas Byrne Edsall and Mary D. Edsall, "When the Official Subject is Presidential Politics, Taxes, Welfare, Crime, Rights, or Values . . . The Real Subject is Race," *The Atlantic*, May 1991, pp. 53–55.

10. George Keller, "Black Students in Higher Education: Why So Few?" *Planning for Higher Education* 17 (1988–1989), p. 55.

11. James R. Kluegel and Eliot R. Smith, *Beliefs about Inequality* (New York: Aldine de Gruyter, 1986), pp. 287–302.

12. Franklin Roosevelt, "Economic Bill of Rights," in *The Human Rights Reader*, ed. Walter Laqueur and Bary Rubin, rev. ed. (New York: New American Library, 1989), p. 313.

13. As quoted by Mwatabu S. Okantah, "In Search of the Real King," *The Plain Dealer*, April 4, 1993, p. 1D.

14. See Howard Schuman, Charlotte Steeh, and Lawrence Bobo, *Racial Attitudes in America* (Cambridge: Harvard University Press, 1985), pp. 139–162.

15. See Paul E. Peterson, "The Urban Underclass and the Poverty Paradox," in *The Urban Underclass*, ed. Christopher Jencks and Paul E. Peterson (Washington, D.C.: The Brookings Institution, 1991), p. 9.

16. Gordon Allport, *The Nature of Prejudice*, abridged ed. (Garden City, N.Y.: Anchor Books, 1958), pp. 251–253.

17. See Chancellor Williams, *The Destruction of Black Civilization* (Chicago: Third World Press, 1987), pp. 320–331.

18. Isabel Wilkerson, "Middle-Class but Not Feeling Equal, Blacks Reflect on Los Angeles Strife," *New York Times*, May 4, 1993, p. A20.

19. St. Clair Drake, *Black Folk Here and There* (Los Angeles: UCLA Center for Afro-American Studies, 1987), p. xv.

20. For example, in *The Signifying Monkey* Henry Louis Gates explored the significant impact of African story-telling styles on African American thought and literature, while in *The Destruction of Black Civilization*, Chancellor Williams argued that the hope for African American unity lies in understanding the great African civilizations and their distinctive values. Henry Louis Gates, *The Signifying Monkey* (New York: Oxford University Press, 1988); Williams, *The Destruction of Black Civilization*.

21. Gunnar Myrdal, *An American Dilemma* (1944; New York: McGraw-Hill, 1964), vol. 1, p. 4.

22. See Anthony J. Lemelle, Review of *From Exclusion to Inclusion, Contemporary Sociology*, 22 (January 1993), p. 63.

23. People for the American Way, *Democracy's Next Generation II*, pp. 48–49.

24. Derrick Bell, *Faces at the Bottom of the Well* (New York: Basic Books, 1992), p. 12. Italics omitted.

25. William E. B. Du Bois, *The Suppression of the African Slave-Trade to the United States of America, 1638–1870* (1896; New York: Schocken Books, 1969), pp. 93–199.

26. Quoted in Emily Morison Beck, ed., *John Bartlett's Familiar Quotations*, 15th ed. (Boston: Little, Brown, 1980), p. 556.

Index

African-American history, 123–24, 324
Afro-Caribbean culture, 121
Afrocentric perspective, 350
Allen, Debbie, 37
Allen, Walter, 95
Allport, Gordon, 19, 21
Alvarez, Rodolfo, 13
American dilemma, 91. *See also* Myrdal, Gunnar
American dream, 9, 33–34, 187, 190, 223, 320, 359–60
American Medical Association, 204
Anomie, 192, 273
Aptheker, Herbert, 281
Ashe, Arthur, 272
Auletta, Ken, 6

Bach, Robert, 219
Bargaining, 44, 235
Bell, Derrick, 363
Bell, Ella, 163
Bell, Peter, 312
Benign neglect, 361
Benjamin, Lois, 13
Bill Cosby Show, 224
Black businesses, 187–222; and 'ole boy' networks, 193–98; construction contracting, 196–98, 201, 210, 214; customers, 212–19; problems of location and capital, 198–204; small, 192;
Black capitalism, 188
Black colleges, 130–31
Black criminality, 48
"Black English," 113
Black middle class, 26–29, 360; and action for change, 346–55; and economic restructuring, 328–30; concern for less affluent, 326–27; defined, 27; goals of, 274, 346–55; survival strategies of, 272–318; view of future, 321–31
Black poor, 42
Black Power, 19, 299
Black pride, 349–50
Black professionals, 204–212; professional connections, 206
Black residential areas, 264–67
Black rights, 42
Black shoppers, 47
Black student organizations, 125–27

Black underclass, 5–9, 341
Blackwell, James, 64, 128
Blalock, Hubert M., 18
Blame-the-victim perspective, 132, 331, 362
Blauner, Bob, 11, 13, 281
Blockbusting, 243–44
Blumer, Herbert, 29, 199
Brittan, Arthur, 19, 316
Brooks, Roy, 327
Bullard, Robert, 267
Bush, George, 74, 325
Business (contracts). *See* Black businesses
Busing, 325
Butler, John S., 132, 188

Calmore, John, 100
Campbell, Bebe Moore, 135
Carmichael, Stokely, 19, 299
Carter, Stephen, 6, 8
Chicago, 140, 188, 271
Citadel, 97
Civil Rights Act (1964), 7, 11, 37, 40, 75, 138, 176
Civil Rights Act (1968), 249, 268
Clark, Kenneth, 157–58
Cobbs, Price, 293
Collective memory, 348
Colleges; black faculty at, 159; bureaucracy of, 128; campus climate of, 93–129; faculty at, 106–29, 159; grading at, 108; "whiteness" of, 133
Collins, Randall, 19
Collins, Sharon, 162
Columbia College, 78
Common Destiny, A, 8, 11, 14, 22, 75, 184, 264
Community pride, 347–48
Competency testing, 101
Complex organizations, 167
Construction contracting business, 196–98, 201, 210, 214
Contending with discrimination. *See* Survival strategies
Coping strategies. *See* Survival strategies
Cuban Americans, 219–20
Cumulative impact of discrimination, 16, 23, 52, 71–75, 145

Davidson, Chandler, 325
Deindustrialization, 328–29
Democratic Party, 9, 330
Denton, Nancy A., 226, 248, 269
Depression, Great, 189, 234
Detroit, 227
Discrimination. *See* Racial discrimination
Discriminatory actions: dimensions of, 20, 312
Double consciousness, 35–36
Douglass, Frederick, 364
Drake, St. Clair, 356
Du Bois, William E. B., 26, 35, 94, 164, 348, 355, 364
Dubuque, Iowa, 252
Duke, David, 122, 329
Durham, North Carolina, 188
Durkheim, Emile, 192

Edsall, Mary, 6, 9, 330
Edsall, Thomas, 6, 9, 330
Education: discrimination in, 78–134. *See also* Elementary and secondary schools; Colleges
Elementary and secondary schools, 80–86; curriculum, 82–83, 335–36, 361; tracking in, 84–85
Ellison, Ralph, 72, 108, 216
Employment discrimination, 135–86; entry stage, 136–43; in performance evaluations, 143–57, in white-collar workplace, 157–64. *See also* Workplace
Equal Credit Opportunity Act, 249
Equal Employment Opportunity, 158, 176
Essed, Philomena, 13
Evans, Jimmy, 312
Excessive surveillance, 255–56

Fair Housing Act, 248
Fair Housing Administration, 226, 249
Fair housing laws, 236
Feagin, Joe R., 106, 112, 127, 130, 196
Federal Home Loan Mortgage Corporation, 249
Federal Housing Administration, 249
Federal Reserve Board, 249
Fernandez, John, 13
Frazier, E. Franklin, 26
Fredrickson, George, 73

Gallo, Carmenza, 198, 220
Gardner, Carol Brooks, 60
Ghetto riots. *See* Riots
Gilder, George, 6
Glazer, Nathan, 6, 219
Goering, John, 268–69
Government action against discrimination, 322–25, 333, 339–41, 343, 354
Graduate Record Examination (GRE), 114
Graduate school, 109–10
Gramsci, Antonio, 30
Green discrimination, 242
Grier, William, 293
Griffin, John Howard, 63
Gutman, Herbert, 304

Hacker, Andrew, 13
Hamilton, Charles, 19
Handel, Warren, 75
Hartford, Connecticut, 80
Harvard University, 70
Hate crimes, 3, 58–59, 73–74, 320
Hate Crime Statistics Act, 58
Hate stares, 63–64, 76, 82, 254
Higginbotham, Elizabeth, 147
Hill, Herbert, 176
Home: as refuge, 224–26
Homeowners, 234–43
Hooks, Bell, 12–13
Horatio Alger dream, 34
Horton, "Willie," 74
Housing, 223–71; city neighborhoods, 247; rental, 228–34; resegregation of, 243–49; segregated, 226–28
Humphrey, James H., 273

Impact of discrimination, 15–18, 20, 23–24, 44, 52, 71–75, 145, 214, 277, 293–302, 318
Institutionalized racism, 3–5, 10, 17–19, 265
Interracial friendships, 105

Jackson, Jesse, 53
Johnson, Lyndon, 333
Jones, Ed, 143, 154

Kanter, Rosabeth Moss, 152, 158
Katz, Joseph, 119
Katz, Phyllis A., 18
Keller, George, 6–7, 92, 107, 132, 331, 342
Kerner Commission, 320
Kilpatrick, James, 74
King, Martin Luther, Jr., 334, 348, 355
Kluegel, James R., 11
Kovel, Joel, 48
Ku Klux Klan, 90, 97, 261, 320, 329

Landry, Bart, 27
Lauer, Robert, 75
Laughter, 104, 286, 288, 301–2, 345
Lawsuits, 290–93
Legal segregation, 68, 217
Lemann, Nicholas, 6
Lenders, 249–52
Life perspective, defined, 17
Los Angeles riot (1992). *See* Riots
Louisiana, 122

McAdoo, Harriette, 303
McClain, Leanita, 29–30, 34, 77, 135, 326
MacKinnon, Catharine, 112
Malcolm X, 348, 355–56

Marable, Manning, 12
Marxism, 183
Massey, Douglas S., 226, 248, 269
Maynard, Mary, 19, 316
Medical schools, 116–17, 127
Mental energy, 25, 277, 295–98, 318
Mirowsky, John, 76, 156
Montgomery, Alabama, 167
Moynihan, Daniel Patrick, 6
Multicultural courses, 83, 336–37
Myrdal, Gunnar, 18, 91, 174, 301, 359

National Advisory Commission on Civil Disorders, 4–5, 270
National Association for the Advancement of Colored People (NAACP), 45, 308
National Black Police Association, 69
National Commission on Minority Participation in Education and American Life, 91
National Council of Churches, 3
National Crime Victimization Survey, 73
National Medical Association, 205
National Research Council, 8, 11,
Negotiation, 19–20, 42–43, 317
Neo-Nazis, 90
New York, 188

Oak Park, Illinois, 248
Obligation to children, 314–15
Olivet College, 105
"Open persons," 60
Opinion polls, 2, 11, 13–15, 22, 79–80, 103, 137, 189, 227–28, 322
Orfield, Gary, 271

Parks, Rosa, 167
Pettigrew, Thomas, 19, 213
Police harassment, 64–71; police brutality, 65
Portes, Alejandro, 219
Prejudice, 2–4, 9, 19, 21–23, 86–90, 232, 262
Professionals. *See* Black professionals
Public accomodations, 38–56; hotels, 51–52; restaurants, 38–46; retail and grocery stores, 46–51, 53–55

Quotas, 232, 325

Racial discrimination, 4; action to change, 346–56; as everyday experience, 15–18; by customers and clients, 177–80, 215–16; character of response to, 20, 24–26; continuing significance of 12–15; cumulative impact of, 16, 23, 52, 71–75, 145; defined, 20; dimensions of, 18–26; energy-consuming aspects of, 25, 44, 277, 295–98, 318; financial resources to fight, 275; future of, 321–31; impact of on victim, 20, 23–24, 44, 214; in educational institutions, 78–134; in hotels, 51–52; in housing market, 223–71; in performance evaluation, 143–57; in police department, 164–65; in public accommodations, 38–56; in restaurants, 38–46; in retail and grocery stores, 46–51, 53–55; in the workplace, 135–86; preparing children to face, 311–16; range of actions, 20, 21–23, 312; responses to, 49–50, 54; self blame for, 104, 298, 315, 318; site of actions, 20–21; strain of, 273, 277, 293–302, 318; street, 56–64; subtle, 100
Racial ecology, 267
Racism: and legal structure, 317; as lived experience, 15–18; collective wisdom about, 313–14; defined, 3–4; denial of, 362; gendered, 105; old fashioned, 24. *See also* Racial discrimination
Racist insults, 175
Racist joking, 98–99, 173, 281–82
Rage, 293–94
Rand Corporation, 8
Reagan, Ronald, 325

Real estate industry, 237–41
Republican administrations, 163, 324–25
Republican Party, 325, 330
Reverse discrimination, 5
Rider College, 98
Riots, 4–5, 18, 320; in Los Angeles, 2, 18, 65, 193, 270, 320, 349
Rodney, Walter, 222
Rollins, Judith, 25
Roosevelt, Franklin, 333
Ross, Catherine E., 76, 156
Rustin, Bayard, 6, 7

Scammon, Richard, 6
Schlesinger, Arthur, Jr., 83, 337
Scholastic Aptitude Test (SAT), 114–15
Scott, Kesho Yvonne, 13
Second eye, 25
Separate worlds, 320
Sexism, 105, 180–83
Shaker Heights, Ohio, 248, 264
Sigelman, Lee, 14
Sillen, Samuel, 273, 298
Slave revolts, 281
Slavery, 217
Sleeper, Jim, 6, 10
Smith, Eliot R., 11
Social support, 302–11; black families, 302–4; black friends, 305–6; black organizations, 306–7, 352; helpful whites, 149, 307–11
South Africa, 126, 334–35, 357
Southern Poverty Law Center, 252
Sowell, Thomas, 6, 187
"Standard English," 55
Steele, Shelby, 6, 7–8, 187
Steering, 238
Stereotypes, 22, 48, 50, 62, 70–71, 86–91, 99–100, 105, 106–14, 139, 147, 153, 257, 332, 342
Supreme Court, 323
Survival strategies, 272–318; alliances with coworkers, 169; avoidance, 275; black solidarity, 349; confrontation, 281–90; laughter, 104, 286, 288, 301–2, 345; lawsuits, 290–93; of parents, 311; overachievement, 297; religion, 299–301; retreat, 279; sharing pain, 316; shield, 294–95; using official channels, 290–93

Taylor, Dalmas A., 18
Theory of rights, 42
Thomas, Alexander, 273, 298
Trump, Donald, 187–88
Tulsa, Oklahoma, 188
Tuskegee, Alabama, 205
Tuskegee experiments, 205

Underground Railroad, 149
U.S. armed forces, 343–44
U.S. Bureau of Labor Statistics, 27
U.S. Commission on Civil Rights, 8, 339
U.S. Commission on Minority Business Development, 199
U.S. Constitution, 1, 359
U.S. Courts, 2, 35; Supreme Court, 9, 323–24
U.S. Declaration of Independence, 358–59
U.S. Department of Education, 129, 189
U.S. Department of Housing and Urban Development (HUD), 229, 268–69
U.S. Department of Justice, 233, 268, 340
U.S. House of Representatives, 346
Universities. *See* Colleges
University of Alabama, 97
University of Maryland, 103
University of Nebraska, 70
Urban Institute, 140

Voting Rights Act (1965), 157, 354

Wards Cove Packing Co. v. *Atonio* (1989), 323
Washington, D.C., 140

Wattenbert, Ben, 6
Wealth, 203, 223
Weber, Lynn, 147
Welch, Susan, 14
White attitudes, 337–45
White racism, 4–5, 10–11, 16, 23
Wieseltier, Leon, 10
Willhelm, Sidney, 13, 328
Williams, Patricia, 12
Wilson, William J., 6, 7, 12, 27, 245, 328, 342
Workplace, 135–86; black managers in, 163; entry stage discrimination, 136–43; interracial alliances in, 169; tokenism in, 143, 160–61; white-collar, 157–63

Zoning, 267

HARM'S WAY

HARM'S

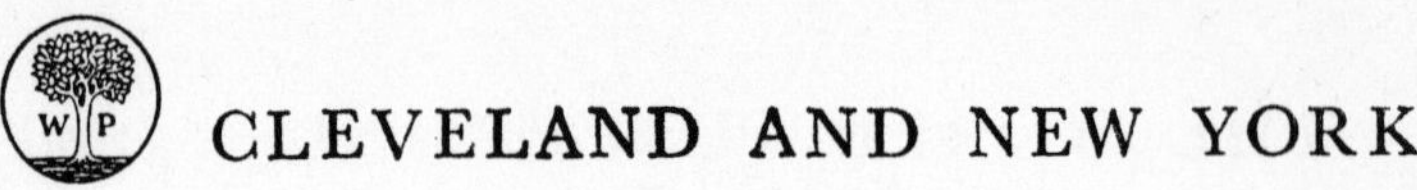

WAY

James Bassett

THE WORLD PUBLISHING COMPANY

PUBLISHED BY *The World Publishing Company*
2231 WEST 110TH STREET, CLEVELAND 2, OHIO

PUBLISHED SIMULTANEOUSLY IN CANADA BY
NELSON, FOSTER & SCOTT LTD.

LIBRARY OF CONGRESS CATALOG CARD NUMBER: 62-21442

FIRST EDITION

WP1062

For my wife, Willie,
who lived through
all these things, and who
loved Admiral Bill Halsey
as much as I did.

Contents

FOUR STRIPES

1. No Longer the Harem Eunuchs! 13
2. No Sea Anchor 40
3. Some Men Play God 60
4. Neither Did the Cruse of Oil Fail 79
5. Toward a Certain Gethsemane 100
6. Who'll Play Torquemada? 119
7. No Man Is an Island 148
8. Too Much, Too Little 168
9. What Lies Beyond a Thing Called Duty? 188
10. The Japs Won't Wait Forever 206

TWO STARS

11. You Can't Simply Order a Man 225
12. Nobody Cares Whether You Live or Die 249
13. Sailors Take Warning 279
14. Be Kind to Your Webfooted Friends 311

15. Season of Falling Stars 333
16. Like a Wolf on the Fold! 360
17. What's Been Started Can't Be Stopped 390
18. The Lock Clicks Shut 417
19. Joss Sticks Bring Good Luck 434
20. No Captain Can Do Very Wrong 460
21. Everlasting Gratitude 494

PRECEDE

IN THIS STORY of naval command during the year that began with Pearl Harbor, on December 7, 1941, certain things occur which never really happened at all. Other things which did take place in that early phase of the Pacific War have been purposely omitted, for the narrative's sake.

Thus, the historical events which form part of this novel's framework have been telescoped to create a microcosm, a bit of everything in miniature, rather than a one-sided view of war's more sweeping macrocosm.

Except for the historical persons whom I have not endeavored to disguise, none of the characters in this fiction are based on any actual person, living or dead. Only the heroes may have subconscious counterparts in the author's mind. Such villains as might appear have been cut from whole khaki cloth.

For there are no villains in war.

Only war itself is the villain . . .

"I wish to have no Connection with any Ship that does not sail fast, for I intend *to go in harm's way . . ."*

—JOHN PAUL JONES, USN

FOUR STRIPES

1. *No Longer the Harem Eunuchs!*

FRAMED by the open weather door of his cabin, where he stood peering through the obscure dawn toward Oahu's invisible shoreline, Captain Rockwell Torrey, USN, was not unlike the ship he commanded: tall, spare, angular, and plainly fabricated out of some hard gray substance that armored both man and cruiser against the weapons of a hostile world.

Although the image he evoked was unmistakable, he would have derided the suggestion that he also resembled an absolute monarch at this precise instant, surveying his domain from a castle parapet, and contemplating what lay ahead for his thirteen hundred subjects, his steel realm, and himself, during the long day that had just begun.

Captain Torrey, feeling neither regal nor infallible, pushed back the frayed sleeve of his seersucker bathrobe and glanced at the waterproof watch on his bony wrist, as if to verify mechanically what he could not confirm visually in that pervasive semidarkness. It showed 0630, four minutes past the "official sunrise" decreed by the almanac. But full daylight would not arrive for another half-hour, when the sun would burst blindingly over Tantalus and Olympus, the canefields would change from somber black into bright yellowgreen, and the twelve-hour gunnery exercise would get underway.

Consciously, with a sense of physical relief, he inhaled deeply, filling his lungs with moist salt air to exorcise the staleness caused by sleeping all night behind the closed ports of his stateroom. The cold metal plating felt good against his bare feet.

For a long moment he remained at the exit to the small veranda deck, where he occasionally sunbathed on peaceful afternoons. It lay just below the glass-windowed navigating bridge, and one level above the cruiser's sweeping main deck. His line of vision toward

Oahu, still hidden in the eastern mists, was impeded by a pair of five-inch/38s. Canvas-hooded against the dampness of the subtropical dawn and the corrosive spray that sifted back from the bow, these lean rifles provided secondary defense against surface enemies and primary protection against aerial attack.

Despite her advanced age, however, the cruiser had never fired her guns in anger, and nagging doubts about what might happen if she were suddenly confronted by an authentic foe were constantly on Torrey's mind.

Scowling, he considered this possibility for the thousandth time in the past week before he rejected it as too improbable, or at least too premature, for valid concern just then. Meanwhile, in the endless pattern of other days, he must try again to wheedle his ship into that desirable condition which the Navy called "maximum readiness." This entailed launching the cruiser's clumsy pontooned aircraft, recovering them, shepherding the minesweep rehearsals of the two ancient converted four-stack destroyers, and shooting at target sleeves towed by patrol planes from Pearl Harbor, a dozen miles away.

Captain Torrey turned slowly as a knock sounded against the inner door that led to the superstructure passageway.

When he called, "Yes?" his voice was as thoroughly neutral, severely accentless, and utterly controlled as only twenty-seven years in the Navy could make it.

"Five bells, sir," the Marine messenger announced softly.

"Thanks," Torrey said. "I know. I'm awake."

"Commander Eddington reports that our first launching will take place at 0700 sharp."

"Very well. Tell the exec I'm coming topside right away. And, Leary, have the galley send breakfast up to my sea cabin. Bacon and eggs. Toast. Black coffee. Some juice. That's all."

"Aye, aye, sir."

He could almost *feel* the Marine's stiff salute through the closed door. Heavyshod feet sounded like a one-horse cavalry charge on the steel plates outside, then faded, as the messenger clop-clopped down the ladder to alert the cooks that the captain was wide awake, hungry, and in one friggin' hell of a hurry to get cracking.

When he swung back toward the open portal, Torrey's grim

expression eased imperceptibly, for he noted that the irrepressible tradewind was blowing lightly, north-to-northeast. This, he reflected, should simplify the always vexing problem of catapulting the scout planes. His grayblue eyes narrowed again as he stared aft, past the 20-millimeter twin mounts uptilted in their steel tubs, past the tall smokestacks and the catapult tracks, past the squat tower that contained the secondary controls (where his executive officer would assume command if an enemy shell obliterated the bridge), and finally past the menacing three-fingered bulk of Number 3 turret with its eight-inch main battery.

Torrey cast a last lingering glance at the ocean, the sky, and his ship before he commenced his Spartan morning toilet.

In this uncertain moment just before the true dawn, which was briefly delayed by a wall of translucent clouds banked wraithgray against the Koolau Range to the east, the cruiser seemed quite alone and friendless on the greenslag sea. Neither graceful nor swift, she plowed stolidly along her prearranged course like an old woman darkclad in widow's weeds crossing a deserted street. Her progress was all the more deliberate, and unhurried, because only a fraction of the 107,000 horsepower generated by her turbines had been summoned into play. Where her sharp prow engaged the easy swells barely a trace of white spume showed.

From clipper stem to speedboat stern she measured almost six hundred feet; from rail to rail she was sixty-five feet broad; her loftiest eminence, the gleaming truck light, was a hundred feet above her main deck; and she drew twenty-two feet of water when fully burdened.

Her "legal limit" of 10,826 tons displacement had been determined by a rather curious treaty signed at Washington, D.C., six years before her keel was laid in 1928. She was, therefore, thirteen years old on this particular morning in December—an age which in the human animal heralds budding adolescence, or the first stirrings of young manhood, but which spells creeping obsolescence in warships.

Torrey realized that all of his cruiser's imperfections were not attributable to age alone. Viewed in silhouette against the glowering half light that filtered across Oahu's volcanic crown, she would betray a noticeable concavity, a downsweptness that was not unlike a bent bow, in the area between her two raked funnels. This odd spinal distortion might have been the result of a designer's whimsical pen slip, or it could have been brought on by overwork during the Fleet's endless war games.

But whatever the cause, from this odd circumstance sprang her nickname which was at once unlovely and affectionate: *Old Swayback.*

Even Torrey used this homely appellation, although he was well aware that *Old Swayback* was rated a proper, if not enviable, command for an officer clawing his way up the career ladder that leads from Annapolis to an admiral's stars. (Or, he reminded himself occasionally, to the limbo of premature retirement for those overage in grade, where you tend a rose garden on some foggy hillside overlooking the fine vessels skippered by your "best-fitted" classmates.) After serving his stint in a heavy cruiser like *Old Swayback,* a senior captain could expect a battleship or even a carrier, provided he wore pilot's wings, as the logical prelude to Flag rank. Always assuming he didn't get bushwhacked in the jungle of high-level Navy politics, he might even wind up with a task force or a Fleet. At the apex of the whole brawling heap stood the godlike figure of CinCUS: Commander in Chief, United States Fleet.

Through the diminishing gloom Torrey could make out the shapes of the antique tincans, burying their needle noses in the moderate swells, and casting aside the graygreen seas the way properly trained spaniels cleave the waters of a duck pond in their eagerness to join their master. It was time to go to work.

Sighing a private sigh, he stripped off his blue-and-white seersucker bathrobe and strode briskly into the tiny head that adjoined his stateroom, where he showered, toweled vigorously, and prepared to shave.

From a worn redplush case he extracted one of seven straight German surgical steel razors, which lay cradled in slots marked for each day of the week. He opened the blade and began to knead it lovingly across a leather strop that was darkpolished from long use and old age. It was his *Sonntag* razor. If calendars had never been invented, he could have kept an infallible chronology with his seven razors. They had belonged to his father. The Old Man had also been a four-striper, although he had stumbled somehow on the penultimate rung of the ladder and had never quite achieved admiral. Nevertheless he'd refused to nurse roses after his retirement, and until the day he died at seventy-three he taught naval tactics at a frowsy little military school on the southern California coast.

Peering into the misty mirror, Torrey searched his unhandsome, yet not quite ugly countenance, as if he were studying the face of a total stranger. He had learned, especially since moving into the monastic quarters aboard *Old Swayback,* that this was the most naked moment of a man's day. All defenses down, he now confronts himself solitary and unarmed, and suddenly conscious of the skin-shell within which he dwells imprisoned and alone with himself, his soul, and his conscience.

Torrey was forty-eight. He might have been taken for fifty-eight; but he would retain this agelessness for many years to come, etched deeply and varnished darkly upon his gaunt, almost equine face by sun sear and wind whip. Four parallel lines were permanently carved across his forehead, and lesser crow's-foot wrinkles spread almost from eye to ear, like mooring lines securing ship to wharf. Even a modified crew cut could not disguise the grizzled grayness of his sparse hair. With a slight feeling of distaste, he noticed that the skin between his lean belly and his prominent clavicle was beginning to acquire an oldish-softish look, like used crepe paper.

Clothed in service blues or in starched whites, which concealed this softness, and when his slightly awed underlings imagined he was beyond earshot, he was known as "The Rock." It emanated as much out of a certain admiration and even grudging affection for this reserved, withdrawn, meticulous man, as it did from the plain fact that he had been christened Rockwell Torrey.

He had no middle name.

When The Rock was born in 1893, his father had already been a struggling ensign for five austere peacetime years. It was a belt-tightening time for the steam Navy, despite Commander Mahan's demand that America heed *The Influence of Sea Power upon History,* and the Old Man said he'd billy-be-damned if any son of his would revel in the luxury of a middle name while Grover Cleveland was substituting torpedo boats for battleships in the dubious interest of "hard money."

As The Rock rose steadily toward the rarefied command plateau which he now occupied, awaiting the moment when he might be sought out for Flag rank, he made it quite plain that he expected—even demanded—of his subordinates this same craggy independence of attitude and action that ruled his own life. Always, of course, within the clear confines of nautical discipline.

They tried.

Torrey placed his razor gently upon the chromesteel edge of the washbasin, mixed lather in a USN coffee mug with a decrepit badger-hair brush, and carefully soaped his face. Legs braced to compensate for *Old Swayback*'s predictable ten-degree roll, midriff pressed firmly against the stand, he began to shave with quick, clean strokes, pausing now and again to deposit bits of stubble-pocked foam on a neat square of tissue. Through the opened port he could hear the metallic clump and rumble of the five-inch twin mount as its crew unlimbered their battery after a night of carefree Condition Three. His eyes, above the ludicrous mask of white lather, compressed into a ruminative scowl.

Old Swayback's daily schedule called for antiaircraft drill as well as surface maneuvers, and lately her marksmanship had ranged from a discouraging 3.2 to a mediocre 3.6, with no perfect 4.0s to brighten her record, nor any gunnery E's for excellence to flaunt from her masthead. With a certain detached grimness Torrey speculated upon what might happen if the target-towing PBYs suddenly metamorphosed into Japs some murky dawn, and came swinging in at five hundred feet with torpedoes hanging loose-as-a-goose. *Old Swayback* wouldn't last twenty minutes.

In his most recent communication with the Pacific Fleet's cruiser commander, The Rock had observed with more truth than diplomacy: "It is difficult to achieve maximum results through dry runs, dummy loading practice, or wardroom discussions devoted to theory. . . ."

Thoughtfully, he wiped the last trace of soap from behind his rather generous ears. By 1700 he would need another shave if he wanted to look properly shipshape, but unless some urgent social function impended he would let it go until next morning.

He replaced his meticulously cleaned razor in its *Sonntag* slot, and took a fresh pair of skivvies and a T-shirt from the steel bureau in his stateroom. Slowly, almost deliberately, he began to clothe his angular nakedness. As he slipped the short-sleeved cotton shirt over his shoulders, his gaze fell briefly upon a small tattoo on the deltoid muscle of his upper arm. He frowned again. The tiny fouled anchor, originally a bright violet, had become almost indistinguishable over the years, but it still symbolized a distant time when he was less sure of himself, less in control. Now he was marked forever by this silly little emblem which he'd acquired during a weekend in Havana on his younger cruise, a whole generation ago.

He checked his wrist watch again before he poked his long legs into his stiffstarched khaki trousers. Inconsequentially, he remembered then that this was the first Sunday of the month.

It was now 0645.

Ashore, in their self-consciously tropical cottages that nestled among the greatfronded shade trees along Nuuanu stream or that sprawled under the sunshine glare of Manoa Valley, the Fleet's officers would be enjoying leave as usual with their families. Some would doubtless be sleeping off too many gin and tonics or rum and Cokes after dollar dinners at the Pearl Harbor Officers' Club. The Rock didn't really care. If *Old Swayback* had been in port that Sunday, he would have remained on board anyway, staying in his bunk until 0700 instead of reveilleing at his normal 0600, and maybe putting off his shave until midmorning, when he would join the cruiser's church services on the fantail.

The ship was his home, just as a dozen Bachelor Officers' Quarters had been home during his earlier tours of shore duty, for he had no place else to go. There was a time, of course, when he might have hurried ashore the moment his ship tied up. But that was long ago and very far away; and now he preferred not to think about it any more, or about the proud, cold woman he had married, and the strange, unfathomable son she had borne him.

Athalie and Jere. Yes. It was one hell of a long time ago . . .

Actually, Torrey supposed, he should envy these brother officers who could shuck off their professional cares so cavalierly during a lazy weekend, when they painted their Lanai chairs or studied the *Advertiser* comics or tuned up their secondhand Fords for a spin around Diamond Head to the lovely windward beaches of Waimea and Haliewa and Kahuku. They'd carry with them basket lunches filled with civilian delicacies like deviled eggs and stuffed celery, and their Thermos jugs would glisten with the delicate sweat of daiquiris.

But The Rock felt no envy. For this, he imagined, was their escape from the tenseness that had gripped the Fleet ever since Hitler triggered the European war in September 1939, and which had a nasty way of erupting into jagged nerve peaks during the periodic false alerts, then dwindling as cooler heads decided you couldn't cry wolf forever.

Now the tenseness was rising again, at least among the upper echelon directly concerned with such ponderous matters. Task force admirals, it was assumed, got The Word almost as soon as President Roosevelt himself; captains of ships received "essential information" necessary to carry out their parochial jobs; but the lesser folk had to be content with illegal and generally unreliable scuttlebutt gleaned from the omniscient yeomen who typed out secret dispatches.

The Rock's intelligence was neither better nor worse than that possessed by his fellow skippers. Locked away in his gray-steel desk safe, and dog-eared from much handling, was a dispatch from the Commander in Chief, Pacific Fleet, which sternly ordered maximum vigilance against possible enemy submarines in American operating areas. Destroyers were told to depth-bomb any hostile contacts. These instructions, naturally, left individual captains carrying a heavy load of personal responsibility. For what *is* a "hostile contact," exactly, when your country's at peace? More or less.

CinCPAC's order bore a November date—the 28th.

A day before this filtered down to Torrey's level, even more sobering Word arrived at Fleet headquarters. But four-stripers never heard about it, because it was too highly classified for perusal by mere captains of cruisers or even battlewagons and carriers.

"THIS DISPATCH," the Chief of Naval Operations radioed to CinCPAC's busy eyrie above the great harbor, "IS TO BE CONSIDERED A WAR WARNING . . . AN AGGRESSIVE MOVE BY JAPAN IS EXPECTED IN THE NEXT FEW DAYS . . . UNPREDICTABLE BUT HOSTILE ACTIONS ARE POSSIBLE AT ANY MOMENT."

It was axiomatic, of course, that any "irresponsible and misguided" enemy (to quote the language of a confidential Fleet letter which also reposed in The Rock's desk safe) would certainly launch its attack against the United States' weak Far Eastern defenses, rather than against the Hawaiian chain. Pearl Harbor lay 3,500 miles from Tokyo, damned wide-open miles as a top-heavy Nip battleship steams; and it was another 2,000 miles to San Francisco. Hence Pearl was a target so difficult to reach, and so thornily protected once you got there, that only a lunatic would dream of such an adventure.

Sometimes Torrey wondered . . .

Unhurriedly, in the mouth-pursed fashion of a bachelor sewing on a shirt button, The Rock took a pair of tiny silver eagles from his wardrobe drawer, and pinned one to each collar wing of his khaki shirt. He considered these neat symbols of his captaincy rather typical of the Navy, and quite unlike the clumsy birds worn by Army colonels. Alongside them in the stud box was a pair of gold pilot's wings, which Torrey ignored.

Fully clad, he cast a final appraising glance around the low-ceilinged cabin. It was also very neat and very precise, and satisfyingly different from the stuccoed warrens inhabited by the Island Command landlubbers at Fort Shafter, whom he occasionally visited under extreme social duress. Nothing marred the sterile orderliness that was the most obvious characteristic of his cabin, which measured 24-by-10 feet, or the adjoining stateroom, which was only half as large. Several nautical books occupied a rack over the metal desk, on which reposed a standard gooseneck lamp, a magnifying glass and dividers, a trim stack of Fleet correspondence, form letters from various naval bureaus, and a clipboard containing flimsies of all incoming radio messages.

Torrey's lips tightened as his eyes strayed across the desk. The topmost dispatch was the shoot-to-kill order in the unlikely event that *Old Swayback* and her consorts encountered any unidentified submarines in Hawaiian waters.

His old cruiser was about as prepared for lurking subs, or enemy surface craft, as a half-blind setter was equipped to tackle a pack of timber wolves. Her mast was devoid of any radar antennae, although this fabulous electronic gear was already standard in the hard-pressed British Navy, and new American ships arriving at Pearl lately had these "eyes" that could pick out an enemy through darkness and fog. Nevertheless, as The Rock clapped his goldlaced cap upon his head and started topside, he was not entirely dissatisfied with his aging vessel. She was at least a ship, by God, and he had possessed her for seventeen months, during a barren time when half his classmates were enviously eating their hearts out for any seagoing command at all.

The black-dialed clock fastened to the bridge bulkhead behind the mammoth ship's wheel now showed 0655.

The Rock went to the starboard wing where his executive officer was overseeing preparations for catapulting *Old Swayback*'s two Seagulls. The stubby little biplanes were perched on their outswung firing tracks like sparrows clinging to a telephone wire, awaiting the signal for launching once the ship reached proper speed into the light breeze. Even above the firecracker sound of the planes' 550-horsepower engines a deep-throated hum was audible in the quickening air as the turbines stepped up their tempo and the cruiser's nightlong fourteen knots accelerated toward a respectable twenty.

The exec waved his brawny right hand.

Instantly there was a puff of white smoke, a sharp explosion, and the first Seagull started down the catapult rail, rapidly gaining momentum. It veered, lurched, dipped, then climbed. After that the exec flagged off the second plane. Both pilots circled *Old Swayback* once, waggling their ailerons, grinning, and shamelessly exposing the inadequate 100-pound practice bombs slung against the underside of their planes' wings.

In the abrupt quiet that followed the launchings, the exec's voice sounded loud and harsh.

"Hell of a way to fight a war, isn't it, skipper?"

"Yes," Torrey snapped, and turned away.

The exec appeared abashed at this curt rejoinder, although he had known Torrey since Academy days, when he was a raw-fannied plebe and the captain was a lordly first-classman wearing the four thin stripes of a battalion commander. Perhaps he should have been smarter than to attempt heavy-handed humor with The Rock at this unholy hour. The captain hated unnecessary chatter at any time, but most of all in the morning watches before his human juices began flowing and he warmed up a bit.

Just now, however, Paul Eddington found it impossible to bridle his tongue: he was suffering from an almost compulsive urge to talk, to say anything that popped into his stupid head, even to the point of discussing the peculiar way those trade-wind clouds were beginning to detach themselves from the serrated peaks of the Koolau Range and drift high and slow over Pearl Harbor.

Eddington had a skull-shattering hangover.

He had acquired it during a couple of hours of steady drinking, alone, long after he bade the wardroom coffee klatsch good night around 0030. Guiltily, yet with a kind of clinical awareness of what he was doing, he had gone to his nearby stateroom, locked the door, and pulled the quart of 100-proof bourbon from his foot-locker, which he kept padlocked. Eddington silently mouthed a prayer before he took his first stinging swallow of raw whisky.

It went something like this: *For Christ's sweet sake give us action . . . any kind of action . . . soon . . . please . . . so a man can become a man again . . . amen!*

His clandestine alcoholism, which was only suspected by his busy subordinates, was a disease that rode him cyclically like the waves of undulant fever. It came upon him during periods of boring inactivity when he had too much time to think and far too little to keep himself occupied.

Normally, Eddington was a quiet man, with something of The Rock's gift for self-possession. His associates prophesied that he would go places in the Navy, if, as they invariably appended, he kept his nose clean. Most of them even acknowledged that he was brilliant, despite a tendency to become a trifle erratic at odd intervals, which they attributed more to his perpetually youthful *élan* than to any real imbalance in his character. As the years passed, however, certain nagging doubts arose in the minds of some highly situated officers. For, after all, when a man's forty-five, you can no longer regard him as a stripling; by then he is presumed to have acquired the seasoning he needs, and achieved the stability inherent in responsible command.

During maneuvers on the battle game board, which was set up every two weeks on a tennis court alongside the Sub Base quays, Paul Eddington proved himself a daring tactician, willing to take the most astonishing calculated risks with the flag-marked bits of painted wood that represented warships. Generally he got away with it. And the old boys smiled tolerantly again, figuring that he was—just as they'd been saying all along—a damned savvy fellow who simply needed somebody to keep a fatherly eye on him.

After these practice sessions, he and The Rock dined together in the captain's secluded cabin aboard *Old Swayback*, and mulled over the day's events. On the days when Eddington had been too exuberant with the toy warships, Torrey would chide him gently for his impetuosity.

"Paul," he said once, talking slowly and gravely around the bulldog briar he smoked on such occasions, "eventually you'll get a ship of your own. Maybe after that a squadron. Then who knows? Even a Fleet, because you're the kind of fellow we'll be needing." Torrey rubbed the pipe against his prominent cheekbone, and inspected its finegrain sheen, before he added: "When the time comes."

"*If* the time ever comes," Eddington corrected him flatly.

"Point is, then it won't be a game any more, but the real thing played with men's lives and a lot of expensive hardware instead of little chunks of pine on a plot board."

"Hell—that's the name of the game, isn't it?"

The exec's wide face, which still bore the marks of an overenthusiastic Academy boxing career, split into a crooked grin. With a curious feeling of distaste, The Rock noted that his expression was too eager, almost wolfish, as if Eddington were relishing some small private preview of Armageddon.

"Command," he said softly, "can also be a damned dangerous business, Paul."

"Danger's our business. It's what we've been training for all these unbloody peacetime years. Isn't it?" The wolfish gaze sharpened. "Look what's happened to us since the war ended in 1918—squatting on our beach-bound arses and pushing around mountains of papers, or out here pretending we're gallant seadogs with ships that couldn't fight their way out of a rain squall." He remembered a scornful Academy phrase, "Like the USS *Tuscarora*—'seven decks and a straw bottom!' And always worrying about what the goddamned taxpayer or some fat-bellied politician's thinking. Hell. You know what I mean. If it's not Guam fortifications, it's too many men in uniform eating their fool heads off." Eddington's abrasive voice ran down like a tired sanding lathe.

The Rock rationed himself a bleak smile.

"Maybe that's what the armchair experts call our 'peacetime mission.' Making do with the widow's mite."

"Sure. Or playing poker against the Nips with a Fleet that's split worse than a busted straight. Right up the middle—from Singapore to Frisco."

"So we've got to keep our wits about us, fella. Hang tough. Stay smarter."

The exec, who chainsmoked his cigarettes, reached for an ash tray that was tooled from the base of a five-inch shell casing. He jabbed the butt savagely into the shallow brass cylinder.

"Meanwhile," he growled, "the Sons of the Samurai will gobble up all of eastern Asia. Great!"

"Only temporarily."

"We should have jumped the bastards when they sneaked into Manchuria. Or when they clobbered the *Panay,* by God!"

"Anyhow, we know what we're up against," Torrey said. "What's the Nip term for it? *Hakko Ichiu.* Pulling all eight corners of the world under one imperial roof."

"So in the bare face of all this," Eddington said, "dear old Daddy Roosevelt orders every fifth combatant ship back to the Atlantic and leaves us with three lousy carriers. Makes a friggin' lot of sense, doesn't it?"

The Rock countered mildly, "That's where the fighting's going on."

"Suppose it starts here, too?"

"You've seen Rainbow 5."

"Sure. I've seen the noble document," Eddington said rudely. "Defensive nonsense!"

Many times before they had debated the Pacific Fleet's carefully tooled war plan, and always they arrived at this same impasse. The exec viewed it with the haughty intolerance of a man whose military lexicon contains only one word: *attack*. Once fighting started, Rainbow 5 aimed to lure the enemy away from the Malay Barrier by quickly establishing a series of beachheads in the Marshall Islands. Even Torrey had to admit that the Japanese undeservedly inherited this choice bit of strategic real estate from the Germans as their reward for having been such pleasant chaps during the Great War.

Scant hours after hostilities commenced, the United States Fleet —wherever it was, in all its components—would get the signal to execute Rainbow 5.

"Do you suppose," Eddington demanded, "that the Nips will hang by their tails from the banyan trees while we move in on 'em?"

"No doubt they've read Mahan, too," The Rock said, "and realize our job would be keeping our sea lanes open, while throttling theirs. Sure. They'd retaliate—violently—whenever they decided war was inevitable."

"Isn't it?"

"We haven't reached the breaking point yet. They're still talking in Washington."

Eddington crushed another cigarette into the ash-tray rubble. "Personally, I'd rather jump the bastards while they're still in their huddle."

"You don't care what the world thinks?"

"Screw the world! With our superiority in planes and pilots we'd wind this thing up before the saintly Joes got their halos adjusted. Then let 'em holler."

Torrey's pipe had gone dead. He relit it, slowly and lovingly, before he said, "No. It wouldn't be that easy. We know the Nips have laid down a pair of battleships armed with eighteen-inch guns. Sixty-thousand tonners. Bigger than anything we've got blueprinted. That's why we're playing for time."

"Wrong!" The exec waved his third cigarette like a marshal's baton. "We *don't* wait. We profit by surprise. All we need is some strategic gizzard. The Nips can't stand a full-scale war and they know it. Maybe they'd last a couple of months. After that—*pau!*"

The Rock's expression mingled sorrow and annoyance. "I grant you the 'gizzard,' Paul. But I'm not sure about your strategy. Or your judgment."

Embarrassed, and visibly angered, the exec growled, "Are you suggesting I've got low savvy quotient, skipper?"

"Perhaps."

Eddington glowered at him. Then he concluded, "Now I'm damned if you don't sound like my sainted father."

"Or mine."

Torrey remembered how the Old Man, stern as an avenging New Testament angel with his shock of white hair, used to prowl their small living room that gazed out upon the Pacific, pausing every so often to remark upon the *duty* which Jehovah Himself had set upon His humble seafaring servants. Responsibility, he rumbled in a basso accustomed to outshouting wind and waves, increased in exact ratio to the eminence which such servants reached in the careers they had selected of their own free will.

Later young Torrey would comprehend what the Old Man meant, although he didn't fathom it in those early days before he'd been baked in the Navy's crucible. For who is to command his fellows? And how? And, especially, why? Are great captains born? Nursed and trained into competency? Or are they merely creatures of lucky circumstance—as politicians often are—and catapulted into crises which test their leadership, to succeed or fail willy-nilly?

Torrey's father had never been really close to this serious, questing son of his; yet both of them seemed to prefer their curiously detached relationship. Without being told, the youth understood that a commanding officer had to remain aloof, remote, even virginal in his dealings with subordinates; and the Old Man was his superior. This doctrine was hoarier than Julius Caesar and fresher than Karl von Clausewitz. It was provable by the way you could stare down a man (because you knew the answers), or bolster the same man's courage (because he knew you knew the answers). Torrey's relationship with the Old Man provided a classic example of the strange filial communication which existed between troops and their colonels, or crews and their captains. At all hazards such command officers saw to it that their men were properly fed, reasonably well bedded, and nursed back to useful health when they were sick or wounded. But they never, never fraternized. If relatively little genuine affection stemmed from all this, in the ordinary paternal sense, there was developed an overwhelming sense of responsibility assumed, and of dependency accepted, which made up for any lack of human warmth.

Or so the boy imagined. Because that's how he was taught.

When he was fifteen and striving desperately to make his high school football team as a too-skinny left end, he was advised by the Old Man to shoot for quarterback instead.

"That's where the power lies, boy. In the hands of the fellow with the ball."

Much later, when he had already been called The Rock for a number of years, Torrey discovered that power also lies in the hard hands of the man who throws the switch, who urges the machine past the point of no return, who figures the deadly odds and then casts the first dice, and with whom the buck stops abruptly, positively, and forever, because there's nobody standing reassuringly beyond him to grab it and say, "Don't worry, mister, let's do it this way instead . . ."

But here was Paul Eddington, looking like hell, plainly hung over, and pathetically eager to talk. Torrey turned away from *Old Swayback*'s biplanes, which were wave-hopping around the tincan minesweepers, and faced his executive officer, whose red-veined eyes and rufous countenance gave him no visible pleasure.

He said shortly, "Let's have a spot of coffee."

Grateful for the reprieve, Eddington snapped his fingers for the Negro messboy. "Two jamokes. On the double. No cream."

When the coffee arrived, the exec cradled the thick porcelain mug in his great paws, as if he could derive some special new life strength from its blistering heat. There were no handles on the cups. Seamen prefer them that way, particularly during the cold and lonely midwatch when the spray lancing across the forecastle can cut a man to the bone.

"I'm sorry, skipper," Eddington muttered.

Torrey understood his oblique offer to do penance.

Speaking softly, so the inquisitive junior officers of the deck could not overhear, he said, "Why do you do it, Paul?"

"Christ only knows. Maybe it's because I see myself growing older —dry-docked—obsolescing like this sadsack ship of ours—with all my chances slipping away."

Eddington's right hand described a small circle that took in the cruiser's rebuilt mainmast and her gunnery director tower. A splash of coffee hit the unpainted steel deck. He scuffed at the stain with his cordovan flight boot.

"What you're talking," The Rock said, "is surrender." His lean jaw knotted. "That's something they shoot a man for in wartime—pusillanimously striking your colors in the presence of the enemy. Remember, Paul, there are all kinds of enemies."

"I know." Eddington's gravelly voice was made harsher than ever by the alcoholic phlegm that caught in his corded throat. "And I ought to be able to look you straight in the eye, Rock, and tell you it's all finished. *Pau!*"

"Can't you?"

"No."

"Why not?"

The exec scratched his unshaven chin. He grinned uncertainly. "Maybe I'm a little crazy. Anyhow, that's what Beth claims."

Eddington's glance roved toward the leeward coast of Oahu, which had begun to shimmer like square-cut jade as the sun mounted, and his face twisted into a self-pitying grimace that was almost small-boyish. The miniature flotilla was rounding Barbers Point. It was 0710 by the bridge clock. Two dozen miles across those cloud-capped mountains, due east, Beth would still be asleep in their two-room apartment on the Ala Wai canal. He could imagine her murmuring fretfully in her slumber because the warm rays would have touched her lovely cheeks through the uptilted venetian blinds, and disturbed the pattern of her nightlong rest.

He suppressed a groan.

Beth was so incredibly beautiful with her tumbled honey-colored hair and gamin face and dusky eyelashes and ripe mouth that never really needed lipstick. (Yet she always protested that he'd ruin her make-up when he came bounding up the outside staircase for a returning sailor's kiss.) And always, too, her nubile body, felinely softfurred in its secret places, tortured him with promises lingeringly offered and then cruelly withdrawn, like food snatched from a starving castaway.

Beth liked to wear little-girl skirts and skintight halters that displayed her magnificent legs and bold breasts. She was only twenty-four, a whole maturity younger than Eddington, and she frequently taunted him about this, calling him "Daddy" less in jest than in deliberate seriousness.

Certain of his more audacious classmates had kidded him about robbing the cradle when he married Elizabeth Havens after her graduation from Sarah Lawrence College. But the fierce frown that swept across his shallow forehead and their belated remembrance that good old Paul once held the Academy's middleweight belt quickly silenced them. Besides, when you got right down to it, he wasn't the first middle-aged seadog who'd snaffled off a pneumatic young piece, although he sure as hell was a damned lucky stiff.

Eddington had met Beth Havens when her Junior League visited the Brooklyn Navy Yard on a mission designed to improve the enlisted men's harsh lot. After they'd seen to the commoners' wants, the charitable young ladies stayed for cocktails and a dinner dance hosted by the Commandant. At that time Eddington was the admiral's aide.

To Beth, who preferred "older men," he seemed marvelously attractive in a rugged, offbeat sort of way. He was, she told him, cute.

Saffron-spinning lights, the melancholy wail of *Deep Purple* played Glenn Miller style by a bluejacket orchestra, and a number of very large martinis mixed five-to-one made Navy life appear every bit as glamorous as Dick Powell's movies had promised back in Bronxville.

Beth struck with the sure swiftness of Cleopatra's asp.

Eddington was allowed certain groping liberties in the commodious back seat of the Commandant's big black Cadillac while the admiral's driver took them on a midnight tour of the Yard. Beth murmured, once, that she didn't care a hang about gantry cranes and graving docks. Her interest tended more toward personnel.

After that it was as easy as falling into bed, although Eddington didn't realize it then, because he had never known anyone like her: so goddamn sweet (he would have said if he'd been able to articulate his thoughts) and so shyly virginal in her surrender. Beth protested a little at his fumbling eagerness. But she *did* surrender. Very convincingly, too.

Like a clumsy and faithful dancing bear, Eddington pursued

Beth Havens through all the intricate terpsichore that led up to their not-quite-society wedding, after which he rather humbly imagined they would settle down like any other newlywed Navy couple in a small rented apartment. Beth would learn to whip up curry dishes for his compeers on Saturday nights, and she would study books explaining how to deal diplomatically with the senior officers' haughty wives.

But it didn't work out that way.

Beth appropriated the Navy Yard Club as her private palace, and its hard-drinking denizens as her courtiers. They took most of their meals there, and Eddington, more often than he liked, found himself blossoming into a male wallflower while his bride, dewy-eyed with the wonder of it all, danced away the night with eagerbeaver j.g.'s who figured that old Paul probably would be grateful as hell for a respite from the newest dance craze called the rumba.

When he was ordered to the Pacific as Captain Rockwell Torrey's exec, Eddington took heart, foreseeing a sea change in their rapidly deteriorating way of life once they reached the enchanted islands.

The exec stared out across the lightening waters from *Old Swayback*'s bridge.

In a few minutes Beth would stir in her bed, languidly stretching tanned arms and flexing sleep-softened tennis muscles, and her pale breasts would tighten, briefly, while their roseate nipples seemed to grow larger and more inviting. At such moments, when he was "home," Eddington yearned to creep like a lonesome child across the mat-strewn parquet floor from his own cotlike *punee* to hers, and bury his battered face between those Chanel-scented mounds of pliant flesh.

He had succumbed to this desire only once. Awakened suddenly from her half sleep, Beth had hissed, "Damn it, Paul, your whiskers hurt. Go 'way!"

After that he never approached her until he had shaved, showered, and donned the uniform that signified the military manhood which had first attracted her to him. She would thereupon accord him a maidenly, almost filial kiss that sent him off to his ship, puzzled and wondering. Females, he reflected morosely, had cunning ways of driving a strong man crazy . . .

Eddington uttered a curse. His free hand doubled unconsciously into a sledge-hammer fist and slammed down hard upon the metal bridge rail. Covertly, he glanced at The Rock to see whether his eccentric behavior had been noticed.

It hadn't.

Torrey finished his coffee, returned his mug to the messboy with a courtly thank you, and stepped across the bridgewing to the stadimeter stand. He was squinting through the eyepiece, double-checking the junior officer of the deck's estimate of the distance between *Old Swayback* and her tincans, which had now eased up to the port and starboard quarters of the cruiser.

When they quickened their stride enough to pace her by a few hundred yards, the minesweepers would stream paravanes through the choppy sea interval, just as keel depth, like finned kites. This fishing for "enemy" mines could be a tricky business. If anything went wrong with the expensive gear, Torrey wanted to know exactly who fouled up, and why, so he decided to oversee the operation personally before retiring into his cramped sea cabin for a solitary breakfast.

Although both destroyers were skippered by regulars, their personnel was mainly reservist. The Rock had a grudging respect for these kids who had to learn so much so fast, but he was also wary of their competence. They'd never faced a real test. Playing at war, he thought gloomily, was akin to dress-rehearsing a badly constructed drama that might never open at all because nobody wanted very much to be on hand when the curtain went up. Except, of course, the Eddingtons of this world. They were kept alive by the grimly joyous prospect of that cataclysmic Opening Night.

Torrey checked his wrist watch for the twentieth time since he had risen that morning. It was now 0730.

Up ahead the lean old tincans had managed to stream their paravanes without getting them tangled up in their propellers or fouling their lines. Through his binoculars he could see black cables extending outward and aft. He nodded briefly. The senior officer of the deck called "all ahead standard," and the throttleman gave the engineroom telegraph handle a gentle nudge. *Old Swayback* slowed to fifteen knots, settling behind her escorts with easy dignity.

Emboldened by the coffee which had begun to heat his blood, and perceptibly refreshened by exposure to the cool postdawn wind, Eddington spoke.

"I repeat, skipper, that it's a hell of a way to fight a war."

The Rock unbent a minuscule fraction. "Yes. It's a hell of a way to fight a war. I agree."

The exec grinned appreciatively. Perhaps he was really forgiven, now, by this avuncular man who rarely seemed to do the wrong thing. If The Rock only knew it, if he could ever get it through his blasted impervious monolithic skull, he needed a guy like Paul Eddington around him to complement those steady-Eddie qualities (so highly admired) which might even (to some) suggest a certain lack of verve, or spirit, or even that ultimate element of character in a fighting man—courage. So the exec thought. And he wished he knew what really lay behind the captain's dryball demeanor, or from what deep wellsprings Torrey drew his imperturbable sufficiency.

Whatever it was, it made Eddington damned uncomfortable. Adolescent. Unsure. A small spark of resentment began to smolder deep inside him. Didn't the captain's tolerance simply cloak a self-righteousness which nobody should exhibit in front of his fellow men, particularly his subordinates?

Almost masochistically Eddington found himself hoping, or somehow expecting, that Torrey would unleash his quicksilver temper upon him, lowering the boom, and thereby resolving all the gloomy concern he felt for his future and all his nagging doubts about Beth. What the hell right had The Rock to be so Christly tolerant of anybody, granting reprieves for failures that were inexcusable when you viewed them coldbloodedly, forgiving and forgetting? It was a weakness. It was unmanly. Eddington felt only contempt for softness of any sort.

If he could have put it into words, the exec would have said he feared neither God, man, nor the devil, in whichever order you chose to list them.

Eddington wore aviator's wings on his khaki jacket, which permitted him to argue with professional validity that the surface Navy would soon vanish into the limbo of round shot and cutlasses. His vast pride in these wings made him view with much bafflement The Rock's refusal to wear his own insignia. Torrey had gone through Pensacola only three years earlier as a very senior flight student. He had asked no quarter from the grinning youngsters who taught the manly art of self-preservation in the thin air above the seabound Fleet. Yet, having achieved his wings, he kept them hidden in the same drawer that contained the Navy Cross he'd won during World War I. The wings, and the snippet of blue-and-white silk appeared over his breast pocket only on formal occasions which (by Navy regs) demanded "full uniform including decorations."

Once, when Eddington screwed up enough nerve to ask him why he insisted on this odd display of modesty, Torrey had replied frostily that he'd wear his wings when they started sprouting out of his shoulder blades. Or when CinCUS in his eternal wisdom saw fit to give him command of an aircraft carrier.

But The Rock betrayed no chauvinistic animus against this new dimension in combat strategy. Actually, he worried openly because the Fleet's aerial reconnaissance showed a number of obvious gaps: whole pie-shaped segments that got only cursory attention from the lumbering PBYs prowling out of Kaneohe and Ford Island. He stood staunchly with the captains and admirals who pleaded for better antiaircraft weapons for their vulnerable ships; and whenever anybody would listen, he reminded them that Rainbow 5 clearly suggested the outside possibility of a suicidal air assault on the Fleet some quiet morning when it was bottlenecked bow-and-stern in Pearl Harbor.

Before he secured for breakfast, Torrey swept the skies one last time with his wide-angled glasses.

Close to the eastern horizon, almost indistinguishable against the grayblack lava outcroppings at the base of the Waianae Mountains, *Old Swayback*'s scout planes wheeled about their humdrum business of searching for hostile subs that weren't supposed to be within half-an-ocean's span of these guarded waters, as everybody damned well knew. Just to keep its hand in, gunnery was dry-running the main battery as well as the patchwork antiaircraft system. Whenever the cruiser altered course, the jug-eared director tower rumbled on its ball bearings, and the long snouts of the big rifles swung slowly toward the banking aircraft.

Nobody pretended to be very enthusiastic about these mundane chores, which had become a matter of glazed-eye rote. They performed them just proficiently enough to keep the skipper off their backs. But no better.

Nevertheless, The Rock had eyes like a housefly that seemed to peer simultaneously toward every quadrant of the compass from his vantage on the exposed bridgewing. He could spot a laggard machine-gun station as surely as he'd notice a badly trained main turret. God's wrath was personified by the captain's icy sarcasm, when you fouled up, and it was no less devastating because it was muted, like a Maxim-silenced revolver.

Whenever the crew bothered to remember that this was a day of rest elsewhere in the civilized world, they wished rather forlornly that *Old Swayback* could have remained in Pearl over the weekend, swinging off her buoy in East Loch. They could forget all about the gunnery drill. Chow would be a leisurely ritual instead of cold horsecock sandwiches grabbed on the dead run, and a man could loll around the sun-warmed deck writing to his girl or browsing through a good western.

Out here it might as well be 0800 Monday instead of the Sabbath, and those few miles of green sea separating them from shoreside pleasures the International Date Line.

The Rock addressed the radio talker.

"Tell the planes to make a pass over us at three thousand feet," he ordered, "so we can draw a bead on them."

"Aye, aye, sir."

Three minutes later the Seagulls started toward the cruiser, climbing swiftly as they came. The A.A. spotters frantically cranked their muzzles into position.

"Slow. Too damned slow," Torrey growled disgustedly. "Like a bunch of rusty-hinged doors."

For a moment he followed the scout planes' passage above his trio of ships, and well beyond, before he swung his binoculars back toward the Island where a much larger formation was orbiting lazily in the vicinity of Schofield Barracks, north of Honolulu. The aircraft were too far away for accurate identification, even through his seven-power glasses, but Torrey estimated their altitude at five thousand feet. He counted two dozen in all.

Eddington was watching them, too, with sharp professional interest. "Looks like papa's got the kiddies up early for squadron exercises." He sounded wistful, as if he wished he were airborne instead of condemned to *Old Swayback*'s endless penal servitude.

"Hell of a strange place for a rendezvous," The Rock growled. "Why aren't they off Diamond Head where they belong?"

"So maybe the soldiers need some ack-ack drill, too."

"Maybe."

But Torrey had little confidence in this pat explanation. He felt vaguely uneasy, nagged by the same sort of extrasensory perception that had assailed him one foggy night in November, when *Old Swayback* was saved from a sideswiping collision with another cruiser by the margin of one thin coat of camouflage paint—just because he'd inexplicably changed course about five degrees. Had he analyzed this odd sixth sense, he doubtless would have concluded that black magic played no part in it at all, for he knew his brother captains were subject lately to this same alchemical edginess. They imagined things that weren't always there to be seen. Nerves were raw. Ganglia exposed. And those few who received Top Secret data continually expected the unexpected to happen, and even seemed a little disappointed when it didn't.

Eddington tried again.

"Halsey's due back this morning with the *Enterprise* task group. Those might be his dive bombers coming home to roost."

"On a Schofield Barracks parade ground?"

"Hell! Halsey'd love to shake the doggies out of their Sunday snooze. Blow some dust in their faces."

Both men continued to study the faraway planes, which had finally completed their orbit and were proceeding due south on their assigned mission, whatever it was. Eddington admired them silently. But The Rock's uneasiness was taking shape now, inchoate and formless, as when you awaken from a nightmare to find you haven't been dreaming at all, but are confronted with something horribly real.

Nothing was quite right about the way that distant formation looked or behaved, despite its slow-moving, peaceful, unhindered progress across the gentle terrain between the Army headquarters and Pearl Harbor.

With the satisfied air of a man who had personally talked the homing aircraft back to earth, Eddington said, "You wanted planes orbiting over Diamond Head? Well, you've got 'em, skipper. At least thirty. And they're all heading for the same barn."

Torrey's thin lips tightened beneath his incongruously large nose. "So I see."

"Still don't think they're Halsey's?"

No answer.

Secure in his knowledge that The Rock was too preoccupied with the riddle of the planes to notice him, the exec shot the captain a glance that blended irreverent amusement and thinly veiled condescension. He guessed Torrey had the williwaws again. Looking under the goddamn bed, like a practical old maid, and cocking his ear for things that go bump in the night.

Eddington gestured shoreward.

"Bogies at five o'clock?" he suggested with heavy facetiousness, indicating that compass point on the horizon.

"No," The Rock retorted. "Antiaircraft fire at four-thirty!"

Even without binoculars, the officers and men on *Old Swayback*'s navigating bridge, a full fifty feet above the slaggy sea, could discern the tiny black smoke puffs that studded the sky over the southern tip of the Waianaes.

The junior officer of the deck made bold enough to ask Eddington what he figured was going on. The exec's confidence was legend among the ensigns of the division watches, and naturally you didn't annoy the captain with such plebe-ish questions, even when he stood right at your elbow. You went through proper channels.

"Man, oh, man!" The exec was squinting through his glasses again. "They're *really* playing war back there."

The youngster nodded wisely.

"It'll shake up the boys along Battleship Row, won't it, commander?"

"Damn tooting. They need it, Mr. Harrison, every day of the week and twice on Sunday." Eddington appealed to Torrey. "What do you think, skipper?"

The Rock started to mutter, "God knows what I think," then stopped.

You don't betray unknowledgeable anxiety in front of your subordinates, particularly when it's apt to be baseless. Captains of ships are Jehovah's deputies in their narrow domain; and Jehovah is never perturbed. Just angry when things go badly. But it occurred to Torrey that Jehovah Himself might wonder why Pearl Harbor hadn't bothered to notify ships operating offshore about these peculiar Sabbath goings-on. If this was an oversight, it was a damned stupid one.

"You're probably right, Paul," he said crisply. "Hell of a comprehensive drill. Better than anything Hollywood could put on."

"What about our own planes?" Eddington asked. "Wind's freshening. If we hold to schedule, they'll never be able to set down out here."

Torrey studied the sea surface critically. He noted for the first time that whitecaps were flecking the choppy swells.

"No." He made a snap decision. "Tell them to swing over Pearl and see what's up."

Eddington's puffy eyes widened.

"Very well, sir."

From the exec's tone Torrey realized that his inward concern had somehow become too evident, so he turned deliberately away from the rail and held up his right hand, pointing at his watch.

"It's 0810. My breakfast will be cold as a damned iceberg."

He started toward his sea cabin where the messboy had laid out his food on a small pulldown table. During night maneuvers he caught whatever sleep he could on a leather transom that was fastened against the bridgehouse bulkhead. This ten-foot cubbyhole was his whole solitary world reduced to the absolute microcosm.

But he never reached the cabin door.

A communications ensign, out of breath and white-faced, tumbled off the ladder that led from Radio Central, picked himself up, and darted across the bridge to the captain. He clutched a dispatch flimsy in a sweaty fist. Wordlessly, as if mistrusting his voice at this awful moment, he thrust the paper into Torrey's outstretched hand.

The Rock smoothed the crumpled sheet.

Gravely, even studiously, he perused the message, while the others waited with undisguised impatience for whatever shattering news it contained. In the interval before he spoke, he speculated why he felt so calm at this climactic instant for which he had been preparing since boyhood. It was as though he were somehow standing *outside* himself, coldly appraising Rockwell Torrey, and waiting for this stranger whom he barely knew to take—what was the Navy cliché?—appropriate action.

Then he turned slowly to the senior officer of the deck.

"Sound General Quarters, Mister Paige. And break out the live ammunition."

The Rock's taut voice carried across the bridgewing and into the wheelhouse, drawing toward him and the paper which he held in his hand every eye on *Old Swayback*'s navigating level.

He handed the dispatch to the exec. As Eddington took it, the GQ alarm's crazy klaxon began to sound.

"FROM CINCPAC TO ALL SHIPS PRESENT," he trumpeted hoarsely. "AIR RAID ON PEARL HARBOR. THIS IS NO DRILL."

The exec stopped, and the klaxon brayed on. Below them, in the quadruple 40-millimeter gun tub that nested atop Number 2 turret, the handlers were already prying open wooden boxes of high-explosive shells. The Rock could see them fondling the heavy clips, a little gingerly, as if they weren't sure of themselves now that they finally might get a chance to fire at a flesh-and-blood target.

Eddington moved close and whispered into Torrey's right ear: "We've got our *cojones* back, skipper. Now we're no longer the non-friggin' harem eunuchs, by God!"

2. *No Sea Anchor*

Naturally it was Commander Archibald Bowen's brilliant idea that USS *Cassiday* should have a fifth anniversary party. As commodore of *Cassiday*'s four-destroyer division, and a man full of soulful nostalgia for the Good Old Days, Commander Bowen considered such a birthday celebration essential to something he called "the morale factor."

Besides, the Sunday *Advertiser* would carry the story tomorrow morning on its society page. The facts, already furnished them, would be duly reported alongside the news that the Island's Number 1 general had played host at Fort Shafter, and that an admiral or two had shot a few rubbers of contract bridge with another admiral or two. With wives. This was the sort of heady company Commander Bowen liked to keep, even vicariously.

Dinner, he ordained, would be served on board *Cassiday,* from whose rakish single mast his pennant flew. After that the officers and their ladies would go ashore to dance at the Pearl Harbor Officers' Club.

Although he was a bachelor, the commodore imagined that he understood his subordinates' domestic problems, and particularly the kind that confronted his married junior officers. Even at a dollar, he was aware, dinner at the Club would strain a j.o.'s budget, when you computed the cost of his bride's meal, a few belts of bourbon before, and maybe a couple of brandies after.

The commodore decreed 1800, which was a bourgeois six P.M. down along the gaudy Waikiki strip, as the dinner hour. He intended his repast to be a leisurely affair, with plenty of good conversation after dessert, rather than the eat-and-run operation that inevitably occurred whenever they didn't get seated until 1930. Furthermore, starched white would be the uniform of the day for the officers. The ladies were expected to wear organdy cocktail dresses which, after their fashion, also constituted a uniform.

Bev McConnel had been "in" the Navy just long enough to discover that independence may not always be a virtue. It can brand you a maverick, start the gossips talking behind their palms, and ruin you socially. Which might be fine if you were just Bev—free, white, and twenty-three, and scornful of such nonsense. But it was pretty darned fierce when you were the fairly freshcaught wife of Lieutenant (junior grade) William Patrick McConnel, USN, Class of '38, and himself a pristine twenty-four.

Bev's latest gaucherie was trying to sew her own cocktail dress instead of buying one at that darling shoppe across from the Royal Hawaiian. Even she had to admit it did look sort of tacky, although she'd saved fifteen dollars, which was exactly the price of the new khakis Mac needed so badly. Trouble was, the homemade gown stamped her as an appalling type who ought to have been wedded to a reservist shoeclerk instead of to an Academy man with a brilliant future.

There was only one redeeming aspect to this whole sorry mess. Mac didn't give a hoot in Hades.

As Bev slipped the garish print over her coppery-haloed head, he said, "Honey, on you it looks absolutely 4.0. Tremendous. I mean it."

Bev jerked the low-cut bodice tight across her small breasts, defiantly, as if she were armoring herself for battle with the Philistines.

"You think so?" she snapped. "Well—*they* don't."

"Hell with 'em."

Mac ran his strong hands across her bare shoulders, which were tan and dustily freckled from the subtropical sun. He let his fingers glide down inside Bev's half-bra, and caressed her breasts.

"Stop it, you oaf!" She pretended to slap at his face as she drew away. "You'll get my Paris original all mussed up."

Bev pirouetted before the full-length mirror which they had bought for the bathroom door in a moment of wild extravagance on their first anniversary. "Perhaps," she offered doubtfully, "I could pin the damned thing up on the starboard side where it sort of droops."

"Allow me to help, ma'am."

"Naval officers can't mend anything but canvas sails. It's illegal.

Besides," Bev said, "you've got that wolf gleam in your baby blue eyes, mister. Go 'way. We'd never make the commodore's party."

"Suits me."

She grinned. "Right now you'd better trot your little self downstairs and crank up the limousine while Beverly repairs the damage."

Mac sighed.

"Aye, aye, skipper. I'll go peacefully."

As he went slowly out the door, into the limpid late afternoon, Bev blew a kiss toward his white-clad back.

Then she sighed, too, because she suddenly felt baffled and whipped by the System. Just two years ago, when she was still Beverly Rawlings, the prospect of becoming a naval officer's wife seemed full of gay adventure, as excitingly different as becoming a movie star's bride. There'd be journeys to exotic places where native servants cost twenty cents a day and you could queen it over a mansion supplied gratis by an appreciative government, and life would assume a dignity which nobody in Beatrice, Nebraska, had ever dreamed possible.

They had met at a Navy dance, back in '39, thanks to Bev's cousin Marty who was engaged that idyllic spring to an ensign on the *Texas*.

That was also the year the Rawlingses decided they ought to expand their horizons by motoring from Nebraska to Manhattan to take in the World's Fair. Bev especially needed broadening, Mom Rawlings wrote her kinsfolk, and maybe a touch of Eastern sophistication. So Cousin Marty esteemed it an act of kindness to arrange a blind date for this uncultured daughter of the midland wilderness.

Marty's fiancé was George Halley. Even then he was better known as Good Old George, owing to a perpetually seriocomic concern for his "future," and his owlish manner of lolling around on shipmates' bunks yarning about such abstruse matters as the effect of the European War on the stock market, the shortage of housing, or the plight of the defense industry. While others dreamed of admiral's stars, Good Old George pondered the delights of latching onto a nice fat block of Du Pont and running his own business, once he got the hell out of the Service. In the bunkroom which Good Old George shared with five other young officers, his engagement to Marty was regarded as his first logical step toward becoming a millionaire civilian. But although they envied his weekly forays into Manhattan when the *Texas* was moored in the Hudson River, nobody was eager to follow his example.

A little gentlemanly seduction—yes; the awful finality of marriage—no.

Of all the j.o.'s exposed to Good Old George's heretical philosophy, Ensign McConnel was closest to becoming a convert. This, however, stemmed more from the fact that he often wondered why he ever got into the Navy in the first place, than from any genuine concern for his economic future. Mac was also damned bored sitting around an ancient battlewagon, day after day, and counting the spires of New York City's skyline across a quarter mile of murky riverwater. Except for a few chance encounters around the Waldorf at the cocktail hour, he had sweated out six months without feminine companionship. This was a deplorable condition for a man raised in the brawny Missouri rivercountry near St. Louis.

He was a pushover for a date with Bev Rawlings that dulcet April evening. Afterward he had several more dates that weren't blind at all, and before Bev returned to Nebraska, he'd persuaded her to wear his Academy ring. They wrapped thread around the heavy gold band so it wouldn't slip off her slim middle finger.

The next June they were married at her home, where his dress whites, epaulettes, and goldhilted sword mightily impressed the natives, and the following year Mac got orders to join *Cassiday* at Pearl Harbor.

Their single-plus-kitchenette apartment on the Ala Wai canal, only three short blocks off Waikiki Beach, was a real fun place, wonderful for having friends pop in for a predinner drink or for lazing around Sunday mornings and—because it was the first time they didn't seem to be camping out like a couple of gypsies—it was also fine for making happy, eager, uninhibited love.

On those Saturday nights before Mac drew the Sunday duty, of course, they usually took things pretty easy. They'd hit the sack (Mac's deplorable phrase for it) around 2200. Taking excessive care not to awaken Bev, he would rise at 0530 and drive out to Pearl City in the fragile predawn mist, where he caught the first morning boat to his ship.

Cassiday was moored by herself in East Loch, close to the old destroyer tender *Dixon,* which appeared to be suckling Commander Bowen's three other charges. Under the prevailing quasi-peacetime conditions, only skeleton crews manned the twenty-odd destroyers that generally lay in the harbor on weekends. *Cassiday* managed with a couple of j.g.'s and a pair of ensigns from the gunnery, engineering, or communications departments.

The skipper, who was a lordly lieutenant commander, liked to go golfing on Sundays, and their two-striper exec had established a comfortable boudoir beachhead somewhere up the slopes of Punch Bowl. Neither spent much time aboard ship during *Cassiday*'s off-duty periods.

When Mac thought about it, he was aware that his pride as acting captain, even for a brief period, came from the absolute authority mandated him to pull the seacocks and scuttle his iron monster if ever he took such a goofy notion. There'd be a hell of a scandal and some admiral would string him in chains off *Dixon*'s big yardarm. But he had the power. It tasted good.

Moodily, almost uncaring, Bev cast a final look at her dress. It still hung crooked. She gave the gaudy aloha-pattern skirt a vicious yank. There was a ripping noise as several safety pins tore loose.

"Damn hell spit," Bev said in a clear voice.

This was starting out to be one of those nights when everything was bound to go all wrong. Obviously. Mac had the miserable Sunday duty so they'd have to quit the Club early, but since she had the curse anyhow that didn't make much difference except it gave her cramps (maybe a shot of straight bourbon would help); and now she would show up at the commodore's party looking like a crummy *hapahaole* washerwoman.

Bev picked up her lauhala-reed purse, and peered inside to double-check the five dollars Mac would hesitantly request for a last round of drinks at exactly five minutes to midnight. She walked out the door with her hem drooping. But her three-inch heels tapped out defiant little signals on the hard asphalt driveway. Anyhow, she had a damned sight daintier feet and shapelier legs than the rest of the *Cassiday*'s wives, or even ladies, and she didn't even need Mac to tell her so.

He was wrestling with the Chevvy when she reached the hibiscus-covered carport. Bev smiled, albeit ruefully, because the decrepit car seemed to symbolize the whole silly rat race. It was five years older than *Cassiday* herself. The sadsack truth was, she supposed, that she just didn't have the stamina, or the brassiness, or the *guts* to be a trueblue Navy wife, or whatever it was that sustained her bright-eyed sisters and kept them merrily dashing around to bridge parties and cocktail parties and dinner parties where you served rice and curry with all the exotic condiments so the senior officers could loosen their belts and pat their plump bellies and reminisce about the grand old days in Chefoo.

Bev managed to cloak most of her distaste for this merry-go-round existence by pretending to psychoanalyze the other wives, and reporting her findings to Mac when they were alone later.

Authentic eighteen-carat naval wives, she decided, fell into two categories: the jaunty finishing school type and the tweedily conservative type. They either had scads of money, or they behaved as if they'd just lost a cool fortune at roulette but didn't give a hang because plenty more would be coming along on the next clipper from the mainland for deposit in the Bishop Bank. Between the Jaunty Ones and the Tweedy Ones, a few simple souls like herself lived a sort of twilight half life, counted their pennies, and mourned the impossibility of ever having a normal family, because they'd married the whole darned Navy instead of one man.

Mac was in a foul mood.

"Damn pigiron wreck!" He kicked the Chevvy's front left tire. "We ought to scrap the beast."

"What have the *menehunes* done to our little beauty this time?"

"Shorted the blasted starter. But it's fixed. I think."

"So's your pretty white sailor suit, sonnyboy."

Mac scowled ferociously at the olive-dark grease smear on his sleeve cuff. "Nuts. I'll tell the commodore it's dried blood. That should make the old goat happy."

"Maybe," Bev said brightly, "it'll remind him of the time he led that landing party ashore to put down the Moro uprising and he got shishkebabbed by a native spear."

"Hop in, Lady Macbeth."

They had to pause at the Ala Wai exit to let a shiny new Ford convertible pull into the parking strip alongside the apartment. An Army Air Force major, whose visored go-to-hell cap was shoved well back on his forehead to display a mop of Byronesque curls, was driving. Because the car's top was down, he was wearing dark flight glasses, and his left hand spun the wheel with indolent expertness as he brought the purring Ford abreast of the asthmatic Chevvy. But he kept his right hand cupped possessively around the bare shoulder of a blond, laughing girl. She waved at the McConnels.

"Hiya, kiddies!"

Bev glanced quickly at Mac before she replied indifferently, " 'Lo, Beth."

"You and Mac making the Club brawl tonight?"

"We're on our merry way right now."

"Then why don't you stash the jalopy and come upstairs with Pete and me?" the blond girl said. "It'd be more fun to go together. You can have a wee drinkie while I'm piling into the glad rags. I'll only take a jiff."

Judging from Beth's moist brightness, Bev figured she'd already had several wee drinkies.

"Thanks. But we're eating aboard ship."

"Fooey! Prohibition stuff." The blond girl wrinkled her perfect nose, and turned to the Air Force major. "See? They're all party-poopers. Real honest-to-God Navy. Just like I told you."

Her escort took a philosophical view of the snub. He grinned charmingly. "So we'll fly solo, Mrs. Eddington."

Bev asked malevolently, "How's Paul?"

"Running around the briny deep, as usual, and playing war, also per usual."

"Oh."

Beth still refused to be embarrassed by Bev's patently upraised eyebrows. "Paul always tells me to have a good time when he's gone."

"And you do, don't you, honey?"

"Damned right."

Mac gunned the Chevvy's rachitic motor impatiently. "We've got to get rolling, Bev. It's after five-thirty."

"Ta ta," Beth called in her emptily cheerful voice.

As the two cars separated, Bev tilted the rearview mirror so she could watch the couple debark from the low-slung convertible and start hand in hand up the studio apartment steps.

"Happy landings, major," she called softly.

"Naughty, naughty," Mac said. *"Honi soit qui mal y pense."*

"Precisely. You read me five-by-five, lover."

Bev's heart-shaped face was thoughtful as she turned away from the mirror, and she said nothing more until they reached the four-laned Pearl Harbor thoroughfare. Then: "You know, dear husband, if all the arguments against this kind of life were boiled down into one little perfumed blob, that blob would be named Beth Eddington."

"She's not that bad," Mac said. "Nor that good, either."

"How would you know, lieutenant?"

"I wouldn't, really. Just testing."

Bev asked seriously, "What is it a ship sometimes needs when it's running before a typhoon—to slow it down?"

"Sea anchor."

"Well, that's what Beth needs. A sea anchor. She hasn't got one . . . and so she's drifting around crazy and loose just like a lot of these other Navy gals I keep bumping into."

"Most of 'em make out pretty well."

"Would you like me to join Beth Eddington's little sin-and-sewing circle?"

He smiled at her paternally.

"Negative your last transmission. Over and out."

"I play tennis with her a couple of times a week."

"That's out of doors. Daylight. It ought to be safe enough."

"Mixed doubles, mostly," Bev said, watching him, "followed by mixed drinks. Also doubles. Husbandless women versus hungry males."

It was already twilight when the Chevvy swung down the steep hill toward the Pearl City landing. The harbor's muddy waters were turning amber-purple as the sun hovered, hesitated, then dipped below the distant horizon, leaving in its red and boiling wake only the bloodied remains of the tradewind cloud bank. Far out along the ocean's rim an inshore patrol four-piper was trying its signal gun, calling, calling, calling, and beyond her loomed the unmistakable downscooped bulk of a cruiser nicknamed *Old Swayback*. Both ships were running parallel to Oahu's southern headlands which, in the thickening gloom, looked like prehistoric monsters snuffling at their water holes.

Cassiday's officer of the deck, who was wearing an automatic pistol slung in a webbed khaki belt over his white jacket, greeted them forebodingly after Mac saluted the taffrail colors.

"Everybody's in the wardroom already, Mister McConnel. You're ten minutes late."

Bev smiled at him. "It's all my fault, Ensign Campbell. I'll patch things up with the commodore."

Daintily following in Mac's wake, she picked her way forward around the cosmoline-smeared torpedo tubes, taking excessive care not to brush against the warlike gear that occupied every spare inch of deck space outside the narrow walkway. The destroyer's wardroom was on the main deck just beyond the superstructure that housed the plotting room, bridge, and five-inch main battery director platform. From door to door, the officers' dining and social quarters was barely twenty feet long, and hardly wider than the parlor of a cheap tract home.

Commander Bowen was a man of relentless habit. Promptly at 1800 he had marched formidably into the wardroom, surveyed his officers and their ladies as if they were midshipmen on parade, noted the McConnels' tardiness, and then ordered brusquely: "Please be seated."

Four officers had brought their wives to *Cassiday*'s birthday party. The exec and a sporting j.o. escorted ladies of the town. Lieutenant Commander Harding, their captain, was alone, as were two other ship's officers and Commander Bowen himself. If pressed, Harding would admit that he was married, all right, but that was back in the States; out here he was on his own, by God. But since he believed in a severe cleavage of business and pleasure, much as Church and State are separated, he never allowed his personal women aboard his destroyer.

When Mac ushered Bev into the wardroom, *Cassiday*'s officers as one man sprang to their feet a split second after the commodore, whose gallantry was too well-honed for juniors to outfox him. Commander Bowen had prepared a cutting remark about the perils of lateness in social affairs, and how such dilatory habits might ultimately lead to disaster in military operations. But the sight of Bev's prettily worried face checked him.

Curbing his acid tongue made the commodore feel very noble.

Bev offered, "I'm to blame, sir . . ."

"Nonsense, Mrs. McConnel," he boomed. "Lovely ladies are always worth waiting for."

Bev dropped him a little curtsy.

Commander Bowen beamed. Then he gave an imperceptible nod. They sat down, still in unison, and picked up their spoons. At each place was a brimming bowl of pineapple, papaya, watermelon, and cantaloupe, carved into delicate little balls.

"I urge you," the commodore said, "to taste this dish carefully. It comes from a very special recipe given me years ago by a chief steward's mate who served with Admiral Winfield Scott Schley."

They tasted.

"Mmmmmm," Bev said, artistically feigning delight, but wondering whether the commodore was a lot older than he looked. "Simply scrumptious. What *is* the secret, Commander Bowen?"

"It would be more appropriate, ma'am, to stamp it 'Top Secret.' For that's how it must remain."

They all pretended vast delight, which pleased their host's gourmet soul, although everybody knew the mystery ingredient in the fruit cocktail was no more complicated than a stiff and illegal lacing of 100-proof California grape brandy. He had thefted the "secret" from a carrier admiral during a dinner powwow of destroyer division chiefs aboard the flagship a month earlier, and changed the airman's scotch to a more effete brandy.

Navy life, Commander Bowen was observing emphatically, provided the finest existence yet devised by thinking man; and he'd never found an officer who genuinely regretted his seafaring career. (Or who, Bev said silently, would ever admit such a heinous thing.) Fiercely, he surveyed his audience, blinking his pale blue eyes, before he added that naturally there'd be moments of self-doubt and inward pain, but by God you can't make an omelet without (Bev futilely screamed *Stop!* to herself) smashing a few eggs.

The commodore tapped his Purple Heart and World War I Victory ribbons, which were even more faded than his red-and-yellow Yangtze emblem, and this led into his favorite yarn about the Moro uprising on Mindanao, when he'd challenged a whole bloody tribe of spear-toting savages with nothing but a boatload of blue jackets, and got pinked in the shoulder by a native lance.

"Was the spear poisoned?" Bev asked innocently.

"As a matter of fact," he said, "it wasn't. But I took no chances. Treated it like any other rattlesnake bite, by Tophet!"

If you hadn't heard it before, the commodore's endless monologue could be rather amusing, like the contrived patter of a folksy night club entertainer. But to Mac, even more than to Bev, the recital was older than Taps. He fought to stay awake by contrasting this pretentious fool with other officers he'd known during his seven years in the Service, and especially those who inculcated in him that warm band-of-brothers feeling which had sustained navymen ever since Nelson's time.

The commodore's salty bombast didn't have this effect, even when the old boy hoisted his coffeecup and trumpeted:

"A toast, by heaven, to a fighting ship! May she always be ready to challenge our country's enemies, come what may!"

He slapped down his cup with a deliberate roughness that cracked it neatly in half, declaring almost tearfully that the proudest moment of his life would come when he led his beloved division into battle, with flags fluttering and guns barking, and *Cassiday* courageously in the van.

Mac's glance strayed to a varnished ebony plaque on the after bulkhead, near the coffee urn, which bore the goldlettered motto: "GIVE ME A FAST SHIP FOR I INTEND TO GO IN HARM'S WAY." Commander Bowen was very pleased with this slightly abbreviated version of John Paul Jones' original plea, for he claimed a certain affinity between himself and the Great Captain.

Noting Mac's interest in the plaque, he said approvingly, "When you've got the duty tomorrow, fella, remember that a destroyer must always stand at the ready, like a pistol hung loose in a well-oiled holster."

Mac nodded.

So did the other j.o.'s.

Commander Bowen was in his finest mentor mood.

In his own Academy years, Mac had been inspired most by a remote taciturn man who seemed to make the least conscious effort to whip up the midshipmen's enthusiasm for their exacting profession, yet who succeeded quite remarkably. Either you had it or you didn't, he believed. Like a well-made ship, a newcomer could be conned into open water where the freshest winds blew. But after that it was up to him, to plow smartly ahead or to foul up and get caught in irons with his airless sails flapping.

This teacher was a senior captain named Rockwell Torrey, who administered a course in naval strategy and tactics during Mac's first-class year. Behind his back, the midshipmen called their ramrod-straight and authoritarian teacher by the same nickname he'd acquired at Crabtown-on-the-Bay so long ago: The Rock. He was, they acknowledged, a pretty cold customer, but eminently fair, who possessed a certain vibrant something which most of the other profs lacked, for all their humanness.

In his classroom dealings, Captain Torrey was an uncompromising stickler for precision and completeness. He seemed to have no personal diversions, hobbies, or otherwise distracting habits which might alleviate this single-minded attention to his present duty, which was pounding military sense into the close-cropped skulls of youngsters whose own forebears probably skinned mules in Missouri or picked ore on the Mesabi Range. Teaching the untried science of modern naval warfare, which everyone suspected had come a long way since Jutland, The Rock strove to engender in them a *zest* for it. He was aided by his own earnestness in seeking out new methods, as well as by his patent regard for those traditions which had served the Navy so admirably since John Paul Jones, Esq., accepted America's first commission as a lieutenant on a desperate December day in 1775.

Torrey impressed Mac, along with certain of his classmates, with the solitariness of high command, and the inexorability of combat decisions which, once taken, must be lived with or died for.

"Jones," he told them, "was a lonely man. He was also a great tactician who never had a chance to become an even greater strategist, because they wouldn't give him the ships.

"Yet Jones had a weakness. It was a very human flaw, and it hurt him deeply, as a naval officer and as a man. I commend you gentlemen against such weakness, even though someday you may mistake it for the very essence of command. Believe me, it is not."

The Rock studied them for a moment with his iceberg eyes.

Then he said, "I am speaking about egotism. Conceit. Arrogance. Nothing in God's world will cause you to fail more miserably than imagining you can't be wrong . . . ever . . . or that your judgment is infallible just because you carry a Presidential commission." He shrugged. "I don't mean you should approach decisions with uncertainty. Don't do that. But never be afraid, either, to be a little humble in the presence of the power that will someday be placed upon you as captains of ships.

"When the moment comes to exercise this command judgment," he concluded quietly, "you might even pray a bit. You'll find it good for the soul . . ."

Although Captain Torrey exhibited none of the vanity which he ascribed to John Paul Jones, he did have the diminutive hero's perfectionist zeal. Even when his students moaned that he was a knuckledusting sundowner, they respected him for it, for somehow he was able to make them understand that he didn't demand flawlessness simply for its own stuffy sake. He required, rather, a sharp regard for those niggling details that could cost a captain his ship through neglect, just as a missing horseshoe nail once led to the loss of an entire kingdom.

Certain knowledgeable first-classmen claimed the secret of all this impeccability lay in the fact that both Jones and The Rock were bachelors, given to the fussiness of their breed. At least, they imagined that Captain Torrey was a bachelor. He lived alone in his four-stripe quarters, and rarely unbent enough to mingle with his peers at the Officers' Club, or to summon a startled group of midshipmen into an off-hours bull session.

Inevitably, of course, cautious rumors arose that The Rock had a woman hidden away somewhere, perhaps in a Manhattan penthouse. Once or twice a year he disappeared for a long weekend, carrying a scuffed suitcase and wearing threadbare civilian tweeds. The few midshipmen who had seen him on the northbound train could report only that he swung briskly aboard at Annapolis, and without a backward look strode directly to the club car, where he sat down, lit his pipe, opened a book (usually geopolitics or contemporary history), and apparently dismissed the outside world until he debarked at Pennsylvania Station in New York. After that, his mysterious journey became completely unfathomable, for he simply disappeared into the crowd outside the terminal, or hailed a cab.

One inquisitive midshipman had the temerity to ask the captain's ultimate destination. Torrey froze him with a glance that gave him permanent frostbite, the youth claimed, as if he'd been adrift all night in a North Atlantic blizzard.

From these excursions Torrey returned looking more withdrawn than ever. Within a few days, however, his students could congratulate themselves that The Rock was back-to-battery. He would relax perceptibly as he stood before the class, swaying gently back and forth on his blackburnished heels, as if the rostrum were an unsteady deck, while he hammered away at the strategic concepts prevalent in those months before the start of another European war.

Item: One expert had written, "Ours is primarily a gunnery Navy: a fleet which depends upon heavy artillery and good shooting."

Item: Mahan himself, who was still the seapower messiah in that interbellum period, urged that the Navy's chief concern was to blockade the enemy by erecting an impenetrable battle line against his exposed harbors, rather than to go dashing off on foolish commerce-raiding expeditions, like Von Müller in his *Emden.*

Soberly, aware that he was skirting heretical shoals, The Rock assured them that both the Mahan and the *Emden* scholastics might be right.

"Until we have a genuine two-ocean Navy," he said, "we've got to meet our commitments in a number of ways. None of them are entirely satisfactory. The airplane has changed our thinking dramatically. Yes—and the submarine, too."

He drew a booklet out of his desk drawer as he spoke, and opened it to a full-page photograph of a capital ship.

"Let me read this caption, gentlemen, from last year's Army-Navy football game program: 'A bow-on view of the USS *Arizona* as she plows into a huge swell. It is significant that despite the claims of air enthusiasts no battleship has yet been sunk by bombs.' " The quadruple lines in The Rock's forehead deepened. "I'm afraid this betrays a bit of wishful thinking, and certainly a great deal more optimism than the present world situation—or the weapons at hand—permits."

He flashed a quick, sardonic smile.

"Of course, it was quite decent of the editor to append what you gentlemen call the 'Jesus factor.' His use of the word *yet,* I believe, is significant."

That same summer, during a fleet problem in the central Pacific, planes from the aircraft carrier *Saratoga* sneaked over Pearl Harbor from a launching point one hundred miles north of Oahu, and after they dropped their hypothetical bombs the referees ruled they'd kicked the stuffings out of that impregnable bastion.

Captain Torrey's blunt estimate of naval strategy stirred up considerable fuss among certain other captains at the Academy whose authority was greater since it came from a loftier rung on the promotional ladder. They admonished him privately, after discovering that he was adamant in his curious views, and not long afterward The Rock was quietly ordered to less sensitive duty where he couldn't tinker with impressionable young minds.

They gave him *Old Swayback* on the theory, doubtless, that once an Academy graduate is commissioned, he's intellectually "safe." Thus the cruiser's officers could ignore Torrey's unorthodoxy, while at the same time profiting by his tactical savvy, which was held in high esteem ever since he'd won a Navy Cross as a tincan skipper in the Big War.

Commander Bowen lurched to his feet, belched comfortably, and patted his ursine belly. It was, he proclaimed, a damned decent repast, although not as elegant as they might have been served on the old China Station. Listening to his fruity, self-satisfied baritone voice, Bev imagined that *Cassiday*'s steel bulkheads were closing around her like the sides of a medieval Iron Maiden. Bulkheads, she reminded herself fiercely, not walls. And those silly little round windows weren't windows, but ports. Or were they portholes?

Then everybody was standing up, and it was time to struggle aft to the quarterdeck where the commodore's gig bobbed in the dark waters at the foot of the accommodation ladder.

Rather pettishly, Bev decided that if dinner aboard the destroyer had been horrible, drink-dancing at the Club would be a darned sight worse, with gales of brittle laughter and too much frenzied guzzling to beat the midnight bar curfew when they all stopped being gallant heroes and beautiful heroines and suddenly turned into tired underpaid little people who'd have galloping hangovers next morning. Sunday. The sin-repenting Sabbath.

She snuggled up against Mac on the gig's crowded transom and laid her head on his broad left shoulder. His j.g.'s boards felt rough against her ear, even through her thickburnished shield of hair.

Bev said, "Damn!" not quite audibly, and inched forward to get more comfortable.

Mac bent his head and brushed her uptilted nose with his lips, casually, in the manner permissible during these informal Saturday night galas.

"Having fun?" he asked.

"Scads."

He sensed her lack of conviction. "Wait'll we get to the Club. Things will pick up."

"That's what I'm afraid of."

"Anyhow," Mac pleaded, "let's enjoy the night. It's an absolute dinger. Check that moon!"

Bev nodded. With a mewing sigh, she tried to relax, aware that even a disgrunted j.o.'s wife ought to give the Hawaiian moonlight a fighting chance to work its subtle magic. It was almost 2000. Across the dim harbor the Club's orchestra would just about be breaking into the first chorus of *Sweet Leilani,* which they'd play a dozen times before the evening ended. Eventually some lieutenant commander's wife would slip out of her chair, kick off her sling-pumps, and start to hula. You could pretty well calibrate your watch by this moment when the amateurs usurped the floor show. It would be about thirty minutes to midnight, with a half-hour left for really determined drinking. You were supposed to applaud, even if the impromptu hula wasn't the world's greatest, especially when your husband was a whole stripe shy of two-and-a-half.

Bev pinched herself savagely on the arm.

"Lieutenant junior grade McConnel," she whispered contritely, "I'm a nasty little itchbay."

"Should I ask why?"

"Don't."

"Okay," he said, puzzled, but willing to let her enjoy privately whatever odd mood had seized her.

They sat silent for a moment, savoring the night, as the gig approached the landing where the Club squatted beneath a grove of ironwood trees. A ghostly, raffish eyebrow was cocked over the moon, Bev noticed, painted there by a crescent-shaped tradewind cloud.

But Mac's attention was caught by a pair of searchlights which had managed to pinion an Army Air Force bomber at the apex of their beams. The twin-engined B-18 looked like a clumsy moth impaled on needle points. Idly, he wondered whether they'd be able to trap a bogey that neatly, if an enemy a lot more elusive than this pot-bellied relic sprang at them out of the blueblack night skies. He doubted it. No matter how often he himself went through gunnery drills, Mac always felt a sense of frustration, a nagging fear that he'd fail, somehow, if a real showdown came. But when he discussed this delicate matter with the skipper, that youthful veteran of no wars at all laughed uproariously and advised him to hold his goddamn water till the shooting started. He'd probably discover that he was a real Annie Oakley with the five-inch/38s. Provided, the captain added meanly, the shells didn't jam up the way Number 2 did on Fleet maneuvers last week . . .

The Officers' Club bullhorn shattered his reverie. *Arizona,* the stentorian voice called as the boats edged closer. *Neosho, Detroit, Dobbin.* Shrill laughter and lusty shouts signaled the arrival of couples from the ancient battleship, the converted oiler, the venerable four-pipe cruiser, and the old destroyer-tender. Station wagons brought others from ships that lay in dry dock.

There wasn't much night work going on, because it was just another peacetime Saturday, and even the hammerhead crane that extended its arm over the dry-docked Battle Force flagship stood as immobile as a disused gallows. Officers and men alike appreciated this weekend quietude. It made it possible to dine comfortably on board your own vessel, unless the yardmen had stripped her down too drastically, in which case you cussed the inconvenience—though only as a matter of form—and tooled off to the nearest BOQ or enlisted mess. Or home.

That night ninety-four ships were in Pearl Harbor, including all eight battlewagons, and even though the hour was still unstylishly early, the Club was already jammed. Sweating messboys dragged in extra tables for unexpected ships' parties, and the dance floor grew progressively smaller, like an eroding coral spit.

Nevertheless, Commander Bowen's imperious manner won them a beachhead under an artificial palm tree near the bandstand. The human-babble, echoing discordantly off the scarred plywood walls and down from the low ceiling, almost drowned out the commodore's authoritarian bellow.

"Drinks all around," he decreed. "On me. Then, ladies and gentlemen, it'll be Dutch."

Bev winced.

But after Commander Bowen brightened things up with one more yarn about an old shipmate who'd won a gambling joint in a crap game down in Santiago, Cuba, only to discover he'd accidentally taken title to a whorehouse, they were reprieved. He suggested that they dance. He'd even launch the festivities by essaying a small schottische with the charming Mrs. McConnel, by God, if the lieutenant didn't object too strenuously.

The lieutenant didn't.

With a forced smile Mac said, "Be my guest, sir. Anything I have is yours."

Bev tossed him her best we-who-are-about-to-die glance as she headed for the dim-shadowy dance floor, with the commodore clutching her tanned right arm in a moist but viselike grip. The orchestra was still worrying away at something Polynesian, earnestly, the way a dog gnaws a bare but nostalgically pleasant old soup bone.

It looked like the start of a long, long session.

Mac decided a rum and Coke might ease the boredom that always hit him around 2030 on Saturday nights at the Club. He managed to finish one drink and order another before Commander Bowen returned, sweating and puffing, with Bev.

She seemed cool as the ice that tinkled in Mac's empty highball glass.

After intermission the orchestra decided to eschew the islands and experiment bravely with some Glenn Miller arrangements. The saxes wailed *The Nearness of You,* more or less the way Glenn recorded the ballad in the dulcet spring of '41.

Mac said, "My turn, please?"

"Gladly."

Bev sounded as if she meant it.

And suddenly Mac thought her tacky little aloha-print looked wonderful, like something royalty would wear if royalty could pour itself into that lowbodiced wisp of size 10 nothingness. Bev's slim body felt marvelously soft and round in his lean arms, as she pressed close against his starched white jacket, playfully tickling the shorthairs in the back of his neck with her left hand, and shamelessly thrusting her small belly against his belt buckle.

They were quite alone in the crazy universe. Nothing else mattered, not even Mac's dawn departure for shipboard duty tomorrow, and for a moment they were free of that pervasive chilliness with which they had lived since the first "war scare."

At 2325, with only thirty-five minutes left till closing, and just as the orchestra sawed into *Sweet Leilani* for the last time, the predictable happened.

There was a smattering of applause in the dim distance near the scuffed black-leather bar. Several uninhibited ensigns without dates, who regarded the whole evening as a colossal carnival staged for their special benefit, wolf-whistled as a blond girl with remarkable breasts approached the tiny bandstand. Her pale blue silk skirt swept up and exposed a generous expanse of deeply tanned thigh when she stepped onto the platform.

She catapulted her wispy sandals toward the crowded tables by high-kicking her legs like a cancan dancer, and stood proudly in the amber spotlight, flashing white teeth at the goggle-eyed males in the audience.

It was Beth Eddington. She was very beautiful and very drunk, although she seemed in full control of her exciting body as she began undulating to *Leilani*'s lazy rhythm.

Beth finished the dance, laughing and breathless, with perspiration gleaming on the rise of her uncupped breasts, and almost physically tasting the applause that rocketed off the walls and ceiling.

Somebody yelled, *"Hawaiian War Chant!"*

Other voices took up the cry. Joyfully, the orchestra obliged, for tonight's amateur talent was something very, very special, and worth cultivating.

Deep-drumming, bass-throbbing, the native beat assaulted the room with its sharply rising crescendo, and Beth moved pantherlike into the pagan rite. With the quickening tempo, her abbreviated skirt flared higher, revealing her golden body, arching, crouching, spinning, and in the wild apogee of the *Chant* her dusky-lashed eyes were tightly shut. She was a woman glimpsed at the climactic instant of passion.

As suddenly as it had begun, the music stopped, leaving the audience stunned and silent, and after an embarrassed pause, they clapped briefly, but nobody requested an encore. Now that the spell was broken, Beth seemed stumblingly awkward, and she had to be led from the bandstand by the curly-haired Air Force major.

Mac whispered to Bev, "That poor dame looks like a sleepwalker."

"*Street*walker."

"No. She's in trouble. Honest-to-God deep-six type trouble."

Bev said quietly, "I told you what ails Beth Eddington. Remember? No sea anchor."

"She needs a psychiatrist."

"Forget it, lieutenant. You're a gunnery expert, not a medico."

"What sort of therapy is the flyboy giving her?"

She smiled wickedly. "The usual, darling, but it won't help her any. On top of all her other problems, Beth's a tramp, and that's a tough extra handicap for any Navy wife."

"How about her poor damned Navy husband?"

"Commander Eddington's had it, I'm afraid. Now pour me one more drinkie and I'll take you home to bed."

"Drinkie?" Mac groaned. "D'you suppose what she's got is catching?"

At fifteen minutes past midnight they headed back toward town. Bev slept all the way home on the Chevvy's tattered front seat, with her head against Mac's coatless shoulder.

An hour later Beth Eddington and the Air Force major named Pete also quit the Club, having downed three more illegal after-hours bourbons on the rocks from a jug which the major thoughtfully fetched along for dire emergencies. The wife of *Old Swayback*'s executive officer had to be hoisted into the Ford convertible, like an inert sack of golden wheat, but the major didn't mind. Beth had a delectable body for lifting, or for laying down, and the remembrance of her satiny thighs started muted little bells ringing somewhere in the alcoholic labyrinth of his brain.

They drove north out Kamehameha Highway toward the barren beaches of Waialua Bay on the windward side of the island, instead of toward busy Waikiki.

It was a moondrenched night as cleverly constructed for love as Beth herself.

And just as marked for death.

3. Some Men Play God

THAT SAME FALSE DAWN which painted *Old Swayback* a gentle purple with its pale, vague light in the open sea twenty miles to the southwest brought into uncertain focus the narrow highway leading toward Pearl City from Honolulu. Still foggy-eyed, although he had remained in bed a disgraceful half-hour after the alarm clock snarled reveille at 0500, Mac kept the Chevvy at full throttle, holding to a stout sixty miles per hour, except when he had to slow down briefly to negotiate the turn near a sparse clump of roadside buildings at Aiea.

His duty began at 0700.

It was a cardinal sin to arrive late, even though this promised to be a murderously dull Sunday, spent drinking too much strong black coffee, shooting the same old breeze with the three j.o.'s who completed *Cassiday*'s minimum Sabbath roster, and wishing to hell he could be frolicking at Haliewa with Bev. There the sands would feel warm to the body, although it was less than three weeks till Christmas, and by midday the northeast trades blowing against the Island's windward slopes would be as mild as a baby's breath, once the six-thousand-foot overcast dissipated.

Momentarily, Mac took his sleepy gaze off the macadam and scanned the crowded fleet anchorage as it unrolled into full view from the Waianae foothills. You'd have to be a real clod, he thought, not to get a boot out of that sprawling mass of seapower, even when it lay so somnolent and smokeless and serene.

First came the destroyers, grouped in threes and fours and fives in the shallow waters of East Loch, with his own ship sitting slim and alone behind the pack, a sheep dog awaiting the master's whistle. For all her 341 feet, *Cassiday* from that distance looked oddly toylike, instead of deadly and full of high-explosive menace.

Astern of the destroyers were the Big Boys, moored fore-and-aft against the protecting flank of Ford Island, where the harbor was only forty feet deep. To a man, the experts agreed that this shallowness wouldn't permit an effective torpedo run, so nobody had bothered to string nets around the battleships. *Nevada* and *California* occupied the rear and van of the stately, immobile procession. *Arizona* shared a berth with a creaky old repair ship, while the remaining four, all of them dating back to the early 1920s, stood in ponderous double harness.

Like fat pelicans that had seen too many winters, a trio of PBYs lumbered off the runways at Ford Island, painfully gained altitude, then headed westward on the inadequate dawn patrol.

A pair of cruisers nestled on the opposite side of the many-fingered harbor from the battleships.

And in the dry docks near the Officers' Club, helpless as anesthetized patients on operating tables, lay another twenty-two vessels. One of them was *Pennsylvania,* nominal flagship of the Fleet, which shared space with a couple of Mahan-class destroyers, sisters to *Cassiday.*

Far away, where the horizon mated uncertainly with the predawn sky, he caught the quick-winking signal light of the same patrolling four-piper he'd seen the previous night. She was condemned to Sunday morning exercises, and still dismally trolling for enemies she knew weren't there at all, just to keep in practice.

While he waited for the dutyboat to make its 0645 call, Mac sauntered across the marshy ground to an abandoned jetty where two small boys were fishing with bamboo poles. A light breeze was corrugating the harbor's graygreen surface, and the sun, about to surmount the cloud-capped Koolau Range and burn off the low-hanging mists, promised a normal Hawaiian day. Hot. Shining. Azure.

"How are you doing, mates?" he asked. "Catching any sharks?"

The anglers stared at him contemptuously, in the manner of all outdoorsmen forced unwillingly to chat with ignorant tenderfeet.

"Nope, lieutenant," said the older of the two. "Just a couple of stinkin' perch."

"Well," Mac said, "I'd like to swap jobs with you fellows. It's nicer to be fishing here than marooned out there on a tincan till dinner time."

The youngster relented. "We've got an extra pole, if you want."

"Duty's duty," Mac said sadly. "I'm bossman of the good ship *Cassiday* today—and here's my boat. Good luck!"

Impressed, the boy breathed, "Gee, lieutenant, you're skipper of that there can?"

"Temporarily."

"Hot dog!" The fisherman's mouth opened in a gaptoothed grin. "If you see any subs, sink one for us."

Mac laughed.

"Thanks, mate, I will. But there's a darned sight more chance of your hooking a hammerhead than *Cassiday*'s bagging a submarine in Pearl Harbor."

Chief Boatswain's Mate Roman Kluzowski, clad in outrageously faded dungarees, with the webbed belt of his .45 cutting a perilous arc beneath his gross belly, saluted Mac at the quarterdeck. He was proud of his brevet status as officer of the deck. And he was even prouder of the fact that somebody had once described chief petty officers as "the backbone of the Service."

Kluzowski lived by this tenet. When the occasion arose, he also fought for it, against gyrene and dogface sergeants, as well as against sundry left-arm Mickey Mouse ratings who should have known better than to tangle with any guy who displayed a bosun's wheel on his brawny right arm. Kluzowski's shipmates called him "Wop" because of his incongruous first name. In several strategic places he wore tattoos that extolled Mother Love and portrayed the charms of naked mermaids.

"Welcome aboard, cap'n," Wop rumbled.

Mac nodded.

Through the vagaries of the Navy's precedence system, he was senior officer for the next twelve hours, thanks to an eleven-promotion-points edge over Tom-Tom Agar, the head of *Cassiday*'s engineering department, who shared Sabbath duty with him and two reserve ensigns.

"Better crawl back into uniform, chief. When the sun comes up somebody off the *Dixon* might see you and figure we've been hijacked by pirates."

Wop was unperturbed. "Aye, aye, Mister McConnel. Soon's I'm relieved for chow."

As he headed for the wardroom, Mac warned himself that Tom-Tom's temper probably would be edgier than ever, for despite his disdain for naval rote, the pudgy little engineer resented playing second fiddle to his Academy classmate every third Sunday. What made things worse, Tom-Tom was a full year older than Mac. Since he had come aboard *Cassiday* immediately upon their graduation in '38, he considered himself a pretty stable fellow, and certainly no bird of passage who'd served in battleships before joining the virile Tincan Navy.

Like Wop, Tom-Tom figured his mission-in-life provided the indispensable warp which strengthened the Navy's woof, for whenever the hellfires faltered in Tom-Tom's sixteen oil burners deep down between *Cassiday*'s appallingly thinskinned flanks and below her two tall stacks, she was no longer a destroyer, but a wallowing creature bereft of any lethal punch, powerless either to attack or escape. Tom-Tom derived immense satisfaction from the fact that *Cassiday*'s engineering record was close to a perfect 4.0, and that during her full-power trials after last month's yard overhaul she'd accelerated from a standing start to her full thirty-six knots in nine breathless minutes.

Mac had guessed right. Tom-Tom was in a foul mood.

One of the lesser bearings had been running hot, he growled, and unless he took a couple of miserably dirty hours off to horse around with it, they could expect real trouble next time out.

For another thing, Bulldog Balch had won a Coke from him through a sneaky technicality involving some obscure aspect of naval history.

Bulldog shook his close-cropped head.

"Nothing sneaky about it. Just the inevitable triumph of science and skill over ignorance and superstition."

Tom-Tom got madder.

Even though his sparse hair was beginning to turn prematurely gray at twenty-six, Ensign Ewing Balch, USNR, had no right to bolster his case with Academy lingo. Take that phrase about science versus superstition. It was genuine Annapolis esoterica. Just because they happened to be former All-American fullbacks, reservists should never forget their inferior status alongside ringwearing Trade Schoolers.

But Bulldog didn't seem to give a hang.

"As America's oldest living ensign and most promising assistant gunnery officer," he said in his flat Midwestern voice, "I know all about history, because I've lived it." He scratched his barrel chest beneath the Kansas State varsity sweater that topped his abbreviated track shorts.

"Balls," Tom-Tom said rudely.

Mac looked around the wardroom, with its duck-covered chairs, green baize table, and untidy transom littered with old *Life*s and *Esquire*s. The destroyer's social center was about as warlike as a YMCA poolhall. Even the music from the beat-up Capehart, broadcast by Honolulu's earlybird radio station, came out disgustingly hygienic. Glucose. Bing pleading for *Just One More Chance.*

"Who's fourth man?" he asked.

"Poet."

"What's the immortal bard doing?"

"Bird-dogging the district's radio traffic," Tom-Tom said. "The air's full of stuff this morning."

That figured.

Even though *Cassiday*'s small communications department was required to monitor only the Fox schedule, which provided a ubiquitous watch service for the Fleet, Ensign Martin Cline, USNR, spent most of his waking hours in radio central high in the ship's superstructure, with his ears tuned to the incessant nautical gabble-gabble that flooded the half-dozen other frequencies audible in the Hawaiian area where communications were handled by the Fourteenth Naval District.

Cline had reported to *Cassiday* late in 1940, about the time Congress got scared enough to vote F.D.R. his two-ocean Navy. He came aboard speaking in carefully cultivated Ivy League accents. Cline, who was twenty-three, admitted freely that he was an aspiring poet whose ensign's stripe derived from a compulsory ROTC course he'd taken to avoid less appetizing military service.

In desperation the skipper had assigned him to communications.

To everybody's amazement, this worked out beautifully, for Cline proved a bearcat with coding machines, didn't mind inordinately long hours, and even kept the notoriously dour comm-office yeoman happy by reciting snatches of original bawdy verse. Thus his nickname: Poet.

Shortly after a lone messboy began serving the steak and eggs that presumably made Sunday duty more endurable, Poet ambled into the wardroom. His tall, scarecrow frame was draped in a brocaded silk dressing gown that might once have been a royal purple, but which now was streakily faded, like an inferior camouflage job.

Bulldog looked up from his plate.

"You missed a whale of an exhibition by crapping out on the commodore's wingding last night."

"So?" Poet daintily buttered a sliver of toast. "Pray tell, Lothario, even though it sounds horribly depressing for a dull Sunday morning."

"You're too young and innocent," Bulldog said.

"Don't let my beardless cheeks fool you, guns. I've seen life in the raw."

"What our aging bachelor friend means," Tom-Tom explained, "is that he's fallen in love again."

"Whom with?" Poet asked precisely, only mildly interested in Bulldog Balch's inexhaustible romances.

"With the O-Club's latest catch-as-catch-can hula champ, who was also pretty blotto and in a mood to teach us some basic anatomy."

"Check," Bulldog said. "That baby was strictly a sacktime *wahine*."

"You're just susceptible to bare female skin," Tom-Tom said. "Furthermore, she's senior officer material. Off limits."

Bulldog demanded incredulously, "This dreamboat's married? What about that flyboy with her—the non-husband type?"

"Her husband's exec on *Old Swayback*. Guy named Eddington."

"He'd better stick around home," Bulldog said. "Or buy this babe a chastity belt. Flyboy wasn't playing pattycake when I saw him last."

Mac gave him the look that Academy first-classmen save for particularly backward plebes, and changed the subject. "How's your correspondence course coming along?"

"Lousy. Stuck on the third lesson, somewhere between torpedo runs and crossing the T," Bulldog mourned. "Maybe I'm too goddamn old for homework."

"You didn't sound that way a minute ago, Mister Balch."

"That was a different kind."

"This sort might come in handy someday, fella, when you're out there in the middle of the ocean all alone and the Jap fleet's bearing down on you at thirty knots."

Bulldog's expression turned warlike. "Another thing—how in hell can anybody concentrate on paper battles when the real thing's happening right now in the Atlantic?"

"If you're talking about the Neutrality Patrol," Mac said, "you've just lost your argument. Those guys know tactics backward, from Zebra to Able."

Nobody spoke for a moment, as they thought somberly of *Greer* and *Kearny,* and especially the four-piper *Reuben James,* which had gone down six weeks earlier with all her officers and most of the crew after a U-boat torpedo atomized everything forward of her Number 4 funnel.

Poet glanced up from his egg. "Somebody's busy in the Pacific. All the carriers are gone."

"'All the carriers,'" Tom-Tom mimicked. "Two! Halsey's got the *Enterprise* and Newton's taken out the *Lex*. Probably on maneuvers again. Bang, bang! Now play dead!"

"How come they left the battlewagons home?" Mac asked.

"How come anybody does anything?" Tom-Tom countered. "Maybe the Big Boys are tired. God knows they're old enough to deserve a rest."

But even he had to admit that it was damned odd for all the battleships to stay in port. These were days when the extraordinary was getting to be almost commonplace, however, so that's how they left the matter. At this subordinate level, far below the CinCPAC staffers and almost as abjectly inferior to four-stripers like Rockwell Torrey, young officers usually dismissed these cosmic issues without comment. Moreover, whatever factors led up to such events as carriers putting out to sea without gunfire support were generally Top Secret, anyhow, and therefore unfit topics for j.o.'s.

Mac displayed a philosophical detachment about all this that bordered on the fatalistic. He thought a lot. But he kept his own counsel. Tennyson summed it up quite succinctly, he believed, as the Light Brigade galloped into the Valley of Death. *"Theirs not to reason why. Theirs but to do and die."* Sometimes, though, he'd fret about his capacity for doing whatever he had to do when the decisive moment came, suddenly and without warning.

None of this affected Tom-Tom.

He regarded high strategy with a kind of silent derision, as a precocious youngster listens to the opinions of his backward elders.

His job was grooming and feeding the 42,000 horses stabled in *Cassiday*'s infernal bowels. Anything else would have to take care of itself.

As reservists, and therefore not entitled to hold any opinions on toplofty naval subjects at all, neither Bulldog nor Poet said much. Once in a long while the assistant gunnery officer lost his temper and berated Fate in bald Midwestern patois, after which he'd stalk off to his stateroom and chin himself twenty times on a bar that a machinist's mate had welded to the overhead in exchange for a case of green Philippine beer.

As they were idly sipping their final cups of coffee, three blacks and a pale Boston for Poet, and speculating on the day's dreary occupations, the watch messenger burst into the wardroom without knocking. His expression was frozen somewhere between puzzlement and fright.

He handed Poet a message flimsy.

"Meeker says this is the ComFourteen dispatch you intercepted at 0654."

The communicator consulted his waterproof stop watch. "Took the kid a hell of a long time to decode it. Damned near twenty-five minutes." But as he scanned the brief message, his tutorial manner swiftly changed.

Tom-Tom gave him a bored look. "More fun and games?"

"Christ, no!"

"Okay," Mac said, "spill it, Shakespeare."

"It's from *Ward*—you know, they've got the inshore patrol—and it says they've attacked, fired upon, and dropped depth charges on a submarine operating in the defensive sea area."

Tom-Tom whistled.

"Oh, brother. Now some poor Joe's got his tit in a wringer for sure. Dumping ash cans on one of our own subs just because it wandered off base."

But Mac wasn't so certain *Ward*'s report was that harmless. Between these patrolling PBYs he'd seen earlier, and the destroyer's spotters, there'd be plenty of sharp eyes and shrewd brains figuring out whether the target was an improbable foe or some blundering friend. They'd also have double-checked operating schedules, knowing damned well that dropping depth charges in error was a capital offense.

He managed to keep his voice calm as he said, "Ask the bridge whether they've intercepted any visual word about this business from Yard tower."

With his preposterous gown flapping around his skinny shanks, Poet scuttled out of the wardroom. He was back in three minutes flat.

"ComFourteen's ordered the ready duty destroyer underway to help *Ward*—and her standby's been told to build up steam."

Mac looked at Tom-Tom.

"Maybe we'd better touch off a few boilers ourselves, matey, just in case . . ."

The engineer hid his own excitement behind a massive scowl that was calculated to impress the reservists. "In case of what?"

"God knows," Mac said. "Call it psychic. But suddenly I've got the damnedest feeling right down here in my gut." He patted an icy area below his ribs. "Want it in writing so the Old Man won't chew you out?"

"Hell, no!" Tom-Tom was outraged. "I just wish you didn't get these notions at chow time, that's all. Maybe you're not psychic at all. Maybe you're just pregnant."

"It's 0725. How soon can we get underway—if we have to?"

"The Book allows an hour. Give me forty-five minutes."

"How about the flat-arsed bearing?"

"We'll fix it."

"Okay."

At 0755 the blue Prep pennant fluttered from the yardarm atop the Navy Yard's tallest water tank, marking five minutes to Morning Colors. Every ship in Pearl Harbor, from garbage tender to battlewagon, dutifully followed suit with its own hoist. When this flag came down, signifying the traditional "execute" command, the immobile Fleet units would break out starred Union Jacks from their bows and Old Glory from their sterns, and across the placid waters would drift the brassy sound of Colors played by buglers on the larger vessels.

On the Small Boys, like *Cassiday,* a bosun's pipe sufficed.

Wop took a spraddle-legged stance on the fantail, close to the depth charge roller-racks, and inflated his cheeks for an almost soundless warm-up with his whistle. This was the happiest moment of his busy day. He felt like Gabriel preparing to let loose a blast on his everlovin' trumpet. Powerful. Nine feet tall.

Eight miles away, crystal tinkling on the still morning air, Honolulu's myriad church bells heralded early services. Wop made a mental promise to drop around to Father O'Hara's late-morning Mass aboard *Dixon*. He'd been pretty lax lately and the padre was starting to give him the old dog-eye when he caught him at the Yard rec hall over a stein of beer. Besides, now that McConnel had dragooned him into dress whites, he figured he ought to do something worthy of all this starched glamour.

That's when Wop saw it.

Cruising almost leisurely, it skimmed the fringed tops of Pearl City's algarrobas, and passed overhead at masthead height.

Ten feet lower and the goddamn idiot would have clipped off *Cassiday*'s truck light.

"Crazy flat-hattin' son of a bitch!" Wop yelled at the plane.

Nonchalantly, the pilot leaned out of his cockpit and gave the bosun a jaunty handwave. Wop could see sunlight glinting off his goggles. Too furious to say more, he waved an impotent fist at the scudding craft.

Then, abruptly, Wop froze.

That friggin' plane didn't have stars under its wings. Those were *meatballs*—bloodred and murderous—exactly like the insignia he'd seen nine years earlier when the Nips came gliding in over Shanghai, without warning, to blast his favorite city into smithereens. The bomber, which he recognized as a Kate, was closely followed by eleven others, all with torpedoes slung beneath their fat, ugly bellies.

The color guard, a lone seaman, waggled his halyards impatiently. He hadn't seen the plane and he was hungry. There were flapjacks for breakfast, and unless they finished this petty chore pretty soon he'd be tail-end Charlie in the chow line and probably wind up with beans instead.

"What's eatin' you, chief?" he said. "Toot the damned whistle."

Wop aimed a stubby forefinger toward the Kates which were banking slowly to starboard over East Loch and obviously vectoring for a broadside run down Battleship Row.

"Those are Japs!"

"Horsecock," the seaman said unpleasantly. "They're Army jokers foolin' around with fake torpeckers. Bet you a buck—"

Wop made his decision.

"Okay, sonny, execute Colors!" He blew an earsplitting blast on his pipe. "Now shag your ass into the wardroom and tell Lieutenant McConnel the goddamn war's started!"

Even before Mac reached *Cassiday*'s bridge, scrambling up the steep ladder four steps at a time, the first torpedoes from the potbellied Kates were driving into their hapless targets, and the initial wave of dive-bombing Vals was shrieking down from the six-thousand-foot overcast.

Chief Quartermaster Ishmael Quoddy, who had the bridge watch, pressed the General Quarters buzzer. In the crazy tumult that was compounded of nearby gunfire and vast faraway explosions the destroyer's klaxon sounded almost fragile.

But it sufficed.

Cassiday's crew were at their battle stations before the last harsh notes died away.

Mac yelled, "Good work, chief!"

Quoddy grunted. Being a Down Easter, he never said much. Now he said nothing. There was work to be done. Somehow, through all this shambles, their static ship had to be brought underway.

The bridge clock showed 0800. Right on the button.

Hidden in the billowing and greasy smoke beyond the harbor's fingerlochs, a new string of signals replaced the blue Prep flag high on the Yard tower. "ALL SHIPS IN PEARL SORTIE," they ordered. To the Fleet signalmen's eternal credit, most of the undamaged vessels promptly repeated the hoist, relaying The Word from ship to ship through the grayblack smudge that rolled from the stricken battlewagons.

Mac spotted the sortie pennant fluttering from *Dixon*'s yardarm. He stepped across the narrow bridge and blew sharply into the voice tube to attract Tom-Tom's attention in the engineroom forty feet below.

"What the devil goes on up there?" Tom-Tom demanded angrily. "Sounds like all hell's busted loose."

"It has," Mac yelled. "Pearl's under attack. Japs. We've got to get underway—pronto!"

"Jesus H. Christ!"

"How soon can you give me power?"

"We're getting her licked. Still wrassling with that goddamn bearing. How's twenty-five minutes?"

"Lousy! War'll be over by then—"

"Twenty?"

"Make it fifteen."

"I'll try, buddy."

Mac fought to keep a frantic note out of his voice. "Do your best, Tom-Tom."

"Roger. Just keep us posted. We're sorta out of touch down here."

"So are we," Mac said grimly. "Also snafued. And it's getting worse by the second."

Cassiday's 20-millimeter Oerlikons had been firing steadily for five minutes, pumping 450 rounds a minute at random targets. Although none of the eight little popguns had hit anything, at least they gave the noisy effect of positive action in that hopeless battle between the stationary ships and the wheeling, swooping, unimpeded Japs.

Mac looked up just as a Kate burst out of the muck, barely thirty feet above the littered surface of the harbor, and headed straight for *Cassiday*.

At that split second, he was curiously unafraid. He could make out with awful clarity the cigar-shaped torpedo hooked beneath the plane's fuselage, and in detached fashion he speculated whether it would detonate fore, aft, or amidships under the bridge where he himself stood.

But now the Kate was a scant two hundred yards off the starboard bow. So what the hell did it matter where *Cassiday* took the fish? She'd never survive a direct hit from that distance.

Suddenly the Number 2 five-inch gun passed a miracle.

Its first fifty-pound shell caught the Kate squarely in her pregnant belly. She was still plunging at the destroyer when her torpedo blew. The plane exploded with an appalling roar and pieces rained into the oil-slicked water. Number 2 kept firing methodically as torn chunks of aircraft metal ricocheted across the ship's slim foredeck.

Stripped to his brawny waist and wearing only soiled skivvies, Bulldog Balch stepped from the blast shield that housed Number 2. His face was black from powder smoke.

"Winged the dirty bastard with one shot!"

Mac howled back at him. "Right in the breadbasket, by God!"

In an oddly disconnected way, he was aware that his own voice was hoarse, too, as if he had been shouting for a long time, and he wondered why Bulldog was handling a solitary five-inch rifle instead of operating the director that controlled the entire four-gun main battery. Belatedly he remembered. Until they got up steam, the apparatus wouldn't have power. So instead of isolating himself high above the bridge, Bulldog was turning his keen football eye and rock-hard muscles to the more immediate task, which was optically aiming and manually firing *Cassiday*'s guns at the invaders.

Mac looked toward the quartermaster.

"Our All-American boy's throwing touchdowns," he exulted.

"Good shootin,'" Ishmael Quoddy acknowledged. "But we should've cranked down the windshield. Concussion busted 'er to bits."

"Who cares?" Mac watched the place where the sundered Kate had disappeared. "We're in the fight. We've drawn first blood, by Christ!"

"Got some on your face, too, Mister McConnel."

"What?"

"Blood, sir."

Mac touched his cheek. It *was* blood. He'd been cut by a shard from the glass windscreen. The jagged gash had begun to hurt.

Then Mac got mad at himself. Stupid goddamn fool! You're supposed to lower the bridge windshield whenever you go into battle. That's what the Book says. Concussion from the forward fives bounces back like a triphammer. You could've caught a splinter in a worse place than your silly cheek. You could have been blinded. In the frightening minutes since the attack began, this was the first vital detail he'd muffed, and it never should have happened. Now he felt apprehensive again, not for himself, but for *Cassiday,* whose future lay in his hands. Neither the skipper nor the exec, who were stranded ashore, would have forgotten to drop the glass screen.

As he issued the orders that would free *Cassiday* from her mid-harbor prison, Mac was only half aware of his surroundings, for some of the things that were happening seemed to occur jerkily, like sequences in old silent movies, while others just hung there, agonizingly, as if frozen into the slowest of slow motion.

That is how the nightmares would come to him later . . . *Arizona,* torn and twisted, with her broken tripod foremast canted at an improbable angle, but with her taffrail flag still bravely whipping in the breeze. *Oklahoma* slowly capsizing, with a stricken whale's movement, until her masts touched muddy bottom and she stopped rolling, keel upward. Only *Nevada*, despite deep wounds from both bombs and torpedoes, making any visible effort to tear loose from her deadly trap astern of ruined *Arizona,* and backing slowly and deliberately like some monstrous, animate creature, as if every movement of her 37,000-ton carcass brought mortal agony.

During an inexplicable lull, Mac glimpsed all of this briefly through a break in the smokepall, and for the first time since the attack began, he thought about Bev, alone in their tiny apartment on the Ala Wai, and maybe scared stiff. Or would she be frightened? No. He guessed she wouldn't. More likely she'd be standing out in the driveway, popping at the Japs with the .22 pumpgun they'd bought on a foolish whim for target practice.

Then the second assault wave engulfed Pearl Harbor and there wasn't any more time to think about matters you couldn't help, anyhow, because *Cassiday*'s survival was all that counted. You went to work, swiftly and automatically, with a strange sureness, as if you and your crew had changed from innocent fledglings into battle-toughened veterans during the thirty-five minutes that had elapsed since the first Kate swung out of the pallid morning sunlight.

The speaking tube whistled.

It was Tom-Tom. Proud as a new papa, he reported that steam was making up fast in all four boilers.

"Five more minutes," he promised. "You'd better start freeing the lines now."

"Good!" Mac calculated swiftly as he peered through the wild gloom along their route to the harbor gate. "I'm going to want 400 r.p.m. just as soon as you can deliver 'em."

"In the channel?" Tom-Tom said incredulously. "Are you out of your friggin' mind?"

"Negative."

Brief silence. Then: "Okay, mister. It's your funeral. But 400 r.p.m. means twenty-seven knots. And that's awful goddamn fast for a hearse."

More to his own private Furies than to the voice tube, Mac said softly, "This is a good day for funerals."

"Can't hear you."

"Nothing, Tom-Tom. Nothing. Just give us those 400 r.p.m."

"Check. I'm wiring the safety valves shut!"

Bulldog Balch was delighted when Mac passed The Word that power would soon be restored. After his stroke of pure luck with Number 2, they might as well have been firing blanks at the Nips. They hadn't hit anything except a derrick barge that strayed accidentally between *Cassiday* and a Zeke fighter bent on strafing the destroyer's fantail and maybe exploding her depth bombs. But the Zeke escaped and the barge ran aground.

Bulldog shambled across the narrow bridgewing and slapped his temporary captain on the shoulder, hard, the way he used to pummel a buckfeverish quarterback just before Kansas State went for broke on the five-yard line.

"We'll make it," he added. Then he appealed to Ishmael Quoddy: "Won't we, chief?"

Ignoring the holocaust that raged around them, the quartermaster was smoking his battered corncob and waiting patiently for *Cassiday*'s turbines to roll. Now he took the pipe from his pursed mouth, and examined the charred bowl as if he might find the answer down among the Bull Durham embers. A brief smile flickered across his leathery face.

"Yep. Reckon we'll make it."

They got underway at exactly 0833. *Cassiday* left a sizable length of bow chain behind her, and a snapped segment of cable trailed crazily from her stern buoy, as she whipsawed free from her fore-and-aft mooring. The crew huzzahed. Let 'em court-martial him, Mac thought irreverently, and let 'em send a bill for the busted windshield, too, and maybe for the whole goddamned tincan in the next couple of minutes.

Who the hell cared? They were moving.

Ishmael Quoddy conned the destroyer downstream with a calm-faced detachment that came from thirty years of experience in tincans. Almost lovingly, Mac contemplated the quartermaster's bony shoulder blades as he hunched over the big helm which controlled the delicately responsive steering system of the 1,450-ton ship. The solid brass wheel could have been a living part of this taciturn man. Mac breathed a small prayer of thanksgiving that the chief hadn't gone ashore last night with the allowable one-third of the crew. At best *Cassiday* was undermanned that winter, but right now her working force was a woeful skeleton. Here on the normally crowded bridge it would be McConnel and Quoddy against the world, performing between them an intricate task that should have been shared by the captain, the officer of the deck, a pair of helmsmen, and the quartermaster of the watch.

Buttoned down tight, with all her ports dogged, her weather doors secured, and her watertight compartment hatches irrevocably sealed, *Cassiday* barreled down the narrow channel at twenty knots, still accelerating, as if there weren't another ship in the hideous harbor. Her scorched guns were silent, momentarily, for the sky was free of enemy planes just then, and there were no targets.

Mac crossed his fingers. In another fifteen minutes they'd be free, with their ship unscathed except for the shattered windscreen, a few minor hull scratches where the Kate had blown up alongside, and a neat dotted line of bullet holes traced across her fantail by the Zeke.

But nothing was ever that easy.

He knew it.

Almost as if he'd been awaiting the man's shout, Mac heard the port side lookout call, "*Dixon*'s hoisting a new signal, lieutenant—'Enemy submarine sighted to starboard.' "

"Horsefeathers!" Mac retorted, unbelieving. "Check again!"

However faulty its aerial defenses, Pearl Harbor was heavily guarded by complex gates and antisubmarine nets. Nothing could get through. *Dixon* must be seeing ghosts.

But Ishmael Quoddy's dry twang cut in. "It's sure as hell a sub, Mister McConnel. Dead ahead."

A second later Mac himself spotted the Thing. It was cruising along slowly, less than three hundred yards away, with its squat gray flanks awash, and looking incredibly evil despite its vest-pocket size. Two torpedo tubes leered from its blunt snout, like barrels of an over-and-under shotgun. They were aimed right down *Cassiday*'s vulnerable throat.

As Mac watched, fascinated, a white spurt blossomed from the midget sub's bow, and became a torpedo wake.

Cassiday careened into a bicycle spin, heeling sharply, and the projectile fled past the destroyer's stern. Mac saw it porpoise twice on its runaway course toward Ford Island, where it exploded harmlessly.

"Now," he shouted, "let's ram the little son of a bitch!"

Ishmael Quoddy kept his imperturbable gaze firmly on course. "Aye, aye, cap'n."

"Aim for the conning tower."

"That's where I'm aimin'," the tall quartermaster said emotionlessly.

He whirled the wheel again, hard left, and *Cassiday*'s sharp stem knifed toward the sub, whose boxy tower was slipping beneath the foul waters. With her second torpedo unexpended, the midget still carried a puff adder's sting if it ever broke free. The Jap's strategy was obvious. Just one Yankee warship sunk in the shallow channel would finish the desperate sortie before it got fairly underway, leaving the Pacific Fleet survivors hopelessly bottled up. Next day the enemy could pick their bones bare.

Mac called to Wop, who had his eye glued to the stadimeter, plotting the distance to their submerging quarry.

"Range?"

"Less than two hundred yards."

"Damn!"

Even at her breakneck speed *Cassiday* couldn't reach the diving sub before it vanished.

"Talker!" Mac yelled.

A curly-haired seaman wearing a headset replied, "Sir?" in a scared sophomore voice.

"Pass the word to the fantail to set depth charges at thirty feet. Tell 'em to drop 'em in twenty seconds."

The boy's tone was firmer now that he had a man's job to do, and he suddenly felt a lot braver.

"Aye, aye."

"Let me know when they're ready."

Inside of five seconds the talker announced, "Chief torpedoman says can of beans comin' right up!"

"Good."

Wop hollered, "Range zero!"

The destroyer's keel grazed the fleeing sub, too softly to inflict any real damage on its hull, then slid free.

Mac counted to ten, aloud, before he snapped, "Roll 'em!"

The drum-shaped charges, each packed with four hundred pounds of TNT, rattled down their short tracks. For the second time that day he offered up a silent prayer. "Scratch the sub . . . but spare the tincan." Even before his soundless lips stopped moving, the charges exploded into giant geysers, horrifyingly close aboard, and *Cassiday* staggered under the impact. Her bridge fell away abruptly, drunkenly, then leaped upward again.

When Mac regained his balance, and looked aft, he saw the fantail crew slowly dragging themselves off the oil-splattered deck. They were wet, dazed, and bedraggled. But the ship seemed whole.

He finished his prayer. Then he added aloud, to nobody in particular, "Now maybe those kids will catch their shark, too!"

As *Cassiday* rounded Hospital Point with a thirty-knot bone flashing snow-white in her sharp teeth, Mac's backward glance was caught by a motor whaleboat racing futilely after them, and he wondered vaguely what in hell the idiots in that small craft had on their minds. For only idiots would stray out into the debris-strewn harbor unless they had urgent business that couldn't wait till after doomsday, or unless they had some protection from the shrapnel that whistled murderously from the darkened skies. Even a destroyer's bridge offered damned little security from those steel fragments. But it was better than an open whaleboat.

The launch fell farther behind in its effort to overtake *Cassiday,* and as the gap widened, somebody in the bow stood up on a seat and waved his arms crazily.

Mac hoisted his binoculars for a closer look.

The man balanced so precariously in the whaleboat's tossing bow was Commander Bowen. He had a golf club in his right hand. Behind him, also gesticulating wildly, was Lieutenant Commander Harding.

The commodore's lips formed the words, "Slow down, for Christ's sake! Let us aboard!"

"We gonna stop for 'em?" Wop demanded incredulously.

Cassiday had already entered the wide-open antisubmarine gate at the harbor's slitted mouth. Once she reached Blue Water, she would have a decent chance of survival and the opportunity to strike back against the enemy. But stopping now, even with the destroyer's twin screws flung into full reverse to stem her thirty-knot surge, would cost them twenty precious minutes.

It might also cost them the ship itself.

Mac turned solemnly to the bosun.

"Do you see anything back there, chief?"

"Me?" Wop asked piously. "Jeez, sir, I'm blind as a bat."

"What about you, Quoddy? D'you see anything astern?"

"Negative, Mister McConnel. Can't see nothin'. But I can *feel* a passel of Nip dive bombers right on our tail."

"How's your eyesight?"

"Real good," Quoddy said.

Mac smiled wryly. The quartermaster was too preoccupied with conning *Cassiday* to freedom to waste any idle backward stares. But he understood his youthful skipper's predicament, and if the lieutenant needed an alibi, by God, Ishmael Quoddy was with him to the bitter end, including a General Court-Martial.

Mac checked the bridge clock. It was 0923.

He addressed the engineroom speaking tube. "You fellows still alive down there?"

"Barely," Tom-Tom's muffled voice responded.

"Live enough to give us thirty-six knots?"

"Roger."

"Then give, Tom-Tom boy. We're clearing Pearl . . . and we're about to go Jap-hunting!"

Cassiday's turbine-tempo, already a high-pitched whine, picked up appreciably as she edged toward flank speed. Her graceful prow rose to meet the first offshore Pacific swells and her wake churned into an arching five-foot wave that marked an ivory path across the clean sea.

Bone-weary, Mac sank into the canvas-backed swivel chair on the windward bridgewing, which had always been the commodore's sacred throne, as realization came to him at this moment of escape that he was in full command, now, and alone with his awful trust.

Like Rockwell Torrey, who was twice his age, he must play God until *Cassiday* returned to port.

4. *Neither Did the Cruse of Oil Fail*

Except for her token escort of four-pipers, *Old Swayback* was alone in the innocent seas beyond Pearl Harbor. None of the frantic messages that crackled out of Fleet headquarters were addressed to her, as she roved Oahu's southern headlands on a seemingly aimless course, like a puzzled bloodhound seeking a spoor. At that moment she was utterly forgotten, or ignored, by the sorely beset high command.

In unwitting imitation of his ship's larger quarterings, Captain Torrey methodically paced the navigating bridge, awaiting The Word that would send him charging after the Japanese. He had already alerted the chief engineer to be prepared on short notice to give him thirty-two-knot flank speed.

Deep in her hull, far below *Old Swayback*'s waterline, shell handlers were readying live ammunition for her eight-inch rifles. The five-inch guns, and smaller automatic weapons, were already loaded, their muzzles trained at 45 degrees, and their unblooded crews nervously scanning the skies for the enemy. Whatever her lookouts could discern from their positions on the forward director platform, a hundred feet above the cresting swells, she could see. But that was all. Once the night closed around her, she would be utterly sightless, without search planes or radar.

This thought lay uppermost in The Rock's mind as he measured eight deliberate steps from the port wing of the steeldecked bridge to its starboard extremity, passing through the doors on either side of the pilothouse on each lap of his endless pacing. It took him just ten seconds to negotiate the narrow passageway. One-sixth of a minute. Time to launch the torpedo or drop the bomb that could murder a ship; time ticking away like Eternity itself. He wished he could be certain—as he should—that CinCPAC's myriad experts, his intelligence Merlins, and his operations geniuses had tracked the foe by now with their vaunted new shore-based radar, or pinpointed his radio chatter with their longfingered direction finders. Soon, too, Halsey's carrier pilots would be relaying some news. And perhaps their own picket subs would relay a clue.

Through the open door to the chartroom, just aft of the pilothouse, The Rock could hear the Honolulu radio urging civilians to dig slit trenches along the beaches, fight stray fires, give their blood, and (above all!) keep calm pending imposition of martial law. Meanwhile the news from Pearl Harbor continued to be bad, the announcer said, for it appeared the Fleet had been completely surprised. Many, many ships sunk or damaged. Casualties in the thousands.

"Stand by," he added earnestly, "for our latest bulletins."

Torrey's thatched brows contracted in a frown, and his temper, kept under leash during ninety minutes of tense waiting, flared briefly. Brushing aside the junior officer of the deck, he stepped to the chartroom door.

"Goddamn it to hell, Paul, why doesn't CinCPAC *tell* us something?" His irate question was purely rhetorical. "Are we supposed to get all our 'news' from civilian radio?"

As if to mock him, the Honolulu station suddenly switched from hysterical bulletins to jazz. The music echoed tinnily off the bulkheads of the cubicle where the exec and the navigator were huddled over a Hawaiian area chart which traced their wanderings since 0758.

Eddington looked up, perplexed. "Radio bother you, skipper?"

"No." The Rock choked back his anger. "Leave it on. Maybe that fellow will accidentally spill something useful."

The exec nodded his rufous head doubtfully. "Burke and I figured we might catch some word about home. That's all."

Now that Torrey's quick wrath had subsided, he felt an unspoken sympathy for his two subordinates. Lieutenant Commander Bobby Burke, he recalled, had returned reluctantly to the ship the previous night, because his pregnant wife was expecting their first child at any moment. Peggy was damned near thirty-two, the navigator explained morosely, so having a baby mightn't be very easy for her.

Burke, who was a small thin man, set down his dividers and lit one of his favorite small thin cigars. He took scant comfort from the exec's easy assurance that since nothing ever happened to

Old Swayback—either good or bad—they'd have him safe in the prospective mother's arms within forty-eight hours.

"They've even bombed the downtown area," he said bitterly. "Hell of a lot of people killed and Christ knows what else."

Torrey was silent.

There was nothing he could say to comfort Burke. No logic would suffice. For it was possible that *Old Swayback* would be ordered into the farthest western Pacific to bolster the inadequate Asiatic Fleet, without returning to base, or just as peremptorily dispatched anywhere along the vulnerable perimeter which the Navy must contrive to hold until reinforcements came.

Burke turned suddenly toward Eddington.

"What about Beth?" he demanded. "Aren't you worried about her?"

The exec's face hardened. "Sure I'm worried, Bobby." (But not because of stray bombs at Waikiki, he told himself savagely. Somebody'd be looking after Beth. Somebody always did.)

At 0935 *Old Swayback* doubled back from Barbers Point into the broad bosom of Mamala Bay and stood a few miles off the harbor mouth, in full view of the vast column of oily smoke that stretched ten thousand feet into the once-clean skies until the tradewind finally scattered it into the endless gray murk. Mamala isn't really a bay at all, but a scimitar-shaped shelf whose blade presses against Oahu's southern shore, and whose handle is Diamond Head. At its outer edge, the coral-bottomed, twenty-fathom shoalwater drops off abruptly to one hundred fathoms or more, although it's another thirty miles to authentic Blue Water, where Fleets can maneuver and where submarines can prowl undetected.

The Rock kept his binoculars trained toward the harbor mouth from which elements of the beleaguered Fleet must soon escape.

At 0940 a destroyer, her knifesharp nose high as she boiled along at formidable speed, appeared at the gap, and set course straight for *Old Swayback*. In less than three minutes the white numbers on each side of her prow were discernible through the glasses.

Eddington riffled hastily through the Fleet roster.

"*Cassiday*," he announced.

"Who's her captain?"

"Rafe Harding."

"Damned good man." Torrey's tired face brightened at the knowledge that a veteran commanded his new consort. "I remember Harding from Fleet exercises last summer. Got credit for scratching an 'enemy' sub. Doesn't have to be told what to do. Solid. Plenty of moxie."

The destroyer slackened her headlong pace and sidled into a parallel course with *Old Swayback,* a quarter mile distant, matching the cruiser's deliberate fourteen-knot advance.

"Ask him what in hell's happening back there," The Rock ordered sharply.

The exec picked up the shortwave voice microphone.

"Cruiser calling Little Boy," he intoned. "Come in!"

Quite unidentifiable, his words distorted by the low-powered TBS (talk-between-ships) transmitter, somebody replied laconically: "Little Boy reporting for duty . . . awaiting orders."

"What's The Word at Pearl?"

"Godawful." The disembodied voice hesitated briefly. "*Arizona*'s blown to bits. Gone completely. We couldn't hang around for a good look, but we saw at least two other BBs sinking. *Pennsy* got it in dry dock, along with a couple of tincans. There must be others . . ."

The destroyerman caught his breath, as if he were overcome by what he had seen, and Eddington wondered why an old hand like Rafe Harding would get the wind up so obviously.

"What's left?" he asked into the TBS.

"Not a hell of a lot," the stricken voice continued. "Maybe a couple of cruisers and a few tincans will get out. But the Big Boys have had it."

Torrey nudged the exec.

"Ask him whether the Fleet's issued any orders we might have missed. Visual signals. Anything."

Eddington relayed the question.

"Just sortie," Little Boy replied bleakly. "That's all CinCPAC told us."

"Order him to set course 70, speed 15, standard zigzag pattern, keeping three hundred yards ahead of us," The Rock said. "We'll remain in this area until the rest of 'em show. And tell Harding to forget the TBS for a while. Might be Jap subs around. We'll use hoists."

Cassiday swung nimbly into her assigned station.

Astern, the tawdry little DMS four-pipers tagged along like mongrel puppies.

As he stared fore-and-aft, assaying the dubious merits of his unimpressive flotilla, Torrey was grimly aware that these four ships represented the sum total of American seapower in Hawaii's sacrosanct waters at that exact moment. It was not a prideful thought.

For the better part of an hour they etched crooked wakes along a bearing that took them past Ewa Field, where smoke still eddied from bombed-out Marine aircraft, and finally beyond the western end of Oahu itself, and into the deepening waters.

Once they were erroneously reported by a friendly but confused scout plane, which was moving too fast and too high for accurate sighting, as "enemy transports." Nothing came of it. CinCPAC was too busy to bother about them. Had they really been Japs, Eddington growled, they could have landed a whole goddamned division on the beaches at Barbers Point without losing a single dogface.

Torrey swore softly but made no comment.

As Oahu dropped farther astern, the exec kept urging a more southerly course, on the assumption that the enemy must have converged upon Pearl Harbor from his mysterious atoll bases which sprawled along the Equator, two thousand miles across the dim horizon.

"Let's stop playing blindman's buff," he pleaded. "Let's go after the friggin' Nips—now!"

The Rock inspected Burke's navigational chart. "Why d'you figure southwest, Paul?"

"Because our subs spotted two of their carriers in the Marshalls only last week," Eddington reminded him. "That's where they always rendezvous."

Torrey was doubtful.

"No. I'm betting they struck from the north, where we'd least expect them. It's been lousy weather up there all week. Perfect cover for a raid. Besides, those subs you mentioned would have intercepted any force large enough to do *that* kind of damage." He stared back at the smoldering Island, and appeared to be grappling for something in the dark waters of his memory. Then: "I think it was just about a year ago, Paul, that old Admiral Yamamoto said he doubted the wisdom of tackling the United States single-handed, but that if he had to take us on he'd 'run wild' for six months or so because he was afraid of what might happen to Japan during a really long war."

"Maybe so," Eddington acknowledged. "But what's the riddle?"

The Rock fished out his shortest briar, which he reserved for smoking on the open bridge, and lit it before he said ruminatively, "I played poker with Yamamoto once, 'way back in the early thirties when we were still romancing the Nips with goodwill visits to Yokohama. He won our goddamn shirts. Skivvies, too, as I recall. Now, as a shrewd card player, he'd also be a hell of a bluffer, wouldn't he?"

"Maybe," Eddington repeated, still unconvinced.

"So Yamamoto decoys us by planting a couple of carriers in the Marshalls. He still has plenty left in case his pat hand gets called. But it doesn't." The Rock's bass voice dropped even lower. "And we gave the Japs chapter and verse on how to attack Pearl Harbor during our Fleet exercises last year. Remember? *We approached from the north!"*

Eddington reversed course. "All right. But what in hell's our job now?"

"Waiting. Period!" To soften his harshness, The Rock added, "It's not easy for any of us. Especially for Burke, here."

The navigator's Adam's apple bobbed convulsively as he swallowed hard. "I'd be happier," he admitted, "if we could get our hands on those bastards."

Almost conversationally, Torrey asked, "Have you gentlemen stopped to figure what the Japs might have used in this crazy operation?"

"Couple of fast carriers," Eddington guessed. "Plus a few escorts."

The Rock reached into the small bookcase over the chart table, and drew out a bluejacketed pamphlet. He flipped open a page. "You should pay more attention to your intelligence reports, Paul."

Eddington looked guilty. Like many combat-minded activists, he was somewhat contemptuous of the Navy Department's intelligence personnel, whom he viewed as backroom sorcerers prone to shadowy theorizing and slopping up too many lunchtime martinis in plush Washington hotels.

"Generally," he muttered, "I do."

"This one's dated November," Torrey said. "It gives our current strength in the Pacific compared to the Nips'." He ran his thin finger down the list. "From the Philippines to the West Coast we've got nine battleships to their ten. Three carriers against ten. Thirteen heavy cruisers to eighteen. Eleven light cruisers to seventeen. Eighty destroyers to one hundred eleven. And fifty-five subs to sixty-four."

"Doesn't quality count for something?"

"What do we know about the Japs' quality," The Rock snapped, "or about their efficiency, either, except what they taught us this morning?"

"They caught us napping."

"You're damned right they did. And frankly, fella, I think they shot the works. At least half their carrier force, plus enough heavy stuff to kick the hell out of anybody that tried to intercept 'em."

The exec's pugilist face, always florid at this critical stage of his secret hangovers, flushed deeper red. But it was no longer mere embarrassment at having been found wanting in such a simple matter as relative seapower. He was seized by a quicksilver rage that stemmed from unpleasant circumstances which he hadn't created, and which he couldn't control.

"Balls!"

As he uttered the expletive in a strangled voice, Eddington drove his great fist against the chartroom bulkhead. The steel rang like an Oriental gong.

"Feel better?" Torrey asked.

Eddington massaged his injured knuckles. "Maybe it's the only way to draw blood," he said stolidly. "Maybe they'll leave us out here forever . . . like that goddamn Flying Dutchman."

The Rock quit the chartroom and resumed his measured pacing. There were, he knew, moments when men as savagely kinetic as Eddington had to flare up. Perhaps this was their safety valve. Certainly it was something born into them. Between such outbursts, however, they were like heavy-duty machines, to be utilized for all manner of brutal jobs. Torrey was aware that this unsubtle difference between himself and Eddington contributed in large measure to a comradeship which appeared so unlikely when viewed from the surface. Although they were almost the same age, he felt paternal, or at least avuncular, toward his impetuous exec; and he was inclined to protect him when Eddington's tongue and temper brought him afoul of the High Brass.

For one thing, there was the exec's unquestioned courage, exemplified by a commendation ribbon for cool-headedness during the *Shenandoah* disaster in '25, when he'd helped parachute the shattered dirigible's hull section to earth, thereby saving most of the crew. Eddington was just thirty that year and already marked as a comer.

Torrey, who looked upon his own Navy Cross as the purest of flukes, signifying nothing, often speculated on how he would react under similar conditions of extreme peril, and reminded himself that one could dismiss a lot of the man's roughness and overzealousness in favor of his proven bravery. Given more time and proper seasoning, Eddington would become a worthy chief of staff to some admiral who lacked those qualities that he possessed in such generous amounts—dash and color—and which, The Rock conceded, were among his own probable deficiencies.

Whereas Torrey was an *inward* man, Eddington faced defiantly *outward*. It may have been inevitable that such a paradoxical friendship would grow during a period when The Rock was discovering for the first time that a man must live with himself, as well as within himself. What Torrey had failed to realize, in the earlier formative phases of his career, as he strove to fashion himself into an apparatus geared solely to the business of command, was that this could also lead to a drying-out of the human juices—a monkishness that might defeat the very thing he sought. Mechanical perfection was not enough.

And yet, in those far-off days when he was still striving for his third stripe, The Rock occasionally found himself envying the easy charm of certain less dedicated though more popular officers, which didn't seem to impede their advancement. But he would have denied that he led a life of quiet desperation, like Thoreau, or that he was indifferent to the world around him. He savored exquisite sunsets and dawns which could only be observed from a ship's bridge; and the sight of a sudden rainsquall marching toward him across green billows, or the rainbow that came afterward, gave him a deep, solemn, inexpressible sense of pleasure.

The first week after he took command of *Old Swayback,* Torrey bought a small motion-picture camera to record these gratifying phenomena. He had thousands of feet of color film showing opalescent twilights against Mauna Loa's smoky hulk, scarlet suns drowning in lonesome seas, and the unblemished white arch of tradewind cloud banks that dwarfed the Pacific itself. But he never bothered to look at his handiwork when it came back from the mainland processors. He was quite content to know that these scenes could be relived if he so desired.

By 1400 the raggle-taggle fugitives from Pearl Harbor were assembled far beyond Oahu, and the worst that Torrey had feared became depressingly evident: *Old Swayback* was the undisputed heavyweight of that meager battle line. Beside her steamed three light cruisers, five destroyers that had joined *Cassiday,* and his original pair of minesweepers. None of the cruisers carried radar. Their scout-plane catapults were empty.

So now, instead of one bat-blinded ship, there were twelve.

What could they bring to bear against the enemy, The Rock asked himself, even assuming they were lucky enough to intercept the Japs in this ocean wilderness? What was their total firepower? He made a rapid calculation. There were *Old Swayback*'s own eight-inch rifles, nine of them; the smaller cruisers' forty-five six-inch guns; and the combined flotilla's fifty-six five-inchers. Add seventy-two torpedo tubes mounted in the destroyers. Finish off with the four-pipers' eight four-inch popguns. That was that!

Encountering the Japs with this insignificant assemblage would be like thrusting one's head deliberately under a guillotine, just to test the blade's sharpness; yet it had to be done. Maybe the tincans could manage a fast torpedo run, and perhaps the cruisers could get off a few rounds from their inadequate main batteries at the enemy battleships before the ax fell. But he wouldn't bet on it.

Torrey stopped calculating.

In military doctrine, certain men and machines must be sacrificed for some all-important objective. Considered academically, and far from a fighting front, this had a noble ring to it. But the present circumstances weren't at all like those which theorists propounded in textbooks, because now the dubious goal seemed hardly worth the cost. The Rock shut his mind to the various alternatives, all of them highly unpleasant, that lay somewhere over the smoky horizon. If there was any comfort whatever in their plight, it came from the rather guilty knowledge that some admiral in one of those newly arrived ships, and not Rockwell Torrey, had the responsibility for making the cold decision which might destroy the lot of them: twelve steel ships and sixty-five hundred exceedingly mortal men.

But even this was shortlived.

Using blinker lights rather than telltale voice radio, the squadron held a hasty round-robin conference which elicited the melancholy fact that none of the latecoming cruisers was entitled to fly a two-starred admiral's flag. Hence the senior captain must automatically assume command.

Torrey, Annapolis '14, knew without consulting the precedence list that he superseded *Brockton*'s Joe Gayley, '15, *Eureka*'s Mike Hammersmith, '16, and *Penobscot*'s Cary Peterson, '17.

Wearily, yet with a pride that superseded the mingled shame and relief he had experienced in anticipation of taking orders from somebody else, he directed a message simultaneously to his three companions: "AM ASSUMING TASK GROUP COMMAND AT 1420 THIS DATE. SET NORMAL CRUISING DISPOSITION WITH FLAGSHIP AS GUIDE. COURSE 010. SPEED 25. GOOD LUCK AND GOOD HUNTING."

After he appended the traditional Navy Godspeed to his brief dispatch, The Rock leaned back in the high swivel chair alongside the wheel, feeling deep inside himself an unaccustomed warmth that couldn't have arisen from simple pride. It was something different, something he had never really felt before, which linked him irrevocably to his own shipmates and to those others in the gray-steel vessels that were now racing to form a tight circle in obedience to *his* orders.

CinCPAC had not forgotten Torrey's Task Group. But he had, in the press of more urgent business, delayed issuing the commands that would give purpose to this remnant of his Fleet, or to others scattered from the Aleutians to Pago Pago, and the West Coast to the Philippines.

Eventually The Word came.

"PROCEED AT MAXIMUM SPEED TO LATITUDE 18 DEGREES 10 MINUTES NORTH, LONGITUDE 162 DEGREES 3 MINUTES WEST WHERE YOU WILL REPORT TO COMTASKFORCE ABLE FOR OPERATIONS AGAINST ENEMY RETIRING TOWARD JALUIT IN THE MARSHALLS."

Torrey took the message into the chartroom.

With his dividers, Bobby Burke stepped off the distance they must cover to join the fast carrier squadron which was now driving northwestward at full speed, after having abandoned some inconsequential peacetime mission in Samoan waters. The Rock inspected the pencil dot that his navigator had placed so neatly on the chart, to represent their rendezvous, and he realized it presaged at least three hundred miles of hullbanging travel, more south than west from their present position—eleven bloody hours of it.

"An exercise in futility," he growled to nobody in particular.

Eddington diplomatically kept silent.

Despite a deep-seated conviction that the supreme command was wrong, however, Torrey was able to commiserate with CinCPAC's plight. He knew that tired communicators could jot down an erroneous compass heading for a radar fix on the Jap invaders. One's own flyers might glimpse a friendly surface force through a momentary hole in the overcast, then report it as the enemy. Harassed planners could even deduce that the foe must surely have approached from the south, because that's where so many of his planes had orbited before roaring in for the attack.

The Rock understood these things. He also understood that there could be no further debate on the subject, even if *Old Swayback* were permitted to break radio silence, since the Almighty had spoken.

The quadruple furrows across Torrey's forehead deepened. He doffed his goldlaced cap and slowly ran long fingers through his grizzled hair, becoming aware as he did so that his scalp was sweating. This evidence of his carefully concealed nervousness annoyed him, and when he spoke to the signalman his voice was brusquer than usual.

"All right, Flags. Hoist our new course-and-speed signal."

During the long dreary afternoon and throughout the night Torrey's Task Group plunged south-southwest deep into the clockwise equatorial current, holding as close to the thirty knots as its brevet admiral dared in the rising seas.

Two hours before midnight the moon climbed mistily above the horizon and silhouetted the ships against the tumbling murk. The Rock was moved by sudden sympathy for the destroyers that were endeavoring to protect the small force's van, flanks, and rear. On

Old Swayback's careening bridge, pitchblack in the translunar gloom except for blue battle lights, accurate information was minimal. But these escorts had none. Theirs was the blindest obedience of all in this blind game, where Chance got most of the breaks and Logic fared so badly.

At 0200, in a triumph of Burke's navigational skill, they made contact with Task Force ABLE.

As The Rock watched the dark blobs take shape and assemble into augmented formation, his melancholy eased. Now they were a genuine battle array. Instead of twelve they were twenty-three. And they had radar to pierce the gloom. Task Force ABLE's great carrier, her slabsided hull towering out of the night like a mobile fortress, was a comforting sight to Torrey's surface-bound vessels as they set hopeful course for the Marshall Islands, where the Japs, fresh and fat from their easily won victory, presumably were also headed.

But the early-morning hours passed without any sign that the enemy was even in the same ocean.

Seized by a growing desperation that was compounded of many things, none of which he could himself regulate, Task Force ABLE's admiral hurled his search planes into the gray skies shortly after daybreak. His request for fuel reports from each of his ships had brought chilling answers. Only Torrey's group was adequately supplied for a stern chase that might last several more days. ABLE's seven destroyers were riding high and rolling with alarming awkwardness, as their oil bunkers drained emptier.

The Rock had napped for an hour in his emergency cabin, and now, stretching and yawning, he cast a distasteful eye at the morning heavens as they turned into ugly scud after a fleeting instant of auroreal glory. An ancient rhyme came back to him: *Red skies at morning, sailors take warning.* Without being told, since the logistics of the situation were too elementary even for discussion, he comprehended what was in store for *Old Swayback* and her consorts.

Nobody approached where he stood alone on the chill windward side of the bridge, hatless in the stiffening gale. Even Eddington understood that the captain preferred to spend this private moment in yogalike solitude, pondering whatever thoughts creep through a lonely man's mind.

Torrey rubbed a hand across his beard stubble. If he hurried, perhaps he could shave before the pilots returned with their search reports. The therapeutic tang of the straight razor (it would be the Old Man's *Montag* blade) against his tired skin might compensate for his eyeball-stiffening lack of sleep.

One by one, like exhausted homing pigeons, the planes winged back to the carrier, and alighted clumsily on her pitching flight-deck. As soon as they landed, the pilots were hustled to air combat intelligence. But it soon became dismally evident that they'd seen nothing—not even a fishing sampan—although they did report the world's meanest, blackest, ugliest storm front at the nether end of their two-hundred-mile sweep, aimed like a dumdum bullet straight at the depleted ships.

On the Beaufort scale the needle already showed that the wind had reached Force 8—"fresh gale" was the disarming phrase for it— and there was every indication that this would soon develop into Force 11. The admiral winced noticeably at the news. His top-heavy destroyers would be mincemeat for the seventy-mile-an-hour hurricane which this portended.

Fortunately for his peace of mind, the logistical experts at Pearl Harbor made the decision themselves, after plotting his progress, figuring his fuel difficulties, and conceding the fact that they could do nothing constructive about it except fetch him home forthwith, since there were no fast tankers within range of Task Force ABLE.

Addressed both to the carrier and to *Old Swayback,* the orders arrived at five minutes after noon on December 8:

"TASK FORCE ABLE HEREBY DIRECTED TO RETURN TO BASE. TORREY GROUP WILL PROCEED AT BEST POSSIBLE SPEED TOWARD LATITUDE 26 NORTH LONGITUDE 160 WEST WHERE REVISED INFORMATION NOW PLACES ORANGE ATTACKERS. POSSIBILITY EXISTS THEY MAY LAUNCH FOLLOWUP STRIKES ON HAWAIIAN BASES. TORREY GROUP SHOULD PREPARE TO ENGAGE ENEMY ALONE IF REINFORCEMENT PROVES IMPRACTICABLE."

The Rock was back on the bridge, cleanshaven and munching a cold ham-and-egg sandwich, when his communications yeoman brought him the decoded message. His first response was quiet satisfaction that CinCPAC had finally accepted his own estimate of the Japs' launching point. (He could not know, of course, that this "revised" intelligence came from a Nip pilot who had been captured by Polynesian natives after crashing his Zero on a tiny islet off Lanai, west of Oahu.)

Torrey was neither shocked nor surprised at his new orders. They were exactly what he had anticipated ever since Task Force ABLE's fuel crisis arose, and he had reconciled himself to this assignment which was outlined so starkly on a single sheet of tissue. He could even allow himself a frosty smile as he savored the elegant navalese. *If reinforcement proves impracticable.* Translated: *It probably can't be done.* Why? Because back in the steaming muck of Pearl Harbor the thirty-six hours normally required to refuel a task force had been doubled or even trebled. Another element to this "impracticability" was the likelihood that any potential relief for his meager force was scattered from hell-to-breakfast around the Pacific, dispersed on the same sort of wild-goose chases that had sent his own ships so far south of Oahu.

Halsey himself might be halfway to the Philippines by now! Or to the South Pole. It made just about as much good sense.

Torrey swore softly as he eased out of his swivel chair, conscious of the damp-induced stiffness in his leg joints. There was work to be done. Lots of it. *Work,* he chanted silently, *for the night is coming.* Just as the Old Man used to sing in the long evenings when Torrey was a little kid . . .

Even at "best possible speed"—another example of nautical jargon that meant anything or everything—his weatherbeaten ships faced seventeen hours of unmerciful pounding before they could reach the designated hunting area.

The Rock gazed out across *Old Swayback*'s squat main turrets, whose guns were canvas-stoppered against the bursting waves, toward the destroyer that had drawn the lead position. Again it was *Cassiday.* As he watched her laboring against the heavy seas, Torrey estimated his own ships' resources. These six destroyers had been operating at high speed for almost eighteen hours, and when they arrived on target at 0700 tomorrow, their furnaces would damned near be sucking air instead of oil. They could stretch their usefulness for as much as five days by slowing to medium cruising rate, but that wouldn't satisfy CinCPAC's "best possible" dictum, which he had decided to interpret as meaning, *go like hell.* While they crawled north at fifteen knots, the enemy might strike again and escape scot-free. That was the awful, inescapable nub of the problem.

Torrey called to the signalman.

"Tell the group to resume formation at twenty-five knots," he said crisply. "Course 010. We'll take the guide as usual."

A few minutes later Task Force ABLE scattered along the ragged horizon, taking with it his two four-pipers whose fuel supply had also dwindled far below the danger mark. And as the homeward-bound flotilla dropped from sight, Torrey's brother captains in the remaining cruisers manfully sought to provide the necessary words of encouragement.

Out of the depths of their own experience, they could appreciate The Rock's predicament, and they were eager to bolster him now that he had to assume the uncomfortable mantle of temporary command, which can be the worst kind of all.

"GAYLEY TO TORREY," flickered *Brockton*'s signal gun. "YOU FURNISH THE TARGETS AND WE'LL SCORE THE BULLSEYES."

Eureka cut in: "HAMMERSMITH TO TORREY. HOW COME ONLY 25 KNOTS? WE'RE WEARING OUR WASHPROOF PAINT."

And *Penobscot* said: "PETERSON TO TORREY. REFER OLD TESTAMENT FIRST KINGS XVII VERSE 12. PUT QUOTE I UNQUOTE IN LAST WORD AND ALSO REFER VERSE 16 SAME PASSAGE. THAT'S US. AMEN."

Torrey smiled wryly.

Captain Peterson had brought his eight-year-old *Honolulu*-class light cruiser through the Panama Canal only a month earlier, after a tour of Neutrality Patrol duty that threw him into frequent contact with the Royal Navy. The Britons' fondness for salting their dispatches with Biblical gems used to fascinate him, and goad him into striving to match their rather affected cleverness. Good old Cary! Even now, here in this godforsaken corner of watery nowhere, he was still trying.

The Rock summoned the junior officer of the deck.

"Ask the chaplain to step up to the bridge," he said. "And tell him to bring a Bible."

The JOD looked stunned. "Chaplain, sir?"

"Don't worry, Mr. Harrington. We haven't reached the last rites stage, yet. I'll let you know when to dive overboard." He showed him *Penobscot*'s dispatch. "See? After this, young man, I want you to make sure the Good Book sits right alongside the code book—as long as Captain Peterson's around." Lightly, yet aware of his unhumorous double meaning, he added, "We're going to need it."

The chaplain, a diminutive Gael who had spent the morning applying spiritual poultices to scared young egos, was manifestly delighted to be called to the bridge. He made quick work of Captain Peterson's cryptogram, even inserting the required "i," and then he recited the verses in a surprisingly deep booming voice.

"'A handful of meal in a barrel,'" he intoned, "'and a little oil in a cruse'. . . 'And the barrel of meal wasted not, neither did the cruse of oil fail.'"

Torrey rationed himself another of his evanescent smiles, and explained the curious text. The chaplain nodded understandingly.

"Good to have men with us who know their Bible," he said. And as he turned to leave, he asked matter-of-factly, "Now—what can I tell those lads down there that might buck 'em up?"

The Rock seemed surprised. "What's your problem, padre?"

"Well—" The wizened Irishman considered his reply carefully—"we've got quite a lot of freshcaught kids on our hands, sir. Seventeen-year-olds, some of them. Maybe a kind of claustrophobia seizes the ones who have to stay buttoned-up all day belowdecks. Or maybe there's such a thing as 'precombat fatigue.' Who knows? But this I'm positive of—they need reassurance after the last thirty hours."

Torrey motioned the chaplain to the far side of the starboard bridgewing, out of the searing wind and beyond earshot of the patently inquisitive afternoon watch standers.

"I wish to heaven," he said, "that I could reassure them, padre. But I can't. Because, frankly, if you'll pardon the profanity, we're in a hell of a spot. I don't know what's going to happen. Nobody does. Except God . . . maybe."

The chaplain asked quietly, "How'd you rate *Old Swayback*'s chances, captain?"

"That depends on whether our luck's good or bad. On how smart we are if a showdown comes. On your Man Upstairs, padre . . . let's say the odds are one-in-fifty if *we* find the Japs. One-in-a-hundred if *they* find us." Torrey looked reflectively across the gray seascape. "And if you were a betting man, I'd give you two-to-one the enemy spots us first."

The chaplain's shrewd Gaelic face was very wise as he observed gently, "Don't you take a certain solace from your understanding of a situation, captain, even when it's as desperate as this one? And some comfort in your own ability to do what has to be done? Those lads fear *unknown* things." He spread his small hands in a placative gesture. "Surely you recall, as a boy, all those terrors that lurked in the dark attic?"

Torrey was silent, thinking, for this wasn't the sort of dread he had felt as a child; rather, it had always been a gnawing fear that he wouldn't measure up to the challenge when confronted by this *unknown* of which the padre spoke.

The chaplain's rich voice went on, as if he hadn't expected any answer, but was simply ruminating aloud.

"Sometimes you wonder at what point a fellow's worry becomes outright fear . . . when his emotions might edge across the line into panic . . . and you wonder how in God's Name you can prevent it."

"What's your prescription, padre?"

"I give 'em autographed Bibles." The chaplain grinned. "They're inclined to confuse me with the Lord Almighty, sometimes, and even the Gideons themselves couldn't have kept up with the demand today. I also remind them that right now they're men—*fighting men!*"

" 'England,' " The Rock quoted ironically, " 'expects every man to do his duty.' "

"Precisely."

The little chaplain's words reawakened the disturbing thoughts that had troubled Torrey during his morning colloquy with Eddington and Bobby Burke. Almost unwillingly, he again found himself balancing something he deemed strong against something else that was soft. Stern and unflinching, you had to set an example. You must be resolute. You personified strength. After that the others would follow where you led.

From the brass bell below the bridge came the four clangs that signified 1400, and the double-spaced notes seemed to be striking in his own perplexed soul.

Torrey halted the departing chaplain.

"Padre . . ."

"Yes, captain?"

"Wait. I'm coming with you."

As *Old Swayback* drove north with her task group, two-thirds of her crew manned their action stations, while the remainder waited belowdecks in varying degrees of impatience, weariness, or apprehension for the signal that would send them back to duty. Gas masks hung in coconutlike clusters from overhead hooks, to be grabbed and donned on the dead run. Unlimbered firehoses snaked along the dimlit passageways. The handrails that made climbing the steep ladders reasonably simple even in rough weather had been removed so watertight hatches could be slammed shut at the first *onk-onk* of the General Quarters klaxon.

Methodically, determined not to omit the smallest interstices where men or machines were at work, Torrey stalked through his battle-ready command, with the chaplain trotting along beside him, sweating and grinning, like a peasant escorting his king around an especially well-kept royal preserve.

He began his inspection tour on the second deck, near the great curved bulk of Number 1 turret's barbette, and made his way aft through shell stowage and powder handling rooms filled with enough explosives to blow the cruiser into bits if an enemy torpedo ever pierced her thin skin at this waterline point; through the Marines' tight and stuffy quarters; through murderously hot drying rooms above the cruiser's furnaces; past the galleys where the soup kettle bubbled for men returning from frigid topside watches; through messrooms that served as off-duty gathering places for the dog-tired, yet sleepless, members of the crew; and finally into the ship's service canteen.

A trio of beardless seamen-seconds were moodily dawdling at paper cups full of ice cream and chocolate syrup, silent and morose, with their redrimmed eyes fixed on some uninspiring vista in the middle distance of the compartment. They looked appallingly young as they squatted against a wire screen that safeguarded small stores against random pilferage.

The Rock paused beside them, and pointed at the cups.

"What do you fellows call that stuff?"

The seamen scrambled to their stockinged feet. There was a painful moment of tongue-tied speechlessness before the tallest youth could respond.

"They're called *gedunks,* sir."

An unaccustomed wave of sympathy for the embarrassed boys seized Torrey.

"Let's have a couple of *gedunks* ourselves, padre. They look interesting."

As Torrey toyed with his sundae, repelled by its sweetness, he studied the three boys solemnly, and noted that the oldest seaman wore a tattooed eagle on his skinny forearm just under the tattered fringe of his dungaree jacket sleeve. In the eagle's beak was a ribbon that proclaimed, "For God and Country!"

"That's a mighty noble sentiment, son," The Rock said mildly. "But I'd recommend against any more tattoos."

"Why, sir?" the boy quavered.

"Because when you get to be an officer it might prove a little embarrassing." Torrey bared his own right arm. "Look!"

They gaped at the tiny fouled anchor that was etched in faded purple ink below his deltoid muscle.

"I had it put there during my youngster cruise to Havana in '12," he explained, "and I've regretted it ever since. Worse than a vaccination scar on a chorus girl's thigh."

With their discovery that the captain was made of ordinary flesh and blood, and tattooable like anybody else, their stricken awe began to ease, and so did their earlier fears. Hell. If the Old Man could leave the bridge and come down to this oppressive steam-heated hole, and even gobble a *gedunk,* maybe things weren't as desperate as they'd seemed a little while ago, when the carrier force haul-assed and left them to the mercy of the Japs . . .

Now the captain was talking again in that rumbling Dutch uncle voice of his, and asking the boy named Marty what his battle station was.

"It's the 40-millimeter quad, sir. You know. The one on top of Number 2 turret."

"Are you a gun pointer?"

"Not yet, sir. Just a loader. But I'm workin' toward pointer. Sometimes they let me practice."

"Good man!"

Torrey remembered seeing this boy, and nine others like him, crouching in the inadequate shelter of the waist-high steel tub which surrounded the four-barreled Bofors, where they caught the full brunt of the icy waves that crashed aft when the cruiser thrust her nose into the gale-swept seas. For them there was no shelter, as on the bridge, where a man could step into the decked-over pilothouse. Before their four-hour watch ended, they were half-drowned and almost frozen.

"Rugged duty," The Rock acknowledged, setting down his *gedunk* preparatory to resuming his interrupted tour. He hoped they wouldn't notice that he had not been able to finish it. "I'm glad you fellows can relax off-watch. Means your nerves are pretty steady." He passed a last critical glance over the nondescript threesome in their non-reg garb. "That's a good sign. Because we've got one hell of a job ahead of us."

"Count on us, sir," Marty said stoutly. "Our quad crew handloads and fires damn near two hundred rounds a minute—and the manual only calls for a hundred and sixty!"

After the captain and the chaplain left, The Word spread rapidly through *Old Swayback*, like gossip in a crowded tenement, about how the Old Man had eaten a *gedunk* with Marty, Joe, and Hank, and how he wore a big tattoo on his shoulder. What kind? Why, a mothernaked babe, that's what kind, who wiggled her fanny every time the everlovin' Rock flexed his biceps.

The chief petty officers, whose supersensitive antennae can detect the minutest details of shipboard life, were owlishly anticipating The Rock's arrival in their quarters above the cruiser's four great screws. He found them sedately drinking black coffee and listening to a shortwave broadcast.

Above the staticky tumult of the radio, which was having reception trouble because of the storm, the chaplain asked genially, "What's the latest news, gentlemen?"

A sweat-rimed chief machinist's mate, unabashed at the grease that matted the hair on his bare chest, rumbled, "Near's we can figure out through this friggin' static—pardon sir!—old F.D.R.'s gonna talk pretty soon. From Washington, D.C."

The gibbering of the radio mingled oddly with the heavy thrum-thrum of the propellers spinning only twenty feet below the steel deck where they stood. As Torrey listened, he thought of the President—an ineffably lonesome man wearing steel braces on his crippled legs—who was at this very instant tiredly studying his penciled notes and watching the creeping hands of the clock, and probably wondering how the shocked country would react to his words.

The Rock felt a curious identification with that fatigued and immobilized man, whose only higher authority was God Himself. Whatever Mr. Roosevelt said in those next few minutes must somehow calm the apprehensions of millions of people who'd be listening to him in their snug little parlors, in beersmelling saloons, in their automobiles, in crowded Army barracks, and on the high seas.

Torrey hoped it would be good.

He turned to the chaplain.

"Padre, ring up radio central and ask whether they can't bring this thing in any clearer. Have 'em hook up the intercom loudspeaker. I've got a feeling the whole ship ought to hear what the President has to say . . ."

Clustered in small groups, from fighting top to firerooms, the cruiser's 1,267 officers and men listened to the grave, mellow resonant voice.

"Yesterday, December 7, 1941—a date that will live in infamy—the United States of America was suddenly and deliberately attacked by naval and air forces of the Empire of Japan . . ."

There were uneasy stirrings as they learned of the enemy's perfidy in talking peace while he was plotting war. Mutterings when the President told how Oahu had been bombed barely an hour before the Japanese ambassador conferred with the Secretary of State.

". . . No matter how long it may take us to overcome this premeditated invasion, the American people in their righteous might will win through to absolute victory," the eloquent voice went on, concluding: *"I ask that the Congress declare that since the unprovoked and dastardly attack . . . a state of war has existed between the United States and the Japanese Empire."*

In the CPO's compartment the taut silence was shattered by a chief gunner's mate.

"Goddamn it!" he exulted. "Now we can sink the sons of bitches —legal!"

5. *Toward a Certain Gethsemane*

ALL THAT WANING DAY, as the afternoon watch merged sullenly into the evening dogwatch, Torrey's Task Group pressed northward toward the Kauai Channel, battling to maintain its constant course despite savage crosswinds that whipped up a quartering sea.

The Rock's dourest expectations about the weather came true shortly after dinner, which he took piecemeal in his emergency cabin, just as darkness threw a strangler's blanket across the face of the small squadron. The gale had indeed howled past Force 10 on the Beaufort scale. In the driving murk the ten ships lost all visual contact with each other, and the formation soon broke into isolated units, each locked in singlehanded combat with the storm.

Torrey was able to transmit only one brief order to *Old Swayback*'s consorts before they disappeared: "TASK GROUP PREPARE FOR NIGHT ENGAGEMENT. PRESENT COURSE SHOULD BRING US WITHIN ENEMY RANGE AT APPROXIMATELY 0600 PROVIDED PRESENT RATE OF ADVANCE IS MAINTAINED. PLACE DOUBLE WATCH ON ALL SKY LOOKOUTS. DESTROYERS KEEP TORPEDOES AND DEPTH CHARGES ARMED. CRUISERS MAN MAIN BATTERIES. GODSPEED. TORREY."

At first his captains were glad that the darkness would conceal their outnumbered flotilla. Always assuming they saw the enemy first, they might demoralize him by a savage attack before he became aware of their real impotence. Officers solemnly discussed this longshot tactic in their wardrooms. Less informed, but far more inclined to pile rumor upon rumor, the crews freely predicted they'd beat the living bejesus out of the Nips before daybreak. Didn't two of the light cruisers flaunt gunnery E's on their stacks—inside, of course, where prying strangers couldn't see 'em, but there nevertheless—for bracketing targets at 25,000 yards? Hell. You don't win trophies by shagging potatoes at beer cans!

But luck wasn't with them. They were, as Eddington observed sourly, screwed from the very start.

Before the first watch was sixty minutes old, with three more hours remaining till midnight, all hope of reaching their destination on schedule vanished in mountainous seas and banshee winds. As an elementary precaution against losing men overboard, or having them maimed against stanchions and bulkheads, the captains withdrew their skywatchers and sent their gun crews below.

Maintaining battle readiness was impossible, unthinkable, in that howling chaos.

Felt rather than observed from *Cassiday*'s crazily pitching bridge, the storm was something animate, to be fought blindfolded in a darkened room. It leaped at the destroyer, wildroaring and barefanged, leaving her precariously balanced in the trough of alpine waves whose crumbling crests bore down with the crushing force of an avalanche. Forward progress slowed from the assigned twenty-five knots to less than nothing, and *Cassiday* slithered sidewise like a frightened crab during the heartstopping moment when her twin-screws flailed empty air.

She strove to stay alive. That was all.

Gripping the captain's swivel chair to keep from being flung against the pilothouse, Mac stared vengefully out into the night, while Ishmael Quoddy conned the tormented ship. The chief quartermaster refused to relinquish the wheel, even for coffee, and now it seemed welded to his clenched fists as he fought to hold *Cassiday* on some semblance of course. Quoddy's eyes flickered between the dimly illumined binnacle, which was the only light on the heaving bridge, and the gyro-repeater that gave an approximation of their everchanging speed. Any other instrument had to be sought out gropingly in the darkness: voice tubes, TBS radiophone, intercom mikes, Verey flares to signal a torpedo attack if zero hour ever came, emergency light switches, and even the buzzer that fetched the bedraggled messboy with more jamoke.

Mac said nothing because there was nothing to say. You simply acted when some desperate need arose. Otherwise you kept silent, waiting and hoping.

Unless, of course, you were Ishmael Quoddy. Then you unbuttoned your taciturn lips and yowled back at the elements, soundless as a figure in an old silent movie, for in that din not even Beelzebub himself could hear a mere man yell. This is how Ahab would have driven the *Pequod*. Right into the teeth of the hurricane.

When dawn finally came, evil and dirty, *Cassiday's* log reported triumphantly that they had "held steady on 010 from midnight until 0600," barring a few detours that even Quoddy couldn't avoid. But the storm's back was broken. Like stray lambs chivvied by an invisible sheepdog, Torrey's scattered group returned to normal cruising order, and on each of the bruised ships life began to quicken again as men appeared on the deserted decks, and guns that had been depressed against the gale returned their muzzles skyward.

"Chow time, Mister McConnel."

Wakened from an uneasy stand-up dream by the quartermaster's hoarse voice, Mac looked at his watch.

"Could use bre'fast. Coffee. 'Specially some goddamn hot black jamoke."

"I'll stand by," the quartermaster said, "till you get back."

"How long have you had the wheel, chief?"

"Goin' on ten hours."

"Jesus!" Mac regarded him doubtfully. "Sure you're all right? We could put one of the kids to work . . ."

"Not them." Ishmael Quoddy heaped scorn on his absent helpers. "They're not ready for this—yet. I'm good for another thirty minutes, lieutenant. Ask 'em to send up a mug of java, that's all. But hot as the muckin' hinges."

"All right."

When Mac started for the ladder, he found that his legs had unaccountably turned to rubber, incapable of supporting him, and for a panicky second he clung to the bridgerail.

"Rub 'em," Quoddy suggested. "Maybe they're just froze."

"They're asleep," Mac said bitterly.

Tom-Tom Agar and Poet Cline were already seated in the wardroom, trying to eat from plates that threatened to leap off the table despite the foulweather racks which were supposed to anchor them securely, but never did.

Mac eased himself painfully into a chair and ordered coffee. Now that the immediate emergency was passed, he felt marrowchilled and numb, like a man coming out of shock. Vaguely surprised, he noticed that his right hand was shaking as he lifted the thick porcelain mug, so he reinforced it with his left. He inhaled deeply the fumes of the chicory-laced brew, savoring its hot aroma, before he joined the desultory morning-after conversation.

Poet was moodily prodding at a grayish mound on his plate, trying without much success to spear bits of something with his fork.

"What's that?" Mac asked.

"De-bloody-hydrated eggs," Poet rolled his longlashed eyes dramatically. *"O perfidious Albumin!"*

Mac ignored the pun. "What's your beef—aren't you as comfy and dry as a pampered poodle? Also alive?"

"Have you seen the color of that stinking ocean?"

"I don't have to see it, Shakespeare. For the past six hours I've been breathing the stuff."

The communicator yawned elaborately. "At a moment like this one is reminded of James Joyce's description of the Irish Sea, lieutenant. 'Snot green.' That's what the goddamn ocean is. Nose-picked by an eyeless dawn . . ."

"Where's Bulldog?" Mac asked.

"Dan'l Boone grabbed a fast bite earlier," Tom-Tom said, "so he could get back to listening for Jap subs."

"In this weather?"

"Hell, yes," the engineer said disgustedly. "The silly bastard stayed with his soundgear all night, even after I told him the sonar couldn't pick up the *Queen Mary* at a hundred yards when we're turning up twenty-five knots in heavy seas. But he insisted."

"Dedicated type, Balch."

Mac took up a cigar lighter that had been tooled from a 40-millimeter shellcasing and ignited one of the absent commodore's green Havanas. There was more sympathy in his face as he turned to Poet.

"How goes the outside world?"

"Godawful." The communicator riffled through a pile of flimsies. "Japs bombed Wake again this morning. Killed fifty-five civilians in a hospital. Charming fellows. And now they're about to invade Guam . . . also the Philippines and Malaya."

Mac grimaced. As he viewed their plight in the midst of a combat theater dominated by the enemy, he could discern no bright spots at all, and when it was narrowed down to *Cassiday*'s own predicament, the situation seemed especially bleak.

"What's our fuel reading?"

Tom-Tom picked at a loose button on his dungaree jacket.

"Lower'n a snake's belly, Mac. Last night drained a hell of a lot out of us. At this rate we'll be bonedry in another eight hours or so."

"Has Captain Torrey requested a report?"

"Not lately. Probably afraid to ask."

Mac demurred. "Not him!" he said, remembering how The Rock had hammered into the plebes' thick skulls an uncompromising creed which required clinical analysis of all the facts that bore on any problem, no matter how distasteful they might be. Torrey wouldn't gloss over their fuel crisis. No. He knew already. Plainly, however, he was resolved to carry out his orders even if it meant hoisting bedsheets for sails.

When Mac last checked *Cassiday*'s position on the watersoaked chart in the pilothouse, they were still one hundred miles short of their goal because of the storm. Ahead of them lay some tricky maneuvering past French Frigate Shoal and into the seas beyond the surfbreaking coral heads which marked the outer reaches of the Hawaiian chain.

Ahead, too, should lie the Japs.

Mac blotted his saltcracked lips with a napkin, and winced at the sandpapery sound and feel of the linen against his two-day-old beard.

"I'm going back topside," he said. "Quoddy's holding down the fort alone. Keep the jamoke flowing. It's getting goddamn tough just to stay awake."

"Better string some lifelines," Tom-Tom said forebodingly. "With our fuel set-up, this tincan's going to start rolling like a fandancer's arse any minute."

"Will do."

Despite the liberal use of aluminum in her upperworks, *Cassiday* was a top-heavy creature once her ballasting oil ran low, for her beam was scarcely one-tenth her slim length. Standing unsupported on the bridge at such times was like trying to balance upright in a pitching hammock. Five-inch guns traced crazy arcs across the sky as the inclinometer needle swung wildly past sixty degrees. From the dipping bridgewing you watched the greasy ocean rising toward you as the ship heeled over in the trough of a swell, hang there for a breathless eternity, and then fall sickeningly away, until only the tattered sky itself was visible.

Idiotically, Mac recalled one of Commander Bowen's longwinded yarns about a four-piper that held the Asiatic squadron's unenviable record for this chancy sport. She'd survived a seventy-five degree roll. But later, trying for eighty, the luckless tincan turned turtle and sank with all hands. Mac tried to erase the garrulous commodore's tale from his fatigued mind.

Maybe it never happened anyhow . . .

At 0940 the sun struggled through the low overcast. The flat monochromatic light was in drab harmony with the increasingly gray spirits of the officers who commanded the ten ships of Torrey's Task Group. There was no longer any profit, even for "morale purposes," in deluding themselves as they waited for The Rock, whose stubbornness far outweighed theirs, to admit his mission had failed. Hell. Nobody could blame him for not achieving the unachievable—not even CinCPAC himself, who'd handed him this assignment. Privately and separately, they decided that CinCPAC should be bloody well glad that Torrey's Task Group *hadn't* stumbled across the Nips. At least now he would get back unscathed a nice little flotilla which might otherwise have been resting three thousand fathoms deep somewhere north of the Tropic of Cancer.

Mac reached this conclusion as he tried to focus his leaden eyes simultaneously upon the jittery seamen who had relieved Ishmael Quoddy, on the binnacle card, on his flanking destroyers, and on the ironhued surface of the sea ahead where at any moment a feathery white flicker might become an enemy periscope wake. Pearl Harbor had warned that these waters were teeming with Jap I-boats, gigantic fleet-type submarines that displaced almost two thousand tons and sometimes even carried small scout planes on their decks.

A haphazard paragraph of journalese he'd seen in a Honolulu paper popped into his mind:

The sheriff's posse was advised to take no chance with the killer who is presumed to be armed and therefore dangerous . . .

An hour later, aware of the calculated risk, The Rock ordered his force to quit zigzagging. Although resuming their arrow-straight course would stretch their depleted fuel supplies, it would also increase the everpresent peril from subs. But this was a danger he was willing to accept if it meant prolonging the chase for an hour or two more, since even the experts were sharply divided on the efficacy of zigzagging. Certainly it was book-doctrine. Yet the convoys that had been plowing crooked furrows across the North Atlantic for months, in hopes of baffling the Nazi wolfpacks, were getting regularly clobbered in spite of the tacticians' fanciest footwork. So who could judge what was right and what was wrong in this instance—especially when it was also conceded that the most skillful *zig* in the world was nullified if your next *zag* carried you right into a waiting sub's torpedo sights?

Torrey had concluded his message by declaring: "SITUATION DEMANDS RENEWED VIGILANCE BY LITTLE BOYS AGAINST HOSTILE SUBMARINES PRESUMED IN AREA."

In the superheated room beneath the paperthin forecastle deck, Bulldog Balch was admiring the preoccupied genius who managed *Cassiday*'s sonar gear.

The soundman, who was barely five-foot-four, was known as "Kreisler," because he had been studying to become a concert violinist when the Navy grabbed him just ahead of the Army draft. Now the nickname had a more practical meaning. His remarkable ears could differentiate between a whale's *ping* and the noise made when an electronic echo bounced off a U-boat's submerged hull, just as a virtuoso could distinguish between the velvet music of a Stradivarius and the cacophony of a bargain-basement violin. Kreisler's tiny head was lost between rubber-covered earphones which left only his face free, and he didn't seem to mind the temperature of the crowded compartment which had forced Bulldog to strip down to his skivvies.

Both men kept their eyes fixed upon a translucent glass plate around which raced a thin band of light, alert for the brighter pinprick within this speeding beam that would signify a contact—fish, sub, or perhaps only an unusually highcresting wave—and give its range from *Cassiday*.

Bulldog also had to catalogue the position of the eight blips rearrange this will-o'-the-wisp pattern on the circular panel whenever the bridge phoned a course change.
that represented the other ships in their formation, and mentally

Torrey's Task Group made the soundmen's work more difficult

by adding the element of speed to the rest of the imponderables which cut down the system's reliability. Even the density of the ocean itself, a whimsical condition dependent on temperature and salinity, could confound the apparatus, despite all its delicate dials and probing sonic moans.

By noon the exhausted crew's struggle to stay awake had become a battle for sanity. Not even the cold-douche excitement of a false alarm broke the boredom of the task group's passage northward. Lackluster skies were barren of planes. Flintgray seas unreeled endlessly ahead, alongside and astern, like an amiably banal film whose very innocence assures its tedium.

Balch, who was feeling the strain like any other mere mortal, ground a fist into his grainy eyelids, and stared unbelievingly at Kreisler. The mousy little soundman was manipulating the knobs and wheels of his complex apparatus as if he'd just arrived on duty, instead of having sat chained to his straight-backed chair since midnight. His only evidence of fatigue was a loud adenoidal breathing. And maybe, the gunnery officer told himself, that didn't indicate tiredness at all; maybe *Cassiday*'s sonic dome had picked up some particularly exotic echo and piped it to Kreisler's batlike ears, thereby quickening his respiratory tempo. It was a hell of a note, Bulldog brooded, matching stamina with a man half your size.

He rose heavily to his sneakershod feet, ducking slightly to avoid a transverse beam, and stood for a moment in the exact center of the small room, scratching his sweaty chest.

Then he shouted toward Kreisler's muffled ears, "I'm going back to my popguns. Can't make any money here!"

The soundman didn't reply. But his breath was coming even more rapidly now, and he seemed completely oblivious to the gunnery officer's presence as he listened to the occult noises that came to him from the outside waters.

Bulldog glanced at the sonar screen, counting the little blips that flickered briefly in the wake of the spinning lightband.

Now there were ten!

The alien pip dimmed, then sparked up brightly when the beam caught it again. Bulldog hastily computed its position—directly off the task group's vulnerable starboard bow.

"For Christ's sake, Kriesler, what *is* it?"

The soundman eased aside a foamrubber earphone.

"Feels like a sub," he said judiciously. "But you never can tell. Might be a killer whale. They're pretty damn big."

Bulldog grabbed for the intercom mike.

"Until it spouts, we'll treat it like a sub!" he yelled. Then: "Bridge? This is Balch. We've picked up a strong contact. Bearing five degrees to starboard at sixty-five hundred yards. Closing fast!"

Mac's voice said, "Kee-rist!"

"Hold everything, skipper," Bulldog added, "I'm coming right up." To Kreisler: "Keep feeding the range to the bridge, champ."

"Damn tootin'!" The soundman showed his yellow teeth in a wispy grin. "That's what we're in business for. And if it's a sub, Mister Balch, murder the c——"

But his epithet was lost in the rising siren whine of *Cassiday*'s engineroom blowers.

Before Bulldog reached the bridge, the destroyer had stepped nimbly from her twenty-five-knot cruising speed to her ultimate thirty-six. The "SUBMARINE CONTACT" hoist, already whipping in the stiff breeze, was followed immediately by "WE ARE ATTACKING" as he scrambled to the depth-charge control station.

At this breakneck pace, they should close the enemy in less than five minutes.

Torrey observed *Cassiday*'s abrupt departure from the formation, even before he caught her frantic signal, and he frowned. Although he was willing to concede the destroyermen understood their trade, and thus were simply executing their duty, this unwelcome diversion was like everything else that had happened during the past fifty-odd hours: deplorably ill-timed and probably just as ill-fortuned.

The Rock had—at that exact instant—decided to abandon the futile quest and set course for Pearl Harbor.

It was 1300. By now even CinCPAC must appreciate their plight (doesn't God know when the lowliest sparrow falleth?) and recognize that they would pass the point of no return in a few more minutes. Obviously there'd be no reinforcements. Their one prospect of refueling, too, had gone glimmering when a commercial tanker hove into sight on the northwestern horizon, pulled close, and then showed her red Plimsoll mark, high and dry, as she hurried southward to safety. She was bone empty.

Heavyhearted, but resigned, Torrey had prepared the order: "CHANGE COURSE TO 110 SPEED 17. RESUME ZIGZAG."

But now because of this annoying new development, the varicolored pennants of the unsent signal lay strewn across the flagbag like Christmas cards that would never be mailed. Instead, *Old Swayback*'s halyards blossomed with curt instructions to the two destroyers on the starboard flank: "ASSIST CASSIDAY IN SUB HUNT."

With graceful, wheeling motions that would have delighted a Nijinsky, they veered away from the formation and raced after their sister ship, speedboat wakes piled high and snowy against the ashen sea. Far astern, the four cruisers and their three remaining escorts slowly fanned out into a better defensive posture.

The Rock appended "RESUME ZIGZAG" to the flagship's hoist, telling himself ironically as he did so that at least one-third of his original signal had been effected.

There was no warning tracery across the tumbled surface of the sea.

There was simply an eardrum-shattering, world-ending thunderclap as the torpedo penetrated *Old Swayback*'s lower forecastle, boring through her five-inch armorplate as easily as a rifle bullet pierces a cheese, and exploding somewhere deep inside her.

Thrown flat on his back by the blast, dazed and hurt, Torrey stared up at a dirtywhite pillar that seemed to hang motionless above the cruiser's bridge. Then the strange tower collapsed in his face, and he was shocked into full consciousness by an avalanche of icy water that inundated the chesthigh bridgewing. He floundered to his feet, coughing to free his choked lungs, dimly aware that his right arm hung uselessly at his side. It must have been broken, he thought, when he was tossed against the steel deck . . .

Eddington sloshed through the flood to The Rock's side. He was limping. Later he discovered that both his ankles had been sprained as the ship's deck fell away under the torpedo blast, then rocketed upward with murderous velocity. He also learned he was lucky. Four men had their legs broken although they were topside and far away from the point of impact.

"You okay, skipper?"

Torrey gripped the rail with his left hand, ignoring the exec's solicitous question, and sought vainly to pierce the mustard smoke cloud that billowed out of *Old Swayback*'s ruptured deckplates. When he spoke, his voice didn't sound like his own. It came from a huge distance.

"Ask damage control where we took the fish."

But as the exec moved toward the bridge phone, a second blast shook the cruiser, and she staggered like a dumdummed elephant.

Torrey felt the cold, bitter, frustrate, almost unbelieving anger that sailors have experienced since primitive man launched the first hollow log, when their ship is mortally hurt—crushed against some uncharted reef, shattered by an unexpected hurricane, or wounded by an unseen assassin. He saw the crew of the 40-millimeter quad atop Number 2 turret struggling to train their barrels to starboard, where the attack must have originated. One of the men hadn't gotten up. Oddly twisted, he lay quite still, as if his spine were broken or he were dead. He was both.

And then The Rock knew that the corpse wasn't that of a man at all, but a skinny kid with "For God and Country" tattooed on his right forearm.

To Torrey's trained ear, this new explosion had a far more sinister and meaningful sound than the first. It rattled *Old Swayback*'s brittle steel bones to their electrically wired marrow, although she continued to plunge ahead, as if she were the victim of some frightful practical joke and determined not to show her agony. It came from deep amidships, from the intricate propulsion system that was the cruiser's very blood-pumping heart. He kneaded his broken arm, which had begun to throb savagely and focused with a conscious effort upon *Cassiday* and her twin helpers. Far ahead off the port bow they were laying down a relentless depth-charge pattern that turned the ocean surface into a sprouting forest of little white trees. Deepmuffled, the clump-clump-clump of the underwater detonations drifted back toward the cruisers.

Although it was bitter consolation, he knew whoever torpedoed *Old Swayback* would never live through that blanket barrage to murder another ship.

Torrey swung away from the rail as Eddington reappeared through the pilothouse door. The exec's crooked face was grim.

"Goddamn phones are dead," he growled. "Can't reach central damage control. Everything's dead. I'm going below to check."

"All right. Send a messenger back as soon as you've located the main problem . . . and judged how bad it is."

Eddington nodded.

For an instant, forgetting the pain that gripped him, The Rock felt a new surge of affection for his homely exec. A fragment of remembered high school Latin flashed across his mind: *Ecce homo!* Despite all Eddington's too-human weaknesses here stood a man—a friend—who calmly flipped an offhand salute as he departed to combat the terrors deep inside *Old Swayback*'s breached hull. It wasn't bravado. It was merely Eddington doing a job.

The exec's immediate destination was central damage control, the nerve center from which repair parties would be fanning out to probe the ship's wounds, and then try to bandage them with steel and tin and wooden shorings, or even with the crew's own mattresses. They literally "read" their way along pitchblack passageways when power failed, by a sort of fastgroping Braille system, touching hatches, ladders, and scuttles. Theirs was brutal, dangerous work. If they kept the ship afloat, they'd have accomplished their purpose; if they didn't they would probably go down with her, trapped in some flooded cubicle without a wharfrat's chance of escape.

Death awaited *Old Swayback*'s damage-control teams behind a dozen leaky doors. Designed by architects who possessed no modern warfare background, the ship was especially vulnerable to undersea attack; and her hull had been welded and riveted together by builders whose craziest dreams never encompassed anything like electric torpedoes, ultra-HE shells, or armor-piercing aerial bombs. The cruiser was an anachronism—obsolete before she ever fired a shot in anger.

But she was worth saving.

Now that the ultimate crisis gripped his ship, The Rock had become a prisoner: condemned to *Old Swayback*'s bridge, sealed off from the fury belowdecks, dependent upon faulty intelligence relayed by his flame-seared and smoke-blinded subordinates, plagued by riddled communications lines—yet trying always to interpret for himself the meaning of the alien noises that reverberated from tortured metal deep inside the cruiser's hurt guts.

He called the officer of the deck and dictated an urgent message to Pearl Harbor: "TORPEDOED AT LATITUDE 24 DEGREES 8 MINUTES NORTH, LONGITUDE 162 DEGREES 10 MINUTES WEST. EXTENT OF DAMAGE UNKNOWN. WILL ADVISE." Torrey consulted some invisible oracle before he added, "TASK GROUP FUEL INSUFFICIENT FOR FURTHER OFFENSIVE OPERATIONS. AM ORDERING GROUP MINUS FLAGSHIP AND ONE DESTROYER TO RETURN TO BASE AT 20 KNOTS."

The OD hesitated.

"Break radio silence, sir?"

The Rock flared. "Damn it, man, don't you reckon the Japs *know* where we are by now?"

So there it was, Torrey told himself, after the humbled OD had departed. Failure spelled out in the dit-dah of International Morse. They hadn't even reached their goal, however empty that achievement might have proved, before disaster struck; and whatever little they had done would hardly go down in naval annals as one of the Fleet's more heroic performances.

As if aware at last that this was no practical joke, and overwhelmed by the enormity of the truth, *Old Swayback* had begun to dip awkwardly by the bow. Her helm responded sluggishly to the quartermaster's urgings. Obviously she was taking water, tons of it, through her subsurface rupture. Worst of all, her forward progress had dropped to eleven knots as hampering seas shoveled aft each time she nosed into a wave-trough. Yet, in her extremity, The Rock loved his illshapen cruiser; and he admired her struggle to live as he might have esteemed the comeback attempt of some crippled, overmatched, and slightly punchdrunk old prize fighter.

A hollow-eyed engineer ensign finally arrived on the bridge with Eddington's report, looking like a courier from Hades, and pouring out his account of the appalling situation in a compulsive torrent.

. . . Yes, sir. Damage-control parties had halted the fires up forward where the first torpecker hit . . . But it was really the exec who'd done it by making 'em let the water keep pouring through a hole big enough to drive a PT boat into until their eyeteeth started floating . . . Thank Christ the flames died down before they reached the eight-inch ammo room . . . Then they'd stuffed mattresses and blankets into that great big hole. Even the crew's lifebelts. . . . When some of the men beefed about this Commander Eddington told 'em flat out if they saved the ship they'd save themselves so what was the friggin' use of worrying about how they'd survive in the water where the sharks would probably chew them up alive anyhow . . . Of course the real trouble was happening farther aft where the exec figured the second torpecker caught us dead amidships . . . And brother that was awful sad because he didn't think the pumps could handle the water that kept roaring through the hull like Niagara Falls. The flood was already edging up toward the fireroom boilers . . . Only thing keeping us in lights and power was the emergency generator but God only knows how soon that'd blow and leave *Old Swayback* cold as a corpse . . . Commander Eddington said to tell the Old Man—sorry, sir, captain that is—he'd better start thinking about a tow . . . Oh, yes, and he wants you to know that casualties are damn heavy . . .

When the ensign finally paused, winded and distraught, The Rock said gently, "Thanks, son. Now you'd better sit down and drag some fresh air into your lungs."

Gratefully, the exhausted j.o. sank against the bridge shield near the pelorus stand, and shut his eyes as if he wanted to forget what he had just seen.

Torrey's craggy face had hardened into a stony mask while the ensign blurted out his story. Now a curious gentleness eased its deepcarved furrows. Yesterday, he remembered, when he'd stepped through the hatches which carried the stenciled warning "Closed during Condition ZEBRA," his only spoken comment was that he hoped they had drilled themselves to dog-down those watertight covers quickly. To himself he had added: *relentlessly,* too, without any sentimental regard for comrades trapped inside compartments which the sea might invade.

There was nothing left for him now but to wait, assailed by a mounting impatience that tested his rigid control, until he learned whether the ship would live, or die, or survive as a crippled derelict. Only Eddington could issue the localized orders that might save *Old Swayback.*

The walls of Torrey's duty-imposed penitentiary closed tighter around him as *Brockton, Eureka,* and *Penobscot* wheeled away from the stricken flagship, forging southward, with their valedictory "GOOD LUCK!" hoists almost indecipherable in the gray morning mist. Only *Cassiday* remained. She hovered a half mile off *Old Swayback*'s dangerously sloping bow like a worried bantam hen, her speed readjusted to match the larger ship's decelerating pace.

They had dropped to eight knots. It was only a matter of time—minutes—before the cruiser would be dead in the water.

The Rock cast an appreciative glance at the destroyer. Unquestionably she had deep-sixed the Jap submarine, because a fountain of Diesel oil pocked with debris from the I-boat's collapsed hull spewed high above the surface after the fifth depth-charge spread, closely followed by several mangled Jap bodies. This skirmish victory gave him a small shred of comfort, particularly since it was coupled with the first optimistic news from Eddington. By working a calculated miracle in the wreckage forward of Number 1 turret's volatile powder stores, the exec had managed to save them from blowing to Kingdom Come the way HMS *Hood* had succumbed to a single salvo from the Nazi *Bismarck*'s guns seven months earlier.

Torrey beckoned to the omnipresent junior officer of the deck, who came bouncing eagerly across the bridgewing with his tin helmet awry.

"Tell *Cassiday* to lay alongside," Torrey said. "We're going to need her."

"Aye, aye, sir!"

The JOD wanted desperately to ask *why*. But he didn't. Instead, straightening his flak-hat, he relayed the order to Flags, hoping as he did so that he looked as nonchalant and emotionless as the Old Man. The Rock, thought Ensign Harrison enviously, didn't have a goddamn nerve in his whole goddamn stringy body!

Bareheaded to the fresh wind, and squinting across the leaden scud, Mac watched *Old Swayback*'s searchlight blink the message.

At first, something like panic snaked along the shorthairs at the back of his sunburned neck when he read the simple orders. Once more, he knew, he'd have to rely on Seaman Hobday's uncertain helmsmanship, for Ishmael Quoddy had gone below, reluctantly and resentfully, to sack out after their engagement with the sub, and now the chief quartermaster was sprawled out like an opium-smoker in his fantail bunk, beyond call of *Cassiday*'s underpopulated bridge.

Laying alongside another vessel in the open sea demands practical skill of a sort you don't absorb from books. It requires what is known as a Seaman's Eye to estimate the span between your own ship and the one you're closing. No handy telegraph poles or crisscross highways lend depth to your perception. You've got to be born with such judgment.

But suppose you're a j.g.—gunnery at that—who happens temporarily to command a warship because of an improvidential series of happenstances, none of them within your small power to govern or even alter. When they were steaming around Blue Water with plenty of margin for error, it had seemed pretty elementary; and Mac looked back on extricating *Cassiday* from the ruins of Pearl Harbor as something done in a dream rather than as a tough nautical exercise. Besides, Ishmael Quoddy had been at the wheel the whole time, immobile and dependable as the statue of that sou'-westerclad fisherman up in Gloucester.

Mac wiped his sweating palms across filthy trouserlegs and tried to choke back his recurrent feeling of inadequacy as he considered all the probabilities of the impending maneuver.

What would the Book say?

Approach *Old Swayback* from astern while you keep checking her course through the pelorus. Pace her. Figure her speed from the pitometer log. Remember—your helmsman's view is restricted, so from the portside of the open bridge you must be his eyes and ears as you inch warily toward the cruiser's starboard lee.

Now step her up five knots and pull alongside. Cut your speed to allow for *Cassiday*'s surge.

And for God's sake, pay no attention to *Old Swayback*'s wounds, or her sodden contour, or her scorched and twisted plates. *Keep your mind on the job!*

Because now you've overshot the mark and it's all engines back full . . .

Mac stopped talking to himself and addressed Hobday: "That's got it, fella!"

Miraculously, *Cassiday* was riding easily beside the cripple, keeping a few yards of tumbling water between the two ships, the way a small cowpony might trot parallel to a huge roping Brahma bull.

Hobday grinned.

"Reckon Quoddy'd give us a passing grade, lieutenant?"

Mac didn't resent Hobday's implication. Suddenly he didn't have buckfever any more. And his palms had stopped sweating.

"Hell, yes," he replied. "The chief would say we've grown our Seaman's Eye."

"I know," the substitute quartermaster said happily. "Son of a bitch is always on my tail to get that 'eye.' Now he's not even around to watch."

From the parapet of *Old Swayback*'s navigating bridge, twenty feet above them, somebody yelled at *Cassiday* through a megaphone. The speaker's face was concealed, but the bassfiddle voice was unmistakably authoritarian, and very familiar.

"Nice work, Harding," it bellowed. "You did 4.0 on that sub."

Mac cupped his hands. "Thanks, sir. We were lucky. But I'm not Harding."

"Where's Harding?"

"Ashore, sir."

Astonishment lifted The Rock's voice a half note. "Who's in command?"

"I am, sir."

"Name?"

"Lieutenant j.g. William McConnel, sir."

"Not the Class of '38 McConnel?"

"Yes, sir."

From the man hidden behind the megaphone came a single expletive: "Jee-sus!"

Mac wasn't surprised at the profanity. He figured Captain Torrey had plenty of provocation, with his cruiser lying almost dead in the water, a sitting duck target, caught in the middle of hostile seas with a lone destroyer escort . . . and on the tincan a pickup skipper who'd been his none-too-smart pupil at the Academy only three years ago.

Torrey's voice resumed, all business. "Can you rig for towing, McConnel?"

"Yes, sir."

"How about transferring auxiliary power to us?"

"That, too."

"Very well, then *Captain* McConnel, carry on!"

Torrey experienced a singular glow of pride as he watched the young officer prepare his 1,450-ton destroyer for the tricky business of taking in tow 11,500 tons of inert pigiron and steel.

The clumsy plebe had become a stalwart man, commanding the ship on which the teacher now relied so abjectly.

Cassiday crept away from the cruiser, paying out the bulky manila hawser through her stern chock, until three hundred yards of green water separated her from *Old Swayback*'s waterlogged bullnose. From his elevated post, Torrey stared down at the smaller ship, contemplating her depleted depth-charge racks and her inadequate A.A. batteries. Despite its brevity, the fierce winter storm had left *Cassiday*'s deck a shambles of gear, smashed guardrails, and splintered whaleboats. Even her torpedo mounts were canted at odd angles. The destroyer's overtaxed crew were just beginning to rectify the damage. Some of them were bare to the waist as they labored, despite the chill of the air; others wore tatterdemalion pea-jackets, blouses, T-shirts, or even, he noted, college varsity sweaters.

The Rock found himself sending up a small prayer for a clear passage home.

Eddington's gravel voice interrupted his musings.

"Don't worry about those kids," he said. "They'll survive. They'll even brag about what they've been through. And believe me, skipper, that tincan's a hell of a lot better off than we are."

Swinging around toward the exec, really seeing him for the first time since he had returned to the bridge, Torrey was horrified at his appearance. A gobbet of bloody skin and torn brow hung down over Eddington's left eye, although the bleeding had stopped, and his sparse red hair had been charred into a grotesque black skullcap. Scorched remnants of khaki uniform covered his squat body. But he managed a grin, and his teeth gleamed white against the carbonblack of his face.

Torrey asked foolishly, "Are you hurt, Paul?"

The ghastly grin faded.

"No. But we've got maybe a hundred guys who *are* hurt bad . . . and fifty or so who're dead. Burned, blasted, or trapped when we had to flood the ammo spaces." Eddington touched his blood-encrusted scalp. "Hell—this is nothing!"

"Both of us are lucky, I guess," The Rock said slowly.

"Depends on what you mean by luck."

"Yes." Torrey was silent for a moment. "It comes in all sizes and shapes, doesn't it?"

"Also male and female," Eddington added incomprehensibly.

"We've got a damned long haul at five knots," The Rock said. "Will she hold together?"

Eddington shut his good right eye, reflectively, as he computed the efficiency of their pumps against the weight of saltwater inside *Old Swayback*'s perforated hull. The power fed back to them from the destroyer wouldn't be enough to maintain top performance. And if the jerrybuilt bulwarks they had erected against the encroaching sea collapsed . . . well, that was the end of the ballgame.

Like that.

He said calmly, "I'd figure less than a fifty-fifty chance of just staying afloat. Better tell that tincan not to jerk us too hard. Our bandage might slip." Eddington regarded the sling on the captain's right arm. "Skipper, you'd have a hell of a time swimming all the way to Pearl one-handed."

Later, of course, the crew were inclined to credit the little Mick chaplain for their miraculous survival, because he'd done such a fine job of concentrated praying once he finished helping the two medics and the four corpsmen with the casualties. He had also pronounced last rites for the forty-nine dead and missing. And after that *Old Swayback*'s foul luck changed, almost as if the Man Topside ordained it, and at 1300 the sun burst out of the grisly clouds and the ocean flattened out like a limitless spread of waving alfalfa, smooth and green enough to satisfy even a homesick seaman-second from Iowa.

CinCPAC tossed the final crumb of comfort just as lambent twilight faded.

"FLEET REPAIR TUG COCKEREL ACCOMPANIED BY DESTROYER GAINES WILL RENDEZVOUS AT 2100," he messaged, "TO ASSUME TOWING AND ESCORT DUTY."

The Rock read the dispatch in his emergency cabin where he was resting, in rumpled T-shirt and skivvies, for the first time in more than three days. Perhaps he should have been pleased with this comforting advice. Even elated. Yet he wasn't. Although he had saved his ship, and was bringing her home for repairs and restoration to duty, a certain Gethsemane had just begun for Rockwell Torrey.

That's the way the Book said it had to be . . .

6. *Who'll Play Torquemada?*

IGNOMINIOUSLY, all glory gone, the remnant of Torrey's Task Group returned to Pearl Harbor late on the afternoon of Wednesday, December 10, creeping toward its berth past the black and twisted shards of the Pacific Battle Force. Twilight had fallen. Through it, low-hanging in the west over The Rock's left shoulder, gleamed a waning sicklemoon, and as he glanced back and saw it from his position on *Old Swayback*'s bridge, he recalled ironically that this same moon meant good luck to superstitious people.

Along the debris-choked shoreline of Ford Island, where the skeletons of charred PBYs loomed against their ruined hangars, the night clean-up crews leaned on their shovels and pushbrushes to stare at the crippled cruiser and the perky little Fleet tug that towed her, and for a moment the nightmare came back to them as this new evidence of enemy ruthlessness emerged out of the gloom.

What was it Spartan mothers told their warrior sons? Return with your shields, when the battle's done, or on them.

Somehow *Old Swayback* fitted neither of these unsparing alternatives. There had been no battle, yet here she came limping home, barely afloat and plainly defeated—if anybody wanted to get technical about it, as certain of The Rock's less charitable peers inevitably would. Torrey knew, even before he stepped ashore, that he soon must confront an outwardly sympathetic but inwardly pitiless minority who would adjudge his predicament to be the natural outcome of his own stubborn refusal during all those lonely years to seek the advice they would have so freely given him. He also knew that jealousy is as fickle as the success which nurtures it.

Motor running and four-star emblem shining, a station wagon waited at dockside for Torrey and Eddington, under the command of a solemn ensign who behaved as though the vehicle were a man-of-war. He saluted when they approached, and announced in a sepulchral voice that CinCPAC wanted to see both of them right away.

When they reached the windswept hill called Makalapa, which was Fleet headquarters, the ensign gave way to a four-striper who beckoned Torrey aside before they entered the graypainted, two-story building.

"There's some damned bad news for your exec," the captain whispered. "We figured he'd better get it from the Fleet chaplain."

"Paul's wife?"

"Yes."

Torrey glanced across the cement walk at Eddington. The exec was looking bleakly down the long slope toward the hulks that lay in the Fleet anchorage.

"I'm not sure the chaplain can do much good," The Rock muttered, "though he can try, God knows . . ."

The CinCPAC officer nodded, walked over to Eddington, and spoke briefly. Immediately the exec spun on his heel, like a boxer caught by an unexpected solar plexus punch, and headed for the stairway that led to the upper level where chaplains, personnel officers, public information specialists, and sundry other noncombatants plied their esoteric trades.

The captain turned back to Torrey.

"Eddington's wife was killed Sunday morning," he explained abruptly. "There was an auto accident 'way to hell-and-gone the other side of the Island. Nasty mess. She'd been on some kind of a wild party with an Air Force major, from the looks of things, and when the attack started they headed back for Hickam Field, both of 'em still drunk as coots. They ran off the road coming down the hill from Schofield Barracks and plowed into a telephone pole at eighty miles an hour. There wasn't enough left to bury, even, after the convertible exploded and burned."

"So there *are* worse things," Torrey said more to himself than to his brother officer, "than court-martials."

"What did you say, Rock?"

"Nothing, Harry, nothing. Just thinking out loud. Poor damned soul."

"The girl?"

"No." Torrey contemplated the stairs up which the exec had fled. "Eddington. Heaven help him now!"

From his deepleather chair, fingers pressed tightly together in churchsteeple fashion, the grayfaced admiral heard out The Rock's uncompromising story of frustration and failure. For a moment after he finished, the only sounds in the room were the exasperated buzzing of bottleflies as they tilted against the unshaded neon lights, and the faraway taptapping of yeomen transcribing the Fleet's endless paperwork. Torrey felt compassion for the ghost-harried man whose sloped shoulders carried most of the blame, whether deserved or not, for Sunday's disaster. Already the High Brass and the politicians were arguing, as they would continue to argue for years to come, over who was responsible for the greatest military catastrophe that had ever befallen the nation.

When the admiral spoke, his habitually soft voice was muted by exhaustion and by his awareness of the unpleasant job that must be done. "I'm detaching you from your command, captain, and assigning you to my staff for temporary duty."

"May I ask what sort of duty, sir?"

They'd have to work something out, the admiral said slowly. At this juncture affairs were in a state of extraordinary flux, and he himself was awaiting orders to Washington, so he couldn't be sure. Fresh blood seemed to be the prescription for the Fleet now. New energy. New ideas. Perhaps (he observed with sudden bitterness) some of the concepts he had urged so long and so futilely would at last be accepted out of sheer necessity.

"We're both in the same boat," he added kindly. "I'll have to tell my story to the Navy Department. Maybe to the President himself. You'll tell yours to a court of inquiry."

"Or a court-martial, sir."

"Possibly . . . although you had only one ship torpedoed, Torrey."

Then, in a businesslike tone, the admiral said Eddington would take the cruiser back to San Francisco for repairs, once she'd been made seaworthy enough for the trip. Perhaps, he offered, hard work might be good therapy for the fellow, in view of his personal problem.

The Rock said nothing. Knowing Eddington's almost psychotic regard for Beth, even after he became convinced of her faithlessness, Torrey doubted whether mere physical labor would eradicate the exec's memory of this strange nymph who goaded him so mercilessly, yet kept him in such abject thralldom. No. The real tragedy was Eddington, not Beth, and now he was a man in mortal danger.

The admiral was saying, "Keep your dauber up, Torrey."

The Rock smiled faintly. "Sir, I guess if you can remain steady through all this, it shouldn't be too difficult for me. Mine's a damned small crisis alongside yours."

"But they're cut from the same miserable cloth, captain. If your ship had carried radar, or if your destroyer screen had been equipped with better soundgear, perhaps . . ."

Torrey waited for a moment, without speaking; but the brief interview had ended. He backed slowly toward the door, found the knob, and opened it. When he left, the admiral was staring at the tightly draped window, as if his tired eyes could X-ray through those thick curtains and see what lay beyond, and far below, where the repair crews' arc-welding torches mocked the blackout in their effort to get the crippled ships back into action.

Nobody at headquarters knew where Eddington had gone after the chaplain gave him The Word. He'd simply bolted from the building, rushed blindly down Makalapa Hill, and then vanished afoot into the night. Without much conviction, Torrey hoped the exec had returned to *Old Swayback,* even if he intended to get drunk. At least that would keep him away from the downtown Shore Patrol, whose regard for rank had depreciated markedly during four days of martial law.

The four-starred station wagon wasn't around anywhere. It had probably disappeared, The Rock guessed philosophically, along with Cinderella's coach-and-four. He waited while a harassed motor pool chief rounded up a dirty Ford sedan to take him back to the dock, where emergency repairs had already begun on the cruiser.

As he paused briefly at the gangway brow, it seemed to Torrey that the junior officer of the deck saluted a split second later than was customary when the captain returned aboard, and there was a speculative expression on his young face which betokened knowledge beyond the necessities of mere deck duty. Without resentment, The Rock reflected that news of his imminent departure from *Old Swayback* must have drifted across the harbor on the kona breeze, somehow, or reached the ship through that unique Navy osmosis which filters bad news a lot faster than good tidings. Your subordinates feel change coming; you can't conceal it.

"Has Commander Eddington come aboard yet?" Torrey asked, after he responded to the JOD's salute with an awkward left hand.

"No, sir."

"Well . . . let me know as soon as he returns."

"Yes, sir."

Torrey started for the ladder leading to the veranda deck where he turned and added: "And I don't care how late it is!"

The OD repeated, "Yes, sir," but a faint flicker of surprise betrayed him for the first time. Obviously he didn't have *all* the answers.

An indefinable sadness, mingled with a sense of foredoom which he could not ascribe entirely to Eddington's plight, assailed The Rock when he entered the long, low compartment that had been his home for seventeen months. He sat down tiredly at the circular table which served as diningboard and workbench. It was an hour past his customary mealtime and he realized he was hungry. He rang for the steward's mate, and ordered a bowl of soup, a ham-and-egg sandwich on whole wheat bread, and a glass of milk. Then he went into his stateroom to start packing his gear until the food arrived.

With his right arm useless in its sling, the task of assembling his belongings, meager as they were, was clumsy and difficult. But he persevered, collecting small left-handfuls of pipes, or books, or photographs, laying them on the bed, and finally stowing them in a plain wooden footlocker on which was stenciled "Capt. Rockwell Torrey, USN."

The photographs were the easiest load to carry across the room. There were only three of them: Athalie (proud and haughty and cold); Jere (stubbornly defiant in his crimson Harvard blazer as he posed for the picture he knew was meant for his father); and the Old Man (in the neck-choking high-collared dress blues he'd worn the day he left the service as a passed-over captain).

The largest single packet, four inches thick, contained The Rock's orders. They dated back to his fledgling duty as an ensign aboard an unstable little gunboat that precariously and ineffectually shadowed British blockaders in the early months of World War I. To a naval officer such orders correspond to a statesman's "personal papers," to be used as crutches for a flagging memory at some gafferish later date when he wishes to mull over his memoirs. Smudgily typed and endlessly "endorsed" from one command to another as he progresses toward Flag rank or premature retirement, they are a biography written by impersonal strangers and strategically placed friends.

What had Rockwell Torrey done since the day he reported aboard the gunboat *Pinder* in that uncertain autumn of 1914?

Precious little, he brooded, when you measured it with history's yardstick. Looking back upon his short, violent service in the first war, he realized with a trace of surprise not unmixed with bitterness, that only then was he temporarily free of the sense of insufficiency or inability—whether real, imagined, or potential—which had nagged him all his life. He remembered again how, as a boy, he'd been so terribly anxious to satisfy the Old Man: the acolyte despairingly aware of his own shortcomings in the master's presence.

Torrey often wondered whether the Old Man felt the same way about *his* Old Man. But he'd never dared ask.

That earlier war was a time of elemental challenges and developing stresses, when civilization was decently bounded by steel bulkheads, decks, and keels. Everything seemed very noble, then, as well as honest and ordained. If an enemy shot at you, you returned his fire. Hidden motives didn't bother a man. Only overt actions.

But after the Armistice, when The Rock came home from Europe with his Navy Cross, he soon learned what every warrior has been forced to learn since Neolithic man agreed to stop throwing stones and go back quietly to his cave. Most men-at-war find it difficult to transform themselves into men-at-peace. A few find it impossible, and gradually come to view themselves as half-men, trapped in a pacific world which regards their profession indifferently, or even disdainfully, once the danger has passed. They aren't ashamed of their trade. But they are deeply perplexed that outsiders cannot, or will not, comprehend their peculiar problems of readjustment, which in their extreme case is not unlike a narcotic addict's withdrawal, with much the same symptoms, but modified and endlessly stretched out.

For these men, unhappily, there is no real cure except another war. Meanwhile they enshell themselves in their Service society, while the world's tide ebbs and leaves them stranded like hermit crabs in a blackwater pool.

Torrey had made his readjustment, more or less; Paul Eddington hadn't.

Rejuvenated by his recall to active duty as port captain for one of the grubbier Atlantic coastal cities, the Old Man was still very much alive when Torrey returned to the States in the spring of 1919, and he hustled up to New York to welcome his son home. But he evinced no sympathy when the young lieutenant gloomed about the Navy's probable peacetime future.

"There are two kinds of people, boy," the Old Man said, pointedly ignoring the fact that Torrey was then twenty-six, as he expounded his favorite philosophy. "Men who serve and men who are served."

Torrey knew that his father's use of the word *men* was deliberately calculated to emphasize an abiding belief that this was a harsh masculine world in which women played damned ineffectual roles, if any.

"Yes, sir," he assented humbly.

"Of course," the Old Man went on, "I don't mean 'serve' in the ordinary sense, the way your wardroom messboy hops to it when you order a cup of coffee. I mean it in the *duty* sense. In our trade . . ."

Torrey hid a smile as his father allowed himself the rare humor of labeling his beloved profession a "trade." Although the *cognoscenti* call Annapolis their "Trade School," the Old Man would have shot dead with his Service .45 any unwashed civilian who applied this same term to the Academy, or to the business of being a Navyman.

He was saying, ". . . the servers dedicate their lives to a kind of duty the servees could never understand, because it's too complicated for them. Or too lofty. Take your choice, boy. Either way, it means you're serving a Cause from which you can't just walk away and quit. Ever. But those fellows can always drop what they're doing. Their civvies make them invisible. Nobody cares. Our uniform makes us marked men." He glowered at his son. "But *men,* thank God!"

And thus ended the sermon.

They went to the Army and Navy Club for a quiet dinner, after which The Rock bought a chair-car ticket on the New York, New Haven & Hartford, and began the first leg of his journey to Boston, where Athalie awaited him.

Perhaps she really should have let the chauffeur drive her down to New York in Papa's new Simplex, which had replaced the Pierce-Arrow. But, as Athalie wrote him, she despised the noise and smell and unspeakable filth of Manhattan even more than she relished the idea of meeting her gallant husband on the dock; and another day wouldn't make a dreadful lot of difference, would it? Besides, Captain Torrey had written her that he was coming in from that odd town in New Jersey, and she just knew they'd have oodles of mantalk to catch up on. Athalie thought this was rather sporting of her, and even self-sacrificing, as if she had given up something she wanted very much to do.

Her letter, written on heavy gray notepaper that bore the Cunliffe crest in royal purple, hadn't surprised The Rock, although it rather depressed him, for he had been hoping that her Laodicean coldness might have thawed, and her heart grown poetically fonder, during his long absence. But why imagine that such Tin Pan Alley nonsense ever came true? Athalie was, well, Athalie. Doubtless she would be properly loving after he moved back into the Beacon Street brownstone which the Cunliffes had given them when they were married two years earlier. Yes. Very properly loving. With annoyed little protestations that he was disarranging her Charles Dana Gibson hair-do, which curved like a pale questionmark across her forehead and down her regal neck, and with meticulous attention for certain hygienic matters even before his kisses had dried upon her cool lips. Sex was a nasty business. One must approach it cautiously, lest it sway one's emotions, and leave one upset and messily sweating like any little South Boston colleen. So it secretly pleased Athalie that she never perspired even at the climax of their infrequent lovemaking, for which she always fortified herself with champagne and brandy. Sherry wasn't strong enough.

There had been one horrid exception: their wedding night. She still hated the memory of it, and felt degraded, because it was the only time in her well-ordered life that she had ever surrendered to animal impulses, or forgotten for a single instant that she was a Cunliffe lady.

It was astonishing, when anyone bothered to consider the matter, that she'd married Lieutenant (j.g.) Rockwell Torrey in the first place.

Or was it such an extraordinary union, on second thought? Their marriage may have been quite in keeping with the Cunliffe creed of stability in all things. The enduring family empire, upon which their comfortable fortune rested as if cemented against Plymouth Rock itself, had been founded by Papa Cunliffe's maternal great-grandfather, Jeremiah Farr. Undecided whether to become a mercantile czar, a shipping tycoon, or a fur-trade baron, Commodore Farr tried all three upon his graduation from Harvard. He was not the least bit astonished that each venture turned to gold in his tight Yankee fist. Nor was he particularly elated. Such things simply happened to the Farrs of this world. Nothing surprised Jeremiah except failure (which was beyond his comprehension anyhow); and during his eighty-nine robust years he was shaken out of his complacency only once, when the youngest of his four sons became a missionary to the Congo instead of joining Farr Factors, Ltd., like a proper gentleman. There was so little profit in saving souls.

Each generation of the Farr-Cunliffe dynasty prided itself on producing at least one "sailor" for the breed, which meant, in their spare New England lexicon, somebody destined to command a Fleet or run the Navy Department for a grateful President. By investing prudently and marrying wisely, they managed to maintain a respectable average: one vice-admiral, one Undersecretary, and a trio of captains whose years-in-grade trapped them before their Farr-Cunliffe talents could be fully appreciated.

After thorough investigation, they assured themselves that Rockwell Torrey was worth a calculated risk—provided dear Athalie wished to consummate a friendship begun in 1915, two years ago, when she had met him formally at a cotillion given in honor of a visiting Naval Squadron. The lad came of stoutly conservative seafaring stock (Maine, to be sure, rather than Massachusetts; yet it would suffice) and he was known to have comported himself quite sedately at Annapolis, without that deplorable flashiness which seemed to be afflicting so many young chaps in these increasingly warlike times.

That summer Torrey visited the Cunliffes at Merrymeeting Bay.

His maturity impressed Papa, although Mama Cunliffe was intuitively troubled by something she couldn't quite lay her patrician finger upon, but which she guessed must be his lack of sophistication. She had hoped for a man who would complement Athalie's own naïveté.

Papa also appreciated the fact that Torrey sported a sound masculine nickname: The Rock.

Like the boy's naval career, this satisfied family tradition, too, for every successful Farr-Cunliffe male gloried in some apt sobriquet. In the City, Papa was known to his banking friends and his Massasoit Club associates as "Crash," a tribute to his prowess as a fullback in Harvard's flying-wedge days, and more recently because he'd sold out ahead of the '07 panic.

Papa convinced Mama that they had damned little time to waste.

At twenty-four, Athalie was already a couple of years older than young Torrey, and since her debut at the Carlton in '12 (memorable because it coincided with the Democrats' return to power after Teddy Roosevelt's Bull Moose tomfoolery) she had done nothing to encourage the few gentlemen who rather halfheartedly besought her bony hand. This scared Mama and worried Papa. Both of them agreed it was high time that good New England horse-sense prevailed, even though it might mean aiming a notch lower on the social scale than the Cabots or the Lowells. So Torrey was, as Papa phrased it in his elegant style, "as welcome as the flowers that bloom in May."

Studying the solemn youngster as he skippered Athalie around the Bay in a sailing dinghy, the family was positive they had made a wise Farr-Cunliffe decision by permitting him to become engaged to their solemn young daughter. Even physically they gave every outward evidence of being the Perfect Couple. Torrey was lean and lank in the approved Yankee mode, and his face, with its long upperlip, had an equine look about it that betokened Cunliffian stability. Athalie was poured from this same dependable mold. When she bore his children, the Cunliffes would have an heir worthy of their proud name. This was a source of abiding comfort to Papa and Mama, since Athalie was an only child—a female at that—and therefore perilously close to becoming the last of their imperial line.

When the occasion demanded, Mama Cunliffe could be as swift and ruthless as a puff adder. She went to work, very subtly and very cleverly, and before The Rock's leave ended he found himself betrothed, to his considerable astonishment and without comprehending exactly what had happened.

Torrey understood that a proper union with the proper woman was an important step in an officer's career, but it hadn't occurred to him that matrimony might overtake him so soon. The Old Man had often expounded upon the necessity of a suitable marriage, without irony or bitterness, although Torrey's mother had never advanced his own fortunes to any noticeable degree. She was a Maine farmer's daughter, pleasant to contemplate, a splendid baker of apple pies, placid-spoken, but utterly devoid of the specious graces that counted in Service society.

That, of course, was the rub.

Obliquely, the Old Man suggested that a girl's wealth shouldn't disqualify her for marriage to an impoverished ensign whose star was rising. He suggested also that beauty was only skin-deep, whereas a noble soul was a desirable commodity to come by in these days when Victorian virtues counted for so little.

The Rock wasn't overly impressed as he listened to his father, although this was the Old Man at his moralistic best. Here, he felt, was a decision which a man must make for himself—little knowing that it had already been made for him by Mama Cunliffe.

Their engagement lasted a decorous two years.

Thoroughly satisfied with this protracted, long-distance courtship, neither of them was in a hurry to conclude an arrangement in which regular letters and periodic visits took the place of the more overt romanticizing expected of betrothed couples. Torrey, immersed in his quasi-wartime duties, and Athalie, who had taken up woman suffrage, had little time for spooning.

Then it was February 1917.

Kaiser Bill had just declared unrestricted U-boat activity against blockade-running ships, including those flying the neutral American flag and operated by Farr-Cunliffe, Ltd., and it appeared (Papa said positively) that damned soon we'd be in this thing right up to our necks. Wasn't it significant that Athalie's young man had been promoted to lieutenant (j.g.) far ahead of the Navy's normal snail'space schedule, and assigned to one of those smart new four-stack destroyers outfitting at Boston Navy Yard? Of course it was!

What the Cunliffes had best do, Papa proclaimed as he paced up and down in Mama's elegant boudoir, was to lay on a champagne-and-caviar wedding at the Carlton that very spring. Once hostilities commenced, President Wilson, who was a bluenosed Scottish Calvinist, would probably declare it unpatriotic or even immoral to spend one's own money for such fripperies.

They selected April 6 for the nuptials.

But as the date approached, looming more baleful and irrevocable with each passing day, Athalie began to panic. She lost her appetite, and her longboned and almost breastless figure became even more distressingly angular. So when Athalie muttered certain doubts about her ability to go through with "this appalling performance," Mama acted again.

"All the child needs," she told Papa, "is confidence. I shall see that she gets it."

Mama Cunliffe's diabolical plot hinged around a bridal shower, whose guest list was handpicked to include the most knowledgeable and sophisticated young ladies within Athalie's circle of friends, or even remote acquaintances. Geography was no handicap. Her final invitation, sent special delivery to San Francisco, contained a round-trip ticket on the Union Pacific for Constance Van Buren, who had been Athalie's best chum at Vassar until Mama herself broke up the liaison because Connie was too "fast." She was known to have gone all the way with at least three young Ivy League gentlemen, who caddishly confirmed the rumors.

In Papa's colorful argot, Connie Van Buren was just what the doctor ordered for what ailed Athalie.

The bridal shower was held on April 5, one day before the wedding, in a private room at the Copley. Mama finally chose the Copley over the Carlton because it was gayer and more worldly. Even the stringed trio plunged into the spirit of the moment and played ragtime, after a fashion, which made everything seem terribly continental and *soigné*.

Looking back on that night, months later, Athalie came to the coldly logical conclusion that she'd been framed by Mama Cunliffe and a handful of false friends. Especially, as she now knew, by Connie Van Buren, whom she'd been so enchanted to see again after almost three years. She'd had certain suspicions even during the party; but the mood of the evening caught her, and so did an abandoned curiosity to learn more from these worldly-wise young ladies.

They chattered about the Turkey Trot and the Bunny Hug and about that slinkyhaired "tango pirate" from Princeton who clasped girls much too close to his bosom (thereby wickedly squeezing theirs) and who always reeked of gin. They wondered hopefully if slit skirts would slit any higher, and they giggled sympathetically when Athalie showed the pearlgray spats that Mama insisted she wear to conceal her ankles. They covered each other's hair with their hands to ascertain how they'd look bobbed, and they quoted vignettes from Mr. T. S. Eliot's slim new book of poems in which he spoke so frankly about the jiggling of women's breasts. ("Imagine! Mr. Eliot's from Boston—isn't it incredible?" It was.)

This, of course, led them to the drama, which was only a short conversational hop to Theda Bara's milkwhite semi-nakedness. Connie Van Buren sniffed derisively.

"For nudity," she opined wisely, "give me Isadora Duncan—dancing in the moonlight and wearing nothing but that silly little transparent spiderweb of hers."

Athalie confessed she had never seen Miss Duncan perform her fabulous terpsichore.

"You have an awful lot to learn," Connie said, "especially about clothes. And men."

Athalie agreed rather mournfully. "I'm scared to death. Simply quivering like an aspen leaf every time I think of . . . *that*."

Everybody knew what *that* was. Everybody nodded wisely, blushing, and got ready to pursue the subject. Connie pulled a package of scented Turkish cigarettes from her handbag and offered them around, nonchalantly, before lighting her own from a wonderful little sparking machine.

Athalie tried one. Just then she felt seductive and crazy and deliciously abandoned.

As if resuming a lecture, Connie Van Buren demanded, "Why not take a leaf from La Duncan's act tomorrow night, dearest child?" She smiled slyly. "Perhaps I should say—a *fig* leaf."

Athalie was horrified.

"Dance naked . . . in the moonlight?"

"Exactly." Smoke dribbled sinfully from Connie's nostrils. "Unless, of course, there isn't any moonlight where you're going."

"It's Merrymeeting Bay," Athalie said. "Our summer cottage."

"O dear God!"

"What's wrong with Merrymeeting Bay?"

"Everything. It's so—so utterly familial. Cold, too, and not just because of that atrocious Maine weather. But you'll simply have to rise above it, dear heart. *Par example*." Connie lifted her skirt above her knees and displayed several inches of silk lace. "Absolutely the latest rage in Paris. They'll put the bloomer people out of business before summer's over, you just wait and see, because they're calculated to drive a man right out of his silly lecherous mind." She gave her hostess a hard look. "Your sailorboy would love you in something like this."

"Rockwell loves me without them," Athalie said unwarily.

Connie shrieked, "Aha! Athalie's gone 'free love' on us!"

"Nonsense."

But their laughter drowned out her protest, and heedless of her almost tearful embarrassment, Connie persisted in describing a bacchanalian night—"*night,* my dears, not just an evening!"—she'd spent once with a tattooed San Francisco sailor who wrote poetry.

"Atrocious verse," Connie admitted cheerfully, "but beautiful sentiment."

To elude her nautical bard, who'd become much too possessive, Connie had fled all the way to Hollywood and stayed there for a whole month, watching those funny people make their funny little moving pictures. Mr. Cecil B. de Mille had offered her a job as an extra, Connie added, but she refused. She didn't mind taking off her clothes, *normally,* but it seemed rather pointless to do it in front of a cinema camera.

Spurred by Connie's deviltry, under the luxuriant cover of the violins and the violas, they drew the net tighter around her. Lure the man, they advised their credulous hostess. Entice him. Flaunt. Beckon. Hide.

"Hide?" Athalie breathed.

"Yes. Run away from your panting sailorboy," Connie explained, "just when he thinks he's got you. Make him hunt for you. Taunt him a little. But when he finally searches you out . . ."

Owing to some warped whim of Providence, their wedding date coincided with the eve of the United States' entry into the war, and it took all Papa Cunliffe's influence to preserve the bridegroom's brief leave. They borrowed Papa's goggle-eyed Pierce-Arrow for the journey to the Edwardian family cottage, which occupied most of a small windswept islet in Merrymeeting Bay.

Unquestionably, there were extenuating circumstances, even for a graduate of Miss Bronson's School and Vassar, for what Athalie did on that early spring night, if one stopped to consider the hypnotic effect of Connie Van Buren's coaching in the true Art of Love. Almost trancelike, she played a coyly contrived game that was as old as Eve, as she fled from her startled husband, and cajoled him into tracking her down through twenty darkened rooms with only her muffled laughter to guide him. When Torrey found her, she wasn't in the vast cottage at all, but outside in the frosty moonlight, and poised statuesque on the rocks above their private cove.

Athalie was mother-naked.

The pallid glow which silvered her thin body also softened its contours, and gave it the illusion of warmth and excitement. Even her flat breasts were caught by this lunar magic as she cupped them in her hands, tendering them at Torrey the way Connie said burlesque queens flaunted their nude bosoms in the Barbary Coast dives of San Francisco.

Stunned, he stared at his transfigured bride, who seemed oblivious to the gaze that swept down her body like a hotly searching hand, touching the surprisingly large brown nipples, fondling the neat little navel which punctuated her concave belly, and finally coming to rest upon the velvety triangle below.

Athalie beckoned to him.

Suddenly he rushed toward her. He caught her up in his arms and carried her into the parlor of the Cunliffe cottage, where he deposited her sprawling in front of the glowing hearth. Her surrender had amazed him. But somehow he managed to order her with mock severity to stay where she lay while he got his damned tight uniform trousers off.

After that, for Athalie, the crazy dream burst apart like a ruptured toy balloon.

Torrey mauled her all over Papa's favorite grizzly bearskin rug, the one he'd brought back from his last hunting trip to Canada, and everything became horrid and messy. It was like wrestling one's way through some awful wilderness filled with the strangest kind of fanged and grasping beasts. But Athalie kept her mouth tight shut and didn't scream at all, thank heaven, by biting her underlip until it bled.

At last Torrey had his way. They lay there in the flickering light of the fire: he exhausted and spent, she as uncomprehendingly stiff as the castiron tongs that leaned against the fieldstone chimney.

Even now, two years later, Athalie remembered how her violated body had shone wetly in the fire-gleam and how for the first time in her puritan life she had smelled the funkiness of human sweat, her own mingled with Torrey's. . . .

When they hurried home next day, pushing Papa's great Pierce-Arrow to the limit of its twelve throbbing cylinders, Athalie felt as if she had been reprieved from a fate that was much worse—as the saying goes—than Death itself.

And when The Rock left for his destroyer, puzzled by her abrupt change into something even colder than the frigid prenuptial Athalie, she took scant pains to conceal her relief. She wished him well, and pecked at his left cheek, dismissing him as unemotionally as if he were simply trotting down to S.S. Pierce's for a tin of flaked codfish, instead of sailing off to war.

Athalie realized he'd return, eventually, and dreaded it. Meanwhile she would have time to collect her troubled thoughts and press them dry as last year's rosepetals between the pages of her hard Cunliffe mind. And, of course, there was always the chance that The Rock might *not* come back at all, especially since he seemed so boyishly eager to go where the fighting was. Guiltily, Athalie caught herself hoping that he would be killed (in suitably bloodless hero-fashion); and even when her latent New England conscience chided her, she found it impossible to bury this morbid wish entirely.

But The Rock didn't get killed.

His ship was one of Commander Taussig's half-dozen "gesture destroyers" that reported to a wornout and despondent British admiral at Queenstown early in May. They drew first blood. Before the desperate spring brightened into a more optimistic summer, they were heroes, almost to a man, and with decorations to show for it.

When the Armistice came, Torrey was a senior lieutenant, full of honors and wisdom and ticketed to go places—always provided *anybody* was going places in the Service now that this war to end all wars had ended.

Papa Cunliffe, having surveyed the situation with his glacial Yankee gaze, decided the Navy held no future for Athalie's husband. It offered neither financial nor career prospects. In a renascent world, banking was the only vocation fit for a gentleman, and the House of Farr-Cunliffe might find it profitable to have an authentic hero on the staff, first as an assistant to the president (Papa) and later as a vice-president in his own right after he'd learned the ropes.

Papa's mind's-eye gleamed at the thought of how he'd impress his sobersided brethren at the Massasoit Club: "Meet my son-in-law, Lieutenant Torrey. Going to join the firm. Hasn't even had time to buy civilian clothes since he left his destroyer down at the Yard. This bit of blue-and-white ribbon? Gentlemen, that is the Navy Cross, second highest decoration given by the Service."

Then Papa would order drinks all around. "Incidentally," he'd add, "people who know this lad call him 'The Rock.' Sort of healthy new blood we need in Boston now that the war's over . . ."

Torrey listened respectfully to Papa Cunliffe, thanked him for his offer of a fine $75-a-week position, and just as respectfully declined it. In his pocket he had orders that would take him to Washington after a decent interval of leave. There, the Old Man had said, the politicians would brawl over the Navy's destiny more fiercely than the sailors themselves had ever fought in the North Sea or along the Atlantic convoy routes. Moreover, since combat duty entitled The Rock to a couple of years ashore, he and Athalie could find a colonial house in Old Georgetown, every bit as weathered and hoary-gray as anything on Beacon Hill; and she'd hardly be able to tell the difference.

Ah, but she could!

Athalie was sure of that. Wild horses—even the neighing brutes that raped poor Europa—couldn't drag her down to Washington, D.C. Or was it a bull? No matter. Europa was carried off, degraded, ravished, and that was that.

Grudgingly, Athalie recognized in her husband's virile strength the same sort of masculinity that exuded from Papa. So be it. She would become the Immovable Object, fastened like a limpet to the four-story yellowbrick mansion that had served the Cunliffes since the Commodore struck it rich, and she wouldn't even return to the brownstone which Papa had given them as a wedding present. There must be something inherently cruel about Torrey, she reasoned, else why would they call him The Rock, like some slope-browed waterfront dock fighter? His primitive power was more of spirit than thews, Athalie had to admit, yet it drove the wedge irrevocably deep between Torrey and herself, and between his inconstant world and her own methodical one.

Athalie gritted her rather prominent teeth. One odious task remained to be accomplished before her husband left alone for Washington D.C. Properly executed, it would guarantee that she didn't have to go away from Boston. Ever! She determined to submit—that's how Athalie phrased it in her own shrinking mind—to Torrey that night, before she had time to brood on the distasteful business, even if it killed her. She would become pregnant. Once the seed was planted, and the baby was on its way, she could argue plausibly that she must remain at home where Dr. Cartmill could care for her, just as he had looked after Mama twenty-eight years earlier.

It never occurred to Athalie to question either her own fertility or the sex of the yet-to-be-conceived child, who would be named Jeremiah Farr Torrey, after great-great-grandfather, and who naturally would attend St. Marks and Harvard College before entering Papa's bank.

All this she foresaw with the same dehumanizing logic which had repelled a dozen suitors before Rockwell Torrey happened along. Some women are afraid of thunder. To Athalie, that was sheer nonsense: she was afraid only of the lightning. She knew that thunder couldn't hurt you, since it was merely the effect and not the cause of the electrical action. She could tell you, and invariably did with a tolerant smile, how far away the lightning bolt had struck—after multiplying mentally the time it took the thunderclap to reach Beacon Hill by the one-fifth mile per second at which sound travels. At sea level.

On all counts except the last, Athalie was prophetically right about Jeremiah Farr Torrey . . .

By 2200 The Rock had finished packing his footlocker. Perhaps because he felt ashamed of this paltry accumulation, the *lares et penates* of an excessively lonely life, he screwed down the wooden lid himself. When his supper came, he ate stolidly, without tasting either the heavy sandwich or the anonymous brown consommé, and trying not to think. But too many memories, some toughly calloused over with ancient scar tissue, some angrily new, came tumbling through a door that wouldn't stay shut.

After he finished his meal, he turned to the task of stowing clothes and toilet gear into a folding canvas suitpack.

When he reached the box containing his seven-day supply of German steel razors, Torrey held the faded redplush case in his hand for a moment, then opened it, and mechanically tolled off the days of the week from the inscriptions on the blades. *Mittwoch.* Wednesday. Midway through an interminable week that had wrecked a Fleet and dozens of careers, including his own, he thought without rancor. He could have remained aboard ship until Friday (*Freitag!*), pending the inquiry, but suddenly he wanted to leave. Get the hell out. Away. So Eddington could assume the new responsibility that might disperse the demons that rode him tonight.

Perhaps, he mused, when the captains of the inquiry board began to probe into the torpedoing, and faced him across the baize-covered table with all their what-ifs and why-didn't-yous, Rockwell Torrey would wake up to the gravity of his own problem. Right now he didn't care very much. Only that hectoring sense of insufficiency with which he'd always lived penetrated his curious numbness.

There would be condolences from brother officers, hollow and hypocritical, like those offered by family friends to the husband of a murdered wife. Even though he hadn't actually slain the woman himself, it seemed to them he'd somehow been accessory after the fact to a crime he should have prevented. A few understanding souls might have the honesty to say—privately, of course—that what had happened to him might also have happened to them, under similar circumstances. But to the perfectionists, *Old Swayback*'s near disaster spelled failure. Torrey's. Despite its illogic and unfairness, The Rock accepted the inevitability of such a decision, for he likewise belonged to that inflexible breed to whom facts were facts, however harsh; and anyone who sought to mitigate them proved himself a moral coward.

That was the unforgivable sin.

In the gray silence of his sterile room, Torrey smoked a pipeful of tobacco, and then prepared for bed. He lay awake for a few minutes, listening to the multifarious deck noises, before exhaustion overcame the pain of his broken arm. He had reviewed every aspect of the unpleasant situation, and since there was no honorable way to alter it, he had resigned himself to whatever his peers decreed.

The last sound he heard was *Old Swayback*'s brass clock chiming six bells—an hour until midnight—from the bridge he would never pace again. His final thought was for Eddington . . .

Somebody shook The Rock's shoulder, gently but insistently, and passed a blue flashlight beam across his face to rouse him. He glanced instinctively at the luminous dial of his watch. It was 0415, barely five hours since he'd turned in, and another two before the time he would normally rise.

"Captain," a voice said apprehensively, "it's me. Leary. The OD told me to wake you irregardless of the time on account he's got word about Commander Eddington."

Torrey was up and donning his khakis before the Marine orderly finished speaking.

"Shut the ports," he said quietly, "so we can turn on some lights."

"Yes, sir." Leary fumbled his way across the compartment. "I'm sorry about—"

"Forget it, son. I left strict orders. Just tell me what the OD said."

"Well, sir, it seems like the exec got into this brawl downtown and clobbered some Army Air Corpse type. So now the SPs have him locked in the brig."

The Rock reached for his black necktie. "Help me with this thing, Leary. I can't tie it with one hand. Then ask the OD to scare up some transportation into town. If Mister Burke's aboard, I'll take him along to drive."

"Mister Burke went to the hospital," the Marine said. "His wife had a kid."

Silent for a moment, Torrey recalled the navigator's fierce anxiety during their westward chase, and the compelling thought came to him of the continuity of mundane lifebreathing things in the midst of the artificial crises which men imagined were so overpowering and vast. Pearl Harbor could blow skyhigh. But Bobby Burke was with his wife at Aiea Hospital and all was right with his world.

"I'd forgotten," he said. "You'll have to pilot me, son."

It took them fifty minutes to drive from Pearl Harbor into downtown Honolulu through the blackout that the military government had instituted for the entire Island. Only the thinnest slits of blued headlamps, which served more as a warning than a navigational aid for the few vehicles on the highway, were permitted, and they were halted four times by sentries before they crawled into a parking space near the Shore Patrol headquarters in the palmfringed civic center.

An elderly commander responded to Torrey's peremptory knock, yawning hugely, scowling, and prepared to visit unshirted hell upon whoever had disturbed him at this godless hour. Then he counted his visitor's four gold stripes, and saw his ferocious jaw line.

"What can we do for you, captain?"

"You've got my exec locked up," The Rock said. "I want him."

The SP commander looked positively relieved. "You mean Commander Eddington?"

"Yes."

"Will you sign for his custody?"

"Certainly."

"Then he's all yours, captain."

"May I see the Shore Patrol booking sheet?"

"Sure." The old three-striper pushed a piece of single-spaced typewriting across the scarred desk, and shook his head in rueful admiration. "This fellow Eddington's a goddamn wildcat. It took four of my best men to subdue him."

"So? I'd have figured at least five," Torrey said unsmilingly, turning to the report.

> . . . Patrol Baker was summoned to Hong Kai Yuk's Tropical Tavern at approx. 2035 for the purpose of quelling a disturbance

when Hong Kai Yuk phoned for assistance after he proved personally unable to handle situation involving subj. officer (Cdr. P. Eddington, USN) and an unidentified U. S. Army Air Force major. It is believed the latter may require medical attention if & when located although he fled scene after sustaining severe beating prior to arrival of Patrol Baker.

. . . According to Hong Kai Yuk subj. officer entered Tropical Tavern at approx. 2010 and asked for "a shot of bourbon." When Hong Kai Yuk informed him that M.G. rules forbid sale of liquor during current emergency period & suggested subj. officer had already imbibed what appeared to be a sufficient quantity, latter became extremely abusive & profane.

. . . Subj. officer said "no g.d. Jap" was going to "dictate" to him, which remark angered Hong Kai Yuk inasmuch as he is of Korean origin and feels very strongly in this regard.

. . . At this point the unidentified USAAF maj. entered the Tavern and proceeded into a private rear room known as the Kona Klub where liquor is dispensed gratis to the management's personal guests, according to Hong Kai Yuk. (Patrol Baker recommends investigation of this.) The USAAF maj. was accompanied by a woman approx. 30 yrs. of age, who subsequently identified herself as Miss Judy Smith, waitress, of Lower Canal St., but alleges not to know the name of her escort whom she had met only 1 hr. previously, other than that he called himself "Jocko."

. . . In a loud objectionable manner subj. naval officer thereupon asked "what in hell is the f—— flyboy doing with that f—— broad in that back room?" He expressed dissatisfaction with Hong Kai Yuk's explanation of the private nature of the Kona Klub & proceeded to force his way into same, knocking down and severely bruising two waiters who endeavored to halt him.

. . . Approaching Miss Smith & her escort in a belligerent manner, subj. officer informed the maj. that he (the maj.) was "a disgrace to the Service" inasmuch as he (the maj.) was plying Miss Smith with whiskey in an obvious attempt to get her intoxicated so he could treat her the way the "g.d. flyboys always treated women." Namely, "f—— them."

. . . But Miss Smith informed subj. officer (Cdr. P. Eddington) she was plenty old enough to look after herself & for him to "screw off."

. . . At this phase the eye-witnesses tend to disagree concerning what exactly happened. One informant claims he heard subj. officer remark re. Miss Smith that "here but for the Grace of God goes

Bess. (or Beth)." Another informant alleges subj. officer declared he would "get every g.d. USAAF b—— if it's the last thing I do in my lousy life." Whereas a third informant believes subj. officer was in a semi-weeping and hysterical condition that may have indicated he suffered from some mental type problem.

. . . In the resultant altercation which began when subj. officer jerked the USAAF maj. off his chair three imitation palm trees valued by Hong Kai Yuk at $25.50 ea. were broken & further damage ensued when Miss Smith took a coconut from one of said palm trees & flung same at subj. officer, missing same but smashing a large bar mirror valued by Hong Kai Yuk at $56.95, installed.

. . . Although subj. officer was approx. 20 lb. lighter than the USAAF maj., & quite inebriated, he administered such a severe beating to same that the latter fled without waiting for Miss Smith after less than 5 mins. of actual fighting. Subj. officer displayed professional boxing ability, according to informants. Several teeth believed to belong to the USAAF maj. are herewith enclosed as evidence.

. . . When the maj. disappeared, subj. officer quieted down & collapsed in a corner of the Kona Klub where he was sick. Definitely in a weeping condition at this time, he sat with his head in his hands prior to arrival of Patrol Baker at approx. 2050, whereupon subj. officer suddenly leaped to his feet saying in a loud voice that "you b——s will never take me alive."

. . . He endeavored to escape but was taken into custody at approx. 2105 by BM1c H. Margolies, GM3c J. Pitney, S1c K. Navarro, & S2c G. Maxwell, who were forced to utilize their nightsticks owing to subj. officer's extreme combat tendencies . . .

The Rock looked up, frowning, when he finished reading the file.

"You arrested Eddington at 2105. Why wasn't I notified for seven hours?"

"Hell's fire, we didn't want the fellow on our hands any longer than necessary. But he wouldn't tell us who he was. All he'd say was, 'Why don't you bastards go away and let a man die in peace?' "

"Didn't he have his identification card?"

"No, sir. He'd lost his wallet. Or maybe he'd been rolled before he made Hong Kai Yuk's dive. There wasn't a scrap of I.D. on him anywhere. Then we got lucky. My morning watch chief used to be a Fleet welterweight and he was interested when Margolies said this fellow acted like a pro fighter. Right off my chief spotted Eddington as his coach on the *Texas* 'way back in '23. Hell of a memory, hasn't he?"

"Hell of a memory."

"Well, that was at 0400. We phoned you just as soon as we found out what ship he was attached to."

"Thanks."

"Aren't you skipper of the cruiser that got torpedoed?"

"Word gets around," The Rock said shortly. "Yes. I am."

The three-striper looked at him curiously. "By damn, that and now this! Your exec can't seem to win for losing, can he? This time he's up against a pretty tough rap."

"Commander, it's a hell of a lot tougher than you think—and it'll get tougher, believe me."

Eddington leaned his bandaged head against the front seat of the station wagon, keeping his eyes tightshut against the gray dawn, as they began the chilly return trip to Pearl Harbor. The Rock himself drove. He had sent Leary ahead in a taxicab. Now he waited for the exec to speak.

"You think I'm a bastard, don't you, skipper?"

Torrey watched the fogbound road ahead.

"No. But I'm sorry for you, Paul. Sorry as hell. I think I know what you're going through."

"Nobody could know," Eddington said in a strangled voice. "Nobody can ever know."

"Maybe not everything. But I do know this, fella, and it comes from hard experience—you can't solve problems with your bare fists, alone, or treat the whole world as a jungle."

Eddington spat out the window.

"Isn't it?"

"Not the way you think. What's happened to you has happened to a lot of other men." The Rock glanced at the exec's averted face before he added softly: "I went through something like this myself . . . a long, long time ago."

Eddington opened his bloodshot eyes. For a moment he groped for words that would cut and hurt. "Did your wife take a powder with an Air Force bastard, too?"

"No. She didn't run away with anybody except herself . . . and our son . . . but no matter how you look at it, it's just as final, and suddenly you're left alone, bitter as hell, and ready to smash out against everybody and everything."

The exec emitted a dry sobbing sound.

"Why in Christ's name did it have to end like this? So ugly. When she was so beautiful. So goddamn beautiful. And no good for herself or for me or for anybody else on earth." His battered face swung toward The Rock. "Or was it just because she was a *woman?*"

"I wish I could answer questions like that, Paul, but I can't, because there aren't any answers."

"All right," Eddington said harshly. "So you've had your own troubles. So I say balls. Look at you. Are you an alcoholic? A weakling? A failure? Christ, no! You're strong . . . and a hell of a lot better man than me."

Torrey shook his head. "Not better. Just different. When this happened to me, instead of fighting back, I ran away from it."

Neither of them spoke after that, for there was nothing more for either man to say.

The Rock supposed that the Navy would forgive the exec, albeit reluctantly, and with a stubborn pride in preserving one of its own. Eddington had taken one of the few missteps to which every officer-and-gentleman is entitled. Much later, of course, when his personal tragedy had been forgotten, and his name came up for captaincy, the Selection Board would admit rather sadly that the circumstances which mitigated the original offense no longer pertained, and they would recoil at the thought of Eddington's ferocious temper and emotional imbalance. Even if he stayed sober as a Methodist chaplain, kept his nose clean, and played for all the breaks, he'd never make that fourth stripe.

It was ironical, The Rock thought, maneuvering the station wagon past the Pearl Harbor sentry box, that both of them had reached this same dead end by such divergent routes . . .

The inquiry into *Old Swayback*'s "unfortunate encounter with a unit of the Japanese Navy," as one highranking board member delicately phrased it, was brief and rather meaningless. Sitting in judgment on a matter that seemed so inconsequential, when viewed in the context of Pearl Harbor itself, inspired none of the board's five officers with any real wish to play Torquemada. Their questions, therefore, were perfunctory. So were the replies.

Was Torrey's Task Group zigzagging at the time of the attack?

Negative: The need for preserving fuel made it imperative that they pursue the enemy in the most expeditious manner possible.

Shouldn't Torrey have broken off the chase earlier?

Affirmative: But this was a discretionary risk taken under orders from CinCPAC. Besides, the visual signal for retirement was ready to be executed at the very moment when *Cassiday* made her underwater contact with the Nip submarine.

Did Captain Torrey have anything further to offer the board concerning the "incident" which might benefit others involved in a similar situation?

Problematical: Until our combatant ships are adequately equipped for modern sea warfare, we might as well recognize that such dangers will continue to exist. The same day *Old Swayback* took her fish, HMS *Prince of Wales* and *Repulse* had fallen prey to enemy aircraft. So if there was any lesson to be drawn from these "unfortunate encounters," it was the simple ABCs of preparedness against three-dimensional onslaughts—surface, aerial, and submarine.

After the hearing, nothing too damaging went into his fitness file. Nothing, that is, except a curt notation that Captain Rockwell Torrey, USN, during temporary command of a task group, had managed to get his cruiser torpedoed, owing to a pattern of events which (in the board's opinion) might not have happened if he had adopted hypothetical Plan X, Y, or Z, instead of doing what he actually did.

Despite its apparent innocuousness, however, The Rock fully understood the deeper meaning of the report, and what they had done to him.

There are degrees of disgrace in the Service. One of the most damaging, because of its exquisite subtlety, overtakes a man as the result of some misdeed for which he's not really to blame. For the suspicion remains, forever haunting him and causing his fellows to whisper: "Poor devil—he just didn't have it in the clutch."

Nobody ever defines *it*. And nobody sentences him to Coventry, either, but this backhanded pity is the worst part of that formless disgrace, and the hardest for a proud man to endure . . .

Inevitably, the Big Brass chose Sunday for launching an abortive attempt to lift the siege of Wake Island, and naturally *Cassiday* drew screening duty with the pick-up task force that was scheduled to clear Pearl Harbor at 1730—the precise hour when Bev McConnel hoped they'd be mixing martinis in honor of her twenty-fourth birthday.

As she guided the Chevvy through the Sub Base gate, Bev said "Damn hell spit!" so loudly and so bitterly that the startled Marine sentry forgot to leer at her as he usually did when she slowed down to show her I.D. card. He just stared. She pulled the dilapidated coupe into a slot labeled Submarine Group Commander. Let 'em sue! Mac said they'd have one hour to celebrate, by darn, and those precious sixty minutes weren't going to be spent hunting for a place to moor this unspeakable wreck in the j.o.'s parking lot.

Mac was waiting right where he said he'd be, with a big package in his hands.

Bev opened the door.

"Happy natal day, old woman." He got in and kissed her uptilted nose. "Hey—that tasted good. More!"

Mac pressed his mouth down hard upon hers. Groping and searching, his hands were exquisitely hurtful and exciting on her breasts, and for a fleeting moment Bev ignored the passing throng of duty-bound sailors, *Cassiday*'s imminent departure, and even how stinking lousy everything was. Then she glimpsed the submarine commander's hoitytoity sign.

"Damn hell spit!"

Mac relaxed against the scrofulous upholstery, blinking his bewilderment.

"What's wrong?"

"Only the whole cockeyed world."

"Oh." He looked relieved. "That. I thought it was something important. Like you. Or me."

"Aren't we part of the cockeyed world?"

"Sure, sure," Mac pointed to the watch on his freckled wrist. "Look, honeypot, we've got fifty-five minutes before I turn back into a khaki-colored rat and Goldilock's coach becomes a '32 Chevvy. Let's don't waste 'em."

"You've got your fairy stories all mixed up." Bev wiped away a rudimentary tear and tried to smile. "I know I'm being an awful dope, darling, but you'd be surprised what living on the edge of a volcano does to us girls. We all behave this way. Runny noses. Sniffles. And trying to keep our chins up and pretend we're a bunch of Joan of Arcs."

"Well, damn it, you are."

"We're real heroines, all right," Bev said disgustedly. "Rolling bandages at the Red Cross. Did you know they've turned the Royal Hawaiian's lobby into a Red Cross center? Starting canteens for The Boys. Wondering when we're going to be shipped home with the rest of the female baggage. Keeping up civilian morale . . . whatever the heck that is. And all the while scared silly whenever *Cassiday* puts to sea."

"Nothing to be scared of, child. I swim like a porpoise."

Bev blew her nose. "William P. for Stupid McConnel! If you only knew. Out there in your poor little tincan with nothing between you and the Japs but a half-inch of sardine lid . . . and most of the Fleet squatting right here in the mud and just as useless as I am . . ." A slow-breaking grin routed her anger, and she added slyly: *"Or was."*

Mac looked puzzled.

"I don't read you very clearly, honey. Too much static."

"Maybe I'll tell you later," she said. "If you behave."

"Heroes don't have to behave."

"Just a figure of speech, sir." Bev drew his hands to her breasts again, squeezing them down hard, and showed the tip of her pink tongue. "See? There are all sorts of behavior patterns, as my old psych prof used to say."

Oblivious to the wolf whistles outside, he kissed her again.

Through her half-closed left eye, Bev watched the repair crew that was reconstructing a midget Japanese submarine salvaged from the harbor bottom. It was the same ugly two-man suicide boat which *Cassiday* had rammed and depth-charged. The sight of the sub started the old, cold train of thought chuffing through Bev's mind, blowing a mournful whistle as it came, and reminding her that the worst damn part of being a woman in wartime was the very nothingness of it all. You weren't a queen bee any more; and you weren't even a decent drone. You were zero-in-skirts.

And that was why she had resolved to do something about it,

whether Mac liked it or not. She would tell him when it was too late for any effective McConnel-brand countermeasures. How did he express it? Sure. What's the use of a guy hanging around a poker game unless he's got a little piece of the action. Bev scrabbled through her lauhala handbag and fished out a black-market Kleenex. She dried her tears. Then she powdered her small nose, and surveyed the wreckage in the rearview mirror.

"Jeepers, lieutenant, I *do* look twenty-four, don't I?"

"You don't look a day over twenty-three," Mac assured her. "You're ravishing. Or is it ravishable?"

"Not here in the commander's personal parking space!"

"When I get back—" He sighed. "They've kept me so damn busy I haven't even been able to buy you a present. But the commodore donated this with his blessings."

Mac unwrapped the package. It was a pint bottle of Veuve Cliquot and a pair of paper cups. When he freed the cork, apologizing for his clumsiness, the champagne made a wonderful popping noise. Mac filled their cups quickly as the wine bubbled out.

"To the woman of my life," he toasted, "who keeps me warm when it's cold, dry when it's wet, and brave when it's frightening . . . even when she's far, far away."

"To my man . . . and please dear God bring him home safe."

Suddenly it was time to say goodbye.

Mac stood beside the Chevvy as Bev struggled with the starter, and when the engine finally uttered the bronchial coughs that meant it was coming to life, she poked her head out the window. The afternoon sun made her hair gleam like something handcrafted from red gold.

He swallowed hard, twice, and waved. The car began to move.

"I forgot to tell you," Bev called back at him, "that I've taken a job with the Island Command. Air-raid spotter at Fort Shafter. Now I'm 'essential to the war effort'—and they can't ship me home till it's all over!"

Mac yelled, "Hey wait—"

But the Chevvy was gone.

7. *No Man Is an Island*

For a professional military man, Purgatory can mean staff duty in an area that is not quite *rear,* and certainly not *combat,* but which lies within the limbo where the fighting forces mingle briefly and somewhat arrogantly with the plans-and-logistical echelons before they embark on their Jason quests.

In the waning winter and the early spring of 1942, therefore, Pearl Harbor was Purgatory for a great many naval officers of high and low degree who yearned for ships instead of desks, and whose hearts weren't really in the business of projecting great adventures for others to carry out. Hawaii was still classed as a "combat area," since the enemy presumably could drive his way across the Pacific any time he wished, and launch another assault on the Island bastion. It was outside the continental limits of the United States, and, theoretically, those who performed on CinCPAC's vast and growing staff were considered as executing "sea duty" for pay purposes. This anomaly entitled them to the same 10 per cent bonus given submariners who ran the Japanese gantlet into Manila Bay, carrier pilots who bombed Maloelap—and the Marines who wouldn't be able to cash their paychecks for a hell of a long while because they'd been captured on Wake Island two days after the sun reached its winter solstice and spring was nothing but a forlorn dream in men's discouraged minds.

At first Torrey accepted it philosophically, and without futile complaint, although he was already experiencing the hollowness, the sense of vacuum, that comes when the absolute authority of high command is snatched away. John Paul Jones had known such a time. Stripped of his naval jurisdiction, beached in Russia after his gaudiest victories, he was reduced to proving his masculine combativeness with shabby little encounters in Muscovite boudoirs. The Rock was not unaware of the lesson to be learned from Jones' tragedy, now, as he found himself virtually a junior officer again after so many years. He was just one of several captains in CinCPAC's

War Plans department, and surrounded by two-star admirals who were, themselves, extremely conscious of their subordinate status in relation to the galaxied High Brass in Washington, D.C.

One thing stood in Torrey's favor. The new CinCPAC, who had quietly relieved the old one on New Year's Eve, remembered him from his Academy teaching days, and recalled the way The Rock had argued for airpower when the battleship crowd was riding so tall in the saddle (an expression CinCPAC himself might have used, being a Texan). Because of his ill-timed enthusiasm, Torrey had come perilously close to committing the Original Sin. But now it wasn't Original Sin any more; it was CinCPAC's only hope for wriggling out of the desperate situation he'd inherited.

"Let's forget recriminations," he said in a twangy drawl that left no margin for nonsense. "When you gentlemen relax over your bourbon and branch, I want you to be figuring out what can be done, instead of regretting what might have been. Understand?"

They understood. And they considered Halsey, whose pair of aircraft carriers represented the whole Pacific Fleet during this painful interlude. He'd pop up at the most improbable places with his small task force, raising merry hell with the enemy; and in the process he'd generate enough headlines back home to lift the country out of its defeatist doldrums for a little while.

That spring The Rock was assigned quarters with two other senior captains in a paintsmelling new frame house on Makalapa Hill. Thrown into close proximity with these officers, he was confronted with the choice of turning completely antisocial, or rejoining what was loosely termed The Lodge—an informal confraternity based on their related staff jobs—since they ate in a common mess and observed certain convivial amenities. To his quiet surprise, Torrey discovered that The Lodge was a rather pleasant place, providing a curative for a loneliness which had lately bordered on melancholy self-pity.

By coincidence, none of them stood headquarters duty on Thursday nights, and they generally spent the evening together, playing poker, listening to the radio, browsing through the multipaged reports that flowed out of Washington's duplicating machines, or just talking.

Larry Moorian cooked their Thursday suppers, wearing a chef's cap over his crisp black hair.

He was the highest ranking Armenian in the United States Navy, he insisted proudly, and thus entitled to special respect. When he quit his father's vineyards in Fresno, California, to enter the Academy, the world lost its last chance to replace the great Escoffier, Moorian declared, because his real love wasn't winemaking, or even the sea, but creating exotic dishes, such as Genoese *burida* made from fresh Hawaiian fishes, Tarascon *pintadeau au porto* made from guinea hens he found God knows where, and Budapest *gulyas* made from everything under the blazing sun. Moorian refused to prepare Armenian specialties. Just thinking about grape leaves, he said, made him violently ill, although he used wines liberally enough in his work. He was short, dark, shining, and wore a tiny penciled mustache along his upper lip.

Moorian's CinCPAC job was routing convoys from West Coast Australia, where the serious build-up for recapturing the South Pacific from the Japs had just gotten underway.

The third member of their household was a reservist captain named Egan Powell, who had joined the naval militia as a lieutenant (j.g.) right after World War I. In peacetime, he wrote mystery films for Hollywood and dabbled in cryptography on the side. Happily, a Bureau of Personnel yeoman had punched the right button after Pearl Harbor, so Powell received orders to CinCPAC Intelligence instead of public information. He arrived with two trunksful of uniforms tailored to his handsome frame, and a dozen autographed pictures of America's best-known film actresses, several of whom he had married and divorced as casually as Torrey changed his khaki shirts. Egan Powell still subscribed to fan magazines. But he worked furiously at some secret occupation which he wouldn't discuss even with The Rock or Moorian. They knew only that it concerned experiments with codes and ciphers in the catacomb office beneath Fleet headquarters.

Sometimes the northeast tradewinds blew raw red dust into their jerrybuilt house from a mountain farther back in Oahu's sudden wilderness, where the earth was being hollowed out to form a bombproof fuel cache. It drifted under doorsills and through cracks in the window sashes, and caused Powell to grumble, "Wouldn't silicosis be a hell of a way for a Navy man to die—even a goddamn reservist?" At other times, after the warm rain gave way to limpid sunshine at 1100 every morning, double rainbows curved across the graygreen hills behind Makalapa, where a perpetual mist overhung the hidden valleys like a pale caul. If he were off-duty, The Rock would get out his camera and solemnly record the phenomena.

Torrey's hobby went almost unnoticed by Moorian and Powell, who guessed that he had found his own antidote for the tedium which affected everyone at Pearl, and which daily grew more oppressive during this interim war-that-wasn't-quite-war.

There were several methods, none of them particularly longlasting or satisfactory, for combating the monotony. Some officers turned to Honolulu's limited supply of unattached women in search of relief. Others played endless sets of mediocre tennis on the Submarine Base's courts, or paddled just as endlessly around the palmshaded swimming pool, until they were exhausted physically and emptied mentally.

And a few combined sex and sports, utilizing the Sub Base facilities as a rendezvous, because the Navy nurses from Aiea were granted weekend swimming privileges. Grudgingly at first. Then wholeheartedly, as the supply of accessible women dwindled under CinCPAC's stern edict that all "nonessential" females must go back to the mainland, and even the drab nurses began looking better. Accessibility, of course, was a matter of academic interpretation. The Island's feminine population appeared to be divided almost evenly between hungry bachelor girls toasting their babyoiled bodies under the hot sun on their off-duty days, and wives who had found war work that allowed them to remain in Oahu while their husbands were gone. They felt hungry, too, sometimes.

Egan Powell readily confessed that he was a sex-and-sports man. Smoothing his waxed mustache, which was bushier than Moorian's token adornment, he urged The Rock one afternoon to accompany him to Waikiki Beach on "a field expedition." It was their fourth Thursday in The Lodge.

"Man," he declaimed, "cannot live by bread alone—not when he's used to the fleshpots of Hollywood."

Torrey smiled, but shook his head. "I'm from Kittery, Maine," he reminded Powell.

"Hell, mister, this is a purely scientific expedition. You'll discover fauna you never dreamed existed."

"I'm not trained for it," Torrey said. "I'd get lost."

"Then let the old professor describe what he means in nautical terms, so you'll understand." Powell tugged pensively at his lower lip. "It's like this, Rock. Some women are like ships in what you'd call standby status. Boilers cold as ice. Then there are the ready-duty kind. All fired up and set to go. It's like a Fleet availability report—you can even draw a graph from it, showing whether a woman's in the mood for romance, or if she can be coaxed into it."

The Rock coughed to hide his embarrassment. It was disconcerting to hear a grown man dissect women in this clinical manner. But Moorian, emerging from the kitchen and mopping his olive brow with his chef's cap, wasn't in the least distressed.

"Tell us more, Captain Casanova," he coaxed. "Just how do you plot this marvelous graph?"

"Easy, logical, and scientific. Let's take a girl lying in front of the Outrigger Club. You compute the exact degree of arch in her back, and if it's a fifteen-degree curve, you're in just as good shape as she is. Ready to roll. Twenty degrees is optimum. But anything under ten," Powell added judiciously, "isn't worth the effort."

Moorian pulled off his apron.

"Keep an eye on the bouillabaisse," he told The Rock. "At 1700, turn it 'way low so it'll simmer. Egan needs a convoy to Waikiki. See you at chowtime . . ."

Torrey thoughtfully filled his bulldog briar after they left, and picked up a Naval Intelligence report he hadn't had a chance to study. For a while he sat reading before an opened window, with the breeze fanning his gaunt cheeks, but he soon found it difficult to concentrate. Feeling a vague uneasiness, that might have been caused by a foretaste of Moorian's rich bouillabaisse, he closed the pamphlet, and idly switched on their communal radio, which was pre-tuned to Honolulu's daytime station. A girl was singing a curiously haunting ballad about seeing her faraway lover in all the old familiar places. For a nostalgic moment Torrey was carried back to another place, long ago, when the song was *Dardanella,* and he suddenly wondered what Athalie and Jere were doing in Boston, where it would now be six P.M.

Because the sidewalk slush on Beacon Hill had already hardened into jagged coldsteel, Athalie would have told the butler to sprinkle furnace ashes over the pavement so Master Torrey wouldn't slip and break his precious young neck when he came home to supper. Not Midshipman Torrey, as it should have been; but Master Torrey, Harvard senior, the future white hope of Farr-Cunliffe, Ltd., and a very earnest young man who lived at home instead of in a Yard dormitory, because dear Mama preferred it that way.

She and Jere had remained in Boston when Torrey went off to San Diego to take command of a destroyer in 1924.

"I do not wish," she told him, "to become a Navy camp follower. When you are granted leave, you may come home. Jere and I will be here, waiting for you, always."

Athalie did not offer her marble cheek for the usual farewell kiss.

For three years, Torrey made his annual month-long hegira to Beacon Hill, enduring her Mona Lisa smiles whenever he mentioned Jere's future, and discerning in the boy himself a strange reluctance to accept him on any terms: son-to-father, man-to-man, or even as polite stranger-to-stranger. It was as if Athalie were both father and mother for Jere, wrapped up into one neat, comfortable, crooning package, and The Rock didn't exist.

When the summer of 1927 came, and his four-week leave was due again, Torrey sat down one evening in the Officers' Club lounge at Coronado and laboriously composed a letter to his wife.

". . . so it would appear to be the wisest course," he finished, "for me to remain here rather than make the empty gesture of visiting you this year. For yourself, I feel only a great sorrow, my dear, because you are a very lost and unhappy woman. But I wish to God I knew what you have done to our son. Whatever it is, I can only hope it is in his best interests, and that Jere will emerge somehow from this cocoon which you have spun around him . . ."

Athalie's proxy reply was penned by the Cunliffe family attorney who regretted to inform the lieutenant commander that Mrs. Torrey was filing suit for divorce, charging desertion. She would waive alimony. All she wanted was Jere.

The Rock scribbled his own answer on a penny postcard. "Terms acceptable. R. Torrey, USN." Then he caught a jitney to San Diego and got royally drunk for the first time in his austere, self-possessed, systematized life.

It was remarkable that Torrey neither hated, scorned, nor even disliked women after their divorce. He merely ignored them.

He didn't go back to Boston for five years. Finally, finding that the scar tissue had healed across the old wound, he resumed his visits on a curtailed basis, running up to Beacon Hill from Annapolis or wherever he was stationed at the time, spending a restless day with Athalie and his son, and then returning to duty. It was highly unsatisfactory. But Torrey felt a compulsive desire to observe Jere's development, however alien it was to what he had originally planned for the boy.

Shortly after he was made captain, in 1936, The Rock enrolled for flight training. He was self-conscious about it—a four-striper taught by kids young enough to be his son—but he persevered and won his gold wings.

He liked flying. A man could think clearly at ten thousand feet, he discovered, all by himself, and as he wheeled lazily over the semicircular beaches of Pensacola, he'd sometimes reflect how easy it would be to push the stick and let the fat little Grumman go screeching down into the gulf, taking care, of course, not to plow through the housing projects along the shore.

But Torrey had no real death urge. He didn't particularly like to recall these brief moments. They still bothered him.

But now it was May 1942, and on the huge chart nailed to the beaverboard bulkhead in War Plans, orange pins that symbolized enemy task units crept relentlessly eastward from their bases in Japan, from the Kuriles, and from the Marianas. Some pointed toward the Aleutians. But most of them appeared to be converging upon the outer reaches of the Hawaiian chain itself, toward the new base at Midway Island.

A preliminary battle had been fought in the Coral Sea, with the result that CinCPAC must face the foe with one less precious aircraft carrier.

Early that month, while the Coral Sea engagement was still brewing, The Rock was called into CinCPAC's private conference room with a half-dozen other captains and admirals. Egan Powell was already there, standing alongside a shrouded easel, with a wooden pointer in his manicured right hand, and looking like an actor awaiting his first starring role.

At a nod from the admiral who headed Fleet Intelligence, Powell flipped the cover off the easel.

"We have here, gentlemen, the complete layout of Operation MI, the Japs' plan for occupying Midway. It is the brain child of Admiral Isoroku Yamamoto. As far as we know, there are no details missing—the enemy's size, his intentions, or his strategy." He paused. "You gentlemen understand why we cannot divulge even in this room exactly *how* we obtained this material. But our knowledge of Yamamoto's purpose is worth at least one fast carrier task group . . . and it may even compensate for the imbalance between the Orange forces and ours."

Torrey gave his whole attention to the easel. The Japanese were committing four large carriers, three lighter ones, eleven battlewagons, fifteen cruisers, forty-four destroyers, fifteen submarines, and a gaggle of lesser ships to their supreme effort. CinCPAC could count on three big carriers, eight cruisers, eighteen destroyers, and nineteen subs.

His jaw tightened. Among those cruisers would be *Old Swayback*, restored to action, outfitted with radar's magic eye, and twice the ship she was when he commanded her. Porky Hamm had her now. He was Class of '18, four years younger than The Rock; and his exec was damned near an infant, when you compared ages, out of '22. Torrey thought of Eddington, who had ferried *Old Swayback* to the West Coast five months earlier with a wooden cofferdam fastened to her wounded flank like a gigantic mustard plaster, and he wondered whether the rumors about Paul's continuing drunkenness were true. He hoped they weren't. But The Rock's one letter to Eddington, while his former exec was still at Mare Island, had gone unanswered.

". . . So, gentlemen, we shall concentrate our forces here, here, and *here!*"

An operations officer had replaced Powell at the easel, which now showed the whereabouts of all the scattered American forces. There was no margin for error, he said, in CinCPAC's plan. If it failed, the Nips could steam unimpeded all the way to Frisco and turn the Top-o'-the-Mark into a sukiyaki palace . . .

When the meeting ended, Egan Powell buttonholed The Rock in the corridor outside the admiral's office.

"What d'you think about the surprise party we're cooking up for the Japs?"

"You've done a hell of a fine job, fella. I just wish we'd had your code-breaking team a few months ago."

'These things take time," Powell said. "We were already working on it then."

"That's great comfort."

"You sound bitter."

The Rock halted in front of Operations, and waited a moment with his hand on the doorknob, before he said unemotionally, "Yes, I guess I'd be bitter if I started brooding over what happened. But it wouldn't help. You can't refight an engagement any more than you can unring a bell."

Powell shrugged in broad Gallic fashion. "Look how times have changed. Now they're giving Navy Crosses to captains whose ships are torpedoed. Like crackerjack prizes. Next they'll be making 'em admirals if they get their ships sunk. You wait and see."

"I'll still be here," Torrey said morosely. "Waiting. And seeing."

"Meanwhile, Rock, what about a little rest-and-recuperation? Friends of mine have a cocktail bash planned for 1700 out at Black Point. It'll wind up before blackout. Could be our last chance at R-and-R before the dam bursts." He grinned. "Man cannot—"

"—live by bread alone."

"Affirmative! You're learning."

Torrey caught a glimpse of blue sky and cottonwhite tradewind clouds through the door at the end of the dim passageway. Now that he thought about it, he did feel stale and tired, and he was haunted by something that could have been the sort of fear that grips a man at night when he awakens suddenly to the realization that whatever it was he wanted from life has eluded him and is fleeing down some gloomy corridor, never to be attained.

"All right, Mephistopheles," The Rock said. "I'll join you."

"Tallyho!" Powell shook his lean hand. "The outside world will amaze you, Rock. Women wear perfume. They smell good. And they can make you forget your troubles."

"Thanks." Torrey smiled oddly. "You'll have to fly wing for me, Egan, because I've lost most of the social graces."

But as The Rock slowly dressed for Egan Powell's party, and inspected the loose hang of the tropical tans he'd bought in San Francisco two years earlier, his old prejudices came flooding back. Maybe he should welsh out now, before he played the fool in front of Black Point's insouciant society, trying to make small-talk and laughing at clever jokes he didn't understand. He tugged at the jacket. Damned tailor had made it too long by a whole inch, so it looked foppishly non-reg, like the coats worn by those Hollywood actors who impersonated naval officers on the screen, or in the reserves. The Frisco tailor, a stickler for pomp, had also sewed his double row of decorations irrevocably above his left breast pocket, along with an embroidered pair of gold wings.

Then Egan Powell strolled into the bedroom wearing a uniform that was even more dashing than Torrey's, with his black-knit cravat tied in a Windsor knot, and his yellow pre-Pearl Harbor ribbon gleaming lonesomely on his coat. He sounded aggrieved, like a small boy waiting for a tardy parent.

"If we're late," he said, "we won't even get into the ballgame."

"You don't mind if I just sit and watch, do you?"

"Suit yourself," Powell said. "Personally, I'm a lousy spectator-sportsman. I like to play." He whistled softly at the sight of Torrey's ribbons. "You look like a goddamn Gary Cooper with that fruitsalad splattered all over your manly chest. And a Navy Cross—"

"Skip it," Torrey growled.

Powell was unperturbed. "If they bother you, I'll swap jackets."

The Rock's embarrassed look faded. "All right, fella, let's shove off. You've got the Fleet guide. I'll take station on you."

They arrived only a few minutes late for the inaugural round of martinis, but a score of Army colonels, bouncing young Air Force majors, pretentiously grimfaced Marine officers, and aloof Navy commanders were already milling around the flagstoned veranda that overlooked Black Point. The more enterprising officers were wasting no time zeroing in on the half-dozen unencumbered women with whom their host, a gregarious Waikiki entrepreneur, always decorated his Service parties. Having all this brass in his elegant house gave him a sense of well-being, and the knowledge that he was contributing something pretty worthwhile to the War Effort.

Egan Powell showed Torrey the bar over which a liveried Filipino presided.

"First chukker's half finished," he said, "and I've got to find me a mount. Maybe that platinum-blond filly in basic black velvet by the rail needs her glass replenished. Take care."

Ironically amused, The Rock watched him glide across the big porch toward the girl. She was surrounded by four grinning officers. Since none of them were Navy, Powell's chances were excellent.

Being alone in a crowd had never bothered Torrey, for he had come to accept this self-imposed condition over the years, and now he made himself comfortable by resting his shoulders against a pillar, and surveyed his host's opulent estate. Below the veranda, on the manicured lawncarpet which descended gently toward the lava seafront that gave Black Point its name, a pair of male peacocks meandered haughtily, their tail feathers outspread like brummagem-jeweled fans. Beyond them the surf thundered against the rocks. Each time the breakers receded, they exposed a section of barbed wire coils, placed there months earlier when it was feared the enemy might try a landing. Past the surf and the coral reefs of Maunalua Bay lay the open Pacific, turning purple as the molten sun declined, a dark backdrop for the lone destroyer patrolling offshore, and for the PBYs wave-hopping back from their afternoon searches toward the Japanese-held Marshalls.

For the first time Torrey became aware that the weather was insufferably hot and muggy, even with the sun setting and a tentative breeze wafting around Koko Head. To make matters worse, his tailored uniform was less porous than regulation khaki, and the coat clung soggily to his rake-thin back.

A young colonel wearing USAF silver wings surmounted by a command star walked past him, wiping his brow.

"Reckon it's genuine bombin' weather, don't you, captain?" he drawled.

Torrey started to agree, but the pilot was already swallowed up by the crowd of laughing, gesticulating drinkers.

Another voice asked, "What's 'bombin' weather,' sir?"

It sounded neither cornpone Southern nor nasal Yankee nor flat Midwestern. It was just a soothing, rather throaty feminine voice, accentlessly cosmopolitan, which fell pleasantly upon his ear without the stridency affected by the other women he'd heard discussing surfboarding, waterskiing, and certain more exotic athletic accomplishments after too many five-to-one martinis.

The Rock turned.

She was a Navy nurse, a two-striper, and quite small. Maybe about five-feet-three without her prim two-inch heels, he guessed, but now she was standing so firmly in her gray seersucker uniform that she seemed taller. She wasn't wearing a cap. Her coif of hair, which was the color of polished mahogany, showed a few strands of gray where it waved over her forehead. She might have been thirty. Or more. Or less.

Torn between treating her with avuncular condescension or superior-officer coolness, neither of which seemed right, Torrey chose the natural approach.

" 'Bombin' weather,' " he explained, "is like 'earthquake weather' in California. It doesn't mean a thing, really. Just that when the weather's hot enough to boil your blood, people get a lot of weird ideas."

"Oh."

Torrey looked around. "Haven't you strayed away from your convoy, lieutenant?"

She appeared genuinely puzzled.

"I don't think I understand, captain."

"There seems to be a rule around here," he said, "that young ladies must be escorted by a minimum of five gentlemen."

"In that case, I'm exempt."

When she smiled, her mouth slanted oddly, giving her a soft sly look that was quite appealing. She didn't use as much lipstick as those suntanned Brünnhildes, either, he noticed.

The Rock heard himself say, "Now it's my turn not to understand," awkwardly, as if this composed woman were *his* superior officer and he was a j.o. trying to create a favorable impression.

"Well, for one thing, I'm damn well not a 'young' lady," she said matter-of-factly. "Because I'm thirty-six. Not size, either. Age."

"You don't look it."

"What *do* I look?"

"I don't know," he said honestly, "but I'd swear you're young enough to be my daughter, if I had a daughter . . ."

"Maybe you've lived a harder life than mine. Though I doubt it." She touched her artlessly coiffured head. "These gray streaks weren't painted on here by a beautician."

"Your hair is fine."

"Thank you, kind sir." She bobbed her head in mock humility.

"Coming from Captain Rockwell Torrey, I suspect that's rather a huge compliment."

"How did you know my name?"

"Spies," she said in a Mata Hari voice. "They tell me everything. Even things like 'The Rock is an awfully tough cooky. Hates women. Thinks they ought to be abolished. Never appears in polite society.' "

Uncertain whether to be amused or annoyed, he asked, "Isn't this polite society?"

"Perhaps you're slumming."

"No. I've wandered a little off course," The Rock said, "and strayed out of my element, that's all."

She gestured with her glass toward the exquisitely gowned women. "So have I. Trying to match beat-up seersucker against sexy chiffon doesn't make much sense, does it?"

"Then why did you come?"

"Our host takes pity on female military types, too, although he prefers us out of uniform. He invited four of us from Aiea Hospital. See those three kids over there? They're my buddies. Emmy, Jo, and Bonnie. They came in mufti. But you'd never mistake 'em for anything except Navy nurses, would you? Feet a little too big. Hands rough. And so damned eager to please the boys they make your skin crawl."

"You seem in control of the situation."

"Got to be. I'm their chaperone."

The Rock saw that her glass was empty. He said, "What are you drinking, lieutenant?"

"Bourbon. Neat. On the rocks." She caught the slight upthrust of his heavy black brows. "It's my early training. You see, I learned to drink on Army posts."

"I don't see it at all."

"Fetch me the bourbon," she said, "and I'll tell you the sad story of my life."

"Agreed." He took her glass. "But first, tell me your name."

"Margarethe Poinciana Suzanne Haynes. Isn't that the damnedest? Mother was going through her Caribbean phase when I was born."

"What do they call you?"

"Maggie. Just plain Maggie."

When he returned, she had moved to a secluded corner of the veranda, under a jungle of tree ferns. As she reached for the drink she said, "Cheers, Captain Torrey."

"Confusion to our enemies, Lieutenant Haynes."

Manfashion, Maggie lifted the glass to her lips with a strong right hand and downed half the whisky in one gulp. The Rock watched closely to see whether the raw liquor brought tears to her eyes, which were a remarkable amethyst color. It didn't.

"My life?" Maggie said in response to his unspoken question. "In one sentence—I was an Army brat."

"Army!"

"Surprised that I turned Navy at this hardened-artery stage of my career?"

"Naturally." He glanced over her slim figure. "But what really puzzles me is why you'd go in for nursing in the first place."

She gave him her twisted smile. He observed that it tended toward starboard and got tangled up with a dimple he hadn't seen before. But it was damned attractive.

"When I was seventeen I got married to escape the General."

"You enjoy talking in riddles, don't you?"

"The General was dear old Daddy. One-star. They gave him a second star after he ran his Stutz Bearcat off Pikes Peak during a race. He wore it very proudly. Also very posthumously, because Pikes Peak put him in heaven, or wherever useless peacetime Army generals go when they die." Still holding her drink, Maggie fished a cigarette out of a shoulderbag with her left hand, and lit it expertly with a mansized Zippo. "I suppose Daddy might have wound up in either place. He was an angel and a devil. But mostly a practicing alcoholic and an eighteen-carat bastard."

The Rock's brows contracted, and again she sensed his disapproval.

"Sorry, captain, but I picked up my vocabulary in the same places where I learned to drink. Army posts. Daddy served in Missouri, once, and I got kind of adopted by the muleskinners. Ever hear 'em talk?"

His frown vanished and he groped for a decently repentant thing to say. "Don't be sorry, lieutenant. I'm a stuffy—bastard."

She regarded him speculatively.

'That legalizes an illegitimate word, doesn't it? Now, Captain

Rockwell Torrey, why don't you loosen up and call me Maggie, instead of lieutenant, so I can stop masquerading in these funny Navy clothes."

"All right." He tried it experimentally: "Maggie."

"Much better."

"Maybe you'd better call me Rock."

"Isn't that pretty *infra dig* for a two-striper?"

"If we ever meet on duty, you may genuflect and refer to me as Captain Torrey."

"Very well, Rock—sir!"

He felt his cheek muscles tighten into an idiotic grin as he looked down at Maggie's upturned face from his greater height, and the random thought occurred to him that Athalie would have fainted dead away if he had ever called himself a "bastard" in her presence. Later, of course, he'd learn that Maggie's candid language went with her uncompromising realism; and he'd also discover that she had a tendency to regard adult warriors as funny little kids playing with explosive toys that might blow up in their faces any minute, and send them bawling after mama. Maggie hated pomposity. Which was rather unfortunate. She was exposed to so much of it.

"Damned near 1830," she said, consulting her stainless steel wrist watch. "Blackout time in a half-hour. I've got to dash back to Aiea and play Florence Nightingale again."

"But you never finished your story."

"Inquisitive?"

The Rock was surprised at his prompt reaction. "Yes, I am."

Maggie surveyed the dwindling cluster of guests.

"My three little chums seem to have disappeared," she said, "right out from under grandma's eyes. Which is par for the course. I'd make a lousy duenna. Anyhow, now I'm stuck with the jeep and if there's anything I hate worse than chaperoning, it's chauffeuring."

"I could drive you to Aiea."

"How'd you ever guess what I was hinting at?"

Maggie lowered her eyes with pretended coyness, and he perceived that her lashes were extraordinarily dark and long.

"Intuition. And I'd really like to hear the rest of your autobiography."

"It's pretty gory."

He tapped his ribbons.

"Ma'am, I am a registered member of the hero's union. See? We never faint at the sight of blood." (Thinking: *What in the hell am I saying, me, Rockwell Torrey? Have I suddenly lost my middle-aged mind?*)

Silent during the long ride back through the twilight, they sat quietly in the parked jeep now, staring down the long hill from Aiea toward the Fleet anchorage where the warships rode dark against dapplegray waters, with no lights showing. Maggie's small face gleamed palely in the dusk.

She spoke first, hesitantly, as if the hiatus in their conversation had made them strangers again.

"I don't know why I even started to tell you all those things about myself. Mostly I keep them locked up. It's better that way."

"Sometimes it helps a man to talk about himself . . . and his troubles."

"Man?"

The Rock's hands, clenched tightly around the steering wheel, showed little white ridges where the knuckles protruded. He said, "Yes. Man. Me. All my life I've held it in. Now I don't know. Maybe it isn't good for anyone to imagine he's completely independent. What did that poet say? Something about an island?"

"I don't read much poetry, Rock, but I have read a lot of Hemingway. He quoted it in *For Whom the Bell Tolls*. John Donne wrote it. 'No man is an island, entire of itself . . .' "

"That's it." Torrey's gaze sought out tiny Ford Island in the center of the manyfingered harbor. "Even if we were 'entire,' I guess we'd be lost without some bigger continent to cling to. Like Hawaii. And a hell of a lot more islands farther west in the Pacific that are waiting for us."

Maggie asked abruptly, "Are you married?"

"Not any more." He didn't seem surprised or offended.

She lit an illegal cigarette, shielding the Zippo below the dashboard in deference to the blackout, and smoked it with the glowing end cupped inside her right hand.

"Neither am I."

"What happened?"

"My mistake was marrying Daddy's personal aide because he was handy. The General got so mad he arranged for us to be ordered to the Philippine backcountry. But Arthur—that *was* my husband—took it like a real man. He started drinking, and after a while, when I thought about my mother's 'marriage,' I said to hell with it."

Even in the gloaming, Torrey could see the tight muscle pads form alongside her mouth as she kept herself under remarkably unfeminine control.

"So that's when you decided to become a nurse?"

"No. That's when I started to help Arthur drink up all the gin in the Philippines."

He said roughly, "What good did that do?"

"Not a damned bit. After six months even I figured that out. So I turned very pukka sahib and volunteered for the native health center." She laughed mirthlessly. "Oh, they called me 'that dedicated little Mrs. Alderton' and they said I was truly helping carry the White Man's Burden. Sometimes I was 'that *poor* little Mrs. Alderton.'"

"Alderton?"

"That was my charming husband's name. After the divorce I became Haynes again, because I preferred it that way. For all his whoring and hellraising, at least the General was genuine. But Major Alderton was a phony. That's what really queered things. I hate phonies."

"Do you always talk so frankly to people?"

"Never."

"Then why to me?"

Maggie's eyes searched his seamed face for a long moment before she replied enigmatically, "Maybe you remind me of somebody I've always wanted to meet . . ."

"How—" Torrey began. Then he stopped, unaccountably afraid to probe deeper.

"I guess I've just had bad luck with my men," she went on. "Arthur managed to kill himself cleaning his .45 automatic. He blew the top off his silly head, and that proved one thing that surprised me. It wasn't filled with sawdust. Brains he'd never used got splattered all over the wall. Arthur wasn't a very pretty sight, even though I'd been exposed to some of the unlovelier aspects of life in the tropics. You know. You've been there. Natives with dripping yaws sores. Scrotums swollen like watermelons from elephantiasis."

"Are you trying to shock an old seadog?"

"No. It's how I talk."

"Always honest like this?"

"Always." She moistened her lower lip with her tongue. "Maybe that explains why I'm a bachelor girl retread after eighteen years."

" 'Retread' is a word that doesn't even have a female gender," he said, trying to lighten her mood. "Only Navymen ever get retreaded —when there's a war on."

"I don't think you know very much about women, Captain Torrey."

"That's true. And now I'm too damned old to learn."

She wanted to ask his age, but he seemed immersed in his own melancholy just then, so she fell silent. It didn't really matter. Whatever it was, she felt older. Much older.

The Rock said suddenly, "I wonder . . . is it possible to be homesick when you haven't got a home?"

"Yes." Her husky voice was very wise. "You can be homesick for something you've never even had. Believe me. I know."

He turned slowly toward her on the cramped canvas seat. "May I see you again?"

"Certainly."

"Soon?"

"Yes. I'd like that."

In the fire-opal glow of the halfmoon that had risen through the eastern tradewind mists, she seemed very beautiful to him, and suddenly he bent down and kissed her full on her mouth. It tasted sweet. For a moment his longing was appeased, and he was content just to hold her lightly in his arms, inhaling the fragrance of her hair.

Maggie's voice sounded faraway. "You're a strange, strange man, Rock."

"Do you still want me to call you?"

"Of course." She looked surprised. "Why do you ask that?"

Torrey pondered the question. Her scent, her softness as she lay in his arms, stirred desires he hadn't felt in years.

"I don't really know why I asked that," he said seriously. "But

I will telephone tomorrow, because you still haven't told me how you became a Navy nurse."

Maggie sat up and found her comb. "That part of the story isn't as bad as the other. It's just dull." She grinned. "Now I'll have to use *my* influence, captain, to get you a ride home. Remember? This is a hospital jeep."

Egan Powell hadn't returned to Makalapa yet, of course, but Larry Moorian greeted Torrey at the door, his round Armenian face expectant, just in time to see the hospital corpsman pull the jeep away from the curb.

"When Powell phoned to tell me he wouldn't make it for dinner," Moorian said, "he sort of hinted you might be a trifle late, too."

"Powell knows too goddamn much."

"He claims you deserted him for a lady lieutenant."

The Rock snorted. "Powell deserts pretty easy."

"Anyhow," Moorian said, "it's nice to know you've rejoined the human race, fella."

"Thanks."

"Don't thank me. Thank the female two-striper."

"I will," Torrey growled, "when I see her tomorrow."

"*If* you see her," Moorian said forebodingly. "Things are clouding up."

"The Japs?"

Moorian nodded. "They're finally moving. CinCPAC may call an Alert any minute." As Torrey started for the stairs, he added: "By the way, there's a special-delivery letter for you on the table. Very chi-chi and scented. Fancy coat of arms on the back flap."

Without speaking, The Rock went into the livingroom and picked up the small gray envelope. The handwriting, stiff and angular, was unmistakable; and the pretentious heraldic gewgaw was the Cunliffe family crest. Moorian's curious glance followed him as he took the letter unopened to his own room.

What the hell, he mused, did Athalie want now?

Sitting on his bed in the airless, blacked-out chamber, with a gooseneck lamp shining against the vellum notepaper like a third-degree spotlight, he read her brief message.

". . . So you've won, after all," Athalie wrote, "and I hope it makes you very happy. I'm not. My heart is broken. Jere's joining the Navy means he won't finish his master's degree at Harvard until this horrible war ends. Perhaps never. What my son has done disturbs me, Rockwell, because it reminds me too much of you, and your insane devotion to 'duty,' or whatever it is you call what you've been pursuing all these years . . ."

Torrey reread the passage. At first Athalie had penned "our son," but then she'd scratched out the *our* and substituted *my,* taking malicious care that the original word remained quite legible.

". . . Perhaps you may meet Jere sometime, out there, because they say the PT boats are to be used mainly in the Pacific. I am not sure that he will wish to see you, although that is entirely up to him, for he is almost a grown man now and I cannot rule his life . . ."

Athalie might as well have appended the phrase *any longer,* since it was inherent in that final sentence. Even at twenty-two, Jere was her pliant creation; and if her will could be exerted telepathically, she would still contrive to shape him to her cold image. He wondered what he would do when the boy's torpedo-boat squadron arrived at Pearl Harbor, as it inevitably must, enroute to a combat assignment after its East Coast training, and he also wondered if Jere hated him.

He supposed he did.

8. *Too Much, Too Little*

LARRY MOORIAN WAS ACCURATE in his warning. Sometime during the night, when the orange pins representing the Japanese task forces reached an invisible "X" on the War Plans chart that was known only to CinCPAC himself, the Hawaiian area went on full Alert status. Within an hour their island world was completely changed, as if an omnipotent lever had been pulled, clanging shut the massive gates of Pearl Harbor, Hickam Field, Kaneohe Naval Air Station, Schofield Barracks, the Marines' windblown aviation facility at Ewa, and all the lesser military satellites that ringed these big bases.

CinCPAC had made prisoners of them all.

Torrey accepted his incarceration with a calmness marred only briefly by a flicker of selfish annoyance. He'd expected it. And until yesterday, restriction to his cluttered War Plans desk, the senior officers' mess, the dusty house he shared with Moorian and Egan Powell, and the few hundred yards of black asphalt road that separated these ends of his triangular cell, would have caused scant change in his mundane way of life. Even in his sidelined status, The Rock was not directly involved with the impending battle, but was working on the tedious details of the *next* operation—which was founded with impersonal confidence upon the assumption that Midway would be an American victory.

Now, curiously, there was a sharp new edge to the frustration that nagged him, although he was unable, or unwilling, to recognize its source.

Several times that morning Torrey went out surreptitiously to the pay telephone in the main corridor to call Aiea Hospital, only to find it occupied by some sadfaced junior officer, with others queued up outside the booth awaiting their turn to notify their wives that they wouldn't be home for dinner that night, nor the next, nor until Heaven knew when, because the Alert was on. The Rock was reluctant to use his CinCPAC line. He suspected the operators weren't above listening to a captain's conversation, particularly now that any morsel of news was more prized than rubies, and he didn't relish having the yeoman pool privy to his personal business.

It was almost noon before he finally caught the public phone out of use. Feeling like a schoolboy about to call his first date, Torrey slipped into the booth. He hoped nobody had seen him.

Maggie's calm tone swept away his puerile embarrassment.

"You're trapped, too?" She laughed ruefully. "So am I. But I didn't think they locked up the High Brass during an Alert."

"CinCPAC captains are a dime a dozen."

"You're worth at least a quarter, Rock. Maybe even fifty cents."

"That's a pretty high rating. I don't deserve it."

"Please let the nurse make the diagnosis, captain."

"Thanks . . . anyhow, it gives me courage to go on."

Her voice betrayed concern. "You sound tired, Rock."

"I shouldn't be," he said, knowing he was, and adding despondently, "unless sharpening pencils and pushing pins makes a man tired."

There was no response from Maggie's end of the humming line, and Torrey wondered if she had hung up. He wouldn't blame her. He was a hell of a dull conversationalist, at best, and now he had nothing to say, except to plead soundlessly for the special comfort he felt she could give him. He was almost surprised when she spoke again.

"You know, Rock, combat fatigue doesn't only affect the people who are doing the fighting. It hits noncombatants, too, especially when they're used to combat themselves. I've seen it. Daddy suffered from it sometimes. Maybe that's what he was trying to escape from that night on Pikes Peak."

"What do you prescribe for noncombat fatigue, Lieutenant Haynes?"

"In your case," she said firmly, "I'd start remembering why they call you The Rock."

"That belongs to another incarnation," he growled, "when I had a man's job to do."

"Sometimes it's a man's job just being a man."

Suddenly humbled, he said, "You should have been a man yourself, Maggie."

"Do you really think so?"

"No."

"Neither do I." The rueful laugh sounded again, and she appended "—usually."

"What time do you go off duty?"

"Nine o'clock. I mean 2100."

"I'll call you then. Do you mind?"

"You asked me that yesterday, Rock. Why?"

"Because," he muttered, "I'm afraid you're just being kind to me."

"If you don't stop this kind of nonsense," she said, "I'll send you a big fat bill for psychiatric advice."

Incredibly, then, he heard himself say, "You're a wonderful woman, Maggie. I wish I'd met you twenty-five years ago."

"When I was eleven?" Now her laughter was genuine. "I was a miserable little monster."

Torrey saw a crew-cut ensign from War Plans, whose name he couldn't remember, pawing the ground outside the telephone booth.

"Goodbye . . . my dear."

"Goodbye, Rock."

He hung up. The ensign jostled past him in his haste to seize the phone before somebody else pre-empted it, then stopped short, staring, as he recognized The Rock. Senior officers never used the public telephone unless they were indulging in sinister private affairs uptown. It was unthinkable that The Rock could be one of this Casanova fraternity. Or was it? You sometimes heard strange things about these close-mouthed captains.

"Sorry to have tied you up, son," Torrey said.

"That's okay, captain," the j.o. assured him. "I'm just calling home."

"You're lucky to have a home."

The Rock strode away, leaving the youngster more mystified than ever.

As the time of battle neared, the Alert tightened around them and their prison became more restrictive. Nights were the worst. Now that the incandescent moon had waned, walking along Makalapa Hill was like prowling molefashion through a tunnel. Even the repairs on the bombed-out ships had stopped and not a pinpoint of light broke Pearl Harbor's unconditional blackout, which was violated only once, deliberately, when a handful of combatant ships returning from the Coral Sea had to be replenished within twenty-four hours. That night the loading crews worked under glaring arc lights to ready them for Midway.

Tin helmets, .45 automatics in stiff new holsters, and snipe-nosed gas masks were issued to everyone, admirals included, along with stern orders to keep this unaccustomed gear handy at all times. Wrecked trucks were arranged helter-skelter at Pearl Harbor's entrances to forestall any enemy attempts to rush through them in the event a landing were made on the Island's exposed beaches. Rifle-carrying Marines searched cars passing through these same gates. And the huge oil tanks in the fuel farm below Makalapa Hill were sheathed in steel strips.

Torrey was positive the Alert and the battle that culminated it would always represent the absolute nadir of his career, assuming he survived the war.

Enviously, morosely, he watched others manipulate the long-range devices which translated strategy into tactics. His advice was asked only once, after a carrier had been badly hit by Japanese aerial torpedoes, and abandoned in apparent sinking condition, only to be discovered miraculously afloat long after her crew had left. Should the ship be reboarded? Towed back to Pearl?

"You've been through all this," a two-star Operations admiral said to him. "What do *you* think?"

Torrey studied the dispatch from the task force commander. Before he replied, he cast a searching look at his interrogator, wondering whether there was any mockery in the question. There wasn't. The admiral seemed genuinely eager for his opinion as he stood patiently alongside his graysteel desk in War Plans.

"Judging from this, her equilibrium's holding steady with a twenty-five degree list. That's not bad." The Rock gave him a wintry smile. "You'd be surprised what a ship can take, until you've been through something like this. She can be brought back alive."

"I'm glad you concur. We're going to try."

"Good."

As the admiral started back toward Operations, he observed, "Weird things happen sometimes, Rock, don't they?"

"Yes," Torrey said, comprehending exactly what the other meant by his cryptic remark. "They do."

One of the cruisers that had taken survivors off the stricken carrier was *Old Swayback,* and *Cassiday* was among the destroyer team that subsequently relocated the great ship. These coincidences merely succeeded in driving the shaft of strange unrequited desire deeper into Torrey's heart, and twisting it.

At sunset, he walked alone down the slope from Makalapa Hill to the Sub Base instead of returning to his quarters, suddenly yearning to get close to the sea again, and to smell it, even if it were only the torpid backwaters of Pearl Harbor. Across the bootlike peninsula which separated the submarine jetties from the main channel, he could hear the first faint notes of Taps, mournfully, played from a ship somewhere in the middle distance: keening for the dead day and for the Dead themselves. In the melancholy twilight *Arizona*'s ruined superstructure and her tripod mainmast also bespoke death, although the sunken battleship's taffrail flag still fluttered in the night wind.

"Day is done . . . gone the sun . . ."

Larry Moorian burst into their Makalapa quarters on Friday night, barely twenty-four hours after the Midway victory, exultantly brandishing a set of orders which freed him from CinCPAC staff duty. They gave him command of the new antiaircraft light cruiser *Moultrie,* bristling with five-inch dual-purpose rifles, sweet, greyhound-swift, and the first of her class. She was an eminently desirable ship.

"Damned wonderful, fella." The Rock swallowed the rancid bile of envy. "It couldn't happen to a better man."

"Thanks," Moorian said, regarding him steadily. "Keep your pecker up. It's going to be a long war. And they're building a hell of a lot more ships—bigger and better than *Moultrie.*"

"Sure," Torrey said. "I know."

Even as he tasted the sour jealousy he'd never known before, he realized its meanness. Like Job, he wanted to cry out. But unlike Job, he was silent, ashamed, as he remembered what Maggie Haynes had told him on the first morning of the Alert, and again that evening. ("Others," she'd said, "are serving while they wait.")

Egan Powell was speaking. He had no hope of command, so he could take a more pragmatic view of Moorian's good fortune.

"Who'll cook our gruel?"

"When *Moultrie* gets to the South Pacific," Moorian said grandly, "I'll send out a shore party to fetch back a Melanesian cannibal who's used to handling tough steaks, and ship him up to you. Then maybe you bastards'll appreciate how good my cuisine really was."

They toyed briefly with the notion of a farewell feast. But nobody really felt like celebrating, even though the Alert had been lifted. Moorian said he guessed he'd grab a bite at the senior officers' mess and then catch a movie, since it might be a hell of a long time before he saw Betty Grable again, and he wanted to store up a few callipygous memories. Powell termed that a splendid idea, and asked Moorian to save a place at the table. He'd be right along as soon as he finished a letter to his third wife, now divorced, who was complaining about overdue alimony.

"How about you, Rock?" Moorian asked.

Torrey's pretense evaporated. "There's plenty of time left for me to contemplate Miss Grable's charms. I'd rather sulk in my tent."

"Okay." Moorian's tone was sympathetic. "But you've got to eat. Check the foodlocker. I think there's a can of terrapin stew saved out of our last batch from New Orleans."

"Any plain pork and beans?"

"Sure—if you want to live like a goddamn Marine."

"Mightn't be a bad idea," The Rock said thoughtfully. "Maybe I'll give it a whirl."

After Egan Powell left, Torrey wandered into the kitchen, and poked around the cupboards for something more appetizing than beans, but less exotic than tinned turtle, which he didn't care for even when it was served fresh from the tidewater Gulf. He found a can of Philadelphia scrapple and two links of wrinkled *chorizo* sausage. As he inspected them unenthusiastically, he knew that the emptiness in his belly wasn't hunger at all but the dull ache of frustration, solitude, and failure.

Torrey squinted at the wall clock. It was 1755. Assuming they adhered to the rigid routine followed by other naval establishments, the nurses at Aiea Hospital would be sitting down to their Friday night fish and chips in another five minutes.

He said aloud, "Don't be a goddamn fool!" unaware whether his admonition was meant to forestall what he intended to do, or to spur himself on, and not really caring, as he went to the telephone that lay on the kitchen table and dialed the hospital number. The Aiea switchboard passed him along to the nurses' quarters, where a bored young voice asked who he was and whom he wanted, please, because it was dinnertime and Heaven only knew if she could catch anybody before they got swallowed up in the messhall where they couldn't be paged.

When he identified himself, she seemed reasonably impressed, and said she'd try to find Lieutenant Haynes.

Two minutes later Maggie came on the line.

"Need a nurse's help again, captain?"

"Yes."

"Want to see me?"

"Very badly." He hesitated, boyishly shy, before he said, "Where do you go when they take you out to dinner?"

"Depends on who 'they' are. Have you wheels?"

" 'Wheels?' "

"Transportation."

"I'll get a staff car—if you can get away."

"You didn't ask me if I have another date."

Suddenly apprehensive, he asked, "Do you?"

"Only Doug MacArthur, Vinegar Joe Stilwell, and Georgie Patton. But I'll stand 'em up if you really insist."

"I insist. To hell with the Army. Join the Navy, Maggie."

"Didn't I ever tell you, Rock? That's what I've already done." Her velvety chuckle delighted him. "Now, there's a wonderful little place 'way on the other side of town, up one of those crazy streams, that has a willowpond full of lazy old carp, and sometimes you can get fairly decent steaks. Owned by a Chinese gentleman. It's called the Chinaman's, naturally. Game to try it?"

"Yes."

"Pick me up in fifteen minutes," she said. "I'll be on the front stoop."

Maggie twirled the stem of her martini glass and watched the tiny pearl-onion gyrate through the colorless liquid. They were seated at a table alongside the pool, in a willow-shrouded patio whose only illumination was the lambent night itself. Neither of them had spoken since Torrey finished explaining, haltingly at first, why he'd waited five days before telephoning again. He found it easier to talk as he went along, as the inhibitions that had always barred him from anything smacking of the confessional seemed to dissipate.

With a curious, almost third-person detachment, he recounted his last days aboard *Old Swayback*, and described what had happened to him after the torpedoing.

At length Maggie said quietly, "I'm nothing but a civilian once removed. What's worse, a female. But all that doesn't sound so awful to me. You weren't running away. You were even willing to be killed."

"Not willing. Just available."

"What does it matter?"

"The way the Navy figures these things, if it brevets you God, in command of a ship or a fleet, you're expected to behave like God. You've got to anticipate everything and cope with anything. Otherwise you forfeit your God-stripes."

"I see."

"Do you?"

"And I also think I see where most of your trouble lies, Rock."

"Tell me," he said seriously. "I don't."

"You've been a Navy captain all your life. Probably even when you were a little kid, because your captaincy was passed down to you like a royal title. And now you're so damned busy trying to present a flawless front to the world that you've forgotten how badly bruised you can get just falling off a throne."

"I'm beginning to find out," he admitted.

"When's the last time you talked like this?" Maggie asked quietly.

"Never."

"Doesn't it help a little?"

"Yes," he muttered. "I guess it does."

"You know, Rock, I've found out a lot about you, lately, because I became curious and asked questions. Maybe that's a bitchy thing to do. But it's me. I even learned what happened to your marriage."

Maggie waited to see whether he would get angry. Torrey took a deep drink of his scotch before he said quietly, "It wasn't much of a marriage, you know."

"Now I'm trying to figure out if you're a misogynist or a misogamist—whether your private bête noir happens to be women in general or just marrying them."

"Hardly worth wasting your speculation on an old crock like me, is it?"

"Crock? At forty-eight?"

"How did you know my age?"

"By shrewdly—what d'you call it—'estimating the situation.' You were Academy '14."

"Maybe I wasn't very bright. Maybe it took longer—"

"It didn't. You wound up twelfth in your class."

"My, my," he marveled, "but you've engaged in an amazing lot of research."

"Nurses get involved in that sort of thing. Research. Rehabilitation. Name it. We do it."

"Maggie . . ."

Torrey paused in mid-thought, obviously having changed his mind about what he started to say, and stared up through the latticed trees at the sunset afterglow.

"Go on, Rock."

"No. Confession's over. At least for now. It's your turn."

She smiled faintly. "You still want to know how I migrated from a native hospital in the Philippines to Aiea?" He nodded. "Easy. After the major 'accidentally' blew his brains out, there was nothing left for me to do but get the hell out, so I caught the first ship for Frisco. Things were booming in the twenties and it was a cinch to wangle a nurse's job at the county hospital." She pantomimed a drawn theatrical curtain. "Suddenly it's December 7, 1941, and little Maggie's all fired up to do her bit. So I volunteered."

"You earned two stripes pretty fast."

"Well, I was head ward nurse at the county hospital, which sounds impressive even to the Bureau of Medicine. They started me out this way."

"How do you like 'fighting' the Battle of Pearl Harbor?"

"No better than you do, Rock. But they've promised me a forward area billet as soon as there's a forward area to send anybody to."

"Could be a hell of a long time, Maggie."

"That's what I've got plenty of—time," she said.

"Everybody has plenty of time here," he said, "but God knows for what."

"What do you really want, Rock?"

"I want to be *doing* things . . . not blueprinting them for others to build."

"So you can be promoted to admiral?"

"Frankly," Torrey said slowly, flatly, "I don't give a good goddamn about those two stars. No. Let me take that back. I do, in a way, because they mean you've done your job in the lower echelons smartly enough to get to the top, where maybe you can really affect the course of the war, one way or another. But making admiral just for the broad stripe and the six side boys you rate instead of four, well, that doesn't mean a bloody thing to me. I've seen too many cocktail commandos who are worth less on the hoof than their gold lace would fetch in a pawnshop."

His seamed face split into its swiftly shaped, quickly passing smile, and he beckoned to the Chinese waiter who was lurking in the weeping willow shadows.

"How do you like your steak?"

"Blood rare."

"Good girl."

"Maybe you were right. Maybe I should have been a man," Maggie responded with her crooked grin. "Because I also like raw whisky, five-to-one martinis, stud poker, pipesmoke, and ice-cold showers."

"I'm still damned glad you're a woman . . . in spite of all that."

When he didn't speak for a long moment, Maggie fished a penny out of her shoulderbag and laid it solemnly on the table in front of him.

"Ransom for your thoughts," she said.

What could he tell her? He could, perhaps, say that she might help bridge two incompatible worlds for Rockwell Torrey: the world of uncompromising, often unfair discipline, command, and duty; and the one where men and women mingled, laughed, conversed easily, and made forthright love. But how could he voice those things which were so dangerously close to love itself? In the cold logic of 20-20 hindsight, his marriage to Athalie had been the sort of error of commission which an intelligent man was permitted only once, and he was resolved never again to make that monumental mistake.

"You wouldn't like my thoughts," he said finally.

"Try me."

"Later . . . maybe."

"Afraid?"

For the first time he looked directly at her, searching her face as if he wanted to memorize every convolution of soft cheek and tilted nose and cleft chin.

"It could be fear," he said slowly.

"Don't be afraid of me, Rock," she pleaded, "ever."

"It's not you, Maggie. It's something I can't explain. Something I thought I'd buried years ago."

They drove in silence around the greatfooted base of Diamond Head, past the spectral treeshapes of Kapiolani Park, and along nearly empty Kalakaua Avenue toward downtown Honolulu. Torrey maneuvered the station wagon through the blackout with cautious slowness, yet skillfully, using only his left hand, and guided by the sparse illumination of the blueslitted headlamps. Maggie remained close to him. She kept her slim palm against his free right hand. Occasionally he squeezed it, hard, as if to voice some unuttered thought.

But when The Rock spoke, his words were matter-of-fact. "Earlier tonight, you told me 'they' had promised you a forward area assignment. Who's 'they'? And what kind of job is it?"

"Blackjack Broderick is 'they,'" Maggie said. "He's going to command Operation Mesquite."

Startled, Torrey withdrew his hand, and said gruffly, "Mesquite's top secret. Even Admiral Broderick shouldn't be talking about it outside of CinCPAC War Plans."

"Don't blame poor old Blackjack. He didn't blab. It was his silly aide, Commander Owynn, who told me about my orders."

"You mean ex-*Senator* Owynn?"

"Yes. That's the one. Neal Owynn. I went to dinner with him last night."

"Well." The Rock let his displeasure show by placing both hands on the wheel. "It didn't take him long to dive into the social swim. He only arrived four days ago."

"You hadn't called me," Maggie pointed out. "Besides, Commander Owynn wanted to explain the scope of my future duties. That's how he put it. Things like lining up adequate personnel for a Mobile Operating Base Hospital." She tried a gay laugh that didn't quite come off. "Isn't that priceless? They call it 'MOB,' as if it was something in an Edward G. Robinson movie. They're setting up MOB Able at Toulebonne where Admiral Brod—"

"Yes, I know," he interrupted. "That's where he'll mount the Mesquite show, from nice, safe Free French territory."

"You're the only person I'd ever discuss this with," she said quietly.

"What about Commander Owynn?"

"People don't discuss things with the Senator. He tells *them,* in several thousand well-chosen words every time he opens his stupid mouth, Rock, because he's a talker, not a listener."

"Sounds as if you've seen an awful lot of this fellow," Torrey grumbled.

"Only twice. But it seems like more. Honest. Commander Owynn doesn't do anything on a whim. In his own horrid way, he's a rather determined guy."

"What do you mean?"

"Well," Maggie explained candidly, "he's looking ahead to when he won't be up to his fat fanny in susceptible women who swoon every time he shakes that wavy senatorial mane at 'em. One of these days Commander Owynn knows he'll be stuck on that-top-secret-place-we-won't-mention-the-name-of and he'll need a female real bad. So like a damn thrifty squirrel, he's storing up a future supply. In this case, they're nurses, and they'll be hoarded away in a hollow tree called MOB Able, to be used as women when the time comes."

"Owynn doesn't strike me as the squirrel type," The Rock growled. "He's more of a rabbit."

"Have you seen him?"

"Only his pictures. That's enough."

Maggie pried Torrey's right hand loose from the steering wheel again, and fondled his hardboned fingers for an instant before she said in mock surprise, "Captain Rockwell Torrey—I do believe you're *jealous!*"

He glanced at her, puzzled, trying to fathom his tangled feelings. He'd been envious of Larry Moorian's acquisition of a fine new cruiser. That was clear enough now. But here was a different emotion that bothered him even more, because he couldn't understand it.

"Am I?"

"You shouldn't be jealous," she teased. "Remember? You're an 'old crock,' and I'm a superannuated Navy nurse. Platonic friends are never jealous."

"To hell with . . ."

"Yes?"

"Nothing," he finished lamely. "Nothing at all."

Next day Commander Neal Owynn, USNR, wearing the triple gold-and-blue aiguillettes that signified his lofty status as aide to Vice-Admiral Jack Broderick, USN, moved into The Rock's quarters on Makalapa Hill. Ironic coincidence had nothing to do with his arrival. Makalapa had become painfully crowded, and after Larry Moorian joined *Moultrie,* it was inevitable that Torrey and Egan Powell would draw as a housemate the first senior officer assigned to CinCPAC, either on permanent or temporary duty. Because of the complicated nature of Operation Mesquite, Blackjack Broderick's medium-sized staff had to work in exceedingly close harness with the Fleet planners, and thus it was that Owynn took Moorian's vacated room.

Torrey was resolved, even before the Senator joined The Lodge, to maintain an open mind on politicos who viewed his beloved Service as a place to recoup their depressed fortunes. He had decided to ignore Owynn as much as possible, and treat him simply as one of the faceless horde of outward-bound adventurers who passed briefly through Pearl Harbor that summer for a couple of months of indoctrination cramming before they moved West. But after his arrival, The Rock found it increasingly difficult to keep his objectivity, and easier to agree with a cynical news commentator who had once said: "If you think you don't care very much for Neal Owynn, wait until you get to know him better, then you'll hate the son of a bitch."

Owynn's presence on Admiral Broderick's staff attested to his ability to improve on the Law of Natural Selection. He and Blackjack were made for each other. But only the Senator was aware of this vital fact.

Blackjack Broderick was known throughout the Service as a play-it-safe operator whose Navy Department file bore a large red "P.I." on its manila cover. This stood for Political Influence. It meant that Broderick, whose second wife was the widow of an ex-Cabinet secretary, never hesitated to use his fortuitous marriage as a lever to pry open doors that might otherwise remained closed to him, and it had been particularly effective some years earlier against the guarded portal which led from captain to rear admiral.

In his own transmogrification from the United States Senate to the United States Naval Reserve, Owynn had looked around carefully for a likely star to which he might hitch his wagon. Blackjack was the perfect vehicle. His three stars guaranteed that any mission entrusted to him would carry adequate prestige—certainly enough to insure that anybody traveling with him would bask in the reflected glory that comes from being around when great deeds are done.

Aware that his wife's inherited influence wouldn't last forever, Admiral Broderick was delighted when this prominent young politician volunteered to serve under his command. Eventually the war would end, bringing with it the inevitable scramble of too many admirals for too few jobs, and when that deplorable time came, it would be comforting to have a statesman securely in your debt. Meanwhile, pending the outcome of his longshot bet, Owynn might be fairly amusing company. You don't often have a staffer who genuinely rates the title of Senator.

Three weeks after Owynn quit Capitol Hill, with the plaudits of his admiring colleagues still echoing pleasantly in the nation's press, Admiral Broderick was tapped for Mesquite—one of the choicest prizes available in a year when prime assignments for Flag officers were dismally scarce. He held full responsibility for mounting an amphibious assault on the Japanese-held island of Gavabutu in the southwestern Pacific, once Cominch and CinCPAC came to agreement on the general outline of the operation. Time, however, began running out for Mesquite even before the planning ended. Soon the equatorial front would envelope the target area, bringing with it tropical rains that would stall jungle fighting in a swampy sea of mud, and the omnipresent threat of autumn hurricanes that could scatter a supporting Fleet like kicked marbles, leaving a newly won beachhead at the mercy of superior enemy ground forces.

Nevertheless, Mesquite was projected as a relatively "safe" move, for as yet the Japs hadn't consolidated their hold on Gavabutu. The planners figured Blackjack could strike fast, seize control within a relatively few days, dig in, and get braced for the next phase of island hopping.

With that in prospect, Torrey had already been ordered to start drafting the tactics of Operation Skyhook. This would be the really *big push,* he was solemnly informed, with vastly more dependent upon it than devolved around the preliminary capture of Mesquite.

Skyhook—or Levu-Vana—was nearly four hundred miles north and west of the Japs' thinly held advance base of Gavabutu. It was a much larger island, encompassing several authentic mountain ranges, a river or two, hundreds of square miles of copra plantations, and plenty of flatland from which the Seabees could hack airfields for future offensives. One of the best natural harbors in the entire southwestern Pacific lay within Levu-Vana's crablike eastern claws, commodious enough to handle the whole Fleet with plenty of searoom to spare.

As The Rock went about this new task, his pride in being nominated head of Skyhook's planning section was mingled with a growing restlessness that bordered on despair. Once again he felt passed over, and once again he was merely proposing the elaborate schemes which his luckier confreres would dispose.

To Egan Powell, the Senator was neither unusual as a type nor unfamiliar as a personality. It was a matter of lasting regret to him that he had encouraged Neal Owynn—the aging boy wonder of the ageless Middle Atlantic hill country—during a quasi-political interlude in Hollywood, when the politician was at the height of his reputation as a super-patriot. Although some of Powell's friends got burned by too-close exposure to the Senator's noisy hellfires, he himself escaped with only nominal scars on his psyche, and after that he contented himself with watching politics from a safe distance, and eschewing causes like aid for the Spanish Civil War loyalists.

For vastly different reasons than Torrey's, therefore, Powell was far from enthusiastic when Owynn joined their ménage. But if the Senator recognized him as the near-miss target of his scattergun foray into Hollywood, he kept it to himself; and, content for once with anonymity, Powell was happy to leave it that way.

Before Blackjack's aide took up residence, however, Powell made certain that The Rock was fully aware of Owynn's background. As a naval officer, he reasoned, Torrey had a hell of a lot more to lose by running afoul of this ruthless man than he himself ever did as a movie scenarist, and it behooved The Rock to recognize the curious rules under which the Senator played, and the wretched things that motivated him.

Now that Neal Owynn was a simulated naval officer, he cut his prematurely ashgray curls a trifle shorter, got fewer manicures, and strove to retool his senatorial glare into the look-of-eagles that shone from those portraits of Stephen Decatur just before he damned the torpedoes in Mobile Bay. Owynn wore his uniform tight across his generous rump, British-style, and his pants stopped too far above his burnished aviator-type boots. Although he had gone to an undistinguished land grant university, regrettably, instead of to Harvard, he dropped his R's as he spoke of his *deah* friend, Blackjack Broderick, and he elided his syllables in describing the *tremjuss* job of building an "invasion team."

After the Senator moved in, the times that exasperated Torrey the most were those intervals of calculated intimacy when Owynn decided his Makalapa companions had something worth adding to his store of useful information. Egan Powell first became aware of the Senator's easy ability to discard his normal superciliousness, briefly, and indulge in a bit of chummy relaxation.

"You know," he said, "if an octopus were mated to a sponge, the result would have a brain like this bastard's. Horrible thought. But that's how he functions. And when you give this octo-sponge the extra advantage of political insight, Rock, all I can say is, get the hell off the beach before it reaches out and grabs you!"

The best way to accept Neal Owynn, they both agreed, was to regard him as one of the more exotic hazards of war.

Three weeks before the Mesquite staff was scheduled to embark for the Free French island of Toulebonne, Admiral Broderick received the final increment to his amphibious invasion team: a squadron of sixteen motor torpedo boats fresh from stateside training. Never one to admit that his own strength equaled that of his adversaries, Blackjack sourly viewed the PTs as final evidence that CinCPAC expected him to do a man's job with boy's help.

How do you fight a war with a handful of plywood speedboats crewed by cooky-pushing kids—most of them from Harvard?

That's what Blackjack wanted to know, even while ignoring the indisputable fact that he already possessed all the support forces that CinCPAC had been able to pry loose from his other vital commitments around the Pacific. Operation Mesquite's ships included the refurbished battlewagon which Rockwell would personally ride to the South Seas, a mixed bag of light and heavy cruisers led by the modernized *Old Swayback,* several small aircraft carriers that had been converted from merchantmen, and nine destroyers. This wasn't the greatest armada that ever set sail, Operations told the reluctant admiral, but it would have to suffice.

That same night—their duty-free Thursday—the Senator elected to favor Egan Powell and Torrey with his company at dinner, and even provided a bottle of Chianti to complement the spaghetti and meatballs which Powell had prepared from a recipe given him by an obliging Italian actress. Owynn's inevitable hidden motive became obvious almost before they finished the wine, and got ready to settle down with their after-dinner coffee and tobacco.

Without any diplomatic feinting, he said abruptly, "You're our Intelligence wizard, Egan—tell me, what do *you* think about the Nips' probable reaction to Mesquite?"

"Light to moderate."

"We figure it'll be a lot stiffer."

Powell flicked an invisible bit of Turkish cigarette ash from his black silk cravat.

"Then why ask me?"

"Because, goddamn it, my boss wants all the facts laid on the line. I've heard him talking privately, fella, and he's not happy. Not happy at all with what the Japs have ready to throw against us."

Owynn pronounced it *agaynst,* in his famous mellow baritone, and he spoke as if the two captains were an audience of ten thousand.

Egan Powell seemed unimpressed. "Maybe you don't need Intelligence. Maybe you'd do better slicing open roosters, and studying the contents of their gizzards."

"Very amusing, fella," the Senator said, gravely, "but not what I'd call teamplay. It's easy for you people back here at Pearl to 'estimate' the enemy's strength. But we're the ones who've got to do the fighting. *We've got to know!*"

"Bucking for a Purple Heart already?"

"Please be serious." Owynn spread his hands placatively. "If Mesquite falls behind schedule, Skyhook's in trouble. That's what is worrying my admiral."

Torrey glanced up from lighting his pipe, quizzically, and observed in a deceptively mild tone, "That worries us, too."

"Then why don't War Plans and Operations give us more support?"

The Rock suddenly lost his patience.

"Look, mister, a damn few months ago we were all in a hell of a lot tougher fix than the one you're imagining for Blackjack Broderick. I don't know what you've got in mind. But I'd just like to remind you that Halsey ran the Japs ragged with nothing but a couple of flightdecks and a few wings and a loud prayer."

"He wasn't mounting an amphibious operation."

"But he was ready to. Anytime CinCPAC gave The Word. Anywhere from Wake to Makin."

Owynn reversed course and asked plaintively, "As Plans chief for Skyhook, Rock, don't you think we should have more leeway between the Gavabutu mop-up and when we hit Levu-Vana?"

"No. Repeat—*no!*"

"Why?"

"What the hell are you aiming at, Owynn?"

"Nothing." The Senator flashed a toothy smile he'd inherited from an old photograph of Teddy Roosevelt. "We lawyers call it serving as *amicus curiae*. Friend of the court. I'd just hate to see your timetable get all fouled up because you fellas misjudged the Nips' potential. That's all."

"That's plenty." Torrey snapped. "If Mesquite doesn't finish right on the goddamn button, Skyhook's in major trouble. There's weather. There's also the fact that the Japs aren't stupid. Eventually they're going to tumble to our next move. Maybe sooner, if they happen onto a lucky tealeaf pattern some afternoon. Or later, when our carriers start softening up Levu-Vana. But when they do, they'll toss in everything they've got to save that piece of real estate."

"So," Owynn said sarcastically, "CinCPAC gives us a PT squadron instead of a new battleship."

"The Peter Tares are doing pretty well in the Solomons."

"Blackjack doesn't want to wetnurse a bunch of unweaned brats."

"It all depends on how they're used," Torrey said coldly. "For Skyhook, we're giving 'em a hell of an important task that's out of all proportion to their size. They could make the difference between taking Levu-Vana in a few days, or getting pinned down for a couple of weeks. It's going to be terribly rough on these 'brats,' mister, and some of them won't be coming home to mama."

"Interesting," the Senator said, "also very romantic. But my boss would still rather have some heavy firepower."

"So would everybody in this man's ocean. MacArthur's screaming for Big Boys to beef up the Seventh Fleet. Halsey would like a squadron or two. Both of 'em make good cases. But we've got to share the wealth—what little there is of it."

Powell, who had remained aloof from their conversation, suddenly yawned and looked at his elegant gold watch. "You gentlemen fight the rest of the war. I'm hitting the sack. It's almost ten o'clock and I've got the morning watch in the goddamn Cave. *Buenas noches.*"

He left.

Bound by a thin vestige of politeness, Torrey refilled his bulldog briar while the messboy cleared the table, and reluctantly prepared to give Owynn exactly twenty minutes more. To pass the time he asked idly, "What's Blackjack doing with the PTs while they're waiting to be loaded for Mesquite?"

"We've got 'em camped in West Loch." The Senator sniggered. "I went up there this afternoon. It's practically a swamp. They'll keep busy enough just swatting mosquitoes."

"Poor devils."

"They're getting indoctrinated into the tropics," Owynn opined professionally, "weatherwise and conditionwise. They can tinker with their little playthings for a few days, and take a few practice spins outside the harbor."

"A PT armed with torpedoes and depth charges is a hell of a toy."

The Senator stubbed out a quarter's worth of Uppmann Fancy Tale and took a fresh cigar from the alligator case he carried in his breast pocket. "Incidentally," he said, "one of those kids has the same name as yours. Torrey. I saw it on the squadron roster."

"What's his first name?"

"I remember that, too, because it had a Biblical ring to it—Jeremiah." The Senator regarded Torrey through the rich smoke. "Is the lad any kin?"

"Just my son," The Rock said quietly.

"Well, sir, now isn't that great? Sounds like we're about to have a regular family reunion."

Torrey ignored Owynn's heavy-handed political jollity. Reunion? He wondered. It had been five months since the arrival of Athalie's caustic letter, and almost as many years since he'd seen his son. The memory of their last meeting still haunted him. Although Jere hadn't put the thought into words, he seemed in his reserved and unbending way to have been charging Torrey with failure, somehow, in the shaping of his young life. Jere never spoke these things. During their infrequent sessions he would simply stare at his father, bleakly, and turn aside when The Rock endeavored to talk with him about his future, or whether he'd changed his mind about going to Harvard instead of Annapolis. No. Torrey didn't understand his strange son.

He didn't even know him!

The Rock brushed a hand across his forehead. He was sweating. "You're damned right," he announced, "there's going to be a reunion. Tonight. Right now."

Then he went to the kitchen telephone, dialed the motor pool, and ordered up a station wagon. It was 2215. The PT squadron probably had already gone to bed. But he didn't care.

9. What Lies Beyond a Thing Called Duty?

ENSIGN JEREMIAH FARR TORREY, USNR, dangled his naked legs over the concave plywood sides of *Miss Brimstone,* a combatant vessel of the United States Navy listed officially as PT 396, and scratched the swollen place on his left thigh where he had been bitten by a mosquito, a loudbuzzing insect of the *genus Culicidae* known parochially as a "Waikiki dive bomber." Bug-repellent didn't faze them. Nothing did. They vectored in the light of the fulgent moon and then swarmed down like carrier planes, choosing their targets with the same unerring accuracy.

All in all, Jere gloomed, undergoing an attack by Waikiki dive bombers was an appropriate climax to a miserable day.

After only forty-eight hours under Admiral Broderick's command, the squadron had dropped its original nickname—"Fair Harvard"—and dubbed itself "Blackjack's Bastards," in the mordant fashion of men who intend to do the job to which they have been assigned, even if they aren't wanted by the assigner. They called their reserve commissions "birth certificates," because as bastards they figured they were damned lucky to have them in the first place.

Jere looked around the bivouac, distastefully, and wondered for the fiftieth time in the past two days why he'd chosen PTs instead of something clean and sensible, like the infantry. A dozen sagging canvas tepees provided halfhearted shelter against the microscopic pink dust that sifted down from the hills by day, the mildew damp that seeped down from those same hills by night, and the showers that fell every morning. Two muddy roads—cowpaths—wandered through the camp, raggedly bordered by chopped sugarcane stalks. Overhead the paraplegic limbs of the algarroba trees made ghastly scraping noises whenever the tradewind blew.

The unredeemed ugliness of their pre-combat base was impervious even to Hawaiian moonlight.

Jere slapped at his right ankle. *Got the little bugger!* Moodily, he inspected the crimson blotch that had been a mosquito, remembering the B movie he'd seen that night, with Bela Lugosi, in which the vampire quenched his thirst with the blood of a choice young damsel. He shivered. Crummy, ill-smelling, hellish West Loch, home of Blackjack's Bastards! Then a philosophical thought struck him, and he grinned back at the moon, bolstered by his awareness that he was still a Rational Man, Harvard '40, and able to surmount these more nonsensical aspects of modern warfare. When he saw his crew at breakfast, it might help compensate for the meal itself: dehydrated eggs which could be cooked only one way (scrambled into a gray mass), Spam (fried), powdered milk (watered), orange juice (canned), and coffee (laced with chicory until it damned near blew the top of your head off).

He'd tell them, "You know, men, when the Almighty finally gets browned off enough to give the world the enema it's been needing ever since the Flood, he'll stick the syringe right here—into West Loch—for obvious reasons!"

Jere was genuinely content only when he was driving *Miss Brimstone*. She was such a lovely, streamlined creature, responsive as a passionate woman to a man's touch, and with her trio of twelve-cylinder Packard engines, she could do better than forty knots in flat seas. Of course, if there was a chop running, she'd throw you right out of bed, unless you hung on tight. *Miss Brimstone* was just a shade under eighty feet long, too small to be called a "ship," yet too big to be hauled ashore like a "boat." As a hit-run weapon of opportunity, she displayed four torpedoes mounted fore-and-aft amidships, four .50-caliber machineguns coupled in pairs and fastened abaft her tiny superstructure, and a smokepot on her fantail to lay a screen when things got really desperate.

She was lightly clad in half-inch plywood. She carried twelve men. They loved her deeply, confidently, and perhaps requitedly.

The muted blue-slits of headlamps, intermittently visible through the algarroba grove, caught Jere's attention from the deck of his PT moored a few yards offshore, where he was on-duty for the night. He wondered idly what godforsaken business a visitor could possibly have with the squadron at fifty-five minutes to midnight. It had to be some stranger, for all the Bastards were present, accounted for, and sacked out. Unwillingly, he slid over *Miss Brimstone*'s sculptured side and into the shallow, muddybottomed water as the car braked alongside the makeshift dock, and waded ashore in his cut-down dungarees to find out what the hell cooked.

A four-striper, whose shoulderboards gleamed dully in the moonlight, but whose face was obscured by his visored cap, was impatiently drumming long bony fingers on the steering gear of a station wagon which had CinCPAC's unmistakable four-star galaxy painted on its front door.

"Where's the officer of the deck?" the shadowy captain asked brusquely as Jere approached.

"I've got the duty, sir."

"D'you always stand watch from your boat?"

"Usually, sir."

"Suppose you got a call from Fleet headquarters?"

"We can't, sir. We don't have a phone."

"I see."

The captain's authoritarian voice sounded curiously familiar, Jere thought, and he wished the visitor would step out into the clear moonglow so he could catch a better look. But the four-striper stayed behind the wheel, still drumming.

"Everybody asleep, mister?"

"Well," Jere said truthfully, "they've turned in. But I wouldn't guarantee they're sleeping. Our cots were salvaged from Grant's army, I think, and every night you have to get used to 'em all over again."

The stranger clucked in mock sympathy. "Tough war, ensign."

Astonished, Jere stared down at his ragged shorts, and wondered how the captain knew his rank, for he was hatless as well as shirtless.

"May I ask, sir, what we can do for you here at Blackjack's Bas—" he began formally, then stopped in midsentence, aghast at his near faux pas. This delegate from Big Brass mightn't have a sense of humor. It'd be a miracle if he did, since the risibility factor seemed to diminish in exact opposite ratio to the number of stripes which a naval officer wore. Jere knew this for a fact. He'd learned it from his own humorless father.

"Well," the captain rumbled, "you might lend me a few minutes of your valuable time, Ensign Torrey . . ."

"Christ Almighty," Jere breathed reverently. "It's the Old Man!" He almost added, "Or vice versa!" because when The Rock emerged from the station wagon and straightened up to his full six-foot-one, he did look like a sort of lean fierce messiah who'd donned Navy khakis just for the Heaven of it.

They found seats on a scabrous wooden park bench which somebody had scrounged from the Pearl City boat landing when the SP wasn't looking. Jere sat at one end. His father took the other, as if wary of the son he hadn't seen for almost five years, and lit his familiar bulldog briar behind hands so skillfully cupped that not a match flicker violated blackout regs. The boy waited. After all, it was the Old Man's gambit, wasn't it? His party. His nickel.

There was a long period of silence while The Rock smoked stolidly, fist clamped over the pipebowl, appraising Jere with his heavily hooded eyes.

Yes. Jere looked even more disconcertingly like Athalie than he'd imagined, with her pale blond hair, and her aquiline features. From the reposeful way Jere waited on his side of the narrow bench, Torrey judged he'd acquired most of her glacial calmness, too, as he grew into young manhood. Yet, contemplating his son, The Rock thought he detected in him an almost apologetic manner, as if Jere wanted to conceal his native hauteur under a cloak of humility.

"Your mother wrote that you'd joined the PTs," he said finally.

"I know." Jere's fine teeth gleamed briefly in the moonlight. "She was mad as hops."

"So I gathered," Torrey said ironically. "Why did you do it, then?"

"Because suddenly last spring I discovered I was twenty-one years old, and hadn't done a blasted thing with my life except write some bad poetry and drink one hell of a lot of tea and bourbon. Which hardly made a career. Funny. When my class at Harvard got together at a reunion, you'd be surprised how many fellows felt the same way. Useless as tits on a boar hog . . ."

"Strange expression for a Bostonian," The Rock murmured dryly.

"My chief machinist's mate gave us that one. He's from Arkansaw. Marvelous guy."

"You sound resigned to being in the Navy."

"Resigned?" The boy looked across the few yards of stagnant harbor backwater toward *Miss Brimstone*'s gently bobbing hull. "No. That's not quite the word. I'd say satisfied. Pleased. Really alive for the first time in my whole goddamn useless existence. These boats did it."

The Rock inspected his pipe. It had gone out. He made no attempt to rekindle the tobacco.

"Why didn't you let me know when you signed up? I might have helped."

"Because," Jere said, "if I'd written, you'd have remembered me as little Master Jeremiah Farr Torrey, dressed up in his Ivy League jacket and highwater flannel breeches, and clutching at mama's apron strings. No, sir. I wanted to wait until you could see me in a man's uniform . . ."

Smiling, The Rock aimed his pipestem at the boy's bare torso. That's a hell of a uniform, ensign!"

"Blackjack's Bastards," Jere said proudly, "consider dungaree Bermudas as good as dress blues. And a lot more practical for our brand of work."

"You'll be in great shape if Admiral Broderick decides to pay you a surprise visit."

"Fat chance!"

Torrey had to agree. He was pleasantly astonished by Jere's realistic attitude toward the Siberian treatment accorded his squadron. Perhaps this philosophical acceptance of things-as-they-are stemmed from his empty years in private schools where a boy's survival depended on something inside himself, rather than upon any outside influences. Jere had even survived Athalie, he thought, not without a tinge of bitterness.

As he looked back upon his own career, listening abstractedly to Jere's eager description of how it felt to con a torpedo boat through the heavy swells with saltspray half-blinding you, Torrey realized once more how hopelessly dry-docked he'd become. Why, he brooded, had this happened to him? There was a destiny in the fact that he was third-generation Navy, he presumed, molded directly by the Old Man, and to a collateral degree by the seafarers who'd preceded him. Only outright rebellion could ever shatter the matrix. But that never happened. Form was a self-perpetuating thing.

The Old Man insisted, moreover, that there was no room within an officer for flabby emotion, even though such emotion might betoken a freer will which could compensate for any unexpected off-course shifts as you progressed along your way. And as a result, Torrey supposed, until this first year of the war for which he had trained so assiduously, he had been like a robot ship pursuing an automatic course, with its wheel tightlashed. But now he didn't know. He had doubts. For there were other things about a ship which robs it of true independence. One day it runs low on fuel. Like man himself, it carries no built-in, self-generating logistical system. It must have help from the outside . . .

What was Jere saying about his own childhood?

". . . After you'd visited us and gone away again, each time, Mother used to raise Cain whenever I mentioned your name, and soon you'd fade away into a dim memory that smelled like shaving soap and tobacco smoke." He grinned ruefully. "But even that didn't last long. Dear Mama fumigated the house to get rid of 'that awful pipe-stench,' because she couldn't stand masculine smells. Every Christmas she'd present me with a big bottle of after-shave cologne that stunk like a French whorehouse, and I'd give it to the upstairs maids. They thought it was great."

The Rock said, "Yet you managed to escape from the mold."

Jere stared at him, puzzled by this seemingly irrelevant remark. "Sir?"

"I think you've avoided both the Torrey and the Cunliffe handicaps, son, and still managed to hang onto what's good in each legacy. There *is* a lot of that, too." He hesitated. "What will you do after the war, Jere?"

"Depends. Teach, maybe, after I get my doctorate. English lit. Unless this thing drags on so long I'm too ancient. Then I don't know."

"Is that what you want?"

"It's all I've got. That or selling bonds for Farr-Cunliffe. *Screw them!* I'd rather peddle Shakespeare than AT&T. And it's a hell of a lot closer to what a man ought to do with his life . . . I guess."

Torrey checked his watch.

" 'Way past midnight, fellow. When do you get relieved?"

"At 0600, sir. We stand a twelve-hour watch when we're on the beach."

"That's rather unorthodox, isn't it?"

"So's most everything about PTs. This way the gang really gets in some sacktime. One of these days nobody'll be sleeping—they tell us." Jere pondered a moment, as if he were assaying a delicate idea, before he added, "Look, sir, we're going to take the boats out around daybreak, which'll be right after I go off-duty. Bucky Farris —he's my exec—usually exercises *Miss Brimstone* when I've had the overnight. But I'd sort of like to get the feel of the Pacific because we haven't much time left before we shove off. Anyhow, sir, what I'm driving at is this—how about going for a spin with us?"

"I'd like it, ensign, very much." The Rock gave him a shrewd glance. "That is, if you're up to piloting your battlewagon after going without sleep for twenty-four hours."

"Thirty-six," Jere said. "Hell, I'm finer than frog hair—that's Arkansaw again—and rarin' to go!"

In the coralpinkness of first light, Jere's PT team looked younger than they really were. His crew chief, a hairy mechanical genius who drawlingly insisted his home was "Admiralty House, Fort Smith, Arkansaw," was the oldest of the dozen men. He was twenty-seven. He had run a rural garage that kept Model-A Fords alive for farmers who couldn't afford anything newer. Jere was next senior in years. His exec, the only other officer aboard, was barely twenty-one. Everything Bucky Farris knew about seafaring he'd picked up secondhand at the Ninety-Day Wonder course in Arizona, where the teachers outlined ships in the desert sand as part of their "indoctrination."

Mincingly, the sixteen boats danced away from their moorings and threaded the twisting corridors that led to Pearl Harbor's now closely guarded entrance. Their triple engines emitted muffled, throaty sounds, like the growling of mastiffs impatient for the leash to be unsnapped so they can hunt down the unknown quarry. Once clear of Fort Kamehameha to port, and Keahi Point to starboard, they revved up fast, and before the sun climbed the Koolau Range, they were racing hell-for-leather across the corrugated surface of Mamala Bay in closeknit formation.

"Thirty-six knots," Jere exulted, "and we're not even trying!"

The Rock nodded, but he didn't try to speak against the wind that whipped aft across the V-faced superstructure which contained the tiny pilothouse and a matchstick radar mast. The force of the slipstream blast brought tears to his eyes.

He was impressed. Jere handled the razornosed craft as if it were an integral part of himself. His expression was ecstatic. The boy's lean cheeks, Torrey noted, had the same woodgrained brownness as his own; and when Jere issued orders, he used the fewest words possible, short, incisive, and crisp. This couldn't have been conscious imitation, for the son had come to maturity without ever having seen his father on a ship's bridge. So if it was familial, it was also instinctive.

Miss Brimstone's captain yelled into the teeth of the sharp gale, "Now we're passing forty knots!"

On signal from their flagship, fifteen plywood dervishes wheeled into a single line for a dummy torpedo run against an enemy simulated by the sixteenth boat.

Bucky Farris kept his eye fixed against the stadimeter.

"Three thousand yards," he called as they bored in. "Twenty-five hundred . . . two thousand . . . fifteen hundred . . ."

Still the rocketing squadron bore down upon the target—which might have been a Jap warship—until Farris was calling the range in hundreds. In actual combat, Torrey knew, such a pointblank attack would be sheer suicide. The enemy would blow most of these tiny craft out of the water with his big guns before they'd closed nearer than fifteen hundred yards, yet here was Farris hollering "four hundred" as they peeled off like a flight of dive bombers and tore past the target PT with unlimbered tubes jutting outward.

Torrey recalled their fatalistic self-estimate: expendable.

After an hour of gutrattling maneuvers, they turned tail for home, proceeding more slowly, and drying their spray-soaked clothes in the early morning sun as they neared the harbor net gate. Conversation was easier now, too, and The Rock let Jere chatter excitedly about the marvels of the PT Navy, without voicing the thoughts that were in his own mind. This was PT doctrine. A beached and barnacled captain had no business offering fatuous advice to the youngsters who had to carry it out. Jere's own attitude contained no hint of bravado. He acted like a kid with his first rifle, eager as hell to find a suitable quarry, preferably one that could snap back. When they finally secured again in West Loch, he looked at Torrey with a broad grin.

"What d'you think of Blackjack's Bastards now?"

"They'll do."

The Rock let it go at that. He was bruised, both physically and emotionally, and he didn't trust himself to say more.

"Once we get to Gavabutu," Jere said, "we'll probably be staying aboard our boats the way Jack Bulkeley's gang did last spring before they were shagged out of the Philippines."

"Sounds cozy, ensign."

"Well, it'll be better than squatting in a tent, at that, because we've got all the comforts of home. Head. Galley. Bunks. Everything our little hearts desire. Hell! You could raise a family on *Miss Brimstone*." Jere grinned. "Can't you see it—'The President of the United States was born on a PT boat,' they'll be saying. They'd probably even put it in the Inaugural Parade. Beats Abe Lincoln's log cabin all hollow for glamour."

"Seems to me Navy regs frowns on women sleeping aboard warships."

"Man can dream, can't he?"

"Where you fellows are going, there'll be damned few females, anyhow, except a handful of Navy nurses."

"They're practically women."

"Some of them *are* women, son, and don't you ever forget it!"

Jere regarded his father quizzically, amazed at the earnestness in his voice. This didn't sound at all like Captain Rockwell Torrey, whose misogyny was famed from Portsmouth, New Hampshire, to Coronado, California.

"You actually know a nurse, sir?"

"Yes." Now The Rock seemed almost shy. "I know a nurse. She's in charge of *all* the young girls who'll be setting up shop with you at Mesquite. Maggie Haynes. Two-striper."

Jere whistled. "Man! Am I ever outranked!"

"Most of her kids are ensigns."

The boy looked wistful. "D'you reckon you could give me a letter of introduction or something that I could use out there? It's apt to be a hell of a long war. We might need a bit of spiritual uplift."

Torrey's reflective expression belied his embarrassment. "If you don't mind early chow, maybe I can arrange something. I've got the overnight duty in War Plans, so it will have to be a sort of hit-run affair."

"That'd be great, sir!"

"Then I'll pick you up at 1730 sharp." He repressed the bitterness that tried to creep into his voice. "It'll be a good thing for you combat troops to get together. Moralewise, as a senatorial friend of mine always puts it so eloquently." Torrey tested his wrinkled trousers. "I guess I'm dry enough now to put in an appearance at CinCPAC headquarters. Thanks for the buggyride, son."

By custom, lately, The Rock telephoned Maggie from the pay-booth in the headquarters lobby to avoid the quidnunc ear of Commander Owynn, who seemed always to be lurking around the Makalapa house whenever he most desired privacy. Torrey was not unaware of his brother captains' speculative interest in his calls to Aiea Hospital, and he had become conscious of certain anticipatory gigglings which sounded off-stage in the nurses' lounge before Maggie picked up the receiver; but these were minor irritations alongside the Senator's fish-eyed curiosity each time he'd asked her out to dinner, for a swim, or to play a game of late-afternoon tennis. Their conversations were brief. The Rock held that idle telephonic chatter was a specious waste of a man's time, and small-talk baffled him. You spoke your piece and then hung up. Period. But Maggie's calm, low-pitched voice never failed to lift his spirits, like an intravaneous shot of some euphoric solution.

It worked now.

As she said, "Hello, stranger," he could almost see her winsome crooked smile and the humor crinkles around her eyes.

The Rock grimaced into the mouthpiece. "Sorry it's been so long, Maggie. But we're really up to our damn ears in this thing."

"I know," she said oddly, "that's what Neal tells me."

"Neal?"

"Yes. The Senator seems to have a lot of spare time to brighten our drab lives. My kids are getting fat as pigs from the candy he brings whenever he pays us a visit—which is too damn often."

Neal Owynn, he thought sourly, could lollygag around Aiea forever and not be missed except when Blackjack Broderick needed an expert cocktail mixed, or a sartorial opinion rendered on his new battle jacket.

"Nice he's so available."

"Sometimes," Maggie said, "I think my main role in the war effort is keeping the Senator out of your hair."

"You're pretty successful. He hasn't been around Makalapa very much."

She pondered this observation a moment. Then: "Why did you really call me, Rock?"

"Jere's PT squadron has arrived."

"Your son?"

"Yes. I'm having dinner with him tonight. I thought perhaps you'd join us . . ." He paused awkwardly. "And maybe you could find somebody for Ensign Torrey—another one-striper."

"But Neal's already asked me."

"Oh."

"However," she confided, "I think I'm coming down with a terrible headache."

"That's too bad—"

"You idiot! I mean, it's a diplomatic headache. Sick-on-purpose. Of course I'll come. And I've got just the perfect little charmer for Jere. Even her name's right for a Boston boy—Annalee Dorne."

He laughed. "I'll come by for you at five-thirty."

"No," she said firmly, "I've got my future to consider. Ensign Dorne and I will—how do you seadogs put it?—proceed independently. By taxicab. So there'll be no danger of having the Senator discover he's been two-timed."

"Damn it, Maggie, it goes against my grain—"

"Remember, sir, I've got to live with this stuffed shirt once we reach that top-secret-place-I-can't-mention . . . figuratively, of course . . . and he can be such an unpleasant s.o.b. without even trying."

"I still don't like it."

"You'll survive," she promised. "Maybe I will, too, if you buy me a rare steak at the Chinaman's."

Torrey capitulated reluctantly. "All right. We'll rendezvous at 1800."

"Affirmative."

When the Rock and Jere arrived at the Chinaman's, Maggie and her ensign were already seated beneath the willow trees by the pool of leaping carp, looking as though they needed a drink but didn't dare order it because of their prim uniforms. Their eyes brightened as the two officers neared their table. Torrey laid his arm lightly across the boy's shoulders.

"My son," he said. "Living proof that I'm exactly what I told you I was—an old crock."

Half serious, half mocking, Jere gave Maggie a formal salute. She returned the honors with stiffhanded precision, but her cheeks dimpled as she said, "Ensign Torrey, meet Ensign Dorne . . . living proof that *all* nurses in Uncle Sugar's Navy aren't 'old crocks.' "

The Rock muttered, "Truce!" and nodded his head solemnly.

Torrey's affectionate gaze, as he adjusted Maggie's chair, perplexed Jere even more than their riddle talk. But the boy said nothing. If the Old Man wanted to turn gooney over a Navy nurse, it might be a good thing: completely improbable, of course, but humanizing. He turned his attention to Annalee Dorne. She was a trifle babyfaced, perhaps, yet fashioned like *Miss Brimstone* herself, and he wondered how she'd look in a one-piece bathing suit, stretched out on the sands at Waikiki. Jere smiled his appreciation at the softscented night. There might even be a decent beach at Toulebonne where a fellow could relax before he charged off to the wars.

After the drinks came, Annalee lifted her rye old-fashioned and regarded him with unstudied shyness from beneath her dusty-black lashes.

"To your health, Ensign Torrey, past, present, and future," she said in an intriguing little-girl voice. "May you never fall into the hands of the MOB."

Jere blinked. "Beg pardon?"

"That's what they call us. MOB Able. Mobile Operating Base Hospital. Isn't it ridiculous?"

"Then I won't drink to it," he said positively. "Maybe I *want* to fall into your MOB's hands."

"But not for business."

"Negative." Jere gave a flickering imitation of his father's split-second grin. "Pleasure only."

Across the fishpond the Chinaman maintained a cleared space where dancing was permitted to the music of an elderly jukebox. It was deserted, now, although Red Nichols was playing *Don't Sit Under the Apple Tree.* Jere motioned. Annalee nodded her head.

They rose and sauntered around the pool, arm in arm, and started to foxtrot with complete unself-consciousness.

Maggie watched them through the early gloom. Her face, usually almost whimsical in its candor, wore an odd expression in which quiet envy mingled with a kind of sorrow.

"My child nurse is lucky," she said.

"To be young . . . and so obviously falling in love?"

"That's only a small part of what I mean. It's hard to put into words. She's so wide-eyed full of crazy ideas about what we're getting into. Look at her. Hell, Rock, look at *both* of them. You'd think God had personally created this island just for them . . . and war had never been invented."

"That must be a good way to feel."

"Sure. But what happens when they wake up suddenly and all the good clean fun's gone?"

"I doubt that Jere has many illusions."

"Maybe so." Maggie brooded a moment. "Still, he's acting awfully let's-be-merry-because-tomorrow-we-may-die, without really knowing what it's all about."

The Rock tried to remember his own youth, a quarter-century earlier, and to recapture his feelings as he went off to war as a buck-ensign. But nothing came back. He supposed it was because he'd never had Jere's insouciance; or maybe it was because he hadn't been young at all, even when he was twenty-one.

"Another thing worries me," Maggie went on. "Girls like Annalee will have to rebuild their lives all the way from cellar to rooftree when this thing ends."

"I don't understand."

"Men never do."

"Explain."

"Out here, even the ugliest duckling gets rushed off her feet, simply because she happens to be a woman in an overpopulated man's world. And where we're going, it'll get worse. Instead of ten men for every girl, there'll be hundreds. More. Can't you picture what this does to the ego of some kid who's never had more than a couple of dates in her whole life? Pretty soon she gets thinking she's Cleopatra, and then she's spoiled forever. Oh, Annalee's charms aren't the greatest—but they're damned nicely arranged up here and down there, you must admit and they could probably drive a man out of his mind if he got hungry enough."

"Isn't that what women were made for," Torrey asked wryly "—driving men out of their minds?"

"Under the proper sporting conditions," Maggie agreed. "But this is different. Tragic, even. What do you suppose happens when these kids sail back through the Golden Gate some fine peacetime day and find out they're not the main course at the banquet any more, but yesterday's cold mashed potatoes, and just about as alluring. *Poof!* Chalk up a couple of dozen more busted hearts."

"How about yourself, Lieutenant Haynes?"

"Hell's tinkling bells! I've gone through this a dozen times, and nothing ever really changes for me. I guess I'm just different. Born to be a housemother."

"Did you ever think about remarrying?"

Maggie's ironic grin vanished. The bluntness of Torrey's unexpected question startled her, although he couched it in impersonal language that seemed deliberately to exclude himself from consideration.

"Marriage?" She pretended to mull over the idea. "Certainly not while the war's on. Maybe never. You know, Rock, two people in uniform getting married and climbing into bed strikes me as being damned near as immoral as those same people cohabiting without benefit of clergy in the first place."

Slowly, treading gingerly over rough terrain where he wasn't sure of his footing, Torrey said, "You spoke about 'two people in uniform!' Did you mean it that way—two particular people?"

"Yes," Maggie said. "I did."

When they returned to Aiea Hospital, The Rock parked the station wagon in their customary spot overlooking the harbor. The sight of the berthed and anchored ships, which were awaiting the signal to depart for Operation Mesquite, unaccountably saddened him, and he pulled Maggie close. Both of them ignored the yearning, striving sounds that came from Jere and Annalee in the shadowy back seat.

Maggie asked, "Will we see each other again?"

"God only knows," The Rock said, "and since He's in charge of intelligence, I guess He's not talking. I hope we can. We'll get The Word tomorrow. But it looks as though we're going to advance the schedule at least four days, maybe even a whole week.

The Big Boss is getting damned concerned because Blackjack won't get moving. He's still 'co-ordinating.'"

"I suppose they'll quarantine us for a couple of days before we sail . . . as if we had cholera or something."

"Security regs."

"Maybe they're afraid I might talk too much—to you!"

"About Mesquite?"

"About anything . . ."

Torrey's arm, resting on the canvas-covered seat, suddenly gripped Maggie's slim right shoulder, hard, and he bent down to kiss her.

"I think I love you," he said, wonderingly.

"Yes. I know. And I think I love you, too, Rock."

Torrey smiled in rather a lugubrious fashion. "We're a couple of pretty cautious people, aren't we? *Thinking* about love."

"Maybe it's safer that way."

"Or perhaps we're just so damned—mature."

"Don't be bitter, Rock, just because you've got gray hair. I like gray hair. I've got some myself."

"There was a time when all that mattered for me was something called 'duty,'" he muttered. "Now I keep asking myself what the hell lies beyond it . . . and how you get there."

He felt Maggie's mouth shape a smile. "When I was in college I remember reading a poem by Keats. Funny. It came back to me just now, sort of paraphrased, when you mentioned 'duty.'"

"Tell me."

"'Duty is truth, truth duty—that is all ye know on earth, and all ye need to know.'" Her smile erased itself against his lips. "But Keats was talking about 'beauty.' Not duty. So what's the use of kidding ourselves . . . duty isn't beautiful at all. If it ever had a color, it would be gray. Damn dull monotonous gray. Like a uniform." Her work-muscled arms grew taut. "And we're both stuck with it. Now kiss me once more, dear Captain Torrey, and then I've got to run—back to my *duty*."

The Rock gunned the motor. As the car rolled downhill, he sighed gustily, and so did Jere, sitting beside him. They both laughed, although the joke wasn't clear to either of them. It was mournful laughter that died away as quickly as it came, leaving them curiously abashed.

Jere asked abruptly, "Where's Conshohocken?"

"Pennsylvania, I believe. Near Philadelphia. Why?"

"That's Annalee's home."

"I didn't think you youngsters had time for idle chatter about home towns. I thought—"

Torrey stopped, peering uncertainly at his son through the nightgloom, and wondering how Jere would take this heavy paternal humor.

"You thought what, sir?"

"That nights before the battle were made for something else."

Jere said seriously, "I don't get that feeling with Annalee."

"No?"

"After all, MOB Able's scheduled for Mesquite just as soon as we can hack out a spot to put it. So she'll be right up there in the forward area, too, getting shot at along with the rest of us."

"Not quite, son. You'll need more than a beachhead for a hospital."

"That shouldn't take long."

"Let's come back to Conshohocken . . . Don't you realize it's clear off the edge of the flat world as far as your mother's concerned?"

"Annalee's left Conshohocken for good."

"What about you?"

Jere's youthful brows knitted in unconscious parody of The Rock's formidable frown. "If I live through this thing, I don't think I'll go back to Boston either. It belongs to people like Mother. Maybe they'd better keep it for themselves—the way they want it."

"Annalee Dorne seems like a nice girl."

"She's different from anybody I've ever met before." Jere snorted. "But probably that's because the Cunliffe-Farr inner circle doesn't include families with seven kids who go to Mass instead of the Presbyterian Church."

"It's my impression," Torrey observed, "that the Irish are about all that keep Boston alive nowadays. There's more than a drop of Mick in our own background. Perhaps you'd serve the cause better by taking Annalee back to Beacon Hill and infusing some new blood into that tired old New England breed."

The station wagon slushed to a muddy halt beside the tent that belonged to the crew of *Miss Brimstone*. The Rock switched off the ignition. He regarded his son curiously.

"Let me know when the banns are posted . . . I'd better be around when you break the news about Annalee to your mother. You may need protection."

"Damn right," Jere promised.

Torrey checked his wrist watch and gave his son a final penetrating glance.

"Just one more thing, ensign, before I shove off."

"Yes, sir?"

"Better wipe the lipstick off your chin. Your squadron commander might disapprove of cosmetics."

Jere pulled a handkerchief from his hip pocket.

"Thanks." Then, slyly, he said, "You're wearing a touch of make-up yourself, sir . . ."

At 0930 next day, with a few twirls of his fountain pen, Rockwell Torrey revamped eighty thousand lives by hastening the moment when the vast pyramidal complex that was Operation Mesquite would get underway. Only ten thousand men were scheduled to go ashore on Gavabutu. But it took seventy thousand others to get them there, feed them, provide fresh ammunition, refuel their airplanes, heal their wounds—and plan their daily destinies while they lived.

What had been D-Day minus forty, now became D-Day minus only thirty—one month to go—as Mesquite was advanced by ten full days.

As soon as the Top Secret dispatches sped by officer-messenger to Admiral Broderick's forces stationed on Oahu, and by coded radio to other elements of his ponderous array scattered throughout the Pacific area, a tight security lid was clamped down upon the personal movements of everyone connected with Mesquite, from the highest brass down to the lowest seaman on the Liberty ships which would ferry the eight PTs of Blackjack's Bastards to their staging base at Toulebonne.

The embarkation was set for 0700, just forty-five and a half hours hence.

Normally Torrey would have drafted the new D-Day orders without a thought for the eighty thousand brains and bodies with which he was dealing, for his part in this massive drama was coldly academic. He was the scholar-monk rewriting the Book of Revelations, updating Armageddon, and warning Gabriel to be prepared to sound his trump earlier than the script had originally demanded. But no, for the first time, the job was different.

The Rock picked up the leather-cased combat telephone which the Island Command engineers had installed for special calls to transient units camped in areas beyond regular line service. He spun the handcrank three times and asked for MTB Squadron Baker in West Loch.

A brisk young voice answered. "Peter Tare base. Commander Norris speaking."

"This is Captain Rockwell Torrey at CinCPAC. May I talk to Ensign Torrey?"

"*Captain* Torrey?"

With his inherited taciturnity and natural reluctance to Talk Family, Jere obviously hadn't bothered to tell his fellow Bastards that he had a legitimate, highranking naval father.

"Ensign Torrey's my son."

"Oh . . . I'll get him."

In a few moments Jere was at the phone, slightly out of breath, as if he had been running.

"Sir?"

"How are you fellows making out over there?"

"Just the way you said we'd be—working our tails off to get the boats cradled for loading on those Liberties." Jere's abrupt laugh sounded. "Funny as hell, sir, taking forty-knot PTs across the Pacific on scows like that."

"It's a long trip, mister."

"How about . . . her?"

"They're writing MOB Able's orders now. She'll beat you there. Probably wave her handkerchief at you from the dock when you arrive."

"Thanks—Dad."

"Good luck—son."

Quietly they both hung up. The Rock turned back to his unpleasant duty. He wanted to call Maggie, too, but Aiea didn't have a combat hookup, and he couldn't use the insecure public system. Perhaps it was just as well. That night he'd write her a note. There are some things which ought to be penned privately and read in thoughtful solitude.

10. The Japs Won't Wait Forever

In no mood for either the tennis or the swimming which CinCPAC had decreed for his sedentary officers, Torrey brooded through the wideflung blackout window of his bedroom, disconsolate, at the mundane world spread out below Makalapa. The steel battens had been removed from the fuel tanks, and the huge cylinders were now painted a mottled landscape green. The access roads to the Hill had been oiled, and they no longer gave off choking spurts of fine dust every time a staff car or supply truck passed. Flags flew correctly from every building, every moored vessel, every authorized frontyard pole. Clusters of sailors in starched dress whites waited alongside the pickup zones for buses, taxis, or Good Samaritan civilians to haul them into Honolulu, where they would get—as they themselves described it—screwed, brewed, and tattooed just as they'd done before the *Attack*.

Everything, Torrey thought despondently, was as goddamn normal as blueberry pie, or whatever it was the advertising fellows claimed the Armed Forces were fighting for. That, he told himself, was also a goddamn laugh. Fighting! He might as well have been in Muncie, Indiana, or Tallahassee, Florida, for all the military advantage his four stripes afforded him. Three square meals a day at predictable intervals. Steak on Sunday. A guaranteed eight hours of undisturbed slumber. Transportation for the asking. The pleasant company of women when you wanted it . . .

He turned from the window and focused on the sheet of paper in his hand.

Maggie Haynes' sixth letter had arrived that morning, full of chatty intelligence about heat rash, the yellowing effects of atabrine, and the attrition that continued to wear away at the troops of Mesquite, due as much to malaria and dysentery as to the enemy's dogged refusal to quit fighting even after he was so patently defeated in that miserable stinking swamp jungle.

But her first letter, penned aboard the transport that carried MOB Able to Toulebonne, had been the best. In it she'd called him a "real live livin' doll" for having written all those precious things to her that last night in Pearl Harbor (and sending it to Aiea by messenger) after he knew they couldn't see each other again because the transports were embarking at dawn.

"Every girl needs a hope chest," Maggie had added. "And I'm pressing your note away with my candlewick bedspread and my monogrammed tea towels and fancy nighties—just in case someday you'll want to recall what you said and prove you still mean it . . ."

One snippet of information especially pleased him in today's letter. Since MOB Able staged on to Gavabutu from Toulebonne, Maggie had seen Commander-Senator Neal Owynn only once, when he paid a hasty visit to Mesquite with Blackjack Broderick. He'd spent most of his brief stay ashore consoling wounded Marines from his home state, while the admiral spun around the battlefront in an armored recon car. Owynn praised her for doing a "simply grahhhnd job," she reported precisely, and regretted that his staff duties made it impossible for him to get up to Mesquite more often.

"What an unmitigated jerk," she opined in her neat, nurse's handwriting.

The Rock idly traced a forefinger across the grimy windowsill. He would gladly have exchanged all his unwanted Hawaiian comforts just then for the minimal four-striper job at Mesquite, including a humble liaison spot with COMAIRRONSOSEC (Commander Air Squadrons Southern Sector), an Air Force prodigy eleven years his junior, who flaunted a major general's two fat stars.

Torrey saw what his subconscious had scrawled in the red dust. *"Maggie, MOB Able."* Guiltily, as if he'd been caught scribbling obscenities, he erased it with the palm of his right hand, and wiped the grime on his clean trouser leg. In another moment, he supposed, he would have appended *"I love you!"*—the way a boy carves his best girl's initials on a tree trunk. He thought of Freud.

And he swore, softly, at the empty bedroom.

Other letters came to The Rock, from classmates who derived a special pleasure from recounting their adventures to deskbound noncombatants, and these always left him feeling even more frustrated and bitter at the circumstances which kept him marooned at Pearl Harbor. Sometimes, with a hypocritical cunning, they would express envy at his CinCPAC staff job. That was even worse. Although Torrey had Olympian advance knowledge of what each operational move would be, it was like a chess game played over and over against an inferior opponent, spiritless and unexciting.

Paul Eddington had finally turned up, too, in Toulebonne, where he commanded the naval air station. Most of his work seemed to involve repairing PBY search planes damaged over Levu-Vana, far to the north of Gavabutu. He wrote once.

"This lovely little island," Eddington reported, "used to be a penal colony. *Tres apropos.* Did you know, skipper, that cocopalms look just like jail bars when they're planted close together and you squint at them through the bottom of a whisky glass? Try it sometime. These Free Frigging French didn't waste a single hectare of land out here, probably because the Japs were the real bosses of this property under a system that let the colonials 'earn' a fancy fee for doing nothing except hand over their proxies. So when we chased the Nips away the FFFs got mad as cheated whores at us for drying up their unearned increment. (Excrement?) . . . The sewers run openly down the gutters of Toulebonne and so do the lovely ladies of this island paradise, with their hands out and their skirts up. The going price is five bucks *Americain.* If you get drunk enough they're worth it.

"As for what we're doing," Eddington continued with the candor of a writer who censors his own mail, "I've never seen such a three-star mess. There's even a new phrase for the operation. Fubar Baker Easy. Which means, 'Frigged Up Beyond All Repair by Experts.' We're getting bled white by a lot of smallbore engagements that cost us a tincan here and a couple of planes there, instead of grabbing the bull by the horns and twisting its goddamn head off. You know what I mean, skipper. We used to talk about it back when we were playing Flying Dutchman with *Old Swayback.* Somebody's got to move. Fast! There's no other way to win. But do you know that our fearless leader has only gone up the line once since D-Day? They ought to change the frigger's name to Yellowjack. . . ."

At this point in Eddington's imprudent letter it was apparent that he was getting very drunk, for his words were running into each other, almost as if he were talking aloud in alcoholically slurred syllables.

". . . Anyhow," he finished, "it's steady work. They don't fire anybody in wartime. They just find you a place where you can rot away quietly and peacefully."

There was a *P.S.:* "Bitchkitty tough about young McConnel and the *Cassiday,* wasn't it?"

Torrey had known about *Cassiday* for three days. Torpedoed in one of those pointless scuffles around Gavabutu to which Eddington had scornfully referred, the destroyer had rolled over and sunk in less than seven minutes, taking with her all but a handful of her officers and men. Commodore Bowen was picked up after a night of drifting in a leaky raft, dazed and speechless for the first time in his life, by a prowling PT boat. But Tom-Tom Agar was dead, trapped in the engineroom; and so were Poet Cline and Bulldog Balch. Lieutenant McConnel was still listed as "missing."

Yes. It was indeed bitchkitty tough. Torrey knew he should have gone that same day to Mrs. McConnel's cottage, high up in Nuuanu Valley, which she shared with Tom-Tom's wife. Or widow. But he had procrastinated, feeling little confidence in his chaplain abilities at such a time, and hoping that Word would come momentarily that Mac had been found. It was a one-in-a-million chance, however, for "missing" was all too often a naval euphemism for "lost" that endless summer.

Now, reluctantly, he went.

Bev met him at the door. Dry-eyed, but unsmiling, she invited him in, and went to put coffee on the little electric stove. She seemed, he thought, remarkably composed.

"Helen Agar isn't here," Bev said, returning. "She's got the spotting duty down at the Fort."

Torrey declined her offer of sugar. "Duty—work—can also be therapy sometimes, I've found."

"There's no avoiding duty," she said quietly, "when you're in the Navy, is there?" Bev pointed toward a bamboo-framed photograph of her husband which leaned against a potted orchid on the coffee table. "Mac always talked about duty, too, especially after he made his two stripes last spring. That's when they appointed him *Cassiday*'s exec."

"I know. I recommended him."

"Mac could have had shoreside duty," she said in the same calm voice. "But he turned it down."

"I know that, too."

"Do you think there's any hope?"

Torrey studied his coffeecup. "They rescued a naval aviator a while back who'd lived for eight weeks with the natives on an island north of Gavabutu. Anything's possible."

"But not very likely?"

He shook his head, "I'm afraid not."

"Then," Bev said in a flat voice, "I wish you'd read something Mac sent me just before *Cassiday*'s last action."

She folded under the final lines of the brief letter, which touched upon matters which might embarrass the captain, and handed it to him silently.

". . . Some macabre joker painted up a big sign and hung it over the top of the accommodation ladder last time we made port," Mac had written. "It said, 'Abandon Ship All Ye Who Enter Here.' Poet Cline claimed that was a Dante dish to set before the commodore. (Pun.) But now it's not funny any more because it's so damned near true. Beats the hell out of me what the Big Brass has in mind. We've diddled and dawdled around here for weeks, now, without any evidence that old BJ knows his fanny from a hot rock about amphibious operations, while every day something else goes down the drain . . ."

The Rock looked up. First Eddington, he thought, and now young McConnel. Each of them in his own way an expert eyewitness to what was happening, or *not* happening, at Mesquite, and each speaking his acid mind without benefit of censorship.

"I don't believe I'd show this letter to anybody else, Mrs. McConnel. It's a pretty rough indictment of Admiral Broderick."

"He deserves it!"

"If affairs are really this bad at Gavabutu, I'm sure there'll be some changes . . ."

"Aren't they that bad?"

Torrey looked into Bev's challenging blue eyes. "Yes. I believe they are."

Seven days after The Rock's visit to the cottage, Lieutenant McConnel indeed was rescued, very much alive but hungry as a werewolf (as Mac himself described it), from a coralspit that didn't even appear on the Fleet's navigational charts. He had paddled ashore in his Mae West life jacket, trailed all the way by a couple of sharks that never quite got up courage to make an all-out assault on him, and then he'd lived for a week on shellfish and rainwater.

The Rock telephoned the great news to Bev.

After she stopped crying, he said, "Now, Mrs. McConnel, take an old seadog's advice and start packing your gear for San Francisco. That's where we're ordering your husband for his survivor's leave. All thirty days of it!"

When Egan Powell came back from the cryptographer's Cave that afternoon, he brought The Word that they were invited to CinCPAC's private quarters at Number 10 Makalapa for dinner.

"When?" Torrey asked.

"Tonight." Powell grinned. "Not much time to primp, your lordship. Just black tie. And clean khakis."

"Maybe we've finally arrived."

"Or they've worked their way down the barrel to the commonfolk who've never seen the inside of the palace."

"Who else is going?"

"That's what baffles even an old code-breaker, Rock. It's topdrawer as hell. Chief of staff. Operations. War Plans. Air. And my own boss—Intelligence."

Nevertheless, the High Command invitation pleased them immensely, for when you went to Number 10, you were assured of three things: a damned good meal, a provocative disquisition on the conduct of the war, and the undisguised envy of your less favored brethren when they heard about it. You were also informally close for an evening to the man—*the* Admiral—in whose huge gnarled hands lay the destiny of a world area larger than any other assigned military sector in the war. The Admiral's command ranged ninety-five hundred miles from the Bering Sea to the edge of the Antarctic, and ten thousand more from the West Coast Sea Frontier almost to the Philippines. You could drop the moon into this portion of the hydrosphere and never miss it. (In fact, some experts theorized that the moon originally came from here, anyhow, wrested out of the Pacific deeps that plumbed to thirty-five thousand feet, and then cast loose into the heavens.)

The Admiral managed to take his awesome responsibilities in stride—a mammoth, loping, relentless gait that exhausted younger men who tried to keep pace with him—and he betrayed his never-ending pressures only by an occasional glint in his blue eyes and by an unwonted stiffening of his Confederate drawl.

At the fieldstone entryway to Number 10 Makalapa, overlooking an extinct, saucershaped volcanic crater, the Marine guard gave them a smart salute. A Chamorro messboy flung wide the front door, goldtoothing his welcome, as their host himself strode across the deepnapped carpet of the sunken livingroom.

"Let me know when 'upstairs' is ready," he told the messboy.

The Chamorro nodded and withdrew.

For a few moments they chatted constrainedly, until the two-star department heads arrived, whereupon the messboy materialized as if on secret signal at the foot of the curving balustrade.

He announced, "The 'upstairs' is now ready, sir."

"Thanks, Hernando."

Seemingly relieved that smalltalk could be put aside, at least temporarily, the Admiral led them up to the second floor and into a modest sitting room. It was furnished sparsely, with eight straight-backed chairs, and a desk on which reposed two decanters, one marked Scotch and the other Bourbon, a pewter bucket of cracked ice, a vial of bitters, a seltzer bottle, the fruit essentials for old-fashioneds, and a tray of simple hors d'oeuvres. Against one wall there was a bookcase, atop which a small stuffed animal, which Torrey could not identify, crouched in a menacing pose.

This was the sacred chamber reserved for prolonged toplevel sessions when the Admiral wanted the rest of the house economically and tactically dark after sundown. It had a big exhaust fan set into its one window, and the noise of the one-tenth horsepower motor sounded like a destroyer's blowers in that confined space. The Admiral secretly admired this evocative noise, for he was an old tincan sailor himself; and he hadn't been to sea for years.

He took one of the chairs. The rest of his dinner party occupied the other seats, primly, as if preparing for a Quaker meeting. They waited for the Admiral to speak.

"Bourbon," he asked, "or 'oke,' gentlemen?"

Torrey and Powell hesitated, deferring to their seniors, who promptly said, " 'Oke,' sir!" Since it seemed improbable that their august host would have gone to the trouble of having native okulehou available unless he meant it to be used, they murmured, "Make ours 'oke,' too, sir." The Admiral chipped off a few inches of frosty grin.

Egan Powell relaxed and nodded covertly at The Rock. They'd passed their first social challenge.

Like a chemist dealing with a highly explosive formula, the Admiral picked up the mendacious Scotch decanter, and measured two fingers of colorless liquid into eight old-fashioned glasses. He added three globules of bitters, a pinch of powdered sugar, a squirt of sodawater, and a slice of orange into each, and then, as if time counted for nothing at this carefree moment, he stirred them thoughtfully, in precise order, with deft clockwise strokes.

As he distributed the glasses, he said earnestly, "Try it. If it's too bitter, I'll put in a touch more sugar. And as soon as you drink some, I'll add a bit of ice."

They sipped. The okulehou had a mule's kick. They understood now why the cocktail hour at Number 10 was never more than thirty minutes long, and why the limit was two to a customer.

"This 'oke' is made especially for me over on the Big Island," the Admiral observed contentedly. "Nearest thing I've ever found to 'white lightning.' It's got real authority."

Authority, The Rock thought vagariously, is as authority does. Isn't it? He wished he could repeat the *bon mot* for Egan Powell's benefit. But Powell, who had been chatting quietly with the Intelligence chief, had moved across the room, and was now staring at Torrey in an odd manner, as if he'd forgotten to wear his pants, or had a smear of lipstick on his cheek, or had committed some other equally heinous social offense.

The conversation proceeded according to the ritual established for such affairs: a few ponderous jests, a word or two concerning the unseasonable kona weather, and some droll remarks about the stuffed creature on the bookcase, which turned out to be a mongoose.

"My cook's an amateur taxidermist," the Admiral explained. "He traps 'em in the hills. This one showed up here the day after I'd had Bill Halsey to dinner—just before the Gilberts raid—and we'd run out of steaks." He uncorked his benign smile. "Never found out what the cook served us. But I recall it was a little stringy."

When it was time for the second round of 'okc' old-fashioneds, the Admiral prepared them with even greater care than the first. As he passed each glass personally to a guest, he said in the gentle magnolia voice that he reserved for such occasions, "Please wait for a little toast I'd like to propose."

Curious, but respectfully silent, the seven officers held their untasted cocktails while he rummaged around in his desk and found a framed sheet of paper, which he held high with his left hand, printed side toward him. He brandished his own glass in his great freckled right fist.

"Ordinarily," the Admiral said, "what I'm about to do gets lost in the daily routine, because only a man's few close friends ever seem to care much about it, or give it the honor it deserves. Yet it doesn't happen to many naval officers. And sometimes it comes to those who least expect it—or who have lost hope that it might ever happen at all."

He looked around the room, savoring the perplexity on their faces, until his gaze came to rest upon The Rock.

"I have here," he continued, "suitably framed for hanging on a convenient bulkhead, Bureau of Personnel's dispatch 031135, which arrived this morning. Without exaggeration, I confess it gave me more pleasure than anything that's come out of Washington in many months."

He read aloud: "FROM BUPERS TO CAPTAIN ROCKWELL TORREY USN. INFO CINCPAC. YOU ARE HEREBY ADVISED THAT SELECTION BOARD THIS

DATE APPROVED YOUR PROMOTION TO REAR ADMIRAL WITH RANK FROM JULY THIRD."

As he handed the framed message to Torrey, he added soothingly, "I suppose we've transgressed some obscure Navy regs by intercepting this dispatch before it got to you, Rock, and holding it back. But I wanted to do it my way"—looking imperious—"and, after all, the Boss has some privileges, doesn't he?"

"Yes, sir," Torrey agreed solemnly.

"Not irked?"

"No, sir."

"That's fine," the Admiral went on, "because this little party was planned for you . . . so I'd have a better chance to mention a few things that have been on my mind for a long time, and outline your new billet." He hoisted his old-fashioned glass like a marshal's baton. "Now, gentlemen, a toast!"

Six more glasses were raised, but The Rock's remained in his lap. His face was an odd study in pride, mystification, and embarrassment.

"To our newest admiral—and to his success on a very tough assignment!"

While the toast was being consummated, Torrey searched the Admiral's blandly innocent expression for some clue that might explain what was meant by his two cryptic references to new duty. Four-star admirals are inclined to behave independently, sometimes with a ponderous and maddening kind of deliberation, yet always with a purpose; and The Rock knew he'd have to await the great man's pleasure. Besides, now it was his turn to respond to the toast.

He arose, feeling as though the eyes of the entire Navy were boresighted in upon him like the torpedo tubes of the Jap submarine that had robbed him of his first major command, and he slowly lifted his half tumbler of okulehou.

"Since I was never called upon to endorse any bad fitness reports you'd prepared for me, sir, I can only assume they were—well—'satisfactory.' Now I know you must have been a lot more kind than I deserved."

The Admiral harrumphed testily.

"All I told BuPers," he said, "was that you were another ruddy John Paul Jones."

Unguardedly, The Rock asked, "Without a ship, sir?"

"That's immaterial," the Admiral said sharply. "It's a matter of where your personal flag flies."

"Yes, sir."

The Admiral, who seemed to have more to say, suddenly dropped the subject. Instead, he reached into his cluttered desk drawer and produced a set of two-starred collar pins.

"I wore these out here in December," he said, "before I had a chance to pick up my four-star insignia. Maybe they brought me luck, although I'm not betting my last dollar on it—yet." His blue eyes gleamed. "Too damned early."

He reached for The Rock's collar, unhooked his eagles, and replaced them with the stars.

Torrey stared down at the tiny silver badges, and for a wild moment he debated whether he should confess the truth: that he'd immersed himself in the complexities of Operation Skyhook because he wished to escape mentally from his Pearl Harbor cell, and not because the immediate task had held any great allure for him. But the moment passed.

He looked up. "Thank you, sir."

"Don't mention it, *Admiral* Torrey. Just hope they do bring luck. You're going to need it!"

As they filed down the semicircular staircase to dinner, Egan Powell gripped The Rock's hardboned shoulder and whispered, "Your trouble, laddie-buck, is that you were born just one year too bloody soon."

"How so?"

"Remember what I told you a few months ago? That when a captain got his ship torpedoed they'd brevet him a two-star admiral before his damned skivvies dried off?"

Egan Powell was right, although he'd oversimplified the case. With the passage of time, realism had set in, bringing with it certain practical shifts in High Command attitudes. Last year's untested experts were this year's blooded participants in an exacting game that tended to make fools out of anybody who imagined he had all the answers, or even a majority of them, because nobody did in this unorthodox war against the unpredictable Asian foe.

Before they entered the diningroom, Powell managed one last word. "What d'you reckon the Big Boss has planned for your fair white corpus delicti?"

"Probably convoy commander," Torrey growled. "I'm ripe for it . . ."

The main course was beef Stroganoff, which the Admiral had discovered during a tour of duty on the Kamchatka Peninsula, when the United States was attempting rather clumsily to set matters straight in Siberia after World War I. Recollection of that abortive Asian operation led him inevitably into a discourse on how not to do things, militarily speaking, if you wish to succeed. He laid down his fork with a small crashing noise and the seven officers gave him their fullest attention.

"Frankly," the Admiral announced, "I'm damned concerned about Mesquite."

His subordinates waited expectantly for him to expand this gloomy theme which they, themselves, had pondered for the past four weeks. They hoped he'd finally pass The Word about what ought to be done to prod Blackjack Broderick out of his potentially disastrous lethargy, and into action, so the Gavabutu operation could get moving again. The Admiral pushed aside his empty plate. Taking excessive care not to spill any tobacco on the damask tablecloth, he rolled a Bull Durham cigarette, ignited it with a kitchen match, and inhaled a leathery lungful of smoke. His eyes closed momentarily. Then smoke burst from his pursed lips like the forerunning clouds of a tropical typhoon.

When the Admiral spoke again, a flat, precise, almost tutorial tone had replaced his drawl.

"Broderick reminds me of a certain Civil War general. I'm sure you gentlemen have studied him somewhere along the way. We've always regarded him as the classic example of military procrastination. Fellow named George B. McClellan. He took over the top Union command at a rather delicate and certainly very desperate time, when Lincoln wasn't having much luck finding a man who could get his Army organized. Abe had tried a half-dozen other chaps. They all let him down.

"Well, this George McClellan—they even called him the 'Young Napoleon' before they knew better—did a whale of a fine job up to a certain point. Then he stalled. McClellan proved to be a fine organizer, all right, only he managed to get himself and his Army so overorganized that they couldn't fight because they were too busy doing paperwork and shining their cannon. Finally Lincoln is supposed to've said, 'Sending reinforcements to McClellan is like shoveling flies across a barn.'

"This 'Young Napoleon' wouldn't stir a finger, by God, until things got so critical he had no choice. Then along came Antietam. He could have scored a decisive victory for the Union, but McClellan dillydallied and didn't follow up his advantage over Lee. So what might have been the real crossroads of the war as early as '62 petered out into a dismal cul-de-sac."

The Admiral scowled ferociously around the small table, and each of his admirals and captains felt a sudden guilt twinge, as if they ought to be someplace where the bombs were falling instead of placidly digesting beef Stroganoff.

"Here's what I'm driving at, gentlemen—after McClellan let him down, Lincoln simply *had* to find a Grant. History demanded it. He had no other choice. 'Young Napoleon' was a fine administrator. All spit-and-polish. Great idea man—on paper. But he wouldn't *move!*"

Still nobody dared interrupt the Admiral's monologue. He had dropped one shoe. They waited anxiously for the other to fall.

"Mesquite," he went on, "has been stalled for almost a month. But I don't have to belabor that point. You read the daily situation reports. Backing and filling. A few miserable miles here, a couple of hogback ridges there, but never the conclusive assault that will secure Gavabutu, so we can get cracking on Skyhook. Meanwhile we're running out of time . . . and weather."

Again the Admiral's glance swept sternly around the table.

"If we haven't launched Skyhook before Christmas, I'd say we're in trouble. Double-damned deep trouble. Because the Japs aren't going to oblige us by sitting on their hands forever. They might even have a few plans of their own." He turned to his Intelligence chief. "What's your latest estimate, Harry?"

"The Nips definitely are up to something, sir. That's certain. Our subs report heavy combatant shipping all down the line from Tokyo to Skyhook—at Pelaka Jima, especially, where they stage into Levu-Vana—and west at some of those bases they grabbed from the British last year. Cape Titan, for one. We know they're storing up some damned impressive power within a few days' steaming range of our next target . . . and they're obviously getting braced to reinforce Skyhook itself, because we've spotted troop transports in the Carolines."

"What's your best guess about their timetable?"

The Intelligence officer had been doodling lines on the tablecloth with his dessert spoon as he talked. When he looked up, his face was very grave.

"They'll strike in a few weeks. Certainly no more."

"After dessert," the Admiral said, nodding, "we'll go up to my chartroom and see what we can see." Then he added portentously, as if he were disclosing something Top Secret, "We're having papaya mousse."

The Admiral's private chartroom, on the second floor of Number 10 Makalapa, just beyond his blackout cubicle, had the lived-in look of a place where an oppressively busy man rides his hobby during his meager spare time. Maps covered all four walls. A large-scale projection of Blackjack Broderick's command—areas occupied and those still to be seized from the enemy—was draped across a drafting table. It was fixed there by an ivoryhilted ceremonial dagger taken from the corpse of one of the Japanese midget-submariners who'd penetrated Pearl Harbor on December 7. A deep-leather chair with a goosenecked lamp alongside it was the only other article of furniture in the cramped room.

"My hideaway," the Admiral explained briefly. "Sometimes when I can't sleep—too much on my mind—I crawl out of bed and read from 0300 to 0500. And do a bit of quiet thinking. That's why I've had this duplicate set of charts made up. I like to see things laid out in black and white, so they can be properly evaluated. You'd be surprised how clear a man's brain gets along about 0400 . . ."

With his great paw he motioned toward the dagger-skewered chart on the drafting table, and the staff crowded in for a closer look.

For some inexplicable reason, although Torrey had studied the topography of Mesquite and Skyhook scores of times before, even memorizing the terrain, it seemed more understandable when it was delineated by the Admiral. Like an ugly wisdom tooth impacted against a second molar, Skyhook's prime target island of Levu-Vana clung to its sister island of Toka-Rota, separated only by a narrow straight called Pala Passage. At its widest, this waterway was barely twenty miles across. Rough as an amalgam filling which the dentist has neglected to file down with his bur-drill, a serrated mountain ridge ran the length of Levu-Vana, rising to a maximum height of slightly more than a mile.

The Admiral set his stubby forefinger against a red arrow that pierced an indentation on the island's east-central coast, marked Lakola Bay.

"That," he said softly, "is it."

Here the Americans—a Marine division backed up by a composite division of Army troops cadged from every command between Port Moresby and Samoa—would make their landing.

Levu-Vana was one hundred and twenty miles long and eighty miles wide. Around the rim of Lakola Bay grew a tangle of copra palms which, abandoned by the British and Australian plantation owners, had become part of the jungle itself. About a quarter mile inland, according to photographic reconnaissance, lay a vague something which Intelligence insisted was a partially finished fighter strip, under clandestine construction beneath nets strung across the tops of the coconut trees.

"If you're right, Harry," the Admiral said, "we've got to get humping. Once the Japs finish that strip, our problem will be doubled. We'll have one hell of a time softening up Levu-Vana by air—if the air's full of Zeros."

"I'd say our problem would be tripled," Harry opined judiciously.

Four hundred crow's-flight miles south of Skyhook was Mesquite. Off the bottom of the chart, indicated by a blue arrow, lay the island of Toulebonne, the Free French sanctuary from which Blackjack Broderick directed the floundering struggle against the enemy on Gavabutu, like a man handling redhot coals with a pair of fireplace tongs, gingerly, and from a too-safe distance.

What did not appear on even the Admiral's map, of course, were all the imponderables, such as faulty navigational aids which had gone unchallenged during the four centuries since the wandering Spaniards discovered this island chain. There remained far too many uncharted reefs. Skyhook's target itself, Beach Red, later would be "found" atop a smoldering volcano seven miles inland from the deserted Crown colony of Anaka, because of the fuzzy reckonings of Don Alvaro de Mendaña, explorer extraordinary, whose taste ran more to bullion than to cartography. Nor did the charts mention anopheles (malaria) mosquitoes, breakbone (dengue) fever, the Gavabutu Trots (dysentery), crocodiles in mangrove swamps, white ants big enough to haul away a man's field boots, or the stench of rotting copra, festering vegetation, mildewed clothing, and the pervasive sense of clammy doom that clung over this green hell which looked so lush and lovely from a reconnaissance plane traveling at a hundred and fifty knots—and three miles high.

The Admiral stared morosely at the blue arrow that pointed toward the invisible Toulebonne.

"I am reminded," he rumbled, "of the essayist Montaigne, who wrote that 'on the most exalted throne in the world we are seated on nothing but our own arse . . .' At least gentlemen, I *think* it was Montaigne. Whoever he was, he uttered a damned perceptive bit of wisdom."

Again they waited.

He slammed his hand against the chart so hard the Japanese dagger sprung loose and fell to the floor, needlepoint first, where it stuck, quivering like a tuning fork.

"Of course," he went on, "we can't pull Broderick out of this business entirely. Shaking him up is one thing. But scrambling his whole command is another. It mustn't be done overnight." The Admiral emitted another derisive snort. "These things can have a damned bad effect on our temperamental allies—as well as giving the enemy some aid and comfort he doesn't deserve right now.

"But—we can remove Broderick from immediate tactical control of Skyhook, and make somebody else responsible for mounting Skyhook. Which is exactly what we're going to do!"

The Admiral looked like a man who'd made a monumental decision that astonished even himself, but one that also gave him considerable satisfaction. He continued: "McClellan needs a Grant to do the dirty work while he administers his 'area.' Good. We'll give him one. He can attend the French governor's fancy tea parties and handle all the social amenities while this other fellow—Grant—spits on his hands and starts digging." He hesitated, then asked ironically, "Did I say *McClellan*? I meant Broderick."

The Intelligence chief generated enough nerve to inquire, "What about 'Grant,' sir?"

"I'm going to have this man—this Grant—report to *both* Broderick-McClellan and to me. Difficult, you say? Certainly it'll be difficult. But not impossible. It can be done by the right fellow . . . who's not afraid to tackle a damned nasty assignment, and who's got a touch of diplomacy to go along with his drive. I'll back him to the limit. And—" he grinned—"I'll let him choose his own staff, a damned small one, so he's sure of loyalty in his own camp."

The Admiral's arctic eye circled the room and, as it had an hour earlier, froze upon Torrey.

"Ever think of growing a beard, Rock?"

"Sir?"

"You'd better get started on it," the Admiral said quietly. "There isn't much time left. Because I'm picking you to play Grant to Blackjack Broderick's McClellan!"

TWO STARS

11. You Can't Simply Order a Man

It was two hours after sunrise in Toulebonne, a cool pale sauterne of a morning below the Equator, when Admiral Blackjack Broderick should have been getting his best Sunday sleep in the hilltop mansion the Americans had liberated from the French island's leading Japanese industrialist. But he wasn't. For at that precise moment, 0705, he was confronted with a most unpleasant task.

Across from him at the breakfast table, unshaven and rather petulant at having been roused from his own dreams of glory, sat Commander Neal Owynn.

Both men gazed intently into their coffeecups, as if they might find some Delphic answer to their special problem among the dark leftover grounds, or because they didn't wish to look at, and comment upon, the typewritten message that lay on the tabletop between them. Outside an open French window a Tonkinese gardener, humming a weird runic ballad, was spreading forbidden nightsoil fertilizer around the rosebushes which Blackjack had ordered flown from California. A two-week-old *New York Times,* also brought by air, littered a delicate Japanese settee beneath the casement. The scene presented all the dulcet aspects of a normal Sabbath in Toulebonne. Later they might motor to Va'tanse beach for a leisurely swim, a bit of suntanning, and a couple of bottles of Budweiser, which the admiral greatly preferred to the 3.2 canned hosspiss supplied by the Army's unimaginative logistical people.

Later, that is, if they could discover a way out of the dilemma presented them by this astonishing dispatch from Pearl Harbor.

Blackjack slammed his fist down hard upon the damask-covered table. The shellthin dishes trembled and tinkled under the sledgehammer blow.

"I'm not going to stand for this—goddamn it!—not for one

bloody minute. Even if I have to go to Ernie Jesus King himself and get it squared away!"

The Senator lifted a manicured hand, placatively, and seemed to be debating how well he'd taught that little halfcaste girl, Saree, to apply nail polish.

"Let's not," he suggested softly, "do anything hasty."

"Hasty—hell! The son of a bitch'll be in Mesquite on Thursday. What should I do? Take this lying down? Be a goddamn doormat with 'welcome' printed across my arse?"

Owynn lit a cigarette. "Maybe we can swing this business to our advantage."

"How?"

"Torrey might just possibly, somehow, goose those bastards at Gavabutu into the kind of action they haven't produced for you, B.J." (This was a secret bit of camaraderie between the Senator and the admiral: B.J. for Blackjack; and it made them feel quite clubby when they were discussing their respective futures.) "So if Torrey makes out—fine! You get all the credit because you're the area boss. And if he screws up—that's *his* tough luck."

Broderick snapped his fingers for more coffee. A midget Melanesian houseboy tiptoed into the diningroom with a silver urn, poured, and the oracular coffee grounds were covered up.

"You goddamn politicians," Blackjack said admiringly.

"You can catch more flies with honey," Owynn observed in his buttery baritone, "than with vinegar."

"I thought you fellows were more apt to use the stuff the Tonk's spreading around the rosebushes out there."

"That, too. But with discrimination, B.J., and with finesse."

The admiral's broad, sunburnt, oddly handsome face stiffened and his heavy brows drew together. "Mesquite's a hell of a long haul from Toulebonne. Take a fellow like Rock Torrey—I know his type—he'll operate in a bloody vacuum and only tell us what he wants, when he wants."

"So we put a 'tail' on him."

"What?"

"Back in Washington," Owynn explained, "we used to have a little trouble sometimes with certain people who didn't behave properly. Radicals. Recalcitrants. Various sons of bitches. So we'd assign a smart committee staffer to watch 'em. It's called 'tailing'—

crowding their tails day and night until eventually they met the wrong guy or shacked up with a broad or pulled some other actionable Brody—and then *wham!*—we had them right by the testicles."

As he spoke, the Senator's spurious Harvard accent wore away, along with his elegant rhetoric, for now he was at his enthusiastic best, scheming to confound an adversary, or destroy him, and all in the name of good clean political fun.

"You could 'tail' Rock Torrey from now until doomsday," the admiral said gloomily, "without catching him doing anything worse than moving the wrong piece in a chess game, and even that'd probably turn out to be an honest mistake."

Owynn inspected his glossy fingernails again. "There are plenty of ways to skin even a clever cat like Torrey."

"Who'll we put on the job?"

"Me."

"You?" Blackjack Broderick's slumberladen eyes widened in disbelief, and he sounded almost ungracious as he growled, "Hell, Senator, you like this layout in Toulebonne too much to go gallivanting up the line to Gavabutu. You've been there. That's no country for a white man."

Owynn coughed lightly. Behind them the houseboy stood motionless, stolid, coffeepot in hand. The admiral, he thought with a fleeting twinge of embarrassment, would never make a politician. Broderick required a lot of careful honing. He needed Neal Owynn beside him, coaching and prodding.

"Beat it, Omoo," the Senator told the native. Then: "A little forward area duty might be good for me, B.J., if you follow my line of reasoning." Blackjack looked so genuinely puzzled that Owynn explained, "After the war, politicians with combat records will be sitting pretty. Hell. Being entitled to sport the right ribbon in your buttonhole should be worth a half a million votes in my state alone . . ."

Broderick nodded sagely. "Yes. Now I see. Which ribbon appeals to you, Neal?"

"Legion of Merit?"

"Done. Cut the mustard at Mesquite, and you've got your Legion. But that means holding Rock Torrey on a short leash, because, frankly, I don't want any hotheads taking over just when we're bringing this operation nicely under control. In a couple of months Mesquite will be signed, sealed, and delivered. After that we'll wait for spring and hit 'em with Skyhook when the weather clears again." He smiled. "This isn't such a bad place to spend the winter."

"I suspect," Owynn said, "Torrey's coming down here with a different timetable."

"That's what I'm afraid of. He's just been given two stars. So he's got to make a showing. Besides," Blackjack added reluctantly, "The Rock has plenty of guts in that goddamned quiet way of his."

"Bad combination. Bomb with fuse."

"All right. You defuse him!"

Owynn drummed with his tapered fingers, making clicking noises with his nails on the tabletop, in tempo to his secret musings. He had seen enough of Torrey during his sojourn at Makalapa to know that "defusing" him, or even keeping him shackled, was going to be a ticklish job, somewhat akin to harnessing a maverick stallion. You'd have to find some other means of controlling The Rock. But a shrewd lad might succeed. *Cut the mustard,* as Blackjack put it so elegantly and so succinctly.

Taking his aide's meditative silence for assent, Admiral Broderick projected his own thoughts toward a warless day when his only battle would be with the Green Bowlers—a special closeknit hierarchy of the Service—for a seat at the overcrowded head table. As he'd reminded himself many times, it would be nice to have a United States Senator on the string. Who could tell? Chap like Neal Owynn might even wind up as President. You could number on the fingers of your left hand the admirals who had ever been intimates of a President, starting with T.R.'s George Dewey and ending with F.D.R.'s Bill Leahy; and that made the notion all the more exhilarating, particularly for someone like Blackjack Broderick who'd need plenty of close-in support when the postwar scrambling started.

". . . I trust," Owynn was saying with elaborate casualness "that you don't have any immediate plans for hauling MOB Able away from Mesquite."

Blackjack asked innocently, "Why, are you about to take sick?"

"Yes. It's an old Capitol Hill malady caused by inhaling too much mimeograph fumes and too little perfume. Lackanooky.

I'm apt to get it so damned bad I'll have to go to bed with a nurse."

Owynn's antique joke amused the admiral, who permitted himself a quick laugh. "Just don't fraternize with the lower ranks."

"This one's due to make lieutenant commander any minute," the Senator said complacently.

"Sounds pretty long-in-the-fang."

Owynn shook his head. "No, sir, she's cuter than a goddamn quail. And a hell of a lot more elusive."

"Gavabutu's a smaller island than Toulebonne," Blackjack observed, "or even Oahu. It might hamper her fancy footwork. Maybe you'll catch her yet."

"Man can always hope."

The admiral signaled the end of their colloquy. "Just remember, commander, where your real duty lies."

"I'll remember . . ."

Tonight, Eddington knew, was going to turn out like all the rest of the Saturday nights in Toulebonne. He'd take Saree to the Officers' Club which the island command had set up in a corrugated-tin and moldering-stucco relic called L'Hôtel Magnifique du Pacifique. He'd belt down five stiff bourbons served in beer cans with their tops cut off and beveled smooth, while Saree daintily sipped a 3.2 beer, and then they'd stroll together down the malodorous street to her room in the Madagascar Hotel. Maybe he'd take his pleasure with her tiny body before he passed out, or maybe he'd collapse into his usual drunken stupor and forget all about her, in which event Saree would undress him and hang up his disheveled khakis. Then she'd sit there at the foot of her brass bed with all those curlicues on it, staring at him and crooning some strange half-Tonk half-Frog lullaby she'd learned from her mother, an indentured Tonkinese day laborer who had died when Saree was thirteen, or from her reputed father, a French petty officer long since fled back to Marseilles.

Shortly before dawn Eddington would awaken groggily, splash lukewarm water over his ravaged face from the basin on the bedside commode, and stagger out in search of the Navy Landing, which somebody always misplaced during the night. Once back at the air station across the limpid bay, he'd grab a fast shot of eye-opening whisky so he could face breakfast, his confreres, and the endless goddamn day.

Impressed by the old stone cathedral, certain quaint odors which he hadn't as yet identified, a couple of frowsy tramp steamers tied alongside the town's collapsing wharves, the hot red blaze of the flame trees, and the shadowy hint of mysterious goings-on behind shuttered windows—unduly impressed by all these, that is, a freshman war correspondent remarked one evening at the Magnifique's bar that Toulebonne was "a chapter right out of Maugham, illustrated by Gauguin." When Eddington heard this journalistic hyperbole, he pretended to throw up; and had he been of a literary mind himself, he'd have corrected the reporter by branding Toulebonne as the quintessence of Dante portrayed by Doré.

Eddington might also have concluded that this ugly French colony was a singularly appropriate place for a man to contrive his own downfall: it was so absolutely, utterly, stinkingly hideous.

It took him only four double bourbons at the Magnifique to get into the mood for Saree's dank little room. Lately, he'd discovered, his tolerance for whisky had diminished, and because of this something like fear stirred in the distant recesses of his brain. Suppose he reached the point where he couldn't drink at all? That would be the ultimate tragedy, to have this nepenthe snatched away, leaving him at the mercy of his dark fancies. Sometimes Eddington tended to forget what had originally caused his melancholia. And sometimes—though much less frequently—he aroused himself enough to realize that he was being witlessly sorry for himself, immersed in a corrosive self-pity that eventually would eat him up, like a bath of sulfuric acid.

Saree led him into her chamber which was just one of a half dozen or so identical rooms that opened off the Madagascar's sagging veranda. The door was unlocked. She bolted it only when she was entertaining. Otherwise there was nothing to steal. Captain Paul was a rather special client. Since he paid her handsomely for the trouble he caused her, she supposed that made things all right, if not exactly moral, although there were times she wished he'd go away, particularly when he fell into one of those *humeurs malheureuses* which changed him from a predictably crude man into a raging uncontrollable animal.

Tonight Eddington took off his own clothes.

Half-crouched on the monstrous brass bed, which was the only furniture in the room except for the lacquered stand on which lay the porcelain washbasin, he studied her tiny face, perplexed and somber, without speaking. His silence was not unusual. Their conversations were carried out laboriously in his dimly recalled French and her recently acquired basic GI English. It wasn't poetic. But it sufficed. What bothered Saree was the intense way Eddington stared at her, as if he were trying to penetrate her small soul. Unlike her jalousied bedroom door, she kept this possession locked up tight, to be contemplated only by herself in the rare hours of the morning when she was alone or when the man beside her was asleep.

Eddington said in his abrasive voice, "She was blond, *bébé,* not dark the way you are. But she was a whore, too, only not like you, either, because she wasn't even an honest whore."

Saree could not comprehend what he was saying. She had been called a whore before, often, yet it didn't distress her. One accomplished one's business. That was that.

"You are sad, *mon commandant.*"

He passed his great fist across his forehead. "Just tired, *bébé,* like Death before it's warmed over."

"You want Saree?"

"Sure." He laughed harshly. "I want Saree. What else?"

She wriggled out of her single cotton garment and slipped gracefully into the feather-mattressed bed. She stretched her arms toward Eddington, placative and inviting, and he threw himself heavily upon her frail body. He lay there, inhaling the faint odor of female sweat that mingled piquantly with the perfume he'd bought her, motionless, like a votary who has flung himself exhausted upon an altar after too much praying.

She shuddered lightly.

Eddington felt the almost imperceptible tremor and abruptly cast himself free. On propped elbows, he let his gaze rove lengthwise down the girl's minnow-slim nakedness, from tiny mouth to budded breasts to halfspread thighs. Then he sighed deeply.

Saree said, "What is the matter, truly?"

"Truly, *bébé,* Christ only knows."

"Is it Saree?"

"No. It's not Saree. It's a goddamn fool named Paul Eddington. But you wouldn't ever understand."

"It is not good to say 'Christ' and 'goddamn' in this manner, *mon commandant.*"

With his right forefinger he traced indolent circles on her taut belly, just above her navel, the way a small boy makes stickmarks on a clean sandy beach.

"You really believe that, don't you?" Eddington said.

"Yes," she replied simply, "I believe."

"You're lucky, *bébé,* because I don't believe in anything. Not a single solitary frigging thing!"

"Impossible!"

"Someday," Eddington said, "when we have a hell of a lot of time on our hands, I'll explain. Right now it's too long a story. And much too sad for an innocent child."

"What is 'innocent'?"

He looked around the room. Even in the fecund gloom it was austerely unfeminine, and rather pathetic, for it was a barren place where nobody could hide from anything, himself or his innermost thoughts. Now his sigh became a groan.

"You're innocent, *bébé,* like a kid who's just been born or snow that hasn't been walked on."

"Snow?"

"Forget it."

Eddington's gravelly tone rejected further talk. He put two cigarettes in his mouth, lit them simultaneously with a Zippo, and they both lay back making the small puffing noises that people make when they try to smoke very quietly. Soon he fell asleep. She took the halfburnt cigarette from his relaxed fingers. After that she resumed her vigil at the foot of the big brass bed, regarding him through the darkness with a look that was no longer inquisitive, but strangely maternal for somebody who was only seventeen.

At midnight a heavy knock rattled the thin-louvered door.

Saree called softly, "Go 'way, Commander Owynn. Tonight I am busy."

Whoever was outside said, "It ain't the commander, miss, it's Yeoman Margolis from the air station, and I've got to talk to the cap'n."

Saree shook Eddington awake.

"It is a man," she said, "who wishes to speak to you, *mon commandant.*"

He glanced at his luminous wrist watch. "Tell the son of a bitch to scram."

But the knock sounded again, more determined this time, as if the intruder meant business. Margolis' voice was urgent.

"Commander, sir, I've *gotta* talk to you. Duty officer sent me. He says you'd skin us alive unless you got The Word we've just received—toot sweet." Cryptically, Margolis added, "He says you've been waiting seven months for this."

Eddington pulled on his shorts. He opened the door, boldly and brusquely, and confronted the luckless yeoman.

"Goddamn it, Margolis! What Christly Word could possibly make the OD send you across the bay at this hour?" He didn't have to ask how they knew he'd be here at the Madagascar; his movements were never secret.

The dungareed sailor shoved a bit of paper into Eddington's incipiently fisted hand. He blurted, "Take it, sir!" Then he half saluted, turned, and sought sanctuary in the night.

"Light me a candle, *bébé,*" Eddington said.

Saree obeyed without comment.

When the tiny flame glowed, he held the paper close so he could read the typed message. It was CinCPAC's dispatch 260116, marked PRIORITY, ordering Commander Paul Eddington, USN, to report without delay as chief of staff for Rear Admiral Rockwell Torrey, USN, who had just been appointed Commander Advanced Tactical Zone South Pacific. Headquarters: Mesquite.

Suddenly Eddington felt very clearheaded. He started to dress, unhurriedly, with special regard for the way his trousers hung and how his buttons fastened, instead of furiously jerking the garments over his nakedness as if he resented their stricturing presence.

Saree touched the message flimsy. "Is good?"

"Is very goddamn good, *bébé*. Is a reprieve from *Monsieur le Gouverneur*. Is maybe even life and hope."

"Oh," she said, "I comprehend."

But she didn't. All she knew was that Eddington's jubilant tone meant that he was going away. And she couldn't tell, inside her small head or within her very large heart, whether she should be glad about this, or sad.

From Toulebonne to San Francisco, a Great Circle Course would encompass roughly one-quarter of the distance around the globe as it arched northeast across the jungled islands of Melanesia (among them Gavabutu and Levu-Vana), the landspecks of Micronesia, the Hawaiian chain, and finally the bleak offshore approaches to the Golden Gate itself. Because such a route spans the International Date Line somewhere south of the Equator, Toulebonne's somnolent Sunday morning would have become San Francisco's vibrant Saturday evening . . .

Bev McConnel caught herself grinning into the pierglass mirror that clung to the old-fashioned hotel wall, happy as a coocoo clam in her new scarlet cocktail gown, and thinking how darned different this was, getting gussied up for a stateside adventure instead of dressing for one of Commander Bowen's creepy old dinners. Thinking of the commander made her remember *Cassiday*. Her smile faded.

Rather guiltily, she hoped Mac would get duty somewhere in the Bay area, like Mare Island or Hunter's Point or the unsinkably granite naval district headquarters downtown, although it really didn't matter. Just so Mac could stick around for a while, close by, where she could hear his bubbling laughter and feel his lean arms around her at night. True, Mac didn't seem to laugh as much as he used to, and there were certain unmentionable moments when it was *she* who comforted *him*.

But tonight they would go to the Top-of-the-Mark and have a few drinks, bourbon on the rocks for Mac and daiquiris for her, and then they'd blow a day's pay for two of Luigi's best dinners, lovingly prepared at tableside, and to hell with the expense. Oh, and afterward *café espresso* in a smoky dive at the foot of some steep street that touched the Bay, where the greenblack harborwaters slapped against a barnacled jetty. Perhaps Mac would forget *Cassiday* for a little while. She'd help him by pretending to be blithe and gay and oblivious to All That.

She peered out the sixth-floor window at the fog that was rolling across the Golden Gate Bridge. That was one thing you could always say for San Francisco: its afternoon mistblanket pushed the sun down over the yardarm so early you could start drinking with good conscience before most cities quit burping after a late lunch, except possibly Great Falls, Montana, or Presque Isle, Maine, which weren't tippling towns anyhow. You could say a lot more for this exciting city that seemed to have been founded just for heroes-come-home and for their brides. But wasn't that what they called redundancy? All war wives were brides in Frisco.

At five-twenty Mac stalked into their hotel room looking sort of hagridden, and flung his overseas cap and coat across a brocaded chair as if he never expected to wear them again.

"Rough day at the office?" Bev asked, hoping she wasn't seeing ghosts.

He smiled faintly at her solicitude. "Tol'able. Market's way off. We dropped a cool million. Otherwise, no sweat."

"I thought I detected a kind of brainwashed aura about you, lieutenant."

"Negative." Mac started to get annoyed. "This is my normal look. I don't have any other."

"But you used to, dear heart. Glad, mad, bad, sad. All kinds of flavors."

"Visiting ComTwelve's talent agency does this to me," he said shortly. "I'll get over it."

"Any Word yet?"

But Mac was pulling his shirt over his head—he never bothered to unbutton it—and apparently he couldn't hear her. Bev shrugged her bare shoulders. They still had eight days, six hours and twenty-seven minutes of survivor's leave before the Navy engulfed him again, so she might as well save her worries for later. When he finally stepped under the shower he was whistling something very brisk and horribly off-key. That was better, for it signified that whatever was eating him couldn't be too monstrous; otherwise his whistle would be nearer the tune, probably that post-Pearl Harbor song about praising the Lord and passing the ammuniton so we'd all go free.

Mac took an inordinately long while to bathe, shave, don his blues, and carefully knot his blackwool tie before the mirror, and when he finally swung around toward Bev, he pretended he was seeing her for the first time that afternoon.

"Who let you in here, miss?" he demanded severely. "I thought this was a *respectable* hotel."

"It was, mister, until they started admitting sailors."

"You like sailors?"

"Mmmmmm." Bev formed her carmine lips into a seductive pout. "I pick 'em up all the time."

He considered her thoughtfully. "You look pretty expensive for a j.o. What's your price, ma'am?"

"Tempt me with a good dinner, lieutenant."

"Luigi's?"

"How'd you guess?"

Instead of going to the Top-of-the-Mark, they went to a hotel across the street where a Hawaiian orchestra was playing in a palmdecked basement, just for the sake of a happier past, and they ordered a drink called a Cobra's Fang. A semi-nude semi-Polynesian maiden danced *Princess Papule*. Perfumed odors that might have been jasmine and ginger wafted through the contrived tropical atmosphere, and it ought to have been romantic as hell. But it wasn't. For suddenly the room was the Officers' Club at Pearl Harbor and the girl doing the hula was Beth Eddington and tomorrow the whole damned world would go bang!

"Let's blow this joint," Mac growled.

Bev nodded bleakly. "Affirmative. It's starting to give me the haunts."

"Me too."

They caught a taxicab for Luigi's. Mac settled into the seat with that odd look he'd worn when he arrived at the hotel darkening his young face again, and now Bev saw furrows around his mouth and across his forehead that hadn't been there before *Cassiday* got sunk.

Whatever weighed so heavily upon his mind would come out, sooner or later, so she'd just have to be patient. She squeezed his hand. There was nothing else she could do. He was still brooding when they left Luigi's for the *espresso* place. But here, with his mouth pressed so close to the steaming coffeecup she had to listen very carefully, Mac finally started to talk.

"I guess you've already figured out what's troubling junior."

"Not really."

"Well, I did get The Word at headquarters," he muttered, "and you're not going to like it, Bev."

She said, "Oh?" in a funny sort of way that was more a sigh than a spoken word, and waited.

"I'm going back out."

"But they can't . . ." she began.

"They can do anything they damn well please," Mac interrupted.

Fighting to keep her voice calm, Bev asked, "What sort of duty is it?"

"Staff."

She relaxed. "That's better. I was afraid it'd be another tincan."

"Maybe this is worse."

"How could it be worse?"

"Easy." He set his *espresso* down carefully upon the redchecked tablecloth. "You've heard of Gavabutu—that island where our guys have been stuck for the last three months?"

"Yes."

"Admiral Torrey has been made bossman for the operation. He wants me as his Flag lieutenant."

Bev sounded puzzled. "Why's it so darned important for you to go 'way out there for a staff job? It seems plain silly."

"Gavabutu's only the start. Once it's washed up, we'll start moving again. And then it'll be the Big One."

Bev said, "Oh," again in a miniature voice, as she tried to recall Admiral Torrey, who'd been only a captain when he visited their house in Nuuanu. She conjured up a fleeting vision of a hawklike face, very stern yet strangely compassionate. She guessed he was a good man. He must be. Mac thought he was God Almighty in khakis.

"I wish," Mac was saying softly, "that I could tell you this'll be a nice soft billet, sweetheart, but I'm afraid it won't work out that way. Not if I know The Rock. Gavabutu's been 'safe' too damned long. They've got to get some action going. Attrition's nibbling 'em to death."

He pulled the typed orders from his inside breast pocket and unfolded them.

"It says 'proceed immediately.' That means within forty-eight hours."

"But we've got eight more days!"

Mac touched her small clenched fist. "Not any more we haven't, honeybug. I'm sorry."

She regarded him steadily. "You *want* to go, don't you?"

"Yes . . . I guess I do."

"Then I'll be a big brave girl, lieutenant, just as soon as I go to the ladies' room and blow my damned nose. Order me another *espresso,* please, and tell the man to put an extra slug of brandy in it."

When Bev returned, she was singularly composed, as if she had come to blunt terms with herself, and didn't intend to let down again.

"Exit crybaby," she said. "Enter mature woman."

Mac wished he could find words to match her jaunty courage. But they wouldn't come. So he simply blew her a kiss.

After they drank their double-laced *espresso,* and had another even stronger one, Bev said meditatively, "You know, lieutenant, I'm going to stay right here in Frisco and get a job typing at Com-Twelve. Free a man for combat duty."

"That's great, Mrs. McConnel." He grinned. "Only let me give you a word of advice—don't call it Frisco. Otherwise you mightn't be here alive when I come back."

Bev tried to laugh. But somehow it wasn't very funny, his telling *her* how to keep from getting killed.

On Makalapa Hill it was midevening, and growing darker as the quick subtropical twilight faded, making it necessary to draw the blackout curtains in the places where men worked, ate, or relaxed off-duty. His restless brain filled with thoughts of his new command, Torrey sat in the gloom of his bedroom, smoking a guarded pipeful of tobacco, and blowing white smoke rings into the breezeless night through the opened window. As a long-forgotten schoolboy memory came to him, he smiled, inwardly amused at the image it evoked. In a way, he supposed, he had now named to his personal staff two of the Three Musketeers whose unquestioning faith was essential for the task which CinCPAC had assigned him with such casual confidence.

Paul Eddington, he mused, was not unlike Porthos in Alexandre Dumas' adventure—that gnarled and hulking musketeer who died a hero's death before the tale was done.

When Torrey had proposed him as his chief of staff, the Admiral's Kriss Kringle eyebrows raised skeptically, but he offered no serious objections. Some of The Rock's peers were not quite so charitable, suggesting none too obliquely that Eddington was washed up, a derelict floating in alcoholic self-pity, and useless except as a minor component in a Fleet that would function just as well if he sank without a trace. Yet Torrey's choice of his former exec had been no sudden whim. Still dormant below the surface of the man's scarred personality, he believed, lay a bold imagination, a thrust, and a zest for combat that needed only a challenge like Operation Skyhook to make it come alive again.

Young McConnel, of course, was the puppishly eager d'Artagnan.

Perhaps it had been a dirty trick ordering the boy to join his staff before Mac's thirty-day survivor's leave ended. A phrase originated by the abbreviation-happy Navy communicators came to mind: SHORE DUT PUB INT. It signified that a particular officer's "shore duty is in the public interest," and whenever he drew a coveted stateside billet, his dispatch orders had to carry this magic jargon as proof that he was needed more urgently behind the guns than alongside them. Conversely, Torrey had never heard of anyone returning to sea with the notation that his combat DUT was in the PUB INT; but in McConnel's case, he was sure it would turn out that way.

Still intrigued by the Musketeers analogy, The Rock suspected he'd have to play the role of the contemplative Athos himself. It was not inappropriate, however, for like Athos he was still prey to moments of brooding melancholy, when the burden of command became too personal a thing to carry easily, and before he had made the irrevocable decision which blotted out all but the strategic effects of such a judgment.

Now only a nimble-witted Aramis was needed to serve as senior administrative aide to Rear Admiral Rockwell Torrey, USN, commanding the Advanced Tactical Zone, South Pacific.

The Rock's inward amusement faded. In the evolvement of this designation, it was hoped that Blackjack Broderick would be mollified, or at least that his face would be saved, since he retained titular control over the area. But The Rock wasn't at all convinced that his nominal superior, a notoriously thinskinned man, would accept any whittling down of his authority without a fight. He wouldn't react frontally. Blackjack didn't operate that way. But his devious response could be damned effective, even disastrous, especially if Neal Owynn's Machiavellian talents helped draw the counterplot. Anybody backing Torrey, who wore only two stars, must brace himself for trouble in such a contest with Broderick, who wore three.

Torrey was unconcerned about his own future. Skyhook might well prove to be the end of the line for him, for it was the forlorn sort of command which often goes to an officer who once showed huge promise, has fallen from grace, and now seeks to recoup his fortunes. Success in the race to capture Levu-Vana would crown a man a hero; failure, whether through his own doing or the intervention of some meddlesome outsider, would ruin him.

Eddington needn't worry. His career was already blasted, and only a miracle at Skyhook could restore it.

McConnel was too humble a target, even as Torrey's Flag lieutenant, for Blackjack to consider seriously.

But whoever drew the senior aide's job—Flag secretary—would inevitably be regarded by Broderick as an archenemy, since his name must appear on every scrap of correspondence that passed between Mesquite and Toulebonne. It was, therefore, necessary that such a man be as impervious to career damage as either Eddington or The Rock himself.

As Torrey weighed this problem, he recalled his first response to the sesquipedalian title that had been created for his command, which the communicators had promptly dubbed COMADTAC-ZONSOPAC.

"It sounds," he had grumbled to Egan Powell, "like a hay fever sneeze."

"No, admiral, I disagree. COMADTACZONSOPAC has the soft, sneaky, sibilant sound of a mother's lullaby—nicely calculated to smooth away Blackjack's cares and make him sleep like a goddamn little babylamb."

"Okay," Torrey had said, but without much conviction. "You win."

"Gracias, señor." Powell bowed elaborately. "I'm glad you approve of my brainchild."

"Yours?"

"All mine. If CinCPAC had awarded a prize for naming your new job, I'd have won it hands down."

Remembrance of this random colloquy confirmed something The Rock had known, but hadn't acknowledged, ever since their night at Number 10 Makalapa. There was only one officer close to him who met the selfless requirements of that third Musketeer: Egan Powell. His reserve status gave him immunity to intraservice struggles. He was loyal. Torrey accorded it a final moment's deliberation. By God, why *not* Captain Powell, the transplanted Hollywood blade, the amiable conversationalist, the spiritual uplifter—who'd work his happy heart out for this project in which he believed?

Yes. He was the perfect Aramis . . .

Torrey went downstairs to look for Powell. A light was burning in the kitchen, and when he pushed through the swinging door he found him sprawled at the table, legs across the top, deeply absorbed in a magazine called *Cinema Spice*. Not at all perturbed at having been apprehended reading such a nonmilitary document, Egan Powell placed a forefinger between two pages to keep his place, and looked up, grinning.

"Wait'll I turn to page thirty-three," he said, "and learn what a heel I really am."

The Rock looked puzzled. "Heel?"

Powell showed him *Cinema Spice*'s gaudy frontcover which promised "Intimate Revelations of Mona Matrice." He grinned disarmingly.

"My third wife. Lovely child. Used to make her mad as hell when they pronounced her name 'mattress!' But they always did, because that's where she did her best acting. Once upon a time I offered to fight a duel for Mona's honor after some gentleman at the Trocadero called her Miss Mattress instead of Miss Mat-reece. Duel never came off. The lady filed suit for divorce before I could confront her traducer behind Hollywood Bowl with my trusty epee." He pointed to the wall clock. "Damned near two bells. You didn't come down here to hear Casanova's memoirs. So what's your problem, admiral?"

"Insomnia."

"Worry-type insomnia? Rank hanging heavy over your head?"

The Rock considered the matter seriously. "No. More the brain-in-a-squirrelcage brand, I guess."

"Mesquite?"

"Is there anything else in the world besides that confounded piece of real estate?"

"Well, there's always Hollywood. But you wouldn't like it. Too much fighting." Then, suddenly serious, Powell tossed his magazine into the kitchen wastebasket. "You've inherited the goddamnedest basket of eels I've ever heard of, Rock."

"It's worse than you think, Egan. Much worse. And yet—somehow—we've got to lick it before the weather and the Japs and our friends get it snafued any worse." Torrey's tone was bitter as he rasped out the word *friends.*

"Did you say 'we' might do the job?"

"Yes."

" 'We' means thee and me," Powell said doubtfully.

"It does. I want you with me at Mesquite, fella."

"I see." The Intelligence officer lit one of his acrid Turkish cigarettes, very slowly, as he pondered this unexpected request. "You're asking old Egan to quit the cushiest billet he's ever had—even cushier than writing screenplays after your option's been taken up."

"That's right."

Powell half shut his left eye and let cigarette smoke dribble past his thin nose. "Of course," he said, "there *are* certain delightful plus factors to this handsome job which the average guy might overlook. Little items money can't buy. Like catching malaria or getting yourself killed or falling in love with a poxy Melanesian native."

"All those," The Rock agreed, "and one hell of a lot of twenty-four-hour days."

Egan Powell continued as though he hadn't heard Torrey's remark: "Then, too, even a literary genius needs to broaden his horizons. See new faces. Taste new foods—Spam and K rations—and experience real-life situations—" He added with a wry smile "—like having your goddamn back against the wall."

"Things aren't quite that hopeless at Mesquite."

"I'm thinking ahead to Skyhook. That'll be rugged enough for a Marine top sergeant with paid-up life insurance."

"Scared?"

"Christ, yes, I'm scared!"

"What kind of 'scared'?" Torrey asked, paraphrasing the other's earlier question.

Powell considered the problem judiciously. "That funny kind

I used to get when we sneak-previewed a movie I'd written and knew damn well it was four-star lousy."

"Not physically scared?"

"No. I just don't like the scenario for this little turkey they've asked you to produce, Rock."

"Maybe that's why I need you. To—what d'you fellows call it?—doctor the script."

Powell stood up, stretching, and thrust out his hand. "All right, admiral. Give me the contract. I'll sign. Even without options."

"I appreciate that, Egan," Torrey said simply. "This kind of job isn't one you can flatly order a man to take on. He's got to come along willingly."

"Like being tapped as a 'volunteer'?"

"No—*being* one."

Powell's mustache twitched. "Combat duty might help recharge old Egan's batteries. My luck's been all bad lately."

"Gavabutu isn't exactly loaded with your kind of glamour," The Rock said. "It's a trifle short on women."

"I know." Powell gave him a curious look. "Mostly nurses, aren't they?"

Maggie Haynes passed a trembling hand across her sweating forehead, shut her eyes for a moment to curtain off the ugliness around her, and then straightened her shoulders preparatory to another hour in MOB Able's receiving shack.

Beside her the medical officer glanced up from the semiconscious Marine rifleman he was attending. "Don't think about it," he said. "Just keep working. That's the only way."

"Sure." Her voice was bitter. "It's the only way."

She scrawled the casualty's name in her admitting records. *BARROWS, HENRY F., USMC. Grenade wounds in abdomen & groin. Condition critical. Major surgery required immediately.* The boy couldn't be more than eighteen. But even if he survived the operation he wouldn't be much use to anybody, including himself, because the Jap explosive had riddled him from belly to knee like a stabbed voodoo doll. Besides, his one-in-twenty chance of survival under ordinary conditions was cut to one-in-fifty by the fact that they didn't have enough medics to handle the cases which were flown back from the combat area in a steady bloody stream, so he'd have to await his turn for the surgeon's scalpel, and would probably die while waiting. Some days the "portable" casualties dwindled down to less than a dozen. When the Nips started exerting pressure along the ill-defined front, near the sluggish Mantaki River, these might jump to almost a hundred. Today was just average. Pfc Barrows was Number 37.

Maggie put down her steelbacked clipboard and helped the doctor hoist the Marine off the stretcher and into a cot. This was supposed to be the corpsman's chore. But he'd gone to dinner, having already missed his noon chow owing to a sudden spate of casualties around 1130. Her back ached. Her head throbbed. Her thigh tendons hurt. And there was a different pain in her heart that came more from looking at this endless, useless drama, than from lifting the deadweight of inert bodies. When she picked up the clipboard again, there was a smear of blood across the space where she had written Pfc Barrow's name.

Two more wounded Marines were unloaded from Red Cross jeeps in front of Receiving before the corpsman wandered back from the messtent at 1625. Maggie collapsed onto a canvas campstool as soon as he relieved her.

The corpsman regarded her solicitously.

"Pooped?"

Distrusting her voice, she merely nodded, and he went on, "Picked up some damned hot scuttlebutt at chow."

"That's dandy."

Maggie didn't evince much interest. The corpsman's gossip was usually unreliable, like most backfence chatter, and he delivered it in such glittery-eyed Ancient Mariner fashion that it sounded even more bogus.

"One of the headquarters yeomen tipped me that CinCPAC's sending a troubleshooter down to Mesquite to find out what the devil's the matter. They're browned off as hell. This fella's supposed to bang a few heads together and start things rolling. That's what the yeoman says."

Maggie wished the corpsman would stop yakking, but she was too exhausted to struggle off her comfortable seat and go away. To keep him happy she asked, "Who's this brassbound genius they're giving us?"

"Guy named Toomey or Torrence or something like that. The yeoman told me but I forgot exactly. Anyhow he's a freshcaught admiral from the Big Staff at Pearl."

"Torrey!"

"That's pretty close. First name's got 'Rock' in it."

"Oh, gee . . . oh, God!"

The corpsman stared. "Heat gettin' at you, Lieutenant Haynes?"

Maggie was out of her campchair, dancing, and suddenly she didn't feel tired any more.

"When's Admiral Torrey due?"

"Tomorrow, the yeoman says."

She tossed the admittance file at the startled corpsman. "You've got the duty, mister. Take over. Maggie's going home to wash out a few little things, on account of there aren't any more shopping days left till Christmas . . ."

But by the time she slogged through the everlasting gumbo mud in her Marine boondockers that were so big they chafed her ankles, and reached the tenuous privacy of her corner of the nurses' Quonset, the feeling of exhilaration had dissipated, like a meaningless rainbow swept away by a new storm. Indeed, now it was raining, soupily, and the slow-falling torrent made a disagreeable toilet sound against the corrugated tin roof. Maggie gazed bleakly through the screened window toward the cluster of drooping tents, thatchtopped shacks, and Quonsets that constituted MOB Able, a miserable amalgam of living quarters, wards, and surgical centers—abattoirs, she thought grimly—clinging to a hillside above the roadstead where a half-dozen supply ships awaited their turn to be unloaded.

Against the cavelike inside wall of the hut somebody had glued a South Seas travel poster, and it mocked her with its barebreasted dancers and its hint of blue lagoon beyond a crescent beach. Annalee Dorne had put it there. Annalee was an incurable, incorrigible romantic, who still found beauty in those ugly kauri pines and sago-palms the Seabees left standing when they built MOB Able. But Maggie wasn't. She'd been cured. She was corrigible. And now she stuck out her tongue at the hulagirls and formed a silent Bronx cheer for those azure waters, while a graygreen gecko lizard stared down at her from the curved ceiling, gelid-eyed, where he clung by his suction feet . . .

. . . Beautiful glamorous entrancing cruddy South Pacific. *SOPAC*. So pack up your troubles in your old seabag and smile smile smile. Maggie Haynes. Real live livin' seabag. Have loin cloth. Will travel. Look in the cracked primping mirror, baby, and see yourself the way he'll see you in a couple of days. Gorgeous. Godawful. Ghastly. Sweat brings out the gray in your hair—doesn't it?—where it's plastered all over your silly yellow face. Yellow's the color of my true love's atabrined face, maybe he'll say, and won't you have your picture taken for my two-star headquarters where it'll hang alongside Rita Hayworth's in her blacklace nightie and give the troops a lift? . . . Calamity Jane. That's what you look more like, baby, a calamity about to happen right here in your Quonset . . . *Oh, life's all right in a Quonset till a gal wuons what she wuons when she wuonset* . . . Go ahead, baby, fling your bare arms around like Katie Hepburn emoting but it's no use because face it kiddo you're a coolie in a man's world wearing a khaki tent four sizes too big and all your female charms hidden inside it . . . Step right this way folks into the back of the tent and Maggie Haynes will take 'em off one at a time khaki britches open-necked shirt dirty-brown woolen socks goddamn boondocker boots and now you're down to your GI cotton panties and your brassiere and that's what all the fellows are waiting for isn't it? . . . Whatever idiot dreamed up that C cup must have figured there's a bovinity that shapes every Service female's ends because he wants your sweet conical little breasts to fit inside his damn brassiere like a baby's ittybitty fist inside a motorman's glove bad joke lousy metaphor but who feels clever today in the stinking rain? . . . Brains and brawn . . . Brains and bra . . . Look at those broken fingernails on those yellow hands holding your breasts hello hulagirl aren't you greenjealous and no polish on them to match the prettypink nipples that aren't so damned bad after all when you get right down to it and wouldn't you like a dollar for every guy that's tried? . . . Oh God . . . His hands were on them that final night remember those strong capable man's hands that probably didn't even know they'd found your breasts because those hands were made for grasping ship's wheels and fighterplane controls and sextants . . . How much sex is extant in a sextant you're not getting any funnier just lewder . . . Daddy's hands were always manicured like that parfit gentle knight's and so are Commander-Senator Owynn's except he's more the tail end of a horse the parfit gentle knight rides would it be a knightmare negative he's a stallion . . . Goddamn you're not slim svelte any more just plain skinny like those nasty nude female carvings the corpsmen buy from the natives to shock us gals with breasts that stick way out paired with males that stick out too and when the senior medic heard about how the corpsmen talked he'd tacked up an allhands notice that he didn't want to hear any more repetitious wholly inapplicable mention of the procreative function or the malodorous residue of digestive assimilation although he agreed that *bastard* and *son of a bitch* have some merit and so do I and try and make me stop Captain Tully bossman or not because a little solid cussing keeps the boys on their toes and off yours . . . Like when you went swimming in those damnfool cotton panties and bra and the gyrene platoon guarding the Mantaki riverbank was so attentive you discovered too late wet GI cotton turns translucent pretty soon a gal hasn't any trade secrets at all anymore like a badly developed dirty snapshot that's been handled too many times naturally when you called them bastards it made sense didn't it although the worst thing wasn't the peep show but the way that slimybrown river stank like warm urine from the swamps or maybe the Japs outside the perimeter used it for a latrine . . . Now why not sprawl out flat on your GI cot in your GI lovelies stop struggling for a while because an hour of midafternoon beauty sacktime is just what the doctor ordered and later of course there's that *haute couture* seersucker gown whipped up by the same damned C-cup designer which you've got to launder with yellowsoap so the mustysour smell will go away in a pig's whistle it will . . . And maybe you'll dream a dream about him and how he's in his plane right now winging south south south only what the hell does he care about you baby his job is something bigger so you'd better keep your chin up because that's how it'll probably be . . . Your cleft chin was nice he said never mentioning that cleft chins are signs of weakness Christ don't make me weak now but strong enough to take it . . . And oh God why can't you be old calm love-'em-and-leave-'em Maggie practical hardheaded mistrusting doubtful suspicious Maggie Alderton-once-removed Haynes damned good questions without answers except what's hidden deep in your hard-bitter career gal's heart that got hardbitter trying to match careers with hardbitter men after nambypamby Arthur ripped your world apart although it wasn't much of a world even before he pulled the trigger remember how he'd want you when he was drunk and try and try and try but couldn't leaving you unsatisfied frustrated dirty ashamed as if you'd suddenly turned into a whore . . . And that's when you built your defenses against anything that might bring back that icecold feeling which wasn't just Arthur in bed but the whole lousyevil world and you'd never let it happen again and dear God now it has and could you ever trust any man again even him . . . *Rock of Ages cleft for me let me hide myself in Thee* . . . Nobody goes home again but how do you even start looking for it that's more to the point because it'd be no good if the old dark-thoughts returned baby that's self-pity why don't you ask does he really need you the way you need him look down look down that looooonesome rooooad before you travel on . . . Keep listening Maggie Haynes what does your heart say are you in love the way you told him back at Pearl and he said so too but maybe it was music and the nightmood and those crazy kids romancing in the back seat Annalee and Jere so damned innocent please God let somebody stay that way unspoiled oh hell here it comes again admit you love this solemn granite puss who's married to the Navy because his flesh-and-blood marriage didn't work any more than yours . . . Where do we go from here boys trap him with female trickways hell that's easy only no answer because now it's all or nothing shoot the works Maggie either you love him or you don't and maybe you'd damnwell better find out if he loves you . . . Wouldn't make more sense but at least there's no law that says you can't fix that frightwig powder that gargoyle mask dig out your last nylons baby those legs could be worse dab on a little Chanel now get along with yez let's see what happens tomorrow who knows who knows maybe happiness and sure as hell worth the old college try . . .

12. *Nobody Cares Whether You Live or Die*

For all her thunderous seventeen hundred horsepower twin engines, the gullwinged, deepbellied Mariner was lucky to be logging one hundred and sixty knots as she approached her mid-Pacific fueling station. A stiff headwind beat against her twenty-five-ton bulk, and she was heavyladen with the accouterments and personnel of a newborn combat command, which was symbolized on her galleon bow by a painted bluestarred flag and the cryptic symbol: COMADTACZONSOPAC.

Dipping sharply, the clumsy flying boat began her steep descent into the tiny island's coralstudded lagoon, passing close above a beached and gutted derelict near the entrance. Because of the chop, they hit hard, bounced twice, and mushed to taxiing speed as they neared the old airline dock where a small VIP welcoming committee was gathered. Admiral Rockwell Torrey emerged first from the Mariner's wideflung hatch, then Captain Egan Powell and then finally Lieutenant (senior grade) William Patrick McConnel, who had never been able to comprehend the logic of a custom that made a senior officer fumble across the feet and legs of his juniors, while entering or leaving a boat. But he dismissed it as added proof that there was a right way, a wrong way, and a *Navy* way of doing everything.

As The Rock followed the island commander, a portly retreaded captain twelve years his senior in age, toward the old Pan Am passenger depot where beer and sandwiches awaited them, he once more perceived the vast gulf that yawns between two stars and four stripes, and he grimaced into the hot whipping wind. Whenever Torrey spoke nowadays, men listened deferentially, as if the mere fact of his admiralship had imbued him overnight with a cosmic wisdom denied lesser beings. Nobody dared interrupt, for now he had The Word on *The Word*. Yet only one number on the precedence list might separate an admiral from a captain; and furthermore, he reminded himself wryly, an admiral continued to draw captain's pay until he passed the halfway mark in grade. Still, it was a comfortable feeling, and balm to his long-bruised ego.

The door of the airconditioned building whooshed shut behind them, banishing the equatorial heat.

Ceremoniously, his host handed Torrey a tall chilled glass of beer, with precisely the right amount of head on it, and gestured the others toward a table laden with punctured cans. There were no other glasses.

"Success to your mission, admiral," he said with ponderous grace, lifting his beer can.

"Thanks." Nettled at his possession of the solitary glass, The Rock sounded more curt than he had intended, so he added in a more moderate tone, "We're going to need all the good wishes we can get."

In the pause that followed their first long draft of beer, the elderly captain observed with unaffected frankness, "You know, sir, I envy you."

"Two weeks ago I'd have envied myself, too, but now I'm not so sure."

"Your island's a hell of a lot different from mine, admiral." This could have been an inane remark. But the four-striper's tone tempered its vacuity, and gave it a curious significance. "Our fellows have invented a name for this place—Limbo Lagoon."

"You've done a good job whipping it into shape to handle planes going through," The Rock said generously.

"Sure. We get 'em through all right." The grizzled captain opened another beer can. "Did you ever hear, admiral, about a thing called 'island stare'?"

"No."

"Well, it's pretty catching. Stick around here for six months and you'll see." He laughed humorlessly. "When I relieved Gerry Hopson as commander, I remember how goddamn stupid he looked, sitting there in his quarters with five pictures of his wife and kids lining the bulkhead, and the phonograph blatting away. He was scratching Rascal's ear—that's the mascot we inherited from the ship you saw at the lagoon mouth—with one hand and flipping records with the other. Then Gerry got sprung. He went back to the States. And one afternoon, by Tophet, I found myself in his old straight-backed chair, scratching that same mongrel's flopear with my right hand and turning those same phonograph records with my left hand, automatically, with my eyes glued on something exactly one thousand yards distant. Whole trouble was, *there was nothing to see* one thousand yards away, except that scrubby kou tree and a flock of gooneybirds, but I didn't even see them! And that's 'island stare' on Limbo Lagoon."

Torrey said quietly, "I've had this 'thousand-yard stare' in a twenty-foot office, captain."

"How'd you lick it?"

"Soul-searching . . . and kicking myself in the fanny."

Once they took off again for Mesquite, The Rock turned in for a nap, and when he awoke, muzzyheaded from dozing through the ascent to their twelve-thousand-foot cruising altitude, he went to the head to refresh himself with a dash of water across the face. It was enervatingly lukewarm. For a fleeting instant he felt a sense of personal affront that the water wasn't ice cold. Then, grinning sheepishly into the bulkhead mirror, he whispered at his reflection, "You've just tasted the first symptom of rank-happiness, mister—watch it!"

Torrey scrutinized his lean countenance, noting that his hair was a trifle grayer than it had been a year ago on *Old Swayback*. Now he was forty-nine. Damned near over the hill, he told himself ironically, and yet here he was, embarking upon a new career after eight chrysalis-months at Pearl Harbor. Fledgling admirals can plummet very far and very fast. There was another fanciful way of putting it, he recalled: the difference between a halo and a noose is only twelve inches. In a military world where distances are measured in flying times rather than in furlongs, ells, or hectares, this was a negligible span. And yet, he reminded himself, inches could be damned important when you reckon there are barely sixty of them from clumsy foot to gaping mouth. For some men it was only twenty-four inches from romantic heart to concupiscent crotch, a measurement which often goes undetected. Most of these gauges vary. But the halo-noose estimate remains as immutable as head sizes. The only difference, he thought soberly as he made his way aft, is what's inside them. He was mildly irked that he hadn't yet acquired his air legs after so long on the ground, because now it was time to go to work.

Torrey shook Egan Powell and McConnel out of their half slumber.

"Reveille," he announced briskly, digging a large folded chart from his briefcase.

Powell groaned. "There was this blonde who was just about to ask me up to her penthouse . . ."

"Tell the lady," The Rock said, after consulting his wrist watch, "that you'll see her at 1700. Maybe if you buy her dinner she'll forgive you for waking up."

"Can't afford it. She prefers the Colony. On captain's pay, that's out."

Torrey ended the whimsy by rattling his map. "Let's talk about Mesquite and Skyhook. When we arrive, by God, I want to land on the dead run. But I also want to know exactly where we're going and how we'll get there." He turned to Mac. "Here, son, you hold this end of the chart—the dangerous north side where the real fighting's apt to happen."

Seen thus, in bird's-eye view, Mesquite-Gavabutu displayed all the unlovely contours of a Sherman tank moving west. Under its right rear tread a redcrayoned semicircle showed the extent of the American offensive to date: abysmally small for the weeks already wasted on the vital effort. And it was a long, long way from the tank's turret, where the main enemy force had dug in.

"That," Torrey observed in an expressionless voice, "was our first mistake. Hitting 'em in what Blackjack likes to call their 'soft underbelly.' An eighty-by-forty-mile island can't possibly have an underbelly, like southern Europe, when it's overrun by Japs. So now we're paying the penalty for this 'safe' assault. It's a choice of slogging across an eight-thousand-foot mountain range, or hiking along the shoreline jungle, with the Nips contesting every goddamn inch of the way."

"Besides," Egan Powell said bleakly, "we don't have the manpower."

The Rock nodded. "After a few more weeks of the losses Mesquite's been taking, we'll be damned lucky if we can keep the original beachhead." He put down the chart. "See what the newest report shows, McConnel."

Mac checked the dispatch file.

"Yesterday's total was eleven killed, forty-six wounded, three missing. That's ground troops only. We also lost three F4Fs in combat and two got creamed operationally."

Torrey's equine face lengthened. Here was another facet of the problem to which there seemed to be no solution. The backbone of Mesquite's slim fighter strength were the Marine Wildcats and the Air Force's Warhawks, neither of which was a match for the Jap Zero in speed or maneuverability. Nevertheless they were making a gallant effort and a lot of the pilots were dying as a result, although those who survived became heroes first-class. Mesquite needed new P-38 Lightnings to beat off the heavily escorted Nip Bettys that bombed its muddy airstrip out of service for several hours every day until the Seabees filled the holes so the planes could fly again.

"Until we take Skyhook, the enemy's got us boresighted, and there's nothing we can do except grit our teeth and accept the punishment," The Rock said.

Aware of his subordinate status, Mac asked diffidently, "Why haven't we used those Marine paratroopers who were in the Guadalcanal show?"

Egan Powell accorded him a benign glance. "Because rain forests are lousy places to jump into. Likewise overgrown coconut plantations. Likewise beaches that are only thirty yards wide."

Stricken by his ignorance, Mac was content to drop the whole idea, but The Rock encouraged him to go on. "What's your thought, son?"

"Well," Mac said, "one time *Cassiday* picked up some survivors from an LST that got torpedoed in the Slot. They were mostly Marine paratroopers who'd been absorbed into a regular ground regiment, and they were pretty pissed off—pardon me, sir—because they felt their talents were going to waste. We yarned with their skipper at mess that night. A light colonel named Gregory. He said they could sure as hell make a pinpoint jump from extreme low altitude if anyone ever ordered it. But nobody did. I remember he had some watersoaked charts he'd been doodling around with, showing little patches of terrain where his battalion might zero in effectively." Mac stopped embarrassed. "Shucks, I'm talking too much."

Torrey shook his head.

"You're doing fine, aide. Now make a note—locate this fellow Gregory as soon as we reach Gavabutu. We'll see if he's still feeling jumpy."

After they refueled in the landlocked harbor of a subequatorial British Crown Colony, which seemed calmly ignorant of the war's quickening pace, they embarked on the final leg of their journey to Gavabutu. The flight steward had The Rock's bunk ready before take-off. Although he had obligingly retired behind the drawn curtains, he stayed awake, thinking and smoking his pipe. They would reach Mesquite at dawn.

Torrey's immediate concern was for his subordinates who would be looking to him for fresh ideas, and for his superiors impassively awaiting the first dispatches that would spell victories along the stalled jungle front. For a tactical commander, he had been given remarkably broad authority, which made it possible—even necessary—to invade the exotic realm of strategy whether Blackjack Broderick liked it or not. Torrey could envisage the blizzard of angry messages that would snow upon him the moment he made a highlevel decision which didn't please the cautious vice-admiral.

Something the Duke of Wellington once wrote to a nagging War Secretary popped into his head: "My lord, if I attempted to answer the mass of futile correspondence that surrounds me, I should be debarred from all serious business of campaigning." Then the doughty general had concluded with more asperity than tact: "So long as I retain an independent position, I shall see that no officer under my command is debarred by attending to the futile driveling of mere quill driving in Your Lordship's office—from attending to his first duty—which is, and always has been, so to train the private men under his command that they may, without question, beat any force opposed to them in the field."

Wellington welcomed command responsibility, wearing it as a proud badge of honor, and he wouldn't part with an iota of his considerable burden, beyond delegating certain lesser duties that might distract him from the greater ones.

No wonder the old boy conquered Napoleon!

One of Blackjack Broderick's weaknesses, conversely, was a reluctance either to move ahead boldly himself, or allow anyone else to advance. Indecision can spread like a virus. Torrey surmised that this disease might already have affected Mesquite's forces, perhaps down the line as far as regimental commanders, and he could only hope it hadn't reached the foxholed companies directly confronting a disciplined enemy.

By now, confident that the irresolute Americans were bogged down for the winter in Gavabutu, the Japanese must surely have drawn up a counterplan; and unless he were terribly wrong, it wouldn't involve a frontal assault against the Yank perimeter. No. What was far more likely, The Rock believed, was a fast build-up at Levu-Vana. By the time the slothful Americans moved again in the spring, Skyhook would have become impregnable.

Perhaps the Mariner blundered into a pressure pocket, or the pilot may have abruptly altered the pitch of her flailing propellers, or whatever, but something shook Torrey awake. When he opened his eyes, he had the uncanny feeling that he was back at Pearl Harbor, stretched prone upon his bed on Makalapa Hill. This odd sense of physical displacement passed as quickly as it had come, leaving in its wake a tangle of thoughts which seemed little connected with the lethal business he had just been pondering.

For all its improbability, the idea came to him that he was going home, instead of plunging into some cheerless unknown, and he found himself considering it rationally rather than emotionally. This ability to stand apart from the corpus of Rockwell Torrey and study himself with complete candor had always pleased him, quietly, and he was glad that the dormant months at Pearl Harbor hadn't dulled this curious faculty. His self-analysis was sharpest whenever he suspected any softening of those fibers which bound him into the tough impermeable package known as The Rock.

What he perceived now troubled him deeply.

There was a time when he'd imagined he had his life figured out, arranged, compensated, as you'd swing a compass to insure its accuracy; and he strode along the narrow course a lonely man takes deliberately, aware that he is alone, wanting it thus, and believing without really knowing that this is the better way. But suddenly doubts had arisen. His snug insularity was being challenged. It was as if such aloofness were no longer safe or even desirable. Had he, in aiming toward mechanical perfection in his naval career, ignored a basic truth—that whatever a man does, or what others do, impinges on all the rest? He had warned Eddington against these things—didactically, he supposed, recalling how he'd spoken—and he'd urged against computing the end while ignoring the means. Yet was he not trained for war, just as Eddington was? And didn't sensitive men placed in sensitive positions tend to agonize too much over harsh decisions, thereby prolonging the ultimate agony of decision itself?

As Torrey listened to the undulant thrum-thrum-thrum of the Mariner's engines, he wondered, but found no answers.

Again he thought: *I am going home.* To an island variously called Gavabutu and Mesquite. Where he would find the only two persons who really mattered in this private world—once-contained and now-crumbling—which he'd been constructing so diligently all his adult life. Maggie and Jere. Beyond them there was nothing.

He glanced through the plane's ovalshaped port. A wisp of nascent moon riding close to the cloud-banked horizon stirred his memory, and he recalled a strange question he had asked Maggie under a similar moon at Aiea: "Can you ever be homesick for something you've never had?" She'd answered yes, because she knew; and then he, Rockwell Torrey, had said he loved her. Ruefully, sardonically, he stared at the moon, remembering still another time when he'd embraced her, and his hand had brushed by chance against her breast. Although this had been accidental, he was instantly aware of that exquisite fleshmound beneath her uniform, and how it grew taut in the cup of his hard palm. Even now this recollection stirred the same feeling of shocked wonderment a monk might have experienced if he were suddenly assailed by carnal desires after half a lifetime of celibate renunciation. An idiotic notion struck him, and he smiled into the darkness of his tiny compartment. Had Lord Horatio Nelson ever behaved in this callow fashion during his between-the-battles romance with Lady Emma Hamilton? He doubted it . . .

At 0615 the flight steward awakened Torrey. They were nearing Gavabutu, he said, and maybe the admiral would like to shave before they landed, since it was a cinch Mesquite's top brass would all be on hand to welcome him aboard. There was an electric razor in the head.

"Thanks, son," The Rock said briefly, "but I'll use my old straightedge blade. Those lawnmowers just flatten my bristles."

As he made his way forward to the little compartment, toilet kit in hand, he was gratified to discover that he could walk surefootedly along the Mariner's swaying aisle. Five hours of slumber at thirteen thousand feet had somehow restored his air legs. He didn't even have to brace himself against the washbasin to shave with his *Freitag* razor.

When he rejoined Egan Powell and McConnel in the main cabin, they were peering through the starboard ports for a first glimpse of the island which was still hidden under a grimy cloud blanket somewhere ahead. Torrey scowled at the overcast. It was an ominous sign that autumnal foul weather was approaching, and that Gavabutu's CAVU (ceiling and visibility unlimited) conditions would become spottier with each passing day, and then cease altogether. Task force admirals enjoyed this cloud cover, because it hid their surface ships from Nip aerial attackers. But for the ground troops it spelled nothing but rain and misery.

Finally the pilot found a hole in the gray scud and nosed the Mariner into it abruptly. As they descended like an express elevator, Torrey thought of the seat-of-the-pants flyers he'd known whose first quick peek at the ground was also their last. Gavabutu's mountainous spinal column could fill those clouds with rocks if the two-striper at the controls misjudged his position, and he was secretly relieved when they broke free of the overcast two minutes later with Gavabutu in plain sight about twenty rapidly closing miles ahead.

By half shutting one eye, so his vision was slightly blurred, Torrey found it possible to imagine that Gavabutu was a segment of lower Pennsylvania's hilly farmland, or a bit of the rolling Shenandoah Valley. Caught in the dull morning light, it had the gently dappled appearance of some peaceful countryside, almost equally composed of darkgreen wooded uplands and yellow-ripening fields. Only the sawtoothed mountain range beyond this deceptively rural foreground impaired the pleasant image, but now its eight-thousand-foot peaks were hidden in the overcast. There was one discrepancy: the incredible palette mixture of aquamarine and emerald shoalwater along Gavabutu's southern coast, marking the coralcapped boundaries of this harborless and inhospitable island, which was punctuated by tiny black commas signifying assault craft wrecked on D-Day.

The Rock's half-closed eye opened as he sought a better look at the airfield which the Americans had hacked out of the raw jungle. He could see the early-morning cargo flights approaching in a steady airborne stream, and diving down for landings after only a token overhead wait while the C-47 ahead cleared the narrow runway and pulled off into the deep mud alongside. Half of Mesquite's supplies arrived in this erratic fashion. Ammo, bomb fuses, mail, replacement tires for aircraft and vehicles, and even propellers for subchasers came here in the stripped cabins of the unarmed twin-engined Douglases that flew by night—just as Torrey himself had flown—to elude prowling Jap air patrols. There had been a desperate interval a couple of weeks earlier when Mesquite's aviation fuel supplies had dwindled to dry rockbottom. The redoubtable ferrypilots lugged barrels of volatile high-test gasoline up from Toulebonne to keep the island's minimal aircover aloft.

When you knew these things about Mesquite, it didn't look as glamorous as the editor of a popular Pacific yearbook (wartime edition) had promised. Tourists would be "enthralled" by the quaint natural beauty of this particular chain, he'd said, assuring them of "plenty of good shooting" along the rainforested ranges. Ducks. Crocodiles. Wild boar. The Rock recalled the idyllic passage with a wan smile. The South Pacific's islands, especially those which bordered the Coral Sea, could bring a lump to your throat with their ineffable loveliness—if you could stop hating them long enough to indulge in aesthetics. Yet for all their beauty, they were as dangerous as a courtesan afflicted with some loathsome and hidden disease.

This was Torrey's new command.

It was a curious jurisdiction for a saltwater sailor: twenty thousand soldiers and Marines, minus the twelve hundred or so who had been killed during the inconclusive three-month Mesquite campaign; an airforce consisting mainly of overworked Marine Wildcats and Army Warhawks, less than fifty of which were airworthy at any one time, to tackle the superior Japanese Zeros; and a small in-and-out squadron of old destroyers and older cruisers that, with his PTs, were supposed to prevent the nightly "Tokyo Trolley" from reinforcing and supplying the thirty thousand Nip troops encamped along the island's northeastern coast.

Gavabutu was rushing toward them at one hundred and twenty knots as the Mariner sloped toward the unprotected roadstead. The seaplane smacked the surface hard as if her young pilot knew they had no time to waste, then lumbered across the remaining expanse of choppy water to the impromptu pontoon dock where a crew of junglesuited handlers slung a gangway into the plane's open maw. Once again a little knot of greeters awaited Rockwell Torrey. But this time they weren't a perfunctory waystation delegation. They were the gaunt and tired defenders of the farthest terminal on the dangerous line.

Rear Admiral Neville Balder shook The Rock's hand first. Class of '12, fifty-two years old, he looked sixty, with a puttygray face and a nervous tic which he unconsciously tried to smooth away each time it flickered across his left cheek. Until the new commander's orders were publicly read, the responsibility for Mesquite was still his. The palm he extended was surprisingly dry, considering the humidity which even at 0630 was becoming unbearable, but there was no strength to his handclasp.

Torrey said simply, "Nev, you look beat."

"Welcome aboard." Balder gave him a wan grin. "Now that you've arrived I feel better already."

"You don't like the glorious tropics?"

"Tropics . . . Hades . . . they're all the same. Stoked by the same devils."

The Rock saw the tic.

"They sent me here on such short notice, Nev, I was afraid you'd be madder than Billy-be-damned—and I wouldn't have blamed you."

"Admiral, I relinquish my baton without regret. Believe me. This is a young man's world."

"Thanks." Torrey emitted a short laugh. "You've got me by three whole years."

"Ever hear of a dog's life?" Balder retorted. "One canine year equals seven for a human. That's Gavabutu. Only it's a goddamn sight worse, because three months here is like being a plebe all over again—in hell!"

Torrey began to feel a tinge of embarrassment, mingled with indefinable shame, at Balder's too-obvious relief at having been spared an onerous burden. To conceal his distaste, he swung on his heel and strode across the steeldecked pier to where the others awaited his pleasure.

Eddington was with them.

He looked trimmer than Torrey had expected. His eyes were clear, and the old wolfish battle grin hovered mockingly on his lips. Only a small tracery of purple veins on his broad cheeks and battered nose, which lent a slightly mottled cast to his complexion, gave away his secret. There was warmth in Eddington's abrasive voice as he greeted The Rock, eagerly, as a castaway might have rushed into the sea to hail his long-awaited rescuer.

"Welcome aboard, skipper."

Torrey regarded the silver eagles on his former exec's open collar. Eddington's captaincy was as much a tribute to the faith which the Navy placed in The Rock's personnel judgment as it was to the fact that his new job rated four stripes.

"Good to be aboard," he said, adding, "with you, Paul."

His rufous face turning redder, and his grin widening, Eddington stepped aside to give his cohorts a chance to speak their brief pieces like schoolkids confronted by a new teacher, or to fawn a little, or just shake hands, according to their several natures.

Last in the impromptu receiving line was Commander Neal Owynn. He had stood alone, unnoticed, behind the others, washing his hands in midair like a fat Uriah Heep, and now he extended his moistlooking palm to The Rock.

"Sorry we didn't have a chance to inform you in advance about my joining your staff," he said. "But, of course, you were already enroute when Admiral Broderick made his decision."

"Which was . . . ?" Torrey growled.

"That there ought to be the closest possible rapport between Toulebonne and Mesquite, sir, which could only be effected by *personal* liaison."

"That was damned kind of Admiral Broderick."

"Thank you, sir." Owynn's smile wasn't combative, like Eddington's; it was hungry. "I'll tell him."

The Rock's voice assumed a sudden glacial quality which signaled danger to those who knew him. "Commander," he said, "as long as you're on my staff you'll do all your communicating with Toulebonne through me. There will be no independent messages originating out of my headquarters. Mail or radio. I trust that's perfectly clear."

Owynn rubbed his bulbous nose. "Quite," he said mildly, "sir."

Neville Balder led them up a marshy path toward the headquarters Quonsets that squatted in incongruous igloo-fashion atop a slight rise. The big corrugated tin huts, with their fiberboard insulation, screenwindows, and wooden floors were the only structures that approached human habitability in this area which the map identified as the village of Atoka. Long since deserted by the British plantation owners, the settlement now consisted of a few moldering shacks and copra sheds, their white paint eaten away by wind and rain, perched on stilts near the waterfront to escape the devouring white ants. Through the marshaled rows of cocopalms Torrey could see the tents of the headquarters enlisted personnel, camouflaged and dankly gleaming beneath the dripping fronds. The ground beside the trail was thickly strewn with coconuts that resembled severed skulls, burst open and rotting. The overall impression was one of gloom, for the massive foliaged trees blotted out all trace of the sky, once you struck inland from the narrow beach, and even on the brightest day there was a sort of greendarkness-at-noon. On this glowering winter-summer day the shree-shree cries of the cockatoos and the mynahs' gabbling seemed to hang low above the humid earth, limp and slack and unmusical. Two scrofulous dogs that had strayed from the nearby native cantonment —an assortment of castoff packing cases and stolen tarpaulins— glared at the passers-by out of redrimmed eyes, refusing to budge and balefully demanding that even admirals walk around them.

There should have been a tingle even in this miasmic air, some hint of important events in the making; but there wasn't. What few GHQ staffers were abroad at this early hour stared at the approaching party with a torpid curiosity that seemed as listless as the heavyhanging atmosphere itself. They looked like men who had given up hope, or who didn't dare hope, that their lot would ever improve. It was, the Rock realized, the same whipped look which betrayed Balder himself.

His scowl intensified, etching the four parallel lines deeper across his forehead and pulling his shaggy brows together above his great hawkbeaked nose. This did not go unnoticed. A Marine corporal drawing water from a lister bag near the command hut caught the grimace.

The preoccupied officers disappeared through the Quonset's swinging door.

Turning to a Pfc who had ambled up for a swig of the foully chlorinated water, the corporal muttered, "Jeez, did you ever see such a mean son of a bitch?" He sighed happily. "Old Baldy looks like a cream-friggin'-puff alongside this joker."

"Who's the new brass?"

"Must be Admiral Torrey—guy they call 'The Rock.' "

"Whoever hung that name on him wasn't foolin'," the Pfc acknowledged.

"You know, gyrene, I *like* mean sons of bitches—for some kinds of work."

"Such as fighting?"

"Ex-friggin'-zactly."

They peered at the screen door of the lowslung hut through which, dimly, they were able to discern the outlines of the High Brass huddled over a long table. Both the corporal and the private wore odd expressions on their atabrine-yellowed faces. Although they'd long since lost any real confidence in the future, for a moment, unaccountably, they felt a hell of a lot better about things. *The Rock*. Tough. Hard. With a puss on him that must have been hacked from a chunk of goddamn Vermont granite, and which by comparison made the fretful Balder look like a wad of used-up kindergarten clay.

When they had filled their canteens, the two Marines walked solemnly down the narrow trail that branched off to their tents. A great thought had come to them. It would be their mission to spread The Word that the toughest friggin' bastard in all Creation had arrived at Mesquite and he'd already started putting the show on the road, plus which anybody who didn't like the way he did things sure as hell had better start swimmin' south to Toulebonne, fast, while the going was good.

By nightfall, which dropped with the casual abruptness of a drawn windowshade over the smoldering island, The Word was passed. With its dissemination came a suspenseful feeling not unlike the expectant lull that follows the dialing of a telephone number—that hushed and breathless interim before some distant bell starts ringing.

Around him, in the semicylindrical GHQ building, Torrey had gathered the officers upon whom he must now depend for carrying out his orders in the critical weeks ahead. He himself sat at the head of the rough plywood table that almost filled one end of the chart-walled, blackboard-laden room. He was sweating, and the unaccustomed heat had even generated a thin film of moisture beneath the crystal of his waterproof wrist watch. Eddington flanked him on the right, Egan Powell on the left, and beyond them were McConnel and Neal Owynn. Admiral Balder's original staff, nine very weary and thoroughly disillusioned men, ranging in rank from lieutenant commander to captain, slumped moodily in their canvas campchairs at the far end of the conference board. Five of them had been asked to stay on. But they seemed quite unimpressed by their good fortune as they waited for Admiral Torrey to explain how he proposed to salvage a campaign which everyone else from Oahu to Brisbane had apparently written off as hopelessly ill-conceived, ill-mounted, and ill-managed—and therefore unworthy of further massive support.

Neville Balder occupied a chair that had been placed discreetly behind The Rock's, as if he wanted it plainly understood that he had disassociated himself completely and without regret from the melancholy affairs of Mesquite-Skyhook.

Purposefully erasing all expression from his rawboned face, Torrey surveyed them quietly, and for a moment the only sounds audible within the crowded shack were the metallic whirring of a pair of electric fans, the mournful croon of a harmonica being played softly in a nearby Quonset, the tentative dripdripdrip from the overhanging palmtrees that hinted heavier rain tomorrow, and the expectant breathing of the officers themselves.

Behind his contrived mask, The Rock's brain teemed with urgent thoughts, all bearing upon their appallingly difficult situation, and none of which was calculated to provide him much comfort. What had seemed so amenable to logical solution at Pearl Harbor a week ago had become a thing of intimate complexity—no longer a geographically removed abstraction to be pondered in safety and resolved at leisure. It was the very magnitude of the challenge that forced him to maintain this façade of competence, lest his personal doubts become evident to these men who were looking to him for guidance.

He regarded Balder's staff with fresh curiosity. Men of certain authority themselves, they had in one fashion or another advanced in their specialties until they had developed stature and know-how enough to be called for this exacting duty.

Take Captain Forrest Tuthill, pensively doodling over there on a sheet of scratchpaper, with his cadaverous cheeks and dark-baggy eyes. He was Operations. His job was arranging the paltry pieces on the checkerboard so they'd appear to be a lot more than they really were, and then move them around fast, before the enemy discovered he'd been duped. The Rock had known Tuthill for twenty years. Hell. Take the wraps off and he'd make a damned good checker player.

Torrey ticked off the four others he intended to retain, as he remembered them, around the table. Captain Fitzhugh Jefferson, quiet and courtly and exceedingly F.F.V., who handled logistics, which was the science of obtaining the unobtainable before it was needed. Commander Max Gottlieb, solemn descendant of a long line of teutonic *herr professors,* whose title was aerologist, and whose job was conjuring up reliable weather forecasts for this region of desolate sea wastes where typhoons and rainstorms germinated in evil secrecy, like an assassin's plot. Commander Willie Lantz, eggbald and cherubic, who managed to keep Mesquite's communications alive despite the dampness that corroded his machines, the jungle rats that gnawed his cables, and the Jap bombs that wiped out whole installations. Commander Clayton Canfil, Intelligence, who'd spent most of his sixty years prowling the treacherous waters of these islands that fringed the Coral Sea, in runty little schooners crewed by Melanesian natives.

Then, as the silence became almost too painful to bear, Torrey addressed himself to Captain Tuthill, "Will you run through your latest situation reports, Tut, so we can see where we stand?"

The Operations officer's fatigued body straightened like a cautiously opened jackknife. Slowly, gravely, he walked across the room to a detailed wallchart of Gavabutu.

"Anybody who draws any comfort from our sitreps" he said bleakly, "is either a blind optimist or a goddamn fool. Therefore I won't try to gloss over the bad news."

The others stirred uneasily. This was a hell of a way to greet the new boss. Tut might at least display a modicum of diplomacy, the way Nev Balder himself had done when Blackjack Broderick visited Mesquite a few weeks ago. Or was it months? Time itself got lost in this confounded morass unless you marked your bedside calendar.

But The Rock's face remained impassive, and he had lit his pipe.

Pointer in hand, Tuthill began patiently to trace the course of the war in the southwestern Pacific. Across the Solomon Sea General MacArthur's forces were locked in combat with the Japs who'd been able somehow to penetrate the slimymatted jungles which continued to baffle their white opponents. Now the enemy was rampaging down the steep Owen Stanley gaps toward Port Moresby itself, the tenuous anchor of the Allies' Papuan beachhead. There'd been a sizable air-sea engagement fought north of the Bismarck Archipelago, however, and the Nips may have been frustrated in their efforts to replenish their New Guinea troops. We'd been clobbered again trying to beat back a smaller Jap attempt to bolster their northern Mesquite perimeter. Moreover, the Nips seemed to have an inexhaustible reservoir of destroyers and motor-barges, backed by cruisers, which enabled them to keep a nightly flow of men and equipment pouring down the oceanic Pass toward their half of Gavabutu. As for the aerial situation—Tuthill spread his hands helplessly—we were outnumbered two-to-one in any category you'd care to mention.

"Today's losses," he intoned, "include seventy-one personnel casualties—Army, Marine, Navy, and Air Force; one destroyer sunk, another damaged, and two PTs destroyed during that fracas in the Pass." Remembering, he added hastily, "Your son's okay, sir. It was the other squadron's duty last night." Continuing: "Four fighter-planes shot down in combat, one missing and presumed lost, three burned on the ground during a Nip air raid; three light bombers downed by Zekes and groundfire while on a mission over Gavabutu . . ."

Tuthill's voice trailed off. Out of the corner of his eye, he'd glimpsed The Rock, apparently lost in meditation and paying no attention to his morose recital.

Torrey put down his bulldog briar.

"Thank you, Tut. It's a real comfort to know things are looking up." A quick smile stretched his compressed lips. "When you're flat on your tail, gentlemen, that's the only way you can look. But we're not going to sit on our fannies any longer. Tomorrow we'll start moving."

Admiral Neville Balder quit Gavabutu at precisely 1635 that same gray afternoon, in COMADTACZONSOPAC's Mariner, eyes straight ahead, as if he feared any rearward glance at his abandoned post might turn him into a pillar of Navy salt. Enroute to Pearl Harbor via Toulebonne, where he'd pay his final respects to the area commander, he was bleakly aware that Blackjack Broderick would demand a full report on Mesquite now that the precarious operation lay in Rock Torrey's thinfingered hands. How in hell did you reply to such a question? With diplomatic caution? Honestly? These were both qualities which Nev Balder had esteemed highly during his career. In this instance, however, the departing admiral reckoned that honesty might be the better policy. For the eventual good of all concerned, it probably would be a salubrious thing to tell Blackjack that the new COMADTAC was patently determined to make some sudden and frantic move against the entrenched Japs—a tactic as yet undisclosed, but certain to be perilous when you considered what Torrey had to work with.

By the time the Mariner bumbled its way below the gray horizon, The Rock had moved his few belongings into Balder's vacated Quonset.

Privacy was the sole luxury that distinguished the Flag hut from a dozen others just like it on the shallow ridge overlooking the seafront. Nevertheless the lowly tentdwellers dubbed this staff colony "Snob Hill," and darkly implied that life there was a continuous Bacchanalian revel. The Quonset's rectangular twenty-by-forty-foot interior was divided by a thin partition through which a doorless gap led to the admiral's bedroom on one side and his workspace on the other. Each compartment had four rustyscreened windows that were protected against the intermittent rains by hinged shutters which did double duty as blackout shields after sunset. The sleeping section contained a bunk and a table, rescued from a cargo vessel which had been beached during a Jap raid, four wooden chairs, and a leather clubchair. This latter had been donated by the charitable skipper of a carrier, who'd perceived the appalling lack of creature comforts during an air-sea-ground powwow at GHQ a month earlier.

The office was equally severe: a plywood desk hammered together by a Seabee cabinetmaker, another fugitive cargo table, a half-dozen canvas stools and straight-backed chairs, and a rack from which depended an assortment of South Seas charts, virginally smooth and clean. The Rock sensed that it wasn't a worked-in room. Nev Balder undoubtedly had preferred the crowded Operations hut, for, unlike Torrey, he was a gregarious man whose courage fed on human company and whose morale was inclined to falter when he had to face harsh truths alone.

The Rock stared pensively through a southern window, listening as the uneasy breeze made small moaning sounds under the opened shutters, and noting that the showers which Max Gottlieb had predicted for tomorrow were still a glum promise on the darkening rim of the world. It was approaching the season of the great rains and winds that would roil the earth into kneedeep mud, and make the unsheltered roadstead untenable for his always reluctant supply ships. He fought back a sigh. Instead he smiled, ironically, thinking of Balder's phobia against being alone, which was really a fear of Fear itself, a childish belief that the cause would vanish if you let others share your apprehensions. It wouldn't, of course. Once you left the crowded room for your own quarters—as eventually you must—Fear would follow right behind you, like an unwanted cur. Yet he could understand Balder's plight, and he hoped he wouldn't fall prey to these same vague terrors after three months' exposure to the problems that had whipped his predecessor. If you let your mind dwell overlong on the enormity of a situation, rather than assessing it coldbloodedly and resolving upon a course of action, perhaps you might fail too. Right or wrong, you had to *do something*.

On Torrey's desk was a buzzer that connected the Flag hut with Operations, Communications, and Intelligence, and with the two

Quonsets in which the upper-echelon staffers lived. This intercom saved much dashing around by messengers. He pressed the button twice.

Three minutes later McConnel knocked at the door of the Flag quarters.

"Come in, Mac," Torrey said, "and sit down."

"Thanks, sir."

Without any prefatory nonsense, The Rock demanded, "Did you contact that Marine paratroop fellow—Colonel Gregory?"

"Yes, sir. His outfit's bivouacked about fifteen miles from here, anchoring the west end of our lines, and he's standing by for your orders."

"What sort of orders, son?"

"I gather, sir, that he'd like something more productive than scratching mosquito bites. Frankly, he sounds raring to go."

Torrey looked at his misted wrist watch. "Have Colonel Gregory report to Operations at 1900."

"Yes, sir."

"And tell the staff to stand by for the same conference. Also the senior Army, Navy, and Marine commanders." He rubbed his darkstubbled chin. "Also, you'd better order up a hell of a lot of coffee and sandwiches around midnight. This is going to be a long session."

Mac saluted and loped off.

After the screen door slammed shut, The Rock turned to Balder's sheaf of unused maps, regarding them soberly a moment before he lifted them from their rack and carried them into his bedroom, where he found a yellow writing pad, a red crayon, and a pair of dividers. In a vain effort to temper the oppressive heat he stripped to T-shirt and shorts. Then, for a half-hour, he checked and rechecked figures, plotted distances on charts, and restudied Mesquite's sitreps, humming softly as he labored over the papers spread out on the bunk, his mind totally absorbed in the task before him, and oblivious to the sweat that poured from his body.

Insistently, something began to intrude upon his preoccupation. Obscure at first, because he wasn't really listening, it provided only a minor disturbance to his train of thought. But it grew louder, and he pushed aside the maps, listening, and prepared to vent his Jovian wrath upon whoever permitted this outrage in the sacred vicinity of the Flag quarters. The nature and source of the noise became clearer. It was the tinny music of a handcranked phonograph in a nearby hut. A woman singer was pitting her vocal cords against the caterwaul of an Ozark hillbilly orchestra. *If I didn't love you,* she wailed, *If I didn't care.* Inexplicably, his anger faded and he thought of Maggie Haynes.

Torrey wanted, suddenly and urgently, to telephone her. He inspected his murky watch again. Almost 1730. The all-important conference he'd scheduled with every key officer on Gavabutu was only ninety minutes away. He muttered an unaccustomed oath in the solitude of his room, because the nearest field phone that could reach MOB Able belonged to Communications, across the headquarters encampment. There was so goddamn much to do and so little time in which to accomplish it. Now he'd have to postpone calling Maggie until tomorrow, and doubtless leave her wondering why he didn't bother to observe the basic amenities even on this Never-Never Island.

The Rock turned back to his work. First thing in the morning he'd tour the Mesquite perimeter, as any intelligent commander should upon assuming his new duties, and his itinerary would naturally include a stopover at MOB Able, three jungled hills removed from GHQ. It was only proper that he should visit the island's casualties. Inspire the troops. Bolster morale. Then he put down his crayon and dividers. Who in hell was he fooling? He wanted to see Maggie Haynes. Period. The rest was simply a ruse masking his real purpose, and a pretty goddamn silly one at that, for a man who wore stars on his collar.

He swore again, louder this time, before he walked slowly and rather disconsolately through the sawed-out portal to his workdesk, where he stood for a moment over the intercom buzzer. He gave the button the single, vicious thrust that summoned his chief of staff.

Eddington lit another cigarette off the guttering end of the fourth he'd smoked since responding to The Rock's call. By invitation he had taken the one leather chair in the bedroom. Sitting there, claycrusted boots propped against a footlocker, he wore a look of fierce contentment which even his piratical skintight haircut couldn't diminish.

"Christ!" Eddington grunted with pure animal happiness. "It's good to be back with you, skipper."

"That goes double, Paul."

"All we need is the goddamn ocean floating past that port over there and the sound of the blowers," Eddington added, "and it'd seem like old times."

"If it's a leaky ship you want, fella, we've got one."

"You brought *Old Swayback* home in one piece."

Torrey paused to fill his pipe. "That was trouble we managed to blunder into all by ourselves. Now we've inherited somebody else's headache."

"It's a bitch," Eddington agreed, looking happier than ever.

The Rock puffed to ignite his gnarled bulldog briar—his "crisis pipe"—and watched the small gouts of smoke rise in the fetid tropical air, hover a moment, then eddy lazily through the screen-windows. From somewhere outside came the raucous sound of a dog barking.

"That's what we need," Eddington said abruptly, "a pooch."

Only Torrey's eloquent eyebrows questioned this odd remark.

"Because," the chief of staff continued, "we're going to need all the luck that was ever invented to pull Broderick's friggin' chestnuts out of the fire. Take those skinny native mutts. Hell. The minute they get fat they wind up as stew in the nearest cookpot. We ought to catch one and take survival lessons from the little bastard."

"Very well, captain. Find us a dog. We'll call him Hard Tack. That's pretty close to ADTAC."

"Speaking of dogs, skipper, reminds me that there's one big advantage to assuming this godforsaken command that's been overlooked."

"Tell me," Torrey said ironically. "I haven't spotted it yet, either."

"After three months of Balder's inaction, the Japs have probably gotten like those stew dogs. Fat and sassy. So used to having nothing happen that when it does—*bang!*—they're apt to fall over dead from sheer surprise."

"Intriguing theory, fella, but it'll take a hell of a lot of proving." The Rock remembered his own tentative thoughts on strategy aboard the southbound plane. "And I figure we have only about ten days to spring our trap."

"Negative, skipper. I make it one lousy week. If the Japs haven't tumbled to the fact that something's brewing—after all the communications chatter between Balder and Broderick during the past few days—then they're a goddamn sight stupider than I think they are."

"All right. One week." Torrey handed him the maps and papers on which he had been working. "Here are a few general thoughts, Paul. I'd like you to study 'em—refine them—before the meeting."

Gottlieb's rain arrived prematurely. It began drumming against the tin plates of the Operations shack shortly before the conferees assembled. Through the quickening downpour the shielded lights of the encampment glimmered fitfully, wavering from time to time as Mesquite's asthmatic generators coughed in the wet night and temporarily lost power. Once they quit entirely. From every hut men emerged with handtorches, which sent feeble beams against the driving gloom, and milled around in the rain, as if they could somehow solve the difficulty simply by talking about it. The six officers summoned by Torrey remained at their places during this untoward blackout, their cigars and cigarettes gleaming redly, awaiting restoration of the interrupted current. This pleased The Rock. He liked to believe that they would behave just as imperturbably if genuine hell were breaking loose.

When the naked overhead bulbs flickered on again, the uncompromising glare etched the Quonset's fittings in stark relief, like a forest illuminated by a lightning flash. Torrey was standing patiently alongside Operations' large-scale wallchart of Mesquite.

"Thanks for sticking around, gentlemen," he said dryly. "You're all needed."

Captain Tuthill responded, "Admiral, after you've been on Gavabutu for a while, you'll find there just isn't any place else to go."

"That's the trouble," Torrey said soberly. *"We've got to find another place."* He turned to the Marine paratroop commander. "You're probably wondering why I took you away from your garrison duties, aren't you, colonel?"

At thirty-one, Dan Gregory imagined he'd reached an age and

acquired a degree of experience equal to any crisis, however unexpected. But he was wrong. His atabrine-ochered face flushed. For a moment he seemed oddly boyish in spite of the lines that cut deeply into his forehead and around his wide mouth. He ran a broken-nailed paw across his crew cut.

"Garrison duties, sir?"

"That's what I call 'em," The Rock growled. "Hardly worth a jumper's time." He indicated the map. "How well d'you savvy this topography?"

"By heart! Hell, I dream about it, sir!"

Torrey's ferrule traced the Japanese perimeter, which lay roughly between a pair of villages called Botan and Torion, on the island's humpbacked northeastern coast.

"Anywhere in that area where a smart Marine chutist could land without getting all tangled up in the jungle?"

Gregory stepped to the map and unhesitatingly drew a small circle with a red greasepencil. "Right here, admiral, we've spotted a meadow that must be damn near five miles in diameter. Level as a tennis court and filled with nothing worse than kunai grass. There isn't a tree around till you hit the edge, and then you've got plenty of cover."

"What's your complement, colonel?"

"Five hundred and forty-three officers and men—as of an hour ago."

"Trained?"

"Maybe they're a bit rusty, sir, but they're eager as hell—and that makes up for it."

Torrey prodded Gregory on the shoulder, surprised to discover that the Marine barely reached to his chin, and motioned him back to the table.

"Thanks, colonel." He faced Clayton Canfil who was watching the little tableau, impassive as a Buddha whittled out of driftwood, with a look of infinite wisdom on his weatherbeaten countenance. "Now I want to pick *your* brain, commander. You know these waters pretty thoroughly, don't you?"

"Sailed 'em since I was seventeen, admiral, which is forty-three years ago."

"Terrain, too?"

"Like a bloody book," the old Intelligence reservist said pridefully. "When I wasn't sailing, I was hiking."

The Rock traced an imaginary line across Gavabutu's mountainous midsection, straight through the eight-thousand-foot Luma Range, from the beachhead at Atoka to the glistening red circle which Gregory had inscribed.

"Could we put a battalion across those peaks?"

Canfil studied the chart. "It'd be tough," he said. "Tougher than dry cow's turds. But not impossible. Right here's a pass that dips down to about six thousand feet, narrow as hell, and tricky footing. If our fellas traveled light and didn't have to lug howitzers, for example, they could make it."

"How far?"

"As the crow flies, maybe thirty miles. Only those boys aren't crows, sir, they're Marines. And that's not quite the same."

"It's better," Colonel Gregory muttered audibly.

Canfil's mahogany-grained face creased into a tolerant smile. "Reckon they could slog across that defile in, say, three days—if I led 'em."

"Suppose," Torrey said, "you could march only after dark?"

"In that case we'd better count on four nights." Canfil's smile faded. "And I'd definitely have to lead 'em."

"How's your wind, commander?"

"Strong, sir."

"Then you've got a job," The Rock said. "Now, gentlemen, let's get down to brass tacks."

By midnight, when two raindrenched steward's mates brought coffee and sandwiches into the shack, Torrey's plan had taken shape. Reluctantly at first, then with mounting excitement as Eddington sketched the details, Mesquite's commanders adjusted themselves to their independent roles. While they talked, The Rock tilted back in his chair, watching them, silently smoking his pipe, with his emotions veiled behind heavylidded eyes.

Operation Rathole—Eddington's term for it—proposed a simultaneous three-pronged drive against the Japanese stronghold across the island. It was, everybody acknowledged, as delicately contrived as a chronometer, and with almost as many parts. To succeed, it would have to function with a watch's split-second accuracy. A single miscalculation could turn Mesquite into a fearful disaster, with the American forces scattered like spent buckshot, and their entire southern beachhead wide open to the onrushing foe.

Yet Operation Rathole also possessed a classic simplicity that would have delighted an old Indianfighter.

Utilizing every seaworthy vessel in the area, including a flotilla of native luggers which Canfil guaranteed he could scrounge without too much difficulty, they would dispatch the main assault contingent on a wide sweep around Gavabutu's eastern tip. After much heated debate, it was agreed that the eight destroyers and two cruisers normally assigned to ADTAC—led by the refurbished *Old Swayback*—could carry two thousand troops. Canfil's raggle-taggle fleet was expected to transport another five hundred. Moving fast, at night, the warships would swing clear of the inshore shoal-waters to avoid enemy patrolships during the daylight portion of their hazardous journey. They'd be escorted by PTs.

Their combined objective was a two-mile strip of sand between Torion and Botan which coastwatchers assured Intelligence had been neglected for weeks by the overconfident Japs. Once in sight of this goal, they would transmit a coded signal and start bombarding the beachhead.

Immediately, a squadron of Douglas C-47 cargo planes would take off with Colonel Gregory's paratroopers for the short hoist over the Luma Range. This, of course, was a bit trickier. Gregory himself had no doubts about his Marines' ability to plummet onto the merest postage stamp, but Toulebonne had become increasingly stingy about airlifting supplies to Gavabutu, so the availability of transports remained a huge question mark, towering over them like a thunderhead.

The Rock received this news from Air Operations without noticeable dismay.

"How many C-47s do we have in the barn?" he asked.

"Nine, sir," AirOps replied.

"Hmmm . . ." Torrey computed mentally. "That'll handle less than three hundred jumpers. We want another seven Douglases."

AirOps gloomed, "Since Toulebonne cut our schedule from ten to six supply flights a week, we haven't needed more than nine planes."

"What happens when a C-47 conks out temporarily—engine trouble, blown tires, snafued instruments, that sort of thing?"

"They send us a spare till we get it fixed."

"Son," The Rock said quietly, "you've just had five C-47s quit on you. Couple of days from now another four will go sour. And if Admiral Broderick's people ask why, tell 'em all nine planes came down with jungle rot!"

"Yes, sir!"

Clayton Canfil, listening to the brief colloquy, thumped his round Buddha belly, as if this was his cryptic method of applauding. Having a boss with moxie directing one of the toughest small-scale military adventures since Marathon made him feel damned good. Especially, Canfil reminded himself, when he personally must lead the march through the passes to surprise the Japs, the way Miltiades had outfoxed the Persians.

Some admirals, he thought, would have the devil's own time melding this handful of Army, Air Force, Marine, and Navy brass. Balder had failed. Blackjack Broderick didn't dare show his beefy face north of Toulebonne. Yet here was Torrey, who sure as hell didn't palaver any more than the law demanded, playing 'em like a pat deal in a game of pinochle. Only one other admiral had ever impressed Canfil this way. Bill Halsey. And he'd told his wrangling commanders that by God they'd better straighten up and fly right or he'd brand "South Pacific Force" across their fannies with a redhot poker. In this parlous world a man like Canfil was under no obligoddamnation to do more than carry out his assigned orders, keep his trap shut, and Beelzebub-take-the-hindmost. Then along comes a Rockwell Torrey and all bets are off. Pretty soon you're up, waving your hand—and *volunteering!*

Canfil thumped his belly again. Harder.

At 0200 they'd finished their planning. Exhausted mentally, yet too exhilarated for sleep, they sat around the table, nursing the villainous dregs of their coffee and nibbling at flaccid ham sandwiches. The rain had eased. Highriding storm clouds would scud past the sickle moon, and for a moment the night would seem less opaquely black. Eddington's dog—he insisted the lonesome mongrel was already his—crawled out of his hiding place to howl at the crescent.

But the euphoric mood didn't last long.

An Air Operations ensign, wearing a pressed-cardboard topee, stepped into the hut. Taken aback by the roomful of Big Brass, he halted, removed his ridiculous headgear, and dropped it to the floor with a clatter.

"Sir," he announced generally, "Washing Machine Willie's loose again."

AirOps took charge. "What's the range and bearing, Peters?"

"Thirty miles, sir, at course 010."

"Just one bogey?"

"That's what we think—"

"Goddamn it!" AirOps' nerves, stretched too fine after six hours in this smokefilled sweatbox, snapped like an old rubberband. "Don't *think*, Peters—*know!*"

Captain Tuthill intervened. "Tell 'em to keep close tabs on our visitor, son, even though it's only Willie." He turned apologetically to Torrey. "We were hoping you'd have a quiet first night aboard, admiral. Little bastard can be annoying. But not really dangerous. Usually drops a couple of hundred-pounders into the boondocks and then limps home."

The Rock refilled his bulldog briar for the tenth time since he'd called the meeting to order.

"You know," he said calmly, "I've got a hunch that Willie's bringing some friends with him this time."

The headquarters air-raid sirens had already begun their ululating wail, and along the eastern edge of Mesquite's defenses the searchlights flicked on, probing the darkness but finding nothing as yet, because the enemy was still far out of range.

Three minutes later the AirOps youngster came back. This time he took his message straight to his chief.

"Mister Bowles says the radar screen's starting to light up like a Christmas tree, sir, and he thinks maybe the admiral and the others better take cover because we're in for an all-night session."

The far-off hum of aircraft was already audible, lowthrobbing and headachy, with the peculiar out-of-synchronization mutter that seemed to afflict all Jap engines.

Torrey scanned the room. According to rules, all "nonessential personnel" were expected to seek shelter in the pre-dug slit trenches. He wondered exactly who on this ineffable island were nonessential, and what were they doing on Mesquite if they were. His companions, obviously, were awaiting his first move.

Presently the ack-ack batteries opened fire around the perimeter. Their exploding shells made soft flashes against the undersides of the rainclouds. Seconds afterward the whump-whump-whump of 75s and 90s reached the headquarters hilltop. The middle ring of A.A. protection took over, and then the anchored ships joined in, and finally the emplacements just below the ADTAC Quonsets blasted loose, and the murky night became an earshattering horror of bursting HE shells and aerial bombs.

From the angle of the little platform that jutted out from Operations' shackdoor, under the dubious protection of a three-foot overhanging tinroof, Torrey watched this unequal duel between the earthbound guns and the oncoming Japs, appraising the action critically, like a veteran firstnighter observing a singularly noisy but embarrassingly bad show. Only he and Eddington were left. The others had preferred bombshelters to protocol.

"I'd give my friggin' right nut for a squadron of Black Widow nightfighters, skipper," the chief of staff said during a momentary lull.

Torrey agreed. "We could use 'em . . ."

"Toulebonne's got some," Eddington sneered, "but they're 'training.' Hell. They'll still be training when Halsey rides into Tokyo."

Down in the unprotected roadstead, now, the high-pitched chatter of smaller weapons overlaid the sound of the heavier guns, as the fat target ships made a last desperate effort to turn back the imperturbable Japs. From the clearings, the beaches, and even from the parked amphtanks in the mobile armored pool came the sound of automatic firing.

"I guess," The Rock said, "it's time for us to hit the dirt, too. They're pitching so close to our heads we might get nicked by a beanball."

Eddington assented reluctantly, and they took refuge in a nearby slit trench, whose inadequate dimensions forced them to lie in a rather uncomfortable embryo posture. With his face pressed close against Eddington's muddy fieldboots, Torrey strove to detect aurally what he could no longer observe visually. But it was useless. The jumbled noises generated both by the attackers and the defenders had merged into a single vast unintelligible roar.

After that there was a brief lull, and then the strafing began, as the Japs swooped low across ADTAC headquarters for a final contemptuous run. Steeljacketed bullets from the unseen planes splatted through the palmfronds.

This was, Torrey thought, a damned humiliating way to come under direct enemy fire for the first time. Every bullet seemed aimed right at him. It gave him an annoying drygut feeling. Later he'd think about this and try to analyze it. But now it was merely an unpleasant constricting sensation which he had never known before.

Suddenly there was a skyrending blast from the beachhead area below them. Even in the foxhole, they felt the concussive force of the explosion which blew out every screen in the Op shack. Flames shot up. And then it wasn't night any more, but a hellish kind of midday, with manmade magnesium and cordite and TNT and hightest fuel feeding the fires of Hades.

Eddington spat out a mouthful of dirt.

"Jesus! It's the ammo dump!"

Torrey peered over the lip of their damp shelter. He nodded grimly.

The raid itself had ended. But the shambles created by the unscathed enemy crackled and flared and exploded for the rest of the night. By dawn, Mesquite's exhausted battalions had barely begun to quell the conflagration. It had been a catastrophic four hours. And if anybody still questioned what had happened, Tokyo Rose dispelled all doubt in her earlymorning shortwave broadcast.

After she'd finished playing a couple of swing records, she addressed herself especially "to those poor misguided boys on Gavabutu." Why not, she cooed, surrender? It'd be so much easier than fighting on against such hopeless odds. Nobody really cares, she added in her sugary-sexy voice, whether you live or die.

Especially Admiral Rockwell Torrey, Tokyo Rose concluded, to whom this raid was dedicated . . .

13. Sailors Take Warning

When dawn finally broke at 0545, it wasn't a buoyant tropical moment of gold and coral and azure, but merely a sullen interlude between pitchdarkness and monochromatic daylight, after the gaudy pyrotechnics of the Jap air raid. Gottlieb's rain was falling steadily again. The men of Mesquite swore it had a discernible *taste* of old burnt rubber and stale horsepiss, which came through your pores even when you kept your friggin' mouth shut and your neck bowed as you worked to repair the night's bomb damage. Torrey watched the birthpangs of the new day through the eastern windows of his Quonset. Haggard, unshaven, he stared downhill toward the waterfront, where the British once had disported themselves on their cricketfield and quaffed interminable gin-and-its in their bamboo-thatched clubhouse. Splintered palmtrees lifted gaunt stumps skyward around the deserted compound. Standing here, long dead, riddled by the naval bombardment that had preceded the Mesquite landings, they were as ugly as unbandaged amputations.

It occurred to him then, as the somber gray turned a half-shade brighter, that the brief period of absolute silence after a major air raid was not unlike the stunned quiet that follows an earthquake. Once, when he had taken his destroyer into a Chilean port in the twenties, this same thing had happened. Still deafened, aghast at the destruction, baffled by their inability to strike back, the quake victims milled about haphazardly for a time, more inclined to discuss the tragedy among themselves in disbelieving terms than to plunge immediately into the task of clearing away the rubble. But this senseless mood doesn't last long. A single whipcracking command fetches them back to their senses.

Inevitably, The Rock knew, the disparate elements of his command, scattered over so many miles of Gavabutan jungle, would equate his arrival with the raid itself, whether or not they'd heard Tokyo Rose. That was human nature. For several weeks prior to his coming they had enjoyed a strange sort of truce. Only a handful of troops actually exposed to the Japs at certain tender sectors along their perimeter seemed aware that a war was indeed being waged. If a man were shortsighted enough—Torrey also knew how quickly the long view gets obscured in such paradoxical circumstances!—he might even conclude that his situation was comfortably permanent rather than temporary, and would resent anyone who brought an end to this pleasant lull.

Torrey hadn't slept.

As soon as the last wave of enemy bombers retreated across the Luma Range, flying high above Mesquite's futile ack-ack barrage, he had left Operations and retired to his own hut. Here he received a steady stream of staffers, all of them exceedingly downcast, and each of them bearing news more doleful than his predecessor's. Simply by the telling of it, however, they seemed to believe they could unload their burden upon Torrey's shoulders.

. . . Ammo dump a total loss. (*Message Toulebonne—URGENT!—that we'll need a shipload of aerial bombs, howitzer and mortar shells, and small-arms stuff no later than next Wednesday. On the double!*)

. . . Three pontoon piers, including the jetty upon which The Rock had landed only twenty-four hours before, blown to smithereens. (*Signal the supply ships to start lightering their cargoes ashore the instant they returned to the roadstead from their all-night dispersal into deep waters; tell the troops to drop their guns and join the stevedore detail because now Gottlieb was predicting a nor'west blow that could stymie unloading for days.*)

. . . Two big Nip bombs impacted in the diametric center of the airstrip's Marston-matting. (*Inform ComAirMesquite this must be operative within three hours—no alibis accepted.*)

. . . Human casualties appallingly heavy. (Guiltily, you recognize that the loss of mere men right now is less disruptive than the loss of equipment the survivors must use during the next couple of weeks. Nevertheless: *Check MOB Able. Find out whether the medics can handle the wounded; see if they've enough morphine and plasma; if they can't and if they haven't, tell Toulebonne we'll need a floating hospital as well as the ammo ship. You might add that Admiral Torrey hopes to visit MOB Able—very soon.*)

Yes. You might . . .

Finally the parade of doomcriers halted. There would be no further evil Word. He'd heard the whole bleak story.

The Rock ceased his moody contemplation of the shattered waterfront. Without haste, he dug a clean set of khakis and underwear out of his footlocker, and found his German steel razors.

Using his *Samstag* blade, he cut away his heavy beard with deft quick strokes, peering critically into a small metal mirror, as if to reassure himself that his gnarled and attenuated face still bore the habitmarks of authority. Even to himself, it was a rather sobering visage at this moment of the early dawn. Fatigue had deepened the lines and grayed the cheeks, until the face might have passed for a slightly inferior Abe Lincoln deathmask. He smiled at his grim reflection. That helped a little. The mask came back to life.

When The Rock stepped from his hut five minutes later, he wore a pair of aviation sunglasses, more to hide any marks of exhaustion than to ward off the nonexistent glare, and despite the rain he also wore his visored cap with the heavy gold-encrusted filigree which identifies an admiral. Both the dark glasses and the goldlaced headgear made him somewhat self-conscious, although he had donned them deliberately, in the knowledge that on this particular morning he must cast a shadow that was longer than his normal six-foot-one. A bit of illusory flair, a touch of drama, was needed, as General MacArthur demonstrated after he'd fled Corregidor last year, smoking his corncob and sporting that bashed-in field marshal's cap.

"Things," Eddington rumbled, "might have been a hell of a lot worse."

The chief of staff was sitting with McConnel in the rear of the jeep, which had just swung away from the ammo dump. A few faint cheers from the Army engineers who were rebuilding the ruined sandbag revetments sounded in the muggy air after the admiral's laconic words of encouragement.

Now Torrey said mildly from his position beside the Marine driver, "Tell me how, fella."

"If the bastards had made one more pass over the supply area, skipper, they'd have finished their job. See? As it was, they missed the fuel stores by a goddamn country mile. We've got just enough high-octane left for Operation Rathole."

"You know," The Rock mused, "we might fire off a dispatch to Toulebonne anyhow. Have 'em fly up a couple of hundred barrels. And then hijack the C-47s once they get here."

Eddington's wolfish grin split his homely face. "Why boss—that's piracy!"

"Also a damn good way to cut down our acquisition time for the paratroop ferry."

As the two-starred jeep neared the airfield, the aviation ratings and engineers, working side by side to fill the bombholes that had put the single runway out of action, looked up inquiringly. Three of Mesquite's precious fighterplanes, a pair of Marine Wildcats and an Air Force Warhawk, lay in a tangled heap just off the tarmac, where they had been bulldozed out of the way like corpses ready for an unmarked mass grave. But the surviving craft stood under the cocopalms, ready to fly as soon as the strip was serviceable again.

An astonishingly youthful Marine brigadier general sloshed across the field.

"Averell, sir," he said. "I'm in command here."

Torrey returned his brisk salute. "Yes. I know. They tell me you did a damn fine job at Guadalcanal."

"Thanks, sir." The Marine was pleasantly surprised that the new boss had heard of his earlier exploits. "This is just more of the same. We hit 'em. They dig out. They smack us. And we dig out."

"How'd you like to change that routine?"

"Change, sir?"

"Arrange it so the Nips couldn't retaliate quite so easily, I mean."

"Try us!"

"We're going to, general. Hang tight to your merry-go-round a little longer. Maybe a week or ten days. After that we'll have a really big assignment for you."

"Action, sir?"

"Action, Averell. We put the finishing touches on the blueprint last night, just before the Japs dropped their calling cards."

Then it was time to head for MOB Able. Staring straight ahead as the jeep maneuvered around a snailpaced file of trucks and ambulances, The Rock found himself taking curious comfort from the presence of Eddington and McConnel at that particular moment. His old feeling of callowness, tinged now with an almost sophomoric embarrassment, had assailed him again, increasing as they lurched up the long slope to the hospital where, he knew, Maggie Haynes was waiting.

They were welcomed at the Admin shack by the chief medic, a middle-aged Navy four-striper who had obviously just come off surgical duty. His gauze mask hung loosely around his neck, and his nicotine-stained hands trembled as he lit a cigarette after they'd exchanged greetings. The Rock wondered how in hell the man could wield a scalpel in his present condition. But he didn't ask.

Captain Tully responded to the unspoken question.

"It's not the shakes, admiral, believe me. It's just the reaction from six hours in Emergency. But we're finally getting a breather."

Torrey said sympathetically, "I know, captain. I went through something like this, myself, once. It's damned rugged."

He followed the stoop-shouldered doctor through a rabbit warren of interconnecting Quonsets to the Senior Medical Officer's headquarters, pausing occasionally to chat with the wounded men, and acknowledging Captain Tully's rather fulsome introduction at each ward with a diffident half salute. He stopped longest before a cot on which a Marine private, whose smashed jaw had been wired shut, was attempting to suck a two-minute egg through a glass straw. It was tough going. But the Marine kept doggedly at this elementary task until the last of the egg disappeared from his cup.

"Excellent," Torrey said with mock gravity. "I'll see that you get a D.S.M. to add to your Purple Heart, son."

The Marine's eyes rolled whitely. He tried to smile. Then he picked up a small pair of wirecutters from his cotside table, and motioned mutely with them toward his pent-up jaw.

"Take it easy, fella. Let the Brass do the talking. We've had practice. You handle the fighting." The Rock turned to his host. "What are the wirecutters for?"

"To chop himself loose in case the egg makes him vomit," the doctor explained. "Otherwise the poor bastard might drown in his own puke."

At this the Marine uttered a strangled, chortling sound, as if what Captain Tully had just said was the funniest thing he'd ever heard. They moved on toward the S.M.O.'s office.

After lighting his fourth cigarette since their tour began, the chief medic relaxed into his canvas chair and uttered the whinnied sigh of a windblown horse.

"That," he said, "is a small sample of what we're up against. When they fetched this kid into MOB Able last Monday noon, he was the seventeenth casualty for the day. Another thirty followed him before midnight. He'll be laid up another three weeks. And all because—if you'll excuse me for poking my long nose where it doesn't belong!—we keep sticking our fingers into the Jap buzzsaw to see if the blade's still spinning." Torrey's eyebrows raised interrogatively, but he said nothing, and the S.M.O. plowed ahead. "I've talked to most of these fellows, admiral, and they'd a lot rather grab that goddamn saw and turn it against the Nips before it does any more damage. It might hurt like hell for a little while. But after that it'd be all over."

The Rock smiled. "Maybe you'd better join my Operations staff."

Like many Navy doctors, Captain Tully was a thwarted tactician, and he seemed only moderately abashed by the admiral's reaction. "I'm available, sir."

"No," Torrey said seriously. "What you're doing is a damned sight more vital right now than the service of another planner. Though you'd probably be a good one. But I can tell you this, captain—we're about to try exactly what you've suggested."

"Magnificent!"

"Let's hope so. It'll be risky, though, and it's bound to increase your . . . business by several hundred per cent. Can you carry the load?"

"We'll carry it, sir, if we have to deputize a battalion of native witch doctors."

With elaborate casualness, Torrey asked, "How about your nurses —how are they standing up?"

"Like Gibraltar." The S.M.O. gnawed at a broken nail. "And it was decent of you to send Commander Owynn around this morning to give 'em that little peptalk. Splendid orator. Quite effective."

The Rock glowered. "Did you say *Owynn?*"

"Why, yes, sir. Seems he was pinked by shrapnel during the raid and needed a little attention. The girls were happy to oblige. They don't get a chance to bandage a senatorial thumb every day."

Eddington cut in. "If it was Owynn's thumb, doc, he probably got wounded picking up a redhot hunk of Jap bomb for a souvenir."

"Well," the S.M.O. conceded, "he did hint he deserved a Purple Heart."

"Fix him up," Torrey snapped. "He'll rate one later—even if it's not warranted right now."

Captain Tully looked puzzled, but he acknowledged saltily, "Aye, aye, sir." Then: "It would be even better if you'd also say a few encouraging words to my nurses, admiral. Sometimes they feel neglected, off here in the tules, and this has been a goddamn rough stint."

"Fine," The Rock said ironically, "if you don't think I'd be an anticlimax after the Senator."

With Eddington and McConnel bringing up the rear, they crossed the ankle-deep mud to the recreation-and-mess hut, and entered without ceremony. Excited squeals and a smattering of applause met Torrey as he stepped inside the screendoor. Grinning uncertainly at this feminine welcome, he cast his eyes quickly around the low-ceilinged room.

Maggie Haynes wasn't there.

Disappointed, perplexed, and almost unconscious of what he was saying, The Rock uttered some traditional words of praise for their services above and beyond the call of duty, told them an even greater challenge lay ahead, and then he motioned to Captain Tully.

"Where's your head nurse?" he whispered.

"Lieutenant Haynes?" The four-striper gave him a surprised glance. "D'you know her?"

"We met at Pearl Harbor. I'd like to say hello."

"If I'd been aware of that, admiral, Miss Haynes would have been here, of course. She's in Receiving, winding up the paperwork on the last batch of casualties."

Torrey summoned his aides. "You gentlemen stay here," he said, "and build a little morale."

He followed the S.M.O. out of the hut. When they reached the admittance shack, The Rock paused, uncertain how he should explain that he wished to see Lieutenant Haynes alone. But a lifetime spent with inarticulate Service patients had given Captain

Tully vast powers of divination, and he withdrew before he was asked.

"Sir," he said, "I'll be waiting in my office when you've finished your visit."

"Thank you," Torrey said gratefully.

Then he opened the sagging screendoor of the shack and went in.

For a long interval, speechless, Maggie stared at him as he stood framed in the inadequate doorway. She, too, was alone. He looked so much thinner—not really older, she reminded herself, but more worn and grim—than she'd remembered.

Why didn't *he* speak?

Finally Maggie murmured, "You're so damned admirably admiralish, Rock . . ."

"But you," he replied gravely and unhesitatingly, "are still beautiful."

She touched her unkempt hair in an age-old feminine gesture, and wrinkled her nose at his obersided gallantry. "Like this?" Maggie indicated her oversized men's khakis, pointing mutely to the stains of blood and sweat and jungle mud that betokened seven hours of charnelhouse duty.

"Just like that."

Suddenly he bent down and kissed her damp forehead. It felt feverishly hot against his lips. She turned in his loose grasp, flinging her tired arms around his neck, and when the needle points of the stars on his collar pricked her throat, she derived a curious pleasure from the small stab of pain.

Close to his ear, Maggie's unpainted mouth whispered, "Hell of a way for an admiral to behave, Rockwell No-Middle-Name Torrey."

For a split second he formed the banal phrase "I love you," but the words refused to come. Because he saw himself standing there in the drab Receiving shack, a veritable Ichabod Crane, peering down into a woman's searching face; and it all seemed too preposterous to be true. Instead, he brushed her small cleft chin with his fist, boxerfashion, and said softly, "I've thought about you a great deal. More than an old sailor should ever confess."

Disappointed, Maggie drew away, and gazed through the grimy

screen at the steaming jungle that spread beyond MOB Able's compound.

"I've thought about you, too, in a dozen different ways . . . all of them quite impossible." She uttered a short mirthless laugh. "Two days ago I was worrying about my hair and my clothes and how I'd look when I saw you. And I was praying there'd be a moon and we could see the Southern Cross." Again the bitter laugh. "Now you're here and it's the middle of a miserable gray goddamn day and that's not how I planned things at all . . ."

Torrey tasted salt tears as he kissed her darkcircled eyes. "Take it easy, Lieutenant Haynes."

She caught her breath.

"Forgive a silly female," she said. "I haven't done this since I joined the Camp Fire Girls. But now it's over. I'm a *man* again."

"Don't—"

Maggie pressed a forefinger against his mouth. "Let me tell you something before I lose my nerve, Rock. It's a thing I've been thinking about till I almost went out of my stupid little mind. Especially nighttimes." He waited. "What I want to say is this . . . Back at Pearl Harbor we'd have been just Maggie Haynes and Rock Torrey, because nothing mattered, really, and neither of us seemed very important. Now it's different. You've got a job that's so big I don't even want to think about it, because it scares me. You're terribly important to an awful lot of people besides this one small Navy nurse." She paused. "You're 'way up on top of a high mountain where I can't even reach you . . ."

"You make it sound as if I were some kind of deity," he said gloomily.

"To these fellows on Gavabutu you are. They're got some idea you can turn their famine into a feast of loaves and fishes."

"Then they're thinking about the wrong Man . . ."

Maggie nodded. "I know. You know. But there's no choice for us. Down here you *are* God Almighty."

Torrey smiled, and his hard grip tightened around her slim shoulders.

"All I want," he said simply, "is to try and find a way to finish this small part of the war, so we can move along to the next chore, and the next, and maybe after that it'll be over."

Trapped by despised self-pity, she could only nod again, frustrated and unaccountably angry. Hot tears carved tiny channels down her dirt-streaked cheeks.

"If I keep blubbering like a damned ninny," she said, "I won't be around to help you celebrate—they'll shoot me first."

"That's one thing I can guarantee won't happen," he assured her gravely.

The unaccustomed warmth of The Rock's expression made his tanned and heavily bearded face almost handsome, Maggie thought, for all its equine gauntness. Her starboard-canted grin suddenly returned.

"Have you got a clean handkerchief, admiral?" she asked. "Mine's all bloody."

"Here," he said.

She dried her eyes. "Maybe . . . sometime . . . you'll find a spare minute to telephone me, Admiral Torrey, just so I'll know you're still alive."

On the drive back to ADTAC headquarters, Torrey sat on his canvas bucketseat, arms folded, looking stonily at the uninspiring countryside. But Eddington and McConnel compensated for his gloomy silence with their voluble appraisal of MOB Able's nurse corps.

"Speaking as an old married man," Mac said, "I'd say these chicks rate approximately 3.2. Passing. But barely."

The chief of staff regarded him across the jeep. "As a former old married man, son, my advice to you is don't be so goddamn fussy. On Gavabutu you'd better be grateful for any little home comforts you find lying around loose."

"Sir," Mac said solemnly, "I shall treasure that advice forever."

"What I have in mind," Eddington went on, "is a certain ensign who seemed to be particularly well-stacked beneath her foulweather gear."

"There must have been a dozen ensigns, captain."

"But not *stacked* ensigns, my boy. As I recall her, this one was a trifle babyfaced, though I'd spot her as over twenty-one, and she had the goddamnedest coalblack eyes I've seen since I romanced a Baltimore gal back in Trade School days. Real Mick eyes."

"Oh," Mac said, "that one."

"Sometime when we've got things under control we'll have to

institute social nights at ADTAC, Mr. Flag Lieutenant, complete with wine, women, and song."

"D'you sing, sir?"

Eddington leered in the darkness. "Negative. And I've also retired from the jug. But I can still handle the other, son, and you can take my word for it—that's the best of the three."

"Since I'm social secretary, perhaps I'd better note down her name for our guest list, captain."

"Can I trust you, son?"

"To the death!"

"Then it's something like Annabelle or Anna-Lou. And her last name's Dorne."

Even wrapped in his Olympian solitude, The Rock heard Eddington's final remark. Wasn't this the girl Jere was so crazy about—the one they'd taken to dinner with Maggie at the Chinaman's? A formless little worry began to nag at him. If she were indeed the same girl, she'd hardly be a match for Paul Eddington, whose brutal unconcern for women had grown harsher rather than softening since Beth's death. Torrey sighed. Here was a problem which an admiral could neither solve nor appear to be aware of, unless it grew into something that involved the sanctity of his command. Within reason, a man's personal life was his own business. You observed covertly. But you stayed aloof.

Known formally as MoTorpRon Charlie, since they were the third PT squadron assigned to the South Pacific, Blackjack's Bastards operated out of a small inlet at the mouth of a stream a dozen miles east of MOB Able. Generations ago this indentation had been christened Strangler's Cove, after the second mate of a British barkentine garroted his first mate during an argument over the favors of some ebonyskinned mary. They might as well have called it Hangman's Cove, for the offender was immediately strung up; and an interested bystander to the whole affair, the third mate, exercised his survivor's *droit de seigneur* upon the not unwilling maiden, then and there, on the pink sands before either corpse cooled. But whatever romance might have accrued from this touching idyll hadn't lasted very long. Strangler's Cove remained exactly as it was before the limeys hove in sight: a treacherous cuplet assailed by crosscurrents, pocked with jagged coralheads, and overgrown close ashore with mangrove roots that made smallboating quite hazardous. But it had a tiny beach, excellent for swimming when a man was off-duty.

Blackjack's Bastards lived on their PTs, but messed aboard a converted four-piper which served as their social center as well as their repair base. Anchored fore-and-aft, this nondescript mothership rode the unpredictable surface of the cove with all thirteen surviving boats of the sixteen-unit squadron tethered like gray sheep from booms extending off each of her flushdecked flanks.

Accompanied only by Flag Lieutenant McConnel, Torrey stepped aboard her after a precarious trip from the swampy beach in a motorwhaler. Almost immediately, as he crossed the brow, he was engulfed by a wave of nostalgia. Although two of her stacks had been removed to accommodate a machineshop, and she no longer was the highfunneled creature he'd known in an earlier war, just visiting a four-stacker again took him back a quarter century. It was a little like reliving a forgotten chapter of his youth, when the physical aches and mental stresses of authoritarian middle age weren't even imagined, much less known. The ancient vessel smelled the same, too, of inefficiently burned crude oil and hot metal and greasy food cooked for too many men in too small a galley.

AG ("miscellaneous auxiliary") 99 was an ugly old crone. But The Rock wished he had fifty more just like her, such as the fifty that had been lend-leased two years earlier to the hardpressed British. Sure. Her torpedo tubes were gone. And her quartet of four-inch/50s had been reduced to a mildbarking pair. With a bit of doing, however, AG99 and her beat-up sisters could be restored to their ancient scrappiness. Best of all, she boasted search radar atop her tall new mainmast. This fact alone made her a valuable adjunct to an undernourished, undersized command like ADTAC, which could utilize her for picket duty, or even for transporting commando raiders.

Torrey proceeded quickly through the double file of six sideboys as the boatswain blew a shrill blast on his whistle in lieu of ruffles, flourishes, and a brassband playing the "Admiral's March."

Jere stood to one side, grinning like a young ape, while his betters exchanged quarterdeck amenities. Then he moved forward and gripped The Rock's hand. As their fingers clasped, Torrey noted proudly that Jere's fist was hard as ivorynut, and his brown face had lost the youthful softness which had been so evident at Pearl Harbor.

"Welcome aboard the *Jungle Junk,*" Jere said. "It's not much, sir, but it's our castle."

They walked through the rainswept darkness and filed below to AG99's wardroom, a dank pigiron dungeon situated under the cutaway bridge, where the skippers of the other twelve boats awaited them.

Dinner was a rather sketchy meal. As he contemplated the unidentifiable blobs of gray meat among the stew on his plate, MoTorpRon Charlie's commodore promised himself to order up a census of the native dogs next morning, and he wished he'd been more insistent that his awesome guest dine tête-à-tête in the stateroom topside. But since the commodore was only a three-striper, and a premature one at that, he was forced to capitulate without a struggle when the admiral suggested chow in the wardroom mess with his son's squadron mates.

After the table had been cleared and the green baize relaid across it, they settled back with their coffee and tobacco, contentedly disregarding the wardroom's fetid heat, and the fact that another cubic inch of smoke might render the tightshut compartment unfit for human habitation. Again, more exquisitely than ever, Torrey savored that lost-youth feeling as he mused over his pipe at their eager, respectful faces, and he tried to imagine how it was to be one of them.

Perhaps it was their rapt expression, a collective look which came uncomfortably close to worshipfulness, that shattered his mood. By his mere two-starred presence he had invoked that deferential attitude, and he could no more change it than he could fly back across the years to the day when he'd puffed his first briarpipe in a wardroom exactly like AG99's, rivet for rivet, paintscaling beam for beam.

When it became apparent that Admiral Torrey wasn't yet ready to explain the war, the squadron skippers fell to discussing the parlous condition of a civilized world which none of them had seen for six months. Their words came lazily through the smoke. Those who were married concluded with much self-conscious melancholia that they'd probably have to court their wives all over again, when the war ended, because a year or so out of a man's life made it damn near immoral to barge through your front door and take up housekeeping right where you'd left off. Or, did it? From the vantage of his extra months overseas, his personal experience, and his nearness to the throne, Flag Lieutenant McConnel held persuasively that these start-all-over-again theorists were dead wrong. In the split second it takes to say, "Hello, baby, I'm home!" the Past turns into the Present, and everything's just as it was. He damned well knew.

Of course, they agreed solemnly, this was strictly academic anyhow, because the war surely couldn't last another year.

Could it, admiral?

The Rock placed his pipe carefully against his coffeecup. "It could," he said, "and I'm afraid it will."

Disbelieving, they asked why.

"Check your charts. They tell the story a lot better than any words of mine." They swiveled around toward the western Pacific map that hung against AG99's after bulkhead, eyes questioning, as he continued: "See—we've barely dented the Japs' Co-Prosperity Sphere. It's a hell of a long way to Tokyo, gentlemen, and I think you'll agree it's high time we got moving."

"Yes, sir," the squadron commodore agreed.

"That's why we're mounting an exercise called Operation Rathole. It's not a mammoth affair. With a little luck and a lot of teamwork, though, it could put the cork in Gavabutu and free us for the really important job—Levu-Vana."

Murmurs and nudges. This was more like it!

"But even Levu-Vana is only the first step toward the real target. Japan. Look!" Torrey stepped to the blue-and-yellow chart. "There's Pelaki, another damn rough five hundred miles north. After that it's the Carolines, the Marianas, and the Volcanos. But they're only the starboard rail of the ladder we've got to climb to the home islands. Off to port there's New Guinea, the Moluccas, Cape Titan, the Philippines, and the Ryukyus. All of 'em held in considerable depth. And the Nips won't give up easily . . . if Gavabutu's any yardstick."

"Sir," MoTorpRon Charlie's commodore said quietly, "we're ready to take off the minute we get The Word."

The Rock returned to his seat. He refilled and rekindled his pipe while the others anxiously awaited his next remarks. "D'you think," he asked between puffs, "that this battlewagon could get underway by noon tomorrow?"

The squadron commander grinned. "She's been sitting here so damn long the barnacles growing off her keel have probably frozen into the Spam cans the cook heaves over the side. Maybe we'll have to send down an underwater demolition team. But we'll sure as hell move her, sir. Just tell us where."

Torrey drew a rough sketch of Mesquite on the back of AG99's typewritten plan of the day, and called their attention to its unmistakable resemblance to a Sherman tank. Strangler's Cove sat just forward of its rear driving wheel. Then he made a small notch halfway up the tank's upward-sloping stern, well around the eastern tip of the island, and at least eighty coastal miles nearer the enemy than their present base.

"If that really were a Sherman," Torrey explained "this would be the exhaust vent. You won't find it on your regular Gavabutu chart. But our coastwatchers tell us Voyon Bay—damned odd they'd call this bathtub a bay!—can handle a four-hundred-foot ship with a thirty-five-foot draft. That gives you about forty feet to spare at both ends, and a full fathom under your keel." He blew a prodigious smoke ring toward MoTorpRon Charlie's commodore. "Provided, commander, you scrape off those barnacles and carry a shoehorn."

"Hot damn!"

"Until we wind up this show," The Rock added, ignoring the commodore's jubilant outburst, "you'll play cat right at the Rathole itself. Just try to remember it's a big rat and it's got damn sharp teeth."

"We'll file 'em down," the squadron leader promised confidently.

Torrey resumed his quiet puffing. Thirteen pairs of eyes focused upon him, hot with speculation, and he knew that if he ordered them to take AG99 into Voyon Bay tonight they'd cheer like lunatics and ring up a full head of steam. The fact that they'd be sitting ducks under the Japs' guns plainly didn't bother them. But inactivity did. Or pointless maneuverings that slowly bled the squadron to death. Impressed once more by the enthusiasm of youth, he glanced covertly at Jere, and saw that his son was as vibrantly eager as the rest.

An irrelevant notion struck him—what the hell would dear Athalie think . . .

Later, The Rock remembered that he'd meant to give Jere a fatherly warning about Eddington's emergent interest in Annalee Dorne. Perhaps it was just as well he'd forgotten, for this had not been a familial sort of evening at all. His son was a warrior now, with a warrior's disregard for softness; and it would have been inappropriate for him to have broached such a frivolous matter.

"Great kids," he muttered. "Lots of guts."

McConnel's surprised look was lost on Torrey. "They remind me of the *Cassiday* gang," he said wistfully.

"That's what I mean."

"Yes, sir," Mac said and dropped the subject.

Plainly the Old Man had fallen into one of his unpredictable moods, and it was best to let him struggle out of this odd humor alone. Mac supposed the admiral's son had something to do with his frame of mind. Among the subjects left untaught by Annapolis was how to consign your own kin to extra-hazardous duty; and yet, he guessed there must have been dozens of Flag officers over the years who'd been compelled to do exactly that.

When they reached GHQ, Torrey debarked from the jeep without returning the farewell salutes of his aide or his driver. Mac stared after the admiral's retreating back. Still puzzled, he scratched his close-cropped auburn head, and then he ambled slowly to the Quonset which he shared with Eddington, Egan Powell, and Neal Owynn. He was pooped as hell.

Although it was after midnight, all four unshaded hundred-watters were glaring. Their harsh light probed every cranny of the hut like a third-degree spotlamp, mocking any attempts to turn the place into something less austere and more livable. Not that anybody cared very much. Bev's picture, in a redleather frame that was already graystreaked with mildew, sat on Mac's footlocker alongside a stub candle stuck into a peanut can. Egan Powell maintained a small semipornographic library, arranged in a fruitcrate and suspended like Damocles' sword above him as he lay in his cot. Owynn's expensive civilian steamer trunk, flown from Toulebonne as part of a shipment of official supplies, stood half open beside the Senator's meticulous bunk, with its cargo of tailored khakis and silk skivvies clearly visible.

Only Eddington's corner gave no hint of its occupant's nature or habits.

The chief of staff had just returned from thirteen hours in Operations, where he'd whipped his planners into a frenzy of effort as they raced the clock against Jap Intelligence, the foul weather, and the danger of being caught with their work unfinished when the admiral pressed his buzzer and said, "All right, gentlemen—this is D-Day!" Dog-tired, he'd stripped off his wet clothes, and now he reclined naked on his rumpled bunk, with his matted barrelchest and heavy belly glistening in the stark light, and his huge genitals unabashedly asprawl. Eddington was fondling an unopened bottle of I. W. Harper, running his blunt hands along its glass flanks and slim neck, sensually, as he might have caressed a woman.

He held it against the light. "Look," he growled. "A goddamn virgin!"

Nobody spoke. The Senator was absorbed in giving himself a pedicure. Snoring gently, Egan Powell lay face up, protected against the bald light by a black cloth eyeshade that fitted him like a burglar's mask. And Mac, who had just entered the shack, was totally unprepared to comment on the chief of staff's remark.

". . . Reminds me of two very important things," Eddington continued imperturbably. "First, the frigging civilians can't get bourbon without paying a king's ransom for the stuff, whereas we heroes buy it for one-fifty a jug, when it's available. Second, I used to be a hell of a drinking man myself." He appealed owlishly to McConnel. "Pretty good reminders—eh?"

"Pretty good, sir," Mac said.

"Also," Eddington went on, "a fifth of whisky's one damn fine barroom weapon. Better than a boarding cutlass. Away back when, maybe I should have used a bottle . . . but that's another story . . . because if I had, I wouldn't be here now."

"You *want* to be here, don't you, captain?"

"I do," Eddington said cryptically, "and I don't."

This was going to be one of those evenings when you'd have to fight your way out of the dismal swampland, Mac brooded. First the Old Man. Now the chief. *Chloe!*

"That's an oddball thing to say." He coughed politely. "I'm damned if I get it."

Eddington scowled up at the .45 automatics, jungle knives, gas masks, and steel helmets that hung from nails driven into the hut's walls.

"Seeing all that crap, there, also reminds me that what we're doing here is *almost* war. But not quite. It's still a goddamn sight closer to being a spectator sport than I like—holding the coats while the other guys do the real fighting."

He squinted one eye to avoid the smoke from his cigarette, and the grimace twisted his battered face into an expression that was almost comic in its ferocity, the more so since it could not be disassociated from his great ursine body.

"Last night's raid sounded damn real to me," Mac countered.

Eddington cut him short with a harsh laugh. "Son, there are only two honest-to-God combat jobs in this man's war. Rifleman and fighter pilot. The rest of us are nothing but spear carriers in the back row."

"Surely you wouldn't call the PTs 'spear carriers,'" Mac protested, remembering his evening on AG99, "or the bomber crews. Or even—goddamn it, sir, I know!—the tincans!"

"They're borderline cases. With them, self-preservation is almost as important as destroying the enemy. What's more important, they never *feel* the son of a bitch with their bare hands."

"Combat riflemen and fighter pilots like to come home all in one piece, too, I imagine," Mac said.

"Not the real ones. Not the guys who understand war. They don't give a frig."

Mac stared at Eddington, who was gazing blankly into a bare lightbulb, and he tried to guess what really lay behind his narrowed eyes. He thought he knew. But it frightened him. Nobody had a right to be so goddamn casual about human life, especially his own. Even as a calculated pose this was wrong, and the chief of staff wasn't posing. He meant exactly what he said. Already, after only three days on a job that brought him within sight and smell of battle, Eddington was discontented. He wanted to grapple with the foe. He simply couldn't remain in what he considered the tactician's craven posture. It cramped and physically hurt him. Watching the chief of staff, Mac wondered how Torrey, for all his own unshakable composure, was able to control this foreboding man who always seemed so perilously close to the bursting point.

Owynn glanced up from his toenails. His face was very red. "If Operation Rathole fails, you're apt to get your wish, captain. Maybe you'd better keep a BAR handy."

"When that happens you'd better start running home to Papa Broderick. I've seen what Nips do to lard-assed captives who happen to look important. And it ain't pretty, mister!"

Owynn squirmed uncomfortably, but he ignored the thrust.

"It does seem to me," he said more mildly, "that Admiral Broderick ought to be informed about your plans. After all, he's still the area commander."

"Frig Broderick—in spades!" Eddington rubbed his groin reflectively. "Let him keep his goddamn meathooks off Mesquite. And I don't want to hear anybody passing The Word to him, either, until Rathole is at least six hours underway."

The Senator felt Eddington's hot gaze boring between his fat shoulders, like a stiletto, as he returned to his pedicure. He also felt cornered. This was one hell of a lot different from matching wits with the boys on Capitol Hill. The chief of staff held all the aces. *And what was the bastard saying now?*

". . . If Toulebonne tries to stymie Rathole we'll know goddamn well somebody squealed to Blackjack. And believe me, commander, I'll find out who it is—and once I get my hands on him you can bet your toga he'll take such a beating they won't know *where* to pin his Purple Heart!" After this oblique threat of mayhem, Eddington appeared content to drop the matter. "Now let's change the subject to something we can all fight about."

Egan Powell hadn't been asleep. He pried up one corner of his ridiculous burglar's mask.

"Such as women?"

"That ought to do it."

"Any particular dame, *mon capitaine*?"

"Well," Eddington rumbled, "there was this plump quail out at MOB Able this morning, who's got the juiciest pair of tits I've seen on a broad in years . . ."

He stopped. Why in Christ's name had he said that? It wasn't

fouled up with an Air Force major. She was killed during the Blitz with her loverboy. After that the poor devil went sort of berserk, I guess, and never really recovered."

Annalee's babyvoice quickened with new interest. "You must have seen an awful lot of the Big Boss back at Pearl—to get him to spill secrets like that."

At first Maggie's only response was a sigh. Then she said, "Not as much as I wanted. And remember, he was only a captain then, which is a damned far piece from being a two-star admiral. Even back there."

"Do you love him?"

As if she hadn't heard the unsophisticated question, Maggie murmured, "Oh, we had a lovely time 'way long ago at Pearl. Just too utterly wonderfully lovely . . ." Her voice faded.

"Are you crying?" Annalee asked, suspiciously.

"Hell, no! I'm just gasping for air under this goddamn oxygen tent."

"Yes," her interrogator decided, "you're in love."

"All right . . . so the Old Lady's in love . . . and if you ever so much as breathe a word about this to the other kids, baby, I'll break every bone in your cute little body, starting with your curly head."

Annalee was horrified. "Me spill something like this—about you and the *admiral*? Never!"

"Okay."

"But I've still got *my* problem, Mag."

"Such as?"

"On account of I'm nothing but an ensign and Captain Eddington's a captain, what do I do if he asks me for a date?"

"Tell him you're afraid of Jap snipers."

"No, seriously, Mag."

"Have Jere Torrey buy you a chastity belt."

"Jeepers!" Annalee sounded hurt. "That's a terrible thing to say. You know I love Jere. We're going to get married, too."

"Did he tell you so?"

Annalee whispered proudly, "I'm wearing his ring—the one with his family crest on it."

"The Torrey crest?"

"Heck, no. His mother's family, Cunliffe."

"Oh, great! Chalk up another reason why you'd better scratch

Paul Eddington off your list, baby. He's especially bad medicine for engaged damsels."

"I'm not going to *bed* with him!"

"Nobody ever thinks she's going to bed with anybody." Maggie emitted a brutal laugh. "Ever hear of the young lady from Niger?"

"No."

"Your education's been sadly neglected, honeylamb. Let me recite it for you:

"There was a young lady from Niger
Who rode on the back of a tiger.
After the ride
She wound up inside,
With her smile on the face of the tiger."

Annalee protested softly, "But I don't get it at all!"

"You'll get it all right," Maggie said forebodingly, "if you start playing around with a four-striped tiger like Eddington. Hell. Miss Niger didn't figure on the beast gobbling her up, either, but he did. Poof! Just like that!"

In the tone she generally reserved for declining a second helping of dessert, Annalee said, "I guess we needn't worry very much anyhow. Not on this stinking island. Whoever gets time for any fun around here?"

"Look," Maggie snapped, "one of these days there'll be a real lull, and when that happens all I can say is 'Heaven help the working girl.'"

"But—"

"Go to sleep, Ensign Dorne!"

Reluctantly, Annalee turned her back, feigning slumber. Maggie lay very still in the fetid darkness, listening to the noises that came out of the night. Sinister scurryings around the base of the Quonset which might have been those monstrous tree rats foraging for food, or worse. Damned native dog barking at the half-hidden moon. Giant crickets thrumming. Brokenhearted weeping of the night-birds. Palmfronds rustling like the rubbing together of an old crone's dryskinned hands. And faraway the guttural roar of the night patrol taking off, low-pitched and rumbling, and making a melancholy sound that reminded her of something she'd read years ago when she was a little girl: the Catskill-echoing thunder of the Little Men's bowling balls that Rip Van Winkle heard before he fell into his long, long sleep . . .

Mesquite was a madhouse.

For forty-eight hours, two-sevenths of the inadequate week which Torrey had allotted them to prepare for the assault against the Japanese, his tightknit GHQ became the focal point of every unit commander in the American zone. All of them wanted to see The Rock personally, to hear his evaluation of the adventure, and to be encouraged in their own integral efforts. Most of them, however, had to settle for a few hours inside the heatshimmering Operations shack where Eddington played host in such astringent fashion. They'd rush into the hut, mull over their part of the overall plan, and then race back to their stations to prepare detailed planlets with their own subordinates. These breakdowns were called *annexes.*

Commander Clayton Canfil set up shop in a tent alongside Operations. Despite his relative lack of rank, he was listened to quietly, and with vast respect, by the two Marine colonels who would lead the overland marchers.

He was particularly esteemed for his ability to deal with the stalwart Melanesians whose knowledge of the tangled Gavabutu backcountry could provide the margin between success and failure when the little force clawed its way across the Luma Mountains. Loinclothed, copperhued, with teeth stained the color of ancient dried blood from chewing betelnut, they crowded under the steaming canvas shelter to exchange information with Canfil in pidgin. Despite his weariness, the dour old island trader lost his patience only once when, irritated by the jostling throng, he snarled at an insistent native, "Skin b'long you 'e stink finish. Call 'im how much time you lose along you wash-wash?" The native showed his evil teeth in a Gargantuan grin and ducked out into the rain for a quick shower. When he returned, Canfil said he smelled a little better, but he'd better stand well back.

Egan Powell, contentedly pinchhitting as Canfil's assistant, solemnly jotted down everything that was said.

Divorce, in pidgin, was "take away mary finish," and he deemed this especially fascinating. It would be a useful phrase in Hollywood, Powell said, because it was even simpler than the perfunctory divorce ritual he'd learned in Tijuana when he shed his second wife.

The promise of a uniform of sorts, a little money (that was considerably more generous than the pittance the British had paid their plantation hands), and the assurance of towering stature among their tribes acted like a magnet for the natives. Before the third nightfall, Canfil had recruited a company of more than one hundred of them to march with his troops, and set up an underground between Atoka and the Jap perimeter upon which he could rely for information.

When Powell wondered about how he would get this intelligence back from those remote areas, Canfil glowered at his ignorance.

"Thought you wrote movie scripts," he grunted. "What's that line you're always usin'? 'The natives are restless tonight.' Some wavyhaired actor in an Abercrombie Fitch bush get-up generally says it to a blonde in a sarong about the time the drums start beating. That's exactly how we do it, Powell. With drums. Surprisin' that Hollywood was so accurate, eh?"

Egan Powell admitted the anomaly. "But can you trust these gooks?"

"Damn right," Canfil said, "if you treat 'em like human beings —and don't call 'em gooks. That was Balder's trouble. Also the Japs'. Balder wouldn't let me use these fellas. He always felt the less truck we had with 'em the better, and since they were dirty and smelly he figured they were also unreliable. That's a fairly common mistake. Meanwhile the Nips were ordering any stray natives shot on sight. Word gets around. We didn't pick up much information, but the Japs still have to travel in pairs like Bowery cops to keep from getting killed."

Canfil's tomtom network brought Word that the enemy was preparing to evacuate the northern half of the island, even before Mesquite's aerial recon spotted the first outwardbound barges. The Nips were burning their supplies, the drums said, and striking camp.

Torrey received the news calmly. "Good. Glad to hear it." He gave Canfil a speculative glance. "But why in hell have they suddenly decided to pull up stakes, commander?"

"Because they've got a damn sight worse attrition problem than ours, admiral. Malaria. Dengue. Jungle rot in general. And they've been having the devil's own time fetching in medical stores. Especially quinine. Our subs have just about wiped out their cinchona bark trade."

The Rock stroked his darkstubbled chin and was silent for a moment, while Canfil watched him anxiously. It would, Torrey knew, be easy just to let the Japs slip away, quietly and bloodlessly, and accept undeserved credit for "routing" them after his predecessor had failed. Hell. It could even start a legend: Enter Torrey, exit enemy. Fearsome reputations had been built on less. But this didn't appeal to him. If the Nips were in a mood to quit, they probably weren't in a mood to fight. Moreover, those who escaped scotfree now would oppose them later at Levu-Vana, healthier, stronger, and a hell of a lot more combative.

Then there was always the possibility that they'd somehow gotten wind of Operation Skyhook itself, owing to the obsessive interest taken in the northern island recently by ADTAC's long-range air patrols, and that they were already sending in reinforcements. He had hoped this next move—the vault across Gavabutu to Levu-Vana—would be too logical for them to accept. Surely they would be looking for something more spectacular, considering their own deviousness, or at least more startling, like an end run around a whole complex of Jap-held islands.

The Rock stopped musing. In a conversational tone he said to Canfil, "All right, commander, let's give 'em a farewell shove."

Both the Intelligence officer and Eddington looked so foolishly pleased by this quiet decision that it occurred to Torrey they'd expected him to adopt the simpler course, and allow the Japs to evacuate without a struggle.

"Same timetable?" Eddington asked.

"No, Paul. With the weather outlook so damned negative, I want to take advantage of this break. Every day saved bolsters our chances for Skyhook. We'll roll on Tuesday."

The chief of staff wagged his head, hesitated, then produced a dispatch flimsy from his breast pocket.

"You'd better take a look at this, skipper."

Torrey took the message. It was Toulebonne's 190925L. In the Navy's alphabetese, the "L" stood for *Love,* which in turn indicated the area's time zone: twelve hours removed from Greenwich Observatory's "A" for *Able*. This perverse symbol—*Love*—had always amused him.

"CANNOT URGE TOO STRONGLY," Admiral Broderick had radioed, "YOUR ADHERENCE TO ORIGINAL SCHEDULE DESPITE RUMORED ENEMY EVACUATION OF NORTHEAST MESQUITE. ANY PREMATURE ACCELERATION OF CAREFULLY DRAWN PROGRAM MAY JEOPARDIZE ENTIRE FUTURE OPERATION BY CAUSING JAPS TO REACT IN OVERWHELMING FORCE. REQUEST YOU ADVISE HEADQUARTERS IMMEDIATELY WHETHER YOU PROPOSE SUBSTANTIAL CHANGES IN ORIGINAL CONCEPT."

Despite the weasel phrases, so typical of Blackjack's unwillingness to grasp a problem, or issue an unequivocal order, his meaning was plain enough. It was apparent that Toulebonne had started to fret seriously about what was happening on Gavabutu. Broderick was playing the old Navy game: obliquely warning a subordinate that anything that goes wrong will be his own responsibility, particularly after the boss had defined the pitfalls.

Torrey wondered how much Blackjack actually knew, and by what osmosis Toulebonne had picked up that knowledge.

One thing was certain. There hadn't been the slightest hint about Rathole in any official dispatches from ADTAC, and there wouldn't be until the expedition was well underway. Later, by stretching a few points, he could defend his unorthodox action as coming within the "original concept" of Mesquite, which was to crush the enemy and secure the island. According to the Service's unyielding code, however, he was 180 degrees off course. Only success could save him.

Torrey put aside the dispatch.

"No—my order still stands." He thought a moment. "Tell Gottlieb I want him. On the double. With all his charts."

In less than ten minutes, puffing and sweating, the aerologist arrived in the hut with an armful of rolled maps. He spread them over the converted messtable rather proudly, as if he, too, believed the headquarters myth that rain or shine, it was indeed "Gottlieb's weather." His broad Teutonic face was solemn.

"What's the verdict?" Torrey asked abruptly.

Gottlieb would have preferred to deliver a lecture. In fact, he was quite prepared to expound upon the vagaries of forecasting in the

South Pacific, the dearth of information out of the weather-cradling northeast where the Japs still roamed unmolested, and the inordinate amount of guesswork that went into his twice-daily reports because of this gap. Moreover, August was a miserably unpredictable month. It might bring thirty inches of rain, turning the skies into an element almost as watery as the ocean itself, and curtailing most normal human pursuits. The summer sou'easters had gone; the season of sudden nor'easters was near, bringing with them vast winds that didn't quite measure up to hurricane velocity, but which were damned destructive to anybody caught unprepared on the high seas or trapped on a narrow beachhead.

It distressed Gottlieb's well-ordered soul that he must now reduce all his lore to a few phrases. But the new admiral didn't seem in a mood for talk, and he instinctively knew better than to test Torrey's temper.

"The weather, sir, is going to be lousy starting Monday."

"Three more days."

"It could even worsen by Sunday night," Gottlieb added gloomily, "although we can't tell for sure. There's been no Word from our sub patrols off Pelaki for a couple of days and—"

"Yes, I know." The Rock's impatience bobbed dangerously close to the surface. "We've all got our troubles, commander."

"I do my best."

"Of course." Torrey relaxed a fraction. "And with damned insufficient tools, too. But there's so much riding on our *best* analysis of what little data we've got, Max, that I want to be sure you're sure. That's all."

"I'm sure, sir."

"Now be specific."

"We're expecting a build-up of this stormfront, admiral, that'll bring high winds and heavy rains for a protracted period. Maybe a week. Enough, anyhow, to make you think this Quonset is a submarine before it's over."

"Reckon we're safe through Sunday?"

"Yes, sir."

"Very well." The Rock went to his humidor and filled his bulldog briar. "We'll launch Rathole at first light Sunday. That'll give us fourteen hours before the front closes in. With luck and a hell of a lot of hard slugging, I think our fellows can cut it. After that we'll all be in the same boat—Japs included—and what's impossible for us because of the weather will be just as impossible for them."

"I'll give you a final estimate at 0700, sir."

Torrey studied his watch. "Better make it 0600, Max. We'll have to notify all hands about this schedule change before noon. Even that's damned short notice, considering what they've got to do to make ready."

"Yes, sir."

As the aerologist gathered up his charts, he found himself genuinely worried about Gottlieb's weather for the first time in months, and wishing he were Jehovah instead of a mere three-striper with a Master's degree in meteorology from M.I.T. Nobody used to be much concerned about flaws in his prognosis at Mesquite, because Neville Balder had proceeded on the comfortable theory that when there was any doubt, don't; and he always postponed action whenever Gottlieb suggested the likelihood of heavy seas or wet grounds. But this man Torrey was a different breed of cat. He made you put up or shut up. Gottlieb wasn't certain whether he should be pleased with The Rock's faith in his qualified judgment, or downright alarmed.

Paul Eddington was delighted at the speed-up.

"This," he pronounced happily, "is how to fight a war. Hit the bastards when they don't expect it—when they figure you're too frigging scared to move."

Torrey said nothing. Eddington's blithe way of oversimplifying complex situations annoyed him, but he let it pass. Once Rathole began, this singlemindedness would be useful, for the chief of staff would then seize upon each emergency as it arose, judge it with split-second clarity, and have his response ready long before a more deliberative man had weighed all the pros and cons. There was no hypothesis about Eddington. Everything was certain, positive, inevitable as the shellburst that follows gunfire.

When Gottlieb fetched his 0600 weather summary, he disclosed that an American sub had reported heavy rainsqualls, accompanied by near-gale conditions, which bolstered his previous gloomy forecast.

The Rock scrutinized the isobar whorls and inkfresh ciphers on the aerologist's map, feeling again the solitariness that comes to commanders who cannot appeal elsewhere for help.

Laconically, with no outward hint of emotion, he said, "Pass the signal to execute, Paul."

Eddington raced for the door.

Within a half-hour The Word was flashed. Tentative orders which had been pondered most of the night by Rathole's scattered components were suddenly translated into furious activity. And after that nothing could have halted their forward surge, because now they were like hurled javelins, arching in trajectory toward the enemy, never to be recalled . . .

The brisk young Navy chaplain did offer one small codicil to the surging inevitability of the moment: affairs now lay in the hands of the Lord Almighty. Somberly, but with confidence, the padre blessed the impending flight across the Luma hump, while Dan Gregory's paratroopers stood around their fleet of C-47s in deceptively negligent postures, awaiting the colonel's embarkation whistle.

Casting secrecy aside, compelled to march night and day under the revamped timetable, Canfil's battalion had left forty-eight hours earlier. The amphibious force had been at sea almost as long.

In the mystic darkness just before first light, which was always blacker than the rest of the night, Torrey listened to the chaplain. He had come with McConnel to bid Gregory's men a personal goodbye on their hazardous journey, but now he wondered whether the chaplain would leave anything unsaid. With a kind of irreverent irrelevance, too, he considered this paradox of prayers before the battle, wherein both sides implore divine assistance, each taking equal comfort from the thought that its private deity will confound the hated adversary's.

It was growing brighter when the padre finished.

Torrey stepped across the tarmac to the lead plane under whose wing the diminutive colonel stood, stamping his bulky paratrooper's boots impatiently, and eager to take off.

"Good luck!"

The Rock was startled by the booming falseheartiness of his own voice, which seemed accentuated by the hour and the dank atmosphere. But Dan Gregory hadn't noticed.

"Thanks, sir," he said simply.

"I wish I were going with you."

Gregory grinned. "Hell, admiral, there's plenty of room!"

"Not for joyriders, colonel."

"You wouldn't be a joyrider, sir. Believe me. Just let me tell these jokers you're coming along—observing—and they'll give a yell that'll raise the roof on the Mikado's goddamn palace!"

The Rock regarded the Marine sharply to see whether he was serious. Gregory meant it. His boyish grin was gone, now, and his eyes gleamed at the notion of taking the Big Boss over the battlefield. It would be, Torrey thought, damned unorthodox. The Book was especially forthright on this score: highranking officers privy to supersecret information mustn't make whimsical tours over enemy terrain, because they might wind up captured. Even admirals, it was presumed, weren't impervious to skillfully applied torture. But occasionally some Big Brass ignored the Book. Halsey was forever going up the line to powwow with his combat commanders, prodding them into action, and getting the physical feel of territory that always looks so deceitfully well-ordered when viewed on a chart.

Even one quick aerial glimpse of the contested area, Torrey knew, might give him an immeasurable tactical advantage if he had to change his plans abruptly—committing more men, shifting his attack points, or pulling his forces out entirely.

Suddenly the idea of accompanying Dan Gregory didn't seem like bravado at all. It made a lot of sense.

"Very well, colonel, you've got yourself a nonpaying passenger. But let's forget the morale angle. I'm coming along incognito."

At Torrey's elbow, Mac made a sound that was at once expostulatory and respectful. "But sir—"

"After I leave," The Rock said serenely, "get Captain Eddington on the combat phone and tell him I'm taking a firsthand look down the Rathole." He took pity on his horrified aide. "Also tell him it's a round trip. I'm not jumping."

"Aye, aye, sir."

Mac saluted forlornly and stepped back as the propellers started to windmill.

Torrey followed Gregory into the belly of the twin-engined plane. After them filed twenty-four Marine jumpers. The big doubledoors closed soundlessly. And then the lead transport began to roll slowly down the long strip, lurching occasionally as its wheels sank into badly repaired bomb craters, until it reached the far end of the runway.

Mac waved as the C-47 thundered overhead. "So long, you wonderful crazy bastard!" he shouted into the emptiness of the spectral morning.

14. *Be Kind to Your Webfooted Friends*

In clumsy wildgoose formation, the sixteen duncolored aircraft swung sharply away from the Gavabutu coast and pointed southwestward, in the opposite direction from their target, which lay a scant thirty miles across the eight-thousand-foot Luma Range.

Thinly escorted by twenty fighters, Colonel Dan Gregory's small armada would then make a wide feinting turn designed to fetch them over the drop point between Botan and Torion on the island's undulating north coast, about an hour before Clayton Canfil's raiders burst out of the uplands jungles and the amphibious troops stormed ashore at Beach Red.

Swaddled in a Marine corporal's olive-drab fieldjacket that effectively concealed his stars, and with his lean body jackknifed upon the tiny shelf of the navigator's jumpseat, Torrey sat very quietly, watching the formation take shape. This was Gregory's show. Despite his rank he was merely an "observer," a polite Service word for authorized kibitzer, and to the paratroopers clustered aft on their bucketseats, he was just one of the colonel's nosyparker buddies, the kind that was forever cadging a "ride up to the front" for a vicarious moment of combat excitement; and if anybody was to ask them, a guy needed a headful of rocks to pull a dumb friggin' stunt like this, anyhow, when he could be safely back at base lapping up a cold beer at some plushlined O.C.

For himself, The Rock again marveled at the ease with which rank lifted a man above the necessity of *requesting,* or once having attained his wants, of even thanking the donor, unless he were of a mind to display his imperial appreciation. Yet the power inherent in his two-stars sobered him. He'd known some officers to whom power became an end desirable in itself, as they rose in rank, rather than remaining a useful tool that could work miracles when properly wielded. Blackjack Broderick was one of these. For such men there seemed to be a kind of diabolical fun in power: to be able to flick the wrist, cock the eye, crook the finger, nod the head, or shrug the shoulder—while your subordinates hunted desperately for the occult meaning behind those fleeting gestures. Military power is the absolute power which even money can't buy. It's denied to politicians, when you get right down to it, unless you rate the President a politician—and his supreme authority comes only in wartime when he's Commander in Chief of all the Armed Forces, and therefore a military man himself . . .

Gavabutu was fading into the early haze, beautifully, the way war-locked tropical islands always fade when you're leaving them, and its barrier reef shone bluegreen and amber where the sea lapped against the live coral. A few toylike surface craft scrawled precise little white V's on the deeper amethyst waters beyond the encircling shoals. From five thousand feet—Gregory's C-47s were still climbing—Gavabutu was a thicknapped green carpet. But when he looked closer, spiky treetops probed through the rain-forest mat, and Torrey found himself wondering how in hell a two-legged man could penetrate this tangled morass.

Clay Canfil had said he knew how to whip this jungle. The Rock hoped so. But he would have to be the most extraordinary sort of Pied Piper to lead fifteen hundred raiders through this steamy labyrinth, and thence across the treacherous Luma defile. For all their rugged commando training back home, these were still youngsters, practically unblooded after four stalled months on Gavabutu.

Torrey glanced back toward the cabin where Gregory and his shocktroops sat impassively, stolidly, apparently lost in thoughts which neither uplifted nor depressed them, oblivious to the empty world rushing past their crowded cylinder like a loud windy dream.

He got to his feet, flexed stiffened leg muscles, and made his way aft.

When he touched Gregory lightly on one harnessed shoulder, the Marine colonel awoke with a shudder, arms outstretched, as if prepared to lunge at an enemy. But he relaxed as he saw The Rock's longjawed face close to his.

"Jumpers," Gregory apologized, "get jumpy around bail-out time."

"Your fellows don't look jumpy to me, Dan. Not half as jumpy as I feel myself."

"But they are. And they'll stay jumpy till we're clear of the plane. After that—well, I wouldn't swap these two dozen guys for a cageful of starved panthers." Gregory reached into a pocket and took out a gnawed square of cutplug. "We can't smoke at night," he explained, biting, "so most of us chew."

"Tobacco does help sometimes," The Rock agreed. "I'm a pipeman, myself."

The Marine colonel glanced at his preoccupied squad. "Now that we're damned near there, admiral, don't you suppose you could take off your disguise and say a couple of words to these kids?"

Torrey's first inclination was to refuse. He felt at ease in his anonymity, and he recalled with a small pang of discomfort his previous attempts at morale-boosting, belowdecks on *Old Swayback,* with the dispirited officers of Mesquite, and before the twittering nurses at MOB Able. Gregory's youngsters impressed him as authentic hero material who didn't need any backslapping. In fact, they would probably resent any intrusion upon their private thoughts at this particular moment by some two-starred bore to whom they'd have to listen out of sheer disciplined politeness.

But there was also Dan Gregory to consider. He'd lived more intimately with his men—his comrades in long-chance missions—than most other field grade officers. Presumably he knew what they wanted.

"All right," Torrey said. "Introduce me to your Mafia."

Gregory rose to his full five-foot-five and blew a whistle to gain the paratroopers' attention above the roar of the twin engines. They looked up, automatically checked their watches, noted that it wasn't zero hour yet, then turned mildly curious faces toward their colonel and the lanky stranger who towered above him.

"Fellows," he yelled through cupped hands, "I've got a surprise for you. Maybe you think this is Corporal Shapiro, because he's got Moe's name stenciled on his jacket. It's not. And he isn't Sergeant Brule, even though Steve lent him his cap." Gregory paused, a tight grin on his sunburnt face, before he added proudly, "Meet Admiral Torrey—who's responsible for getting us into the air again!"

Like an emcee satisfied with his night's work, he dropped back into his bucketseat. He was right. His men cheered their frigging heads off.

"Thanks." The Rock acknowledged their greeting with a touch of embarrassment. "I'm afraid Colonel Gregory's right. This little affair was my idea. But"—he regarded them intently—"if any of you men are asking yourselves, 'Is this trip necessary?' the answer is *yes.*"

This reference to civilian travel warnings drew a brief laugh.

"As far as I'm concerned, though, my chief of staff will probably cut my *cojones* off—that's a favorite expression of his—for joyriding with you Marines." Torrey frowned. "Actually, I'm not in favor of Big Brass junkets, either, because they take up cargo space that might be used a hell of a lot more profitably in other ways. But today's is a short hop. We've got no fuel problems. And, frankly, I've become damned unsatisfied with trying to calculate the situation from charts tacked to my Quonset bulkhead." He studied the unreeling topography through a nearby window. "Maybe what I learn this morning will help all of us next time . . ."

"You jumpin' with us, sir?"

Torrey smiled at the young paratrooper who had dared ask this bold question, and shook his head. "That, son, takes your kind of training. Even admirals can't compete with you experts." Suddenly solemn, he concluded, "Now, although your chaplain's said just about everything there is to say, I'll wish you fellows God's luck . . . and happy landings."

The flak started just west of the Japs' perimeter outside the ruined village of Torion, quavering up at them, black and ugly, like bursting toadstools. A pair of near-misses staggered Gregory's plane, but the C-47 shook its brown wings and kept doggedly on course for its target run. Torrey scanned the airspace below and alongside them, figuring that by now the Zeros ought to have jumped the formation. This was a damned ticklish moment. For all their resourcefulness, twenty Yank fighters would be a poor match against the sixty-odd Zeros that Intelligence had last reported at Botan airfield.

The Rock supposed that what he felt was Fear. Clotted deep

and hard and glacial in his belly, it wasn't a pleasant sensation, and it was a different sort of fear than he'd experienced that first night at Mesquite, or much earlier when *Old Swayback* was torpedoed. He tried to taste Fear as a connoisseur might sample rare wine, to determine why this kind was worse than others. Then he knew. Without even the hard heft of the plane's controls to sustain him, he was suspended aloft in an element that was far more unnatural than the quietly murderous jungle or the sea itself, as a mere weaponless spectator. He watched the paratroopers fondle their BARs, and for a claustrophobic instant he wished he were jumping with them, so he could change a coldly impersonal war into a hotly private affair between himself and the enemy. Paul Eddington had this same urge to charge the foe with his naked fists. But there was a vast difference, Torrey knew, between his own momentary combatant impulse and what the chief of staff felt. He was certain that Eddington had never really known physical fear.

Resolutely, he turned his full attention to the immediate situation.

The kunai-grass plain lay almost below them now. It looked terribly small and difficult to hit. Gregory was standing by the wide-open hatch with his hand poised for the bail-out signal, and the Marines had given their webbed harnesses a last loving adjustment.

It was zero minus one minute.

As a sudden atavistic inspiration seized him, Torrey thrust his right thumb against his hawklike nose, wagging a derisive greeting to the unseen Japs two thousand feet below. The grotesque gesture made him feel better. Although the chilly lump remained in his belly, at least fear hadn't degenerated into cowardice.

The jumpers looked at each other. The admiral was, you had to admit, pretty goddamn gung ho for a brass-friggin'-hat.

Later nobody would ever be able to convince Gregory's paratroopers that Admiral Torrey's presence hadn't scared the bejesus out of the Nips and sent them hightailing for the tall timbers. Sure. Everyone knew that Little Dan himself was shot-in-the-ass with good fortune. It was fairly reasonable to expect they'd come out of this brannigan more or less in one piece, barring the loss of a few unlucky bastards whose numbers were up anyhow. But even Gregory's luck wouldn't account for the fact that only a few score of bewildered slanties greeted them when they hit the deck . . .

Alone in the reverberating cabin of the C-47, which had promptly scuttled back to five thousand feet, The Rock observed the small force establish its perimeter defenses, and then start fanning out toward the edge of the jungle. In a few minutes even the ack-ack was silenced as the Marines had rushed the emplacements, only to find them undefended except for their skeleton guncrews. But the Jap gunners had little stomach for a last-ditch struggle now that their comrades had fled.

Torrey's wrist watch showed barely 0800, a full forty-five minutes before Canfil's raiders were due. He went into the cockpit.

"Is your TBS working?" he asked the pilot.

"Yes, sir."

"Contact our fighter cover," Torrey said, "and tell 'em I want two planes assigned to us. Corsairs. The rest can shepherd the formation home."

His eyes widening in surprise, the pilot looked up and nodded. "What'll I say about us, admiral?"

"You can inform the major we're staying around for a while to see how the ground troops make out." The Rock crowded against the pilot's flopeared Air Force cap for a better view of the terrain through the forward windshield.

They were passing over the empty airstrip, now, and its adjacent livingspaces gave unmistakable evidence of a hasty evacuation. Even from this altitude littered fuel tins and bombcasings were visible, as if the Japs had started loading them on trucks for the short haul down to the waterfront, and then had thrown up their hands and decided the hell with 'em.

The Rock indicated a point on the pilot's Gavabutu chart where two trails crossed.

"Head there, skipper."

"Check, sir."

To the co-pilot, Torrey said, "Why don't you let the Old Man take your seat so he can get in a little air time, fella, otherwise they mightn't honor my flightskins this month."

The incredibly youthful second lieutenant scrambled out of the starboard chair, noting for the first time the admiral's gold Navy wings when he doffed his jacket because of the cabin's rapidly mounting heat.

"Want the stick, sir?"

"Thanks."

The C-47 felt vast and unfamiliar in his hands, and Torrey found himself fighting the controls until his long-neglected airmanship returned. After that it was easy, even effortless, to guide the fifteen-ton craft toward the almost invisible notch at the edge of the upland jungle where Canfil's marchers were scheduled to appear. Arriving there, he nosed the transport down sharply, until it was close to treetop level, and throttled back far as he dared. The plane eased to a bumbling hundred knots while he strove for a glimpse of the fronded mountain trail.

He spotted it at the very instant Canfil's column reached the last clearing before the route debouched onto the kunai plain. From four hundred feet, the sweatshiny faces of the raiders loomed white in the morning sun, upturned in stark disbelief toward the low-flying aircraft. Torrey joggled his aileron controls and the C-47 seemed to beckon at the earthbound troops. Their mouths opened in a soundless cheer.

He turned to the pilot. "Got any supply chutes aboard, lieutenant?"

"Plenty, sir."

"Ask your sidekick to fetch me one. Then take over. I'm going to drop Canfil a message."

The Rock reached for the transport's flight log, found an empty page, inserted carbon, and began to write. "NIPS HAVE VAMOOSED. YOU'VE GOT A CLEAR TRACK AHEAD. CONTACT GREGORY ON THE DOUBLE THEN REPORT TO RED BEACH FOR CLEAN-UP DUTY. MY PLANE WILL RETURN TO JAP AIRFIELD AT 1000 TO TAKE COMMANDER CANFIL BACK TO BASE FOR PERSONAL REVIEW OF SITUATION." He paused and added: "WE MUST LIVE RIGHT! TORREY."

The message drop was perfect.

He saw the old Intelligence officer's stooped figure detach itself from the little knot of men near the head of the momentarily halted contingent, and trot toward the collapsed parachute, as the C-47 executed a final lazy circle overhead. Canfil read the note hurriedly. Then he waved a vigorous affirmative.

"Where now, sir?" the pilot inquired.

"Head for the barn, mister."

Torrey descended the spindly aluminum ladder, and walked across the coralsand apron toward the group of officers who obviously were awaiting his arrival in the shade of the Administration hut. Only Eddington and McConnel had greeted him at the bottom of the ramp.

"Glad you're back safely," Eddington grunted. "Hope you enjoyed yourself."

"Thanks, Paul. I did."

"That's goddamn good, then, because there's a little surprise package for you over by the Admin shack."

"Visitors?"

"Affirmative."

More to confirm his own dour suspicions than anything else, for he had already observed the three-star command plane parked in a revetment off the strip, Torrey asked: "Broderick?"

"It ain't," the chief of staff said impiously, "nobody else's butt."

"Who are the others—staff?"

"Christ, no!" Eddington spat into the dust. "Newspapermen. Brought 'em along to show how he's winning the frigging war."

"We've got our own correspondents," The Rock said mildly.

"Sure. But ours stay where the fighting is. These guys are Blackjack's personal claque. Reluctant goddamn headquarters dragons. The only risk they take is getting ink poison from handling too many communiqués."

"I see."

"Broderick arrived just about the time you were taking off, skipper, but I figured you wouldn't have turned that planeload of jumpers around for the Almighty Himself, so I didn't bother to send a message."

"Not even for CinCPAC," Torrey agreed. His deep voice was still gentle as he added, "I didn't miss a dispatch alerting us to the admiral's visit—did I, Paul?"

"No, sir. He didn't even knock. Just dropped in."

"Is he here because of Rathole?"

"Check."

"Have you briefed him?"

"Didn't have to. Blackjack seems to know all about our project."

"That's great!"

The Rock's voice had lost its controlled mildness, and when he reached the Admin hut he was blisteringly angry. But he kept a checkrein on himself as he gave Broderick's sweating hand a quick formal shake. "Glad you could find time to look over our shop, sir," he said with measured sarcasm.

Blackjack matched his irony. "Looks like I picked a rather busy day."

"They're all busy."

"It's good *you* can still find time for a joyride, Rock . . ."

For a moment Torrey choked back his fury at this gratuitous insult, which was doubly galling since it echoed his own initial response to Dan Gregory's invitation. Finally he said, "With a competent team like ours, admiral, there's not much you can do once you've pushed the button that starts the machinery."

Admiral Broderick smiled. He was not an unimpressive figure at first glance, until you inspected him more closely, and thereby discerned the redveined eyes and the nicotine-stained fingers which told of too much nervous drinking and smoking. He had a hearty voice. But it suggested the uncertain quality of a bass horn that had been manufactured to sell too cheaply. Although Broderick was taller than The Rock by a full inch, he actually seemed shorter. Possibly this odd illusion was psychological, or maybe it was due to Torrey's manner of standing ramrod straight, whereas Blackjack tended to slouch a bit, favoring his potbelly. Someone had once observed, "Jack Broderick has all the outward attributes of a hero, but deep inside he's nothing but a damned poor grade of cornmeal mush." Which just about summed it up.

"We have with us," he said meaningfully, "the press."

Torrey scowled. "So?"

Eagerly, as if he had the solution to a riddle that stumped them all, Owynn stepped forward from his modest place in the background. "I believe, sir, that these gentlemen would like to ask you a few questions about Operation Rathole."

"Is there anything they don't already know, Owynn?"

"Maybe I'm dense," the Senator said, flushing, "but I don't think I understand—"

Eddington cut in. "You'll understand pretty soon, mister, because I'm going to make it a point to educate you."

Bewildered by this exchange, Blackjack Broderick complained, "For Christ's sake, Rock, let's get up the hill to your digs. I need a cold beer so bad I can taste it. I've lost thirty pounds of sweat already." He added placatively: "Matter of fact, I lugged along a case of goddamn good Aussie schnapps just for you. Tasmanian bitters. Absolutely magnificent!"

Torrey ignored the overture.

"Admiral, I'm also in one hell of a hurry. But not for beer. If you'd care to join me in Operations, I'll run through our situation for your benefit . . . after I recheck the dispatches."

*"Re*check?" Broderick's voice wasn't conciliatory any more. It was downright nasty, betraying his desire to cut this maddeningly calm subordinate down to convenient trampling-on size. "I wasn't aware you'd stayed at the wheel long enough today to make even a preliminary estimate of the situation."

The Rock saw the correspondents nudge each other delightedly. After four months of cloying noncombativeness, they were enjoying this encounter between the two Flag officers, and they hoped something would explode.

"Gentlemen," he said gravely, "since you've requested a press conference, you'll get one. It's now 0945. Meet me in my personal quarters at 1100. Meanwhile, relax and enjoy our fine scenery, which you may find somewhat different from Toulebonne's."

As Blackjack limped into ADTAC Operations, tenderly massaging his jeep-bruised buttocks, his mood was fouler than ever. Torrey's composure baffled and infuriated him, and he was further incensed by the placid atmosphere of the Op shack itself. The half-dozen officers on duty greeted their three-star visitor respectfully, but without noticeable enthusiasm, as if these drop-ins were as commonplace as Gavabutu's rainfall. Then they returned to their charts and dispatches.

The Rock ambled across the dusty boardfloor to Captain Tuthill's desk, with Broderick tagging along behind him like some particularly large and unwanted stray dog.

"Have Gregory and Canfil joined forces, Tut?"

"Yes, sir."

"Where?"

"Right on the button!" Tuthill touched his dividers against the redcircled paradrop target. "Now they're both hightailing it for the beachhead—as you ordered this morning."

Broderick scowled his disbelief. "How'd you manage to issue orders when you weren't even on deck at zero hour?"

"I delivered them to the raiders," Torrey snapped, "personally."

"Before they left here three days ago?" Blackjack twisted the words into a sneer. "Wasn't that dangerous . . . premature . . . in case Colonel Gregory's jump aborted?"

"Gregory jumped at 0730, admiral. I gave my instructions to Canfil at 0840." Torrey tendered the carbon copy of the message he'd scrawled on the C-47's logbook. "Care to see a duplicate dispatch?"

"Damned unusual procedure for an operational commander to take over in the field," Broderick grunted.

"It's an unusual war, admiral."

Tuthill sought to change the touchy subject. "We estimate our ground teams will contact the amphibs at Beach Red in about thirty minutes. They're meeting minimum opposition."

"I know," Torrey said. "The Japs decamped last night—bag and baggage."

Broderick tried another gambit. "Where were your patrol forces, fella, while the Nips were hauling ass?"

"As you're well aware," The Rock said coldly, "Mesquite's 'patrol forces' consist of two overaged cruisers, eight destroyers, and a dozen PTs. Not a very formidable fleet. Last night they were busy escorting the amphibious team from Atoka to Beach Red."

"You should have asked for more ships."

"We did. Several times. But as my late revered Old Man used to say, it was like spitting into a gale. Very unsatisfactory." Torrey shrugged. "Now, if you'll excuse me, admiral, there are a hell of a lot of dirty dishes to be washed before our next meal."

He propped his bare elbows on the table and began to study the spread-out maps, chin in hand, while Tuthill and his lesser Operations officers stood by. Broderick lowered himself carefully into the hut's only swivel chair, a tiptilted wooden monstrosity with broken arms, and nursed his injured fundament in stony silence. His ego was also hurt. But the press conference would be held soon, and he guessed he could wait another half-hour to assert his godgiven three-star superiority.

War correspondents are a queer breed. Unimpressed at finding themselves at the nether limits of a wartorn world, they roar like lions, scrounge like packrats, plot like foxes, and frequently display the courage of Bengal tigers as they prowl in search of eyewitness stories. To some commanders they are a necessary evil, akin to childhood measles, which you must suffer in order to gain immunity from worse ailments, such as a visit from a Cabinet undersecretary demanding to know why the people's representatives have been getting such shabby treatment. Other commanders ignore them entirely, even barring them from the front, on the theory that the military should be allowed to fight their war in privacy and tell the civilians nothing until it's finished. Still others play upon the press like a cathedral pipe organ, and with the same sonorous effect, so that what comes out sounds like a *Gaudeamus Igitur* paean composed by and for the commander himself.

Blackjack fell into the third category.

Upon joining his command, a correspondent promptly learned to dateline his copy WITH ADMIRAL BRODERICK IN THE PACIFIC COMBAT ZONE, which not only evoked a splendid image of Blackjack striding a blazing quarterdeck, but gave the admiral himself a sense of being always in the thick of things. For a time this had been an illusory feeling; but now it seemed so authentic that he was inclined to believe it himself.

Neal Owynn managed to cut in before the first reportorial query. "You men know the groundrules. Same ones that govern Big Headquarters briefings at Toulebonne. Remember security. Nothing that gives aid or comfort to the enemy. And no improper questions about current operations."

Torrey's glare, aimed at the Senator, melted into a grin as he faced the correspondents who were seated in a semicircle around his desk.

"I've always held," he said, "that there aren't any 'improper questions' from anybody, including the press. Just improper replies from brasshats. Your job's asking. Mine's answering. So let me worry about the results. Shoot!"

Broderick stirred uneasily on his swivel chair against the wall.

What the devil ailed The Rock? Allowing these fellows to grab the ball could only lead to trouble. He'd been through all that. Give the bastards an inch and they'd take a mile. They were slick conniving s.o.b.'s who must be hauled constantly into line lest they start writing dangerous claptrap about "lush rear-area living" and "the forgotten enlisted man." It was only through the sternest repressive measures, disguised as paternalism, that Blackjack managed to achieve decent treatment from them. He was damned certain of that. And now here was Torrey, who'd been a mere three-striper when Broderick made admiral, hellbent on wrecking everything . . .

The Rock was solemnly repeating what sounded like a pretty banal question from a *Time* magazine man: "What kind of war from here on out?" He indicated the wallmap of the Pacific. "There's only one kind, sir, and that's a tough, fighting-every-inch-of-the-way war, until we get more men and more tools. Then we can start rolling. But not before."

"Bull Halsey predicts it'll end by New Year's Day," the AP man said.

"Did the admiral specify *which* year?"

Leaning back in his straight chair, arms akimbo, he smiled benignly at the polite laughter which greeted his modest sally. The interview went on. From the tenor of the questions, it was apparent that the correspondents had been thoroughly informed about Operation Rathole, with one salient exception: Blackjack had overlooked the little matter of who'd be responsible for its failure, or praiseworthy for its success, an omission which left Torrey in a heads-you-lose, tails-I-win dilemma. If he failed—you could almost see Blackjack's suety shoulders droop in eloquent impotence—well, longsuffering Admiral Broderick once again would have known the bitterness of making do with second-rate personnel.

The *Collier's* man had a complicated query: "Admiral Broderick has been telling us for weeks, now, that this area is the 'stepchild' of the war, because it's never been given enough ships, troops, or planes to mount the really big offensive that's needed to shake the Japs loose from their southern islands. I'm wondering, sir, how this squares with your own thinking—as the only tactical commander currently engaged in active combat operations?"

While the reporter was posing his lengthy question, Torrey lit his bulldog briar, astonished that Blackjack had revealed such private woes to his headquarters Boswells. Any honest answer to this loaded inquiry, he knew, was bound to offend his haughty superior.

At length, having gotten his pipe drawing smoothly, he observed, "Both Admiral Broderick and I believe that you must cut your cloth to fit the pattern."

This was a classically equivocal response, which would have to satisfy the *Collier's* man. It didn't.

"But what about Rathole?" the correspondent persisted. "This is a major push, isn't it? How did you manage without substantial reinforcements?"

Torrey said stiffly, "We utilized what was available. No more. No less. We're aware that Admiral Broderick has many commitments in an area as large as this one."

The United Press man elevated his hand. Torrey blew a smoke ring and nodded at him.

"Somebody told us you had your neck stuck out a mile."

From the rear of the Operations hut came Eddington's harsh stagewhisper: "Better make that five miles!"

The Rock's cold smile was lost in a scowl. "We may have extended ourselves beyond a normally 'safe' margin. But it worked. As far as Gavabutu is concerned, the Japanese are no longer a factor."

"What's next on the schedule, admiral?"

"That, sir, is a trade secret." Torrey looked significantly toward Blackjack, and added, "Unless higher authority chooses to brief you fellows on future strategy, too."

The Senator stepped into the diplomatic breach, coughing loudly to gain the correspondents' attention. "I'm sure that Admiral Broderick would like to take this first opportunity to commend Admiral Torrey for executing his orders with such diligence . . . and against such overwhelming odds."

Blackjack's face turned crimson. It was evident he didn't relish his Invisible Man role in the press conference.

"Let me handle the honors, Neal," he snapped. "I'm quite capable."

"Yes, sir," Owynn replied humbly.

Like a potentate surveying his supplicant masses, Broderick managed a benign simper. "When we conceived Rathole," he said, "we knew we were taking a long chance. But, gentlemen, isn't that the very nature of our profession? Accepting risks?" His simper became a grin, and he waved his right arm toward The Rock, grandly. "It's to Admiral Torrey's everlasting credit that he didn't hesitate when he was instructed to clean out the—hah!—rodents."

But Torrey hadn't caught Blackjack's imperious gesture. Instead, his attention was focused on the Quonset entrance, and the gnomelike figure in mottled jungle camouflage leaning against the doorjamb.

"Hello, commander," he said. "Welcome home."

Clayton Canfil, who had been watching the tableau with a look of undisguised scorn on his leathery face, replied, "Howdy, sir," in a flat, dry voice.

Torrey swung back to the newsmen.

"You'd better meet the fellow who genuinely deserves praise for Rathole. Commander Clayton Canfil—the man who led the raiders across the Luma Mountains."

The Intelligence chief touched his grizzled mustache in lieu of a formal salute. "It was damned nice of you to send your taxicab after me, admiral."

"These fellows are the Toulebonne headquarters press, Clay, and I'm sure they'd like a fill on what you've been doing. Especially," The Rock appended sardonically, "since they couldn't accompany you in person."

"It was like round-up time in Texas, sir. My gang and Dan Gregory's grasshoppers and the amphibs all hit the beach at damned near the same minute. Only the Nips were a pretty sick bunch of dogies."

"Splendid teamwork," Blackjack interjected. "Typical of our whole command."

Canfil's redrimmed eyes narrowed as he stared first at Broderick, then at the correspondents. "At the risk of being busted back to third mate on an inter-island schooner, I'm going to let you fellas in on something that's Top Secret . . ."

The reporters looked up.

"Rathole," he went on, "was conceived and executed by one man —Admiral Torrey—after a lot of other people had sat around moaning that it was impossible. It's his baby. Abso-goddamn-lutely his and nobody else's."

Visibly annoyed, Torrey growled, "You must excuse Commander Canfil's enthusiasm, gentlemen. He's been under quite a strain lately and it may have warped his judgment." He stood up. "Thanks for visiting Gavabutu. I'm sure your frontline representatives will provide you with the details as soon as we establish regular communications with the other side of the island."

There was a moment of strained silence in the Quonset after the correspondents departed, and then Blackjack guessed aloud that he'd better get washed up for chow.

"Through that partition," Torrey said, pointing, "you'll find a jugful of water and a basin. Primitive. But adequate, admiral."

The Rock waited until he heard splashing sounds from the next compartment before he motioned Eddington to his desk. "I've got a little chore for you, fella."

"Sir?"

"I want to know how Broderick caught wind of today's operation."

"I already know, skipper."

"How?"

"From a fat little senatorial bird named Owynn."

"Are you sure?"

"Positive. Son of a bitch sneaked an unauthorized guardmail letter to Toulebonne the night we conceived Rathole."

Torrey clenched his lean fist and stared at it thoughtfully. "See that Owynn is aboard Broderick's plane when it leaves Gavabutu, Paul."

"That," said the chief of staff, "will be a pleasure!"

Crotch-itch never killed anybody. But when this annoying jungle rash reaches the more private area of a man's anatomy, it tends to shorten his temper and make him jumpy as a singed cat. Captain Eddington had a galloping case of crotch-itch against which nothing, not even blue ointment, could prevail.

He was scratching his inflamed groin when he came upon Neal Owynn.

The Senator saw him heading across the staff compound, baleful eyes and purposeful, and he sensed immediately that all was not well with the truculent chief of staff. Never one to allow valor to stand in the way of discretion, Owynn started for the dignified shelter of the palmthatched Officers' Club, whereupon Eddington stopped scratching and quickened his own pace. From close range, premeditated murder was visible on his marred countenance.

When he spoke, his gravelly tone matched his homicidal expression. "Slow down a second, mister, I want to talk to you."

"I'm terribly busy, captain."

"Belay that—*wait!*" Eddington roared.

Ignominiously, the Senator cut and ran for it, past the O.C., down the rutted bank, through enlisted men's country, around the burlap-walled and evil-smelling latrines, and into the jungle beyond the ADTAC perimeter. Several times he stumbled against rotting coconuts, and twice he fell, soiling his impeccably tailored uniform on the slimy ground. Strange forest creepers snatched at his face. He lost his goldbraided cap. But like a fleshy two-legged tank, Owynn plunged on, with his implacable foe closing upon him, panting and cursing. Finally he found himself trapped in a cul-de-sac formed by a sheer rock wall, a forty-foot precipice, and a tangle of fallen logs. For an instant both men stood toe to toe at the trail's end, breathing hard, and oblivious to their weird surroundings.

Eddington said, "At least, by Christ, I can get my hands on *one* enemy . . . and I'm not so goddamn sure you aren't as bad as the frigging Nips."

"You wouldn't dare—" Owynn began.

But the chief of staff's vast right fist stopped him. It smashed into the Senator's mouth, breaking two front teeth, and snapping his head back like a balloon. Owynn collapsed on the dank ground, where he lay, bloodily sobbing.

"Stand up," Eddington snarled, "and pretend you're a man."

His wounded mouth agape, Owynn stared up at the chief of staff, terrified, but refused to speak.

Eddington regarded him contemptuously. "You've heard of total war?" he asked. "That's the kind I fight because that's the only kind that wins. But it also means total loyalty, mister, to the guys you're working with. We came down here with a job to do and by God we're going to do it. Neither you nor Blackjack Broderick nor anybody else is going to screw it up. Understand?"

For a trembling split second Eddington's fieldboot poised over the Senator for a kick. Owynn nodded desperate assent. The chief of staff relaxed.

"One more thing," he said. "You're leaving with Broderick. You can make up any goddamn excuse you want. But get to hell out!"

Owynn nodded again.

Then Eddington swung on his heel and strode back toward the distant base.

Cautiously, after making sure his assailant was gone, the Senator arose. Holding his handkerchief against his battered mouth, he started down the brushcovered trail, staggering blindly, and still weeping. But now that the terror had passed, they were angry tears, and his only thought was revenge. Navy regs were all on his side, by God! Striking a fellow officer was a heinous offense: yet he, Owynn, had judicially refrained from hitting back. So Eddington was wide open for a general court-martial. As Owynn's present patron and future protégé, Blackjack would see to that. Son of a bitch wouldn't have a goddamn leg to stand on.

By the time he reached ADTAC's boundary, however, certain doubts had begun to assail him. Suppose Eddington countercharged that he, Owynn, had disobeyed lawful orders in sending that letter to Admiral Broderick? It was preposterous, yet possible. As a once-passed-over commander who'd barely made captain by the grace of his own patron saint, Rock Torrey, Eddington had certainly given up any hope of making admiral. So what the hell would *he* care about a GCM? For Senator Neal Owynn, though, it was a far different matter. When peaceful politicking resumed after the war, even an acquittal might deter the ignorant electorate, who tended to go along with the sea-lawyer thesis that a GCM defendant "must be guilty or he wouldn't be here in the first place." Yes. It could be a nasty business. Worse than a senatorial inquisition of some foredoomed witness. Without counsel.

Perhaps cooler heads should prevail.

And maybe he'd best tell Blackjack that an overripe coconut had dropped from a tree and struck him in the mouth . . .

Egan Powell sipped his highball delicately. There were two lumps of ice in it, and this pleased his soul the way a good dinner at Prince Mike Romanoff's used to soothe his psychic aches. With his left hand, he was idly flipping the pages of a month-old fashion magazine sent him by a fading Hollywood queen who felt she'd better renew some old contacts, just as postwar insurance. Powell was in a mellow mood.

"Here's a hell of an item," he said, "about a rayon manufacturer who printed V for Victory in Morse code on two million yards of dress material. Only he got it all screwed up. It turned out dah-dit-dit-dit instead of dit-dit-dit-dah. B for Bictory."

Eddington, taking his usual naked siesta before he returned to the Op shack, snorted irrelevantly, "Or V for Vitch."

"You hate women, don't you, *mon capitaine?*"

"Only as people."

Clayton Canfil made a walrus noise that lifted his artilleryman's mustache. "Now that you've ruled out women as well as liquor, Paul, there isn't a hell of a lot left, is there?"

"Who's ruled out women?" Eddington demanded. "Powell asked a simple question. I gave him a simple answer. You've heard the saying, 'Love 'em and leave 'em,' haven't you? Well I just operate on the theory that you don't have to love 'em in the first place. Makes the leaving a hell of a lot easier, too."

Canfil took a swig of neat gin from the bottle he kept under his bunk, holding the liquor in his mouth while he fished in his breast pocket for a quinine capsule. He refused to take the Navy's newfangled atabrine tablets. Gin and quinine had always been the sovereign tropical remedy. He intended to stay with it.

Eddington twisted his shaven gargoyle head toward Egan Powell. "Read us some more from that floozy magazine," he commanded.

"My pleasure, sir . . . How about this? 'Cosmetics that shout, "The country *needs* your loveliness!"' Or face powder that 'hides war worries.' And by all that's Minsky—'Civilian nude' rayon hose for sexier legs!"

"Those homefront jokers are taking friggin' good care of the female trade," Eddington said dourly.

Powell nodded. "It's all summed up right here, Paul. 'Only the fair deserve the brave.'"

Eddington uttered a body-functional expletive. McConnel looked up from the clipboard on which he was penning a letter, and asked plaintively, "Sir, how can an innocent young boy write to his bride in this poolhall atmosphere?"

The chief of staff looked away. Mac grinned uncertainly. He

hadn't intended to stifle their afterdinner nonsense, and as usual he'd managed to stick his big fat foot right into his big fat mouth, because you didn't talk about brides when Eddington was around, any more than you lit matches in an ammo dump.

He resumed writing to Bev:

> . . . So now Gavabutu's a darned sight safer than the Golden Gate Bridge at rush hour. Starting tomorrow we'll have open-air movies, and the Supply Officer outdid himself by booking Turner, Grable, and Hayworth into ADTAC for our first showings. Sunday I'm going pompano fishing with Commander Canfil, that old island skipper I told you about in my last letter, out by the purple reef I also mentioned. Son of a gun uses a line that's finer than the thread you sewed your last *holakou* with. Canfil's the only man I've ever known who can smoke a pipe in a shower. He sticks it in his mouth upside down. He wants to sell us a "nice piece of bottomland" he knows about on an island up the way, for our second honeymoon.
>
> . . . But first we've got to recapture that next island, Bevheart, which is what we're starting to work on now. What the Boss has in mind will make Gavabutu seem like a skeet shoot by comparison, but it'll bring this g.d. war one aitch of a lot closer to an end, believe me. He's still a wonderful guy to work for, incidentally, with facets to his personality you'd never dream existed, just from looking at that rimrock phiz of his. During the Big Push yesterday, after he'd checked over the dispatches and barked out a few orders, he sat down in one corner of the Op shack and read an old *Life* magazine. You've never seen anybody appear so doggoned alone—or more as if he wanted to stay that way. Even Admiral Broderick who'd come up to "observe" the action didn't dare bust in on him then. Yet The Rock doesn't stand on a lot of r.h.i.p. First thing he did was get rid of a special one-holer which the former COMADTAC had made the Seabees dig for his private use, that even had two stars cut in the wooden door. Now he squats with us commonfolk.
>
> . . . I guess I mentioned last time that the chief of staff worries me a little. He acts like a guy who's got to be *doing* something every second or he'll explode. When he had to "stay home" during the last operation (the Boss pulled a quickie on all of us and went with the paratroopers) he damn near flipped his wig. Now he's tacked Halsey's favorite quote on the Operations bulkhead—"The Only Good Jap Is a Dead Jap"—and he read it out loud every

morning before breakfast just to work up an appetite. Eddington also has this dog I told you about. They growl at each other. Honest. Only the chief sounds a damsite worse than the mutt, which is more frog than dog, because he really means it.

. . . But enough psychoanalysis. Canfil helped me find something for your birthday, babygirl, that's indigenous to this everlovin' island. An elegant pearl shell. And I've also located a tame Seabee who's going to fashion it into a comb for your crazy red hair. So wear it in good health, darling, because one of these days I'm coming home and then I'll properly salute your anniversary by paddling your pretty little round fanny twenty-five times . . .

Mac put the letter away in his footlocker. He'd finish it tomorrow, before the mailplane left for Pearl Harbor.

Egan Powell was talking again. " 'Way back before Rathole, didn't we promise ourselves one hell of a wingding when the shooting stopped?"

"Beachparty," Eddington affirmed, "with dames."

"That's what I thought. As your hospitality chairman, I'm proud to report that it's all fixed. Food. Beer. Beautiful Technicolor beach."

"And dames?"

"And dames, *mon vieux*. For thee and for me and for junior over there."

"I'm scared of dames," Mac said. "Just let me crank the ice-cream freezer."

"Yours," Egan Powell assured him, "is a very harmless type. All teeth and feet. You'll hate her."

"That's different."

Eddington massaged his blackhaired belly with his right hand, gingerly, because his bruised knuckles still hurt. "Who'd you get for me, glamourboy?"

"Damsel you've been lusting after ever since we hit these delectable shores, old cock. Ensign Annalee Dorne."

Eddington gave his huge belly a final loving caress. "Well done, Captain Powell."

"One final word of caution. Lieutenant Haynes insists on chaperoning her harem."

"Doesn't trust officers-and-gentlemen?"

"Affirmative."

"I believe," Eddington said meditatively, "we'd better arrange a diversionary action for Lieutenant Haynes."

"Such as?"

"Convincing the Old Man he needs a spot of sunshine and seawater himself."

"He does look a little gray around the gills," Powell agreed. "But what if he won't buy our prescription?"

"He'll listen to Maggie Haynes," Eddington said, "especially when she issues him a personal invitation—giltedged on a palmleaf."

"Bravissimo!"

Mac sighed. For him, the beachparty shaped up as an unmitigated pain in the tokus, and a bore to boot. He wished Bev was six thousand miles closer. Here. She collected characters. She'd think it was a ball.

Outside it was raining again.

But this didn't seem to bother the ADTAC Marines, sloshing back to their tents after downing their beer rations, and bellowing at the top of their leatherlungs:

"Be kind to your webfooted friends—
For a duck may be somebody's mother!"

15. Season of Falling Stars

Refreshed by seven hours of uninterrupted sleep, Torrey awoke next morning with a thoroughly unscheduled sun shining full upon his upturned face. Max Gottlieb, he knew, would be chagrined. This looked like a damned fine day, one in which he could even forgive Blackjack Broderick's meddling, ignore the three-star admiral's inherent threat to his own security, and turn to the real mission he had been sent down here to accomplish: Operation Skyhook, the amphibious invasion of Levu-Vana, four hundred miles north-northwest as the bomber flies.

On his way to the officers' communal washroom, toothbrush and towel in hand, Torrey passed a half-dozen Marines in battle gear, clustered around something on the spongy turf just off the narrow path. At first he intended to squeeze past them, avoiding the formality of a salute, for he felt self-conscious in his old gray bathrobe which didn't quite cover his thin shanks. It was hardly a proper costume for an admiral at 0630 on a sunlit morning. Then a whim seized him and he quietly joined the small group, curious to see what could possibly compel such rapt attention on their return from seventy-two hours on the Luma trail.

A colony of white ants had subdued a huge green bottlefly, and were now engaged in dragging it toward their hillock. Despite the inequality of the contest, the winged insect retained a dying will to resist, for it lashed out feebly with its long legs; but each time it became quiet, apparently gathering strength for another kick, the attackers would converge upon it from all directions, as if under orders from some ant in command. Half of them pulled and the other half pushed. Slowly but inexorably the bottlefly edged closer to the anthill's traplike maw.

Fascinated, the combat-hardened Marines observed this struggle between a tired Gulliver and the relentless Lilliputians, their sympathies clearly with the graceful ants. The ugly green fly was the enemy. It had to be conquered. And since this was total war, the conquered thing also had to be destroyed.

Mankind's greater conflict stood still, briefly, while they watched this infinitesimal one.

Once, the ants seemed to tire of the fray, and drew back from the flailing bottlefly as it lurched groggily to its feet.

A Marine corporal groaned. "C'mon, you friggers! Papa's got six bucks ridin' on this fight!" He bent down.

"Lay off them goddamn ants!" The Marine standing next to the corporal sounded aggrieved. "Who d'you think you are—God Almighty?"

"They need a little goosing, is all."

"You touch them ants, Gabe, and I'll goose you so hard with this here M-1 it'll jar your friggin' teeth loose."

"Who're you for," the corporal demanded righteously, "ants or flies?"

"Ants, unless I've got six bucks says flies gonna win."

He spat a quid of juicy tobacco within an inch of the wavering bottlefly. The corporal named Gabe started to protest. But the ants, invigorated by the nicotine, suddenly swooped upon their prey and wouldn't let go. Its kicks subsided. For a moment the bottlefly clung to the steep sides of the anthill, and then it disappeared, dragged to its doom by still more ants waiting inside the tiny tunnel.

The Marines let out an exultant whoop.

"Gimme the six bucks," Gabe said.

"De-friggin'-lighted."

Gabe pocketed the money. "How come you bet on that goddamn meanlookin' bug, mac?"

"Gimme the right odds," the loser explained with a wise grin, "and I'll bet you the old Rock'd sing 'Mother Machree' in the noncom mess at high noon dressed in his skivvies."

As Torrey started to leave, very quietly, the Marines' preoccupation gave way to their customary awareness of things around them. Six hands flicked upward in frenzied salute as they recognized his gaunt bathrobed figure.

"You wouldn't win that bet, son," Torrey said gravely. "I've got a horrible voice. Never sing in public."

His enigmatic smile hidden from the flabbergasted Marines as he proceeded along the path, he wondered if the Japs ever paused in their own lethal occupations to watch ants fighting bottleflies. He doubted it. If they did, this might be a different war: more predictable, less savage. His smile faded. That was a stupid thought. What the hell sort of war *wasn't* savage?

When Torrey reached Operations after his solitary breakfast, he found Eddington deeply engrossed in the preliminaries of Skyhook with Captain Tuthill, Egan Powell, Commander Canfil, and Brigadier General Averell, who had jeeped over from the airfield to give a firsthand report on the airworthiness of his planes. Tuthill seemed more cadaverous and baggy-eyed than ever as he listened to the flyer's melancholy story.

"Eighty-nine serviceable," Averell said. "Maybe a hundred if I can lay my hands on enough chewing gum and bailingwire."

"How many bombers?" Eddington asked.

"Twenty mediums."

"Balls!" The chief of staff slapped an unfurled chart which depicted the entire ADTAC area from Gavabutu to Levu-Vana. "It's four hundred lousy miles to Skyhook and another five hundred to Pelaki, where the Japs have squirreled their ships. Eighteen hundred miles roundtrip. That won't leave your Mitchells a goddamn spare cupful of fuel."

"True," Averell gloomed. "What's worse, those babies come in like bats out of Hades. If they're running low on gas they'll be hotter than ever, and we'll lose half of 'em against the palmtrees at the far end of the runway."

The Rock interrupted in a mild voice. "Better start extending the strip, general. I've got a hunch we're going to inherit some B-17s damn soon."

Averell's eyes widened. "Honest Injun, admiral?"

"Toulebonne doesn't know it yet," Torrey added, "but those big babies have just about finished their checkout training."

Eddington growled, "You working Pearl Harbor by telepathy, skipper?"

"No. But CinCPAC may be interested to know that we're ready to mount Skyhook just as soon as we finish softening up Levu-Vana and Pelaki."

"Finish?" Averell sounded as if he hadn't heard Torrey correctly. "Sir, we haven't even started."

"It's always been my belief that whenever an order's given, the action has officially commenced." Torrey indicated the bulkhead clock. "It's 0730. Let's assume you've had your instructions since 0700. Okay?"

"Okay, admiral."

"We'll hit Levu-Vana first," Torrey said, "with everything in the Book."

"Yes, sir."

The Rock smiled reminiscently. "And I'll bet you five-to-one the Big Boss will agree that we should have a squadron of Fortresses up here within the next ten days."

There was a pause while they digested this morsel of prophecy.

Then Clayton Canfil said quietly, "I'd like to slip a couple of fellows onto Levu-Vana by submarine for a closer look at what's cookin' up there."

"Your regular coastwatchers letting you down?"

"They've been off the air for three days, admiral." Canfil looked grim. "Don't ask me why."

"Very well. Handle it."

"Thanks, sir. We'll leave tonight if you can whistle up a sub."

" 'We'?"

"Well," Canfil said gently, "I figure since Captain Powell, here, has learned everything I can teach him—even pidgin—he's ready to take over. I'd like to go along."

"That right, Egan?"

"I'll never replace the Old Master, sir, but I'll give it a real Hollywood try."

"Nobody," Eddington said sourly, "could ask for anything more than that, captain."

For a moment, their immediate duties forgotten, they stared at Canfil. He seemed unconcerned by their frankly admiring glances as he bundled up the set of maps he intended to study in his own hut. Canfil would pore over them until Levu-Vana's weird terrain was printed indelibly on his brain, to be recalled in detail when he crouched outside the Jap perimeter, or prowled their lines when the moon was down.

Torrey watched Eddington. The chief of staff's face was a study in repressed envy. The distasteful prospect of remaining statically *here* while the real action occurred *there* once more had drawn the parchment too tightly across the fury that always seethed inside him, ready to boil over. It was a little frightening to know Eddington as well as he did, and to be aware that his outward assurance was like the deceptive brick shell of a burnt-out building which masks the gutted blackness inside. He stifled a sigh. Perhaps after this next show he'd have to find Paul a fighting job.

But Skyhook's immediate problems required Eddington's combative, antagonistic zest. Before it concluded, the whole Jap fleet might come thundering down around their ears, because their stratagem was diabolically open to just such an off-chance. The Nips could gather at Pelaki, which boasted a harbor big enough to shelter a major task force, or they could also concentrate a striking force one thousand miles to the northwest at Cape Titan, the commodious base they'd wrested from the British just a week after the war began. Moreover, the enemy had ships aplenty for such a two-pronged retaliation against any attempt to storm the beaches of Levu-Vana, despite their shellacking in the Coral Sea and at Midway, whereas the hardpressed Americans, with a whole globe to police, felt keenly the losses of *Lexington* and *Yorktown*. Hell. At last accounts Bill Halsey had only *Enterprise* and a couple of light carriers, and the Galloping Ghost herself reportedly was hoisting planes to her flightdeck with one elevator, the other having been clobbered by a lucky Nip bombhit.

Torrey's naval forces comprised *Old Swayback*, now riding clumsily at anchor in the roadstead below the hill, seven destroyers, and the nine surviving PTs which were stationed across the island at Botan, now that Gavabutu was technically "secure." But that was it. Period. Dear CinCPAC, Torrey brooded, for Christmas give me a division of battleships (even old ones will do!) and another division of ack-ack cruisers (like Larry Moorian's elegant *Moultrie*) and a squadron of tincans festooned with search radar; and into my black stocking—the one with the big hole in it—you can slip a squadron of heavy bombers and another group of those Corsair fighters that make monkeys out of the goddamn Japs. Thank you. Goodnight. *Amen.*

The planning session broke up at noon after The Rock said he expected all hands within forty-eight hours to produce some definite ideas on how best to pluck the Skyhook nettle.

Uninvited, Eddington accompanied Torry back to the Flag hut, and still without a bidding went with him through the Quonset's screendoor. The Rock was mildly surprised at the chief of staff's presumption, which actually bordered on familiarity, if you were to regard it from the viewpoint of strict Navy protocol. Even old comrades don't intrude unasked upon the privacy of their superiors.

"Something big on your mind, Paul?" he asked.

"Couple of things."

"Sit down."

"Thanks, skipper."

"Spill it."

Eddington picked at a callus on his thumb for a moment, with grave industriousness, before he asked, "Were you just blowing up a gale for those fellows?"

Torrey seemed puzzled. "I don't follow you."

His sandpapery voice accusing, Eddington said, "You *ought* to know what I mean, skipper. That's what you hired me for—shooting from the hip so you could play judge and jury in front of the staff." A deprecatory grin took the edge off his sharp words. "Hell, I don't mind. That's always been my job where you're concerned. Only this time you grabbed the gun. You did the shooting."

" 'Ain't I the captain?' " Torrey said ironically, quoting a shopworn Service joke. " 'Get out of that lifeboat!' "

"Sure, you're the boss. That's why I'm worried. When you told Tuthill and Averell and the rest that we're kicking off Skyhook right now—even yesterday—they believed you. It's not like something I might have fired into the air. It's the real goddamn McCoy."

"That," Torrey said, "is exactly how I want it to be, Paul."

"Jesus Christ!"

"All last evening, alone in this hut after Broderick left, I thought about this thing. What in hell are the Japs up to? Why? How? Where do we lace up our frayed shoestrings next? And the more I wrestled with it, the more I became convinced that we've got to move fast, while they're still off-balance."

Eddington forgot his callus. "What makes you think the buzzards are off-balance, skipper?"

"Faith," The Rock said. "Also a large helping of hope and charity."

"Then you've got a hell of a lot more faith than I have."

"But not quite as blind as it sounds, fella. This faith has damned shrewd eyes. They belong to Clay Canfil and Company, who'll be birddogging the Nips in person. And the first Fortresses that arrive won't be bombers at all—they'll be long-range photo recon planes."

"They will?"

"Yes. CinCPAC's a detail man. He'll understand that."

"I feel," Eddington grumbled, "like a high school kid whose old man has suddenly started pitching for the home team."

"Don't, Paul. Goddamn it, all I've done is throw out the first ball. You've got to catch it, check it over, and start giving the signals for the next pitch." The Rock gazed through the window at the gently waving tops of the palmtrees. "We're due for more rain. This game might have to be won before the fifth inning . . . in case the umpire decides the grounds are too wet. We're racing against time, fella. And it's pretty touch-and-go."

"You're not the desperate type, skipper."

"Perhaps," Torrey said, "you don't know me as well as you think, Paul."

"Where does Blackjack Broderick fit into this picture?"

"I've got a hunch he's about decided to run up to Pearl for a tête-à-tête with CinCPAC. That's another reason I want a definite plan ready to lay down in front of the Big Boss. If Broderick's with him, they'll get our proposal together—'action' for Blackjack, 'info' for CinCPAC. So it'll have to be good. Foolhardy, maybe, but foolproof. D'you read me?"

"Five-by-five."

"We'll load our Skyhook message with requests for everything we could possibly need, from beans to bombs, and then maybe they'll give us half of it."

"CinCPAC's got a hell of a lot of things going right now," Eddington said doubtfully. "Central Pacific's busting wide open. And the Aleutians . . ."

Torrey had started to fill his thinking briar. He left the chief of staff's caveat hanging momentarily in midair while he got the bowl packed to his satisfaction, struck a kitchen match against his khaki trousers, and ignited the tobacco, which smelled astonishingly fragrant against the fetid jungle's olfactory background. He knew all this. However brilliantly ADTAC plotted the Skyhook assault, he would have to settle for the scrapings from CinCPAC's limited barrel. Nevertheless Skyhook was an integral part of the whole, and a lot more depended upon it than even the Big Boss might discern in his remote grandeur. It had to be done. But it had to be done in The Rock's own fashion. Otherwise they might as well resentence him to Makalapa and substitute an admiral who'd behave differently. More cautiously, perhaps, or more deliberately.

He laughed aloud. That was something for you—replacing Rock Torrey because he'd become too rash!

"I'm glad there's something funny left in this friggin' world," Eddington said dourly.

"Not funny, Paul. Fantastic."

"Okay." Eddington let it be. "Anyhow, now that I've caught the bridal bouquet again for the ninety-ninth time, I'd better get cracking. Honeymoon's apt to start any minute. Shoes and rice. That's the ticket. Tons of the goddamn stuff!"

Torrey eyed his chief of staff speculatively. "You hate to see other fellows get the glory, don't you?"

"Glory-my-ass!" Eddington's tone was despairing. "What gravels me is having to stay home and fight secondhand . . . It's like washing your feet with socks on . . . or like screwin' with—"

The Rock cut in. "You want to feel your fists against somebody's jaw, don't you?"

Eddington contemplated the knuckles of his right hand, still bruised from his brief encounter with Neal Owynn, and said thoughtfully, "I guess you're right."

"Then pull on a new pair of socks this one last time, Paul, and wash your feet real clean. When Levu-Vana's secured, I'll find you a combat job that'll singe what's left of your hair."

"Shake!" Eddington offered his sore hand and didn't wince as The Rock gripped it tightly. "Consider the foot-washing as good as done. But how," he asked slyly, "about the other?"

"Your private life, captain, is your private affair."

"Gracias."

Torrey nodded. "You said there were a couple of things on your mind. What's the second?"

Eddington grinned. "A few of us are staging a little picnic. Sort of a delayed celebration for Rathole. We figure it'll have to be today—this afternoon, before we're up to our necks in Skyhook."

"Sounds fine. Have fun."

"...And we all agreed you've been working too goddamn hard, skipper, and need a touch of R-and-R yourself."

The Rock relit his pipe. "I'd cramp your style, fella."

"Negative." Eddington's voice turned crafty. "We've taken care of that."

"So?"

"There's this head nurse at MOB Able, name of Haynes, who'll be there. She thinks you're a hell of a guy, skipper."

"Does she?"

"Affirmative." Eddington pressed his meager advantage. "She's going to invite you personally."

Considering the matter objectively, Torrey realized that the exhilaration engendered by the sunshiny morning had waned, leaving him feeling tired and doubtful again. Worn. Almost as stale as he'd been during those last months at Pearl Harbor after Midway. He longed, in a disconcerting way, to see Maggie Haynes again. He yearned to talk with her. Savor her whimsical wisdom. He wanted many things. And if rational excuse were needed for joining his staff's brief period of rest-and-recreation, here was Eddington himself, tensing up and preparing to return to the Op shack, who must be nursed along like a highstrung racehorse until Skyhook's course was successfully run. Eddington seemed sincere in his invitation. It might be good therapy to humor the man.

"Tell Lieutenant Haynes to save her postage," he said. "I'll come along."

Egan Powell had acquitted himself nobly. He bartered two bottles of vile Australian whisky for eight thick sirloin steaks which the ADTAC commissary steward had been hoarding against a hungry day (his own), a dozen ears of native sweet corn, two mammoth heads of lettuce, dishes, silverware, and a ten-gallon barrel of ice for chilling the canned Budweiser.

All hands agreed that Strangler's Cove was the best beach—

"judged the finest in the world," Egan Powell sneered, "by people who have never been anyplace else"—as well as the most accessible.

They settled upon 1700 for the rendezvous. Nobody ever did much real work between 1700 and 1800, which was the caulk-off hour before dinner. And since chow took up another sixty minutes, you could soothe your conscience by figuring you wouldn't have done anything constructive during that time, anyhow. Later, when it got dark, they could powwow over strategy around the bonfire if the Old Man insisted upon his pound of flesh.

Because there were eight in the party, Egan Powell decided they'd better take a whaleboat instead of a recon car, which he elected to pilot personally to avoid the services of some wiseacre enlisted coxswain with an eagle eye and a long memory. Before Torrey joined them, however, he warned that somebody else could damned well steer home. By that time he and his date probably would have reached an understanding, and he'd need all his hands. Her name was Ensign Meredith Howell, he said, but everybody should call her Merry. Get it? Merry Howl. They got it. She was svelte, blond, and frightfully surprised to find herself in the United States Navy rather than on the cover of *Harper's Bazaar,* Powell further explained, because she really belonged there, being somewhat bizarre herself.

"Merry's making the best of a bad bargain," he concluded with an enigmatic leer.

"Who'd you get for me?" Mac asked suspiciously.

"I believe," Egan Powell said, "you'll find I didn't exaggerate when I promised to find you a real spook."

Then The Rock arrived and they had to belay the foolishness. He sat in the back seat of the jeep with Eddington, pensively quiet, as Mac drove them down the ADTAC hill to the landing. During the preliminary boat trip to MOB Able, Torrey had little more to say, other than to acknowledge their greetings and respond absently to a few tentative pleasantries. Egan Powell caught Eddington's eye, and the chief of staff shrugged helplessly. Both of them wondered if they'd made a gruesome mistake urging the Old Man to come.

A two-starred Navy blanket can get pretty suffocating during the course of a long evening, particularly when it's wet, Powell reminded himself morosely.

Maggie Haynes waved as the whaleboat chuffed toward the hospital dock. Marshaled in the rear like schoolgirls on firedrill, her three subordinate nurses also waved, dutifully, aware of the covetous glances aimed at the moist backs of their seersucker dresses by MOB Able's stay-at-homes. This was the first authentic party ever held at ADTAC, and if the miserable war lasted another hundred years, they'd still be the social pioneers, as famous as Dodge City's dancehall girls, and every bit as much to be envied.

The Rock answered Maggie's gay signal with a clumsy half-wave. His gesture seemed to epitomize the paralyzing shyness he always experienced during these initial moments of their infrequent public encounters. It washed over him again. His face must have turned beet-red in the dwindling afternoon sun, he knew, and he felt like a mawkish goddamn fool.

"This is *indeed* a pleasant surprise, Admiral Torrey," Maggie said with wicked formality when he stepped from the bobbing whaleboat onto the tiny pier.

He bowed. But even that simple gesture was maladroit. "My pleasure, Lieutenant Haynes," he mumbled wretchedly.

Maggie stared at him for a moment, as if disbelieving what she'd heard, before she burst into laughter.

"Oh—poop!"

Her juniors blanched, waiting for lightning to strike her dead. But it didn't. When Torrey spoke, his voice was hardly thunderous at all.

"Hello, Maggie," he said.

"That's a lot better, Rock." She turned to her companions. "Kiddies, this scary-looking man wearing an admiral's stars happens to be a right guy. I've known him for about a hundred years—ever since last spring—and he's especially kind to animals, women, and Navy nurses. You've already met the others. Captain Eddington and Captain Powell. Both bachelors, so be careful. And Lieutenant McConnel. He's married and off-limits, although he's sort of yours for the evening, Sabrina."

They shook hands around, gravely, and then everybody paired up.

Mac had to admit Egan Powell was right. Sabrina (if she had a last name he didn't catch it) was square cut and on the shadowy side of thirty, with a bullhorn voice, an unquenchable thirst, and a downy mustache. She quivered with the unrequited passionateness that afflicts all homely nymphomaniacs.

Annalee Dorne felt Eddington's hard palm close over hers, and she let him clasp it a few seconds longer than protocol demanded, gazing up into his battered face as he squeezed her small fingers.

"Hiya, baby," Eddington said.

"Hello, captain," she whispered.

"It's Paul, baby. Remember that."

She stared at the eagles on his collar. ". . . I'll try."

His low-pitched growl sounded just like Clark Gable's did when he talked that way to Scarlett O'Hara in *Gone With the Wind*. Rough and mean and bedroomy. There'd been fellows like Captain Eddington—Paul—at Conshohocken, but mostly they'd hung around poolhalls downtown or driven big flashy cars. She had never met any of them, although she'd speculated often enough how it would be, going around with somebody who wasn't the All-American Boy type that Mom and Dad approved so enthusiastically. Annalee hoped this wasn't being disloyal to Jere Torrey—just thinking such goofy thoughts—especially when they were going on a picnic to the exact same dinky little cove where his PTs had stayed only a few weeks ago. Jere himself was an All-American Boy, for sure, freshfaced and grinning and crew cut. Her parents would have just doted on Jere. But right now that handsome Hollywood captain named Powell who looked something like Robert Taylor only an awful lot older was gunning the whaleboat's putt-putt motor and coaxing them aboard . . .

"Come on, Annalee," Eddington said.

"Okay—Paul."

Aided by their watchful escorts, the three junior nurses clambered down the steep ladder, giggling and showing much bare thigh, while Maggie and The Rock stood solemnly awaiting the seniors' privilege of boarding the craft last. Two spaces in the stern sheets were reserved for them. These were the best seats, and once the whaler emerged from the scanty shelter of MOB Able's wharf, into the offshore chop, they would also be the driest.

Eddington barked, "Shove off, coxswain!"

Dexterously, Egan Powell swung the double-ended launch away from the pier, pleased to be able to display the skill in smallboat handling he'd acquired during his Healthful Outdoor Living Period at Malibu, seven years ago.

Maggie untied the bandanna that bound her head, and the breeze caught her hair and whipped it back like a battleflag. As they headed toward the barrier reef where the whitewater tumbled, for the life of her Maggie couldn't have explained whether it was the bowspray or the glint of the waning sun or something different and deeper that caused it but her amethyst eyes were sparkling, and there were happy tears in them.

Seated beside her, The Rock appeared content merely to check Egan Powell's course for Strangler's Cove, and she was unable to fathom his expression, because his own eyes had narrowed into thin slits, and he was looking straight ahead.

Maggie nudged him gently. "If you stand up in the boat," she said, "maybe somebody'll paint your portrait, General Washington."

He turned toward her with a slow grin. "Didn't anyone ever tell you it's dangerous to stand up in small craft, Lieutenant Haynes?"

"I guess my education was faulty," Maggie said, "because that's one danger they forgot to warn me about."

More seriously than in jest, he asked, "You know about *all* the others?"

"Every damned one!"

They beached the whaleboat on the firm sands of the small crescent bay. As they stepped ashore, they were seized by a holiday spirit, and the last lingering sense of truancy left them. None of the others would allow the Admiral or his Lady—as Egan Powell ceremoniously phrased it—to assist in unloading the gear, hunting driftwood for the fire, shucking the corn, or broiling the steaks.

Mac handed them each a glistening can of beer.

"Sir," he said, "that fat cocopalm over there, the one that slopes like the back of a captain's chair, has got your name on it."

Torrey felt a sudden expansive warmth. "Well done, thou good and faithful aide."

With Maggie stepping daintly beside him, he crossed the twenty yards of white sand, which was turning opalescent as the red sun dipped, and they sat down against the palmtree. If they huddled close, they discovered, its thick bole provided an ample backrest for both of them. The Rock looked at her and smiled. His earlier embarrassment, he found, was gone now.

It promised to be one of those wildly primitive sunsets, whose colors would nevertheless be warm and rich as mother's milk despite the chill breeze that had begun to blow out of the northeast. The lower sky was pale bluegreen, with mare's-tail clouds wisping across the horizon, and the last rays of the sun fanned out through them like the bloody spokes in the Japanese flag. The man and the woman, admiral and nurse, reclined against their palmbole, neither speaking, and contemplated through half-closed eyes the scene that stretched upward and outward beyond them, framed only by the limits of their gaze, from the warm sands at their feet to the vaulting indigo above the tradewind cloud bank. Observing the small waves roll creamily across the narrow lagoon from the formidable reef, they saw how the jade paled where its coral bottom shelved abruptly upward into the beach. There were living creatures, too, passing along the revolving screen of this enormous diorama. Sandsharks, hardly larger than goldfish at this distance, darted along the surface of the middle shoalwaters, while a tern swooped above them like a disembodied sprite, its forked tail brilliant in the dying light. Once a formation of fighterplanes passed overhead in compact echelon, etched black against a white cloud, and there was a velvet interval of darkness before the moon came out.

"I wish," Torrey said softly, "that I had my camera here."

"Camera?"

He told her about his secret cache of filmed sunsets and sunrises. "Sounds silly, I suppose, for a grown man to be shooting nature movies for his own private enjoyment."

Maggie's canted smile mocked him gently as she asked, "How much of your enjoyment is that way—private—like all the rest of your life?"

His own smile came more slowly, "This isn't private enjoyment. Us, I mean, here. Is it?"

She glanced across the strip of beach that separated them from the others, who were getting the fire started with much laughter and horseplay.

"No," she whispered. "This isn't very private."

"Shall we take a walk, Maggie?"

"Later . . ."

Sabrina sniffed the night air excitedly, like a tethered mare, and opined that the jasmine smell of frangipani was enough to drive a girl out of her everlovin' mind. She pronounced it *franggi-panggi,* as if it were something that might get stuck in your teeth if you chewed on it. Mac shuddered. He'd finished collecting the firewood, and now he had to attend to his grimmer obligations. Sabrina, ankledeep in the surf, might have passed for a defrocked grammar school principal, if it weren't for the beer can which she held manfashion in her right fist.

"Let's go swimming," he suggested hopefully.

She bawled out to Annalee and Merry, "The lieutenant wants us to take a swim before chow. Anybody think to bring suits?"

Nobody had. So the three nurses watched mournfully as Mac, Egan Powell, and Eddington plunged with loud animal shouts into the lagoon, wearing only their khaki shorts.

"How's the water?" Sabrina asked.

Mac splashed a tepid handful in her direction. *"Wunderbar!"* He hoped that was the socially polite thing to do.

"At least I'm going wading," she announced.

With her bluegray seersucker skirt hiked high around her Ionic thighpillars, Sabrina marched purposefully into the shallow water. But this felt so good she kept plunging deeper until it reached her thick waist, and after that she plainly didn't give a damn, for she peeled off her soaked blouse and skirt, and flung them back upon the beach.

"So what the hell's the difference between this outfit and a two-piece swimsuit?" Sabrina demanded.

There was a considerable difference. As Maggie had learned much earlier, the prim cotton underclothing which the Navy issues to nurses and WAVES was made of unsubstantial stuff, and hardly designed for aquatics. Sabrina's turned translucent. One startled look at the way her hairy Amazonian physique burst into sculptured focus caused Annalee Dorne to change her mind about joining them in the water. Merry Howl didn't mind, though, and she pranced into the small surf like a model who'd graduated from Minsky's instead of Conover's, peeling off her outer garments as she advanced.

Annalee wished she weren't so darned inhibited. But Conshohocken does that to a person, she supposed, and she shook her blond ringlets sadly when Captain Eddington taunted her for being such a fraidycat.

Later they stood around the driftwood fire, which burned with a pleasant salty seaweedy smell, drying their wet clothes, and later they devoured the steaks Egan Powell had barbecued over the open blaze, and got butter all over their faces from the huge ears of native corn. It was, everybody agreed, the best damned meal they'd had since San Francisco, where you have to pretend to be a gourmet or get ridden out of town on the nearest shishkebab skewer. As the flames dwindled to a placid glow, they burrowed like surfeited jungle cats into the mellow sand.

Sabrina wanted to neck. But the mere thought of her square-beamed frame, heavythewed as a wrestler's in the clinging GI panties, and her vast darknippled breasts bulging from the damp brassiere, would have discouraged Mac, even if the image of Bev's slim body hadn't intruded just then. Sabrina belched politely a couple of times and dropped off to sleep. She was trying to be a Good Egg, she said amicably. That's all. Mac slapped her wet rump in brotherly fashion to show that he didn't have any hard feelings either.

This ought to make a hell of a funny letter, he told himself, and Bev would probably bust a G string laughing when she read it.

Or would she?

Near the end of the bowshaped beach of Strangler's Cove, a tiny peninsula jutted into the lagoon like a sharp rise on a feverchart, thereby creating a detached and very secluded strip of coralsand before the jungle again closed in. The privacy of this beachlet was further enhanced by a screen of cocopalms, wildgrown and thick, which left only a narrow path between the water and the trees. Only the reflected gleam of the dwindling bonfire showed faintly against the palmfronds to mark the campsite's location.

Torrey found a lava outcropping just beyond the peninsula, and knelt to run his hand along the base. It had the unyielding texture and severe contours of an Oriental couch.

"Try this," he invited.

Gracefully but with caution, Maggie obeyed, and sank slowly against the lava backrest. "You've a nice eye for furniture, Rock," she said. (Thinking: *Idiot! Next I'll be gushing that he'd make somebody a good husband because he's so damned domestic. God deliver me from female clichés!*)

"It's also a fine place for a man to smoke his afterdinner pipe," Torrey was saying.

She scratched a cardboard match, touched it to a cigarette, and offered it to him. He shook his head.

"Two on a match isn't bad luck," Maggie said.

"Pipes take a lot of lighting," he said. "You need kitchen matches."

She watched him draw the bit of sulfured wood across the lava, and noted how expertly he shielded the small flame against the nightbreeze. Somehow this simple ritual depressed her. It was so exclusively masculine, so goddamn symbolic of all the things men could do but women couldn't.

The Rock peered into the cherryred bowl of his pipe, and apparently the gleam met with his critical approval, for he gave a satisfied nod, and set the stem between his strong teeth. He leaned back, staring at the dark arch of the sky, quietly smoking, while Maggie studied his moonlit profile. There were new hollows in his cheeks and the furrows across his brow had deepened, she perceived, although the hard brown hand that clutched the bulldog briar was as steady as when he'd grasped her shoulder and drawn her close to him on Aiea Heights above the ruined harbor, so long ago.

He took the pipe from his mouth. "Clayton Canfil says the natives call this 'The Season of the Falling Stars.' Actually, we're just passing through the Perseid Shower."

Maggie looked upward. It was true. Once her eyes became accustomed to the delicate nuances of dark and light in the glowing lunar sky, she could see the thinbright meteors, dozens of them, that seemed to hang for an instant on the abyss of night, then plummet into the void. They wept and flamed as they fell through Heaven. When each one vanished, burnt to nothingness in the earth's heavy atmosphere, it was like a tiny cry dying out in a vast silent room.

"God's tears," she murmured.

He turned toward her. "Odd. That's what the natives believe, too, and Canfil says they consider the 'Season of the Falling Stars' a sad time." Torrey rubbed the pipe against his hawk nose. "Of course it's all because of the foul weather . . . unhealthy as hell . . . but now's also their burying season."

Maggie wondered if this mournful man himself had ever enjoyed a happy season, and she meant many things when she said, "Poor devils."

"The war's made it worse than ever for them." He grinned ruefully. "Somehow I've got to account for 7,693 native cattle, 236 goats, 171 pigs, 97 horses, and 17 mules that have been 'liberated' either by the Japs or our own Marines."

"Falling stars *do* serve a useful purpose," Maggie mused. "You can wish on them."

"Athalie always did."

"You've never told me anything about . . . her."

"Athalie was a Boston romantic. She believed in things the way natives believe in them."

"'Was?' Did she die?"

He pondered her question. "No. Not exactly, that is, although I suppose it was pretty much the same as dying—what she did." And seeing Maggie's puzzled expression, he added, "Athalie became a ghost, I guess, haunting Jere, and haunting me."

"But you've both escaped."

"Yes," he said. "Jere's grown up—away."

"And you?"

His voice was icecold. "I've grown scar tissue."

"Oh."

Maggie searched for another cigarette, found it, and tore a match from a folder. But the evening moisture had made the cardboard match useless. Torrey produced a kitchen match and struck it against his thumbnail. Behind his cupped hand it shone like a footlight, turning his craggy face into something hewn from dark hard stone. She drew a lungful of acrid smoke, very deliberately, and released it a little at a time through her nose. Athalie wouldn't have smoked in this firesnuffing dragon fashion, Maggie supposed. She was a goddamn lady. She probably used an ivory holder so she could keep her aromatic Turkish cigarettes at arm's length, like everything else in her life, but unlike Margaret Haynes ex-Alderton, who'd never held anything at arm's length in her whole candid thirty-six years. No. Thirty-seven. Last month she'd had a secret birthday.

The Rock was speaking again, and now his voice was warmer, as he asked, "Looking for more falling stars?"

"Not more. Just one special star."

He pointed suddenly. "There's the granddaddy of 'em all—just above the palms beyond the peninsula."

With her eyes tight shut, Maggie blew a kiss toward the meteorite. But when Torrey wanted to know what she'd wished, her mind went blank, and she didn't trouble to explain that wishes-spoken were wishes-lost.

"I guess," she said distractedly, "it was about the war."

"That it would end soon?"

"What else?"

"Funny," he was saying, "Jere's PT squadron asked me when the war would end, right here in this very cove, just a little while ago."

"Did you have a better answer for them than you had for me?" she inquired, not really caring.

Torrey shook his head. "I told them it would last a hell of a long time, Maggie. Years, probably."

"It sounds," she said bitterly, "as if MOB Able's going to be in business forever."

"Nothing lasts forever. Not even a war."

"Sometimes I think you Big Brass would rather it didn't end."

It came to him with a muted sense of shock that Maggie's cynical observation might be true, that he really didn't care if peace ever came, because for him there was nothing beyond the day of victory. No plans. No hopes. Not even formulated desires. He'd experienced one world war "triumph," and the exultation had crumbled to dust before his eyes, like a Dead Sea apple.

"Are you like that Big Brass?" Maggie persisted.

"You wouldn't understand the reasons," he said honestly, "but sometimes I don't want it to end."

"Neither do I."

Startled, he swung around to look at her. She was crouched with her knees drawn close to her small cleft chin, and in the moonlight her hair seemed jetblack and mysterious.

"I've got reasons," Torrey repeated, "but you—"

She flared, "What happens for me when it ends? When I go home? Where I'll be the elderly girl failure, carving a fine fat career out of smelly bedpans and greasy enemas and watching my teeth grow longer and hearing my arteries crackle. But being Lieutenant Maggie Haynes is different. Out here I'm *somebody.*"

"Haven't you forgotten something?" he asked with gentle irony.

"What?"

"How you told me—back at Pearl Harbor—that you'd been through all this a dozen times, but it never bothered you, and nothing changed, because you were the 'housemother' type?"

"Yes," Maggie said, "now I remember." She confronted him, smiling uncertainly. "But that was long ago, and in another country—and besides the wench is dead." Discerning his bewilderment, she added, "Maybe I didn't quote it right. But it tells the story. That old Maggie *is* dead. I want her to stay buried."

"I liked the old Maggie."

"You never knew her!" She moved closer. "And you'd have hated the wench. She wasn't even human."

He reached for her hand. "You're the humanest person I've ever known, Maggie."

"There's no such word as 'humanest,'" she said. "Besides—maybe I'm just one bitchkitty of a fine actress."

"Are you acting now?"

Maggie closed her eyes as if she'd felt a stab of pain. "No. I'm not acting now. But I wish to God I were."

"Then I'm glad."

Torrey kissed her eyelids. They quivered beneath his lips. He found her mouth. She clung to him making small moaning sounds as he pressed her against the harsh lava with his hands on her shoulders, memorizing her face.

"Keep holding me," she said "—tighter!"

"I will."

"I need you, Rock."

Wonderingly, he said, "Nobody ever needed me before," and saw the elfin smile break swiftly across her lips.

"Someone had to shatter the jinx, dear heart."

Torrey wanted to say much more. But the old premonitory feeling had returned, hinting that it might be indecent after so many cenobitic years to expose his naked emotions, or to reveal his personal Self. He had tried to elude that Self, too, knowing he couldn't, for always it was lurking there, around the corner of the Operations shack when a lonely decision had to be made; or in his footlocker where his one suit of civvies had lain packed in mothballs since his final visit to Athalie; or in the sad sound of an accordion played by a homesick Negro messboy; and most of it was in the bleak sight of himself in the morning mirror, each day growing a little older and a little more doubtful, and forever fighting to throw his shoulders back and step more lightly on the balls of his tired feet, and thus to conceal both age and doubt. What was that Kipling poem the Old Man always quoted when the world closed around him? *Down to Gehenna or up to the Throne, He travels the fastest who travels alone. . . .*

"I suppose," Maggie said quietly, "we'd better go back before your staff thinks I've kidnaped you."

She got up and brushed the sand from her damp skirt, while he remained seated, brooding toward the dim place where the moon had sunk below the invisible horizon.

Then he arose, too, and looked past the tiny peninsula. "Yes," Torrey said, "we'd better go back. Even the fire's gone out."

Only Mac and Sabrina were at the fireside when they returned. The aide was nursing a can of beer, and yearning blankly out to sea, across the burnished ebony waste that led ultimately to God's country and Bev McConnel. Sabrina slept like a grampus, sweat-bathed in the furry tropical night.

Ten minutes later Egan Powell and Merry Howl materialized out of the jungle that fringed the beach. They were supremely nonchalant. Powell said they'd been hunting wild orchids in the moonlight, but hadn't found any because the damned trees kept getting in their way and made it dark as Hades. Merry Howl, wearing a Mona Lisa smile, said nothing at all.

The Rock demanded impatiently, "Where's Eddington and Miss Dorne?" He checked his watch. "I want to put Canfil aboard the *Tarpon* at midnight—personally—and time's getting short."

"Maybe they're orchid-hunting, too," Mac suggested.

"Not Paul," Egan Powell said. "He doesn't appreciate the finer things of life. He's a true clod. More likely a grunion-hunter, I'd say."

Merry Howl's Mona Lisa smile turned into an all-purpose smirk. "Annalee might educate the man."

"Or vice versa," Powell said darkly, emphasizing the *vice*.

It was barely an hour until midnight when the missing pair appeared, walking very slowly along the water's edge, and deep in conversation. In the gloom that followed moonset, Annalee Dorne's natural blondness had taken on a curious pallor. She was limping, and as she brushed a vagrant lock of damp hair from her solemn babyface, her hand shook. Maggie's shrewd eyes discerned at once that she'd been weeping. It was equally obvious that Captain Eddington didn't give a hoot about the poor kid's upset state—the four-striped, two-legged beast!

There was blood on Annalee's torn seersucker skirt.

"I'm all right," she said in a small dead voice. "We just went too far."

"Meet some stray Japs?" Merry Howl asked. "You look like you'd been in a fight."

Eddington explained coolly, "Annalee fell down on a piece of coral and skinned hell out of both knees, that's all. Lucky we've got so many nurses on deck."

"Damn lucky," Maggie said, appraising him with open hostility.

Torrey started alone for the whaleboat.

Mac called hastily, "Party's over, ladies and gentlemen—let's roll!"

Annalee was glad they had to undress in the dark so they wouldn't disturb the unfortunates who'd missed ADTAC's first Big Party. Slipping on a chunk of wet coral might alibi her scratched knees and a bloody skirt. But it wouldn't account for those ugly bruises on her inner thighs and on her breasts, and it certainly wouldn't explain away how she'd lost her GI cotton panties and her GI cotton brassiere. Nothing could explain away those things, least of all to Annalee Dorne herself, unless maybe Captain Eddington wanted to discuss it some more in that urgent husky voice of his, the way he'd talked out there in the crazy damned treacherous moonlight.

She folded the ripped skirt and blouse and hid them in her footlocker. Tomorrow she'd burn them. Then she crawled into bed and muffled her face with the pillow so Maggie Haynes wouldn't hear her tight little sobs.

What *could* she say that wouldn't make Maggie smile knowingly in that lopsided way of hers and observe, "I told you so, baby, God knows I told you so!" Sure Maggie had told her. But it was like those Keep Off the Grass signs that don't add Positively. Sometimes you took a few steps anyhow, just to see what might happen.

Behind the sheltering pillow, Annalee closed her eyes tight, but even that didn't shut out the pervasive image of Captain Eddington. He wouldn't go away. He stood there in the darkness above the khaki netting of her bunk, staring down at her with all the speculation gone out of his bold gaze, and a wicked smile twisting his mouth. She choked back a moan, remembering how this ugly man had seemed so excitingly masculine when they'd met on MOB Able's sunlit wharf, with that black mattress of chesthair spewing from his unbuttoned shirtfront as if to compensate for his horrid shaven head, and his powerful male smell, and those tremendous thighs bulging against his khaki shorts, and his flattened pugilist's nose which hinted at all sorts of reckless battles he'd fought in his lifetime and probably won. She hadn't even minded his brutal way of talking, nor the outrageous suggestions he whispered into her ear when the others weren't listening. It was fun. It was a thrilling game that made her feel very adult and intrepid.

But there weren't any rules to the game Captain Eddington played.

As if he knew all the time exactly what he was doing, he'd taken her elbow and guided her down the beach, and when she protested that the coral hurt her bare feet, he just seized her up in those enormous arms of his and kept carrying her away from the others, until they seemed to be miles distant where she could have screamed her silly head off and nobody'd hear, before he set her down.

Perversely and unwisely, then, she had taunted him.

"You're nothing but a big bad wolf, Paul Eddington," she said, "and you can huff and you can puff but you'll never blow my house down."

He laughed harshly.

"Want to make a bet, baby?"

"I haven't got anything to bet," she said. "My purse is 'way back at the fire. I don't even have my comb or lipstick."

"Maybe I'd have to trust you."

"That's a funny thing to say."

"I'm a funny guy."

"Did you bring your cigarettes?"

"Sure."

"Light one for me, captain."

In a way that was thoroughly familiar to him, though quite foreign to her, he put both cigarettes in his mouth and lit them simultaneously.

"That's cute," she said.

"Always aim to give service, ma'am."

The place he picked for them to watch the waning moon was soft and grassy, although it hadn't much of a beach. But here the lagoon was especially limpid and inviting, and for once the rustle of the palmfronds didn't sound to her like creeping Japs.

"Tell me why it's called Strangler's Cove," she said.

"You're too young."

"Please," she coaxed.

So he told her all about the square-rigger sailor and the native wench and the fight and what happened later, without sparing any of the gory details, including the horrible way they'd mistreated that girl afterward.

Annalee shuddered deliciously. "What a dreadful story!"

"You wanted to hear it, baby."

"Do you always do what women ask?"

"Always," he said in his Clark Gable growl, "and sometimes what they don't."

If he meant what she guessed he meant, it'd be a lot wiser to change the subject. Also safer.

"Was the water cold when you went swimming?"

"Negative." His battered face leered at her in the moonlight. "Why don't you try it?"

"Same reason as before, Paul. No bathing suit."

"Maybe I shouldn't have kidded you about that," he said. "You'd look a hell of a lot better than those two other dames. They're real bags. One's too fat. Other's too goddamn skinny. You're perfect."

Annalee dimpled. "Aren't you gallant, though?"

"I've got eyes in my head, baby, that's all."

"It does look awfully nice . . ."

"Have some."

Daringly, almost instinctively, she asked, "If I go into the water, promise you won't peek?"

". . . Officer-and-gentleman," he assured her.

"Turn around."

After he'd averted his head, so all she could see was his immense bullneck, she unbottoned her blouse and unzippered her skirt and took them off. The warm night air was like a caress. On sudden impulse she stripped off her cotton GIs and dived naked into the lagoon. He was right. It was warm as a bathtub. Annalee wished she'd brought a bar of soap. She hadn't had a real bath since leaving Pearl Harbor.

For a few delectable minutes she paddled around in the tepid water, keeping her body modestly below the gentle surface, for she was acutely conscious that Eddington was watching her now from the bank. Then the tiny red glow of his cigarette disappeared, and he was gone.

Alarmed, she called, "Paul?"

Hoarse laughter sounded from somewhere in the tall grasses that marched almost to the lagoon's edge. "Don't be scared, baby, I'm not leaving."

"Stay where you are, then, because I'm coming out."

"Depend on it," he said.

Annalee emerged from the lagoon and ran to the tuft of bunchgrass where she'd left her clothes. But they were gone. Standing in the weird silver nightglow like a dripping figurine sprite, she clenched her small fists in exasperation and tried to control the fear in her voice.

"Damn you, Paul Eddington—that's a mean dirty trick. Bring my things before I shriek."

He came out of a jungle thicket, still laughing, and stepped quickly toward her before she could retreat into the sheltering water.

"Screaming's no good," he reminded her. "Besides, dirty tricks are my business. Officially. Twenty-four hours a day. By The Rock's own orders."

Annalee tried to twist away from his crawling stare. "Please let me alone," she implored, shielding herself with her hands.

"You *are* beautiful, baby."

He seized her arms and wrenched them away from her breasts, spinning her small body around, so that it was pressed against his rough clothing. She tried to break loose from the trap. But it was useless. Instead, she found herself being forced back toward the marshy turf, slowly and remorselessly, as if Eddington relished this unequal test of strength and didn't want to hasten his victory.

"Please let me go, Paul," she whimpered. *"Please!"*

He'd stopped laughing. "Later, baby." His strangled voice wasn't like Clark Gable's any more, either.

Suddenly his great hot hands seemed to be all over her body, pushing her shoulders against the ground, clutching at her breasts, tearing at her soft underthighs. She lashed out at his groin with her right knee the way somebody'd said you could foil an attacker, but he just grunted and thrust his own knees against her legs, until she was spreadeagled beneath him.

Annalee screamed once, despairingly, although she knew her cry would be lost in the empty night.

"Jere!"

Eddington slapped her open mouth.

Stunned by the impact of his hard palm, paralyzed even more by hopeless terror, she ceased struggling, and lay back supine and weeping, while he methodically raped her. When he had finished, he left her sprawled upon the crumpled saltgrass, and went to fetch her clothes. He dropped them over her writhing naked body.

"Get dressed," he said flatly, "and take this handkerchief to stop the blood."

She staggered to her feet. He remained there, smoking calmly, while she put on her skirt and blouse. She didn't bother with the other things. She just wanted to cover her nakedness.

He removed the cigarette from his mouth and offered it to her. She shook her head.

"I want to go home," she said dully.

"Okay, baby." He flipped the half-smoked cigarette into the lagoon where it hissed out like a spent rocket. Then he asked, "Who the hell's Jere?"

"Jere?" She repeated his casual question mechanically. "Why are you asking about Jere?"

"Because that's the name you yelled, baby. I'm curious. Women sometimes yell the damnedest thing when they're getting laid."

"He's just a fellow I knew."

"Boyfriend?"

"Not any more."

"Navy?"

"Oh, yes, Jere Torrey's Navy."

"Torrey!"

"Admiral Torrey's son," she said. "With the PTs. Across the island."

"Why the Christ didn't you tell me?" Eddington growled disgustedly. "It would have made a hell of a lot of difference."

"You didn't ask me," she said, "any more than you asked if I was a virgin . . ."

She started to run blindly along the coralstudded edge of the lagoon through the deepening moonset darkness, faster and faster, as if by running she could kill the pain and cleanse the filth.

His harsh voice called, "Wrong direction, baby."

She paused in midflight, and when the agony knifed inside her again, she collapsed. Eddington picked her up.

"My knee is bleeding," she said dully.

"Better put something on it," he advised. "Live coral's poison . . ."

A cool hand touched her forehead. The pillow was gone. Maggie Haynes' quizzical face peered down at her through the mosquito netting.

"Want to talk, honey?"

"Later," Annalee said. "Now I just want to sleep."

"I know."

"Do you?"

"Yes. I think I know all about it."

"Nobody could know—" Annalee said "—ever."

"Except another woman who's known a lot of men herself, babygirl. All kinds. Even some like that bastard who raped you tonight."

"Oh, Maggie . . . Maggie . . ."

"But believe me, sweetheart, he'll pay for what he's done. Somehow. You wait. You'll see."

16. *Like a Wolf on the Fold!*

WITHIN TWENTY-FOUR HOURS the soft moonlight of Strangler's Cove was exposed as a false harbinger, and the nor'westerlies which Max Gottlieb had been predicting for so many days finally locked around them, vile and wet and blustery. Torrey endured it in stoical silence for more than a month before he summoned the aerologist to his quarters for a showdown conference.

How long, he demanded testily, would this abominable condition prevail?

The weatherman's owlish face was impassive as he shrugged his heavy shoulders. When the South Pacific's topsyturvy springtime rolled around, maybe by April, things would settle down—and then he could accurately prophesy nothing but an endless succession of steady rains. But forecasting now at this point was worse than playing roulette against a crooked house: the wheelman controlled all the odds. Just be glad, Gottlieb urged, that we're out of the hurricane zone.

Torrey studied the meteorological estimates gravely.

If he waited until spring before launching Skyhook, it would mean at least a twelve-week delay, with always the chance that spring itself might prove to be just as miserable as winter. Meanwhile the Nips were enjoying relatively decent weather at Levu-Vana, four hundred miles north; and at Pelaki, another five hundred miles farther up the line, Mesquite's recon pilots reported continual CAVU.

In his mind's eye, The Rock could see the Japanese laboring frantically under clear skies to extend Levu-Vana's airfield, building revetments for the bombers that would soon be ferried down from Tokyo, and erecting pillboxes along the beaches against the day of reckoning. Gloomily, too, he visualized their teeming base at Pelaki Shima: cargoships slipping past the Yank submarine cordon, unloading men and materiel by the regiment and by the ton; their snipe-nosed aircraft carriers and their pagoda-masted cruisers—perhaps even battleships—riding confidently at anchor and awaiting The Word to sortie against the invasion fleet they knew was bound to come.

Worst of all, Torrey felt sure that any opportunity for surprise had evaporated. The most arrant strategic blockhead among the Nips, given one quick glance at a Pacific chart, must figure that the next blow would fall somewhere in the Levu-Vana area, which marked the obvious limit of American capabilities in this arena of the oceanic war. CinCPAC was stirring around in the Central Pacific, planning some massive thrust; MacArthur had set his sights on breaching the Japs' defense line along the Bismarck Archipelago; and there was talk of action in the Aleutians.

Result: precious little equipment left over for the laggard, seemingly uninspired Skyhook operation.

None of these correlated matters bothered Blackjack Broderick. From his sanctum at Toulebonne, he fired off a series of messages to COMADTAC which added up to just one thing: *relax*. Some of these soothing dispatches, Torrey knew, possessed sharp hidden teeth. They weren't suggestions. They were implicit orders to postpone the Levu-Vana assault until spring, when the southeast trades would blow again, and when the composite force of veteran Marines and green Army troops would be more unified. Some of the men assigned to Skyhook were still drilling on the idyllic sands of remote South Sea atolls that hadn't even heard about the war until the Yanks arrived, and it would be a major undertaking—said Blackjack's logistical experts—just to ferry them into the combat area.

Contemplating all this, a man less inured to the problems of improvisation than Torrey might indeed have relaxed as ordered. Such a course would have been as safe as it was simple. If he were criticized for dilatory tactics, he could have made a respectable case for himself on the grounds that he'd merely obeyed a mandate from his superior: Vice-Admiral Broderick. But Rear Admiral Rockwell Torrey couldn't relax, particularly with Captain Paul Eddington beside him, forever driving, prodding, scheming.

Brigadier General Averell handed Torrey CinCPAC's dispatch as soon as he entered the Op hut. His remarkably youthful face was sorrowful.

"Damned tough luck, sir."

The Rock read the impersonal message. It was regretted that the

B-17 squadron currently in training at Toulebonne must be diverted to MacArthur's Fifth Air Force, and would thus be available for support of Operation Skyhook only upon special request, and with General MacArthur's express approval.

"You should have taken my five-to-one odds, mister," Torrey said unemotionally.

Averell shook his head. "All this proves, sir, is that those fellows in SouWesPAC have more muscle with the Joint Chiefs than we've got."

"Aren't you going to protest this friggin' outrage?"

Torrey looked at Eddington, who was glowering at the offensive bit of paper, and rubbing his balled fist. The chief of staff wore a small bandage over his left cheek, he noted.

"No." He stifled the bitterness that had begun to edge his voice. "If there's any appeal, it's up to CinCPAC. But I doubt if he'll agree. Washington sees the Big Picture a lot plainer than we do. They've got reasons, I suppose . . ."

Averell asked, "Shall we keep working on those runways?"

"Yes. Same schedule. I want 'em ready in ten—no, now it's only nine—days." Torrey beckoned to his Air Operations officer. "Find out how soon we can equip some Wildcat fighters with pontoon wingtanks for long-range photo missions."

AirOps' pallid face turned a shade paler, but he said, "Yes, sir," and headed for the telephone.

The stubby Grumman F4Fs had a normal flight radius of about five hundred miles. Unless they were launched from a carrier that had maneuvered into close range, the standard Wildcats would be exceedingly ineffectual during Skyhook preliminaries. With wing-tanks, however, they might make the roundtrip from Gavabutu to Levu-Vana—if they didn't tangle with a pack of Zeros. Should that happen, you could kiss your Wildcats goodbye, because the extra weight of their auxiliary tanks would mean eliminating most of their defensive armament.

Captain Forrest Tuthill stomped across the narrow room from his drafting table.

"We need that high-altitude photography damned bad," he said. "Our charts have more holes in 'em than a wheel of Swiss cheese."

Torrey agreed. "Photos—and some on-the-spot reports from Clay Canfil's outfit."

Egan Powell glanced up from his desk in the farthest corner of the Quonset. "The old boy ought to be reporting any day now—if his luck holds."

"Better order the chaplain to start praying round the clock," Eddington advised him.

Noticing the chief of staff's bandaged face for the first time, Powell inquired innocently, "Bucking for a Purple Heart, fella?"

"Negative," Eddington rasped. "This is a friendly wound." But he didn't elaborate.

The Rock walked back to the table with Tuthill, and stood there for a moment moodily surveying the spread-out charts. Levu-Vana seemed farther away than the moon itself, and just about as unexplored, for their chosen beachhead at Lakola Bay was less clearely defined than the Crater of Copernicus. Months ago, lulled by Admiral Broderick's own procrastination, Neville Balder had delayed fullscale aerial reconnaissance until some later date when the heavens presumably would be bluer, or the Japs less threatening, or the mysterious portents on which he based his infrequent decisions more favorable. Now he, Torrey, was paying dearly for Balder's hesitancy.

"Lakola Bay," Tuthill observed, "looks like a damned poor place to commit a fullscale gunfire support group, even if we knew every square inch of shoalwater, which we sure as hell don't."

The Rock said dryly, "Unless we get more ships that problem may be purely academic, anyhow." He swung toward the blackboard on which were listed the major combat vessels currently available to ADTAC. *Old Swayback*'s name still stood alone, its questionable majesty dimmed by the smudginess of the original chalked lettering, but the number of destroyers had dropped to four. "Why?" he asked.

"Convoy escort," Tuthill said dourly, "*back* to Pearl."

"What's your best estimate of our needs for Skyhook, Tut?" Unhesitatingly, in the manner of a valedictorian delivering a much-rehearsed speech, the Operations captain intoned, "A four-carrier division to soften up the beachhead before the landing . . . one of those brandnew battlewagons for close-in shore bombardment . . . plus a couple of heavy cruisers, and one of the light A.A. types like *Moultrie,* to stay with us through the whole operation."

"I know *Moultrie,*" The Rock mused. "Larry Moorian's got her. Damned fine ship."

Tuthill pursued his script: "We'll want another pair of cruisers—heavies—lying offshore in case the Nips try anything fancy. There ought to be at least six escort carriers standing by, too, after the Big Boys leave. And I haven't mentioned the tincans. It'll take a full twelve-ship squadron to give adequate support and screening, plus what's already on hand."

"Sounds pretty modest, Tut."

"If I were a dreamer instead of a practical man, sir, I'd double that list."

"Yes," Torrey said, "but we'd still be waiting and dreaming a year from now."

"Exactly, admiral."

The Rock bent closer to scrutinize a small indentation on Levu-Vana's east coast. This marked the innermost segment of Lakola Bay. Skyhook's payoff. Here the troops would storm ashore, while a dozen or more transports and cargoships of the amphibious force nervously awaited their turn to unload their irreplaceable cargos of weapons, ammo, vehicles, and foodstuffs upon the jumbled beach.

Tuthill was right, as usual, he concluded.

Lakola Bay was too restrictive for a fastmoving gunfire support squadron to maneuver efficiently, and it would be a hell of a lot worse for those helpless auxiliary vessels. Still, you did what you could with what you had, or you did nothing. The longer Torrey dallied now, after all the months of dalliance that had preceded his arrival at Gavabutu, the more likelihood there was of a show-down battle with the enemy in which Skyhook's woeful forces would be an odds-on favorite—to lose.

He straightened up. "Paul!"

Eddington moved to his side.

"Yes, skipper?"

"Assuming Canfil's intelligence and our photo recon provide the right answers, I want this thing ready to roll within eight weeks."

"We'll roll," the chief of staff grunted, "if we have to start 'em *swimming* toward the friggin' island!"

Admiral Broderick was less than ecstatic when he learned that his nominal subordinate at Mesquite had taken it upon himself to advance Skyhook's timetable by one full month. Yet he was also in a quandary. Aside from a certain small success in acquiring a supply of California table wines and Haig & Haig pinchbottle, Blackjack's mission to Pearl Harbor had been a failure, and now he was back at Toulebonne, nursing a compound-fractured ego.

Raising his scotch highball, he peered meditatively through the clear crystal at the Senator, who sat across from him in the breakfast nook which became their private bar once the sun crept below the yardarm. The prismed amber shrank Owynn's florid face into something that might have hung on an Amazonian headhunter's trophy wall. In spite of his dolorous mood, he grinned.

Then he sobered again.

What had the Big Boss said when he'd complained about the Nips' wholesale exodus just before Operation Rathole?

"Although Torrey didn't catch all the rabbits," the Old Man had drawled in his annoyingly placid way, "there were plenty left over to make a doggoned tasty stew. And that's mighty enjoyable after a man's gone hungry for such a long time." He'd looked out the windows, then, toward the glistening harbor, before he murmured, "Perhaps Torrey didn't exercise the fullest possible restraint. Maybe he should have kept you better informed. But you know, admiral, here we've got a fellow who's willing to move, and I don't think we'd better throw any roadblocks in his way . . . just for the sake of protocol."

Blackjack had blinked pretty hard at that one.

All right, he'd told himself, no roadblocks. But there'd also be no more nasty surprises like Rathole, and the credit henceforth would go where it belonged—to the Senior Officer Present. True enough. Toulebonne was two hundred miles down the watery pike. Yet Vice-Admiral John Henry Broderick, USN, who was senior to Rear Admiral Rockwell Torrey, USN, by one full star and seven long years, technically ruled as SOP for the area.

. . . Neal Owynn was addressing him in his soporific baritone. "Personally, B.J., I don't think Torrey can meet his ridiculous schedule. He's no Halsey. He can't work miracles. And now that MacArthur's grabbing our Fortresses, his reconnaissance is all shot to hell. So what can he do? Stick his head out the Quonset door and ask the Japs what's cooking?"

"Torrey doesn't stymie easily," Blackjack said petulantly, giving the devil his due.

"This time he's got problems he doesn't even know about yet." Owynn took a sip of heavily creamed coffee from a three-starred cup. "Even the command structure he's inherited with Skyhook would be enough by itself to drive a Mexican general out of his mind. I know about these things, B.J., because they're political. Joint Chiefs okay the overall Pacific strategy—provided it doesn't screw up their European picnic—and then Cominch relays it to CinCPAC, who bucks it along to you, and after that you pass it to Torrey, whose job is selling the mess to all three Services under his tactical control. Four—if you count the Marines separately."

As the Senator considered this unwieldly arrangement, a gleam of admiration lit up his fishblue eyes, the way an art dealer's shrewd gaze brightens at the sight of some long-lost masterwork.

"Hell," Broderick snorted, "what you've outlined is strictly normal procedure."

"Ah, but it isn't!" Owynn said triumphantly. "This is only the lid on Torrey's kettle of eels. Wait'll Torrey starts asking for help *outside* of that chain of command. He'll sit around on his duff for a week before MacArthur's Fifth Air Force provides a support bombing mission. Central Pacific's carriers may be busy the very day he needs a major strike. And now even the British are in the act—with their two-bit Aussie 'navy.'"

"I've wrestled with this same set-up for seven months," Broderick pointed out, "and not unsuccessfully either."

Sure, Owynn thought, it's worked fine because we haven't done anything except smooth ruffled feelings and keep people happy. But he said ingratiatingly: "Unlike yourself, B.J., Torrey's a lousy diplomat. And he's surrounded by a damned hotheaded bunch of guys who'll get him into trouble. Wait and see."

"Waiting," Blackjack said complacently, "will be a distinct pleasure."

The Senator lit a thin Havana. He felt in an expansive mood, despite a tender spot on his jaw that still ached after eleven days. Sometimes it was good to serve as mentor to a three-star admiral.

"I'm reminded," he observed, "of a situation that once came up in the United States Senate. My public affairs subcommittee had been digging into subversion in Hollywood, and we'd unearthed some rather interesting stuff, when along came a House group that alleged we'd jumped their claim. Actually, it was more a matter of method than of jurisdiction, but those fellows got mad as hell. They'd been fighting subversion for years, they claimed, and knew all the ropes. D'you know what finally happened? Nobody did a goddamned thing."

"I don't see your point, Neal."

"Look at it this way—Torrey's chairman of the new 'committee' that's getting set to launch Skyhook. He wants things his way, which is pretty unorthodox, you've got to admit. But there's this *earlier* 'committee' already on the ground, and it figures he's full of theoretical crap. So they're set to make things tough for him. You know. Marines who don't like Navy brass telling 'em where to hit the beaches. Army Air that resents the hell out of being ordered around by gyrene flyboys. Infantry jealous as hell of paratroopers. Even civilian freighter captains balking at too much pressure from ADTAC operations."

Owynn's full lips formed a pouting circle and a ring of rich Havana smoke punctuated his last remark.

"Maybe we'd better do something about it," Blackjack suggested.

"My advice," the Senator said, "remains the same—wait."

"How long?"

"Until the Skyhook snafu gets so goddamn bad it stinks from Gavabutu to Oahu."

"And then?"

"Then they'll have to send for the Old Master, B.J. Guy named John Henry Broderick . . ."

That late autumn there was a macabre guessing game played throughout the Pacific, wherever strategical or tactical staffs got together to plan new amphibious adventures, called *How Many Casualties When We Get There?* Usually it was played by the men who had to translate the paperwork into action—the combat types—although sometimes the staffs themselves joined in the fun at academically safe long range. Since ADTAC was one of those command anomalies, however, which combined fact with theory, there was an immediacy about The Game as played at Mesquite that didn't pertain at Pearl Harbor, Brisbane, Toulebonne, or even at Nouméa, where Halsey flew his flag.

Carrying their clumsy new wingtanks, the single-engined Wildcats howled out of Gavabutu just before dawn every day, to scout a forty-five-degree quadrant lying roughly between north-northwest and north-northeast, and extending outward some seven hundred miles. When they straggled home, their pilots were hustled directly to the Op shack to make their eyewitness reports while their films were being processed and their memories were still green.

The redhot Billy Mitchell bombers and the lesser Douglas Dauntlesses serviced a Milk Run between Gavabutu and Levu-Vana, but loaded with bombs instead of film, keeping the pressure on the Japs as best they could.

Always at the same thirty-knot speed, ADTAC's overworked destroyers every night swept up the Pass that led to Levu-Vana and thence to Pelaki Shima, three at a time, in search of Jap convoys. It was risky, rugged work. Before the first month of Skyhook's gestation period ended, The Rock's meager six-ship squadron had been whittled down to five, and two of these were operating below par, with smashed gunmounts, jammed torpedo tubes, battle-damaged controls, and sundry other mishaps to show for their nocturnal ramblings.

Occasionally Torrey received help from far-distant SouWesPAC, but not often for it was an eighteen-hundred-mile roundtrip between the Fifth Air Force's Fortress field and Levu-Vana. Meteorological conditions had to be ultra-favorable before they'd make the attempt. Gottlieb's weather was anything but perfect. It stank in spades. So two of the three Fortress missions aborted, and the full burden of softening up Levu-Vana was thrown back on Averell's slim shoulders.

Day after day Torrey watched his aircraft strength dwindle. He'd started with less than two hundred serviceable planes of all types. Now the big blackboard in the Op hut proclaimed 157. Despite this costly effort, however, the Nips kept right on building their shrouded airstrip on Levu-Vana, bolstering their garrison, cementing their beachhead defenses.

At 0400 one lowering predawn, when it was still black as a witch's caldron, Clayton Canfil slipped back into Mesquite as supercargo aboard a searacked submarine. Going directly to headquarters, he demanded to see The Rock forthwith, regardless of the unseemly hour.

Impressed by Canfil's fierce Old Man of the Sea intensity, the

ADTAC duty officer, who was new in the area, swallowed his apprehension, and ordered a Marine orderly to escort the dirty, unshaven, weatherbeaten Intelligence officer across the darkened compound.

Canfil let out a disgusted snort. "D'you know where I've just come from, sonny?"

"No," the OD said, "I don't," appending a belated "sir" in case this grizzled apparition carried more hidden rank than his own two stripes.

"Picnicking with the Nips at Lakola Bay."

"Oh."

"So," Canfil growled, "I sure as hell don't need a guide to show me where Admiral Torrey hangs out."

The OD smiled faintly. "Yes, sir. I just didn't want you to get shot as a prowler."

"That's just another chance I'll have to take, lieutenant."

Canfil strode unerringly to the Flag quarters, and knocked boldly on the screendoor. A dim light flicked on. The Rock, yawning but already alert, came to the entrance in his tattered bathrobe. If he was astonished to find Canfil there an hour before sunrise, he kept his feelings well under control.

"Come in, Clay."

"Thanks."

"Smoke?"

Canfil shook his graycropped head. "No, sir. I've gotten used to chewing tobacco during the last few weeks. I'll stick to twist, if you don't mind."

Torrey motioned toward a canvas campchair. "Sorry the leather job's gone," he said. "I got rid of it. Too damned soft."

Canfil grimaced. "Good thing, admiral. After what I'm going to tell you, maybe you won't want to sit down again—ever."

"Shoot, fella."

"Okay." Canfil reached into his shirt and brought out an oilskin-wrapped package. "My map," he explained, unrolling the small bundle and spreading the chart across the stained galley table. It was drawn in pencil on thin drafting paper.

Torrey switched on another light so he could scrutinize it more carefully, and as he absorbed the details of the crude topographical sketch, he emitted a long, low whistle.

Canfil said in a wry tone, "See something you don't like?"

"Plenty," The Rock muttered. "If you're right, Clay, we're up to our Plimsoll mark in trouble."

"I'm right." Canfil affirmed. "But I'd respectfully suggest that we're away *past* the Plimsoll mark and takin' water—fast."

Mouth pursed, nodding, Torrey returned to the map.

The Jap airfield, which had defied accurate photo interpretation because of the sheltering cocopalms and its camouflage netting, bore Canfil's notation: "Three-fourths complete. Est. 6,000 ft. when ready. Hard surface. Revetments for appr. 200 planes." Along the nippled indentation where breastshaped Lakola Bay touched the enemy's base, he'd scrawled: "Heavy log emplacements. Concrete ready to pour. Deep trenches. Barbedwire stockpiled." And across the bay itself was the bleak legend: "Coralheads cleared for major anchorage."

When Torrey looked up, Canfil said almost apologetically, "That's only part of the bad news, sir."

"Keep shooting."

"The Levu-Vana natives told me the Nips are bringing hundreds of troops into Toka-Rota every bloody night. They march 'em across the island to Pala Passage, where they're ferried to the main island, and stashed in isolated bivouacs so they won't be so conspicuous. In the short time I was up there, they must have landed five thousand men."

"At that rate," Torrey said, "the one division they've assigned us won't be worth a damn in another few weeks."

At best, an attacking force should outnumber its dug-in opponent by two-to-one, he knew. Maybe better. After the Americans had established a beachhead on Levu-Vana, even if they managed to liquidate its defenders in the first couple of days, there was always the chance the Nips would try a major amphibious comeback. Without reserve forces to back up his committed assault troops, Skyhook could change from triumph to disaster overnight.

Canfil had removed his muddy moccasins and was rubbing his bare feet.

"Couple of nights ago, just before that pigboat fetched me off Levu-Vana," he said, "I was havin' dinner with some Nips. Only they didn't know it. They ate rice and fish around a campfire while I gnawed on K rations out in the darkness where they couldn't see me. After a while they got high as Oriental dragon kites on sake, and started yammering about the big clambake that was going to take place at Pelaki Shima. My Japanese won't win any prizes, admiral, but I savvied enough to figure out what they were driving at. These fellers had only just arrived so they knew the score up north."

He paused, and Torrey demanded testily, "What was the score?"

"A whole goddamned fleet is slated for Pelaki—carriers, battlewagons, transports—the works!"

"Did your Nip friends reveal when this rendezvous was going to take place?"

Canfil tried to stifle a yawn. "Soon. That's all."

Suddenly Torrey's annoyance eased and the acid went out of his voice. Here, he realized, was an old man—a damned gallant weary old man—who deserved his old man's privilege of bothersome garrulity.

"Hit the sack, Clay. I want you to brief the staff in my quarters before noon chow."

"One thing's certain as Max Gottlieb's friggin' rain," Paul Eddington growled, after Canfil finished his report. "We can't let Pelaki go unobserved for a single day."

"It'll cost us plenty—" AirOps began.

"I don't care if your reconnaissance planes have to taxi the whole goddamn nine hundred miles. *They've got to keep us posted!*"

AirOps looked beseechingly toward The Rock, hoping for a reprieve from the chief of staff's harsh orders, but the admiral's stony countenance gave him no encouragement. So he said: "We've hesitated to ask SouWesPAC for operational support this early. They might think we're crying 'Wolf!' Maybe we'd better try 'em for size, anyhow."

"Beggars," Eddington remarked sourly, thinking of the Fifth Air Force's two abortive missions over Levu-Vana, "can't be choosers. Wrap your S O S around a tincup."

Torrey had been listening reflectively to their exchange. Now he spoke. "CinCPAC's kept a submarine watch on the Nips' base at Truk for weeks. We'll get advance warning from Pearl of any real southward push."

"But suppose they reinforce Pelaki from Cape Titan instead of the Carolines?" Eddington demanded. "We're thinner than the Gavabutu Trots up there. Chances are ten-to-one they'd sneak a task force all the way into Pelaki before they got spotted."

"At last accounts," Egan Powell said, "all they had in Cape Titan were some old battlewagons and one carrier."

Eddington snorted. "If they pulled a fast one and replenished their cupboard out of Formosa, they could lay a whole bloody fleet into Cape Titan and nobody'd be the wiser."

"What d'you suggest, Paul?" Captain Tuthill asked.

"That we don't depend on a goddamn soul. It's our baby. Nobody else is going to squander any affection on the little bastard. Let's quit kidding ourselves. Sure. We'll give humble thanks for anything Dug-out-Doug or the Big Boss can spare. But let's count it as gravy—not the main course."

"Speaking of gravy," Tuthill said ironically, "here's a small spot for your vest—it came from Toulebonne just before the meeting."

He handed the message flimsy to Torrey, who read it aloud:

"EIGHT LANDING SHIP TANKS (LST) HAVE BEEN ASSIGNED ADTAC FOR TRAINING PURPOSES AND FOR FUTURE AMPHIBIOUS USE. SHOULD ARRIVE IN AREA WITHIN ONE MONTH. FOUR WILL BE SENT YOU FULLY COMBAT LOADED WITH FIRST INCREMENT OF MARINES FOR SKYHOOK EXPEDITION. OTHERS WILL REMAIN HERE PENDING FORMATION OF ARMY ASSAULT TEAM AND WILL FOLLOW IN APPROXIMATELY SIX WEEKS. URGE MAXIMUM UTILIZATION OF THIS NEW TYPE CRAFT WHICH HAS PROVED EFFICACIOUS IN MEDITERRANEAN OPERATIONS PARTICULARLY SINCE CONVENTIONAL ATTACK TRANSPORTS MAY BE IN EXTREMELY SHORT SUPPLY WHEN SKYHOOK IS MOUNTED NEXT SPRING . . ."

The Rock spread the dispatch over an ancient catsup stain on his worktable. Eddington picked it up by one corner, as if the paper contained live typhus germs, and he cocked his bullethead to reread the message.

"LSTs!" Scorn increased the rasp in his voice. "Frigging shoeboxes!"

"I don't know, Paul . . ." Torrey looked through the Quonset's downslope window toward the roadstead where a pair of Liberty ships were awaiting their turn at ADTAC's overworked dock facilities. "This mightn't be as bad as it sounds. They're ugly brutes. Slow as molasses, too. Maybe ten knots when they're scared. But from all accounts they've done a hell of a job for the British—and our crowd's counting on 'em for the North African show."

The chief of staff dusted the microbes off the dispatch. " 'Conventional attack transports may be in extremely short supply when Skyhook is mounted next spring,' " he mocked. "Why doesn't Blackjack say what he means—that we haven't a chance in Hades of getting anything better than these Mickey Mouse contraptions?"

"Admiral Broderick hates to hurt people's feelings," The Rock observed with mild sarcasm. "Besides, Paul, didn't I hear you say just a minute ago that we can't depend on a goddamn soul?"

Eddington's ferocious scowl faded. "*Touché,* skipper."

"At the risk of sounding like an Academy prof again," Torrey said, "let me remind you that LSTs proved their worth one hell of a lot of years before this war was ever thought of. The Greeks used something like 'em in the Peloponnesian fracas. They're the original amphibious vessel. March your troops aboard at the point of departure, march 'em off again at the beachhead. Simple as that." He reached for his tobacco jar and filled his bulldog briar. "I suspect LSTs might be damned good economy vehicles for us peasants who might have to pack up at a moment's notice to escape the bill collector." Torrey paused to light his pipe before he concluded: "We've given ourselves eight weeks to prepare for Skyhook. But suppose the Nip sheriff shows up with an eviction notice in—say—seven weeks? Do you gentlemen get the picture?"

"Yes," Eddington admitted with unusual humility, "we get it."

The Rock rewarded him with a generous smile. "Then let's send Toulebonne a priority message requesting those LSTs at their earliest convenience." He added emphatically, "But don't bother to insert the usual 'practicable' before 'convenience,' because that'll give Broderick's sea lawyers too much leeway. Just say we want to spare them all the fuss and feathers of training those ships. We'll exercise 'em up here . . ."

It was raining when the staff left the Flag hut with Clayton Canfil to walk across the compound for lunch in the officers' mess. Standing in his Quonset doorway, Torrey wished he could join them while they jovially extracted the juicier details of Canfil's reconnoitering exploit from the saturnine old Intelligence officer. Sometimes he dined with his staff. But more often he was the prisoner on the bridge, whether afloat or ashore, traditionally isolated from commonfolk, and compelled to sup alone, just as he thought alone.

After the steward's mate unloaded his tin tray, The Rock regarded the victuals distastefully. Standard brown Navy soup. Mammoth ham-and-cheese sandwich between two hunks of grayish bread. Pot of black coffee. The uninspiring menu, he told himself, was in perfect accord with the weather, his own feelings, and the responsibility he bore for an operation as ill-favored as Skyhook.

Chewing pensively, hardly aware of what he ate, Torrey found himself speculating on how Maggie Haynes would respond if he gave voice to such melancholy musings. She'd probably tell him to go soak his damnfool head until he came to his proper senses.

There had been time for only a couple of brief telephone calls to MOB Able after he triggered the planning for Skyhook, and they were highly unsatisfactory. Maggie had seemed preoccupied, remote, and when he pressed her for an explanation she claimed the nurses were simply up to their ears preparing for "all that new business" he planned to send them. Rather cryptically, too, she'd asked him how Captain Eddington was getting along.

"Working his tail off," he informed her.

"Tough as ever?"

"Tougher."

"I'm not surprised," Maggie said in a chill voice. "Just keep the man busy, Rock, and away from MOB Able."

Recalling this curious admonition, Torrey again tried to fathom her meaning. He supposed it had something to do with whatever happened between Eddington and Ensign Dorne at their picnic. Since the night at Strangler's Cove, he was aware that Eddington's savage drive had quickened, until it became a compulsive thing, like the efforts of a caged animal to claw its way to freedom. The Rock was deeply concerned by this manic mood, especially now that he needed the roughhewn counsel which only Eddington had the frankness to impart. In war, as in politics, every staff must include at least one No man among all its conciliatory Yes men. This was Eddington's prime function.

Gottlieb's weather continued to harass them, turning Gavabutu into a murky, muddy slough and keeping even the nimblefooted

Wildcats grounded except for a few precarious photo missions they managed to fly between the onslaughts of wind and rain. By the end of the first week they had gleaned little information beyond the firsthand intelligence brought back by Clayton Canfil. There was virtually no enemy activity in Lakola Bay, the exhausted recon pilots reported, other than the goings-and-comings of the Nip tincans that ran the persistent Tokyo Trolley—thereby forcing ADTAC to keep a destroyer division constantly patrolling the long passage between Gavabutu and Levu-Vana.

As The Rock watched the outlines of the operation take shape, he could imagine that he was standing alongside a single-tracked railroad trestle while two trains thundered down upon each other from opposite directions. It was a fascinating experience. Awesome. Horrifying. The point of impact was Beach Red, Lakola Bay, Levu-Vana. If ADTAC's train were the stronger, it might derail the Japs'; if it weren't, he told himself fatalistically, they'd both have one hell of a plunge into the abyss that yawned beneath the bridge.

Nevertheless, when Captain Tuthill brought him his latest "minimum" list of their seaborne requirements, Torrey rejected it out-of-hand.

"We think this is bare-bones," he said. "But you can bet a year's sea pay the Big Boss will claim we've drawn up blueprints for a new Spanish Armada."

"Where'll we whittle it down?" the Operations officer asked hopelessly.

"All along the line. Carriers, battleships, cruisers. Even those attack transports and cargo vessels. No. Wait. Belay that, Tut. Let's keep bidding for the fast carrier striking force. Perhaps CinCPAC can spring 'em loose for a quick pass at Levu-Vana along about D minus five."

"We can always hope," Tuthill grumbled.

Eddington, who had stalked across the Op shack, suddenly snarled, "Hope, hell! You can't kill Japs with hope."

Tuthill gave The Rock an appealing glance. "Maybe Pearl will lend us one of those new battlewagons for preliminary shore bombardment."

"I wouldn't hold my breath till that happens, Tut."

"So how do we plug the gap?"

"Like this." Torrey handed him the notes he'd made. "We'll double up."

As his trained eye scanned the revamped roster, Tuthill's cadaverous face turned more funereal than ever. This was trimming away fat where fat didn't exist, he thought dismally, until Skyhook's white skeleton shone through.

"You mean the same ships will have to conduct the inshore barrage," he exclaimed, "then hightail it back to sea to cut off any Nip retaliation attempt?"

"Yes, Tut. Except for those escort carriers we've been promised. We'll leave the baby flattops out there with a small destroyer screen till the shooting's over."

"Suppose the Japs decide to move down in force from Pelaki Shima?"

"Then," Torrey said, "we'll have a devil of a scrap on our hands." He finished dryly, "But it'll be convenient—won't it?—to fight it right in our own backyard?"

Mainly because nobody else wanted her—certainly not in the areas where the bulk of the Pacific Fleet was operating—a lone Australian cruiser was ordered to join ADTAC's thin line. Her improbable name was HMAS *Diadem*. Although her presence posed some new logistical headaches, The Rock accepted this mismatched warship without hesitation, and he reversed protocol by visiting her captain less than an hour after she anchored in the roadstead off Atoka.

Diadem's skipper turned out to be a potbellied, spindle-legged, gaptoothed Aussie who resembled a cinematic version of Captain Bligh, but whose explosive laughter and boundless optimism gave an immediate lift to their drooping spirits when they gathered in the smokefilled wardroom for warm Antipodean beer and a tot of Holland gin.

Plaques on her teakwood bulkhead recounted the glorious battle history of the cruiser's ancestors all the way back to Trafalgar. Portraits of the Royal Family smiled down reassuringly. Outside on the steamy deck, redcoated despite the heat and wet, His Majesty's Marines ruffled and flourished as if this were still the eighteenth century when the British raj reigned comfortably supreme over all the lesser breeds without the law. Yet it was strangely comforting. Torrey and his aides returned ashore late that night, feeling less alone, and exhilarated by something more than the alcohol that was dispensed so generously aboard the Aussie warship.

Only Eddington appeard unmoved by the presence of the boxy little *Diadem* in the flat gray waters below ADTAC headquarters.

"Friggin' limeys," he rumbled. "More trouble than they're worth."

But then, the staff figured, Eddington didn't drink any more, and perhaps his unwonted sobriety dulled his appreciation of the finer things of life. They sighed a collective sigh. For some obscure reason which nobody could divine, the weather affected Eddington more than the others, and as the gloomy days passed, his patience shortened and his temper flared at the smallest provocation.

They learned that there was no escaping either Eddington or the rain itself, which probed wet fingers through the battens in hut windows and down ventilator gaskets, depositing dirty puddles on the Quonset decks and turning carefully drawn charts and memos into a sodden mess. Often the rain was accompanied by howling winds. Then the cocopalms would tremble and bend under the gale's thrust until their fronds stood straight as slatted boards against the wild graygreen skies. At such times Eddington's depression plumbed the depths, and his subordinates tiptoed cautiously around him, hoping to avoid the tongue lashing that followed his inevitable discovery of the least misplaced comma or undotted "i" in an Op plan annex.

Although The Rock generally remained in his own aloof quarters, receiving progress reports from ADTAC department heads, or summoning into private conference those officers whose specialty happened to bear upon the business at hand, he was not unaware of Eddington's mood. But he was at a loss to understand why his chief of staff would surrender now to the sort of despondency that had engulfed him in the past only during periods of galling inactivity.

A week later, when the chief of staff came to him early one morning asking permission to fly a Wildcat photo assignment, Torrey gave his reluctant consent. The risk might be worth it, he reckoned, if the man's turmoil could be eased by a brief exposure to physical danger. Eddington rushed off to his Quonset to get his flight gear, and even the sight of the grayfuzzy mold that sprouted from his disused boots and helmet failed to dampen his delight. He returned to The Rock's quarters armed cap-a-pie for the mission, with an automatic pistol strapped to his muscular right leg, and a fresh chart of Levu-Vana under his left arm.

In spite of his misgivings about the adventure, Torrey grinned paternally at Eddington's enthusiasm. "You look like Lindbergh, before he hopped the Atlantic."

"I feel more like a schoolkid who's taking it on the lam to go catfishing."

"Don't let any Nip truant officers catch you," Torrey said. "As your lawful guardian, I'd have a damned tough time explaining things."

"Trust me." Eddington suddenly turned serious. "This won't be a joyride. I'm worried as hell about those recon reports. Something's *got* to be happening up the line. It's too friggin' quiet for comfort. Maybe I won't spot anything either—but I won't be satisfied till I see for myself."

"I understand." The Rock gave him a sympathetic glance. "I used to be young myself once."

"You'll always see me as a snotnosed plebe, won't you, skipper?"

Torrey shook his head sadly. "Not really. But in a lot of ways you've never grown up, Paul. Perhaps you never will."

"Is that bad?"

"Only when it affects other people."

"You mean the staff?"

"Yes."

"Have they been talking?"

"No."

"I didn't think they would." Eddington stared at his mildewed flightboots. "They're a hell of a fine bunch, skipper, and I'm an unmitigated bastard. As usual."

"In that case," The Rock said, "an eight-hundred-mile flight at fifteen thousand feet might legitimize you."

"Twenty thousand feet ought to be even better, don't you reckon?"

"Possibly. Just don't push your horizontal luck too far—beyond Levu-Vana."

"Trust me," Eddington said again.

Then he threw back his shoulders and swaggered off, whistling "Anchors Aweigh" like an out-of-key calliope, while Torrey stared after his bandylegged form with an expression that was both affectionate and regretful. He wanted to call him home. Cancel this superfluous mission. Demand that Eddington return to his maps and worksheets like any normal chief of staff, leaving this sort of nonsense to younger and more expendable fellows.

But he mustn't interfere with Eddington's therapy. Sighing, he went back into the hut, to reread the scrawled note that had arrived an hour earlier on the trans-island guardmail plane from Botan, where Blackjack's Bastards now made their permanent base.

If the admiral could spare the time, Jere wrote, he would appreciate a few minutes of his sagacious paternal counsel when he flew down this afternoon to see Annalee Dorne. Torrey hadn't talked to his son for several weeks, and he wondered idly what was on the boy's mind. He supposed Jere was lonesome enough for female companionship to make the grueling journey by boat, jeep, and plane that would permit him a few minutes of hurried romance in some shadowy corner of MOB Able's recreation hut.

The Rock admired Jere's youthful determination. He was also a little envious . . .

After breakfast, Torrey checked the early-morning dispatch board which the Op shack orderly brought him with his coffee, and studied Tuthill's overnight situation report. Nothing had changed in the past eight hours.

The Japs were still lying doggo, inexplicably, as far as their sketchy recon flights could discern.

CinCPAC might be able to spare one fast carrier task group for a strike against Levu-Vana—provided COMADTAC guaranteed him targets that made it worth diverting these valuable ships from other vital duties.

Toulebonne hoped the first LSTs would be ready to move north in about ten days; but reminded COMADTAC that neither ships nor crews were fully trained, so both would need considerable indoctrination (whatever the hell *that* was) prior to combat assignment.

SouWesPAC's Fortresses had essayed another mission against Levu-Vana, but bad weather had forced them to reverse course at the halfway point . . .

Idly sipping black coffee while he read, The Rock had been giving only partial attention to this mundane file. But now he set down his thick mug and seized SouWesPAC's dispatch with both hands as its final sentences snapped him alert.

. . . Fortunately, the Fifth Air Force radioed, the B-17s' excursion wasn't a total washout because enroute home to their Papuan base they'd laid a few eggs on Cape Titan, where the Nips seemed to have concentrated more shipping than usual. Although the Fortresses made their pass at twenty-two thousand fee to escape heavy flak, their bombardiers positively identified one battleship of the *Haruna* class and two carriers . . .

Torrey stepped to the chart on the Flag hut wall. Cape Titan occupied the apex of an attenuated triangle whose lower points were Levu-Vana on the east, and Papua on the west. For weeks it had been even more barren of combatant shipping than Pelaki Shima. But now, if the Japs had finally decided to mobilize here, the pincers movement he'd anticipated—*feared* was the better word—might already be underway.

The key was still Pelaki itself, however, and nobody had the faintest idea what the enemy proposed there. Unless, Torrey told himself without much conviction, Eddington's mission revealed something.

After a last mordant glance at the map, he donned his oilskins, swung his bulldog briar upside-down to keep the rain out of the bowl, and walked bareheaded across the narrow compound to the Op shack.

Tuthill met him at the door, looking unhappy. "Did you know the chief of staff's off on a recon flight?"

"Yes." Torrey shook water off his raincoat. "He checked in with me shortly after dawn."

"Eddington picked a hell of a time to go flying," Tuthill grumbled. "Have you read that Cape Titan sighting report?"

"I've seen it, Tut, and it's bad." The Rock relit his pipe, carefully, before he added matter-of-factly, "Paul has a bee in his bonnet that Averell's kid pilots don't see too well in spite of their twenty-twenty eyesight. He wants a firsthand look at Pelaki."

"Or," suggested Tuthill ironically, "maybe he's just getting antsy like the rest of us."

"Eddington was born antsy," Torrey agreed. "Let's just hope his hunch pays off. We need that Word from up north."

Tuthill regarded him curiously. "You think a hell of a lot of that fellow, don't you?"

"He's an old friend. We've seen some tough times together."

"But it must be more than that."

The candor of this remark surprised Torrey. Despite his habitual sarcasm, which spared nobody, Tuthill was a stickler for the amenities, and until now he'd never presumed upon the professional relationship that existed between department head and admiral. Tuthill's sudden departure from protocol was significant. He deserved a fair answer.

"Yes," The Rock said slowly, "it's a damned sight more than mere friendship." He paused, then asked abruptly, "Have you a son, Tut?"

"Three, sir. One's in Annapolis."

"Proud of your midshipman?"

"Like a peacock."

"In a way," Torrey went on, "I suppose that's how I regard Paul, even though he's only three years younger. He's the kind of fellow I'd always wanted to be—back when my Old Man was climbing the Navy ladder himself."

"Eddington was only a class behind me at the Academy," Tuthill said. "I still remember him from those days. Hell of a guy. Always driving. And always up to his ugly ears in trouble."

"Paul's sin is commission. Not omission. Nobody ever faulted him for taking the easy way out, or for sitting tight, until Pearl Harbor." Tuthill raised his eyebrows, but remained silent. "After his wife was killed, he went to pieces, just as if he'd held his own court-martial and sentenced himself to oblivion. With a whisky bottle."

"I've heard about that," Tuthill said.

"Then I got the brilliant notion that Paul Eddington could be saved—for himself and the Navy—if he could be kept busy doing things he liked, so he wouldn't have a chance to brood." Torrey examined his pipe. "He was worth saving, Tut."

"But now Eddington's learning that staff duty can be damned boring, too, and he's headed for trouble again, isn't he?"

"Several kinds. Right now he's halfway to Pelaki Shima!"

By Air Operations' best reckoning, Eddington would reach the point of no return in his Wildcat fighter at 1245. Provided he was flying a straight course, his wingtanked recon craft would be about one hundred miles north of the Jap base at Pelaki Shima at that turnaround hour.

It was unlikely, Torrey knew, that Eddington would break radio silence to contact Mesquite unless he were spotted by the enemy, or unless he chanced upon something so fantastic it couldn't wait until he got back.

The Rock watched the brass hands of the Operations clock clench at noon, and he sweated out another thirty minutes before he arose, pulled on his soggy oilskins, and went down the hill to AirOps, where any news from Eddington would arrive first.

In another quarter hour, he knew, the chief of staff would have run out his string, and if he didn't reverse course, he'd soon face the unpleasant choice of crashlanding on some equatorial island or ditching at sea. In one instance Eddington would unquestionably be captured by the Nips; in the other, he stood a one-in-a-thousand chance of being scooped up by an itinerant Yank sub—assuming he pancaked the Wildcat delicately enough to allow him to inflate his liferaft before the plane went down like a piece of wet coral.

There was a third alternative which Torrey didn't even care to consider: Eddington might fall prey to a Pelaki Shima fighter patrol in his defenseless recon craft.

Most of AirOps' officers were huddled around the shortwave loudspeaker when The Rock entered the Quonset, and they didn't hear the screendoor slam. Senseless crackling noises from the frequency assigned Klondike, which was the code name for Eddington's mission, filled the hut.

"Any news from our wandering boy?" Torrey asked. It was an inane remark, he knew, but he had to say something, because the tension in the shack was almost physical.

AirOps turned, saw the admiral, and scrambled to his feet.

"Not a peep, sir," he said. "It's quiet as a tomb." He stopped, embarrassed by his inept simile.

". . . Crazy damned fool," Torrey muttered.

"Sir?"

"Not you, commander. Captain Eddington."

"Yes, sir," AirOps said, relieved, and privately agreeing with The Rock.

For another ten minutes they strained toward the frying-pan gibberish that emanated from the loudspeaker. Crouched at the panel and wearing a headset, AirOps' chief radioman fiddled gingerly with the tuning knobs. It was now 1250.

"Eddington should be heading for home," Torrey said, "with the Word."

AirOps nodded sententiously. "No news is good news, sir." He tapped the radioman on the shoulder. "Keep listening, Howard. Now's when Klondike will report—if he's going to speak at all."

"We're right on him, sir."

There was a renewed burst of static from the loudspeaker and the radioman winced as his earphones caught the full brunt of the disturbance. When the airwaves cleared, the gibberish seemed to be making more sense. It sounded almost human, although it was still unintelligible.

AirOps peered over the radioman's shoulder. "What the hell is it, chief?"

Instead of replying, Howard began writing furiously on his clipboard.

"Klondike to ADTAC, Position 4 deg. 12 min. N., 150 deg. 2 min. W. Enemy surface contact. Many ships. Two carriers, three battleships, six cruisers, eleven destroyers. Making good speed on course-175 . . ." For a moment the radioman stopped scribbling. Then he meticulously appended Klondike's final words: *"All for now. Nip patrol sees me. I'm heading for cloud cover—and the frigging barn!"*

Torrey jammed his right fist hard against his left palm, in unwitting imitation of Eddington's favorite gesture at moments of great stress.

"Stay with Klondike," he told them, "and pray him in, though I doubt if he'll open up again. I'm going up the hill. We've got work to do!"

Within thirty minutes a dispatch had been written, coded, and sent Most Urgent to Pearl Harbor, giving the Japanese Fleet's whereabouts and its obvious destination: Pelaki Shima. So CinC-PAC wouldn't miss the Papuan Fortresses' revelation of enemy combatant tonnage at Cape Titan, this intelligence was also embodied in the message.

"CONSIDER MAXIMUM AIR STRIKE AGAINST SHIPS BOUND FOR PELAKI SHIMA ESSENTIAL," The Rock concluded, "TO REDUCE ORANGE THREAT AGAINST SKYHOOK WHICH IS CURRENTLY SCHEDULED FOR DECEMBER FIFTEENTH."

As the grammarians put it, *currently* was the operative word, since the enemy appeared to be on the move in such overwhelming strength against ADTAC's outnumbered forces. Unless the Nips' seapower could be scaled down, Torrey knew, he might as well postpone the Levu-Vana invasion until spring, just as Blackjack Broderick wanted. There was no element of surprise left, now—that is, except what might be derived from an unexpectedly bold counterattack so far ahead of schedule that even these formidable Jap squadrons would be caught off-base.

"Tut!"

The Operations officer glanced up from the chart on which he was plotting the enemy contact and estimated advance north of Pelaki Shima. "Sir?"

"When's that second batch of LSTs due?"

"Third of December."

Another goddamn week! Undoubtedly the Japs would hole up at Pelaki Shima for a few days before they struck south again, although even this was a chancy assumption. Suppose they intended to reinforce Levu-Vana? In that case they'd come down the way the Assyrians did in Byron's poem—how did it go?—"like a wolf on the fold." Byron's grandfather was an admiral, Torrey recalled, whose nickname was "Foulweather Jack." The old seadog would have appreciated this situation, in which foul weather was such a prime factor, and he wouldn't have wasted a minute signaling for action. Those were simpler days when you drove your fleet at the foe without knowing much about his strength until his fighting tops came in sight along the horizon, after which you set your strategy with your sails. Maybe that was better. It eliminated one hell of a lot of agonizing.

Torrey said, "When those LSTs are halfway between Toulebonne and here, we'll issue 'em standby orders."

"Sir?"

"Maybe we won't bring 'em into Gavabutu at all."

"Where, then?"

"We could stage a high seas rendezvous, Tut, and send the whole caboodle straight to Levu-Vana."

"Without final rehearsals?"

"Yes."

"You'd be risking a monumental foul-up, admiral. Those kid-skippers are green as grass. Mostly reservists. And I doubt if the troops have had much amphib training."

The Rock smiled glacially. "It's like your first parachute jump. You can't rehearse that, either, but if it works, you walk away from it."

Tuthill considered the admiral's proposal judiciously. "We would pick up a couple of days, of course, doing that," he mused aloud.

"And those two days," Torrey said, "might give us just the bare margin we need—to establish a foothold on Lakola Bay before the Nips arrive."

Tuthill's hollow cheeks tightened as he picked up his dagger-sharp pencil, T square, and dividers, and turned back to his cherished map. Approvingly, Torrey saw that he was adding a new element to the fine-line tracery on the acetate: the probable point along the four-hundred-mile route from Gavabutu to Levu-Vana where ADTAC would knot the shoestring that tied his meager forces.

At 1400 they sent out for coffee and sandwiches, but nobody stopped working.

An hour later their revised plan for Skyhook had taken form like a Guy Fawkes gunpowder plot, hatched in dark secrecy, yet with a paradoxical calmness that arose from the awareness that now they'd also reached the point of no return, and must plunge ahead regardless of the enemy's superior numbers.

Torrey raised his head, astonished, as Jere walked into the Operations hut. Then he grinned. In his preoccupation with their new strategy, he had completely forgotten his son's impending visit.

"Hello, lieutenant."

" 'Lo, sir," Jere responded in a flat, dull voice. "You seem pretty tied up. Maybe I'd better beat it."

The Rock caught the stricken look on his boy's face, and sought to rally him. "Hell, no! Today's business concerns you, too, fella, and your whole gang."

"It's stopped raining, sir. Can we step outside for a minute?"

"Certainly," Torrey replied, puzzled.

Together they went out into the gray afternoon. Jere guided his father toward a secluded spot behind the Quonset, where three cocopalms formed a natural bower.

"I just didn't want to talk in front of all those fellows," he said unnecessarily.

"Problems, son?"

Jere nodded bleakly. "I came down here because I hadn't heard from Annalee for damned near three weeks. She wouldn't answer my letters. And then yesterday I got *this* in the guardmail." From his watchpocket he pulled a small gold ring, which Torrey recognized as the Cunliffe crest. "So I figured right then I'd better find out for myself what the hell's the matter."

"And what did you discover?" The Rock asked gently.

"Nothing, sir. Absolutely nothing. Annalee just says we'd better forget the whole thing."

"She won't tell you why?"

"No."

"Perhaps her work—"

Jere interrupted coldly, "Work never bothered her before, sir. We always managed. And nobody's so busy she can't write."

Torrey regarded his distraught son for a moment without speaking, wondering what he could say to comfort him. (What had he, himself, done when Athalie left him? He remembered. He'd gone on a skullshattering bender which didn't help a bit. But he hadn't turned to anybody else for comfort, because there hadn't been anyone else.)

Finally he said, "It's rough, son. Damned rough. Especially since you're hardly in a position now to court the young lady all over again . . ."

Jere had been staring out toward the steelgray seascape. He turned. "You must have read my mind, sir. I was going to ask if I couldn't get a couple of weeks' temporary duty at ADTAC headquarters."

"Sorry, fella." The Rock's tone was kindly, but firm. "It's out of the question."

"One week?"

"I'm afraid not. This afternoon—barely an hour ago—we pulled the pin on Skyhook. Your squadron's right in the middle of things —with a damned tough mission to fulfill. They'll need every man. When you return to Botan tonight, I'm going to make you officer-messenger for the PTs' operating orders." He regarded Jere shrewdly. "I don't think you'll have much time to worry about Annalee till this affair's wrapped up. Then maybe we can find a T.D. spot for you here."

Jere shrugged. He seemed strangely, almost fatalistically, content with The Rock's decision.

"Okay, sir."

"There's a rugged month ahead for you youngsters," Torrey said. "We're going to load your boats on LSTs and turn you loose on the high seas until we can smuggle you onto the beachhead. After that . . ." He shrugged, too.

"Maybe we'll get a crack at some big stuff for a change," Jere said hopefully.

"You'd like that, wouldn't you?"

"It'd sure as hell take my mind off my troubles."

The Rock clapped Jere on the right shoulder, and was pleased to feel the iron in his muscles. He had a back like the stroke on an Academy crew, and his narrowed eyes had taken on a stubborn glint that was a damned sight more Torrey than Cunliffe.

When they returned to the Op hut, Tuthill was waiting impatiently with a fresh dispatch in his hand.

"Pearl Harbor didn't waste any time," he said.

Torrey read the message: "FAST CARRIER TASK GROUP 48.3 WILL STRIKE PELAKI SHIMA AT DAWN IF SURFACE CONDITIONS PERMIT REFUELING TOMORROW. REGRET CANNOT RELEASE THIS GROUP FOR EXTENDED OPERATIONS YOUR AREA. AM FORMING SPECIAL TASK UNIT 48.9.1 TO REPORT TO ADTAC TUESDAY INCLUDING LIGHT CRUISER MOULTRIE, ESCORT CARRIERS EAGLET, CHICKENHAWK, AND FALCON (CVES), AND SIX DESTROYERS OF SQUADRON 213. HEAVY COMMITMENTS ELSEWHERE PRECLUDE ADDITIONAL SUPPORT AT THIS TIME."

Tuthill watched him closely. "I hope," he said, "we don't choke on these rich crumbs off the Central Pacific table."

"We won't," The Rock assured him. "Acknowledge with thanks. And send a separate dispatch to Captain Larry Moorian on *Moultrie*—'WELCOME TO SUNNY SOUTH PACIFIC. LOOKING FORWARD TO WILD GOAT SHISHKEBAB.'"

Much later that night Eddington came back. Unshaven, incredibly weary, he shambled into Torrey's quarters after a perfunctory knock, and gratefully accepted a straight-backed chair. The Rock greeted him quizzically. "It took you a hell of a lot longer to get from the field than it did to fly down from Pelaki."

Eddington's expression was inscrutable. "AirOps met me when I landed," he said. "After the usual brainpicking session, I figured I'd better grab a bite before I tooled back up here."

"I'm glad you're home, Paul."

"Thanks."

Torrey overlooked the chief of staff's reluctance to admit his own pleasure at returning safely. "You may have saved our bacon, fella."

"That remains to be seen," Eddington rumbled. "The frying pan's goddamn hot."

"CinCPAC is throwing a strike at Pelaki on Thursday."

"With everything he's got?"

"With one task group."

"Four lousy carriers!" Eddington snarled. "Probably two heavies and a pair of lights."

"We're lucky to get those."

"Crap!"

"You're tired, Paul," Torrey advised quietly. "Hit the sack. Things won't look so black in the morning."

"They'll look a hell of a lot worse," Eddington retorted. "By then those Nips will be holed up at Pelaki like a bunch of curly wolves in a cave—just waiting the right moment to spring."

"Maybe we'll spring first, fella," The Rock said. "While you were out playing hide-and-seek with the Japs, we were pushing pencils. Skyhook's ready to go."

"Without support?"

"With whatever CinCPAC and the good Lord provide us during the next ten days."

Slumped against the straight chair, Eddington seemed whipped, as if he didn't care any more, and his bloodshot eyes were half-closed. "Okay. Tell me all about it tomorrow." Then he shook himself awake and lurched to his feet.

"My son Jere was here this afternoon," Torrey said. "I'm sorry you missed him. He figures you're quite a hero."

"I'll friggin' well bet he does!"

The Rock was still trying to fathom this cryptic remark as the chief of staff, his broad back bowed with fatigue, shouldered through the screendoor and disappeared into the night. His puzzlement wasn't diminished next day, either, when AirOps observed casually that Jere and Eddington had exchanged hellos in the airfield snackbar before the guardmail plane left for Botan.

17. What's Been Started Can't Be Stopped

For some occult meteorological reason which baffled even Commander Max Gottlieb, the skies cleared after three unrelenting weeks of utter foulness. Coral dawns returned. Sunsets dripped blood. All day long the tropical sun shone brazenly upon the men —and the handful of women—who had transformed Mesquite into a teeming jump-off point for Skyhook, and the air was filled with powdery dust as the bulldozers finished their chores on Gavabutu before being herded aboard the gape-mawed LSTs.

Watching them, and breathing the crimson pumice that filtered down through the dry palmfronds, Torrey railed inwardly at the lack of heavy construction equipment for Skyhook. Even by robbing Peter at Gavabutu to pay Paul at Levu-Vana, they wouldn't have enough earthmoving machinery to complete an airfield and produce a network of passable roads before the Japs struck back, particularly if they had to work under fire. For this reason he secretly hoped the Nips would finish their clandestine fighter-bomber strip before D-Day. It would be damned accommodating of the bastards, he thought, to serve up this nice meal for somebody else to eat.

Because of a woeful lack of assault landing craft, most of the rehearsals were dry runs, with Marines and infantrymen leaping out of simulated landing barges—etched crudely in the damp sands with pointed sticks—and rushing pellmell up the slopes and into the graygreen thickets beyond the surf.

Meanwhile the second echelon of four LSTs was wandering around on the high seas, sketchily convoyed by a couple of AD-TAC's precious tincans, and awaiting The Word that Skyhook was officially underway. Torrey hoped the landlubber troops wouldn't be too seasick, or too brittle from their protracted sojourn afloat, to come storming out of these elephantine craft at zero hour.

When you considered this business in all its unpleasant ramifications, he told himself dourly, there were damned few encouraging aspects about it. None, in fact. As a practical man, who had never construed himself an optimist, The Rock had calculated their chances coldly, aware that a longshot gamble was inevitable. Once he'd placed his chips—a single combat division with its scanty reserves, ADTAC's meager air force, and whatever ships the high command finally vouchsafed him—the cosmic croupier's rake would reach out, ready to scoop them into the house stack the instant the little ball slowed down and dropped into the wrong slot. It was up to Torrey, of course, to guess the right *puka.*

Everything possible had been done to prepare for this D-Day which had been set and reset three agonizing times: once by Blackjack Broderick, who timorously wished it delayed until spring; once by The Rock himself, after computing his own strength versus the enemy's; and now more unwittingly by the Japanese, whose abrupt resolve to reinforce Pelaki Shima and Cape Titan had cast an ominous new light over the whole operation.

Zero hour of D-Day would come, Torrey suddenly realized, barely a dozen days hence, almost on the first anniversary of the Pearl Harbor attack!

Special Task Unit 48.9.1 reached Gavabutu at daybreak on Tuesday, as promised, with Gottlieb's weather according them an unseasonable hero's welcome. The resurgent sun rose blindingly over the eastern rim just as the last warship of the flotilla dropped anchor in the roadstead below the headquarters hill.

Up since 0400, a full hour before they came within voice-radio range, Torrey watched *Moultrie* lead the heavier vessels into the anchorage, paced by a pair of destroyers that minced gingerly through the encircling minefield. Although it was the largest sea force that had put into Gavabutu since the initial landings four months earlier, Task Unit 48.9.1 wasn't an overly impressive sight, viewed through his powerful binoculars, as it lay there in the pink-and-amber dawn.

The carrier escorts *Eaglet, Chickenhawk,* and *Falcon* had only recently joined the Fleet. Converted from cargo hulls, they displaced little more tonnage than the ack-ack cruiser's own fully loaded seventy-five hundred, and they carried less than two dozen aircraft apiece. Unaesthetic as three billboards seen broadside, low-lying, manifestly thinskinned and fragile, they squatted now in the middle of the motionless formation, ringed round by the six tincans of Destroyer Squadron 213.

Her sixteen five-inch/38s trained skyward, *Moultrie* crouched lean and bristling nearest the gap in the barrier reef through which they had just paraded single file. She was a handsome ship, built like a destroyer, and she was calculated to be especially useful for desperate infighting since she also carried a destroyer's complement of torpedo tubes.

As if ashamed of their own tawdriness, the six ships of ADTAC's original complement swung from their moorings at a discreet distance from these shiny newcomers.

Torrey could have sworn that *Old Swayback*'s spine was more outrageously curved than ever, either from overwork or antiquity. With her squared bow, ducktailed stern, and odd arrangement of two thin smokestacks bracketing one fat funnel, HMAS *Diadem* might have been something left over from Dewey's triumph at Manila Bay. Like the four resident tincans, these mismated cruisers looked as tired and weatherbeaten as junglefighters who'd been too long on frontline duty. Their upperworks showed bare patches where their camouflage had started to peel, and The Rock knew that the weedy bottoms of all six ships should be scraped and covered with the Navy's marvelous new antifouling paint which wasn't yet available in sufficient quantities for the hinterland forces.

Overhead, a quartet of barrage balloons bobbed in the early-morning breeze, tethered to the sterns of the LSTs whose shallow-draft bows seemed glued to the beaches at either side of the pontoon wharfs.

This whole scene, Torrey thought glumly, was more reminiscent of some weirdly disorganized menagerie than an array of fighting ships. Any minute now, old Noah would blow his bosun's whistle and they'd all go lumbering into his super-colossus of an Ark, and that's the last he'd ever see of them. He replaced his binoculars in their mildewed leather case, shrugging, and went back into his Quonset to press the buzzer for Lieutenant McConnel.

Mac came promptly.

"Inform the task unit's commanding officers," The Rock said, "that it won't be necessary for them to pay their respects to COMADTAC. I'll see 'em all this morning on board *Old Swayback*. Make it 0930. No honors. Strictly business. I'll take you, the chief of staff, Captain Tuthill, and Egan Powell. Tell Tut to bring along enough copies of the Skyhook Op plan for everybody."

"Yes, sir."

Torrey thought he detected a troubled expression on his aide's face as he turned to leave. "What's bothering you, son?"

"Nothing really," Mac said, embarrassed. "It's just that *Old Swayback*'s got a brandnew skipper—somebody I know damned well."

"Is that bad?"

Mac hesitated, trying to gauge how far he could trade upon his quasi-filial relations with this admiral whose whimsical regard for protocol sometimes baffled him. "You remember my *Cassiday* squadron, sir. Its commodore was Commander Bowen—Archibald Bowen—and he made captain early this year. Couple of weeks ago BuPers gave him *Old Swayback*."

"I was aware of that," Torrey said gently. "I sent Bowen congratulations at the time. Maybe I should have made it a sympathy chit, considering what he's inheriting, but I didn't. Bowen's practically my vintage, you know. Class of '19."

"Yes," Mac said, "I know."

"*Swayback* will have to carry our flag—she's the only cruiser available with staff quarters."

Mac nodded gloomily. At least, he consoled himself, Captain Bowen would dine alone when he wasn't occupying his emergency cabin behind the navigation bridge, so they'd be spared those endless reminiscences about the China Station. But the thought of going into battle with Bowen at *Old Swayback*'s helm was pretty disheartening. The manner of *Cassiday*'s demise hadn't given Mac much faith in the commodore's abilities, although when you came right down to it, their outnumbered squadron had fought hard, and the destroyer-leader herself had gone to glory bravely enough. It was just that Captain Bowen, so round and bland and pallid at forty-five, never exuded that magical aura which fostered confidence in others, and which Admiral Torrey possessed in such quiet abundance. Bowen's indecisiveness hid behind a cloak of noisy bravado, and it came as a hell of a shock to learn that, for all his theatrics, he was really a hollow man.

"I wish," Mac said unguardedly, "that Captain Moorian could command the flagship."

Torrey's mouth tightened. "There'll come a day, fella, when we'll need *Moultrie* worse than our own right arm. When that happens, you'll be grateful to look across a few hundred yards of blue water and know that Larry Moorian's in charge of her. Hell. *Moultrie*'s apt to be our right arm!"

Suddenly humbled, Mac replied, "Yes, sir," and departed.

After the screendoor slammed shut, The Rock picked up a roster, and began memorizing the names of his ships' captains. When they gathered aboard *Old Swayback* in a couple of hours, it would gratify the reserve two-stripers who skippered the LSTs to have the Big Boss greet them personally. Torrey paused, frowning, as he came to Archibald Bowen, and reached for his bulldog briar. Although it would have been the worst kind of impropriety to have acknowledged Mac's estimate of the captain's character, young McConnel was absolutely right: the man was a monumental windbag whose bombast was known throughout the Fleet, and the notion of riding into battle as a passenger aboard his old cruiser, with Bowen in command, appalled him.

By 0925 the last of the twenty-two commanding officers, including the commodore of MoTorpRon Charlie who'd flown down from Botan for the occasion, had mounted *Old Swayback*'s mahogany ladder, saluted the quarterdeck, passed through the impressive double line of sideboys, and filed forward to the wardroom where Tuthill had set up his charts.

The Rock himself was early.

Cursing under his breath at Captain Bowen's perfidious quarterdeck honors, he went straight to the long narrow portside cabin which he would occupy when they went to sea. It was a duplicate of the starboard cabin assigned to the captain, which he knew so well, and it also had a smaller adjoining stateroom, complete with shower, washbasin, and head. The furnishings of their two quarters were identical: circular work-and-diningtable, straight and easy chairs covered in white drill, bookcase, buffet, desk—all constructed from the same impersonal gray steel. Outside the open veranda deck door a twin-mount five-inch/38 gleamed dully in the uncompromising sunlight. Torrey caught the odor of hot oil on its gears and bearings. Both the sight and the smell of the weapon pleased him, for they were exactly as they'd been a year ago when he commanded *Old Swayback*. Nothing about the homely warship had changed.

Nothing, he amended critically, except himself.

At length Mac arrived at the Flag cabin door to announce that the captains were attending his pleasure in the wardroom. Torrey followed him below.

There was a momentary hush as they entered the low-ceilinged compartment which extended forty feet across the entire beam of the ship. Then Captain Bowen bellowed " 'Tenshun!" in a bull-horn voice, and the officers scrambled to their feet with a vast scraping of chairlegs across the unpainted steel deck.

"Sit down, gentlemen," The Rock said, irritated at Bowen's pretentiousness. "Let's forget ceremony."

He surveyed his audience briefly. Most of them were strangers to him, either youngsters who had attended Annapolis long after his time, or reservists who hadn't gone to Trade School at all. Their expressions were respectful, some almost worshipful, as they returned his appraisal. Had *Old Swayback* been crafted of oak and canvas instead of steel and brass, Torrey thought, they might have been Horatio Nelson's stalwart Band of Brothers gathered for their admiral's final instructions before Trafalgar.

Paul Eddington, his barbaric face shining sweatily under the harsh wardroom lamps, sat at Torrey's right, just as Captain Hardy himself had stood beside Lord Nelson.

From a frontrow chair, Larry Moorian observed his former messmate through jetblack eyes, with a quizzical expression on his swarthy countenance, as if he were awaiting some unexpected words of wisdom.

The snaggletoothed Aussie who commanded *Diadem* was still in kneelength shorts, The Rock noted, and he appeared cheerfully unconcerned that they were tied pirate-fashion around his ample girth with a piece of manila hemp. His name was Terence Mann.

Earnest, vibrantly eager, the escort carrier captains, John Rudyard, Murray Cagle, and Bushnell Parrott, occupied the rest of the front row. Their ships were *Eaglet, Chickenhawk,* and *Falcon;* and they were all under forty. Their gold naval aviator's wings were very bright above their left breast pockets.

The eldest brother in Torrey's augmented band was Captain Samuel Greenough, USN (retired), who had been retreaded for active duty at the age of fifty-nine, and given command of the reservist-manned LSTs, an assignment that would have tested the patience of a nautical Job, which Sam wasn't. When a Navy medico had wrongly diagnosed some obscure minor ailment as diabetes, he'd quit the Service to become a successful Manhattan stockbroker. Now that he was back in uniform, his socialite wife was giving him long-range fits because their landlord had threatened to cancel their penthouse lease after a novelist who lived downstairs complained about their pet schnauzer's moonlight barking; and Captain Sam wasn't home to do anything about it. The considerable distance between Mrs. Greenough and the commodore of LST Squadron Baker constituted, in his jaundiced eyes, one of the few plus aspects of a billet that had all the charm of straw-bossing a WPA sewer gang.

Youngest of ADTAC's captains was Kyle Bannion, leader of Destroyer Squadron 213. At thirty-eight he had made his fourth stripe months ahead of his class, thanks to certain daring exploits as commodore of an eight-ship division that heckled the Japs from Guadalcanal to Rabaul and back again, always at teethjarring flank speed. Torrey was delighted to have him around to inspire the prematurely aged youths who skippered the tincans. If they considered patrolling the Slot and the Pass as extra-hazardous duty, he reflected glumly, they hadn't seen anything yet. They hadn't even imagined it! Nor had the others.

While Captain Tuthill sketched the sweeping movements of Skyhook on a hydrographic chart, they cast covert glances toward this admiral who had now become the arbiter of their destinies, speculating on what lay behind the implacable geology of his face. Divining something of their emotions, Torrey took wry comfort from the knowledge that Operation Rathole had given him a name for initiative and courage which was all out of proportion to the facts of the matter as he viewed it.

Larry Moorian had sent him a marked copy of a news magazine which hailed "this new Farragut." With a savage pertinacity for which the periodical was famed, the writer had researched Torrey's whole life, discovering in the process that this modest Flag officer shyly concealed his possession of a Navy Cross; that he had married and divorced the heiress of one of New England's most fabulous shipping fortunes after they'd quarreled over his career as a Depression Era Navyman; that he'd taught a prewar generation of Academy kids, one of whom now served as Torrey's aide; and that the admiral's young son, Jeremiah Farr Torrey, an effete lad of great financial expectations, had quit Harvard to join The Rock as a devil-may-care PT-boater.

Now, with twenty-two pairs of eyes questioning him, Torrey strove to hide his singular discomfiture behind a ferocious scowl. If these fellows wanted heroics, they could have Paul Eddington, whose reconnaissance beyond Pelaki Shima was fast becoming legend in the Fleet. Eddington was manufactured out of unalloyed hero stock, and not from some clever publicist's synthetic materials.

Captain Tuthill was concluding his dryvoiced remarks: ". . . Based on our best estimates, gentlemen, I would place our firepower odds at approximately one-to-two against the Japanese. We believe they have in the Pelaki area at the present time no less than three aircraft carriers, five battleships, seven cruisers, and eighteen destroyers. They have additional strength at Cape Titan, although weather hasn't permitted SouWesPAC to reconnoiter that base, so we don't really know. We have reason to believe that they'll stage an amphibious force out of their northern islands in the very near future—with every intention of beefing up Levu-Vana."

He glanced toward The Rock, who nodded imperceptibly and stood up. The glare of the unshaded overhead lights seemed unaccountably brighter just then, and the tropical heat that shimmered through *Old Swayback*'s thin deckplating had started sweat cascading down Torrey's lean back for the first time since he entered the wardroom.

His frown deepened.

"Tuthill's given you the facts. Blunt. Unvarnished. They're not very pretty, I'll admit. But we figured you should know precisely what we're up against, so we can tackle this thing as a single-minded unit, without any illusions about our situation. It boils down to this—the Nips have Levu-Vana; we want it; they know it; we're going to take it; and they'll do their damnedest to throw the blocks to us." Torrey let this sink in before he added, "What's more to the point, I suppose, is the fact that we can't expect much outside help from here on out."

After the lull that followed, Eddington's voice struck them like a shovelful of gravel. "Admiral Torrey means," he said, "that we needn't look for as much as a goddamn extra kayak once we jump off."

"That's about it," The Rock agreed. "Any questions?"

One of the carrier captains raised his hand diffidently. "Parrott, sir, *Falcon*."

Somebody sniggered at this ornithological coincidence. The carrier-man flushed. But Torrey said gravely, "Bushnell Parrott, '23, isn't it?"

The youthful skipper expressed his gratification with a broad grin. "Yes, sir!"

"What's your problem, Bush?"

"Captain Tuthill discussed tomorrow's strike against Levu-Vana by Task Group 48.3. I'm wondering—will they be in a position to follow up their attack?"

"We're just one of the Fleet's commitments," Torrey said. "Right now, with the Central Pacific campaign brewing, and with Halsey hitting the Solomons, it's stretched thinner than a tired rubber band. No. I wouldn't count on a second strike up there."

As a veteran carrier pilot himself, Parrott tried to calculate the odds favoring a clean sweep by the eighty-or-so bombers of a single task group, and they weren't encouraging. He sat down, looking glum.

Captain Rudyard of *Eaglet* wigwagged and was recognized. "How about us?" he demanded brashly. "We could toss a few punches at that island."

Torrey shook his head. "Sorry, John, but that's out. You know why. Your CVEs couldn't turn up better than twenty knots if you fueled 'em with nitroglycerine. You'd be sitting ducks for the Japs. Besides, we've got other chores for your brood."

"Just softening up the beaches, sir? That's pretty tame stuff."

The Rock studied Rudyard's disappointed face for a moment, silently appreciating the man's courage, before he replied kindly, "Let's hope it stays that way, fella—nice and calm and uneventful."

But the *Eaglet*'s skipper had touched the tenderest nerve in the whole sensitive ganglia surrounding the Skyhook venture. Not only were the ships committed to it inferior in firepower to the growing enemy concentration at Pelaki, but they were also slower and less agile. Since no fleet can move faster than its slowest member, any task force unit built around the escort carriers would be limited to their maximum speed: nearer eighteen knots than the twenty which Torrey had diplomatically accorded Rudyard. In her present condition, too, it was doubtful whether *Old Swayback* could approach her rated thirty-two knots, and he suspected she'd be lucky to produce twenty-seven. That Australian monstrosity, *Diadem,* was an unknown quantity. Twenty-five knots? Maybe. But this accounted for only the combatant vessels. All the way up the Pass to Levu-Vana they'd have to adjust their advance to the bargelike LSTs whose top speed, loaded, was ten snailpaced knots!

The Rock shook hands with each of his skippers as they filed out of the wardroom, and for each he reserved a private word applicable to the man's command. When MoTorpRon Charlie's three-striper reached him, he asked, "Are your Davids supplied with enough stones for their slingshots, Ben?"

Commander Benjamin Franklin Norris grinned. "Hell, yes, admiral. All we need now are a few Goliaths."

"You'll have 'em!" Torrey's expression was inscrutable. "How's my boy doing?"

Norris paused. When he replied, he seemed to be choosing his words delicately. "Jere's 4.0—now that he's gotten over that little personal matter—and he's become one of my best skippers. A real tiger, sir. Rather be driving *Miss Brimstone* up the Pass than eating. Or playing bridge. And he's a hell of a bridge player."

"That's what I figured," Torrey said. "Keep him busy."

"Even with our full complement of sixteen boats, admiral, work's the most important thing we've got."

The Rock saw Larry Moorian standing aloof, beyond the farthest baize-covered messtable. He called, "Too exclusive to join my receiving line, mister?"

"Just waiting," Moorian said, "for the rabble to clear out."

Together, they walked slowly to the door that led from the wardroom to the cruiser's sunbaked weatherdeck, still chatting, and seeking to regain their old bantering mood. But it was no use. In the months since Moorian had taken command of his smart new ship, leaving Torrey behind to pick up the scattered pieces of his career, a gulf had widened between them that was not of their own making. Then Moorian had been the envied man, Torrey the pitied one. Although neither envy nor pity remained, now, something else had intervened: the fixed relationship of subordinate and superior. As long as this pertained, they could never quite recall their old camaraderie, for they would be captain-and-admiral, rather than man-and-man. It was not unlike the remarkable change that occurs when a President is elected, and even those who knew him most intimately must put familiarity aside and defer to his lofty office.

"It was great," Torrey said, "to see *Moultrie* drop the hook this morning."

"She's an elegant piece of machinery," Moorian agreed.

"It was also damned good to know you were on her bridge."

"I wish *Moultrie* had Flag quarters," Moorian said.

"So do I."

"There's a new dish I've learned, admiral. *Balatoni fogas à la Rothermere*. It'd be an honor to prepare it for you."

The Rock looked sharply at Moorian to see whether this was irony. But the captain's dark Armenian face was earnest, and it was obvious that his invitation had been made in all sincerity.

"What's this 'balogna fogey'?" Torrey growled.

"Balatoni fogas. Filet of fish boiled in sauterne. Magnificent." Moorian rolled his eyes whitely. "Aboard *Moultrie* we use Spam and vinegar."

"War is hell, captain."

Suddenly Moorian was serious. "Rock—I don't envy your job one goddamned little bit."

"Why?"

"Those fellows in there—I watched them as you were talking after Tuthill outlined the problem. They've set you up as a miracle man."

"Yes," Torrey said dryly. "They must have seen the same clippings you sent me, Larry. Pretty fanciful stuff."

Moorian's magnificent teeth glittered beneath his tiny mustache. "Maybe so. Nevertheless, Rock, you're holding the buck that can't be passed, right in your hot hand. And they know it. Sometimes dependence colors a fellow's view of the guy he depends on." His smile faded. "One thing's certain—I'm glad you've got that buck, and not Blackjack Broderick."

"Technically he's still in command," The Rock pointed out.

"Don't kid me!"

Moorian tossed him a smart salute and headed aft toward the quarterdeck. Alone, except for Lieutenant McConnel who was standing discreetly in the middle distance, Torrey watched the squat figure of *Moultrie*'s captain disappear around a five-inch mount. Then he beckoned his aide.

"Let's go, son."

"Yes, sir." Mac delayed a moment. "Admiral, there's something over here I wish you'd see before we leave."

Torrey's brows lifted inquiringly, but he re-entered the wardroom and followed Mac to the forward bulkhead where a small ebony plaque was affixed just above the senior officers' table. Its gold letters urged: "GIVE ME A FAST SHIP FOR I INTEND TO GO IN HARM'S WAY." The sign, he saw, was streaked and faded as if it had been exposed overlong to sea and sun, then revarnished and regilded.

"This same plaque used to hang in *Cassiday*'s wardroom," Mac said musingly. "Funny. It was the commodore's totem. He called it his *tiki,* and claimed it'd bring us good luck. He must have rescued it when we got hit."

"Pretty risky thing when your ship's going down."

"That's what surprises me, sir."

"People never cease to astonish me, Mac," Torrey observed.

But he was still pondering John Paul Jones' nautical appeal when they reached the quarterdeck. *Old Swayback* was a singularly inappropriate vessel in which to hang such a motto, for her likelihood of blundering into trouble was a thousandfold greater than if she'd truly been a fast ship. Yet they were indeed going into harm's way. Deliberately. Coldly. And in the somewhat less inspired words of the Navy's prosaic dispatch writers, his prospects of acquiring a swifter flagship, or getting additional ships to lead against the enemy, were rather unencouraging. In fact, they were nil.

The Rock wished he had Captain Archibald Bowen's faith in that bit of warped wood as a fortuitous omen for clumsy *Old Swayback*.

By 0800 next morning the initial strike reports from fast carrier Task Group 48.3 began to trickle into Mesquite. First to arrive on target, the scout bombers had spotted three battleships within the sheltering arms of Pelaki Shima, as ADTAC Intelligence predicted they would, along with four cruisers and a dozen destroyers.

But their radios insisted doggedly: "NO—REPEAT—NO JAP AIRCRAFT CARRIERS."

Even before the group's preliminary sunk-and-damaged score reached the Op hut, Eddington had flown into a towering, frustrated rage; and within an hour he was storming around the Quonset, kicking at chairs, pounding tables, and raising what Captain Tuthill mournfully called "unshirted hell." But it did no good. By 0945 the single punch air-strike was over, every pilot had been debriefed, and the South Pacific might as well have swallowed up the three big Nip carriers—flightdecks, planes, and guns—for all anybody saw of them that hectic morning.

There was another worrisome omission in their tabulation: hadn't Task Group 48.3 shortcounted the rest of the enemy flotilla anchored at Pelaki?

Eddington ground his fist against Tuthill's plotting board. "No carriers!" he snarled. "And now we're missing a pair of battlewagons, three cruisers, and a whole friggin' division of tincans! They're up there—goddamn it!—I saw them myself."

Egan Powell ventured a foolhardy suggestion. "You were awfully busy with those Zeros, Paul. Maybe you counted a couple of 'em twice."

The chief of staff seared him with a glance. "Whenever I make a mistake, fella, it's because I underestimate the sons of bitches—not overestimate 'em." He yelled for more dispatches. "Goddamn it to hell—*where are those carriers?"*

Aroused by Eddington's profane appeal, Torrey left his chair in a secluded corner of the room, and ambled slowly toward Tuthill's unpartitioned sanctum, hoping to soothe the aroused chief of staff by his own deliberateness.

"Those Nip carriers can make thirty knots," he observed quietly. "They could be halfway to the Philippines by now."

Unappeased, Eddington demanded, "If they had such all-fired important business elsewhere, why'd they leave their battleships?"

"If we could read the Japs' minds," Torrey countered, "we wouldn't have stumbled into this war in the first place."

For a moment Eddington seemed nonplussed by this deflationary rejoinder. Then he said stubbornly, "Those bastards are up to something, skipper."

Torrey studied the chart upon which Tuthill, stolidfaced and silent, was plotting the results of the carriers' attack as Group 48.3 transmitted them. Two battleships hit, one believed in a sinking condition. Three of the four cruisers damaged, two presumed sinking. Four destroyers apparently sunk.

He frowned at the equivocal language of the strike report, trying to weigh words like "believed" and "presumed" and "apparently."

As they sought to dodge enemy ack-ack while rocketing over Pelaki's harbor at 230 knots, pilots might be forgiven a few slight errors of observation. Waves of bombers launched from other carriers of the task force would normally plug such intelligence gaps during follow-up strikes.

But now there wouldn't be any follow-up, he knew, because this morning's assault was executed by a single carrier group—one quarter of a full task force—that had been told to hit Pelaki Shima hard and then get the hell back to its primary duties far to the northwest. Thus, whatever report its admiral radioed to Mesquite must either be accepted as gospel, or somehow reassessed by Torrey's own experts, nine hundred beclouded miles away from the scene itself. From hard experience, The Rock rated this kind of remote appraisal as sheerest mumbojumbo, and not much better than scanning tea leaves or counting unhatched chickens.

If you accepted Task Group 48.3's optimistic report at face value, of course, the Japanese at Pelaki Shima now had only one battleship, one cruiser, and eight destroyers in shape for an immediate sortie, which meant ADTAC would stand a fighting chance if the two forces met. But this reckoned without the flyers' all-too-human error, and that's where logic failed. It also ignored the inescapable fact that a powerful enemy contingent, including carriers and battlewagons, was mysteriously loose on the high seas, headed God only knew where. What might be even worse, it failed to take into account the B-17s' sightings of another probable Jap surface concentration at Cape Titan.

Shortly after 1100 the final Word crackled into Gavabutu from the withdrawing American carriers: "AFTER RE-EVALUATING PILOTS' REPORTS CONSIDER EARLIER STRIKE ESTIMATES ACCURATE TO GREATEST PRACTICAL DEGREE WITH POSSIBLE EXCEPTION OF DUPLICATE DAMAGE REPORTED ON TWO OF FOUR MOGAMI CLASS CRUISERS HIT IN FIRST WAVE. GLAD TO HAVE BEEN OF ASSISTANCE."

Eddington crumpled his copy of the dispatch into a compact wad and hurled it angrily across the Op shack. "Balls . . . balls . . . balls!" His tone was mincing as he quoted, " 'Glad to've been of friggin' assistance!' "

"They did all they could," The Rock pointed out mildly.

"Balls!" Eddington repeated. "Those pilots weren't wearing sun goggles—they were looking through rosecolored glasses that magnified everything double."

Ignoring the chief of staff's new outburst, Torrey addressed himself to his Operations officer. "Alert all hands that we'll commence Skyhook next Wednesday, Tut."

"That's advancing it another four days, admiral," Tuthill said doubtfully. "We're already crowded for running room."

"I know." The Rock's tired voice was deep and toneless. "But we've got to take advantage of whatever our carriers did this morning. The Nips won't lose any time patching up their cripples. A few days—maybe a week—and some of 'em will be ready for sea again. You've seen it happen before. Remember Midway?"

"You're the boss," Tuthill said, glad that this critical decision wasn't his responsibility.

"I'm afraid so," Torrey replied wryly. As he turned to leave the Quonset, he added, "Let's be damned sure to inform Admiral Broderick. We wouldn't want him to read about it in *Time* magazine."

"Yes, sir."

"Just one more thing, Tut—tell AirOps to step up his recon flights."

The chief of staff laughed harshly. "You suppose those four little Wildcats will spot the missing carriers?"

"No, Paul. But I want to know how soon they repair the damage at Pelaki."

"Christ!" Eddington blazed, "if they'd only give us a long-range photo plane—*just one!*" He scowled at the Skyhook chart. "We should be scouting a fifteen-hundred-mile radius . . . damn near twice as far as the string on our toy kites will reach."

He was still brooding over the map when Torrey carefully shut the screendoor.

Twelve hours after The Rock had alerted every command on Mesquite, from the meanest port battalion to General Averell's harassed air groups, all of whom were already working round the clock, it was apparent that far too little time remained to accomplish too much.

Tuthill kept the growing list.

Item: Replenishing their seaworn ships' stores of food, fuel, and ammunition.

Item: Loading assault troops aboard their transports, stepping up photo reconnaissance of the Levu-Vana beachhead area.

Item: Cajoling SouWesPAC's heavy bombers into a few last high-altitude strikes against the target.

Item: Producing a new set of combat maps which, thanks to Clayton Canfil, had now correctly located their volcanic landmark five miles inland rather than the middle of Lakola Bay.

Item: Eleventh-hour briefings with unit leaders over the air-sea-ground aspects of Skyhook's amazingly complicated Op plan.

Final item: Ascertaining whether MOB Able could handle the heavy casualties that were certain to result between D-Day and D plus two when Torrey figured they'd better have secured the beachhead—or else.

None of these tasks seemed to be consummated exactly as ordered, or on schedule, and The Rock was aware of a thinly disguised yet mounting pessimism among his subordinates. Most of their dire predictions were uttered in the semiprivacy of the Officers' Club, or whispered during bull sessions held in their personal quarters, but they reached his ears, nevertheless. Even Eddington seemed to have joined these doomcriers, although his dejection came more from his feeling that the Japs were ready to spring a trap than from a belief that Skyhook itself was being launched prematurely. In fact, the chief of staff complained they should have driven north right after their victory at Rathole, while the Nips were still trying to recover.

From Toulebonne, too, Torrey received a spate of precautionary suggestions, couched in such Navy clichés as "impracticable," "unfeasible," and "inappropriate"—all of them adding up to the one word which Admiral Broderick himself hesitated to set down in black and white: *Don't!*

Once Blackjack became convinced that The Rock was adamant, however, he reluctantly released two transports and a pair of cargo vessels for Operation Skyhook. Now they waited off Atoka with the rest of the assault force, while landing craft shuttled throughout the night between the docks and the ships, loaded to the gunwales with supplies, and working under arc lights in bold defiance of an enemy sneak air raid.

Aboard the newcomers, the crews wondered what the hell was the hurry. They'd barely arrived from Toulebonne after a ridiculous high-speed run. They were thirsty. Yet Admiral Torrey had sternly forbidden all shoreside liberties, and he'd even shut down the enlisted men's beer garden and padlocked the Officers' Club. But their addition to The Rock's slim force permitted him to detach the four LSTs already in port, and send them around Gavabutu to pick up Commander Norris' sixteen PTs.

Blackjack Broderick's reluctant generosity was taxed most sorely by a final demand from Torrey that he order a hospital ship to Gavabutu as a standby for MOB Able, whose facilities were deemed inadequate for the bloody traffic ahead.

Losing USS *Charity,* a dilapidated World War I vintage floating hospital which had lain off Toulebonne for seven weeks, meant a very special deprivation for Broderick. *Charity*'s nurses had brightened the island's social scene in a way that the snobbish French women of the town never could. Two of them were regular visitors to the admiral's mansion, where they administered certain therapies to Commander Neal Owynn and himself, and he hated the thought of their departure.

"Goddamn it!" Blackjack exploded. "Torrey doesn't need *Charity.*"

"Not the way we do," the Senator agreed ambiguously, "but he might—later."

"You think it would look bad if we turn down Torrey's request?"

"From several viewpoints I'm afraid it'd be tactically unsound." Owynn studied his glossy fingernails for a moment. "But there's no reason why *Charity* can't proceed north with a couple of vacancies in her officer complement. It wouldn't cripple her."

"Her skipper mightn't take kindly to losing his chief nurse," Blackjack pointed out.

"He'd get over it, B.J., once he learned that MOB Able's first lady was her replacement."

"Your little friend?"

"She's more like Admiral Torrey's 'friend,'" Owynn said delicately, "from all I hear."

"You're a devilishly bright lad, Senator."

"Just trying to keep in practice." Owynn lowered his eyes modestly. "Shall I draft Lieutenant Haynes' orders?"

"Yes."

"With information copy to Torrey?"

Blackjack Broderick grinned. "Let's not bother him with fussy little details at a time like this . . ."

Now it was Friday. Photographs from the Wildcat recon flights over Pelaki Shima proved conclusively that the Japs had completed repairs on one of their least injured battlewagons and a pair of cruisers, and that two of the destroyers "presumed sunk" were still very much afloat. Tendrils of smoke eddying from the funnels of these miraculously restored warships indicated they wouldn't remain dormant much longer. Pelaki's three airfields also evidenced a build-up of Nip skypower, and when the latest photographs taken over Levu-Vana were processed, the secret landing strip was shown almost ready to receive planes. The heavy cloud cover which impeded aerial reconnoitering had played neatly into the enemy's hands. The runway was twice as long as ADTAC Intelligence had suspected, and quite capable of handling medium bombers.

Other debits crowded Torrey's red-inked ledger.

Because of recurrent foul weather, SouWesPAC's Fortresses managed to hit Pelaki Shima only once, with what they euphemistically termed "minimum results" from twenty thousand feet. They never located Levu-Vana at all.

Pearl Harbor radioed that it could spare only two old battleships—fourteen-inch-gunned antiques which had been commissioned the same year Torrey graduated from Annapolis, plus a partial division of four tincans. But CinCPAC warned they must be returned in good shape to Central Pacific as soon as the D-Day bombardment was over.

Eddington, who screened the dispatches before Torrey received them, read this last message through eyes redrimmed with weariness and exasperation.

"With that sort of gunfire support," he snarled, "we'll be softening up those beaches from now until Christmas!"

"Don't forget *Moultrie, Diadem,* and *Old Swayback,*" The Rock said placatingly.

"Who the hell could forget those friggin' bathtub toys?"

There was a ruminant gleam in The Rock's hooded eyes as he said softly, "Maybe you've got an idea, Paul. It's just possible we'll be bombarding that beachhead longer than the Big Boss imagines."

Eddington brightened. "More piracy, skipper?"

"No," Torrey said. "It'll simply be 'impracticable' to return those battlewagons for a few days. Isn't that the proper word?"

Shortly before noon on Friday, an enemy sighting was relayed to ADTAC from an American submarine skulking off Cape Titan. It was a belated report, because the sub couldn't break radio silence until darkness fell, that she'd spotted the Nip squadron heading roughly south-southeast seven hours earlier: five destroyers, two light cruisers—as well as the biggest goddamn battleship the awestruck pigboat lookouts had ever seen. She carried nine rifles in her triple turrets and she must have been ninety-nine miles long, they marveled.

Egan Powell was summoned from the Intelligence shack to evaluate the report. His handsome face tightened as he studied the message.

"That could be *Yamato,*" he said, "down from Manila."

"Heading our way," Captain Tuthill added rather unnecessarily.

The Rock forced a grin to mask his own concern. "We should

be honored at all this attention. The Nips haven't trotted out *Yamato* since Midway."

"They've been saving the bastard," Eddington said savagely, "for our Sophomore Prom!"

Of all the weapons in the Japanese arsenal, *Yamato* was the most formidable. Completed just in time to participate in the great engagement of mid-June, she hadn't been observed since, and although her fearsome 68,000-ton bulk was out of sight, it was never out of mind of the American planners. Her sistership *Musashi* was ready, too, and together they made more than a match for any combination of new *Iowa*-class battleships available. *Yamato*'s nine eighteen-inch guns fired thirty-two-hundred-pound projectiles. Any one of her triple turrets weighed as much as a normal destroyer, and her side armor was sixteen inches thick.

Nobody would ever build a bigger battleship. Nobody would ever want to. She was considered invincible in this last of the personal wars.

Torrey remembered the Nazi battlewagon *Bismarck*—smaller than *Yamato*—and what it had cost to bring her to justice in the dark spring of 1941. Even after she was cornered in the North Atlantic, the British had to fetch up an aircraft carrier, two battleships, two cruisers, and five tincans before they could overpower her. And *Bismarck* had been alone!

Now that the Cape Titan force had been spotted, obviously moving into his area, he had a clearer idea of the overwhelming odds they faced: five Nip battleships, led by the horrendous *Yamato,* pitted against the pair of World War I relics he would unlawfully retain after the D-Day barrage; three heavy cruisers against *Old Swayback*; five light cruisers against *Moultrie* and *Diadem*; and at least twenty Jap destroyers against his fourteen. There were, of course, his three escort carriers, but he had scant faith in their ability to impede the southward drive of the foe. While the rest of Torrey's thin line steamed deliberately into harm's way, merely keeping the CVEs out of the Japs' clutches would pose a major problem. These converted merchantmen were as slow as they were fragile, and *Yamato*'s speed was reliably reported to be almost double that of *Eaglet, Chickenhawk,* or *Falcon.* One salvo from the Jap's behemothic main battery would penetrate their paperthin flanks like a bullet going into hot butter.

". . . We think," AirOps was saying hopefully, "that the Nip carriers and battleships which sortied from Pelaki Shima before Task Group 48.3's raid have departed north—gone for good."

"What about the cruisers and tincans?" Eddington demanded.

"They'll be back, sir."

Torrey nodded agreement with AirOps' estimate. He had already counted on this eventuality, for it wasn't likely the Japs would keep their carriers in the restricted waters around Levu-Vana if they imagined the Yank task force was still lurking in the vicinity. No. They'd be a lot more apt to pull a typical Nip stunt—running their carriers north as a decoy to entice the Americans away from the beachhead, which they could then overwhelm with easy impunity and in their own sweet time.

More than ever, The Rock knew, it was essential that Skyhook proceed on its new "impossible" schedule.

"Gentlemen," he said, "let's meet again at 1700. Until then, I want you all to be thinking about how we can pass a miracle next Wednesday. And I'll personally nominate for sainthood the man who produces the best answer."

Torrey was smiling determinedly as he left the Op shack, but when he reached the open air and found himself alone, he sobered. Gottlieb's weather had turned dismal again. A telltale drabness along the horizon, and the breeze that whipped the dusty palms, boded another storm. It probably meant that Averell's midafternoon recon flight would be the last for several days. Or longer.

A Marine Pfc, policing the ADTAC grounds in punishment for firing his BAR too accurately at a native sow, glanced up as The Rock passed him on the path that led to Flag quarters. He dropped his rake and saluted. But the Old Man stared right through him with an expression on his kisser that would have frozen the milk in a friggin' coconut.

When the Marine returned to his labors he wasn't whistling any more. He looked as if he'd just brushed elbows with a ghost.

There were no miracles at 1700, only threadbare suggestions. Captain Tuthill said they'd better fire off an S O S to Pearl Harbor for help. Egan Powell remarked unconvincingly that the Japs might all head north instead of south, for their long-heralded showdown with the Pacific Fleet. At this, Commander Canfil sluiced his cutplug into a coffee can and retorted that Captain Powell—if he'd pardon a flunky's temerity—was romancing again, because the only time the enemy ever bugged out in the face of lesser odds was in the movies when the Seventh Cavalry rode up with Technicolored gonfalons waving in the desert gale, and the Indians skedaddled. AirOps merely confirmed what The Rock already knew: unless the weather improved, tomorrow's photo flights were off. Max Gottlieb capped it by predicting they'd be socked in for at least two more days.

Without much conviction, Torrey had been hoping that his chief of staff would emerge with some radical course of action that might be modified, tempered, or otherwise honed down for use in their extremity.

But Eddington was inexplicably absent from the meeting, and none of the other staff officers had the faintest idea where he had gone. Although lately he'd been a.w.o.l. from the minor skull sessions that were held after dinner for specialized departmental planning, it wasn't like Eddington to ignore a conference of this magnitude. He viewed his role as The Rock's confidant with a jealous pride, and he took spleeny delight in watching the shocked faces of the more sedate staffers whenever he offered some especially outrageous tactical suggestion.

"Last time I saw Eddington," Egan Powell said, "he was sacked out taking his noonday siesta."

McConnel demurred. "He wasn't there when I went back to the hut for my oilskins. And his own raingear was gone."

"Maybe he wanted a firsthand look at Averell's situation down at the air base," AirOps said. "That's more likely."

"Call General Averell," Torrey ordered brusquely. "Tell him I need the chief of staff here right away."

Mac went to the combat phone, cranked the handle, and asked for the air wing commander. Their conversation was brief. Eddington hadn't been around all afternoon.

After that the meeting seemed to bog down.

Tuthill added one lugubrious paintstroke to the gloomy picture: anytime the Japs wanted to move south, they could reach Levu-Vana from Pelaki Shima in two days, figuring their rate of advance at twenty knots along the circuitous route they'd undoubtedly take to avoid coastwatchers, whereas ADTAC's slower forces would require twice that long to travel from Gavabutu to the Lakola Bay beachhead. And the LSTs needed even more time, so they'd have to be dispatched well ahead of the main body.

"Of course," he mused, "if the Nips decide to gather somewhere above Skyhook—pulling together all their hardware from Pelaki and Cape Titan—they might take four days."

The Rock grunted. "Sure. But they could also proceed separately." He stood up. "Finish loading those LSTs, Tut, and get 'em started."

"Yes, sir."

Torrey bent over the chart on which the convoy's proposed route was limned in heavy blue ink. With his right forefinger he indicated a spot two inches below the molar-shaped target island's longest root.

"We'll make this Point Able," he said. "The faster ships will join the LSTs here."

Tuthill looked pained. "That's only a hundred miles off Levu-Vana, sir. They'll be right under the Nips' noses when they rendezvous."

"It's a chance we've got to take, Tut. Just be damned certain we assemble at dawn, so those puddle-jumpers will have all night to close the island."

"Yes, sir," Tuthill acknowledged stoically.

The Rock prepared to leave the Op shack. "When the chief of staff gets back from his mysterious mission," he said, "please ask him to see me in my quarters."

But this time, as he departed, Torrey wasn't shamming a smile. Eddington's failure to show up for this critical session was tantamount to deserting his post on the eve of battle. His dereliction worried Torrey almost as much as it angered him, for it gave a measure of truth to what Eddington's detractors had been hinting at for months: that his basic instability would some day jeopardize them all. This explosive potential, if that's what it was, had heightened in the last few days. But whatever ailed him, he didn't want to talk about it, and all Torrey got for his solicitude on one occasion was the savage retort that Eddington would be okay if the frig-heads would just leave him alone to work out his own salvation.

When the steward's mate brought dinner, The Rock found his food more unappetizing than ever, and his loneliness more encompassing. This was a night when he might have invited Eddington to share his meal. They would have mulled over Skyhook. Dissected it. Laid it under a microscope. And finally the chief of staff would have reached the conclusion, with some innocuous guidance from Torrey, that all that was required to pull this colossal chestnut out of the fire was guts. Yes, by God, combative guts and a will to win! Afterward Eddington would have strolled jauntily out of the Quonset, smiting the air with his sledgehammer fists, and mouthing great oaths against their distant enemy.

Torrey picked up his coffeecup, inspected the contents, then set it down untasted. To hell with coffee. Even though his wrist watch showed barely 2100, he wanted to hit the sack, drug himself with sleep, and forget about Tomorrow until it came.

Just before he snapped off the light, he saw the date on the wall calendar. Tomorrow was the fifth. Sunday the sixth. *And Monday would be December seventh!*

. . . Shrill, insistent, as if somebody had been trying to reach him for a long time, knew he was there, and wouldn't quit till he answered, the ringing of the combat telephone beside his bed jarred him out of his dreamless slumber. He reached automatically for the gooseneck lamp on the nightstand, found the switch, and then checked his watch. Almost 0230. At this hour nobody would dare rouse the admiral unless some four-alarm emergency had broken loose, such as an impending Jap air raid, a ship torpedoed in the roadstead, or the unexpected sortie of the enemy from Pelaki Shima.

He jerked the telephone from its horsehide sheath. The ringing stopped abruptly. He snapped, "Torrey here," and waited for the bad news.

It was Maggie Haynes. Her voice was taut, unnatural, heavy with crisis, and she didn't bother to apologize for awakening him.

"Annalee Dorne committed suicide," she said abruptly, not sparing him. "Sleeping pills."

"Good Christ!"

"I found the poor kid in her bed when I came off watch at midnight. We tried everything. But it was too late. She died a half-hour ago."

"But why—"

"Annalee left two notes," Maggie went on flatly. "One's for Jere. The other's for Captain Eddington. I've got them here. They weren't sealed up in envelopes. So I read both messages. They're very brief. Would you like to know what she wrote to your son?"

"Yes."

"'Beloved Boy—It broke my heart to send you away without telling you what was wrong, or how I felt about you. I couldn't tell you then and I can't tell you now. But somehow you must believe that I love you, Jere, with a love that will outlast my worthless body. Please forgive and pray for me. Forever. Annalee.'"

"What did she tell Eddington?" Torry asked tonelessly.

Maggie read in the same flat voice: "'Paul—After you saw me this afternoon I finally knew what I had to do. You might have saved me. Instead you laughed at me. Now I'm going away with that horrible sound still in my ears. Someday maybe I can come back and haunt you. I hope so.'" Over the humming military wire he heard her sudden dry sob. "Annalee didn't sign that note with her name. I guess she was ashamed. She just signed it with an 'A'—in red ink—like the Scarlet Letter."

"There must be more to it than that," Torrey said doubtfully.

"Annalee was pregnant."

"Oh."

"She'd been raped by Eddington the night of the picnic . . . and he wouldn't do anything about it . . . and I guess Annalee figured this was the only way out."

"I'll come over as soon as I get dressed."

"It would be better if you didn't. Nobody knows about these notes. They don't even know I'm calling you. Besides, there's nothing you can do, Rock. Nothing. Not now."

"But you need help."

"I'm a nurse," she replied stoically. "I'm used to death."

"Not this kind. Annalee was your friend."

Suddenly her voice was bitter as wormwood. "And Paul Eddington's yours!"

Torrey paused. He knew what had to be done. But even now it was a difficult decision. Then: "Trust me, Maggie, when I say that I'm going to take care of Eddington."

"That'll help," she said bitterly. "That'll help one hell of a lot, won't it?"

"Maggie . . ."

"Why do you need this man, Rock?" Now her tone was imploring. "Except for you, Eddington's nothing. He's never been anything. He's evil, that's all, something monstrous and wicked. Sooner or later he'll ruin himself the way he's ruined others. And I just hope to God he won't destroy you at the same time." She added frantically, "Please, Rock, make him go away . . ."

"He'll go away," Torrey promised in a dead voice.

"Thank you, Rock." She hesitated. "What shall I do about Annalee's notes?"

"I'll get them in the morning," he said, "when I visit MOB Able for my final inspection."

"But I won't be here," she said.

"You won't?"

"No. I'm going aboard *Charity* at dawn."

"Charity!"

"They suddenly needed a new chief nurse."

"Who ordered you?"

"The dispatch came from Toulebonne." She gave a mirthless laugh. "Somebody down there seems quite interested in my naval career."

"Apparently." Torrey paused. "About the notes—put them in an envelope marked 'personal' and leave it with the officer of the day. I'll send Lieutenant McConnel."

"Yes, Rock." Her voice was barely audible. "When will we see each other again?"

"I don't know, Maggie. Things are entirely out of my hands now. What's been started can't be stopped. When it's all over . . ."

"At least," she said, "this way I'll be closer to you."

"Goodbye, Maggie."

"Goodbye . . . dearest."

Torrey imagined he'd heard the soft sound of a kiss before she hung up. But he couldn't be certain. Military telephones aren't made to transmit such tender nuances. He replaced the receiver into its leather casing, very slowly, reluctant to break the spell cast upon him by Maggie's last words.

Then he stood up.

And all at once his cold fury at Paul Eddington's treachery—there was no other word for it—overrode every other emotion. What he felt wasn't ordinary wrath. It sickened him, wrung him dry, and left only a bleak urge to visit justice upon a faithless comrade.

He picked up the phone again. When the ADTAC switchboard came on, Torrey asked for the senior staff quarters, and presently McConnel's sleepy voice answered.

"It's Admiral Torrey, Mac. Has Captain Eddington returned yet?"

"No, sir. His bunk's empty. It hasn't been slept in."

"Get dressed and meet me in the Op shack."

"Five minutes, sir."

"Better make it three, Mac."

"Yes, sir!"

18. The Lock Clicks Shut

Even when a hazardous new adventure impended, Operations was slowpaced and tranquil during the early-morning hours, and its tempo wouldn't accelerate until the eve of battle, unless some emergency occurred. A senior Operations officer and a j.o. tended shop by themselves, but one of them generally sacked out on the mosquito-netted Army cot when business sloped off after midnight.

Whoever stayed alert handled the scattering of dispatches from nearby ships which weren't bothered by radio silence, from Pearl Harbor and Washington, and from local commands marooned on nearby islands who merely seemed anxious to keep their oar in. Occasionally a message required an answer, or caused a flag-topped pin to be moved, or extended one of the hentracks on the master Op chart that gave the whereabouts of friendly shipping and made a number of shrewd guesses about the enemy's.

Mostly, however, this active duty officer doodled with paperclips, started writing home on the communications typewriter that printed only in capital letters, reread ancient picture magazines, dreamed alternately of genuine peace or a real shooting war, cursed the wet, munched a bonedry cheese sandwich, washed it down with his eleventh cup of black coffee since the watch began, wished the scrawny bellyscratching yeoman were a WAVE, and finally finished his letter to the States.

Once in a while a Nip submarine would catch a Yank vessel napping, but not very often, because the enemy's undersea fleet had been pretty well bottled up. Then there'd be a brief flurry of activity while Ops got ready to provide assistance if the torpedoing happened within ADTAC's defense zone. Even more sporadically a major Japanese surface movement would be reported by some nightprowling plane or sub, whereupon all the Op lights would glare again, Captain Tuthill would be summoned, and if he deemed the sighting important enough, he'd call the chief of staff—who must make the awful choice of rousing the admiral.

By the luck of the draw, Tuthill himself had the senior duty tonight. He was only half awake when Mac entered the shack, followed by Egan Powell and Commander Canfil, but their wildly non-reg appearance snapped him out of his torpor. Startled, he stared at Powell's lavender silk pajama tops which showed above wrinkled khaki pants, Canfil's muddy carpet slippers, and the usually impeccable aide's capless head.

Tuthill's recurrent dyspepsia hit him like a time bomb. "What's the matter—you fellows going to an all-night costume party?" he asked testily.

"No, sir," Mac said, "we're here at the Old Man's orders." This wasn't quite true, of course, since only he had been told to stand by. But the others insisted on joining him, and there wasn't much use fencing with Captain Tuthill. "The chief of staff's missing," he finished bluntly.

"Christ," Tuthill said, *"Jesus H. Christ."*

As the Operations officer started to probe for details, Torrey strode into the hut, meticulously uniformed beneath his dripping oilskins, and the stormcloud expression on his gaunt face discouraged further discussion.

The Rock greeted them brusquely. "Thanks for rallying around."

"Mac gave us The Word," Egan Powell said.

"Then I won't disguise it, gentlemen. We've got one hell of a mess on our hands."

Tuthill summed up their unspoken fears: "Has Eddington cracked up mentally, admiral?"

Torrey gave him a stony look. "Mentally . . . emotionally . . . I suppose it's the same." He paused. "But I want him found if it takes the rest of the night—and I'd prefer we didn't throw the whole island into an uproar in the process."

Tuthill nodded understandingly. "We've got four phones, sir. We can call in relays. We'll check every unit on Gavabutu—starting with MOB Able in case Eddington's been hurt."

"That won't be necessary, Tut," The Rock said in an odd voice. "I've already contacted the hospital. He's not there."

"Very well, sir. Scratch MOB Able."

Tuthill separated an ADTAC directory into four equal segments.

He kept one and gave the others to Mac, Powell, and Canfil. Stark-faced, silent, they went to their telephones.

It was, they knew, a delicate mission: ascertaining whether the chief of staff of a major Pacific command had been seen in such improbable places as the paratroop camp, galley shack, motor pool, ack-ack battalions, loading wharf, or even at MoTorpRon Charlie across the island where the boats were already loading aboard their LSTs—at the inconceivable hour of 0300. Moreover, in the course of their inquiries, they had to be casual. Revelation that Eddington was absent without leave four days before Skyhook might inspire some Nervous Nelly to hit the panic button, and Gavabutu already had more than its quota of jittery types as D-Day approached.

Egan Powell, who had drawn the PT Squadron base, put down his telephone gingerly.

"Commander Norris," he said, "wants to know how in hell we figure anybody could get from ADTAC to Botan in this goddamn rain unless he'd grown his own wings?"

Tuthill, keeping score on their wearisome quest, put a check-mark beside MoTorpRon Charlie. He had to admit that querying the base was rather futile, considering the weather. But they didn't want to miss a bet, even a slim one.

"What about the airfield?" he asked Canfil.

"Zero-zero. Nothing's moving."

It was nearly 0500 before Tuthill ticked off the last name on the ADTAC roster—Weather Central—but nobody had seen the chief of staff. Nothing remained now but a dragnet sweep through the Gavabutu jungle by Marine patrols—if Torrey saw fit to order up such a desperate measure.

Commander Canfil's assigned telephone rang at 0530. It had stopped raining, temporarily, and the first frail sun's rays were just struggling over the puttycolored eastern horizon. The airfield OD was on the line again. He sounded deeply troubled as he asked if they were still interested in Captain Eddington's whereabouts.

The Intelligence officer exploded. "You're goddamn right we are!"

Audibly shaken, the OD explained in an injured tone that he hadn't been sure that they wanted him to call back if the chief of staff showed up later.

"Spill it, fella!" Canfil snapped. "Is he there now?"

No. Captain Eddington wasn't here now. But about twenty minutes ago he'd walked into the control shack and demanded one of the wingtanked Wildcats, like he'd used on that first flight of his. Remember? The OD had been reluctant to assign him a plane because he looked so disheveled and wildeyed after hiking through the storm. But, after all, this *was* ADTAC's chief of staff, wasn't it, and he'd made that spectacular recon hop, so what the dickens could a mere two-striper do in a case like that, anyhow?

"Stall him!"

Too late. Captain Eddington had brushed aside the abysmal weather reports, borrowed flight gear, fueled the Wildcat, and taken off like a bat out of hell, if the commander would pardon the expression.

Clayton Canfil turned to Mac. "Better tell the Old Man we've located his lost blacksheep."

"And where shall I say we found him?"

Canfil jerked a gnarled thumb skyward. "Up there!"

As the uncertain dawn broke over Gavabutu, Torrey, unable to sleep, lay awake pondering Eddington's crime, and weighing his own harsh task as judge, jury, and executioner. He no longer felt the icy anger which had engulfed him when he learned of Annalee Dorne's death. Instead, he had a fatalistic awareness of what he must do when they found the chief of staff. If there were any analogy for his role, it was that of a governor sitting before an open telephone line while attorneys for a convicted killer frantically marshaled their last arguments to save the man's life. The state's executive alone possessed the authority to reprieve, pardon, or finally allow him to be executed.

But such a parallel would not be complete unless the murderer crouched in that Death Row cell were also the governor's best friend.

Thus it was almost with a sense of relief that The Rock received Lieutenant McConnel's report, delivered with much trepidation, that Eddington had strongarmed his way aboard a single-seated Wildcat fighter, and was now aloft somewhere in those wild gray skies.

"We're trying to raise him on the photo recon frequency," Mac said, "but so far—no luck."

The Rock glanced up at the dirty clouds scudding just above the tops of the tallest palmtrees. "Very well. Keep trying." But he didn't sound hopeful. He wasn't. The man on Death Row had built his own gallows.

"What do you reckon the captain has in mind, sir?"

"God knows, son." Torrey swung away from the open window and regarded his aide gravely. "Eddington isn't as simple a man as he appears. Sometimes even I can't fathom his thinking, although I've known him for twenty-five years. He isn't a person you can get close to—easily."

Easily? For all their service together, despite their exposure to common dangers, The Rock realized he'd never really come close to Eddington at all; and he wondered if Eddington had felt the same way about him. He supposed so.

It was 0600. Saturday. December 5.

Regardless of the crisis engendered by the chief of staff's unauthorized flight, the task of getting Skyhook underway still confronted them, more relentlessly than ever. Throughout the rainy night the LSTs had been loading, both at ADTAC and at Botan across the island, and now they awaited only The Word to shove off. All four attack transports and cargo vessels had signaled their readiness for immediate departure, and the destroyer quartet assigned as convoy escort were already hustling back and forth outside the gap in the barrier reef, sniffing for stray Jap subs. They were only a couple of miles away, yet they were lost to sight in the morning's unnatural darkness.

It was what the airmen called "bird-walking weather," when the seagulls themselves were grounded.

"Has Captain Tuthill turned in?" Torrey asked Mac.

"Yes, sir. He left an 0800 call, though."

Forgetting his own lack of slumber, The Rock wondered how the cadaverous Operations chief could struggle through the day on two hours' sleep, particularly now that he'd be shouldering Eddington's chores as well as his own.

"How about yourself, son?"

Mac grinned stoutly. "I'm okay. But sometimes I worry about you younger officers, admiral."

"Thanks." Torrey hesitated an instant. "After breakfast, fella, I want you to run over to MOB Able and pick up an envelope that Lieutenant Haynes left for me with the OD. It'll be stamped 'personal.' "

"Yes, sir," Mac said, making a valiant effort to conceal his curiosity at this unusual request.

"While you're there, you might inform the senior medic we may be calling on his services sooner than we'd anticipated."

"Shall I tell him how much sooner, sir?"

"No. We'll have to wait and see."

Mac nodded. "Very well, sir," he said, and left.

Torrey flexed his stiff shoulder muscles, seeking to wring the bonedeep tiredness from his lean frame, before he walked across the Quonset to his worktable. There he unrolled his personal sheaf of charts, found one that spanned the vast triangular waste bounded by Gavabutu, Cape Titan, and Pelaki Shima, and anchored the unruly paper flat with a half-empty coffeecup, his tobacco jar, and an ashtray.

For a moment he stared blindly at the geodetic markings and the convoluted tracery of the map. He felt more than mere weariness. He sensed defeat.

Then he rubbed his grainy eyes to bring the chart back into focus. It was, he noted, at least fifteen hundred miles from Gavabutu airfield to Cape Titan, assuming you took a slightly doglegged evasion course; and it was another eight hundred or so miles due east from the remote base to Pelaki. Under the most favorable circumstances, reconnoitering both of these Japanese strongholds out of Mesquite would call for a four-engined aircraft capable of a thirty-two-hundred-mile sustained flight. But ADTAC didn't own such a plane. Moreover, flying conditions couldn't have been worse. A stiffening breeze was blowing from the northwest, which meant that anybody aiming for Cape Titan must buck a twenty-knot headwind before he got past Levu-Vana.

What was that wingtanked Wildcat's range? Something like two thousand miles, Torrey thought grimly—or barely enough to complete two-thirds of the mission.

As Torrey rolled up the charts, he wondered why he was so

positive Eddington would attempt this foolhardy venture. He sighed. When you looked at the matter coldly, it really wasn't foolhardy at all: it was downright suicidal.

Monotonously, endlessly, pleadingly, the powerful shortwave transmitter at the airfield kept beaming its message into the barren skies: "Rover . . . Come in, Rover . . . Do you hear us, Rover . . . Please acknowledge, Rover . . ." But if Rover were still aloft, he wasn't talking; and if he were flying a straight route, every hour set another two hundred miles between him and home base

Rover was Wildcat Dog, fourth of the souped-up F4Fs, and its lone pilot was Captain Paul Eddington, USN, whose a.w.o.l. status was beginning to be suspected by the vainly listening radiomen on the ground at Gavabutu.

Although he would have preferred to join this vigil, The Rock remained resolutely in the Operations shack on headquarters hill, where Tuthill, plainly fighting exhaustion, was drafting the final orders for the Skyhook sortie. When he could, he helped. This temporary reversal in their positions didn't bother him. There was work to be done. A key man was missing. *Ergo:* the admiral would pinchhit as a four-striper until the job was finished and the orders were translated into dispatch navalese.

But he'd told General Averell to notify him the instant they raised Rover. Like the hypothetical governor's communication system, the line was kept open to the airfield, and Torrey's two-starred jeep waited outside the Op hut, its driver drowsing at the wheel. All in all, he told himself sardonically, it was a macabre little comedy they were playing—pretending the chief of staff had simply gone off on another of his heroic junkets—and it wasn't fooling anybody.

Averell had asked: "Did Captain Eddington say what course he'd follow, admiral?"

"Check him toward Cape Titan, general," The Rock said, evading a direct reply. "That's our best bet."

"Cape Titan!"

"I'm afraid," he acknowledged, "Eddington's bitten off a pretty big chew this time—but that's about the size of it."

Averell muttered, "Jesus Christ!" in a tone that hovered between reverence and incredulity, and put down his phone. Five hours passed before he returned to the line and demanded the admiral personally.

"Yes?" Torrey asked.

"We're getting something," Averell reported. "We don't know exactly what. It's garbled as hell. And damned faint. But we think it's English."

"What's the bearing?"

"Three-three-oh, sir."

Torrey set down his own receiver and plotted the compass course rapidly on Tuthill's big chart. If it were Eddington, this reading would place him several hundred miles southeast of Cape Titan, in the area where enemy surface forces had last been sighted by the picket sub.

"Stay with it," he commanded, "I'm coming right down."

By the time Torrey reached the airfield, they had positively identified the distant signals as coming from Rover. His spasmodic messages were filtering into the air command's radio central even more faintly and feebly now, because the Wildcat had reached the limit of its shortwave range, and might have flown a hundred miles or so beyond it, according to Averell's communications officer. He spoke learnedly of such abstruse matters as bounce-back from ionized atmospheric layers and the peculiar properties of low-frequency transmission which sometimes could be read five-by-five, but which at other times sounded like a kid trapped in a deep well.

Nobody cared much about AirCom's electronics lesson, though. Rover held their undivided attention.

After three unsuccessful tries they got the plane's position: 240 miles SSE of Cape Titan. Having made a wide swing after arrowing straight toward the Jap bastion, apparently, Rover was proceeding on course-110, along a route which would bring him somewhat south of Pelaki Shima.

He'd spotted a hell of a lot of sampans, he croaked weakly, but no warships.

Several times AirCom told his radioman to relay ADTAC's insistent command to Rover—"Return to Mesquite immediately!"—but got back only a burst of static for his trouble.

Rover plainly intended to do all the talking. As far as his receiver was concerned, he might have been stone deaf.

"Eddington has ears like a fox," The Rock said flatly. "He's either got his two-way turned off, or he can't hear us because of the distance."

Around 1300, Rover called again.

His scratchy whisper, struggling through the atmospheric crackle, contained a new note. Despite the tremendous expanse of island-studded sea between the lonely Wildcat and his listeners, they could detect the excited timbre in his voice.

He'd glimpsed a Nip battlewagon through a hole in the overcast, he said, accompanied by a pair of light cruisers and five tincans. She looked about four friggin' city blocks long, broadbeamed as Rockefeller Center, and she sported more guns than the Maginot line. Rover confided that he was holding his Jap warship recognition book balanced on his knees right now, and that after studying the topside views, there was absolutely no doubt about it: *This was Yamato!*

But he expressed puzzlement at the Jap flotilla's course. Instead of moving south toward Levu-Vana, they were steaming along, very slowly and very majestically, almost parallel with his own flight line. Rover said he'd shadow the Nips for a while to make certain of their direction before he prowled on ahead to see what they had in mind. Although he thought he knew, he wanted to be goddamned sure.

One salubrious thing about this set-up, Rover confided, was the total absence of any aircraft carriers. The Japs couldn't chase him away.

Another hour dragged past.

Pacing AirCom's double Quonset the way he once strode back and forth across *Old Swayback*'s bridge, Torrey steadfastly held his impatience in check, letting the young communications three-striper run the show, while he kept for himself the passive role of observer. But as he strove for Rover's next message, watching the plotting team shape the enemy formation on the huge plexiglass circle that stood in the center of the hushed room, he learned that passivity didn't come easy. Unable to reach out and assist Eddington with counsel or encouragement, he felt the frustration of a bedridden paraplegic whose mind was still acute despite his useless limbs.

At 1420 Rover's miniature voice spanned the void once more, like the tinny accents of a child's talking doll.

He'd dropped down to less than a thousand feet so he could stay under the rainclouds, he confided, and this precarious altitude reduced his visual range to a thin semicircle directly in front of him. The *Yamato* squadron was a couple of hundred miles aft, now, but up ahead he thought he'd sighted the pagoda masts of still another force.

Rover said he was barrel-assing over there for a closer look.

At 1435 he announced laconically that they sure as Christ were Nips, all right, about a dozen of 'em. He counted aloud. Two battleships. One heavy cruiser and what looked to be a pair of lights. Maybe six destroyers.

Torrey waited patiently while the new sightings were crayoned upon the plexiglass. Then he said, "That's got to be the outfit which sortied before Task Group 48.3 hit Pelaki Shima—minus the Jap carriers."

General Averell's narrow, youthful face was glum. "Those flattops have got themselves a godawfully big ocean to hide in."

"For Eddington's sake, let's hope they stay hid."

Averell agreed. "But still, I'd hate to have this 'X' quantity staring us in the face while we're launching Skyhook, admiral."

"My guess is that the Jap carriers are long gone," Torrey said, "and for keeps."

"Where, sir?"

"North. Probably even north of the Philippines. They'll try to keep our own fast task force busy up there while they clobber us down here with their surface guns."

"They're taking a hell of a risk, admiral."

"Are they?" The Rock countered. "Even if you combine all our CVE planes you'd hardly wind up with one real flattop deckload. Less than seventy. And what's our landbased strength, general?"

"About a hundred and sixty operative craft," Averell said forlornly.

"How many bombers could you throw against a Nip fleet?"

"Fifty." The Marine airman sounded unhappier than ever when he amended truthfully, "Of course, the Mitchells haven't had much experience with evasive targets like ships—even twenty-knot battlewagons." He brightened. "But we've got a squadron of Dauntlesses. They're hotter'n two-dollar pistols."

"They'd better be," Torrey retorted, just as Rover came back on the air.

Right over the muddygray horizon from this second Nip force he'd sighted a third contingent that looked like the granddaddy of the whole bloody tribe!

What's more, Rover said, they've got air cover—a flock of snub-nosed Zeros.

Torrey forgot his spectator role. "Climb back into the clouds, Paul, for Christ's sake!" he shouted at the useless transmitter.

But Rover's squeaky voice went on unperturbed, mechanically, as he started counting again. Two more friggin' battlewagons. Three cruisers. Only this time the order was reversed, because there were two heavies and one light. Plus the usual quota of tincans. One, two, three, four . . . ten of the little bastards.

Almost conversationally, Rover relayed his belief that the hovering Zeros were land-types, probably from Pelaki Shima, which wasn't much more than three hundred miles north-northeast of them at this point.

And he still sounded unruffled when he reported they'd spotted him.

"Take cover, Paul!" Torrey yelled.

Although he'd dropped his empty wingtanks, Rover opined calmly, his Wildcat couldn't cope with these onrushing Zeros, and it looked like the meatballs would be all over him before you could spell *sukiyaki*. He doubted if he could elude them. Wasn't it a hell of a note, Rover asked rhetorically, that Uncle Sugar couldn't provide his aerial Boy Scouts with stuff that matched the Nips' in speed and maneuverability?

But now he'd have to shut up.

He was too friggin' busy.

The sons of bitches Japs were on his tail . . . snapping at him like starved jackals . . . and those sheltering clouds looked a million miles away . . .

Rover's voice seemed to fade away.

Frantically, AirCom ordered his radioman to squeeze the last ounce of juice out of the overworked receiver, but nothing came. Only the undulating waves of static, building up and receding, echoed through their earphones and ricocheted across the low-ceilinged Quonset from the loudspeakers, like the noise of surf against coral.

Rover had gone dead.

It was Averell who broke the silence. He said in a shocked, unbelieving voice, "Eddington's bought it."

The Rock nodded dumbly. For what could he say now? Eddington's last act, like Eddington himself, was blunt and direct and disarmingly simple. Staring at the foolishly crackling shortwave receiver, he speculated whether even Eddington would have admitted its simplicity, however, or imagined that restitution came that easily. Perhaps vengeance itself was a simple thing, and certainly Eddington had been a demonic practitioner of revenge against the imagined Furies that wrecked his life. But after vengeance has been gained—what then? Eddington's inability to recognize that revenge merely triggered a succession of related events was the fatal flaw. Torrey wondered if Paul had learned this before the Zeros caught him.

His face was expressionless when he finally spoke.

"Prepare an official report on Captain Eddington's flight when you get time, general. List it as an authorized mission."

"Yes, sir." Averell waited a moment then added diffidently, "Eddington rates a Navy Cross for this job, admiral. Maybe even a Medal of Honor. Shouldn't I include a posthumous recommendation?"

"Eddington wasn't medal hunting."

"I understand, sir."

"Do you?" The Rock snapped. "Do you *really* understand, general?"

Averell looked uncomfortable, but he said nothing. For a Flag officer whose imperturbability was almost notorious, the Old Man was behaving rather queerly. Yet who could blame him? That goddamn crazy Eddington, whom the admiral had carried like the White Man's Burden for so long, had finally flipped. This insane adventure proved it. For all his casual disregard for his own safety, even Eddington should have known he couldn't pull it off.

Yet, Averell supposed, the guy *had* pulled it off, when you came right down to the heart of the matter, because if it weren't for his harebrained stunt, the Japs might have come rampaging down within a day's steaming range of Levu-Vana before anybody spotted them. Now their surprise quotient was as negative as ADTAC's. They'd probably mill around while their land-based scout planes fruitlessly scoured the skies beyond Pelaki Shima, and thus grant Skyhook a little more precious leeway.

The general found his voice. "Sir, we've already phoned the contacts to Operations. Captain Tuthill says he'll have 'em all plotted by the time you get back."

"Very good, Averell." Torrey beckoned to his aide. "Come on, Mac."

For the first time in weeks, Captain Tuthill's situational chart resembled a finished work rather than the preliminary sketches for some surrealistic coffeehouse mural.

Now, on this midafternoon of Saturday, the fifth of December, they knew precisely where the enemy lay, and that great space north of Levu-Vana no longer yawned emptily from the plotting board. Having combined his own sagacity with Eddington's eyewitness reports, Tuthill was computing where the Nips would be tonight, tomorrow, and even the following Monday. But his prophetic draftsmanship didn't create a very handsome picture. The extruded lines all aimed straight at Lakola Bay. *Beach Red.* Skyhook's target had likewise become the target for these three Japanese surface forces, whose movements he had just marked with crimson crayon, and what they'd suspected for many days had come bleakly true.

The Nips weren't going to oblige the armchair experts like Blackjack Broderick and hibernate until spring. Nor would they supinely withdraw to some remote defensive position while the Yanks moved unhindered into Levu-Vana.

Tuthill's chart showed them rendezvousing slightly south of the point from which Eddington had sent his valedictory message, then sweeping southward as a single unit in the grand tradition of Trafalgar and Jutland.

Torrey shook his head.

"Tut, I hate to spoil your masterpiece. But I just don't think it'll happen that way."

The Operations officer, who had been behaving with grave circumspection in the face of The Rock's bereavement, suddenly bridled.

"And why not, admiral?" he inquired stiffly.

"Because the Japs know damn well what we've got on hand to oppose 'em with—and I doubt if they're much impressed," Torrey said. "They've certainly discounted our fast carriers as a factor in whatever they're cooking up. Otherwise they wouldn't be exposing their battleships so openly."

Still nettled at the cavalier dismissal of his estimate, Tuthill grumbled, "Then what d'you reckon will happen?"

"I think they'll split up and come at us from two directions, Tut."

"Divide their forces?"

Tuthill was shocked by the heretical notion that even the despised Japs might contravene naval dogma in this fashion. You kept your fleet intact. You smashed at the foe with everything you had. That was the Book. If you needed proof, wasn't every fast carrier in the Pacific Fleet welded into mighty Task Force 48 at this very instant, while he and Torrey were arguing doctrine? And didn't ComTaskFor 48 refuse—unless the skies literally fell in—to break up this powerful team? You're bloody well right he did!

The Rock continued dispassionately, "Either half of that Nip armada would be sufficient to neutralize our strength—" adding deliberately "—on paper."

Tuthill couldn't curb his skepticism. "So you look for a pincers movement?"

"Exactly. They want us to commit ourselves. Get our forces all neatly laid out. Then they'll jerk the noose." Torrey moved closer to the chart. Midway between the Japs' rendezvous and Levu-Vana lay a smaller island called Marate. It was, he recalled, one of Clayton Canfil's coastwatching stations. He pointed. "If my theory's sound, the first crowd—let's call 'em Bandit One—will swing close to the west side of Marate here, and head for Lakola Bay through Pala Passage." He fingered the strait that separated Levu-Vana and its sister island, Toka-Rota. "That's where we've got to stop them."

"And what will Bandit Two be doing all this time?"

"Still theorizing, Tut, but I figure 'em for a wide end-run past Toka-Rota, and then a quick dash for our beachhead."

More candidly than apprehensively, Tuthill observed, "We need help, admiral."

"We won't get it," The Rock said, glowering at the chart. "Task Force 48's to hell and gone up north. Away out of range. We're strictly on our own."

Traced in blue on Tuthill's situation map, one small spurline jutted north from Botan, indicating the LSTs that were ferrying MoTorpRon Charlie to the beachhead. Another, curving around the eastern extremity of Gavabutu, depicted the rest of the slow-moving LSTs. In apparent pursuit of this second contingent of LSTs, a third line betokened transports and cargo ships, along with their escorting destroyers.

At midnight Tuesday they'd all converge at that heavily blue-crayoned circle labeled "Point Able" prior to their final drive into Lakola Bay.

A cluster of indigo dots placed considerably south and east of Levu-Vana showed where the three baby flattops and their tincans would wait until Torrey flashed their planes the signal to hit Beach Red, along with the old battleships which, as yet, weren't close enough to show on the chart.

Meanwhile the cruisers—*Old Swayback, Moultrie,* and *Diadem*—were still anchored in the roadstead off Atoka. Because of their relatively higher speed, Torrey had been holding them there until the last possible moment, as insurance against certain dire emergencies which he'd only been able to surmise before Eddington's flight. But now the guesswork was over.

"We're going into Lakola Bay fast," he said, "and unload those cargo ships even faster. Then we'll sucker the Japs away from the beachhead and keep 'em busy while the troops dig in."

Tuthill shook his head mournfully. "By Wednesday the Nips will be swarming around us like wasps after their nest's kicked over."

"Wednesday, Tut?" Torrey asked innocently.

"D-Day, sir."

"No, Tut, Wednesday *was* D-Day. Now it's Tuesday." Torrey stood up. "Tell those LSTs I want 'em assembled at Point Able by midnight Monday even if they have to get out and push!"

"Yes, sir."

"Inform all the others—the CVEs and the transports—that our schedule's been advanced twenty-four hours."

"This could leave the battleships too far behind to do us much good, admiral."

"Let's be diplomatic, Tut. Advise the BBs that the LSTs have challenged 'em to a race. Last one into Lakola Bay has to buy the beer."

Tuthill's tired face twitched into an approximation of a smile. "Yes, sir. That might do the trick. Those battlewagon skippers have a hell of a lot of pride."

"As for ourselves," Torrey concluded, "we'll board *Old Swayback* tonight. I want the cruisers underway before first light tomorrow."

"Should I notify Toulebonne, sir?"

The Rock's shaggy eyebrows raised in mock reproof. "Why, Tut, I'm surprised you'd even ask such a question. Naturally we'll keep Toulebonne posted. I'm sure they'd like to know how we propose to match Japanese rope with American shoestring."

Within six hours Admiral Broderick reacted sharply—and predictably—to ADTAC's concise summary of the situation. Torrey was in his quarters, gathering up his personal papers, when Mac brought him the message.

He read it slowly, savoring the classically Blackjackian phraseology: "MOST URGENTLY SUGGEST YOU DELAY MOUNTING SKYHOOK AND AWAIT ARRIVAL OF REINFORCEMENTS WHICH I REQUESTED IMMEDIATELY AFTER ENEMY FLEET SIGHTING. PROSPECTS OF ADDITIONAL SURFACE SUPPORT FOR YOUR OPERATION EXCELLENT IN NEAR FUTURE. HAVE ASKED TASK FORCE 48 FOR MINIMUM OF ONE FAST CARRIER GROUP WHICH COULD REACH MESQUITE AREA WITHIN THREE DAYS IF PROMPTLY DETACHED FROM MAIN BODY. APPRECIATE PROBLEM BUT URGE EXTREME CAUTION IN VIEW PREPONDERANT ENEMY STRENGTH. YOU HAVE OUR FULLEST CONFIDENCE."

Torrey looked quizzically at his aide.

"Do you know what 'suggest' means, lieutenant? Or 'prospects' and 'could' and 'if' and 'caution'?" He crumpled up the dispatch flimsy. "Add 'em all together, fella, and they still don't mean a bloody thing except pull in your horns."

"Yes, sir," Mac agreed humbly.

"Admiral Broderick knows damned well Task Force 48 is too far away to do us any good. From all indications it'll be a lot farther away tomorrow, chasing those Nip carriers. Yet he wants us to 'delay' until reinforcements reach us. Hell. There aren't any uncommitted combatant ships south of the Equator." Torrey dropped the wadded dispatch into his wastebasket. "Our only chance now lies in speed—with a force that includes ten-knot LSTs."

"What do you want to tell Toulebonne, sir?"

The Rock consulted his watch. "It's now 2100. Advise Admiral Broderick that I'm hoisting my flag on *Old Swayback* at midnight, and that we'll sortie at 0300."

After the aide left, Torrey stared bleakly around the Quonset, from which his sparse belongings had already been removed, and thought once more about Blackjack's equivocal message. He was well aware that it represented a way out: a last chance to avoid this perilous game, and creep off to the safety of the sidelines. By obeying Toulebonne's oblique order, he would be secure, and so would his frail Fleet, until the enemy discovered his reluctance to fight. After that—well, after that, Gavabutu might fall, and Toulebonne itself could be threatened.

But Broderick's empty promise of aid came too late. Like everything else, it was too goddamn late. He closed his strongbox. The lock clicked shut with a blunt finality, as if he'd barred a door that could never be reopened.

He wondered what Paul Eddington would say now . . .

19. Joss Sticks Bring Good Luck

Six clear notes, smartly paired, clanged from the brass bell below *Old Swayback*'s navigation bridge. They signaled 0300. Three hours past midnight. Three more hours till dawn. As they echoed across the dark waters of the roadstead, a 2,100-ton destroyer of the doughty Fletcher class eased silently toward the break in the barrier reef.

Her name was *Perigore*. She was marked for death.

Spectral in the faint moonlight that rewarded them after two unremitting days of Gottlieb's rain, the remainder of Admiral Rockwell Torrey's flotilla followed *Perigore:* three cruisers and three destroyers. All the other vessels of his command lay scattered like flung coins across twenty thousand miles of South Pacific, from the friendly region above Gavabutu to the dangerous No Man's Land below Levu-Vana.

One destroyer in particular contributed to the vast distances that separated his surface units. At this moment she was churning up thirty-two knots on a course which by midmorning would place her far to the northeast, alone upon the barren open sea, and out of range of any landbased aircraft. Her mission was simple. She had orders to open up boldly with her shortwave radio and simulate a fast carrier task group racing to support the Skyhook landings. Her name was *Crandall.* Unlike *Perigore,* she would live past the week.

From the port wing of his ancient flagship's signal bridge, The Rock surveyed their deliberate progress through the anti-torpedo nets, past the treacherous shoals, and into the deep waters beyond.

He was in a singular mood. One deck above him, seated in his old canvas-covered chair on the navigating bridge, Captain Bowen ruled *Old Swayback,* leaving Torrey a mere inhabitant of the cruiser he himself had once commanded. Set apart by his stellar rank, he was forbidden by custom and tradition to issue orders that might conceivably snatch her from disaster—unless such orders involved her as a unit of his entire force rather than as an individual ship. *Old Swayback* was Bowen's sole responsibility. For Torrey she was simply a mobile headquarters, now, and his relation with her was no different than with the seven other cogs in the floating apparatus he'd designated as Task Unit ZEBRA because it was the last to quit Mesquite.

Rather morosely, The Rock contemplated the sickle moon which clung to *Old Swayback*'s starboard quarter, throwing her superstructure into bulky silhouette with its pale incandescence. He should, he supposed, derive some consolation from the knowledge that Bobby Burke, his small thin erstwhile navigator who smoked such small thin cigars, had finally earned his third stripe and been promoted to exec. Burke was a predictable quantity, a link to the familiar past. During the engagement to come, Burke would take his station in secondary controls, a boxlike auxiliary bridge that was perched above the radio shack, the emergency combat information center, the carpenter shop, and the empty hangar. (They'd drained the aviation fuel bunkers and left their scout planes home as extra precaution against the sort of fires that devastated the American cruisers in the hit-run Battle of Savo Island the previous August. If an enemy shell obliterated the navigating bridge, Bobby Burke would guide *Old Swayback* from here, like a mahout squatting too far back on his elephant's rump.

In the moonglow, Gavabutu looked strange and unreal as Task Unit ZEBRA shaped course along its southern coast. Only a few hooded lights marked the limits of Yankee military civilization on this savage island. Yet Gavabutu was technically at peace. Its turmoil had ended; and now the war was reaching out toward another remote bit of sand and coral and marshland called Levu-Vana, which nobody in Sedalia, Missouri, or Machias, Maine, or Walla Walla, Washington, had ever heard of—and wouldn't, either, until late Tuesday morning, West Longitude Time.

Shortly after daybreak they swung north.

Receding aft and to port, Gavabutu appeared a little darker and hardly more substantial than the hot, blue, watery sky, which gave only a vague promise of still more rain to come. A couple of Wildcats fandangoed over the formation as it drove ahead at a steady twenty knots, and a greenmottled Catalina described endless circles above the ships, hunting Jap subs. All three turned tail for home after about an hour. Until its rendezvous with the escort carriers late Monday night, somewhere south of Levu-Vana, Task Unit ZEBRA wouldn't see any more planes.

General Quarters sounded at 0615.

The Rock, who had been standing with his elbows against the rail, half-asleep on his feet, was shaken into consciousness by the klaxon's bray. For a moment he was assailed by the same sleep-drugged, sweatdrenched sensation which used to grip him after too many hours on *Old Swayback*'s bridge. He blinked hard. Five hundred yards to starboard *Moultrie* appeared to be pulsating in an odd fashion, like a large panting dog, and he stared at her for several seconds before he realized that it was an optical illusion caused by his own fatigue.

This was, Torrey told himself angrily, one hell of a way to approach a battle. Seeing mirages. Unnerved. Dead beat.

He called, "Mac!"

Lieutenant McConnel trotted out of the Flag plot where he'd been killing time until the admiral finished his solitary Sabbath communion and evinced a desire for human company.

"Sir?"

The Rock rubbed his eyes. "I'm going below for a quick nap," he said. "Wake me at 0900."

"But that's only three hours," Mac protested.

"I know. You may have to use dynamite. But wake me."

"Yes, admiral."

"Meanwhile, pass The Word to *Diadem* and *Moultrie* and the lead destroyer—I want their skippers here for a conference when I get up."

Torrey reached for the perpendicular ladder that led to the upper deck where his cabin was located. The cold steel bars felt rubbery against his hands. He hoped he'd make his bunk before he blacked out. And when he did, somewhat to his astonishment, he flung himself across the bed and shut his eyes, without bothering to undress. Perversely, then, he couldn't sleep.

Outside his stateroom, audible through the open port, the operators of the twin-mount five-inch/38 were cursing each other amiably, as gunners are inclined to do when they're not shooting or cleaning or tinkering; and this small distraction caused him to reflect upon the magnificent companionability of a cruiser's gun crew. Working together in their cramped steel box, manning the levers and hoists and gears that aim, load, and project the shells, they have little choice but to be comradely, for theirs is the special kinship which comes from knowing that what happens to one happens to all.

It was curious, he mused, that men could ride into battle so calmly and even elegantly in a machine that weighs thousands of tons: some of them writing letters in their private rooms and quietly pausing now and again to study the photographed faces of their wives, or reading philosophy, playing acey-deucy and pinochle, drinking Cokes, eating *gedunks,* rolling dice, wrestling, yarning, or—as in the case of this five-inch/38 crew—experimenting with fancy new cusswords.

In a few hours the chaplain would wrest them away from these worldly pursuits, pray a bit, and leave them all with a sober awareness that now-we're-getting-on-with-it-at-last.

Torrey tried to remember who said, "There are no foxholes in the ocean," but the name wouldn't come. It was damned true, though. You just kept shooting, and eventually either you or the enemy vanished beneath the waves, because there wasn't any surrender at sea, either.

He dozed.

What awakened him finally was *Old Swayback*'s bugler blowing Church Call. He listened a moment to the sad, soft sound, in which was some of the haunting quality of Taps, some of the sweep of Tattoo. Then he arose, went to the washbasin, and doused his face in lukewarm water. Now it was time to tell his captains how they'd fight the Battle of Levu-Vana.

Moultrie crept smoothly alongside *Old Swayback,* converging on a course that wasn't quite parallel until only thirty yards of frothy sea separated the two vessels. A chief bosun fired a heaving line whose weighted end was quickly seized by a couple of seamen on the approaching cruiser. They used the thin length of hemp to drag a breeches-buoy across the watery chasm, and then, hand over hand, they hauled Larry Moorian from his sleek and fashionable command to Admiral Torrey's deplorably outmoded flagship. This maneuver was repeated for Terence Mann, the barbarous master of HMAS *Diadem,* and finally for youthful

Kyle Bannion, commodore of the four destroyers that accompanied Task Unit ZEBRA and of the other workhorse tincans that were presently safeguarding transports, jeep-carriers, and LSTs all over —as he rather bitterly phrased it—*mare nauseam*.

As each of the three captains was fetched aboard *Old Swayback*, sputtering from unscheduled duckings, his ship resumed normal steaming formation, briskly and accurately, and quite undisturbed by the temporary loss of her skipper.

Torrey and his staff were waiting for them in the commodious Flag quarters. Discreetly aidelike, Mac occupied a chair placed well behind the circular table in the center of the room. Tuthill and Egan Powell flanked Torrey. Only Clayton Canfil was missing. He'd remained on Gavabutu to prod his coastwatcher network into one last monumental effort to discover what the trifurcated Japanese fleet was up to.

When he perceived his guests' bedraggled uniforms, Torrey smiled sympathetically. "Mac will pour you gentlemen a spot of coffee."

"Coffee!" Terence Mann rattled the cups with his cockney roar. "We should've met in *Diadem,* admiral! Then it wouldn't have been coffee, by God, but dark Barbados rum—the only bloody way to splice the main brace before a man faces shot-and-shell!"

Egan Powell stepped into the breach. "We Yank teetotalers fight all the harder, captain, because we've got to win the battle before we can get back to our officers' clubs for a wee dram."

"Damned debatable theory," Mann muttered, aiming a distasteful grimace toward the coffee urn.

The Rock figured they'd adequately observed the niceties. "You all know about Captain Eddington," he said in a changed voice. "It's because of his reconnaissance that we're at sea somewhat sooner than I had planned. We'll have to complete our strategy in the saddle, so to speak."

He could, Torrey supposed, have phrased it a lot stronger: lauded Paul Eddington's heroism, stressed the urgent nature of their impromptu discussions this morning, and solemnly warn them about the perils that lay ahead. But these were intelligent men. Their cognizance of the desperate situation would neither be lessened by understatement, nor improved by hyperbole.

After they'd accorded Eddington a brief silent tribute, Torrey added, "Tuthill, here, is my new chief of staff. He'll brief you."

Moorian said, "Congratulations, Tut."

Tuthill acknowledged him with a succinct nod. "Now, gentlemen, I'll run through our strategy for Levu-Vana—and your tactical part in the set-up." As he unfurled his ubiquitous charts, the freshly breveted chief of staff said, "If these seem hastily drawn—and rather ragged—forgive me. They are. Admiral Torrey doesn't believe in sleep. Nevertheless, I think you'll find them an adequate rendering of what we propose for the phase immediately following the Skyhook landings."

Mann cast a startled look at the intricate markings on the map, and then turned to study Torrey, as if he were trying to equate this inscrutable man with the fantastic plan which Tuthill was explaining.

"Bloody well incredible," he said, showing snaggled teeth in what might have been an admiring grin. "But also a fair dinkum one-way ticket to immortality."

"I thought," said Tuthill, "that you Aussies thrive on longshots."

"Ah, captain, we do. *We do!* But I doubt there's a bookmaker in Sydney who'd take this one—even at a hundred-to-one odds."

"Got the wind up, captain?"

The redfaced Australian sat bolt upright in his chair, with a prodigious display of hurt pride. "My dear fellow! You misjudge me. My quarrel's with those gutless bookies in Sydney." He fetched out a capacious kangaroo-skin wallet, flung it jauntily onto the tabletop, and surveyed his fellow captains. "Matter o' fact, any of you coves care to cover a bet, I'm offering even money we'll pull it off!"

"Hell, Terry, I'll go you one better," Moorian drawled. "I'll lay you *Moultrie* against *Diadem*—and those are pretty goddamn generous terms."

"Done!"

"What would you do with a Yank cruiser, if you win?" Egan Powell asked dubiously.

Mann chortled. "That cute little toy of Moorian's? Why, I've got thirty thousand acres of bush in the Queensland outback—I'd put wheels on *Moultrie* and use her to hunt kangaroos."

Reluctantly Torrey called a halt to the jest. He admired their easy lightheartedness, and he didn't care if it was real or feigned. It bore out Nelson's dictum that all men are brothers in the face of the enemy. But Skyhook lay before them, ominous even when contained on a vellum chart, and there was no time left for pleasantries.

"Tomorrow midnight we rendezvous with the amphibious team at Point Able," he said. "At that same hour the escort carriers will start their run into Lakola Bay, and the battleships should arrive off Beach Red to start their bombardment simultaneously with the air-strike—if their boilers hold up." He tapped the chart lightly. "The transports, cargoships, and LSTs all have strict orders to unload and get the hell out . . . *muy pronto* . . . leaving behind only MoTorpRon Charlie and her mothership."

"I gather we divide forces about then," Moorian remarked conversationally, the way he might have commented on a peculiar new spice in somebody else's *sauce Béarnaise*.

"Yes," Torrey said, "assuming our coastwatchers on Marate and our final recon flights give us The Word we're expecting—that the Nips are figuring to bracket the big island."

They gazed somberly at the map. The crimson line which represented the Japanese separated several hundred miles above Levu-Vana, like a truncated coral snake, and its components wriggled southward toward Pala Passage, which ran between Levu-Vana and Toka-Rota, and thence toward the unimpeded high seas east of Levu-Vana itself.

"How wide is this strait where it bottlenecks into Lakola Bay?" Moorian asked.

"Twenty miles," The Rock said, "but most of it is uncharted shoalwater. They won't have more than a dozen miles to maneuver in."

"And that's where we ram the cork!"

Torrey nodded. Nobody voiced the thought uppermost in their minds: it was an appallingly delicate cork. It might hold. But on the other hand, it was a damned sight more apt to blow sky-high under pressure from the volatile Jap force, splintering bottle and all. This uncertain stopgap was composed of the two old battlewagons, *Moultrie* and *Diadem,* eight destroyers—and sixteen plywood motor torpedo boats. The cork was called Task Group HORATIO, and although it wasn't clear whether Torrey meant to memorialize Lord Horatio Nelson in this manner, the name fitted, so they let it go at that.

Off to the right, tentatively, Tuthill had drawn another series of blue lines to indicate the projected whereabouts of a second American force—Task Group JOHNPAUL—during HORATIO's vigil at Pala Passage. (Obviously The Rock was thinking of the revolutionary captain when he christened this flank of his inadequate armada. Or, they wondered, was he? Perhaps "Paul" subconsciously stood for someone else.) Again, however, the captains preserved respectful silence, waiting for Torrey to speak. Their quietude was enhanced by their sobering discovery of the even scantier composition of Task Group JOHNPAUL: the three paperskinned CVEs, a half-dozen destroyers, and only *Old Swayback* to provide fire support against an enemy line that would surely include battleships.

"I'd hazard a guess," Torrey said calmly, "that the Japs will arrive sometime Wednesday night."

As a conservative New Englander, not given to wild surmise, The Rock would have based his calculations upon the best available Intelligence reports, they knew, so his guess was probably correct.

"Fortunately," Moorian observed, "I've got one damned fine chaplain on *Moultrie*."

Everyone understood his seemingly irrelevant remark. It was already Sunday noon. Approximately sixty hours remained for them to plan, prepare—and pray.

"We Aussies travel light," Captain Mann said. "Aboard *Diadem* I am the padre." His broad pink countenance gleamed with sober pride as he added, "Perhaps you've forgotten that your fine hymn 'For Those in Peril on the Sea' was composed by a staunch Church of England man. When the going gets sticky I find it most useful indeed."

"Do you know the last stanza?" Torrey inquired seriously.

"Yes, sir."

"Then I'd be most obliged if you'd recite it to close this conference—Chaplain Mann."

The Australian didn't seem astonished at the request. After the briefest hesitation, he asked them to bow their heads, and then he intoned the verse in his curiously nasal, yet not unpleasing voice:

"O Trinity of love and power!
Our brethren shield in danger's hour;
From rock and tempest, fire and foe,
Protect them wheresoe'er they go;
Thus evermore shall rise to Thee
Glad hymns of praise from land and sea."

That night the sky cleared, and when the sea turned unexpectedly calm, Max Gottlieb grew emboldened enough to predict decent conditions for D-Day. Task Group ZEBRA drove north-northwestward, now, seeking the invisible mark on the fallow ocean which was labeled Point Able, where the transports and the LSTs would soon be gathering like replete cattle awaiting the herdsman.

From his tall swivel chair on the signal bridge, Torrey peered out at the darkrushing waters, noting the lucent ivory V that foamed endlessly at the flagship's prow. They were making damned satisfactory progress, he thought approvingly, and looked upward to confirm Gottlieb's fair weather promise. But what he saw was the moon half-veiled in a wisp of cloud fabric which seemed to accentuate its soft glow, rendering it almost sensual, like warm flesh glimpsed through black lace.

He turned away, strangely irritated, as he speculated upon what random emotion might have impelled his foolish conceit, and whether others on the quiet bridge viewed this fleshly moon as he did. Then he smiled. It would be amusing to tell Egan Powell about it, and watch his satyr face when this depraved phenomenon was described by the staid and juiceless admiral. But, of course, he couldn't.

Glancing seaward again, he made out the dim shapes of *Moultrie* and *Diadem,* flanking the flagship to port and starboard, and it struck him that this black and soundless ocean had somehow been created for him alone to brood upon, here on the lonely bridge. He felt disembodied: a wraith, an island; a strange and unapproachable man in sweaty khaki, tasting the warm night breeze and listening to the muted sound of voices from the blacked-out Flag plot.

The Rock wore a railroad engineer's cap which Powell had given him on some frivolous occasion, and now he drew it low across his brow. If he wished to seize forty winks, nobody would be the wiser, for the great-billed headpiece would protect his secret . . .

Lieutenant McConnel slipped out of the plotting room and walked carefully past the somnolent admiral on his way to the starboard bridgewing. The Old Man wasn't being very communicative tonight, Mac thought. Even less so than usual. Probably worried about Tuesday. Or their rendezvous with those goddamn slowmoving oatburners tomorrow. Or the Japs. Only one thing was certain about his taciturnity, Mac knew: The Rock never paid an instant's tribute to anything personal. His life was Navy. Chop him open and you'd find Diesel oil in his veins and gunpowder in his gizzard.

A silvery glint on the sea caused Mac to glance upward at the moon.

It formed a perfect crescent, with an eyebrow-shaped cloud tipped quizzically above its peak. Suddenly a vagrant memory nagged him, and he frowned in concentration. Funny. He'd seen just such a moon once before, a very long time ago, at Pearl Harbor when Bev was with him. Wasn't it that last weird night before the blitz? It was. Mac removed his garrison cap to wipe his moist forehead. It was almost midnight. He hated to go below, but he figured he'd better get off a letter to Bev before he caught a little sleep under the steamy airblower. Maybe he'd tell her about this oddball lunar coincidence. She'd get a boot out of the fact that the same moon was shining here, in the godforsaken middle of nowhere, halfway between Gavabutu and Levu-Vana, which had illuminated Pearl Harbor exactly one year ago—on December 6!

There wasn't much cooking in the wardroom. Bobby Burke, the exec, was lackadaisically rolling dice for dime cigars with the little Irish padre, who deemed this innocent game of chance good practice for the incomparably larger gamble his flock was heading into. Two j.g.'s were shooting a game of cribbage, but they seemed to be gabbing a lot more than they were playing, as if all they really wanted was an excuse for an amiable argument.

Off in one corner of the gloomy compartment the shortwave radio yammered away all by itself, with the dial tuned to Tokyo Rose. As usual, she was bragging about the incipient annihilation of the Yankee fleet; and she was being specific about it, too, for she kept talking about Admiral Rockwell Torrey and how he was finally going to get what he deserved. You had to admit, Mac mused, that Tokyo Rose had a goddamn sexy voice, and when she said "finally" she didn't mangle her *l*'s. Most Nips would have said "finarry" like regular comedy Orientals. But not Rosie.

One of the cribbage players called across the wardroom to the chaplain. He wanted to know if the padre aimed to get in a few extra licks on their behalf tonight.

The chaplain's simian face clouded.

"You'd better restate your own case, son, because if you haven't done your homework by now, it's a trifle late." Then he relented. "However, I *am* going to have a few words with Him before I hit the sack. I'll see what I can do for you."

Mac finished his letter. He'd toyed with a juvenile impulse to toss in a few foreboding hints about their anticipated engagement with the Japs, but he resisted the urge, and after he'd sealed the envelope he felt pretty noble about the whole thing. Bev would simply stew around and worry, and it was always possible the battle would never happen anyhow. These alarums and excursions had a way of evaporating, he'd learned. Belatedly, too, he remembered that his letter would still be sitting right in the ADTAC pouch if they got into a fight, for there weren't any spare tincans to send back to Mesquite with the mail.

He rose from the wardroom table. It might be wise to take the letter up to Egan Powell for censorship right now. The captain was a decent Joe. He "read" a guy's correspondence simply by passing his hand across the envelope to make sure it didn't contain HE, LCVPs, BARs, or PTs. Besides, Mac figured he ought to go topside for one last look at the dispatch board before he turned in.

He was damned glad he did.

Lightning, to employ a phrase which always intrigued Paul Eddington, had hit the craphouse. Only in this instance it was Flag plot, a small, ill-ventilated cubicle that normally was inhabited only by a couple of watch officers, a communicator, and the indefatigable Tuthill. There wasn't enough air for more than four people, the captain proclaimed sourly, so itinerants were expected to enter, state their business in a hurry, and get the hell out. But now Flag plot was jammed. Egan Powell, AirOps, and Commander Gottlieb stood cheek by jowl with the chief of staff, and the two Operations duty officers were squeezed flat against the swingdown plotting table.

Admiral Torrey himself held the floor, with a dispatch clutched in his lean brown right hand.

"If Canfil's report is right," he was saying, "then our strategy couldn't be more on the beam."

Tuthill eyed his charts glumly and shook his head. "Except for one thing, sir."

"What's that, Tut?"

"You figured the Nips would split their forces down the middle. Even-steven."

"Didn't they?" Torrey asked blandly. "Remember what we used to say in the First War? One horse, one rabbit. Fifty-fifty."

Tuthill was in no mood for badinage, not even the two-starred variety, and he shook his cadaverous head. "The way I read Canfil's message, admiral, Bandit One is coming down the west side toward Pala Passage with only two battleships, while Bandit Two's keeping the other three. And their cruiser strength is even more unbalanced—three-to-five."

"Look, Tut." The Rock gesticulated impatiently with the dispatch which had arrived from Gavabutu ten minutes earlier. "This simply confirms our earlier conjecture. Don't you see?"

"I'm sorry, sir, but I don't."

"Our fellows watching the mouth of the strait—Task Group HORATIO—have got to halt the Japs at all costs."

"Granted."

"They'll still be outgunned to beat hell, Tut, but under these circumstances they'll stand a damned sight better chance."

"What about JOHNPAUL?" Tuthill said bleakly.

"In a case like this, Tut, we might as well be outnumbered five-to-one as three-to-one. Our job's luring 'em away from the beachhead till our friends rejoin us."

"Then you don't want to revamp the disposition of HORATIO and JOHNPAUL—balance them off better?"

"Leave 'em lay, Tut, just as they are."

"Yes, sir."

The Rock bent over Tuthill's chart which plotted the prospective encounter with these twin Japanese forces, computing quickly the sea distances involved in the early phase before the battle joined.

It was evident that Bandit One would confront HORATIO at the "bridge" several hours before the larger Bandit Two came within range of any intercepting American flotilla. Thus the encounter in Pala Passage would unquestionably turn into a nighttime melee, while JOHNPAUL's affair loomed as an action that must be won or lost in the candid light of day. Perhaps one hundred miles would separate the two engagements. With luck, JOHNPAUL might expect support from HORATIO's victorious survivors by midmorning Wednesday.

As he regarded the twisting strait through which the Nips must steam, Torrey found a sliver of comfort in the fact that HORATIO held a tactical edge, although it was the sort of narrow advantage accorded a very small hunter who's waiting for a very large bear to emerge from its cave. Of course, he reflected, a well-armed hunter might improve his position by crawling into the cave itself, and catching the beast as it unsuspectingly rounded a blind corner.

But this took a hell of a lot of moxie. It could also prove slightly fatal to the hunter—if the hunted ever got its claws on him.

Abruptly he straightened up.

"When we lay our defensive minefield off Lakola Bay, Tut, I want enough eggs held back for an extra little experiment in Pala Passage."

"Pala Passage!" Tuthill's baggy eyes gaped wide.

"Right here." With the point of his dividers Torrey made a pinprick about twenty miles beyond the strait's cornucopia mouth. "They'll have to negotiate this turn in single file, so we might be able to nail a couple of 'em before they get untangled from the mines."

"Just how do you propose to sow this field, sir?"

"We'll send MoTorpRon Charlie's mothership up there ahead of HORATIO's main body. She's been damned near everything else in her career. Now she might as well learn how it feels to be a minelayer."

"And the PTs?"

"They'll accompany her. When the Nips hit the minefield, maybe those boats can get in some useful licks too."

Meditatively silent, Tuthill rubbed a pendulous earlobe as he contemplated the tiny hole which Torrey had punched in the chart. He muttered, "You're putting those kids in a hell of a tough spot, admiral."

The Rock was already parting the blackout drapes that shielded

Flag plot's lights from the weatherdeck. He swung slowly around. "Nobody," he said quietly, "knows that better than I do, Tut."

Then he was gone.

Tuthill waited until the heavy curtains had fallen back into place before he turned to Mac, shrugging helplessly. "Either that man's a coldblooded genius, or he's the victim of a suicide complex that involves all of us . . . including his own son."

Mac reflected upon this statement. It didn't sound at all like Tuthill, and yet, he reasoned, it might be his fatigue speaking. The ponderous bulges under Tuthill's eyes had a smoky look—if the captain were a woman you'd have sworn his mascara had run after a siege of weeping—and he was taking no pains to blunt the sarcasm that always hovered close below the surface, somewhere between his spoken words and his latent temper.

Mustering up his courage, Mac said, "If there's anything Admiral Torrey hasn't got, sir, it's a suicide complex."

He braced himself for a devastating blast. But suddenly Tuthill seemed to relax.

"Hell, McConnel, don't you suppose I know that?" He leaned wearily against the plotting table. "Sometimes you have to play devil's advocate in this business and argue the wrong side just to make damned sure the Old Man's mind is really made up. When you decide it is, then you button your lip and do what he wants, exactly the way he wants it. Paul Eddington was a pretty good devil's advocate, too, although every once in a while he tended to confuse himself with Satan—and then he'd carry his case too far."

Mac gave the captain a frankly speculative look. "D'you agree with the admiral's strategy, sir?"

"It's almost hopeless," Tuthill said, "but I agree with it." He flashed his nervous smile. "Too bad we can't break radio silence. I'd like to fire off a message to our decoy tincan right now."

"What would you tell *Crandall*?"

"To fake a whole goddamn fleet—not just one fast carrier task group!"

Monday, December 7, was deceptively uneventful for Task Unit ZEBRA.

The cruisers topped off the destroyer's oil bunkers, after bringing them alongside like calves that had skipped to mama at mealtime, and feeding them from great black rubber teats slung between the larger ships and the smaller ones on either side. Torrey sat impassively on the signal bridge while Archibald Bowen directed the replenishment of two tincans. Considering the rising wind and sea, *Old Swayback* behaved quite decently, and he was pleased to give the captain a passing grade for demonstrated skill in this tricky task.

Bowen's dexterity was a good omen, he thought.

Shortly before noon, The Rock granted all seven ships permission to blow out their stacks. As the compressed air blasted upward through the funnels of the three cruisers and the four destroyers, great clouds of loosened soot burst into the pallid sky. Some of it sifted back onto the decks like fine black rain, causing a few cynical souls to suggest they'd been given a preview of the Gaelic padre's vaunted hellfire.

Gun crews dismantled their 20-millimeter and 40-millimeter mounts for the last time, oiling and limbering the mechanisms, and caressing the dullgleaming barrels the way Davy Crockett must once have fondled his Tennessee longrifle.

The doctors solemly distributed morphine syrettes to all hands in case they had an arm or leg blown off, without much explanation beyond a shouldershrug and a fatalistic leer. One saturnine medical j.g. urged, "Use 'em in good health!"

On the acetate sheets spread across their plotting board, the Operations duty officers kept track of the Japs' reported movements. Watching the red columns probe ever southward, Egan Powell observed they resembled the Five Fickle Friggin' Fingers of Fate, minus three, but he didn't draw a chuckle. Captain Tuthill opined nastily that even a Hollywood scenarist ought to be able to come up with something funnier than that.

A yellowgreen female parrot belonging to a gunner's mate second class escaped from her cage inside Turret Two and flapped up into the crosstrees of the signal halyards. There she perched for six hours, squawking evilly and pecking at a shackle, while the GM2c debated ways and means of retrieving her. Somebody suggested he ought to shoot the bird to stop the hideous noise. But the heretic was promptly shushed with a reminder of what happened when the Ancient Mariner plugged an albatross.

The wardroom bridge game acquired a breathtaking new

wrinkle: you could only bid a grand slam. Put up or shut up!

In the CPO mess, an earnest debate developed over whether they'd rate another battle star on their Pacific-Asiatic Ribbon if they bumped into the Japs. But the argument dwindled when the chief watertender reckoned he didn't give a good goddamn, because too many guys were earning battle stars who never left Waikiki. How? Scroggin' dames. It was like the flyboys' Air Medal. Five missions and they gave you another one. Crackerjack prizes!

A tincan sidled up to *Old Swayback* to deliver a lengthy message from *Moultrie*. She sported five meatball flags, seven sampans, and a Nip DD, painted grandly on her bridge, and she also displayed a printed sign that said: "We Haul Anything—Buy More War Bonds." As the destroyer came alongside, an irreverent torpedoman third class sitting astride one of the twenty-one-inch tin fish like a cowpuncher gawked up at the cruisermen, and yelled with feigned incredulity, "Don't tell me you guys draw *sea pay* for ridin' around in that hotel!"

Rubber flashcovers were issued to all hands to lay across their bunks so the bedding wouldn't catch fire if or when a shell exploded in the living compartments.

Since *Old Swayback* stayed in an absolute condition of combat readiness—condition Zebra—with her ports dogged shut, doors and hatches buttoned up, and her blowers silent, the 'tween-decks area was almost uninhabitable. Coffee erupted into sweat before it reached the stomach; and those silver I.D. bracelets which a lot of fellows self-consciously wore because their sweethearts had sent them developed an annoying tendency to blacken the wrist.

By dawn Tuesday they were near enough to Lakola Bay for their skytop lookouts to discern the brown powdery bursts which meant that the bomb-equipped Avengers from the CVEs were already on the job, blasting away at the Nips' shore defenses, and a half-hour after sunrise the two old battlewagons loomed large on the flagship's radar screen. Pretty soon the skywatch announced they'd made visual contact, too.

The veteran battleships emerged ponderously from the early-morning mist near the mouth of Pala Passage, veered slowly to port around a smallish cape that sheltered Beach Red, and positioned themselves for the bombardment. They were deliberate, cumbersome, and very dignified, as befitted their extreme age;

but their fourteen-inch shells exploded with lovely precision against the enemy's cocopalm-and-concrete fortifications along the shore.

Taken all in all, the Japs seemed to be absorbing a hell of a lot of punishment.

With *Perigore* still pacing the destroyers and *Moultrie* taking the cruisers' van, Torrey's flotilla edged through the faultily charted shoalwaters, past a gaggle of minor islets that didn't rate names on the map, toward the debarkation area off Beach Red. As this anonymous cluster of sandspits dropped astern, The Rock scowled back at them beneath his railroad cap, wishing they didn't look so goddamn much like the bars of a trap just before it clanged shut.

When the soundsman on *Old Swayback*'s bow sang out twelve fathoms, he figured they'd come near enough, and he signaled the transports to drop their hooks. But the LSTs, which had blown ballast until they drew only three feet forward, drove inexorably ahead. They touched the beachhead at 0700. Twenty minutes later the Marine regimental combat team, storming ashore through the LSTs' portcullis gates, had mortars set up, foxholes dug, and was braced for the Nips' anticipated counterattack.

But it didn't come.

The enemy's pillboxes were thoroughly demolished during the combined air-surface barrage, all right, but this had been a useless exercise. They were quite empty. As supplies piled higher on the narrow beach, and while tanks, halftracks, jeeps, trucks, and bulldozers churned the soft white sands into a mocha mess, the foe continued to lie doggo somewhere back in the greenleafy jungle.

Torrey held his three cruisers as close inshore as he dared, to provide assistance in case the fire-support squads on the crowded sloping beach radioed for help on their walkie-talkies. But no call came.

At 0800 the Nips were still invisible, still mysteriously refusing to fight back. By midmorning the entire division had been safely ferried ashore, the general's command post established and camouflaged under the trees, and a certain semblance of order was beginning to emerge from the confusion.

The Seabees managed to erect a pontoon wharf shortly after noon. After that the chore of landing a ton of food, ammo, and equipment for each of Skyhook's eleven thousand men was considerably less burdensome.

Coughing blue exhaust smoke, MoTorpRon Charlie's sixteen boats left their LSTs and tied up at a shellshattered pier toward the far end of the three-mile beachhead. Their ancient mothership AG99 dropped anchor nearby.

As the quick tropical night fell over Lakola Bay, all four combat transports and supply ships were ready to clear the hell out of these uncomfortable waters. There troop quarters and cargo holds were empty as Mother Hubbard's cupboard. They awaited only The Word from Admiral Torrey to haul-ass.

Ruminatively, silently, The Rock paced *Old Swayback's* signal bridge, fingers gripped in his webbed belt, trying to analyze the premonitory sensation that had enveloped him ever since the first Marines hit the sand. It had been too simple, too easy, too harmless. At last accounts, they'd lost only seven men killed and thirteen wounded, and most of these were victims of landmines or booby-traps. He'd expected the Japs to rest on their oars pending the outcome of the sea battle they knew was coming, but he hadn't fore-seen a fullscale withdrawal, and it worried him. He could imagine them now, squatting on their haunches along the ridges beyond Beach Red, peering myopically down at ADTAC's meager fleet, and probably laughing like goddamn miniature Oriental hyenas while they tanked up on hot sake.

Still, he supposed, he might as well accept this inexplicable situation philosophically, even gracefully, and be thankful that he could now take his handful of ships into action unscathed.

With an almost wistful sigh, Torrey walked around the signal bridge to the open door leading into Flag plot. Although the black-out curtains had been pinned back, the steelclad compartment stayed as torrid and airless as ever, and Captain Tuthill's stringy back was bathed in sweat as he bent over his board, writing.

"Got 'em finished, Tut?"

The chief of staff glanced up. "Just drafting the final set of orders," he said. "Telling Commander Norris to join Admiral Tollafson's Task Group HORATIO with his PTs at midnight."

The Rock nodded. "Good work, fella."

"We're sending 'em out as fast as they're ready, sir, both TBS and blinker. Double insurance."

"How did Tollafson take the news?"

"Damned well. So enthusiastically, in fact, that I suspect he's looking forward to something besides potshooting at cocopalms and coralheads."

"He didn't balk at delaying his departure for Central Pacific?"

"No, sir." Tuthill grinned tiredly. "Tollafson knows that whatever happens, it'll all be over within twenty-four hours anyhow. He figures CenPAC can wait that long for his antiques."

The Flag plot chronometer showed 2000. In another four hours HORATIO would form up, slip past those nameless islands in Lakola Bay, and take station off the mouth of Pala Passage. Then JOHN-PAUL would steam slowly toward the enigmatical northeast, like a lamb being led into the middle of a trackless meadow as tethered bait for timberwolves.

"Signal the transports and cargoships to clear out, Tut."

"Yes, sir."

"Tollafson can execute his orders at midnight. We'll follow at 0100." The Rock glanced hastily at his watch, as if doubting the accuracy of the infallible ship's clock, and beckoned to McConnel. "Order a boat to stand by, Mac. I'm going ashore to turn over the operational command personally to General Aylott."

Mac saluted. "You'll find the division's CP about a hundred yards inland from the pontoon dock." He looked ineffably wise as he added, "And, admiral, MorTorpRon Charlie's at the southern end of Beach Red."

"Thanks," Torrey said gravely. "You're very helpful."

But he appreciated his aide's understanding, nevertheless, because precious little time remained before the PTs and their four-piper mothership weighed anchor for Pala Passage. Their orders had already gone out, setting a 2100 departure hour, and it would be a damned tight squeeze, visiting both the Marine's GHQ and the boats. Yet it was worth the effort. Commander Norris and that reserve fellow who skippered AG99 probably needed a bit of last-minute handholding.

There was also Jere . . .

Seated in the sternsheets of the LCVP that served as his Flag barge, oblivious to the tepid spray cascading back from its spoon-shaped bow, The Rock thought about his Academy classmate, Major General Arthur Aylott, USMC. Twenty-eight years earlier, when Torrey was winning debatable fame as the worst two-miler in Annapolis history, Aylott was achieving more authentic renown on the gridiron. He stood five-foot-seven, then, and weighed 210 pounds. Only dynamite could blast him out of the pathway of an opposing halfback. Thus his nickname: Stumpy. He was, the sportswriters unanimously agreed, the toughest offensive guard in the country.

It would be damned good to see Stumpy Aylott again, Torrey mused. Because of the last-minute crash arrangements for Skyhook, they'd been forced to maintain liaison through delegates shuttling between their two staffs, and by means of impersonal dispatches and scribbled guardmail correspondence. There hadn't even been an opportunity for the usual pre-assault confab. As a result, they'd rushed pellmell into the landing like an unrehearsed football team that wasn't permitted to huddle during its opening game. But somehow it had worked.

At least, The Rock told himself grimly, it had worked so far. But now came the really crucial moment. Stumpy would have to be cast adrift—or, rather, marooned—while HORATIO and JOHNPAUL endeavored to stem a Jap tide that might well turn into a disastrous tidal wave. If that happened, he'd hate to be in Aylott's field-boots, because the isolated troops on Levu-Vana would confront something a damned sight worse than sudden death in the high seas.

Torrey left Mac to scrounge for a jeep to use for their visit to the PTs, while he plowed on foot up the steeply shelving beach toward Aylott's command post. The poorly defined trail was already ankle-deep in sandy mud spewed up by the bulldozers, as they struggled to widen this token road that would become as important as a man's jugular before the fighting ended—or began.

Once he passed a yellowfaced Marine lieutenant cranking despondently at a field telephone, and cursing Alexander Graham Bell, but when Torrey inquired about his problem the lieutenant said, "Hell, sir, this is the only way to get these friggers to work. It's hooked up to a mortar battery—over past that row of cocopalms—and I'm just trying to make contact in case we ever have to start shooting, which doesn't look likely for some goddamn reason."

Aylott's divisional command post, an outsized tent gleaming with fresh green-and-brown camouflage, was pitched over a slit trench.

The Marine general was waiting for him at the entrance flap.

"You old bastard!" Stumpy yelled delightedly. "So you finally decided to come ashore where the fighting is!"

"Fighting?" Torrey exhibited vast astonishment. "This looks like wives' night at Camp Pendleton."

"Stick around a while, Rock."

Suddenly grave, Torrey nodded. "Sure. I know. This thing can explode any minute." He regarded Aylott critically. The old goat weighed 250 pounds now, if he weighed an ounce, but Stumpy still looked like the original Immovable Object as he stood there with his gigantic legs spraddled and a .45 automatic strapped around his vast belly, every inch the All-American guard. The Rock shrugged toward the murky bay behind them. "Have you considered your situation in case we sailors get our ears pinned back—out there?"

Aylott's sweatglistening face hardened. "Old buddy," he said, "I gave the matter exactly one minute of my valuable time, and after that I stopped thinking about it. When you own a gut as big as mine, you don't want ulcers."

"Let's put it this way, then, fella. How long could you hang on without reinforcements—without extra supplies—if Levu-Vana gets cut off?"

"Maybe a week," Aylott said bluntly. "Maybe less." His voice was devoid of rancor as he added, "It all depends on whether you swabbies blow it so badly the Japs can sneak a bombardment force into Lakola Bay past our offshore defenses."

"That could happen, Stumpy—we *are* the offshore defenses."

"Hell's fire! We stuck it out on Guadalcanal when Kelly Turner had to haul-ass right after D-Day. We lived through Savo Island. And when those Nip battlewagons blistered our fannies in October—well, we survived that, too." Aylott grinned ironically. "Probably that's why I drew the short straw and got Skyhook. I'm just slap-happy enough to appreciate this kind of nonsense." He stopped grinning. "You've asked a hell of a lot of questions about our chances, Rock. What about yours?"

"Want an honest answer?"

"Christ, yes!"

"They're damned poor."

"That's what I figured," Aylott said calmly. He probed into a canvas knapsack that hung from the tentpole and extracted what appeared to be a handful of extraordinarily long matches. "Know what these are?"

"Negative, Stumpy."

"Joss sticks. Swiped from a Shanghai temple. Goddamn impious Nips used 'em to perfume their stinking blockhouses."

Torrey looked puzzled. "So?"

"You've forgotten your Chinese, admiral. Joss sticks bring good luck when you burn them. After you shove off, I'm going to touch a match to this whole friggin' bunch."

"Save a couple for yourself, Stumpy."

"Hell," Aylott said serenely, "we've got millions of 'em!"

The Rock's visitation to MoTorpRon Charlie, tantamount to the unheralded descent of a god from Mount Olympus, caught Blackjack's quondam Bastards completely off-guard. Stripped to their waists, the officers and men of the squadron's sixteen boats were deep in the greasy throes of tuning up disused engines and repairing the damage done to hulls and deck equipment during four rugged days aboard the LSTs.

Commander Norris, oilsmeared and anxious, rushed across the ruined wharf to greet the admiral.

"We didn't know you were coming, sir," he panted. "Nobody gave us The Word."

"Relax, Ben. There wasn't any Word. This isn't an official visit."

Norris tried to conceal his amazement. Social calls on D-Day were about as appropriate as tuxedos at a dog fight, to his way of thinking, so the admiral must be joking. Unquestionably this was an impromptu frontline inspection, to see whether the squadron, which had been caught with its collective pants down by the accelerated schedule, had managed to recover its aplomb.

"I'm sorry the boats are in such a mess," he apologized. "They took a hell of a beating. But we'll have 'em operative by 2100. Depend on it!"

"Ready to tackle Goliath?"

"Yes, sir!"

"You understand what you're up against, Ben?"

"Yes, sir." Norris repeated staunchly. "Admiral Tollafson sent one of his staffers ashore to go over things with us personally."

"We've handed your outfit a nasty job, mister."

"Well, sir, isn't that exactly what we've been training for?"

Behind its ludicrous mask of greenblack grease, the PT commander's countenance shone with boyish enthusiasm, and Torrey stifled a sigh at Norris' unawareness of the hazards he faced.

"I suspect the fellows who wrote your training manuals never anticipated anything quite like this—or reckoned on these odds," he said.

"The more ships," Norris said reasonably, "the more targets."

Torrey slapped his broad shoulders. "You're 4.0, Ben. Give 'em hell!"

"Yes, sir."

The Rock squinted across the lagoon toward the berth where AG99 was loading her delicate cargo of contact mines. Even in the darkness it was evident that the venerable tincan was almost ready to get underway. "I gather that Tollafson's people also briefed you about the minefield mission," he said.

"Chapter and verse, admiral."

"In that case, I think I'll pass up a call on AG99. She looks competent to take care of herself."

Norris grinned. "She's plenty old enough."

"There's just about time enough left for me to say hello to Jere. Where's the young rascal?"

"I imagine you'll find him in *Miss Brimstone*'s engineroom—up to his fancy Harvard ears in grease like the rest of us. D'you want me to send for him?"

"No, thanks, Ben. I want to surprise the lieutenant."

"You sure as hell will, sir," Norris agreed. "I don't imagine he's expecting company any more than I was."

Torrey picked his way gingerly along the sagging dock until he found Jere's boat. Saluting, he stepped across the gap to the miniature quarterdeck, and went below. He'd forgotten how vulnerable, how bereft of protection, and how utterly naked these toy warships were. They couldn't be much stouter than the fishingboats that used to ply the Maine coves when he was a kid. No. They weren't even that rugged. Aside from their mighty powerplants, which practically made them airborne at top speed, they couldn't hold a hurricane candle to those lapstraked Down Easters.

Jere and his chief machinist's mate were crouched beside the sleek twin Packard engines, like consulting surgeons studying the results of a particularly complex, but deftly handled operation. As Torrey's footfall sounded on the steel grating that led to the engine well, Jere looked up, scowling fearsomely, and prepared to vent his captain's wrath upon whoever dared invade these sacred premises without permission.

But The Rock beat him to the punch. "Hello, son," he said casually.

"Dad!" Jere dropped the lugwrench with which he'd been tightening the starboard Packard's twelve cylinderheads under the chief's critical gaze. "What the hell!"

"Excellent question, lieutenant," Torrey observed. "Since I happened to come ashore for a powwow with General Aylott, I thought I might as well drop around and see how you're making out."

"We're all set, sir."

"So your skipper tells me. I'm glad. *Miss Brimstone*'s headed for a damned rough party for a lady. More of a brawl, I'd say."

"Commander Norris explained the problem, sir. Nobody figures it'll be a pink tea party." Jere straightened up as far as the engine-room overhead would permit, and regarded his father with a steady gaze. "He also told us what you'll be doing while we're up in the strait."

"Everyone's going to be busy," Torrey admitted cautiously.

"From the looks of it, sir, you'll be the busiest."

The Rock swept a quick glance around the boat's cramped quarters, noting its exposed ribs and slatted flanks. The insistent sound of waves breaking against the mahogany hull was audible in the dim little compartment.

"Possibly," he acknowledged.

Their conversation faltered. There wasn't much more to be said. Stooping low to avoid the beams that supported the thin decking, Torrey started to leave, but Jere's hesitant voice stopped him.

"Did—did she send any word? Annalee, I mean?" Guiltily, The Rock thrust his right hand into his trouser pocket, and felt the crumpled bit of paper he'd put there before leaving *Old Swayback*. He'd forgotten all about Annalee Dorne's tragic farewell note.

"Son . . ."

When he paused, undecided, Jere pressed, "I thought maybe Lieutenant Haynes might have relayed some message."

"She did."

The boy brightened. "What did Annalee say?"

Torrey took his empty hand from his pocket. "She wanted you to know," he said carefully, treading on the razor edge of truth, "that she was sorry about everything . . . that she still loved you."

"Honest, sir?" Jere looked troubled.

"Honest, son."

"Women are sure funny." Jere smiled sadly. "You know, she never wrote me."

"MOB Able's been damned occupied with getting ready for Skyhook."

"Or maybe her letter got fouled up in the mail. We've been sort of at the end of the world, you know." Jere was making a positive effort to discern reasons for Annalee's long silence. "Now we *are* at the far corner." As he lifted his lugwrench and prepared to attack the cylinders again, a wry thought struck him. "Anyhow, sir, it's not often a two-striper gets his officer-messenger mail delivered by an admiral."

"That's democracy, fella," Torrey said, trying hard to sound offhand and whimsical, yet sensing failure.

Jere's smile widened. "If you see Ensign Dorne before I do, sir, tell her I'm keeping our signet ring nice and shiny . . . and ready."

"I'll tell her." Torrey extended his hand across the gleaming twin Packard. "So long, lieutenant. Keep your powder dry."

"Goodbye, dad," Jere said. "Good luck . . ."

Preceded by their mothership, which was burdened to her scuppers with the lethal array of mines racked upon her fantail like balls on a pooltable, the sixteen boats of MoTorpRon Charlie slipped stealthily out of Lakola Bay only nine minutes behind schedule.

Three hours later Task Group HORATIO proceeded northward at slow speed, bound for the mouth of Pala Passage.

Torrey saw them assemble just beyond the barrier islands—two antiquated battleships, two light cruisers, eight destroyers—before they were swallowed up in the midnight gloom. By now the transports and cargo vessels were far below the invisible horizon, beyond *Old Swayback*'s radar range, and for the next thirty minutes the only blips on the translucent screen were caused by HORATIO's dozen ships, steaming toward their rendezvous with an enemy called Bandit One, and by a pair of tincans that would escort the flagship away from this ominously quiet beachhead.

JOHNPAUL's trio of baby-flattops waited east of Levu-Vana. Their planes were stowed below. They were prepared for an all-night run.

The Rock checked his watch. In another thirty minutes *Old*

Swayback would get underway, too, and after that, Stumpy Aylott's Marines would be on their own.

Now the deed was done. Having split his already insufficient forces into two much weaker segments, Torrey's situation was not unlike that of General George Armstrong Custer's at Little Big Horn, when part of the Seventh Cavalry galloped right, and part of them left, with Yellow Hair in lonely command of the inadequate center. Custer, of course, had never questioned the wisdom of his fractionary tactics, although he had woefully miscalculated Sitting Bull's numbers, and thus he met disaster. So here the analogy failed, for Torrey had far more self-doubts than ever assailed the cavalryman, and he did not underestimate his adversary.

Another melancholy thought occurred to The Rock: on the day Larry Moorian arrived at Gavabutu, he had predicted that *Moultrie*'s captain might become his own good right arm. Now he had cut off this essential member, deliberately, because of the Japs' reputed lack of aircraft carriers. *Moultrie*'s formidable A.A. fire wouldn't be needed by JOHNPAUL, he knew, but her prickly five-inchers might prove devastating against the Nip destroyers, which would outnumber HORATIO's tincans twelve-to-eight when they met in Pala Passage.

He smiled mirthlessly into the night, reminding himself that even Moorian would have been only a substitute right arm, since he'd always depended upon Paul Eddington for support where fists and biceps counted. Hadn't he? Torrey considered this for a moment, before he asked himself, in all candor, how urgently he needed Eddington's animal presence on the eve of battle. Or his harsh counsel? Or abrasive assurance?

Eddington hadn't participated in the judgments which led up to this moment, thirty minutes past midnight, Wednesday, December 9, *anno Domini* 1942—had he?

Ask again, Torrey, and you'll find it was yourself, alone, unaided, even opposed by those around you, who made the decisions . . .

The Rock was roused from his somber thoughts by the sharp sound of *Old Swayback*'s brass gong, ringing twice, and by a simultaneous quickening of the blower's whine as the cruiser shook free of her three-hour lethargy and gathered momentum for the all-night dash into the dark, dangerous and unknown northeast, beyond the protective capes of Toka-Rota, where they must meet the enemy.

20. *No Captain Can Do Very Wrong*

BONY ELBOWS PROPPED against the chart table, his drawn face ghostwhite in the hooded lamp's gleam, Captain Forrest Tuthill pondered the irrevocable decision which the admiral had just issued so offhandedly, even calmly, and with every outward indication of confidence. For better or for worse, this judgment was epitomized by a blue-penciled "X" eighty miles due east of Toka-Rota's longest beckoning landfinger, one hundred miles from the mouth of Pala Passage where HORATIO now stood at the "bridge," and another one hundred and twenty miles from Levu-Vana's unguarded beachhead.

Tuthill supposed The Rock had weighed the possibility of errors in the data provided them by Clayton Canfil's Intelligence center on Gavabutu, which was the reporting funnel for isolated coast-watcher units, itinerant native spies, planned recon flights, haphazard sightings by transport planes that gawked and fled, patrolling subs, or an occasional captured Nip who turned talkative after writing himself off as officially dead in the eyes of the Mikado, his bushido gods, and his family.

Torrey's assumption that they'd intercept the enemy at this precise "X" was riddled with Jesus-factors, despite all his careful reasoning. It was based on the thesis that Bandit Two, their own special foe, would continue southward at the same swift rate of advance—twenty-five knots—and on the same 190-degree compass course he'd pursued for almost twelve hours. But if the Japs altered either speed or direction, choosing instead to creep alongside the treacherous coastal waters of Levu-Vana's companion island, they might elude Task Group JOHNPAUL entirely, and pounce upon the naked Sky-hook beachhead before they were apprehended by radar.

"There's an awful lot of empty ocean between us and the blasted Nips," Tuthill observed gloomily.

You couldn't improve on that cryptic summary, Egan Powell

thought, scanning The Rock's immobile countenance for some reaction to the open doubt which Tuthill's tone made no effort to conceal.

Torrey simply shrugged. "Even though our CVEs slow us down, we're closing those babies at forty-three knots, Tut, and that uses up Blue Water pretty damned fast."

When he swung again toward the chief of staff, Powell saw that his saturnine face had turned noncommittal.

Forty-three knots! That was a hell of a combined collision speed for two battle forces: like deliberately driving a Sherman tank into a concrete abutment and hoping you'd find a soft spot. Or, Powell remembered shudderingly, like clipping a Sunset Boulevard lamppost at a cool sixty m.p.h. in a Cadillac convertible, as he'd done once and somehow lived to tell the tale to the desk sergeant. Sure. He'd walked away from that one. But nobody walks away from a naval battle.

Egan Powell's unhappy eyes circled Flag plot's sixteen-by-eighteen feet of paintscraped steel, bolted steel tables, steel bulkheads, and stumplike segments of steel mast that marked the forward and after boundaries of the cluttered room. Beneath his elegant tailored khaki shirt the sweat felt unaccountably cold; and for the first time in his heedless life, Powell knew that he was afraid. With fear came shame. Why didn't Torrey—or that nervous walking corpse of a Tuthill—act scared, too? What Christly sort of inbred courage made them stand there, unruffled and unperturbed, with nothing more on their goddamn Trade School minds than at what point their ten hopelessly outclassed ships would collide with the enemy's three monstrous battlewagons, two heavy cruisers, and nine destroyers? Unhumorously, he recalled one of Paul Eddington's favorite exhortations, borrowed from a Marine topkick in World War I: "What's the matter—you bastards want to live forever?"

Egan Powell did. He had a lot of unfinished business to attend to, a lot of life to live, even though Admiral Rockwell Torrey and Captain Forrest Tuthill apparently didn't concern themselves with such silly trifles.

The Rock's deep bass voice was just audible above the insistent hum of *Old Swayback*'s blowers.

"If we maintain twenty knots," he said, "we should intercept the Nips about half-hour after sunrise."

Tuthill agreed so quickly it was obvious he'd already estimated the converging tracks of Bandit Two and JOHNPAUL. "I'd make it 0700."

"Hold course-and-speed steady, Tut."

"Yes, sir."

"And order Captain Rudyard to launch a ten-plane search just before dawn," Torrey said. "Due north."

"First light may be a bit delayed, admiral," AirOps put in. "It's still raining."

"In that case, commander, schedule the launch for 0615 sharp."

"Whether we've got visibility or not?" AirOps asked, looking worried and figuring that the baby-flattop pilots probably hadn't been checked out for night take-offs.

"Yes." Torrey turned to Max Gottlieb. "What's your prognosis, Mr. Weatherman?"

"It'll clear—partially, sir."

"When?"

"Maybe by morning. Certainly before noon. But it'll stay rather misty, with a light breeze out of the southeast—and we'll have a few rainsqualls somewhere in the vicinity."

The Rock tamped a full load of shagcut into his bulldog briar. "Good," he said softly. "We might need 'em for cover."

Still fascinated by the menacing "X" on Tuthill's chart, Egan Powell sought to ease his own misgivings with a quip. "The way a stripteaser uses feathers to stay legal," he suggested. "Task Group SALLYRAND." But the ill-conceived joke fell flat. Nobody laughed.

"Nice try, Powell," Tuthill muttered ironically.

Torrey blew a fat cloud of tobacco smoke across the hushed compartment. He yawned prodigiously. "It's now 0200, gentlemen," he said. "Five hours until our guests arrive for the party. I'm going to turn in. Call me at 0430, Mac, unless things start popping sooner."

For a moment Torrey paused outside the door, waiting for the pupils of his eyes to expand in the pitchblackness, and listening attentively to the familiar night sounds of a ship at sea. Their variety never ceased to beguile him. To his left the infrared signal gun that was only used after dark made a small dry clicking noise as The Word about tomorrow's planes flickered to the close-knit task group. Somewhere aloft a faint whistling meant the headwind, compounded from their twenty-knot advance and its own twelve-knot force, was taking Aeolian pleasure in the flexible steel rigging. An occasional rumbling atop the superstructure, seventy feet above him, attested to the eagerness of the crew manning the five-inch director—or perhaps it signified nerves drawn too taut—as they probed this way and that around the blind skies with their massive revolving apparatus. Once in a while a vagrant ninth wave would shatter against the cruiser's bow as she cut steadily through otherwise moderate seas, suddenly making Torrey conscious again of the ocean wasteland that encompassed them.

As if they respected the silence of the night itself, or were apprehensive that their voices might carry too far across the rolling waters, the handful of men on the aftersection of the bridge carried on their business in hushed, almost reverent tones.

The Rock heard a seaman-second who had brought the sunrise order to the chief signalman whisper guardedly, "Looks like the Old Man figures to tackle the whole goddamn Nip Navy." A mirthless grunt was the only response.

Instead of going directly to his cramped quarters, Torrey circled the weatherdeck so he could pass the outjutting platform on which the two communications ratings were huddled.

"Finish sending those messages, Flags?" he inquired mildly.

The signalman scrambled down from his tiny parapet. His cat's vision immediately identified the admiral. Aggrieved at what he considered an implied slight against his professional skill, he said, "Yes, sir!"

"You're damned fast," Torrey complimented him.

"Been in the business twenty-eight years, sir."

"That's quite a coincidence. So have I."

"Jeez," the signalman marveled, "and I thought I was the oldest son of a bitch in this friggin' Navy."

"When the sun comes up, chief, we senior sons of bitches will have a special responsibility. You know that, don't you?"

"Yes, sir. I've read the Book."

The Rock grinned confidentially. "Start teaching it to your young friend, here, so he won't worry so much about having to fight the 'whole goddamn Nip Navy.'" He glanced at the apprentice's pale, scared face. "We're not alone in this thing, fella."

"A fellow sure *feels* alone sometimes, sir," the boy said.

"Look across at those carriers," Torrey commanded gently. "They've got sixteen Wildcat fighters and a dozen Avenger torpedo bombers apiece. That's eighty-four planes. They can do an awful lot of damage. And just remember—the Japs haven't any aircraft at all."

The seaman relaxed an iota. "I reckon you oughtta know, sir."

"Yes," Torrey said, "I ought to . . ."

Turning slowly, he made his way forward through the tepid rain, until he came to the deserted bridge shelter. Here he stopped again. Perceived dimly through the wet-streaked windshield, the dark sea that surrounded the flagship seemed unreal, as if glimpsed in a dream, and the ships comprising JOHNPAUL's vanguard and flanks were barely visible.

Captain Kyle Bannion led the formation in *Perigore.* To port and starboard, *Eaglet* and *Chickenhawk,* their five-hundred-foot rectangular flightdecks untenanted in the shrouded gloom, were making a dogged effort to hold to the prescribed twenty knots, while the third jeep-carrier, *Falcon,* lumbered along four hundred yards astern. The remainder of the destroyer screen—five slim, sleek vessels—formed a semicircle around the perimeter of the small force.

It occurred to The Rock, brooding on his chair near the windshield, that the approaching engagement was shaping up like the nebulous battle he had sought but never found just a year ago.

On that earlier December night he'd computed the firepower of his twelve-ship pick-up squadron, and now he found himself figuring again: three baby-flattops carrying twenty-eight planes in each of their hangars, with a single five-inch rifle mounted on their decks more for morale than utility; six destroyers whose combined main batteries totaled thirty five-inch/38s, plus their sixty torpedo tubes; and *Old Swayback* herself, modernized in haphazard fashion, equipped for surface action with nine eight-inch guns and eight five-inch/38s.

Unlike his earlier will-o'-the-wisp flotilla, to be sure, JOHNPAUL had plenty of search radar. But this was rather perverse comfort. It simply meant they might catch an electronic flash of what hit them before the ax fell; and chances were that *Eaglet*'s dawn patrol would transmit the sad Word long before the radarscopes picked up the enemy blips. He grimaced into the enveloping murk. Aside from the Japs' astonishment at finding such a trivial force barring their seaway to Levu-Vana, there'd be damned little surprise this time. It was all laid out, cut-and-dried, familiar, like the choreography of some well-rehearsed and oversimplified ballet.

The Rock eased himself down from his chair. He was exhausted. Those two and one-half hours' sleep he had rationed himself had now dwindled to two, and it was plain idiocy to stay awake any longer, because he couldn't do another bloody thing. Nothing. Except to wait and pray, and hope that when Mac awakened him at 0430 he'd be ready, confident, and grinning, with some immortal phrase that men would remember long after *Old Swayback*'s steel bones were barnacled rust.

When he'd closed the door to the cubicle that served as emergency Flag quarters, Torrey switched on the shaded bulb above the built-in desk which paralleled his bunk. He intended to leave it burning while he slept. If an urgent message arrived, he wanted no fumbling delays while he grappled in the darkness for the orderly's flashlight. As he started to turn away, ready to collapse fully clad across his narrow bed, something on the dropleaf desktop caught his eye. It was the triple set of photographs which he'd always kept secreted in his footlocker: Jere's, the Old Man's, and Athalie's.

But the face that smiled at him from the last frame wasn't Athalie at all—it was Maggie Haynes.

Suddenly he remembered. He had taken her picture one pleasantly indolent afternoon at Waikiki almost eleven months ago. When it turned out better than they'd expected, he had slipped the snapshot over Athalie's haughty replica, and stowed the album away in his sea chest where it had lain forgotten until this moment. He held the small portrait close, studying it in the meager light, savoring Maggie's impish, crooked grin.

Perhaps he should give his Chamorro steward's mate the devil for presuming to unpack an item as sacredly personal as a photograph, and, what was even more felonious, exhibiting it here on this desk. Then he relented. How could the Chamorro realize that Admiral Torrey never put pictures on his workdesk, or that he considered such a display pure affectation?

Tomorrow he'd tell him to take the album below and repack it under the dress whites in his footlocker.

Tomorrow?

Hell.

It was already tomorrow.

And he had to admit that Maggie Haynes' whimsical face—tip-tilted nose, cleft chin, lopsided smile and all—was damned comforting, in an odd way, as it viewed him quaintly across the narrow compartment. Maybe he'd humor the steward's mate and leave it there. Like the rest of his sentimental brethren, Torrey supposed, the Guamian boy doubtless figured this pictorial array was a proper familial reminder to bolster the Old Man in his hour of peril—just as any normal admiral, ensign, or sailor would be heartened by the images of his loved ones, whether framed in goldtooled leather or treasured in sweatstained wallets. He set it back on the desk.

Beneath half-closed lids, Torrey contemplated the three photographs.

The portrait Jere resembled not at all the determined, maturing youth with whom he'd conversed seven hours ago in *Miss Brimstone*'s engineroom. This Jere, glaring so defiantly at the camera, was somebody else, who had never really existed except in Athalie's closed and frigid mind.

It was 0300, now, and the real Jere would be conning *Miss Brimstone* at quarter-throttle along Pala Passage's tricky, convoluted shoreline, trying to make as little noise as possible, and waiting for the pagoda bulk of the Jap battlewagons to loom out of the swirling mist. AG99 should have finished sowing her sketchy minefield. She'd be hightailing it back toward safety, leaving her wooden charges to oppose the giant foe with nothing more than their four torpedoes apiece, their little smokepots, and their forty-knot elusiveness.

The Old Man's rugged countenance regarded him from the middle frame. Somberly, Torrey returned his father's steadfast gaze, thinking how the classic naval situation which confronted watchful HORATIO might have delighted him.

"Cross their 'T' as they steam out of the strait," the doughty captain would have rumbled, "and the yellow devils won't stand a bloody chance!"

Jere's PTs would have puzzled the Old Man, however, and unquestionably annoyed him. Child's play. Minor diversionary action. Heckling. That's how he'd have characterized MoTorpRon Charlie's role in the coming Battle of Pala Passage.

Rather distractedly, The Rock tried to imagine how the Old Man might have behaved if he were in command, and had committed his own son to such a fateful gamble. But instinct had already provided the answer. The Old Man would have penned the orders calmly, transfixed the youthful lieutenant with a glacial stare, and curtly dispatched him on his way. What he'd do thereafter in the sanctity of his private quarters was anybody's guess, although Torrey suspected the Old Man would address himself to the fierce Jehovah who handled the affairs of fighting men, and ask Him earnestly to pay a moment's special attention to this idiotic adventure.

Torrey's approaching crisis with Task Group JOHNPAUL would also have left the Old Man in a state of angry bafflement.

"Why in the name of all that's holy," he'd bark, "did you split your forces, boy?" And he'd dismiss the jeep-carriers as cockleshells that shouldn't have been let loose on the high seas in the first place, unworthy of association with capital ships that could toss a one-ton armor-piercing projectile fifteen miles, knowing it would find its mark.

Only one facet of JOHNPAUL's strategy might have appealed to the craggy old battleship sailor. He believed unswervingly in Nelson's stark prescription for a properly conducted surface engagement: "No captain can do very wrong if he places his Ship alongside that of an Enemy." This had happened at Trafalgar. It could happen again.

The Rock shut his eyes. In the past three days, he remembered, he'd managed precisely nine hours' sleep . . .

But even this minimal rest was cut short. At 0410 he was awakened personally by Captain Tuthill. More pinchfaced and haggard than ever in the obscure light of the seacabin, the chief of staff stood beside the bunk, waiting while Torrey struggled to fit numbed, swollen feet into shoes that seemed to have grown too small while he slept.

Tuthill held a single sheet of paper in his clawlike right hand. "It's started," he said simply.

"Dick Tollafson's crowd?"

"Not quite, sir. The PTs. But Admiral Tollafson relayed this message from MoTorpRon Charlie. He's working 'em by voice."

"Read it to me, Tut."

"SIGHTED LEAD SHIPS OF BANDIT ONE. TWO DESTROYERS. HARUNA-CLASS BATTLESHIP. MOGAMI-CLASS CRUISER. AM ATTACKING. NORRIS."

"Nothing about damage to the enemy from AG99's mines?"

"Not a goddamn word."

Torrey lurched to his feet and tightened his belt. "You know?" he reflected aloud, "I wouldn't put it past young Norris to have ordered that torpedo run *before* the Japs reached the minefield just to confuse the buggers."

"If that's true," Tuthill growled, "he's got a hell of a lot more guts than I have."

The Rock gave him a look of saturnine sympathy. "In a couple of hours, Tut, your guts may have a workout too."

As they walked the short distance around the weatherdeck to Flag plot, he noted that the rain which bathed his hot forehead wasn't rain at all any more, but a lightly swirling mist. The eastern skies were darkmottled with ragged clouds, through which the expiring moon shone fitfully, and the sea had calmed, bearing out Max Gottlieb's prediction of a gentle southeasterly breeze. From a purely meteorological viewpoint, it promised to be a good day—one that would delight any landsman with nothing more on his lubberly mind than a drive across the placid countryside with his family.

Flag plot was unwarrantedly crowded. As the braincenter toward which all communications flowed, from time to time it had to accommodate messengers from the coding room one deck below, as well as from Captain Bowen on the navigating bridge above them, and from the various staffers concerned with the conduct of the entire task group. But now, emboldened by Tuthill's absence, these couriers had tarried longer than usual, and when the admiral and his chief of staff elbowed their way through the blackout drapes, they found a dozen-odd officers jammed around the chart table.

Tuthill surveyed them sourly.

"Get back," he rasped, "and let's give the patient a little air."

Abashed, the kibitzers retreated, and then one by one they faded unobtrusively into the night.

Egan Powell held out HORATIO's latest decoded message.

"THREE MTBS ATTACKED AT 34 KNOTS," it said, "CLOSING TO POINT-BLANK RANGE FOR TORPEDO LAUNCH. LEAD BOAT HOLED BY ENEMY DD FIRE WHICH EXPLODED ON BRIDGE. CASUALTIES UNKNOWN. BELIEVE ONE JAP DD DAMAGED. MAIN ENEMY FORCE CONTINUING THROUGH PALA PASSAGE."

Three minutes later Tollafson radioed that a second PT section had roared out of the darkness to claw at the thickskinned foe, but had been driven off by gunfire from the two Nip light cruisers. They'd fled in a gust of their own smoke. During their headlong retirement, one of the boats had run aground; and now its crew was marooned somewhere deep in Pala's gullet, where they coolly announced they were establishing their own beachhead with machineguns pried loose from the splintered craft.

Four more PTs joined the unequal fray at 0425, expended their torpedoes, and reported seeing the Japs' heavy cruiser falter momentarily, and then pull out of formation. But as they withdrew, two of the boats crumpled under a concentrated five-inch barrage from the enemy's flanking destroyers. They sank immediately.

That left six PTs.

At 0433 a messenger arrived from radio central with Tollafson's final accounting of MoTorpRon Charlie's valiant attempt:

"REMAINING TWO SECTIONS INTERCEPTED NIPS AFTER ENEMY STAR-SHELLS ILLUMINATED FORMATION 18 MILES BEYOND MOUTH OF STRAIT. FIRED ALL 24 TORPEDOES WHICH RAN HOT AND STRAIGHT AND NORMAL. VIGOROUS JAP RETURN FIRE PREVENTED ACCURATE ASSESSMENT OF RESULTS ALTHOUGH NORRIS REASONABLY CERTAIN AT LEAST ONE POSSIBLY TWO DESTROYERS HIT AND SOME EVIDENCE OF DAMAGE TO HARUNA-CLASS BATTLESHIP. TWO MORE PTS LOST. BANDIT ONE NOW ENTERING MINE-FIELD. KEEP FINGERS CROSSED. WE SHALL ENDEAVOR TO DO SAME TO ENEMY'S 'T.' TOLLAFSON."

The Rock returned the dispatch to his chief of staff. "It was a damned good college try," he said. "Those kids did the best they could. They may even have slowed the Nips a little. Got 'em snafued."

"It's expensive, admiral."

"Yes, Tut, it's damned expensive."

Another fifteen minutes passed. Implacably. Endlessly. Crouched over the plot board, on which Tuthill was transcribing data from HORATIO's fragmentary running accounts, Torrey sought to comprehend what was happening almost one hundred miles to the invisible southwest. But it was like watching a sportswriter charting the far downfield movements of a football scrimmage that could be perceived only vaguely through a heavy snowstorm: it was unsatisfactory, confusing, and it made damned little sense.

The brass hands of the bulkhead clock were nearing 0500 before radio central sent along Tollafson's next report: "BANDIT ONE HAS CLEARED MINEFIELD. AG99 OBSERVED PASSAGE FROM ADJACENT COVE AND ADVISES RADAR SCREEN SHOWS ENEMY MAY HAVE LOST TWO SHIPS INCLUDING ONE HEAVY TYPE. JAPS APPEAR DISORGANIZED WITH RATE OF ADVANCE PERCEPTIBLY SLOWED. ESTIMATE THEY WILL ARRIVE OUR VICINITY APPROX 0530."

There was another brief message clipped beneath HORATIO's dispatch. Tuthill, who had adopted Eddington's practice of reading incoming radio traffic before it reached the admiral's eyes, scanned the brief typewritten flimsy.

He looked up, grayfaced, and tendered the slip of paper to The Rock without speaking.

Even before the words came into focus, Torrey knew what they would say, and he was curiously prepared, as if Tollafson's appended personal note were something he had been expecting for a very long time.

"DEEPLY REGRET TO INFORM YOU THAT PT 396 LIEUTENANT JUNIOR GRADE JEREMIAH FARR TORREY COMMANDING WAS BOAT CITED IN MY EARLIER DISPATCH. ALL HANDS ON BRIDGE INCLUDING YOUR SON INSTANTLY KILLED BY ENEMY SHELLFIRE. THIS REPORT CONFIRMED BY SURVIVORS. CAN ONLY ADD THAT LIEUTENANT TORREY ACQUITTED HIMSELF GALLANTLY ABOVE AND BEYOND THE CALL OF DUTY. PROFOUNDEST SYMPATHY. DICK TOLLAFSON."

He returned the message to the chief of staff, and started to leave.

"I'm sorry, sir," Tuthill began.

"Thank you, Tut." Torrey's bleak expression deterred the captain from further condolences. "There'll be nothing more from HORATIO for another half-hour. Notify me when he checks in. I'll be on the bridge."

They watched him depart, silently, and with a peculiar dignity. But his ramrod back seemed bowed for the first time from weariness that came more from the spirit than from his overtaxed physique. Nobody spoke for a moment after the blackout curtains dropped into place.

Then Tuthill said slowly, "There, my friends, goes a *man!*"

Alone, his face to the breeze that blew through the opened windshield, Torrey sat in his tall swivel chair and stared into the murky night across *Old Swayback*'s rifle turrets. He felt strangely composed, as if whatever peace he must make with himself had already been made, aware that self-lacerating grief, now, was a wasteful luxury. It was futile to will the past again, or even to imagine that the future could be different if he were granted another chance. Because he knew the circumstances would be the same, and so would be the orders he must issue—and the inevitable outcome of such commands.

Later, when there was more time to think, he might mourn. But it would be lament for what could have been rather than for what had actually existed. He had lost something which he'd never possessed, although it had come very close to him in these final days. That, of course, was the real tragedy.

An irrelevant thought nagged him.

Why, he wondered, had he called the PTs' forlorn venture a "college try," as though it were a harmless game from which the participants would emerge, a bit battered, perhaps, but still grinning pluckily, and eager for next Saturday's contest? It was a stupid metaphor. You didn't need much imagination to picture what must have happened during that ten-mile running fight in the narrow, twisted, smoky pass. Jere's squadron had flung themselves against the impervious steel flanks of the Japanese cruisers and battleships like so many moths assaulting a blowtorch, and a lot of them had perished the same way, crisped in the devastating blaze of five-, eight-, and even sixteen-inch gunfire.

What had they gained?

Torrey tried to recall HORATIO's sketchy damage reports: three Nip destroyers, a cruiser, and a battleship—possibly hit; another cruiser and destroyer—presumably sunk.

But the Japs were uncannily survival prone, as the many-lived

Haruna had proved from Mindanao to Midway, and when Bandit One finally reached the mouth of the strait it would probably be damned near intact, barring a few dimpled plates and notched keels.

Yes. It had been a hell of a college try, all right, only for Jere there wouldn't be another Saturday . . .

Determinedly, then, The Rock erased Pala Passage from his mind, and stopped thinking about the unthinkable. He had an immediate job to accomplish. It couldn't wait. In another ninety minutes JOHNPAUL might be fighting for its own life.

Lifting his nightglasses, he peered through the mistblown darkness on the starboard side of the flagship, where the boxy shapes of two of their three escort carriers were faintly discernible. Captain Rudyard's *Eaglet* was closest. Tiny human forms were scurrying around her flightdeck, pursued by abnormally large shadows, which he knew were the CVE's torpedo-laden Avengers.

Rudyard was spotting his planes early for the mandatory dawn take-off. That was good. It meant he was eager for action.

Diffidently, as if reluctant to intrude upon the admiral's private anguish, but knowing that he must, Mac materialized out of the gloom, and now he stood beside him, with a fresh dispatch in his hand.

"Sir, I hate to bother you," he began, "but HORATIO—"

"That's all right, son."

"They've sighted Bandit One."

Torrey read the message in the dim red beam of his aide's flashlight:

"RADAR CONTACT AT 33,000 YARDS. JAPS ADVANCING IN STANDARD BATTLELINE. FIFTEEN SHIPS AT SPEED 18 KNOTS. WE WILL CLOSE TO 17,000 YARDS BEFORE COMMENCING FIRE. CLOSE RANGE NECESSITATED BY SHORT SUPPLY OF ARMOR PIERCING SHELLS. WILL USE HIGH CAPACITY SHELLS TO CLEAN UP CRIPPLES AFTER DISPOSING OF BIG BOYS. TOLLAFSON."

The Rock passed the flimsy to Mac, over his shoulder, and continued to stare through the windscreen.

"So we got only two Jap ships," he muttered, "in spite of everything."

"Captain Tuthill's afraid they're only tincans," Mac said unhappily.

"He's probably correct."

"Damned rugged, sir . . ."

Torrey's chair made a small squeaking sound as he turned toward his aide. He understood what Mac meant, and why he couldn't say more to the father whose deliberate gamble had cost his son's life.

"Thank you, fella."

Mac swallowed hard. "The chief of staff wants to know when JOHNPAUL can start communicating on voice radio."

"We'll open up with our TBS," The Rock said, "the minute we spot the Nips on radar. No sooner. I don't want to take a chance on a skipwave bouncing our signal across the horizon and alerting Bandit Two."

"Yes, sir."

"It's about 0545, Mac. They're still a hundred miles away—give or take a few miles we might have miscalculated—and I'd like our planes to surprise 'em before breakfast."

As Torrey spoke, there was a vague auroral lightening of the eastern gloom, like something sensed rather than seen by a hiker lost in a labyrinthine cave, and he noticed that only one rainsquall remained. It was dancing a mournful graveside jig far off to starboard.

At 0550 *Eaglet*'s bloodshot signal light winked toward the flagship, and kept winking for a long time, as if it had a tic that caused an endless series of long and short eye twitches.

Tuthill himself brought the message to The Rock.

"Rudyard's feeling antsy," he said. "He's requesting permission to launch his full strike instead of a search mission."

Torrey considered briefly. Even assuming the baby-flattops succeeded in getting their entire complement of thirty-six Avengers airborne with fighter cover, they still wouldn't add up to a very impressive array. Nevertheless, he thought, plagiarizing a bitter Eddington phrase, they sure beat the hell out of no planes at all. Having none, the Japs were tied irrevocably to the surface. But with their three giant battleships, their pair of cruisers, and their half-dozen destroyers in excess of JOHNPAUL's meager line-up, they weren't likely to worry too much about the henpecking administered by the jeep-carriers, any more than Bandit One had fretted about the gnatlike PTs. It troubled him to commit his paltry air strength in this fashion, blindly and completely, before he knew the foe's exact whereabouts. But time was getting short. And the Japs were fearfully close. Surprise was the essence of this preliminary phase of JOHNPAUL's strategy.

"Granted," The Rock said crisply.

For once Tuthill didn't demur. He, too, could hear the ticking away of the precious minutes before they would sight the enemy.

"Shall we keep a fighter screen here?" he asked.

"What for, Tut?"

"Nip subs."

Torrey grinned tiredly, "Yes. I guess I'm getting punchy. God knows I should have remembered the possibility of submarines—me, of all people, and on this ship! Hold back a few Wildcats. Just in case."

"Yes, sir."

Moments later *Old Swayback* returned *Eaglet*'s nervous blinking with a curt "AFFIRMATIVE."

Almost immediately, as if Rudyard had been stamping around on his carrier's bridge, expecting a favorable reply but cursing the delay, the lead Avenger began rolling down her short flightdeck. The snubnosed, potbellied craft gushed blue flame as it was catapulted aloft against the faint breeze. After her, like pips shot from a blowgun, came another and another torpedo bomber, until *Eaglet*'s twelve-plane contingent was airbone. Acting under Rudyard's tactical control, *Falcon* and *Chickenhawk* launched their single-engined craft in quick succession.

Torrey watched them congeal into three compact echelons, pick up their fighter patrol, climb sharply, and then head into the glowering north. He flipped the pilot's traditional thumbs-up sign toward the vanishing planes.

"That," he remarked, "is that."

Tuthill gave a solemn nod. "I'll wager this is the first time that all the eggs in one basket ever hatched simultaneously—and took off."

The Rock acknowledged his irony with a brief grin. "Now, Tut, let's see if we can't browbeat that goddamn closemouthed radio of ours into giving us some more Word from Dick Tollafson . . ."

But HORATIO was already on the circuit when they entered Flag plot.

His picket destroyers had romped into the midst of Bandit One's startled vanguard, fired four dozen torpedoes from port and starboard, and dashed back to safety through their own smoke. They left behind them a mortally wounded Nip battlewagon, the burning hulks of two enemy tincans—and utter chaos. Follow-up torpedo runs by Tollafson's right and left flank destroyers slowed down the second Jap battleship and demolished another tincan.

Despite his evident confusion, however, the Nip admiral was game. He plunged ahead with his crippled force until he'd closed within twenty-two thousand yards of HORATIO's slowly steaming battleline, apparently unmindful of the horrid fact that Tollafson had him boxed, with his "T" precisely crossed.

Both of the old American battleships commenced firing at 0620, joined scant minutes later by *Moultrie* and *Diadem,* and by 0635 they had shoveled more than a hundred rounds of fourteen-inch shells and a couple of thousand rounds of five- and six-inch projectiles into the luckless Japs, who had obligingly paraded single file into the slaughter like lambs crowding down an abattoir chute.

It was all over by 0655.

Tollafson radioed: "NIP REMNANTS INCLUDING ONE LIGHT CRUISER AND FIVE DESTROYERS ATTEMPTING ESCAPE VIA PALA PASSAGE. BANDIT ONE LOST BOTH BATTLESHIPS ONE HEAVY CRUISER ONE LIGHT AND SEVEN DESTROYERS. OWN CASUALTIES TWO DESTROYERS. THAT'S ALL. ASSUME YOU NEED HELPING HAND FROM BROTHER HORATIO RATHER THAN MOP-UP NOW THAT BRIDGE HAS BEEN SECURED."

Torrey looked at the bulkhead clock. It was 0658. If his calculations were correct, JOHNPAUL should be raising Bandit Two within the next ten or fifteen minutes. His gaze descended to Tuthill's worktable, and to the thumbtacked chart on which the routes of all four opposing forces—two Jap, two Yank—were marked in red and blue.

HORATIO was one hundred miles astern. This meant at least four and one-half hours at flank speed for Tollafson's ancient battlewagons, if they were ordered immediately to the scene. But modern sea fights didn't last that long unless they were conducted at long range by fast carrier squadrons. Whatever engagement confronted him, therefore, was far more apt to resemble the action at the mouth of Pala Passage than the Battle of Midway, or even the Coral Sea; but with one monumental exception, he reminded himself, for JOHN-

PAUL's situation was precisely the reverse of HORATIO's. He had no battleships, no fortuitous opportunity to cross a bewildered enemy's "T," and no escape or hiding place in this open expanse where the swifter enemy could maneuver around him at will.

Long ago during a dull tour of duty at Great Lakes Naval Training Station, he'd once visited the noisome Chicago stockyards, and now he wondered: how long does it take the butcher to recapture a sheep that's temporarily eluded his ax in that maze of pens and runways? Five minutes? Twenty? A half-hour?

Tollafson's onesided donnybrook had consumed barely an hour and a quarter.

JOHNPAUL, Torrey brooded, mightn't survive half that time unless somewhere there existed a more benevolent Fate, looking down and taking pity this morning, than he'd encountered in all his previous years.

"Have Tollafson join us at best possible speed," he said wearily. "He can pick up the pieces."

"What'll I give him as a rendezvous point?" Tuthill asked.

The Rock scowled at the rapidly converging lines on the plot that indicated where JOHNPAUL and Bandit Two should meet.

"We can't open up yet, Tut. But he'll keep tuned to our frequency. When we break radio silence, tell him to head for point 'X.' I still figure that's the best bet. Afterward Dick will know what to do if we go off the air prematurely—maybe he'll start unlimbering some extra liferafts."

"Yes, sir," Tuthill said glumly, turning to the Air Operations officer who stood in the doorway that led from the radar room.

"What I can't understand," AirOps complained helplessly, "is why we don't hear from our goddamn strike."

Torrey mentally agreed. The Avengers should have reached their target long ago, dropped their loads, and returned for more. But he said merely, "It's a hell of a big ocean, commander, and they're only forty-eight planes."

"That's true enough, sir." AirOps' frustrated expression deepened. "And it's still damned muddy outside."

Although daybreak had officially come thirty minutes earlier, the overnight rain had left behind it a thin, low-lying blanket of mist that could play hob with aerial reconnaissance. Looking for a moth hole in its ragged gray surface, the Avengers could have easily overshot their mark. Or, Torrey knew, an estimate like his, which depended so heavily on pure hunch sense, might be haywire by a hundred miles—or even three hundred, had the disobliging Japs decided during the night to change course and head directly for Lakola Bay.

If that were the case, he told himself, Dick Tollafson would get the surprise of his life.

But it wasn't.

At 0720 *Old Swayback*'s radio central picked up something that sounded suspiciously like the barnyard cackle of many Nip voices, and a DF fix placed its source almost due north.

"I'll monitor it for a few minutes," Egan Powell said, starting for the door, "and see whether my Jap lingo's improved any."

Five minutes later he came back, looking grave, with a hastily scrawled translation in his hand.

"It's Bandit Two all right," Powell said. "And the head brigand's passing The Word to all the little pirates." His lip curled. "D'you know what the bastard's telling the brethren? 'Let us now attack, trusting in divine guidance.'"

Tuthill snorted.

For a moment, Torrey wanted to suggest that correcting the enemy's theological errors was the chaplain's prerogative, since he handled *Old Swayback*'s relations with the Almighty, but a shout from the radar room interrupted him. AirOps dashed through the connecting door into Flag plot.

"Surface contact at twenty-two miles, clear as a bell on the screen," he announced breathlessly.

"How many ships?" Torrey asked.

"At least fifteen. Maybe eighteen."

"Keep feeding us the range, fella."

"Yes, sir!"

Almost immediately the phone that linked Flag plot with the navigating bridge rang peremptorily, and Tuthill snatched up the receiver.

It was Archibald Bowen.

With tension quivering in his usually oracular voice, he reported that *Old Swayback*'s skytop lookouts had spotted anti-aircraft puffs along the northern horizon, and he wanted to know whether the admiral intended to maintain this collision course now that Rudyard's Avengers had gotten into the show. Maybe, Bowen hinted anxiously, JOHNPAUL should stand off and observe for a little while.

Tuthill relayed the captain's suggestion.

"Tell him we'll stay tight on course-350," Torrey said. "I want to give the Japs a good nibble before we jerk away the bait. Otherwise they might head west without even seeing us."

Bowen digested this reply for a few ruminative seconds before he came back doubtfully, "We've got a damned light line for sharkfishing, sir."

"It's more sporting that way, Archie," Tuthill assured him with a jauntiness he didn't really feel.

Old Swayback's brasslunged klaxon was already caterwauling General Quarters by the time the chief of staff recradled the intercom phone.

"There's one exception to course-350," The Rock said, as the chief of staff went back to his plotting board. "The carriers. Turn 'em south—as fast as their little legs will carry 'em!"

"Yes, sir."

Torrey reached for his visored linen shooting cap and slipped it over his lean head, letting the padded earflaps hang loose. When the gunfiring began, he would tie the chinstrap tight so they'd protect his ears against damaging concussion from the eight-inch main battery—particularly Number 2 turret which lay just below the signal bridge—and from the excessive noise that tended to scramble a man's thoughts at key moments. Then he affixed circular foamrubber pads around the eyepieces of his binoculars. The *whump* of big guns had blacked many an unwary eye, and he'd have to use the glasses during the coming battle.

"Advise Rudyard he's on his own, Tut. No destroyer screen. We're keeping the tincans with us." As Torrey stepped to the weather door, he called over his shoulder: "Set up shop on the Flag bridge, gentlemen. Our customers have arrived!"

The TBS loudspeaker was gabbling furiously when The Rock reached his chair, for even as *Eaglet, Chickenhawk,* and *Falcon* began to swerve away from *Old Swayback* and the six destroyers, their Avenger pilots were checking in with strike reports, which Captain Rudyard dispatched promptly to the flagship.

They had missed the enemy force cold on their outward leg—just as Torrey feared they might—and only a freakish whim of Gottlieb's weather allowed them to glimpse the Nips at the very instant they were starting their homebound descent. In the ensuing melee the Avengers figured they might have laid a couple of fish alongside a battlewagon and pinked the fantail of a light cruiser, although they couldn't be sure, because the accurate intensity of the Japs' A.A. fire surprised the bejesus out of the attackers.

They sacrificed seven planes trying to penetrate that virtually solid steel umbrella so they could get at the ships underneath. Finally they were forced to withdraw after launching their torpedoes from distressingly long range.

One Jap battleship in particular astonished the Yank pilots. She'd sprouted ack-ack from every pore. The only Avenger that drew close enough for a decent look saw its tinfish explode harmlessly against her underwater armorbelt after a hot-clean-true run, as if the lethal electric torpedo were nothing but a kid's Fourth of July cherry salute.

Within another ten minutes the pagoda masts of Bandit Two's capital ships came into faint view along the horizon, still many miles distant, but blackly ominous to the spotters in the flagship's main top. Seconds later a series of tiny flashes was visible along the sea rim. The Japs' hulls were still below the earth's curve. Yet they'd opened fire!

Methodically, like a doctor taking a patient's pulse, The Rock counted the seconds that elapsed between the faraway flicker and the shell splashes which erupted in huge green geysers between the fleeing baby-flattops and *Old Swayback*. He gave Tuthill a meaningful glance. The Nips' introductory probe had been unpleasantly accurate.

"Twenty-nine thousand yards," he said with reluctant professional admiration in his tone.

"And goddamn big splashes," Tuthill added "—from eighteen-inch rifles."

"*Yamato!*" Torrey shrugged philosophically. "We've drawn the jackpot, Tut. No wonder those torpedoes didn't hurt her. She's hedged with sixteen-inch armorplate."

Glancing quickly over the flagship's starboard quarter to check the jeep-carriers' progress, he perceived that luck, for once, seemed to have favored JOHNPAUL. The flattops' tangential runaway course had taken them almost directly into the wind, so the returning Avengers and Wildcats were able to land without impeding their motherships' withdrawal. Flaps down like tailfeathers, wheels lowered like outstretched birdfeet, they dropped gratefully onto their flightdecks.

Several miles to the southeast Torrey could see the arching darkness of the last persistent rainsquall remaining from the night before. Chased and prodded by the inexorably advancing shellbursts, the three little carriers were hastening toward this precarious sanctuary. And yet, he figured pessimistically, it was damned doubtful if they'd find shelter behind those clouds before the enemy fire caught up with them.

Any extraneous maneuvering by the CVEs might easily prove to be their undoing.

He picked up the TBS mike, pressed the talk button, and asked for *Eaglet*.

Rudyard's voice responded at once. Across that riddled sea gap, it sounded amazingly unruffled, as if the youthful airman weren't in the least concerned by the prospects of sudden annihilation by a well-placed battleship salvo.

"Eaglet to *Swayback,"* he drawled. "Over!"

"Jack—this is Torrey. We're going to tackle the Big Boys in a few minutes and we'll need your help."

"Name it, sir."

"It may slow you down," The Rock said carefully, "but I want another strike against those battlewagons."

Rudyard seemed surprised and a trifle pained that the admiral would even have to ask. "Hell, sir, we're already started refueling our birds. They'll be airborne in fifteen minutes."

"Can you make it ten?"

"Affirmative."

"God bless you, fella."

"Thanks, admiral."

"And Jack . . ."

"Yes, sir?"

"Better remind 'em that Skyhook's their alternate 'airfield'—just in case."

"Roger," *Eaglet* replied stoically. "I understand."

Torrey could envisage Rudyard perched on his ridiculously small flying bridge atop the carrier's token superstructure, glowering down at the meager expanse of flightdeck below him, and probably estimating what a couple of rounds of high explosive might do to his eggcrate vessel. If Rudyard were smart, though, he wouldn't be wasting time worrying about the battleships' fourteen- and eighteen-inch weapons. Even a few five-inch hits would render a baby-flattop's take-off surface useless, jam its pair of elevators, or blast the lone catapult to smithereens.

Each jeep-carrier knocked out, The Rock told himself, reduced JOHNPAUL's insignificant air-striking power by one-third.

He put the TBS mike back on its hook beside his chair, picked up his binoculars, and resumed his taut vigil.

The Japs were clearly limned on the horizon, bearing down upon his small force in what appeared to be a curiously disjointed formation. He pondered this phenomenon a moment. They had, he supposed, begun to deploy into a traditional circle-defense against the earlier air attack; but when their own skytops glimpsed the Americans, the Nip commander must have hoisted the signal for a full-scale surface assault. In their rapid transition from defense to assault, they'd neglected to establish a proper battleline, and now they were spaced out like beads on a cheap necklace, tenuously and unevenly. The awkward maneuver had euchred their destroyers far to the rear where they wouldn't be of much use either as a screen against Kyle Bannion's upcoming cavalry charge, or for a torpedo run of their own.

This was a minuscule crumb of comfort.

But it might prolong the inevitable.

Torrey reached for the TBS mike again. *"Swayback to Perigore,"* he called.

The destroyerman responded vigorously. "Roger!" His voice was more tense than Rudyard's, and a little higher pitched than usual, but its timbre betrayed no real nervousness.

As The Rock issued his next order—a tough, inflexible assignment for Bannion's half-dozen 2,100-ton ships—he fleetingly hoped his own tone didn't divulge how he felt: chilled, sad, and doomed.

"Go after 'em, Kyle!" he said tightly. "Three at a time!"

"Aye, aye, sir."

It was that simple. No further instructions were necessary. The circuit between flagship and destroyer clicked emptily, and an instant later a gaudy string of signal flags fluttered from *Perigore*'s yardarms.

"SMALL BOYS," they spelled, "TO THE ATTACK!"

Torrey watched the first section skate nimbly away from their screening duty, form a fanshaped triple file, and raise their bows as they accelerated toward the onrushing Jap battleships and cruisers.

They looked incredibly small. They also looked like the staunchest warriors he'd ever seen.

Closest to the enemy, on the racing right flank, *Perigore* commenced to lay a smokescreen. Oily black gouts of engine exhaust billowed from her raked funnels, and cottonwhite clouds streamed from the chemical pots on her crouching fantail.

Behind this gauzy shield, boldly and insouciantly, the tincan trio galloped against the foe with every one of their combined 180,000 horses cast loose.

At this juncture Bandit Two was still twenty-two thousand yards away, according to the flagship's rangefinder, but closing fast when the gallant charge began.

Rudyard's second carrier air-strike hovered over its target.

And now it was time for *Old Swayback* to lend the weight of her nine eight-inch rifles to the desperate endeavor.

In the split-second interval before her outswung main battery cut loose with its initial salvo, The Rock cast a searching look at the faces of the three men closest to him—physically and professionally—at that climactic moment, as if he wished to dry-etch them forever on his memory. To his right stood Captain Forrest Tuthill, bone-thin, desiccated as an autumn oakleaf, but without the leaf's color. Behind him was the omnipresent Lieutenant McConnel, strangely assured in his rubicund youth, a distant look in his eyes as if (Torrey imagined) he were giving a last thought to that brave young wife of his whose name was so confoundedly like Beth Eddington's. Then there was Egan Powell, dashing, handsome, full of lively juices, and plainly scared as hell, although he was making a stubborn effort to conceal his fears as this unequal battle joined.

Looking at his comrades in arms—the old man, the boy, and the cavalier—Torrey speculated how he himself must appear to them. He wondered whether his own desolate feelings showed, and he found himself wishing to hell he could see Rockwell Torrey as they saw him.

Suddenly he felt an enormous compassion for everyone aboard *Old Swayback,* and in all of Task Group JOHNPAUL, that embraced the stonyfaced quartermaster clutching the flagship's great brass wheel and the lowliest junior officer of the deck, as well as her absurdly pompous captain and the juvenescent carrier skippers—because he had brought them to this pass, coldbloodedly, intentionally, and fully aware of the hopelessness of the enterprise itself.

Torrey knotted the linen cords of his earmuffed helmet just as the cruiser's Number 2 turret shattered the windy silence a scant fraction before her forward and after guns opened fire . . .

Flattened like greyhounds against the roiled green water, Bannion's destroyers gamely seized advantage of the flattops' follow-up air-strike to plunge within ten thousand yards of the leading Jap vessel, a skyscraping heavy cruiser of the *Mogami* class, where they dispatched their first torpedoes. They spat high explosive from their five-inch popguns all the way in.

Perigore herself rocketed straight into the enemy's steel teeth—to a pointblank five thousand yards—before Bannion squeezed the trigger that unleashed her full ten-fish spread.

From *Old Swayback*'s lofty bridge, Torrey saw the destroyer-leader careen wildly to port as the torpedoes sprang free and burrowed into the waves. Then she scrambled to put a little more margin between herself and the appalling barrage which thundered down from the enemy vanguard at such short range that the Jap gun muzzles were depressed toward the sea's surface.

Perigore had been hit several times during her approach. One of her funnels hung at a crazy angle, and there was an oddly misshapen look about her superstructure.

Mac breathed a fervent "Jesusgod!" as she vanished behind a monstrous graygreen wall of water thrown up by the concentrated fire of the battlewagons' fourteen- and eighteen-inch rifles, the cruisers' eight- and six-inchers, and the distant Nip destroyers' five-inch guns. *Cassiday,* he remembered with a flash of bitterness, had been murdered a hell of a lot easier.

Perigore reappeared briefly from behind this barrier. Aflame from bow-to-stern, she was still throwing shells into the Nips' faces with her twin-mount fives. But she was plainly done for.

Behind her, as she slowed down to die, she left a heavy cruiser circling helplessly, holed by four torpedoes and listing badly.

The TBS crackled. It was Bannion. "*Perigore* to Little Boys," he called, talking slowly and rather disjointedly, as if he'd been hurt, "continue attack . . . we will cover for you . . . as long as we're able . . ."

"Roger," assented another, stronger voice. "I'm going after their lead elephant."

Torrey caught the bluesteel glint of the destroyer that leaped out of the smokescreen created by *Perigore*'s funeral pyre. She whirled toward the behemothic *Yamato* like a fox terrier sprinting to tangle with a mastiff, closely pursued by the third tincan of Bannion's indomitable outfit. The guns behind their thinclad splintershields—designed to repel aircraft, subs, and sampans—barked impudently at the pagodas, and sometimes they bit.

They were making thirty-five knots. They were forever committed. They couldn't possibly reverse course now, even if The Rock had ordained it.

Mac's sweaty hands, gripping the back of Torrey's chair, were whiteknuckled talons. He breathed another "Jesusgod!" as the tincans drove ahead . . .

"Sir!" The officer of the deck nudged Tuthill. "The bastards have started bracketing us!"

It was a classic redundancy, but starkly true. Tuthill nodded. From several ships deep in the enemy ruck, which hadn't yet been engaged either by Bannion's riddled section or by the second echelon of destroyers, rumbled the neatly spaced shells of regular salvos: eight- and fourteen-inch projectiles coming at *Old Swayback* with the sound of a fast freight highballing down a steep mountain grade. Earlier broadsides had fallen short and wide. But the range was narrowing, and the Jap marksmanship had diabolically improved.

Torrey glanced at Tuthill.

"Let's feed 'em a couple more rounds ourselves, Tut, then head southwest, away from the carriers." He smiled wanly. "By now they must know we're here."

"If they can see us," Tuthill said, "behind all those splashes." He passed the message to Captain Bowen, who had climbed from the navigating bridge to the more advantageous battle lookout, from which he was now conning the flagship. There was no need to signal the rest of Task Group JOHNPAUL, for *Old Swayback* was quite alone, and if any tincans lived through the next few minutes, they would follow. The baby-flattops had reached the sheltering rainsquall with reasonably whole skins.

"How did Archie sound?" The Rock asked.

This wasn't an idle question. They were utterly dependent now on Bowen's skill and morale.

"Chockful of piss-and-vinegar," Tuthill said. "He surprised the hell out of me."

"You never know, Tut."

Torrey squinted through his glasses at the havoc that was unfolding fifteen thousand yards ahead of them. One of the Jap light cruisers had been penetrated by a torpedo from the second attack wave, and was gushing flame and smoke. A *Haruna*-class battleship had developed some sort of steering trouble, although her fourteen-inch battery kept thundering, even as she traced a slow, stately crescent wake away from the main Nip line.

To his amazement, *Yamato* seemed to be pulling back. Her stern was aimed directly toward *Old Swayback,* leaving only her after turret free to lob its massive shells toward the solitary cruiser.

Had The Rock been more of an optimist, and less the raw realist he was, he might have taken encouragement from this inexplicable reprieve. Instead, he ascribed *Yamato*'s apparent withdrawal to the sacrificial efforts of his destroyers and to the insistent probings of the carriers' Avengers which were now concentrating heaviest on the super-dreadnought.

Momentarily he expected to see *Yamato* wheel around and come barreling toward *Old Swayback* and the flattops.

Thus far the flagship had demonstrated her heritage of clean living, as Eddington would have said, for she'd sustained only minor damage to her starboard catapult—which was a useless appendage, anyhow—and she'd taken a near-miss alongside her hull below Number 3 turret aft. Casualties were also light.

But Torrey knew these glancing blows were merely a small foretaste of worse to come.

He stepped to the portside of the signal bridge, where two seamen clad in flashgear were keeping tabs on the enemy with pelorus and stadimeter. Although this same data was fed to *Old Swayback*'s main and secondary batteries electronically, their constantly iterated cries of "Ship bearing zero-three-five!" and "Range eleven thousand!" provided an immediate reference for emergency maneuvering. From this unimpeded parapet, he peered aft to ascertain the whereabouts of the rainsquall into which Rudyard had led his vulnerable carriers.

But the protective cloudshield had dissipated in the treacherous early-morning sunshine!

Exposed in all their shaven nudity, *Eaglet, Chickenhawk,* and *Falcon* were vainly trying to stretch more precious searoom between themselves and the implacable Jap gunfire. The shell splashes were stalking them like tall white banshees after a trio of scared schoolboys who'd ventured too near the graveyard.

It was obvious now why the Nips hadn't yet bothered to administer the mercy stroke to *Old Swayback*.

Above all else, they wanted to dispose of those carriers.

Jack Rudyard's *Eaglet,* on the nearest flank of the frantically galloping troika, was already in deep trouble. What appeared to be four-gun salvos, tightly patterned and spaced only sixty seconds apart, had begun to fall around her.

In frozen, helpless fascination, Torrey watched as these quadruple bursts advanced two hundred yards each time the Japs' battery let loose, creeping remorselessly closer to *Eaglet,* and certain to catch her with all four shots when they finally connected. Once, the carrier executed a sharp change in course, which stymied the next two salvos, but the third spread after that found her rudder, flightdeck, and island superstructure—all in one devastating triphammer series.

Before Torrey could suck in his breath, bright flames were dancing out of *Eaglet*'s exposed hangar, fed by volatile aviation gasoline, and the flattop fell away into a mushy turn that had the flailing, uncontrolled look of a wounded animal's death throes. Smoke poured from her wrecked navigating bridge. The man at *Eaglet*'s helm, he guessed, was already dead.

The Nips showed no mercy, although none was beseeched.

As *Eaglet* dropped further behind her sisterships, succeeding salvos punctured her supine body with monotonous regularity, until all that remained of her was five hundred feet of blasted, twisted, burning flotsam. She was still afloat. But she floated lifelessly, drifting on the easy swells, and soon she'd lie face down like the violated corpse she was, rolling over once before she sank. Torrey saw a couple of rafts tumble over her starboard rail, which was almost awash, followed by a pitifully small cluster of survivors. Some of them were on fire as they leaped into the sea.

He turned away from the scene.

He felt nauseated, not so much by the carnage itself, but because the short fight had been so grossly unfair, and because Rudyard never had a rat's chance of retaliating—except with his preposterous little five-inch rifle which kept spitting away at the mockingly distant attackers until it, too, was drowned in the oily reek.

When his mind cleared, Torrey remembered that *Eaglet*'s demise had cost him twenty-eight of his eighty-four planes, which must now wing back to the captured strip at Levu-Vana. By the time they could refuel and rearm, the battle might be over. Might? Hell! At this appalling rate, it would be finished within the next half-hour and JOHNPAUL's gamble would be lost, leaving the Japs free to pounce unmolested upon Stumpy Aylott's beachhead division.

He glanced at his watch. Unbelieving, he noted that it showed only 0755, which would mean they'd been under fire less than twenty minutes. And then he saw that the crystal had smashed and jammed the hands.

Probably, he thought erratically, he had banged his wrist against the bridgeshield when *Old Swayback* cut loose with her first eight-inch salvo. She'd swung hard to starboard in order to bring her full broadside to bear, and she'd careened pretty sharply for a dignified dowager.

It must be at least 0830 . . .

Actually, it was 0815.

Forty seconds later the flagship received her initial direct hit from one of the enemy's battlewagons: a fourteen-inch armorpiercing shell that ripped through her Number 1 turret wall, burst with a horrendous roar, and wiped out the entire guncrew. The mangled steel barrels of this forward mount lay twisted across her forecastle like fingers that had been caught in a hydraulic press.

Old Swayback's main battery was now reduced to six rifles.

At 0818 another two-shell armorpiercing spread riddled her afterstructure, turned the carpenter's shop into an inferno, and sent flames rolling down through her bowels past ruptured safety hatches and blown bulkheads.

Before Bobby Burke could telephone the extent of this new damage from his station in secondary controls above the blazing scene, the after engineroom whistled into the voice tube, and the Black Gang chief informed Captain Bowen in remarkably composed fashion that his men might have to quit their jobs if it got any hotter.

Bowen transmitted this disturbing intelligence to the Flag bridge from his post on the toplofty battle lookout.

Tuthill relayed it to Torrey.

The Rock simply waggled his helmeted head in confirmation. There was nothing to say. On a straight line drawn through *Old Swayback*'s complicated guts, the after engineroom was less than one hundred and fifty feet from his swivel chair, yet the decision to abandon that hellish spot was strictly up to the two-striper in charge of the machinists, electricians, boilermen, and metalsmiths who were now struggling to quell the flames and keep the shafts turning. Even the far greater decision that might come any minute —to abandon *Old Swayback* herself—wasn't Torrey's to make. He might suggest it. But Archie Bowen would have to order what remained of his twelve hundred crewmen over the side in his own good time, after he'd concluded that nothing more could be done to save his cherished 10,826-ton possession.

A few moments later Bowen notified the Flag bridge that secondary controls had blown up.

"Burke's dead," he said in an oddly repressed voice, "and the auxiliary con's been smashed."

The Rock spoke into the tube himself. "Keep all those chins up, Archie. We're counting on you!"

"Yes, sir," Bowen said stolidly.

At 0823 the main superstructure took its first shell from a *Yahagi*-class light cruiser which had crept impudently close to the flagship's port bow, and was starting to pepper her tall upperworks with six-inch high explosive that burst on contact rather than slicing through her steel epidermis.

The fourth shell rocketed noisily into the battle-lookout platform three levels above the signal bridge where Torrey now stood, away from his chair, and wishing to hell he had *Old Swayback*'s command. Bits of metallic debris clattered past the open windshield upon the exposed 40-millimeter tubs below him. There wasn't time to look. But he knew from the screams that followed this shrapnel rain that men were hurt.

The voice tube uttered a blurry, strangled sound, as if its throat had been cut.

Tuthill shouted, "Flag bridge!" and somebody responded in awed accents that he was the only friggin' guy left alive up there in battle lookout.

"Who *are* you?" Tuthill demanded.

"Yeoman Bragg. Chief talker."

"Where's Captain Bowen?"

"Right here, sir—what's left of him."

"Christ!"

"What'll I do, sir?"

The Rock had heard the frantic exchange. He touched his chief of staff on the arm. "Tell him to stand fast. I'm going up," he said.

"Yes, sir."

As Torrey started for the small door that opened into the mainmast's hollow core, where a series of handrails ascended to battle lookout, he paused and gave Tuthill a curiously warm look.

"You're a damn solid citizen, Tut."

"Thanks, admiral."

"If anything happens, take over . . . you'll be the last of the Mohicans."

"Yes, sir. Depend on it."

"I do, Tut." The Rock beckoned his aide. "Come along, Mac. We're going climbing."

Mac's teeth suddenly gleamed white against his cordite-and-cork blackened face. "Anyhow, sir, that'll put us a lot nearer Heaven." He stopped, embarrassed, for it was an idiotic statement to have made. But he'd been staving off pantswetting nervousness all morning, and now he had a desperate urge to talk, even if what he said made no sense at all.

Torrey didn't seem annoyed at this fatuous remark. He grinned, too, and prodded Mac out onto the heaving, earsplitting, devastating emptiness of the bridgewing.

Unlike the weather openings on the lower decks, the mainmast door had been only lightly shut when the battle joined, since it was assumed—quite logically—that anytime *Old Swayback* careened far enough to immerse her signal bridge she wouldn't stop there, but would keep revolving until her great keel gaped.

They spun the door wide, grasped the ladder rungs, and clambered upward like a pair of rubberclad monkeys.

Battle lookout was a grisly shambles.

In the occluded light that filtered through the viewing slits in the heavysteel splinter shield, and through the larger hole made by the fatal shell, Torrey could see five bodies—he supposed there were five, although they were so bloodily tangled there might have been more, or less—flung in gobbety heaps against the bulkheads.

Archie Bowen was recognizable only because his blastgear had been stripped away from his beefy upper torso by the explosion, exposing the silver eagles on his collar. But he didn't have any head, and nothing much below his fat belly.

The yeoman talker was in a state of complete shock, ashenfaced, speechless, and trembling.

"Take it easy, Bragg," The Rock said calmly. The boy nodded his head in dumb response. "Mac, take the kid's phone set, and tell Tuthill I'm assuming command. He can pass The Word to whoever's on the navigating bridge . . . they'll get their course-and-speed orders from here."

"Yes, sir."

As Mac obeyed, *Old Swayback* was staggered by a fearful new succession of direct hits. The triphammer had stopped. These latest punches were administered by a piledriver that crunched through the cruiser's plates as if she were made of cardboard, not tempered steel. But somehow, in spite of the concatenate blasts that followed, he managed to slip the earphones over his head, and raise the signal bridge.

Tuthill answered in a harsh, unnatural voice. "Tell the Old Man we just caught one in Flag plot," he said. "Radar's gone." Mac heard him turn away and speak to somebody else. Then: "The goddamn shell exploded downward into radio central. That's wiped out, too."

Torrey accepted the news in stoical silence.

Stooping to bring his eyes level with the thin perforation in the forward bulkhead, which permitted only a limited view ahead, he contemplated the nightmarish vista spread out before the battered flagship. A dozen or so Avengers were still wheeling waspishly above the Jap force, darting down every so often to sting and run. The lone Yank survivor of the two destroyer assaults was crawling groggily away from the enemy, firing ragged salvos from the twin fives on her stern. Two Nip cruisers seemed dead in the water. One was burning peacefully. The bow of the other had dipped sharply into the graygreen sea. And a *Haruna*-class battlewagon, listing to port, also appeared to have other things on her mind than fighting.

For some still incomprehensible reason, *Yamato* had pulled back even farther toward the rear of the disordered Nip array, and she wasn't shooting, either.

Torrey thought he saw a signal hoist flickering from the battleship's maintruck. But he wasn't positive. She was too far away, and it was too smoky.

Both the remaining enemy battlewagon and heavy cruiser, however, continued methodically about their slaughterhouse chores, pumping salvo after salvo into *Old Swayback* as she limped at reduced speed along the edge of the battlezone, and into the two crippled baby-flattops which lay out of Torrey's restricted visual range. Barely discernible through the drifting multicolored haze generated by the gunfire, by the burning warships, and by the remnants of the screen laid down by Rudyard's suicidal destroyers, a formation of Japanese tincans was girding for a torpedo run against the survivors of Task Group JOHNPAUL.

They'd find goddamned slim pickings, The Rock thought savagely—one stricken Yank cruiser that had been born with a crooked spine; two converted merchantmen which needed only a nudge to send them plunging into twenty thousand fathoms with their silly makeshift flightdecks and their pathetic five-inch rifles; and one ruined destroyer that probably wouldn't last until they got there.

Almost academically, then, Torrey wondered what had happened to *Crandall,* the decoy he'd dispatched three days earlier into the unpatrolled waters three hundred miles east of this sorry battleground. By now she should have started sending out her diversionary messages—pretending she was a fast carrier task group, promising prompt succor to his beleaguered ships.

Maybe she'd fallen prey to a wandering Jap sub.

It wouldn't surprise him.

This was the day his luck ran out.

He swung around. "Ask Tuthill," he shouted above the crazy tumult, "whether we've heard from *Crandall!"*

Mac gave him a startled look. "Sir, the radio's dead. Don't you remember?"

Fumblingly, Torrey passed his hand across his sweating, blackened face. Yes. Now he remembered. They were deaf, blind, dumb; and soon they'd have no hands, arms, legs, or feet.

"Sorry, fella. I guess I'm tired . . ."

Mac gulped at something deep in his throat. It could have been his heart.

The Old Man looked like a goddamn greasy ghost. Absolutely beat. Finished. Kaput. Except for those iceberg eyes of his, which glittered fiercely from beneath his shadowing visor, and that uncompromising granite jaw. Christ. Anybody who could reach this point and simply say, as The Rock did, "I guess I'm tired," deserved an award for all-time understatement, along with the posthumous Medal of Honor they'd send his widow. Mac giggled irrationally. But Admiral Torrey didn't *have* a widow, or wife; and after Pala Passage he didn't even have a next of kin. So around whose neck would President Franklin Delano Roosevelt hang the paleblue watered silk ribbon of the Medal? Lieutenant Maggie Haynes'? Possibly. Charming neck. And right now, Mac reminded himself owlishly, she was chief nurse aboard USS *Charity,* which lay not more than fifty miles over the heavenly horizon.

He wondered what the hell Bev would do with *his* first and only medal . . .

But now The Rock was speaking in his low, sad voice, summoning the yeoman talker and his aide.

"Let's go below, gentlemen. There's nothing more we can do here. I think it is time to abandon ship."

At 0847 the flagship of Task Group JOHNPAUL, while in the process of evacuating the remnants of her crew, received her deathblow in the form of a torpedo spread from a *Shimakaze*-class destroyer. Her wounds were such, of course, that she would have succumbed without this final touch. But for the Jap tincan, it was excellent practice, and the skipper had contemptuously closed within a thousand yards before triggering his lethal apparatus. He stood by, grinning his pleasure, as the four electric fish arrowed toward *Old Swayback*'s tender midriff.

Torrey saw the torpedoes approaching, from his own bridge. Their journey across the narrow expanse between the two ships—executioner and condemned—seemed to take an eternity, although they were driving through the warm sea at fifty knots. There was a sickening lull before the oxygen-fueled projectiles bored through the cruiser's frame just below the waterline.

And then four thousand pounds of TNT blew up.

Old Swayback was disemboweled from wardroom to crew's mess. For ten terrible seconds she arched in agony, convex against the azure sky for the first time in her ill-shaped life, and then she came apart in a welter of shardlike pieces.

Torrey had flung himself flat upon the buckled deck just before the impact, hoping somehow to avoid the worst of the marrow-melting concussion he knew must follow; and he waited for the wall of green water to thunder down upon him, just as it had when the cruiser underwent her baptism of fire a year earlier in a faraway corner of the Pacific.

But now, as he glared futilely toward *Old Swayback*'s rent superstructure, instead of water he saw huge chunks of torn steel slowly, almost lazily, begin to sheer away from the tower above him, and fall toward the twisted plates where he lay.

Had Torrey been a profane man, he might have cursed, railed against God, damned Fate. But he wasn't. As he said, he was very tired. He shut his eyes as the blow struck . . .

21. Everlasting Gratitude

He was awake at last.

But time had no meaning for him. In his semidelirium, his thoughts mutinously refused to marshal themselves in proper military array; and they strayed with his heavylidded glance around the dimly lighted room in which he lay upon a sterile white bed.

Mostly he stared straight upward, for it was easier that way, with his head swathed in bandages as cumbrous and thick as a caracul shako. The ceiling of the small room had been painted and repainted so often in a yellowish creamcolor that now, in the slanting beam of the nightlight on his bedstand, it took on a bas-relief effect, which added to the curious torment assailing him.

There were moments when he imagined he saw continents and islands and seas, weirdly shifting, always in flux, across which were drawn the Operations Orders for some vast enterprise whose scope and nature always frustratingly eluded him just as he thought he understood their import. They had been charted by a spectral hand that looked like Paul Eddington's, although he could never quite perceive what was beyond the man's great hairy wrist. They contained grievous errors—strategical mistakes so plainly visible that he wanted to cry out and correct them—but when he opened his swollen lips no sound emerged; and so the plans remained there, absurdly wrong, patently doomfilled, and ready to be executed by ships he commanded yet couldn't control.

At other times he believed the clownish ceiling was Heaven itself, from which familiar constellations gleamed down upon him: Centaur, Wolf, Dragon, Phoenix, and the five-starred Southern Cross. This sky spun dizzily, patternless, and there was no orderly polestar, nor meaning to anything. But he should have known, he admonished himself distantly, that the immovable, dependable polestar—the mariner's beacon—was never seen by those who sailed the Southern Seas.

Then the steelraftered overhead became the pages of a giant ledger on which were inscribed the names of admirals who'd forfeited their Fleets through stupidity, caused them to be sunk, and thus betrayed their trust. Soundlessly, he wept. For now the ledger was a casualty list that contained only one name, repeated again and again: *Jere Torrey, Lieutenant, USNR.*

With a terrible effort, he willed back the whirling constellations, and Jere's name mercifully vanished.

All this, as he lay motionless upon his bed, seemed to occur just below the level of comprehension: it was fathomed rather than understood; it was alternately frightening and exasperating; and it hurt his bandaged head to think . . .

For a little while he slept again.

When he awoke, it was day, and the nightlight's sculpture had given way to a curious shimmering glow that danced and eddied across the pallid ceiling. Now he was conscious of sounds, too. Through the thick bulkhead beside his bed he could hear the groans and mutterings of other men in the adjacent compartment, and of still others in rooms beyond them.

As he turned his face away from this dolorous medley, hoping to mute the sound, his gaze fell upon the open port, past which were visible the grotesque trunks of shellblasted cocopalms, a steepsloping beach, and the rampant flanks of Mount Tamapali, greenverdured and smoking lazily in the morning mists. The sun's rays, reflecting off the harborwaters, caused the undulating light-swirls on his ceiling.

And then he knew where he was.

From what The Rock could observe through the comfortable, landlubber window that opened onto *Charity*'s promenade deck, the beachhead seemed secure enough, although the rumble of howitzer fire echoed from the distant hills, betokening the enemy's lastditch resistance. He sighed. By now, he supposed, The Word was out, and replacements would soon be coming for the ships he'd gambled with and lost. He hoped they would arrive before Stumpy Aylott had to tackle the entire goddamn Japanese Navy, Army, and Air Force by himself, here on Levu-Vana.

Painfully, Torrey strove to recall what had happened after *Old Swayback* was hit, to compute the time that had passed since he'd blacked out.

But it was futile.

He remembered only the cruiser's collapsing superstructure, the grinning Jap destroyerman, and the relentless enemy force that gave no quarter because, of course, he'd asked for none . . .

For some unfathomable reason, through some inexplicable quirk, he knew that he himself had been saved. Providential? He laughed bitterly, alone in the barren room. What in hell did Providence have to do with anything? Half a fleet sunk, Jere dead, and who could measure by what margin the war had been shortened? If, indeed, it hadn't been lengthened.

His brain throbbed dully, constantly, and he wanted to sleep again. But sleep wouldn't come. So he tried a homely insomniac remedy which someone had prescribed for him many years ago: composing all the members of your body, one by one, until their relaxed deadweight hugs the bed, nerveless and unfeeling, while you float dreamily above what used to be your physical self.

Directing his head to rest was simple enough. Enveloped in its vast gauze helmet, it could only swing to port and starboard, about ten degrees each way.

His right arm, Torrey discovered, was encased in plaster of Paris, so it had no choice but to lay supine, as a restful example to its uninjured mate.

Buttocks composed.

Right leg, ditto.

Left leg—

Torrey tried to straighten his left leg, to fetch it close against the right. But there was something agonizingly wrong about his motor reaction: as if, like his cracked and battered lips, the leg would not obey the brain's command. Disregarding the pain that knifed through him, he used his one good arm to lever himself into a sitting posture, and stared down at the empty place beneath the sheet where his left leg should have been.

His lips moved.

He uttered a terrible cry.

Christ! It was gone! They'd amputated his goddamn leg!

Suddenly Maggie was there. As if she had anticipated his cry, she stepped across the narrow threshold to his room, and now she stood beside him, compassionately enduring his wild, feverish, reproachful gaze.

"Why did they do this to me, Maggie?"

Her own eyes brimmed with tears. "They had no choice, Rock. None at all. Otherwise you'd have died."

"Then they should have let me die."

She brushed a kiss across his unshaven cheek. "Do you think *I* would have let you die?"

"One-legged, one-armed," he said bitterly, still contemplating the emptiness beneath the rumpled sheet. "A goddamned basket case."

"You'll keep your arm, Rock. It's badly smashed. But you won't lose it."

"No steel claw to match my wooden leg?" he demanded crazily.

Maggie pushed him gently back against the pillow. He struggled weakly for a moment before he surrendered and allowed himself to be stretched out straight upon the bed. His eyes were tight shut. She smoothed the tangled covers. Sighing, she reached into the pocket of her uniform skirt and drew out a hypodermic syringe which she deftly inserted into the hard, hot flesh of his upper left arm.

He groaned once.

After that he slept, with his drawn and melancholy face turned toward hers.

She dragged a wickerchair across the room, placed it near the head of the bed, and sat there for a long time, listening to his ragged breathing. Occasionally he would clench his uninjured fist, and try to raise it into the air, as if even in his drugged unconsciousness he was still hurling defiance at someone, or something, somewhere.

At length he grew less troubled.

Torrey slept until early evening. When he finally awoke, still bemused by the massive injection of morphine, it was pitchdark outside, and the window had been lowered to seal out the miasmic dampness of the tropical night. A 60-watt light bulb cast its small glow upon the square glass pane. Clumsily, he raised himself upon his left elbow and sought to peer into the black void beyond the window. *Somebody was staring at him through the closed port!* Deepset, somber eyes regarded Torrey from a face that seemed oddly familiar, like that of a person he'd known long ago, but had forgotten in the passage of time. It was a gray, seamed face, sad beneath its gleaming white officer's cap.

Suddenly, then, Torrey recognized this solemn stranger who pinioned him with his implacable gaze.

It was the Old Man.

Torrey was shocked by his father's expression of undescribable weariness, and by the tired droop of the once-broad shoulders. For a long moment, voiceless, he looked at the Old Man.

At last he ventured, "Sir?"

The Old Man didn't speak, although his lips moved, and his stern features seemed to relax a little.

"I tried, sir," Torrey muttered defiantly. "Christ knows I tried." When the ancient captain continued to brood at him, he added, "But I let you down, didn't I?"

The Rock waited for the gruff reply, which would be couched in uncompromising terms like, "Duty seen is duty done," or, "Judgment, boy, is what distinguishes men from animals—so exercise it!"

But his father remained silent.

"A hell of a long time ago," Torrey whispered, "I warned Paul Eddington about faulty judgment." He gave a mocking chuckle. "But I was talking about *your* kind of judgment, sir, and not God Almighty's. I'd forgotten all about that."

It was true.

In his fatuous self-sufficiency, he'd supposed that rational judgment excused everything. You charted your course. Then you accepted the consequences because you'd done what had to be done, having faithfully obeyed the Book and carefully translated orders into action. But now he wasn't sure any more. He remembered, too, how he'd chided Eddington for playing too jauntily with those wooden pawns on the Sub Base maneuvering board before the war. Secure in his monumentally untested wisdom, he'd reminded the exec that those tiny lengths of pine board represented "men's lives and a lot of expensive hardware."

Torrey shut his eyes to blot out the Old Man's forbidding image. He wished his father would speak. Even the harshest words would be more supportable than that bleak stare. When he opened his eyes again, the Old Man was still there, pitiless as ever, and just as immobile.

The Rock pounded the mattress with his clenched left fist. *"For the love of Christ,"* he shouted at the spectral figure, *"say something!"*

"Rock!"

He turned painfully. Maggie, who had been slumbering on the big chair cushion, stood at his side. Her tousled hair brushed his feverish cheek, and she was coaxing him back against the pillow.

"You scared me half to death," she said.

Torrey pointed. "He's here—the Old Man."

Maggie's voice was kind. "Nonsense, you've just had a morphine hangover. Happens all the time."

Eluding her gentle grasp, he regained his half-reclining stance, so he could look into the mirrored surface of the window. Only his own reflection leered back at him. For several seconds he studied the gaunt apparition that was Rockwell Torrey, chilled by what he saw, as understanding gradually came to him.

"Now do you believe me?"

"Yes," he said dully. "I believe you."

"Then please obey the nurse's orders, sir, and lie down like a nice admiral."

Torrey allowed himself to be lowered into position so Maggie could readjust the tumbled sheets. Her lips were twisted into their oddly canted grin. As she reached across the bed, the gesture urged her small breasts tautly against the starched uniform. She was very young and very sweet, Torrey thought, and just watching her kept his mind off the pain that flooded his tormented body like a hot lava-flow.

With his uninjured hand, he caressed her soft hip, and her lopsided grin widened. "I'm a lousy patient," he said awkwardly.

"You'll get better."

Torrey's glance traveled down to his amputated leg. He essayed a shrug. "Will I?"

"Yes."

"That's very comforting," he said ironically. Maggie's smile faded, and he was suddenly repentant. "Forgive me. I'm a bastard."

She pressed his hand. "When you fell asleep," she said, "I was terribly afraid."

"For me?"

Touched by the humble incredulity in his voice, she murmured, "In this whole wide unblessed world, Rock Torrey, you're my only concern. To hell with the rest of 'em!"

He stared at the strangely sculptured ceiling. "Why, Maggie?"

"Because," she said, "nurses are always falling in love with admirals. It's that simple."

"I don't think it's simple at all."

Maggie's grin flashed again. "It isn't."

"Nothing's simple any more," Torrey said. "Not even the things I learned from the Old Man. 'The fundamentals of being a man,' he used to call them when he was 'indoctrinating' me." The Rock frowned in painful concentration. "Christ! I don't even know what day it is . . ."

"It's Saturday, darling."

"Saturday!" He started to rise again, but Maggie seized his shoulder. "Then I've lain here for three whole bloody days—like a goddamn mummy—while my command's been going to hell in a handbasket."

"Please try to understand," she urged. "The hell's all finished."

Torrey ignored her entreaty. "How did I get aboard *Charity*?"

"They brought you aboard Wednesday afternoon after one of Admiral Tollafson's destroyers fished you out of the water. You weren't in very good shape, Rock, and you were babbling like a goofy little kid. Delirious. But Lieutenant McConnel had sense enough to tie a tourniquet around your leg so you wouldn't bleed to death."

He asked quietly, "Was anybody else saved from the Flag bridge?"

". . . I'm sorry, Rock."

"Egan Powell, Tuthill—all of them?" The Rock drew a deep breath. Then he said flatly: "Gone."

"All except a funny little Chamorro steward's mate who kept insisting he had to look after the 'Old Man.'" Maggie paused. "He meant you, didn't he?"

"Yes." Torrey looked toward the window. "Now I'm the Old Man." He added, "Where's Mac?"

"Just down the corridor. He's got burned hands. Fractured ankle. But he's ambulant."

"May I see him?"

"Certainly."

Diffidently, almost shyly, Lieutenant McConnel hobbled into The Rock's private room on crutches, and managed a crude salute with his heavily bandaged right hand.

Torrey waved toward the bedside chair. "Sit down, fella."

"Yes, sir."

"How do you feel?"

"Happy to be alive, sir," Mac said quietly. "Surprised, too."

"I know." Torrey massaged the dark stubble on his chin. "Sometimes a man finds himself wondering why, doesn't he?"

"Yes, sir."

"There seems to be a seventy-two-hour gap in my memory, Mac, which only you can patch up."

McConnel nodded sympathetically. "You got a hell of a clout on the head, sir. Besides, your leg . . ."

The Rock was silent, thoughtful, trying through pulsating waves of pain to frame the question that would elicit the information he needed. The room was spinning again. It was very difficult to concentrate.

Finally: "Why didn't the Japs finish us off when they had the chance?"

Mac seemed astonished. "You don't really know, sir?"

"Does anyone?"

"It was a hell of a mystery, admiral, until we picked up a couple of Japs who'd been paddling around in the water ever since their light cruiser sank. One of 'em was a communications ensign—or whatever they call ensigns in the Imperial Navy—and since he figured he was legally dead anyhow, he was willing to talk."

What the Nip survivor told Intelligence, Mac went on, mightn't exactly prevent the experts from debating the tactics of the Battle of Toka-Rota for the next few generations, but it would help. *Old Swayback*'s refugees were bobbing around in the ocean, beating off sharks and taking their turns riding the few liferafts they'd been able to launch, when damned if Bandit One didn't abruptly veer away from the area, and head straight north, right back where he'd come from. This wasn't accidental. It was deliberate. Because with blinker light and signal hoist, the Jap flagship—*Yamato*—ordered abandonment of the unequal chase just as her two tincans flattened their tails for a run toward the two baby-flattops that were still afloat.

The men in the water cheered like lunatics, and the sight of the Nips haul-assing gave them just enough courage to hang tough till *Falcon* and *Chickenhawk,* aided by Admiral Tollafson's destroyers which had preceded HORATIO's main body, plucked them out of the ocean.

"What," Torrey asked patiently, "did the Jap ensign say?"

Mac grinned. "Right from the start, sir, the Nip admiral must've figured he had tackled the outriders of Task Force 48. He was pretty gutless, I guess, because he mistook Captain Rudyard's jeeps for fast carriers, and he never did get wise. What's more, he apparently had the wild notion that you expected a potful of landbased planes from Levu-Vana, and he knew all about the pasting his friends took at Pala Passage."

Torrey's cold eyes, barely discernible beneath his turban, grew warmer.

"Did *Crandall* ever send her message?"

"You goddamn right she did, sir!" Mac grinned. "I saw a copy of her dispatch on the tincan that rescued us. 'AM LAUNCHING 200-PLANE STRIKE,' it said, 'FROM POINT 100 EAST. GOOD LUCK. HANG ON.' Hell, it's something I'd never forget. But neither will that Jap admiral. The thought of Tollafson hitting him from the left, and TF48 from the right, must have given the bastards the heebie-jeebies. He felt—according to the Nip ensign—like a filbert caught in a nutcracker."

"I'm glad of that," The Rock muttered. "*Crandall* did her job. So did Dick Tollafson. At least something went right."

Mac leaned forward tensely, earnestly, in the wickerchair. "Admiral Torrey, everything went right!"

"Old Swayback?"

"She did her job, too, sir."

Another painflash traveled through The Rock, starting from his mutilated thigh and knifing toward his skull. He fought back nausea. But he wanted to explain about *Old Swayback,* because Mac plainly hadn't understood.

"What I meant," he said through clenched teeth, "was that we didn't have a decent 'fast ship' for the mission . . . Hell, I loved that clumsy old tub . . . But Archie Bowen's luck ran out—that's all—and this time he couldn't save his John Paul Jones plaque, his ship, or himself." Torrey waited for the pain to ebb, afraid he wasn't making sense, before he added, "But God knows we went in 'harm's way,' because that's all we could do . . . I suppose . . . though maybe there might have been something else . . . a different way . . ."

"What other way?" the aide demanded, oblivious to the admiral's rank.

"Taking Blackjack Broderick's advice. Staying put. Keeping our necks safely tucked in."

Scornfully, Mac said, "Imagine the motto we'd have hung in *Old Swayback*'s wardroom—'Give Me an Anchored Ship for I Intend To Park Here Forever on My Fanny!' "

The Rock smiled wanly. "You're all right, son," he whispered.

As Mac struggled out of the sagbottomed chair, it occurred to him that Torrey had called him *son* less offhandedly than usual, and that when Torrey uttered the word an oddly wistful expression had flickered across his equine face, then vanished. Mac gazed down at the wounded man on the bed. Torrey had shut his eyes.

Very quietly, taking particular care not to scrape his unwieldly crutches on the bare deck, he left.

But The Rock was not asleep.

Locked in the dark penitentiary of his own thoughts, he heard the door close behind McConnel with a faint metallic click. He remained there, sightless and motionless, seeking to comprehend what had happened. He was no longer concerned with the elementary facts of the battle. Those were clear enough, now, and Torrey took pleasure in imagining the Japanese admiral's discomfiture when he finally learned how he might have annihilated the lesser Yankee task force, if only he hadn't fled from a phantom. It was good to realize that these mystic little men also fell prey to hobgoblins, sometimes, because in the desperate subequatorial summer-winter of 1942 too many timid planners were crediting the Japanese with an invincibility they didn't really possess at all.

Blackjack Broderick typified this breed. Wrapping his moral cowardice in a cloak of self-righteousness, however, he haughtily insisted that you don't make a move until you are "certain of success beyond a reasonable doubt" (as if this were a matter of guilt or innocence!), or until you could assure your superiors of "minimum casualties."

The thought of Broderick's reluctance to invoke a command decision caused Torrey to writhe angrily on the sweaty hospital bed. How many golden opportunities missed, he wondered, had actually extended the war? How many more paltry sequences of "minimum casualties" would have to be played before the foe was brought to heel?

As Torrey reflected upon that ultimate day, his anger changed to despair, and his left hand crept almost of its own volition down the sheet to his truncated limb. The demand for peg-legged admirals, he reminded himself, was considerably less than bullish in the United States Navy. They'd beach him somewhere in some backwater job, or retire him outright. Or maybe they'd send him on tour, he thought bitterly, so he could flaunt his honorable wounds to shame civilians into buying War Bonds. Wasn't that what returning heroes always did?

The Rock emitted a blasphemous phrase.

Hero, hell!

Twenty years hence, he guessed, naval history books would cover the Battle of Toka-Rota in a brief footnote: *"RAdm. Rockwell Torrey, USN, '14, commanding a small task group, engaged a superior enemy force in a minor engagement which later was deemed both inconclusive and unnecessary. American losses totaled one heavy cruiser, one escort carrier, and five destroyers . . ."*

For a moment this odd conceit loomed very real. He wondered why historians so rarely bothered to chronicle human casualties in such inconsequential affairs. Perhaps it was simply too much trouble to ferret out the facts. Or possibly machines were intrinsically more important than men, since a battleship's gestation period was two long years, and a human being's just nine short months. But that couldn't be the entire answer. It took seventeen years to transform a boy into a man capable of loading, aiming, and firing a gun; he'd have to wait another four before they'd let him vote; (yet anytime at all he could die a death that was (unlike the Battle of Toka-Rota) very conclusive and still (like that engagement) very unnecessary indeed. It came to Torrey, then, that he'd also been thinking far more about machines than about men, as he weighed the events of the bloody week; and suddenly he knew why.

Deliberately, consciously, he had been endeavoring to erase the memory of Jere. He wanted to thrust aside the brutal fact that he himself, at forty-nine, was the last link to the Torreys' seafaring past, and a sadly broken link at that. He supposed he'd have to write a *Dear Athalie* letter, now, regretting to inform her that their boy was dead, but assuring her that Jere had acquitted himself in a gallant manner which would have delighted Commodore Farr's piratical old heart.

The Rock knew exactly what Athalie would say when he told her that Jere had steamed into hopeless battle at his bidding.

In her precise yet angular hand, the message would arrive by return airmail: *"You have killed my son!"* And her one real regret would be that she couldn't engrave this terrible indictment upon his quivering heart with the nib of her platinum pen.

As he lay in his sterile bed, eyes open and staring at the weird bas-relief above him, Torrey felt a savage loneliness that exceeded anything he'd known before, and which was intensified by his immobility and by the knowledge that there was nothing left to do. Mordantly, as if he wished to tear at an old wound, he mused upon the nickname he'd borne all his professional life. *The Rock*. Scratch its granite surface and deepdown you'd find nothing but dark basaltic strata, igneous and fused and ancient, because he was the flinty product of three decades of trial by fire, and there could be no softness in him.

Yet, in the aftermath of this battle for which he had been so long trained and toughened, he found no exultation, no sense of destiny fulfilled. Instead, he was spent and humbled, and strangely insecure . . .

Maggie gave his left shoulder a tiny shake and he awoke at once.

"Hello, nurse."

She kissed his unshaven cheek. "Hello, my darling."

"I must look romantic as hell," he grunted, "with this scraggly beard."

"Some of it comes out gray." Maggie viewed him critically. "But some of it's damned near red."

"One time my Old Man sported a real nautical muttonchopper," Torrey remarked, "and it was red as a two-cent stamp."

"I think I prefer you without whiskers."

"So do I."

"Later," Maggie said, "you'll get a shave. Right now you've got company. If you're up to it, that is."

He grimaced. "Depends on who's calling. I don't feel very damned social."

"General Aylott."

"Stumpy?" Torrey brightened visibly. "Send the old tramp in!"

As she started for the door, it burst open without warning, and the behemothic Marine came plunging into the small stateroom.

Maggie got mad.

"Even generals are expected to obey hospital rules," she snapped.

Startled, Aylott looked at her like a honey-hunting bear that had stumbled unwarily into a swarm of angry wasps. "Who's this?" he asked.

" 'This,' " mimicked Torrey, "is Lieutenant Haynes, *Charity*'s chief nurse, and my own best reason for being alive."

Stumpy thrust out a gigantic paw. "Delighted, miss! If you've got The Rock thinking along those lines, by Hector, more power to you!"

"You flatter a girl, general," Maggie said primly.

He gave her an appraising glance. "Hell, lieutenant, stone-puss here's the one who ought to be flattered. By God—what's keeping him in the sack? Why isn't he out dancing with you in the moonlight?"

"Because," Torrey growled, "there's no moonlight, Stumpy, and I've lost my goddamn leg."

"I think I'll leave," Maggie said abruptly, heading for the door. It slammed behind her.

Aylott was unruffled, either by The Rock's reference to his amputated leg, or Maggie's departure. He'd lived too long with sudden death to worry about a mere missing limb. And fiery women impressed him. He turned back to Torrey, grinning. "Walks damned nice, too, you sly bastard. Easy movement. Like a chronometer—all wheels and balances and little things that jiggle." He might have gone on, if The Rock's fierce scowl hadn't silenced him, and he finished lamely, "But maybe you're serious, for God's sake . . ."

Torrey relented. "Yes, Stumpy, I guess I'm serious. You see, I've known her all my life."

"Well, I'll be go to hell," Aylott said in an awed tone. "All your everlovin' life."

"Since last December."

The general looked baffled, but he let it pass. Poor bugger was probably off his rocker from morphine shots. He said: "You planning to do anything about it?"

Torrey nodded absently. "There are a couple of little matters to clear up first, Stumpy."

"Such as?"

"Growing me a new leg . . . and the court-martial."

Aylott's ursine eyes widened in disbelief. "Court-martial? Are you out of your friggin' mind, mister?"

"You don't sacrifice seven ships without having somebody lower the boom," The Rock said. "I know. That's the Book."

The general deposited himself into the wickerchair, which sagged dangerously beneath his vast weight, and settled the webbed pistol belt comfortably across his belly. "Maybe it's a damned good thing I jumped the gun and paid you this visit while you're still batty," he rumbled. "You sound like some joker who hasn't heard The Word."

Torrey regarded him stolidly. "This isn't much of an Intelligence center. We're sort of isolated from the outside world."

"Mostly," Aylott said, "you've been cut off from being conscious. Otherwise I'd have dropped around sooner." He fished a dispatch flimsy from the breast pocket of his tentlike khaki blouse, and thrust it into The Rock's unbandaged left hand. "Here—read it!"

Torrey began to scan the brief message. Then, unaccountably, a sudden mist seemed to cloud his vision, and he returned it to Aylott.

"Perhaps you'd better read it to me, fella."

Stumpy cleared his throat. "COMMANDER IN CHIEF U. S. FLEET TO COMMANDER NAVAL FORCES SKYHOOK," he began.

"Hell, I know that," Torrey snapped. "What does Ernie Jesus King *say*?"

"YOU DESERVE THE EVERLASTING GRATITUDE OF YOUR COUNTRYMEN FOR HALTING THE ENEMY AT A CRITICAL MOMENT IN OUR PACIFIC CAMPAIGN IN A MAGNIFICENT ENGAGEMENT WAGED AGAINST OVERWHELMING ODDS—"

"That's enough, mister!"

"But there's more."

Torrey's lips curved in an odd smile. "No. All I wanted to know was whether they'd rewritten the footnote. They have."

Aylott stared at him. "What 'footnote'?"

"You wouldn't understand, Stumpy. It's a private matter between me and my conscience . . . and maybe my immortal soul."

"Are you thinking of your kid—Jere?"

"That's part of it."

Clumsy in his unaccustomed attempt at sympathy, Aylott muttered, "Goddamned shame, Rock."

"Yes." Torrey seemed to be addressing somebody else, as if Stumpy weren't even in the room. "But we've all got to keep moving along, don't we?"

"Sure," Aylott said uncertainly. "There's a hell of a lot of work left, even after we mop up this blasted island."

"That, too."

"You saved our arse, you know, Rock."

"Thanks, fella. That was the basic idea. Saving twenty thousand arses while we lost a few hundred."

Aylott coughed his embarrassment. "They tell me you're going back to Frisco for a yard overhaul."

"Am I?"

"In a special ambulance plane," Stumpy said, gratified that he'd finally found a safer topic, "with a private nurse and an aide of your own choosing. You're leaving tomorrow."

"That gives me just time to pack," Torrey observed dryly.

Aylott heaved himself to his mammoth feet and started for the door, where he paused, turned, and said, "My Seabees have gone into the joss-stick business, Rock. I'll send you a whole shipload!"

"Much obliged, fella."

"They work a hell of lot better than the Nip kind," Stumpy assured him. "Ideal for guys growin' new legs. Miracles guaranteed."

The Rock forced a grin. "Will they also get a one-legged sailor a job?"

"You're goddamned affirmatively tootin'!" Aylott readjusted his cartridge belt. Then added wolfishly, "Hell, all an admiral needs is a fat fanny so he can squat in his bridge chair and issue orders to a friggin' task force."

"So long, fella."

"*Adios,* Rock. Meet you in Tokyo."

The door slammed. Torrey wondered if he'd ever see him again, or where, and he fought against the feeling that Aylott also had an aura of predestined doom about him, for all his unbounded exuberance and taurine zest. Stumpy would have laughed at such a crazy notion. He'd have opined that a man's got to go sometime, and that the world was too full of damned fools anyhow. Stumpy was a hell of a fine Marine . . .

That fact, The Rock brooded, after General Aylott's bullvoice had faded down *Charity*'s long passageway, explained a lot of things. Marines lived so intimately with violent death that they got callous about it. They were inured to battlefield odds, which weren't very favorable during the initial days of an amphibious landing, as the casualty lists bloodily attested.

Stumpy couldn't conceive of inactivity—even for a man who'd had his leg blown off.

The brief exhilaration that had come from Aylott's visit was gone now, and it was succeeded by a savage awareness of his own plight.

It wasn't difficult for him to imagine all his future years of aimless puttering around in little coastal villages, where he'd help provide proper heroic atmosphere for Fourth of July celebrations, or those annual hegiras to Washington for a check-up at Bethesda Naval Hospital and a few rounds of drinks with the other dry-docked gaffers at the Army-Navy Club on Eye Street. Sure. Horatio Nelson had managed with one arm. But he inhabited the eighteenth century. This was the brawling twentieth. Half-men weren't needed any more.

Carefully, cautiously, Maggie seated herself on the edge of his disarrayed bed, near his left shoulder, and reached for his clenched fist. She pried it open, and laid her cool palm against his hot dry hand.

"Now that you know that you're not a failure," she said, "you'll rest better."

"And when I'm rested," Torrey responded lifelessly, "what shall I do? Peddle pencils from a wheelchair in front of the Navy Department?"

Maggie gave him a probing glance, as if she were debating exactly how to reply to this forlorn plea. When she finally spoke, her own question sounded deliberately cruel.

"You reckon the whole world's come to an end, don't you?"

He blinked his surprise, feeling the hot brine of self-pitying tears on his gaunt cheeks.

"I guess," he said abjectly, "that's about the size of it."

"Well, admiral, it hasn't."

He forced a weak grin. "Wipe my damned eyes, Maggie. The ashes from that volcano irritate the hell out of them."

She passed a washcloth across his face. "Better?"

"Much."

"Neither the world nor the war has ended, Rock. But the shooting will stop someday—and then we'll still have the world, whether we like it or not." She paused. "Anybody can fight. Even me. The big trouble's going to come when it's all over."

Torrey shrugged. "I know," he said, recalling his earlier gloomy thoughts.

"Mac's told me more about you, Rock, than I've ever learned from yourself. Things you'd never have explained because they're all locked up inside that lonesome mind of yours. But I'll unlock it, darling."

"What did McConnel tell you?"

"About your classes at Annapolis . . . and how those youngsters looked up to you, as if you had the answers to every problem on God's green earth."

"I didn't have the answer to a goddamned thing."

"But you did. You just didn't realize it."

With conscious irrelevance, Torrey muttered, "You must love me a hell of a lot."

"I do," Maggie said simply.

"For Christ's sake—why?"

She kissed his torn lips. "I just do. It isn't a very complicated emotion, Rock, but I'm awfully sure of it."

"Oh."

"Besides," she concluded, "I've been one of Rockwell Torrey's star pupils, and I want a postgraduate course when you start teaching again. It might take an awfully long time . . ."

All that night, and well into Sunday morning, The Rock slept soundly, without a painkilling injection. He was awakened by the clear clean notes of Church Call. The mellow sound of the well-blown bugle, heard through the open window from *Charity*'s distant fantail, was marvelously soothing. When Maggie came with his breakfast tray, he grinned at her from the ferocious shrubbery of his four-day beard.

He sampled the powdered eggs.

"You, Lieutenant Haynes, are a splendid cook."

"I can sew, knit, launder, and do a lot of other amusing things," she said.

"Ever shave a man's face?"

"You'd be surprised," she replied, "what nurses know about shaving."

"Probably with those dinky little safety razors," he said scornfully.

Maggie reached into the nightstand drawer and drew out a worn, watersoaked redplush box. "Recognize this, admiral?"

Torrey fondled the familiar case. His cherished German straight-blades were polished, sharpened, honed, ready.

"How?" he demanded simply.

"Your Chamorro boy," Maggie said. "From the loving way you always used them, he figured they were some sort of good luck charm. They were wedged under his lifebelt. Which one do you want me to use?"

"Take the one marked *Sonntag* . . ."

ABOUT THE AUTHOR

James Bassett has been pondering *Harm's Way,* his first novel, for twenty years, and actually writing it for the past two. During World War II, Mr. Bassett was a staff officer intimately associated with the late Fleet Admiral William F. Halsey, and handled his press relations from the Guadalcanal campaign to the Japanese surrender in Tokyo Bay. Although he won the Bronze Star with combat clasp, he is proudest of this inscription on a photograph of the famed "Wild Bull": "To Jim Bassett, tried wartime comrade, shipmate and friend." Mr. Bassett holds the rank of captain, USNR (Ret.).

California-born, Mr. Bassett attended Bowdoin College, where he was elected to Phi Beta Kappa. In 1934 he entered the newspaper profession with the Los Angeles *Times,* for which he is now political analyst. He has also been city editor and assistant managing editor of the Los Angeles *Mirror*. On leave from the *Times,* Mr. Bassett has participated in four national political campaigns, and was former Vice-President Richard Nixon's campaign director in 1956, and planning director in 1960.

Mr. Bassett lives with his wife Wilma and fourteen-year-old daughter Cynthia in Glendale, California.

This book was set in

Granjon and Caslon True Cut types

by Harry Sweetman Typesetting Corporation.

It was printed and bound at the press of

The World Publishing Company.

Design is by Larry Kamp.